Enter to Learn

Writing and Research at BYU

Gary Layne Hatch

Danette Paul

Cover art:
Greek (Archaic Period) Double Portrait Bust of Hermes/Hercules
by Wayne Kimball

Address orders to:

English Composition
Brigham Young University
3110 JKHB
Provo UT 84602
Telephone (801) 378-3565
Fax (801) 378-4720
http://english.byu.edu/composition/comp.htm

ISBN 0-8425-2450-9

COPYRIGHT ACKNOWLEDGMENTS: Grateful acknowledgment is made to the following sources for permission to reprint material copyrighted or controlled by them:

Elouise Bell. "Reel Goddesses." Reprinted from *Only When I Laugh,* by permission of the author and Signature Books Inc., Salt Lake City, Utah.

R. Kirk Belnap "Scones, Anyone?" Reprinted from *Proceedings of the Deseret Language & Linguistics Society,* 1993. Used with permission of the author.

John Bennion. "The Burial Pool." Used with permission of the author. First published in *Christmas for the World,* an anthology of Christmas stories printed by Aspen Books.

Alvin K. Benson. "Geological Upheaval and Darkness in 3 Nephi 8-10." Used by permission of the author and BYU Religious Studies Center.

Allen E. Bergin. "Life and Testimony of an Academic Clinical Psychologist." Reprinted from *Expressions of Faith: Testimonies of Latter-day Saint Scholars,* edited by Susan Easton Black. Used by permission of the author and Deseret Book Company. Photocopies prohibited by law.

Grant Boswell. "The Narrative Logic of 1 Nephi 7: A Textual Analysis." Used by permission of the author.

William S. Bradshaw. "I Would Be a Purveyor of Mysteries." Reprinted from *Selected Essays,* 1986, by permission of the author.

Bonnie Brinton and Martin Fujiki. "Communication Skills and Community Integration in Adults with Mild to Moderate Retardation." Reprinted from *Topics in Language Disorders,* 1993, 16.4: 9–19. Used by permission of the authors and Aspen Publishers Inc.

Brian Dean Christensen. "Veiled Door." Used by permission of the artist.

David L. and Delys Cowles. "Living a Miracle." Reprinted with permission of the authors and *Brigham Young Magazine.* Copyright © August 1995 by David L. and Delys Cowles.

Paul Cox. "Conflict." Reprinted from *Nafanua.* Copyright © 1997 by W. H. Freeman and Company. Used with permission of the publisher.

Chris Crowe. "Self-Disclosure and Freshman Comp." Reprinted from *BYU Today,* July 1989: 48. Used by permission of the author and *Brigham Young Magazine.*

Garold and Norma Davis. "The Bombing of Dresden." Reprinted from *Behind the Iron Curtain.* Dorothea Speth Condie. "Let's Follow Dad—He Holds the Priesthood," reprinted from *Behind the Iron Curtain.* Used by permission of the authors and *BYU Studies.*

Richard Davis. "Preserving or 'Pickling' the Constitution." Reprinted from *BrighamYoung Magazine,* May 1995. Used with permission of the author and *Brigham Young Magazine.*

Kathryn Smoot Egan. "Writing from Real Life: Why Writers Keep Journals." First published in *Rough Draft,* Spring 1994. Used with permission of the author.

Eugene England. "Why More Utah Mormons Should Become Democrats: Reflections on Partisan Politics." Reprinted from *Making Peace: Personal Essays* by permission of the author and publisher. Copyright © 1965 by Signature Books Inc., Salt Lake City, Utah.

Earl H. Fry. "Canada—US Economic Relations: The Role of the Provinces and the States." Reprinted from *Business in the Contemporary World,* August 1990. Copyright © 1990 by John Wiley. Used by permission of the publisher.

Edward A. Geary. "Grandpa's Place." Reprinted from *Goodbye to Poplarhaven: Recollections of a Utah Boyhood* (Salt Lake City: University of Utah Press, 1985) and originally published by *Dialogue: A Journal of Mormon Thought,* by permission. Reprinted with the permission of the publisher and the author.

James D. Gordon. "Legal Writing." Reprinted from *Law School: A Survivor's Guide,* pp. 38–45. Used with permission of the author and HarperCollins Publishers, Inc. Copyright © 1994 by James D. Gordon III.

Jon D. Green. "Picasso's Visual Metaphors." Reprinted from *The Journal of Aesthetic Education,* Winter 1985, with permission of the author. Illustrations used with permission from SPADEM, Paris/VAGA, New York, New York.

B. Kent Harrison and Mary Stovall Richards. "Feminism in the Light of the Gospel of Jesus Christ." Reprinted from *BYU Studies,* 1996-1997 36.2. Used with permission of the authors and *BYU Studies* 1996–1997.

Gary Layne Hatch. "Logic in the Black Folk Sermon: The Sermons of C. L. Franklin." Reprinted from *Journal of Black Studies,* 26 (1996): 227–244. Published with the permission of the author and the *Journal of Black Studies,* Sage Publications.

Douglas Henderson. "The Misadventures of a NAFTA Scientist." Repinted from *Molecular Physics,* Vol. 86, pp. 551–565, 1995. Used by permission of the author, *Molecular Physics,* and Taylor & Francis Group.

Susan Elizabeth Howe. "To My Brother in His Casket." Reprinted from *The Literary Review,* Winter, 1990. Used by permission of the author and *The Literary Review.* "Gringa" copyright © by Susan Elizabeth Howe. Used by permission of the author.

Richard H. Jackson. "The Demise of the Drive-In Theater: A Small Town Landscape Feature Slowly Disappears." Used by permission of the author and *Small Towns Institute.* Copyright © by *Small Towns Institute,* PO Box 517, Eldensburg, WA 98926.

Cardell K. Jacobson. "Black Mormons in the 1980s: Pioneers in a White Church." Published originally in the *Review of Religious Research,* Vol. 33, No. 2 (December, 1991), pp. 146–152, and reprinted by permission of the Religious Research Association, Inc., 108 Marist Hall, Catholic University of America, Washington, DC 10064. Copyright © Religious Research Association, Inc.

Tyler J. and Heidi B. Jarvis. "Gambling: A Lie and a Snare." Used by permission of the authors.

Richard E. Johnson. "Wealth and Poverty." Reprinted from *BYU Today,* Sept 1990. Used with permission of the author and *Brigham Young Magazine.*

Bruce W. Jorgensen. "A Song for One Still Voice." Reprinted from *Ensign,* March, 1979. Used with permission of the author and *Ensign.*

Kate Kirkham. "Managing in a Diverse Workforce: From Incident to 'ism.'" Reprinted from *The Diversity Factor: Capturing the Competitive Advantage of a Changing Workforce*. Copyright © 1996 Irwin Professional Pub. Used by permission of the publisher.

Phillip R. Kunz. "Ice Cream Preference: The Relationship of Cost and Quality." Reproduced with permission of author and publisher. *Perceptual and Motor Skills,* 1985, 61, 229–230. Copyright © *Perceptual and Motor Skills* 1985.

Lance Larsen. "Nest," first published in the *Paris Review,* 143, Summer, 1997. "And Also Much Cattle," reprinted from *Salmagurdi.* Copyright © Lance Larsen. "Throwing Papers," reprinted from *Best of Writers at Work,* 1994. Copyright © Lance Larsen. Used by permission of the author and the publishers.

Suzanne Evertsen Lundquist. "Renewal through Reciprocity." Reprinted from *BYU Today,* May 1992: 31–37. Used by permission of the author and *Brigham Young Magazine.*

Sandra Mangum, Charlene Lind, H. Gill Hilton, and Carolyn Garisson. "First Impressions of the Nurse and Nursing Care." Reprinted/adapted with permission from *Journal of Nursing Care Quality,* June 1997: 11.5: 39–47. Copyright © 1997 Aspen Publishers Inc.

John J. Murphy. "Defending Polonius: A Response to Plummer's 'Ophelia Syndrome.'" Used by permission of the author.

Leslie Norris. "Peaches," "Christmas in Utah," and "Bridal Veil Falls, Early Winter." Reprinted from *Collected Poems.* Used by permission of the author and Seren Press, Bridgend, Wales. Copyright © Leslie Norris.

D. Kelly Ogden. "A Sampler of Biblical Plants." Reprinted from *Ensign,* August 1990: 35–39, with permission of the author and *Ensign.*

Joseph Evan Ostraff. "Kupesi 'O Tonga (Patterns of Tonga)." Used by permision of the artist.

Dennis Jay Packard. "Growing Up: From Peter Rabbit to Rabbi Goldman." Reprinted from *BYU Today,* April 1983: 14–17. Used by permission of the author and *Brigham Young Magazine.*

Pablo Picasso. "Bull's Head," "Still Life with Chair Caning," and "Guernica." Copyright ©1999 Estate of Pablo Picasso / Artists Rights Society (ARS), New York.

Danette Paul. "Creating Chaos." Used by permission of the author and Penn State University Press.

Louise Plummer. "First Things First." Reprinted from *Thoughts of a Grasshopper: Essays and Oddities,* pp. 1–5. Used by permission of the author and Deseret Book Company. Copies prohibited by law.

Thomas G. Plummer. "Diagnosing and Treating the Ophelia Syndrome." Reprinted from *BYU Today,* January 1991: 25–39. Used by permission of the author and *Brigham Young Magazine.*

Rex C. Reeve, Jr. "Dealing with Opposition to the Church." Reprinted from *The Book of Mormon: Alma, the Testimony of the Word.* Used with permission of the author.

Charles Schulz. PEANUTS cartoon. Reprinted by permission of United Feature Syndicate, Inc.

Royal Skousen. "Piecing Together the Original Manuscript." Reprinted from *BYU Today*, May 1992. Used by permission of the author and *Brigham Young Magazine*.

Steven P. Sondrup. "The Psalm of Nephi: A Lyric Reading." Used by permission of the author and *BYU Studies*.

Madison U. Sowell. "Why BYU? Education and Much More." Used with permission of the author.

John Sears Tanner. "The Real World." Reprinted from *College English,* October 1981, Vol. 43 No. 6. Used with permission of the author and the publisher.

Douglas Thayer. "Opening Day." Reprinted from *Under the Cottonwoods and Other Mormon Stories,* pp. 17–38, 1977. Used with permission of the author. Copyright © Douglas Thayer.

Jacqueline Thursby. "Folklore, Ethics, and Conflicted Narratives." Used by permission of the author.

Robert H. Todd and Takuto Tamada. "Quest for Relevance: Roles for Academia and Industry in Japan and the U.S." Reprinted from the *Journal in Engineering Education,* October 1997. Used by permission of the authors and ASEE.

Steven C. Walker. "Jonah as Joke: A Glance at God's Sense of Humor." Used with permission of the author.

C. Terry Warner. "An Open Letter to Students: On Having Faith and Thinking for Yourselves." Reprinted from *The New Era,* 1971. Used by permission of the author and the publisher.

Clayton M. White. "The Power of Landscape and Place: Inarticulate Speech of My Heart." Copyright © Clayton M. White, Professor of Zoology, Department of Zoology, Brigham Young University.

David D. Williams and William D. Eiserman. "Expanding the Dialogue: Service Learning in Costa Rica and Indonesia." Reprinted from *The Michigan Journal of Community Service Learning,* with permission of OCSL Press and the author.

Alan L. Wilkins and Michael P. Thompson. "On Getting the Story Crooked (And Straight)." Reprinted from *The Journal of Organizational Change Management* vol. 3 no. 3 1991 pp. 18–26. Copyright © MCB University Press. Used by permission of the publisher.

Bruce H. Woolley. "The Latest Fads to Increase Muscle Mass and Energy: A Look at What Some Athletes Are Using." Reprinted with permission from Woolley, B. H. *Postgraduate Medicine* 1991; 89 (2): 195–205. Copyright © The McGraw-Hill Companies.

Acknowledgments

The creation of *Enter to Learn* demonstrates two things that we hope our students will learn about writing. First, writing is a social act, often done best in collaboration. Perhaps, nothing demonstrates the collaborative nature of writing better than a collected edition such as *Enter to Learn.* Second, academic writing occurs in communities, where the audience consists of interested and committed individuals in the process of creating and evaluating knowledge. We want to thank our colleagues across campus who have generously shared their talents, writing, and research. Their contributions invite entering students to join the academic discourse in our BYU community. Thank you for your hard work and generosity.

Creating this book also confirms something that our students already know. Writing involves a great deal of work. The one person most responsible for seeing that this work continued at a steady pace (and a rather clip one at that!) is Karen Edwards Pierotti, our Composition Office Administrative Aide. Karen kept us and the staff moving along, tirelessly editing and managing this project. We simply cannot thank her enough for her dedicated work. We also had wonderful help in the form of insight, advice and editing from our colleagues in the Composition Office: Kristine Hansen and Penny Bird. We had a very fine editorial staff, whose help was invaluable: Ed Whitley, Matt Hall, Kent Minson, Linda Van Orden, Jeff Niekamp, Pat Madden and Brooks Briggs. In addition, we would like to thank the staff of the Reading/Writing Center for their help in editing and proofreading various drafts of the articles. We are particularly grateful for our Composition Office staff Carrie Standifird, Chantelle Turner, and Katie Willey for their work on this project.

The final lesson about writing that we can learn from the creation of this book (that all teachers of writing must know) is that the best writing comes in environments where there are feedback and support. Therefore, we would like to thank Jim Bell for reviewing this collection, and we would like to thank our colleagues in the English Department, particularly our Chairs, Jay Fox and John Tanner, for their support. Finally, we would like to thank our friends and families for their support throughout this process.

Gary Hatch, Coordinator of English Composition
Danette Paul, Associate Coordinator of English Composition

Table of Contents

Looking Forward and Back: An Introduction

DANETTE PAUL

On the cover of this book is a lithograph entitled "Greek (Archaic Period) Double Portrait Bust of Hermes/Hercules" by BYU art professor Wayne Kimball. This print invites us to ask questions about the relationships between the items in the print and about the relationship between the print and this book. The first question we might ask is, What does a broken Greek statue have to do with education? That is a good question because it asks about relationships. Our answer: While this print does not represent your 115 class, our interpretations of the issues it explores reflect the university's dualistic experience and other important issues that you'll encounter in negotiating your educational experience. A closer look at Professor Kimball's print may illustrate our argument or may lead you to ask additional questions. In this introduction, we'll try to show the relationship between the print and education by asking a series of questions: What does the Janus figure (the double head) mean? Why name the faces Hercules and Hermes? What is the relationship between the classic figure in the foreground and the screen and green plants in the background?

A JANUS MOMENT: ENTERING TO LEARN

First, who is Janus and what is he doing in the print and on the cover of this book? In visual representations, location indicates relationships and values. The Janus figure in the print is in the middle of the foreground, making it literally front and center. Therefore, Janus, the Roman god of entrances, doorways, and beginnings, is the central figure in Kimball's print. In Roman mythology, Janus is the god of beginnings because he is the father of the gods and the creator. So what is a Roman-god figure doing on a Greek statue? Perhaps, it has to do with his role as creator. Why? First, Janus is the god of beginnings. That interpretation is still present, in our language. Janus is the root for "January," the beginning of the year, and for "janitor" as the guardian of doorway or entrances and keeper of the keys. Second, our culture most often attributes the birth of our western civilization (including art, mathematics, philosophy, and rhetoric) to first the Greek and then Roman empires. Third, the title tells us that the artistic style of the statue represents work from the Archaic Period. While the word "archaic" may imply a value judgement, for artists, the Archaic Period is a distinct period of time in Greek art history. This time period immediately precedes the Classical period, which is considered the height of Greek art. In addition, the root of the word "archaic" means beginning. Therefore, the Archaic Period also seems to represent origins. Finally, the statue of a Janus figure is a creation which represents a creator, indicating a relationship between the origins of and the act of creation and the creator's relation to both. Like Janus, the artist seems to be looking back to the origins of art and looking forward to its creation and trying to negotiate his relationship to both.

Entering freshmen find themselves in a similar Janus-like position. Every time we begin a new part of our lives, we quite naturally pause for a moment and look back. And then, we look forward, peering into the distance, trying, in some sense, to see our future. In fact, the desire to look in both directions at once may be so strong that we feel as if our head is spinning. If stopped at that moment, as if frozen in time, we might appear like the Janus figure on the cover of this book—a head with two faces, one looking forward, one looking back—a moment of decision and indecision, of future and past.

While arriving at college with these opposing perspectives might make you feel slightly off balance, the university actually tries to bridge this gap, by attempting to understand the past in order to shape the future. The bridge between past and future is an ongoing search for knowledge. Kenneth Burke, a modern philosopher, describes the search for knowledge as a conversation. The members of the academic community participate in a long conversation that started long ago and will continue in the future. This conversation takes place face-to-face, in print, and over electronic media such as email and the net. To join in the conversation, we read, conduct experiments, listen to lectures, engage in discussions, and surf the net, trying to understand the past. At the same time, we try to push into the future by asking new questions, explaining unexpected results, and trying new research methods. As we write, we envision the future—in journal articles, lab reports, proposals and books. Not surprisingly then, reading and writing are central to our attempts to understand and analyze the past and to explore and negotiate the future.

Those entering the conversation (like new students) must try to understand and explore various positions or relationships both within the university community and the larger community outside the university. They must look back to their origins or the origins of their education and look forward to their future education. After all, Janus's two faces, according to Richard Carlyon, signify "past wisdom and future knowledge" (189). Therefore, new participants in the academic conversation must first look back to their "past wisdom" then look forward to future knowledge. On the threshold of your college experience, you may not feel that you possess any past wisdom. However, there are different ways of knowing. Past wisdom is not necessarily defined as high school or even college experiences. All knowledge does not come out of a text book or even out of school. For instance, we know things by reading, by experimenting, and by our own experiences.

In the *Enter to Learn* section entitled, "Telling Our Stories," faculty members share the past wisdom that they have gathered from their experiences both in and out of the university. These stories relate experiences that help the authors to make decisions that shaped their future, such as their choices of professions, of spouses, of belief. The writers also look to past genre traditions to help them negotiate the balance between form and content. Therefore, the level of artistry (i.e., the relationship between form and content) varies depending on both the author's purpose and the genre. Some are transcripts of oral accounts; others are highly crafted poems. Finally, the writers must negotiate between the actual event(s) and the story they wish to tell in order to create new knowledge. In each case fiction or nonfiction, the authors strive to tell a story that acts as an invitation to respond—just as the print invites our response.

Hermes and Hercules: Words and Actions

The next question we might ask about Kimball's print is, Why does the artist call the two faces Hermes and Hercules? Why not call it/them Janus and be done with it? These questions are even more interesting when we see that the portraits—both in profile and both with a broken-off nose—are practically identical. So why give each face a different name and why these particular names? We can begin to answer these questions by considering what we know of Hermes and Hercules. While most of us are familiar with Hercules, especially with the recent Kevin Sorbo and Disney versions of the Greek hero, we may be unfamiliar with Hermes. Hermes's only appearance in pop culture is as the FTD Florist symbol and then only as the Roman version, Mercury. Hermes is a Greek god known for his speed; therefore, the gods used him as the divine messenger when they wished to communicate with mortals. To improve these communications, Hermes invented language. This invention, however, did not always make for clear understanding because language must always be interpreted. While Hermes is associated with speed and communication, Hercules is associated with strength and actions. Hercules is the son of Zeus and a mortal woman, giving him superhuman strength and eventually immortality. To win the favor of Zeus's wife, Hera, Hercules performed twelve "impossible" tasks, known as the labors of Hercules. Considering this information, the contrast between the two characters couldn't be greater: speed and strength, talk and action.

Yet by joining these two faces together, the artist invites us to explore the relationship between these characters and these concepts. Furthermore, the similarity in the portraits, the similarity in these names and the fact that the names are not assigned to a particular face invites us to see them as similar. Creating and naming these faces seems to link interpretation (the message) to creation (the act). Kimball seems to be implying that interpretation and creation are reflective practices. In other words, the two practices are inseparably connected—like reading and writing—you can't do one without the other. An artist cannot create without interpreting the world around him, any more than a scholar can interpret without creating or recreating the art in her own analysis.

In the university, scholars take on both the task of interpreting Hermes's messages and the Herculean labor of doing research. Naturally, interpretation and research are also reflective practice. Whether working in an archive or a lab, scholars must research to interpret and interpret to research. In *Enter to Learn,* the section entitled, "Listening to Others," is a collection of texts that focus on interpretation. While all these interpretations are in the form of written texts, not all texts are written. Therefore, in "Listening to Others," we start with texts that we commonly interpret—the scriptures—and take an academic look at them. Then we look at a variety of texts for analysis that includes paintings, movies and academic genres. In each case, the author is looking at past wisdom (embodied in the texts they study and the historical context in which the text was produced) and trying to understand it in light of our present knowledge.

The articles in the section entitled, "Creating Knowledge," begin with present knowledge, then push the borders of that knowledge to create future knowledge. In this section, we try to present the variety of both the types of research questions asked and the methodologies used to answer research questions. Here too, we start with items of local interest and move to a more global perspective. Although textbooks sometimes imply that knowledge is static or fixed, in academic discourse, knowledge is fluid and changing, like a conversation. Scholars must look around (with the help of listservs, conferences, articles, and books) and interpret the current state of knowledge in their field. In doing so, they determine what questions have yet to be answered—looking forward to future knowledge.

Negotiating Relationships: Going Forth to Serve

The final question we must ask about the print is, What is the relationship between the Janus figure and the other items in the print? In the print, the Janus figure in the foreground as we have argued above seems to represent the origins, history, practices and interpretation. This combination seems to imply a classical, perhaps, traditional approach to art. It may even encompass an academic approach to art and the creation of art. In the background is a green, vibrant plant. Traditionally, in literature and the fine arts, green plants (even the color green) represent life, growth, and nature. In contrast with green plants, are we to see the ancient, white, broken statue as enduring or as archaic (perhaps, the title provides a clue)? Are we to see the artificial (as in crafted), but enduring statue as greater (of more value) than the natural, but temporal plant? Is it just another way of looking to the past and the future? Or is the statue a remnant of an archaic—old-fashioned—approach that is dead and colorless when compared to life?

The plant and the statue are separated by a third item or items, a matching pair, filling most of the print. What are they? How do they mediate the representions of the plant and the statue? These long rectangular shapes rounded on the top look like stone tablets, church windows, or tombstones. Does this imply that the screen is associated with religious practices? Are they acting as a screen or as doors? Are they opened or bent? The texture of these items looks like stone, perhaps wood. What is their function? If it is a screen, is it protecting civilization from the jungle or is it shutting out life? Or does the screen provide a compromise between nature and art, allowing both a place? As can be seen by these questions, the relationship among the screen, the statue (the Janus figure) and the plant is central to negotiating meaning. Perhaps, this very negotiation represents the question the print poses but does not necessarily answer.

In your education and career, you will have to negotiate three approaches: those of traditional education, religion and the "real" world. You will have to determine the relationship among your traditional liberal arts' education (with its origins in ancient Greece), your religious standards and practices, and your obligations to the "real" world. In the final section of *Enter to Learn,* we examine how other scholars have negotiated these relationships. We look at several methods of entering the academic discourse in ways that are both productive and ethical.

All of the articles in this book invite you to enter the conversations and learn. We hope as you look forward, peering into your future, you will negotiate your educational and professional opportunities so that you may go forth to service.

Work Cited

Carlyon, Richard. *A Guide to the Gods: An Essential Guide to World Mythology.* New York: Quill William Morrow, 1981.

Cover Art:
"Greek (Archaic Period) Double Portrait Bust of Hermes/Hercules" by Wayne Kimball

WAYNE KIMBALL *is a professor in the Department of Visual Arts, where he teaches courses in lithography, drawing, and color. His bachelor's degree was earned at the College of Southern Utah (now Southern Utah University), he received an MFA at the University of Arizona, and became certified as a master printer at Tamarind Institute, University of New Mexico. His prints have been exhibited widely in solo exhibitions and in competitive and invitational groups shows. Although his work is very carefully drawn and reflects his fondness for Flemish detail, its structure and development derive from processes associated with Analytical and Synthetic Cubism. This print is no exception, being a collection of widely disparate visual elements gathered from various sources and assembled into a tightly structured visual collage.*

Telling our Stories

Telling stories is an integral part of life. As folklorist William Wilson explains, a "swirl of stories . . . has surrounded us since we were born—stories we listen to or tell about the events of everyday life and the worlds we occupy."[1] While we may have grown up loving the bedtime stories Mom read or the funny stories Dad told about our family, we don't often associate stories with the rigorous academic standards—accurate, factual, and important. However, stories are an important part of the academic conversations. They are found in many forms, such as oral histories, narratives, memoirs, poetry. They serve many functions. They serve as evidence, examples, enlightenment, even entertainment. For example, Alan Bergin tells a series of stories to explain the relationship between his spiritual and academic life. Clayton White tells stories to show how nature enlightens him while Chris Crowe entertains us with his attempts to become a writer. The most important function stories perform is to build a relationship between the storyteller and the audience, which we call *ethos.* The right stories can help the audience to trust and to understand the author while making the point of the argument more clear.

In this section, we provide a variety of academic genres for telling our stories, beginning with the forms or genres that seem more natural, such as Kate Egan's essay on journal writing and Dorothea Condie's oral history of the bombing of Dresden, then moving to progressively more crafted pieces, ending with the highly stylized poems of Lance Larsen, Susan Howe and Leslie Norris. To tell your own stories in academic settings, you must learn the appropriate forms and functions. Then, your stories will bring your voice into the academic conversation that shapes our world and our understanding of it.

[1]"In Praise of Ourselves: Stories to Tell," *BYU Studies*, Vol. 30, Winter 1990, p. 6.

Writing from Real Life: Why Writers Keep Journals

KATHRYN SMOOT EGAN

Kathryn Smoot Egan has had a long-time interest in pioneer diaries. As she has read and studied these diaries, she has come to understand how diaries can help a writer when creating a work of fiction. She says that, essentially, "life is a fiction." This particular article came out of a workshop that she gave to adults designed to help them write creative works using their own diaries as a base. Egan encourages writers, when looking over their diaries, "to transcend the personal to find the parts that really matter." She says that doing so will greatly enhance creative writing and will "make living life creative." "Writing from Real Life" was first published in Rough Draft *in 1994.*

All writing is autobiographical. Writers craft stories based upon their own experience, both real and imagined. If the story is based on fact, the writing becomes a matter of selection. A journalist selects from the facts of a situation the ones she needs to tell the story she wants to report. That act of selection is one thing that makes reporters necessarily non-objective.

Art, in this case fiction, also is a matter of selection. Just as a painter chooses which tree he will paint to depict the entire forest, so the writer selects, carefully, the details from real life that will be used to make a story. Details from reality are moved around, blown up, metamorphosed into shapes that may not resemble anything in the author's reality, except as symbol. The foundation of imagined stories is still experience—the writer's—and is, therefore, autobiography.

Journal keeping provides a tool for collecting and tracking experience. Whether the journal is the writer's or someone else's, it becomes a cache of human realities, complete with characters, historical information, background, emotions, and even plots. The writer's work is to make fictional sense of what's there. That's easier to do with someone else's journal than one's own.

Beginning writers may benefit from Annie Dillard's perspective:

> I don't think you can write to express what you want to say. You write when there's something you want to make, an object into which you can pour all that's deepest within you, but not directly. The focus must be outside yourself.

Pam Houston, author of *Cowboys Are My Weakness* (W. W. Norton, 1992), says people accuse her of writing ten days behind her own life. If so, she's a master at perceiving the meaning and the symbolism in the events and people that pass through her life in realtime, while the events are taking place, while the people are right there. Ten days for rumination about "what does it all mean?" and the story pops out on her word processor.

"The natural world is like us," Pam said at the Writers at Work conference last year in Park City. "I'm thinking 'see how much you are like the dog? Isn't the world just like you?' But I don't say this. If it comes to the surface and is too obvious I should throw the writing away."

In her stories, people Pam knows might become dogs. Or lovers. But they are not just any dogs or lovers; they become real in her fiction because of the detail she selects. In her short story, "Jackson is Just One Of My Dogs," she writes:

> While Jackson is clearly a human being trapped in a dog's body (one day he lost his senses and buried a bone in the yard and I was no more embarrassed for him than he was for himself), Hailey knows what she is and is proud of it. What she likes to do, more than anything, is to get her belly wet and then lie around in the dirt. Jackson is athletic, graceful, obnoxious, and filled with conceit, while Hailey is slow, a little fat, and gentle to her bones.

I don't know whether Pam keeps a journal; if not, her memory for detail, at just the time she is writing her story, is phenomenal. But then Pam is relatively young. If one is going to write from time and distance, a journal helps keep the details fresh—and useable as symbols.

Writing Fiction from Other People's Journals

My two published novels are based on other men's and women's journals and my own. I also read newspapers and magazines from the period I described, including *Godey's Ladies Book* to get the hair styles and fashions right. I read the *Salt Lake Tribune* from 1889 to 1898 to get the dates and a sense of language to describe polygamist trials in Utah in the late 1890s. My own journals helped me describe towns, landscapes, and the feel of sitting in weeds next to a river in late August, and the dust-covered trunks in my grandmother's attic in Provo, Utah.

One line from a journal of a life the writer probably thought quotidian can evoke a world or an emotion. Some examples:

From Jane Richard's diary from 1846: (She was sick, alone, her husband in England, her two-year-old daughter dead from sadness and starvation, her newborn son dead from hardship. Jane had just been told by Brigham Young, "It shall be said of you that you have come up through much tribulation.")

> I only lived because I could not die.

Patty Sessions, pioneer mid-wife, wrote April 6, 1846:

> I rode behind the man and through mud and water some of the way belly deep to the horse. I found the sister that I was called to in an old log cabin. Her child was born before I got there. She had rode 13 miles after she was in travail.

My own journals are difficult to fictionalize. I'm too close to the people and events. I tried writing about them anyway, and the writing resembled *True Confessions*, when I talked about relationships, and *National Geographic*, when I described the setting. What happens when you try to write from journals and you aren't Pam Houston—you are too entrenched in your people, too traumatized by the events—is that you write several versions (drafts) based on the material. The writing evolves from static to fiction when you gain objectivity, and when you write from the subconscious so that real things become something else ("metaphor" here is too high fallutin').

I did what many women in my situation have done: I wrote about myself as victim. Because passive characters, like passive language, are boring, they do not make good fiction. As Bob Shacochis, author of *Swimming in the Volcano* (Scribners, 1993), said, "Nothing could be more undesirable than being a victim." He claims that although bad things happen to the characters in his novel, all but one chose the circumstances that lead to tragedy. That makes them, Shacochis says, casualties, not victims.

My victim draft served a purpose: it was cathartic. The "husband" in my book, however, was two-dimensional and strident. I hadn't achieved the psychological goal in my personal life—forgiveness—that would provide the objectivity I needed to write the "husband" as three-dimensional, which means he had to have a good side. The "wife" had to have a blind side to make her real. Those changes came three drafts later. I define "drafts" here as completed, novel manuscripts. Yes, I started over—as in new people, new approach—four times. I am now on my fourth draft. "Audrey," the main character, has become "Sheila," which means blind. She is no longer me. The children are no longer my children. The husband is someone I made up—from experience with three husbands. All mine.

Which suggests another problem: sometimes life is too grandiose, too fantastic, and dramatic to make good fiction. It might make a great soap opera script—but even for a soap you must tame what goes on. You cannot simply report what "really happened." Truth must be distorted, stretched, minimalized, shoved to the subconscious, in order to become convincing as story. The best place for reality is a journal. Recorded in daily passages, you can go back to it again and again. What you find is that over time, the event you thought was sealed in stone, like cuneiform, changes. You see it differently, even though the words are right there in ink. It's like reading someone else's story. You bring to the reading your own new circumstances, and even more important, your understanding of what things mean.

That's the foundation for creating fiction from reality, from experience.

Writing Fiction from Your Own Journal

In *The Principle*, I wrote:

> "We were never allowed in the parlor," he said, as they stood at the edge of the ornate carpet, surveying the carefully-kept room, the one with the carved lion heads on the chair arms and the gleaming black piano. "So this is where I hid most." He showed her a place in the alcove, in the corner behind the massive table that held the family Bible. The alcove was just big enough to hold a coffin and allow people to walk around it, for it was intended as a viewing niche. Just behind the Bible was a perfect place to hide.

The description of the parlor is from my journal, which I have kept irregularly since age eight. The parlor is in my grandmother's house, which is the setting of the novel. I did not know until I studied the architectural drawings of the house, and talked to a historical architect at the Utah State Historical Society, that the niche I thought of as a "reading corner" (because that's what my grandmother told me) was intended as a viewing niche for the deceased. Funerals took place at home in the 1890s. The knowledge added considerably to the tone of my story. That's how new experience adds to old. That's how new understanding adds layers and makes the story fiction.

ORGANIZING AND KEEPING A WRITER'S JOURNAL

I keep my journal in 9" x 6", 3-ring binders. One binder per year. I write in it nearly every night. Whatever comes to mind as I'm going to sleep goes into the journal. Sometimes it's a bad experience or worry I'm trying to sort out. Other times it's something wonderful that happened that day. The entry might describe a person or event, a scene I saw from the bus window.

The problem for me, the writer, is in trying to retrieve the specifics when I need them. So I have learned to categorize some of the entries. Following the general "journal" tab, which is the bulk of my writing, are other tabs that divide my binder into sections. There is a "character" tab, a "settings" tab, a "story plots" tab, and sections for "new words," "background," and "technicalities." Each year the journal section is stored in its binder. The writing sections go into next year's binder; they cumulate over the years. I now have a large section on characters, for example.

I collect characters. I see them wherever I go and make up stories to go with them. I once described a woman at the hospital where my daughter was in a croup tent with pneumonia:

> Fat, white lady, sitting on a stool talking on the phone. Blond short mannish hair, wearing ballet slippers with white socks, white bulging pants, like a huge elastic support stocking. Hung up phone, put on cowboy boots. Informed those of us waiting on couches, waiting to hear from someone about a patient, that if the phone rang she'd be in 452.

What this does for the writer is: make waiting in airports and hospitals productive, and provide a file of people descriptions that may suggest a character for a piece of fiction. It also provides practice in descriptive writing, which a writer never gets enough of. The fat, white lady description is still in my journal. I used her in a short story about my son, whom I had to keep awake overnight for an EEG test the next morning. The woman became a hotel guest, and my son became a girl. The narrative voice is that of a nurse.

That sort of transmogrification is one of the tools for making real experience fictional. You have to do that with the people in your stories; real people who become characters must have traits exaggerated beyond everyday recognition. One way of changing real life to fiction is to change the gender of the person you are writing about. Or the age. Or, make the bad guy from your experience the good guy in your fiction.

Settings are different. They can be taken, as is, and set into stories. I take my journal wherever I go so that I can collect settings. I pack blank, lined pages in a manila envelope—easier to carry than a three-ring binder—which I keep next to my passport. It's that important to me. I have described the Acropolis and Delphi in Greece, petroglyphs on a hill-side in Northern California, and a watercress encrusted pond, before and after a herd of cattle walked through it. The blue hole I walked to—through stickers and sharp lava beds—on Cat Island in the Bahamas is as significant as a character in my young adult novel, *Chandelle*.

"Facts" and "technicalities" are also categories that remain as-is, from real life into fiction. I collect facts. Right now I'm enamored of the chaos theory and its boundaries, and the idea of creating something wonderful from seemingly unpredictable pieces of floating debris—in organizations or universes. My favorite writer is Stephen Hawking because he makes my mind soar. I was once a medical science writer. Concentration on the science, the facts, allowed my subconscious free reign. I can't be Michael Crichton, never Stephen King, but maybe I could create a motherly character who solves social problems innovatively. How about a romance novel based on the quantum theory of reality: everything is reducible to light or matter, whatever it is that you are looking to find. The ultimate irreducible "thing" in the universe is relationship. Relationships are what count. Facts are groundwork for fiction; a phenomenon might serve as a sort of singularity for an explosion of an idea.

Some facts I have set down in my "technicalities" section:

• The invention of weaving made life possible in climates north of the Mediterranean.

• Wheat made families possible.

• The most popular kind of writing among women of the upper and middle classes following Gutenberg's invention of moveable type (and therefore printing) were romances.

• Stephen Hawking's explanation of the Big Bang theory does not account for what happened in the first nanosecond before the singularity exploded; therefore he has not disproved God.

WHY MOTHERS WHO WOULD BE WRITERS KEEP JOURNALS

Parenthood, full or part-time, has its frustrations, especially for would-be writers. Writing while caring for children can be done. Judith Viorst wrote columns for *Redbook* while waiting in physician's offices, in traffic jams, while doing housework. She wrote children's books based on her insights from being with her boys. Not all of us can be Judith. I tried—I even knew about her process and couldn't hack it. I got up at 3:00 AM to finish *The Principle*. It was the only time I had to myself.

I also kept a journal during those days of joy and frustration. Now I have the experiences set down in ragged writing (I write in bed, last thing before I go to sleep) but in detail I can use. The entries evoke memories clear as today's in full color and animation. I remember the smells, the feathers flying around our kitchen the first time my husband plucked one of our chickens. The experience of birthing pups. Of saving a calf. The day I had to help the vet geld our yearling horse. The moment I realized my children were arguing about who got to say the A&W lines for a commercial on our radio station—and they were live, on the air. And they'd locked the door to the radio station's control room.

I wish I had known then that writing about the events in my journal, as ungrammatical and poor as the writing was, would preserve the day. Knowing that could have saved me from frustration, could have made my time with my children more pleasurable. So I pass this along to anyone who wants to write but believes she is prevented from doing so because of her children's needs: keep a journal now. Get it all down. As with grapes and investments, passing years are good for journals. Time will make stories from real life.

KATHRYN EGAN *is an associate professor of communications at BYU. She is the author of two works of fiction,* The Principle *and* Starlight, *which are based upon the journals of women who lived in plural marriages. She also writes a bi-weekly column for the Sunday* Salt Lake Tribune *called "Media Watch." She received her doctorate in instructional technology at the University of Southern California, her master's degree in journalism from Northwestern University, and her bachelor's in journalism at the University of Utah.*

Questions and Activity

1. Why does Egan argue that all writing is autobiographical? Do you agree?
2. Egan argues for both selection and detail. How does she work out this potential contradiction in her essay?

3. Compare Egan's idea that "sometimes life is too grandiose, too fantastic, and dramatic to make good fiction" to Louise Plummer's "First Things First."
4. Begin making your own "writer's journal" for your personal narrative paper. Do things like: draw a map of your neighborhood and mark the places where things that were important to you occurred; go through old photographs and write about the day when the photo was taken. Include things such as details about the people involved, the feelings you experienced, the way it changed your life; keep a journal of how you feel right now and relate it to things you've experienced in the past.

The Bombing of Dresden

Garold and Norma Davis

Garold Davis transcribed the following story, "Let's Follow Dad—He Holds the Priesthood," from an interview he conducted with Dorothea Speth Condie, and then included it in a collection of stories he compiled with his wife, Norma Davis, called Behind the Iron Curtain: Recollections of Latter-day Saints in East Germany. *The Davises chose this story for their collection because they knew that Condie was a teenager in Germany during World War II. Her story is, as the Davises say, "in many ways representative of the experiences of Church members throughout Germany." In May 1945, a few months after the bombing incident in Condie's story, the Soviet Union occupied "East Germany." In 1949 they formed the "German Democratic Republic." "Let's Follow Dad," preceded by the Davis's introduction to the collection, is about Condie's experience with a bombing raid in Dresden, Germany, in 1945 in which she shares how their family was spared because they chose to follow her father as they sought refuge from the fires.*

Dresden was the oldest area of The Church of Jesus Christ of Latter-day Saints in the eastern part of Germany. In 1939, at the beginning of the war, two branches thrived, one located in the older part of the city, the *Altstadt Gemeinde,* and the other located across the Elbe River in the "newer" part of the city, the *Neustadt Gemeinde.* In 1945 toward the end of the war, these two branches persisted in Dresden in spite of the loss of many men who were away serving in the German army.

The bombing of Dresden on February 13–14, 1945, was as unsuspected as it was destructive. Because of its location far to the southeast, Dresden had been spared the bombings the German cities further to the northwest had experienced. By 1945 the war was essentially over. The German armies were retreating rapidly. The German air defenses were gone. The Russian armies were closing in on Berlin and were at the outskirts of Dresden. But then the unexpected and unthinkable happened. The "Florence on the Elbe" was destroyed, and with it went one of the branches of the Church. The following eyewitness accounts of the bombing are in many ways representative of the experiences of Church members throughout Germany.

Let's Follow Dad—He Holds the Priesthood

Dorothea Speth Condie

February 13, 1945, is an unforgettable day in the lives of thousands of people who were living in Dresden, Germany. World War II was in full fury, with armed forces on all sides pushing towards the German borders trying to end this terrible war.

We felt quite safe in our city of Dresden, the "Florence on the Elbe," with its many cultural, historic, and architectural treasures. Surely no one would try to destroy these. There was no heavy industry in the region, and this late in the war the population consisted primarily of women, children, and the elderly. However, burgeoning numbers of wounded and sick and thousands of refugees arrived daily from the German settlements beyond the Polish border. Even though all the other major cities of Germany had experienced numerous air raids, Dresden had been spared this terrible destruction.

It was 10:30 that February night when we first heard the dreadful sounds of the sirens and the roar of hundreds of planes and the explosions of the first bombs. When my father looked outside, he noticed strange-looking lights in the shape of Christmas trees lighting the dark sky and the darkened city. These were the flares used to guide the bombers.

We lived on the fourth floor of an apartment building and quickly realized that we needed to get downstairs, to the basement, which served as our bomb shelter. The first air raid lasted about forty-five minutes, and many homes in our neighborhood were set ablaze. But the area hardest hit was the inner city, where every building seemed to be engulfed in flames. For the time being, we seemed to be safe, but with the electricity, gas, and all communications cut off, we decided to remain in the basement for the rest of the night.

Around 1:30 AM, we realized that the planes had returned and that bombs were exploding all around us. Would a bomb hit our house? Would only some or any of us still be alive in one minute or ten minutes or when this air raid ended? It was a terrifying experience! But when the silence finally returned, we were all still alive.

We were alive; however, we were trapped in the basement. One of the first bombs of the second air raid hit our corner house at an angle, setting the ground floor on fire so that the building started burning from the bottom upward. The stairway, our only exit, was already blocked by the fire.

The only way out was a hole in our basement wall connecting the basement with the house next door. The hole had been made for this very purpose, but it was barely big enough to crawl through. We couldn't take anything with us. Our family and an older couple who lived on our floor managed to escape through this hole.

Most of the homes in our area of the city were now destroyed or burning, and the few that remained would soon be on fire. We all realized that we needed to get away from the burning houses immediately! Walking on the streets looked very dangerous because a firestorm with the force of a hurricane was raging, sending thousands of sparks and burning objects flying through the air, fueling and spreading the fires. In the streets, there were also many huge bomb craters adding to the danger.

Once outside, we gathered as a family and quickly held a council. My family consisted of my parents, my two older sisters, my twin sister, and myself. It was imperative that we not get separated as we set out to reach the Elbe River. The Elbe with its wide banks would be a perfect haven from the fire and the smoke that was starting to sting our eyes.

For the last time, we all looked at our house and all that we owned in this life, knowing that the flames would soon reach the upper level. We lived on a very nice wide street leading directly to the river, which was about four blocks from where we stood. For safety, we did not all walk together. My father took one of my older sisters and my twin sister and began to lead the way. My mother, my oldest sister, and I were to follow as closely as possible. As my father started walking, he headed towards a narrow side street instead of choosing the wide street which led directly to our goal, to the river. Mother stopped, not wanting to follow down the narrow, burning street and began calling Dad to try to persuade him to turn around and take the more direct route along our street, which seemed so much safer and quicker. But due to the firestorm, Dad could not hear her plea, and he continued walking along the narrow side street.

With each passing second, the distance between us increased, but Mom was still not willing to abandon her plan. Then I heard my older sister plead with her, "Mom, let's follow Dad; he holds the Priesthood!" With this reminder, we started to move quickly, trying to catch up with Dad, who led us safely in a roundabout way down to the river. We followed several other people into an old hospital building, where we could finally sit down, rest, wait out the night, and be protected from the firestorm and its terror.

After we had been there a short time, a neighbor lady entered the building. She and her elderly husband had lived on the top floor of our building for many years, and they had become our very good friends. But now she was alone, extremely upset and crying. As soon as she regained her composure, she told us that after she and her husband had left our burning building, they decided to walk straight down the wide street to the river. Her husband, tall and slender, walked very quickly leading the way, but she, somewhat short and heavy, could not follow so quickly and lagged behind. Suddenly she saw her husband burnt alive in front of her eyes. Unknown to anyone, liquid phosphorous from one of the bombs had covered the street. It could not be seen but was immediately ignited whenever anyone stepped on it. There was nothing she could do to save her husband, she could only turn around and save herself.

We did what we could to comfort her and then said a silent prayer of thanksgiving that we had been spared. If we had not followed our father, we would have walked right into that liquid phosphorus. I learned that night how important it is that we follow the priesthood.

When daylight finally arrived, we started to walk along the river away from the death and destruction. We were part of a pilgrimage of thousands of people who were tired and homeless and in shock after what had happened. The injured remained behind, lining the path. These are images one can never forget! The smoke was so thick and stung our eyes so badly that we had to wet our handkerchiefs and put them to our eyes to relieve the burning sensation.

Thoughtful neighbors, whose homes had survived the destruction, offered us refugees warm drinks and sympathetic smiles. We really did not know where to go, but we decided to stop at the home of some Church members to let them know that we were alive. We arrived at their house in Leuben around 12 noon, just at the end of another air raid. The Dünnebeil family greeted us with tears of joy in their eyes to see us alive and took us into their apartment, where we enjoyed the luxury of a bath and a bed to sleep in and an opportunity for some much needed rest.

Sister Dünnebeil, her son Dieter, and Grandpa Dünnebeil, with their big hearts and love for the gospel and their fellowmen, had opened their home to several of us homeless families. Their three-bedroom apartment had welcomed the Deus family—a mother, grandmother, and four children—and Sister Sawatzki and her two young children—both refugee families from the East—and now our family of six. At night, to make things a little less crowded, my father slept on the couch at the home of an older couple, Brother and Sister Meyer, who lived close by. My mother and one of us children walked a few blocks to the home of an older sister who had an extra twin bed. Everyone else slept wall-to-wall on Dünnebeils' living room floor, thanks to some more good neighbors who helped with the bedding.

How long could we live this way? This was a temporary, not a permanent, solution. Were there any vacant apartments in this destroyed city with tens of thousands of homeless people? Only a miracle could make this dream come true, but "with God nothing is impossible!"

After about two weeks, a knock came to the door. A good friend of ours asked us to follow him. Herr Hubold was not a member of the Church, but his wife and two children were baptized and were very active in our little branch. He also attended meetings quite often. He was on the board of directors of a private housing development which had survived the bombing. After that terrible night in Dresden, the housing board held a special meeting. Several families who had small children had temporarily left their apartments in order to seek safety in the country or with relatives in other parts of Germany. The question was raised, "Should not some homeless families, even if only temporarily, be invited to occupy these empty apartments?" But how does one select a handful of families out of tens of thousands in need? Herr Hubold asked for permission to invite his friends to move into these vacant dwellings. Permission was granted, and we and three other LDS families who had lost everything had a place to call home, fully furnished.

They were modest apartments with only one big bedroom, but we were deeply grateful and felt richly blessed. None of us had to leave the apartments at the end of the war, since none of the families wanted to return to Dresden and live in the Communist-occupied territory of East Germany.

When the Russians came in, they decided, for some reason, to set up their camp right there on the street where we lived. The Russian soldiers did not have a good reputation with young girls, and there were about four or five teenage girls in the LDS families living there, including my two older sisters. They all came to our house because my father was the only priesthood holder at the time and they didn't feel safe alone. It was about 10:00 at night, and everybody was afraid. When those Russian soldiers come and knock on your door, there is nothing you can do about it. You just have to let them in. At about 10:30, we noticed they were packing up. They were leaving. Near the apartment complex was a big racetrack. That was a good place to set up a camp, so at 10:30 at night they suddenly decided to move over there and set up. Afterward, we were told that one of the big communist leaders in Dresden, who had greeted the Russian army with a white flag, lived in that apartment complex, and he had a young teenage daughter. Even though he was a Communist, he was also a father and didn't like the soldiers camping right in our neighborhood. He used his influence and got them moved.

A few days later, the Russian soldiers received permission to go into any German home and take whatever they liked. They could plunder the homes and do whatever they wanted. I remember when they came into our house. You could hear them coming up the stairs in their big heavy boots. I think there were about three of them who came into our apartment. Of course, we didn't own much. I remember that after the bombing in which we lost everything, we received a second set of clothing and an extra pair of shoes, and that was about it.

We put anything that we didn't want them to take on the couch and put a blanket over it. Then my sister and I sat on the couch playing, trying to hide these things. The Russian soldiers looked through the apartment. One thing my mother had somehow saved from the bombing was an 8 x 10 picture of my brother, who had been killed during the war. It was the only picture we had of him, and he was in his uniform. The picture was hanging on the wall, and the Russian soldiers didn't like that—a soldier in a German uniform. They wanted to take the picture, and my mother really got upset. Somehow she got the message across to them that he was her only son who had been killed, so they didn't take the picture. They ended up taking one of Dad's suits and a pair of shoes, and then they left.

During World War II, we always had enough to eat, and we still had enough of a variety of things to eat. Things were rationed, but we still had enough sugar, we still could buy some chocolate, and we still had meat at least for Sundays or once during the week. We always had enough bread, and we always had enough potatoes. I never remember being hungry. But after the war, when the Communists, the Russians, came in, then we really went without. We ate bread with nothing on it and sometimes potatoes. There just wasn't enough to eat. I can remember going to bed hungry at night. When I got up from the table, I never really felt like I had had enough to eat.

After about 1948, when the food shipments came from the Church, then, at least, we had enough potatoes and bread again. Those food shipments were very much appreciated. They really saved our lives. That is one thing I will never forget.

Shortly after that, my father died and was buried in Dresden. After Dad died, my mother had to go to work to support the family. First she worked cleaning off old bricks so they could be used again. Of course, it took years to get rid of all that rubble. Then she went to work on a street crew. She helped pave the streets, and they didn't have the machines like they have today. They had to do a lot by hand, spread the tar, make it even. My mother worked mostly with women. There weren't many men left after World War II. They needed women to help in those kind of jobs, and my mother had been raised on a farm and thought she was strong enough. The funny thing is she enjoyed it. I think it was partly because she enjoyed the association with the other women. They really had a good time. My mother would come home from work and tell us how much fun they had. They worked hard, they really did, but she enjoyed it. Then the last few years, in the mid fifties—she was close to sixty then—she went to work in a factory.

Eventually my sisters and I, one by one, escaped to West Germany. Our mother lived in the same apartment until 1958, when she finally left Dresden and came west to live near her children. She is buried in Stuttgart.

After leaving Dresden for the West, DOROTHEA SPETH CONDIE *worked as a registered nurse. She served a mission in Stuttgart, where she met her husband, Elder Spencer J. Condie, of the first quorum of the Seventy. She has had many callings in the Church, including wife of the mission president in the Austria Vienna Mission. She is currently serving with her husband in Europe where Elder Condie is serving in the area presidency of the European North Area.*

GAROLD DAVIS, *professor emeritus in the Department of Germanic and Slavic Languages, received his PhD from Johns Hopkins in 1962 after receiving his MA and BA from BYU.*

NORMA DAVIS *received her MA and BA in humanities from BYU and taught humanities at BYU until her retirement in August 1998.*

Questions

1. How does the introduction help contextualize the story told by Condie?
2. Why did the Saints in Dresden think they were safe from the bombs? Were their assumptions reasonable?
3. What figurative language does Condie use to describe the experience?
4. Given her structure and the points she emphasizes, what is the purpose of this story?
5. Think of this story as a script for a movie. What scenes would you focus on? Write one scene that shows rather than tells the experience.
6. Compare this essay to Richard Johnson's "Wealth and Poverty."

Life and Testimony of an Academic Clinical Psychologist

Allen E. Bergin

Allen Bergin's "Life and Testimony of an Academic Clinical Psychologist" was, in one respect, an assignment. Susan Easton Black, Professor of Church History and Doctrine at BYU, asked him to write an essay sharing his thoughts on being both a faithful member of the LDS church and a clinical psychologist. Bergin decided his primary purpose was to convey that it was possible to "be a person of orthodox faith combined with first-rate scholarship and be respected by your profession." This was something he already believed, but nevertheless felt that the process of writing this essay "crystalized some feelings" about his role as a person trying to bring a spiritual perspective into the academic world. "Lots of ideas in the social sciences aren't in harmony with the gospel," he contends, "but it's not insurmountable by any means. [An LDS perspective has] something to offer the social sciences on human nature as well." "Life and Testimony of an Academic Clinical Psychologist" was originally published in Expressions of Faith: Testimonies of Latter-day Saint Scholars.

In 1955, at the age of twenty, I became a Mormon.[1] Now, in 1995, at the age of sixty, I have been honored by a request to reflect upon my life and testimony. Nineteen fifty-five seems like yesterday. My decision then was difficult because I loved the scientific method and believed that observation, experimentation, and reason were the most useful avenues to truth. My high school academic training in Spokane, Washington, was devoted especially to science and mathematics. The arts, humanities, and other intuitive disciplines seemed "soft" and unimportant. Religion seemed chaotic and confusing, though intriguing.

My freshman scholarship at the Massachusetts Institute of Technology (MIT) was a dream come true. The trip to Cambridge was a pilgrimage. There I was, a poor boy from an uneducated family, the first to finish high school, putting my luggage down on the sidewalk outside the MIT rotunda, pausing to absorb the drama of the moment. That memorable pause marked an epochal transition for me as I entered the high-powered world of the secular intelligentsia.

Our studies ranged from Thucydides to Einstein. Our exposure included daily contact with famous scientific contemporaries. Modern microwave radar had been developed there during World War II; Norbert Wiener was discussing cybernetics; my chemistry teacher had worked on the first nuclear fission reaction at the University of Chicago; and my ingenious roommate was working on one of the first modern computers, a giant three-story machine that we could walk around in. (It literally had bugs in it!) Our informal contacts spread to Harvard and the myriad centers of learning in the Boston area. There was intellectual excitement in 1952—virtually more than a down-home boy could absorb.

Oddly, the MIT experience was so thorough an immersion in hard science that I gradually became saturated with it and found myself surprisingly unhappy with its inadequate attention to the human dimension. I was puzzled by the purpose of it all and spent time with a research psychiatrist who was studying group dynamics, a campus rabbi, and a Catholic roommate who seemed very clear about his beliefs.

As the year drew on I found myself searching harder to redefine myself, my purposes, and the meaning of life. I dipped into psychology and philosophy books. Once I prayed the agnostic's prayer: "Dear God, if you are there, let me know what this is all about." When I discovered that MIT had joint programs with some outstanding liberal arts colleges, where I could concurrently obtain a BS from MIT and a BA from the designated college, I decided to enroll. Reed College in Portland, Oregon, was my choice. I knew Portland and had been admitted to Reed the previous year.

Though it seemed impossible, the year in Portland was even more dramatically transforming than the one in Cambridge had been. Intellectual debate on the major issues of human history and contemporary life was endemic and epidemic. Radical dissection of every belief, value, and cultural norm was our daily bread. Some vulnerable people became suicidal over it; others thrived and won Rhodes Scholarships. I wavered between depression and exhilaration. It remains the single most intellectually stimulating year of my life—a year of intensive philosophy and psychology courses, in addition to my standard fare of math and science. Reed brought me past the scientific method to a level of logical and philosophical analysis that soared beyond the technical wizardry of MIT. I came to love analysis of ideas as much as science, and the idea of God seemed even more remote. Now I had both science and philosophy—the keys to knowledge. But another drama unexpectedly intervened, and nothing has been the same since.

I met a young woman at Reed by the name of Marian Shafer. A Mormon from Alberta, Canada, who had just finished high school in Utah, she was on a creative writing scholarship. She was seventeen and had won an award for a short story that was to be published in *Seventeen* magazine. She seemed to have everything—intelligence, good looks, a vivacious personality, and clear religious convictions. She was an anomaly at Reed, having only the first of these traits (intelligence) in common with most of the students.

Our relationship started at a dance just before school began and gradually developed through fall semester. Her Mormon habits were different, but her theology was out of this world. Certainly, I had been searching for a frame of reference, but the disjuncture between modern revelation and secular empiricism was dramatic.

Though I had grown up in a family mixture of nominal Protestantism and Catholicism, my Christian convictions had been learned largely by osmosis and then had gradually faded away, although the Bible continued to resonate faintly in my mind. Mormonism suddenly put new light upon religious history and upon my sense of the world. My knowledge of this new faith slowly grew while my relationship with Marian continued to evolve. Both of these objects of interest provoked approach-avoidance tendencies, but by the end of the year I was hopelessly entangled in both theology and romance. Could I ever disentangle the two?

My opportunity came with summer and an offer from my father, a construction superintendent, to join him on a project in Alaska. I collected a box of books on Mormonism, evolution, philosophy, and eastern religion and headed north. Before leaving Reed, I read every anti-Mormon critique I could find in the library, of which there were many. I also found a used 1920 edition of the Book of Mormon in the Reed Bookstore, which I purchased for fifty cents and packed with my other items. I still have this little volume, with notations I wrote in the margins during the summer of 1954.

One of these notes was written in response to 2 Nephi 33:5, which says "no man will be angry at the words which I have written save he shall be of the spirit of the devil." I had written beneath this: "Then, I am." The dogmatic certainty of Nephi's words flew in the face of my scholarly devotion to tentativeness and care in making strong assertions. But, ironically, I later found Nephi's testimony powerfully convincing, and eventually I wrote a tribute to him.[2] It surprised me later to find that Marian possessed an identical 1920 edition of the Book of Mormon given to her by her aunt, Marjorie Wight, in February 1946. In the back of the book Marian had written: "Started July 21, 1946. Finished reading it December 21, 1946." She was ten years old.

That summer in Alaska I read the Book of Mormon thoroughly, along with the Bible, the other LDS scriptures, and several volumes of speeches and writings by Church leaders. This intensive effort was spiced by a great variety of other, contrary readings. However, the key events of this time concerned my efforts to pray. This activity was new to me, but I went alone into the Alaskan wilderness on many occasions and prayed with youthful energy that God would reveal to me the truth about these matters and his will for me. There, on the banks of the Tanana River, my heart and mind were opened to a new way of experiencing the world. I felt things I had never felt before. The spirit of God came upon me undeniably. At moments, my awareness of spiritual realities became transcendent. Sense perception and reason were no longer the only sources of light and wisdom. My heart overflowed with a sense of goodness and warmth. My test of God, the Prophet Joseph Smith, and the Book of Mormon (Moroni 10:3-5) yielded far more than I had anticipated.

Despite such powerful manifestations of the sacred world, I was so steeped in a secular way of looking at things that I frequently reverted to it and questioned everything I had experienced. Conversion, for me, would eventually require a thousand checks and double checks on whether I was engaging in wish-fulfilling self-deception, which I believed most of humanity was duped by. My year of psychology and philosophy had crystallized an already skeptical nature.

Equally important, I missed Marian and we corresponded frequently and in depth. Toward the end of the summer she made the surprise move to transfer from Reed to Brigham Young University, a school about which I knew nothing. So I traveled to Utah for a visit with her and to see BYU. The university and its setting had a magnetic effect upon me, and Marian's presence there cemented my motivation to transfer too. Fortunately, I was able to gain immediate admission, go back to Portland and Spokane for my belongings, and make the switch.

The fall of 1954 was tempestuous. I began to love Utah and the new gospel as much as I loved Marian; then, however, we had personal and emotional differences and split up. Our friend and mentor, Robert K. Thomas, became our counselor. (A young English professor, he later founded the BYU Honors Program and ultimately became academic vice-president.) He was a Reed College alumnus, and we felt immediate rapport with this man of prodigious intelligence, great human warmth, and an unwavering faith in the restored gospel. His Book of Mormon class became a weekly challenge to my views. It was difficult to maintain skepticism in the face of one who was simultaneously so spiritual and so intellectual. His advanced training at Columbia University combined with his degree from Reed had equipped him with a formidable spectrum of secular knowledge. I had to ask myself: "How does he contain both of these in the same mind?" I also had to ask: "If he can do it, can I?"

It was during this turbulent fall semester that I first attended BYU devotionals and the LDS Church general conference. I was also studying, praying, and testing the LDS lifestyle. My mind was open to the messages and the witnesses of General Authorities. I listened intently and felt things that took me beyond the earlier experiences along the Tanana River.

At the same time my study of psychology intensified and I immersed myself totally in Robert Howell's History of Experimental Psychology course. History shows that psychology as a discipline arose out of a marriage between philosophy and science. So I was back again reviewing the history of philosophy and the rise of modern science, but this time with the focus on human behavior. I loved this course, as many dimensions of my recent experience came together.

During this period when I was deeply exploring psychology and the gospel on two separate tracks, my relationship with Marian was on hold on a third track and mostly out of mind. Later I realized that this turn of events allowed me to grapple profoundly with my whole life—intellectual, spiritual, and emotional—without the distractions and disturbances of romance. It also provided an acid test of the sincerity and objectivity of my conversion process, disentangled from the biasing effect of loving a person who was identified with the beliefs I was assessing. My deep interest in her had focused my attention upon God and his will. Now I had to face him alone on his terms.

Doing so was a struggle. I already held perspectives that made religious belief difficult, if not impossible. The conversion process became a self-study, a jockeying between opinions—all in my own head. What was I to do with the Book of Mormon, the testimonies of the authorities, the faith of Bob Thomas? What about the secular searchers for truth whom I had studied and respected who had chosen a life of uncertain open-endedness blended with positive human valuing?

The decisive moment came when I realized that I had not given God a full and complete test. I had never totally given myself, entirely and consistently, to spiritual inquiry comparable to my intellectual devotion. I scanned again the numerous invitations and bold challenges throughout the scriptures and in the words of contemporaries that specified, like an experiment, how to approach God. Once again, the Book of Mormon set forth a provocative and powerful recipe (see Alma 32; Moroni 2, 10; Nephi 9, 33).

As I began to sincerely pursue this, a tremendous feeling of peace came over me. My being began to settle into the orthodox Mormon frame of reference. I began to know God and to walk in his ways and feel his Spirit. The scales of secularism fell daily from my eyes. A whole new way of seeing the world was being grafted into my intellect. Unlike my previously analytical outlook, this one was accompanied by warmth and hope, and it colored all relationships and aspects of life.

Coincidentally, Marian came to visit and we began to talk and to review our feelings for each other. Also, psychology was gripping my soul as well, since its blend of both the deeply personal and the objectively scientific seemed congruent with my changing orientation to life.

Thus it was, as the fall semester drew to a close in December of 1954, that a momentous transformation occurred. I accepted Mormonism as a faith, chose psychology as a discipline, and asked Marian to be my eternal companion. The rest were details: plans for baptism in March 1955 by Bob Thomas, marriage in June to Marian, and a doubling-up of psychology courses in order to catch up on this new major by the end of my junior year.

All of the preceding context is important because it shows that spiritual knowing is multidimensional. It touches everything and is touched by everything. Detached intellectual knowing is one-dimensional and incomplete: such inquiry cannot reach into the godly realm, and its effects upon relationships, lifestyle, and values are often negative. The eternal principles of living and the values that guide their application are learned by a composite of studious examination, careful life testing, critical ratiocination, and opening of self to the intuitive free-flow of spiritual communion. There is a balance among these ingredients that leads to the good, the true, and the beautiful. Omitting one of these factors from (or entering too much or too little of a given factor into) the equation for one's life orientation results in a failure to equate.

Another two and a half years at BYU seasoned and strengthened my formulation of what life and truth were all about. It also resulted in a master's degree in psychology, our first two children, a marriage anchored in the restored gospel and its associated lifestyle, and an invitation to work on a PhD in clinical psychology at Stanford. Thus, I recycled into the powerful world of the secular intelligentsia but with an entirely new and vibrant perspective. The next fifteen years became a profound odyssey.

I had spent so much time evaluating Mormonism and scrutinizing it with the Reedian blend of scientific objectivity, philosophical analysis, and skepticism that no challenge from secularized Stanford professors or naturalistic psychological theories came close to undermining my new faith. On the contrary, I began slowly then, and continue to the present day, to turn my mental and spiritual skills upon psychology—dissecting and reorienting it for myself, hopefully improving its capacity to reach the broad spectrum of human phenomena, including the spiritual. Psychology had abandoned religion at the turn of the century. Unfettered by superstition, the discipline was supposed to become the wave of an enlightened secular future. Colleagues wondered why I wanted to return to the "myths of the past."

My view was very different. I did not consider it necessary to include the erroneous baggage of religious history in order to restore a spiritual dimension to behavioral science. Indeed, I agreed with many of the criticisms of religious traditions. The restored gospel provided abundant advantages in such an effort. Nevertheless, my efforts to include spirituality in psychology were muted by consistent rejection from many prominent and powerful professors I encountered as a graduate student at Stanford, a postdoctoral fellow at the University of Wisconsin's Psychiatric Institute, and a junior faculty member at Teachers College, Columbia University. Though there was mutual respect, virtually all expressed skepticism toward my views.

Thus, for fifteen years—three at Stanford, one at Wisconsin, and eleven at Columbia—I found some of my keen interests difficult to express. Clearly I, and everyone like me, was boxed in by a coercive ideology that pervaded the great universities of western civilization—an ideology that was laced with mechanistic, naturalistic, humanistic, and secular themes.[3] I understood this very well and could even sympathize with it because the yoke of ancient religions and myths had so often stifled freedom and the search for truth. To a degree, I thrived in the modernist atmosphere because I had the right tools of analysis and method. Indeed, I thoroughly enjoyed and became well-known for my psychotherapy research on understanding and changing psychological disorders.[4] Although I was unable to bring my deep interest in moral values and a spiritual perspective to fruition, I was able to achieve some satisfaction by including material on the topic within my own classes at Columbia. Still, it was frustrating to regularly face the undercurrent of opposition from students and faculty. In addition, there was little literature or research to draw upon from the mainstream of professional scholarship. It is true that there were voices of support over the decades, such as those of William James, Carl Jung, Gordon Allport, Viktor Frankl, and others, but the core direction of modern psychology was essentially unaffected by them.

I did have many deep discussions with faculty members and some of their families over the years about my faith and its basis. These discussions were penetrating and mutually respectful. I often identified the

Book of Mormon as a powerful evidence in support of the restored gospel. It is a tangible object, observable by the senses. Where did it come from? Was Joseph Smith a prophet? Some were intrigued and investigated to a degree. Very few were convinced. Most were honest enough to acknowledge that they had no answer for the book. These were brilliant and sincere individuals who made their peace with this evidence by choosing an honest course of benign avoidance. When I read contemporary critiques of the Book of Mormon, I am amazed by their inadequacies. Many of the more sophisticated doubters tend to leave it alone lest they risk their reputations against a document inspired by the mind of God.

Although I became a tenured full professor at Columbia and received offers from many universities to further pursue psychotherapy research, I chose to accept an invitation to join the BYU faculty in 1972. This created many professional difficulties for me, but it opened the way to pursuing spiritual issues in a more concerted way. Despite opposition among various scholars, including some at BYU, there was enough support to provide me and like-minded individuals, such as Victor Brown, Jr., the freedom and opportunity to explore the spiritual side of emotional distress and treatment. This was truly a breath of fresh air provided, paradoxically, by a university thought by some to be too parochial. My experience had been the opposite. It was the major research universities that were, from my perspective, parochial and entrenched in conceptual tradition.

There were several years of transition at BYU during the 1970s, characterized by starts and stops, trial and error; but for the past fifteen years (1980-95), the spiritual force in psychology and related disciplines has grown abundantly and has gained a place of respect. My own work[5] has earned national awards from three organizations, including the American Psychological Association (APA); those of us who desire to put spirituality back into understanding and healing the psyche have made tremendous progress in gaining recognition for our viewpoint. One of my papers[6] elicited more than a thousand responses, including letters from many prominent professionals, some of which are excerpted below. They imply a strong but hidden interest in these issues that has since become public.

> I congratulate you for saying what I believe has needed to be said for a long time. . . . I very much hope that this paper will, in retrospect, be considered one of the most

important to have been published in the area in the new decade.

—Ellen Berschied, professor, Department of Psychology, University of Minnesota

I think this is a landmark article that says several things that many people must have been thinking for years. You have done us all a great service.

—Ted Lorei, Veterans Administration, Washington DC

[I] am extremely sympathetic with the hypotheses you describe.

—Lisa Wallach, lecturer, Department of Psychology, Duke University

I commend you on your excellent article.

—Karl Menninger, the Menninger Foundation, Topeka, Kansas, Past-President of the American Psychiatric Association

On the whole, I am very much in agreement although we may differ on some aspects. . . . Major values in human relations are woven into various religious systems, and they seem to be universally true regardless of what a therapist's attitude toward a Supreme Being might be.

—Hans Strupp, distinguished professor, Department of Psychology, Vanderbilt University, Past-President. APA Division of Clinical Psychology

Whether it be the role of religious values in the science and practice of psychology, humanism, radical behaviorism, or social learning theory, such ideas touch the lives of people in the field because certain proponents were willing to state them, whatever the reactions of others might be. It is through writings such as yours that religious values will receive greater consideration in psychotherapy.

—Albert Bandura, professor, Department of Psychology, Stanford University, and Past-President, APA

> I don't disagree as much as you might think. . . . I do believe there is some kind of a transcendent organizing influence in the universe which operates in man as well. . . . My present, very tentative, view is that perhaps there is an essential person which persists through time, or even through eternity.
>
> —Carl Rogers, Center for Studies of the Person, La Jolla, California, and Past-President, APA

These new trends did not occur in a vacuum. People gradually became more supportive throughout the discipline. BYU and other religiously sponsored institutions provided a safe haven for the incubation of a new trend in psychological thought. A broad cultural shift also occurred in western culture during the 1970s and 1980s that was evident in resurgent public interest in spiritual matters, along with steady growth of organizations, publications, and conferences devoted to such matters. Religious social scientists and mental health professionals have led the way. I share common spiritual feelings with many of these people. They come from diverse persuasions, but we have high regard for each other's perspectives, and we share the conviction that there are God-given, universal moral standards.

Symbolic of this new trend is a book on religion and the clinical practice of psychology to be published by the APA; the book includes a chapter I coauthored with BYU faculty members Reed Payne and Scott Richards.[7] Success in this effort is already challenging us to demonstrate that these new views will make a positive difference unattainable in other ways. The chance to rigorously bring this to pass is a great opportunity and responsibility.

I am proud of my colleagues around the world who are engaged in this movement,[8] including many at BYU who are making names for themselves as competent, original, and provocative thinkers. There are too many to name individually, but of the centers for new thought about human behavior, BYU has to be considered a leader.

This is all refreshing and rewarding to me. I am excited about the future as cadres of younger faculty and students have their own visions of what can be done. They have an open field, relatively unfettered by traditional obstacles. Beachheads have been won and a new day is on the horizon—one that I believe will be marked by open faith in religious truth as it guides us to new ways of thinking and living anchored by spiritual subspecialities in the behavioral and mental health fields. As this happens, younger spiritually oriented social scientists might consider the following points of advice:

• Become competent and establish professional credibility in at least one area of nonspiritual specialization or expertise. This will provide your passport into the academic or professional world.

• Build all spiritual inquiries on a solid base of scholarship and be willing to absorb negative evidence about your views. Don't make a career out of attacking other people's positions; positively pursue your own. Be caring toward others, including academic authorities who disagree with you. Militancy may win battles in the short run, but in the long run we all have to live together—peacefully, we hope.

• Seek divine inspiration in your work and your life; if you receive specific direction, keep it private. Let your scholarly products speak for themselves as a witness of your insight and creativity.

• Be courageous in holding to your beliefs and moral values despite derision or opposition.

• Be gracious in giving credit to others for helping you advance your goals for the field, including those whose views differ from yours but from whom you have learned much.

Let me return, in closing, to the quest for faith with which I began this essay. I have never found my hard-won new faith to be wanting. I only find myself wanting in my ability to keep up with its momentum as it courses forward into a new millennium under the leadership of the Lord and his servants. Naturally, like others, I see some defects in the culture of church and university that cause me a measure of consternation. I believe that, despite its imperfections, this religious culture is the embryo of the kingdom of God on earth. The deficiencies are part of the human condition and are not fundamental. The cure is not to make a career out of criticism. The cure is to do our own duty well—creatively, with compassion and inspiration.

The key for me, as I look back to my conversion forty years ago, in 1955, has been to give the revealing will and Spirit of God top priority in the ways of knowing. Research and reason are essential allies in the search for truth, but if either of them becomes dominant, God's natural order is upset. We become, to paraphrase Emerson,[9] professional monsters—a good analyst or thinker, a great methodologist, or a penetrating writer, but never a whole human being.

At the same time, I glory in the academic. Universities, research centers, writing, study, and publication are my world. But I have discovered that Bob Thomas was right. It is possible to contain spiritual conviction and academic excellence in the same mind. I am thankful that my church generously supports Brigham Young University, an institution dedicated to a knowledge of Jesus Christ and his ways, and to truth in general. I hope the future brings even more support and more freedom with which we can explore the whole truth of every subject in innovative and inspired ways. To the extent that our inquiries are absolutely penetrating, they can become absolutely revealing.

I know, however, that if every academic trapping were stripped away, I would still thrive, because of more important things—my family of nine children and twelve grandchildren, my eternal marriage with Marian, and my faith in God. I know that God, our Eternal Father, lives. His influence is a daily spiritual experience for me. Nothing is more precious. It affects everything else. There is no trial or doubt that can displace or subsume this conviction of the holy.

His Son, Jesus Christ, is not an abstraction to me. He is real. He has commissioned his church and sanctioned its leadership. He is my Redeemer. I have faith in him whom I know through unseen experiences. He has guided me during forty eventful years. I feel his love and aspire to be his disciple. My feelings for him are beyond words, and my knowledge of him is priceless.

Given such a foundation in spiritual knowledge, additional truth flows abundantly. Albert Einstein said, "I want to know how God created this world. I am not interested in this or that phenomenon. . . . I want to know His thoughts, the rest are details."[10] Becoming attuned to the mysteries of God opens the way for discoveries that transcend ordinary inquiry. I hope for such at BYU and among the community of faithful scholars everywhere. May we conduct our inquiries with an eternal vision that embraces whatever is honest, true, chaste, benevolent, and virtuous. Then, we shall know by personal experience that "to be learned is good if [we] hearken unto the counsels of God" (2 Nephi 9:29).

As a professor and former director of both the clinical psychology doctoral program and the Values Institute at BYU, ALLEN E. BERGIN *has championed peaceful coexistence between psychology and religion. Before coming to Utah, Bergin was a professor of clinical psychology at Columbia University in New York City for eleven years. He has received numerous awards for his research, particularly in religious psychology, and has been president of several professional societies and associations. His continuing interest in values, religion, and mental health have led him to study the "spiritual and mental health" of BYU students.*

Notes

1. An earlier version of this article was delivered as the Kenneth and Mary Hardy Annual Lecture, a Brigham Young University Psychology Forum address, March 28, 1995.

2. Allen E. Bergin, "Nephi, a Universal Man," *Ensign*, September 1976, 65–70.
3. Allen E. Bergin, "Psychotherapy and Religious Values," *Journal of Consulting and Clinical Psychology* 48 (1980): 95–105.
4. Allen E. Bergin and Sol L. Garfield, eds., *Handbook of Psychotherapy and Behavior Change* (New York: Wiley, 1971).
5. Allen E. Bergin, "Values and Religious Issues in Psychotherapy and Mental Health," *American Psychologist* 46 (1991): 394–403.
6. Bergin, "Psychotherapy and Religious Values."
7. E. Shafranske, ed., *Religion and the Clinical Practice of Psychology* (Washington, D. C.: American Psychological Association, 1996).
8. D. B. Larson and S. S. Larson, "The Forgotten Factor in Physical and Mental Health: What Does the Research Show?" (Arlington, Virginia: National Institute for Healthcare Research, 1992).
9. Ralph Waldo Emerson, "The American Scholar," delivered at Harvard University in 1837. In *The Complete Essays and Other Writings of Ralph Waldo Emerson*, ed. B. Atkinson (New York: Modern Library, 1950), 45–64.
10. Albert Einstein, quoted in Ronald W. Clark, *Einstein, the Life and Times* (New York: World Publishing Company, 1971), 19.

Questions

1. What are useful avenues to truth? What does Bergin's essay indicate concerning kinds of knowledge?

2. What does Bergin's metaphor, "the trip to Cambridge was a pilgrimage," imply about education and knowledge?

3. Why does Bergin tell us he still has the "used 1920 edition" of the Book of Mormon?

4. How is the metaphor of seeing important to this story?

The Power of Landscape and Place; Inarticulate Speech of My Heart[1]

CLAYTON M. WHITE

Adapted from an essay soon to be published in New Genesis: A Mormon Reader on Land and Community, *Clayton White's essay began as a list of "spiritual experiences" he'd had outside of a religious context. When the list was finished, he had almost 40 examples. Much like early American essayist Ralph Waldo Emmerson, White realizes that nature can be profoundly spiritual, and consequently decided to share his experiences with his children by writing them in a letter, which eventually grew to become an essay. White explains that he has attempted "to express the notion that the meaningful experiences you have in your short life take place as you intereact with landscapes and environments." Such experiences, he emphasizes, "cause you to reflect on the emotional and personal relationships in your life."*

The first year that I drove the Alcan Highway out from Alaska may have been the first time I experienced true solitude. I did so in the autumn of the year 1964, accompanied only by our Siberian husky. The fireweed still carried some bloom; aspen and birch leaves were turning red, yellow, and subdued earth tone colors. The air was crisp and invigorating, snow topped some of the mountains in northern British Columbia and the Yukon Territory, and the sky changed constantly from crystal clear to rolling thunderheads. I had plenty of time to think since the trip took about eight days. Solitude was great. There was something about being in that particular landscape, and the various forms that landscape took, that helped me learn the value of solitude—of just total concentration on thought. Solitude enables one to reevaluate beliefs and values and I think some of mine relative to man's place on the planet were refined. I started to form my values of stewardship. I redefined my sense of landscapes and the contours they take without really knowing what landscapes were in the broadest sense. I think I came to the conclusion to always "preach" landscape stewardship but use few words.

It was several years later that the writings of Barry Lopez introduced to me a uniquely satisfying and convincingly honest manner of viewing what he called landscapes. He gave the word, landscape, at least two meanings; one is that which is outside, for example what we see around us in the visible world such as birds, dying grass, and frost—the other is inside one's self and is made up of the shape of a persons character, thinking, and feelings, which are largely determined by where one goes, the input of culture, and what experiences they have on the earth. Lopez also suggested that landscapes are marvelous and mysterious aggregations and one must simply accord them the standing that one grants the mysteries, as different from puzzles, of life. Ultimately, it seems to me that the internal landscape dictates how we view and treat all other landscapes. In fact, Simon Schama[2] in *Landscape and Memory* went so far as to suggest that landscapes are culture even before they are nature and that they are constructs of the imagination projected onto wood and water and rock. Personal experiences with landscapes are, of course, perceived differently by each person. Thus, my notions of landscape have been further broadened and in this essay I would like to explore the way in which landscape and culture have influenced me.

My feelings about landscapes can be best described as "spiritual" ones. Spiritual feelings are something I really can't define precisely nor quantitatively but they are to me those which stimulate and educate the senses. That feelings about landscapes are spiritual was nicely articulated by Ansel Adams's statement about Half Dome in Yosemite Park: "[Although it] is just a piece of rock . . . there is some deep personal distillation of spirit and concept which moulds these earthly facts into some transcendental emotional and spiritual experiençe."[3] Ansel Adams was, as many of us have, experiencing nature and landscapes directly. When we experience directly a landscape that has the dominion, rather than us, we come to value it. A poet colleague, Leslie Norris, told of an event in his childhood in Wales. During a blustering storm his school master had all the students go outside, a few at a time, to join hands surrounding a large tree. They each pressed against the mighty trunk, laid their heads on the bark, and listened for a moment. Back in the classroom the school master said, "Now you know how a tree feels in a windy storm." That direct experience to him had a spiritual quality and one that he has not forgotten to this day. The landscapes I have come to know have been manifested directly in a variety of experiences and it is those experiences that define perspective. Particularly important to me are the peak experiences that have punctuated the landscapes here and there. These peak experiences are the "trails" I have travelled. My most spiritual feelings along these trails usually take place as I am relating with or being absorbed into both the inside and the outside landscape, frequently in the autumn of the year as birds are migrating south, earth tones dominate the vegetation, and the quite solitude of winter is approaching.

I keep a short flask of small pebbles I have picked up from the countless unnamed beaches, gravel bars, and streams I have explored in my travels. When the routines of life becomes stressful I finger the pebbles and remember how I picked them from bits of landscape where few have set foot and I gain self-renewal. Several pebbles in particular came from beside a bit of melting glacial ice, cast upon a beach, and were in its temporal passage there. The ice was from a glacier in Prince Williams Sound, Alaska where I was during the Exxon Valdez oil spill. It was old ice with age numbered in thousands of years. It had seen a lot of history, and now was seeing its last as it was peacefully being absorbed into the cold stark waters of the sound; it caused me to ponder my own passage through life. Yi-Fu Tuan put my thoughts nicely when he said, "Satisfaction with life consists largely of taking pleasure in form and expressiveness—in sensory impressions, modified by the mind, at all scales from the smile of a child to . . . [environmental] theater[s]."[4] Life's trails have achieved a certain meaning that I can only pass on in words and thoughts that come from the heart but are difficult to articulate in a concise and meaningful manner. Perhaps it is the combined influence of heart-felt emotion and thought that we call conscience—that still small voice within. It is that voice that has given some of the best sermons about landscapes that I have heard, all prompted from the pulpit of memory—to an audience of one, to paraphrase Neal A. Maxwell. This then, is from whence I take the second part of my title: a song about inarticulate feelings of the heart by the singer and composer Van Morrison which I listened to as I was travelling one of those spiritual trails.

I started to think about spiritual trails one night in January 1993 while I was with a long time friend and colleague Bill Emison, who first worked with me on the USA's underground nuclear testing programs in the Aleutian Islands in the late 1960's. Bill and I were working again together on some research with parrots in western Victoria, Australia. We had finished a day's work, the sun's rays drenching the clouds were all but gone, and sounds of night had begun. It was hot and humid. We were lounging on the porch of a cabin on a ranch drinking cold pop. We were casting about experiences we had enjoyed together and trying to find meaning in them. For whatever reason, both of us had some forms of emotion close to the surface. It was in the late hours during that evening, with night birds such as frogmouths and nightjars and the chorus of frogs and insects calling, that I jotted down a couple score of events (spiritual trails).

If my trails can help you find a spiritual meaning in expressions of life's landscapes then they will have had some value. As my emotions carried me through those trails I thought of the words of Rachel Carson in *The Sense of Wonder*.[5] She tells of a child's world, all full of wonder and excitement. She observed that it has been our misfortune that the clear-eyed vision for what is beautiful and awe-inspiring is dimmed and even lost before we reach adulthood. She remarked that if she had influence with the fairy godmother who presides over the christening of children, she should ask that her gift be a sense of wonder so indestructible as to last throughout life, as an antidote against boredom and disenchantments of later years. It is not half as important to know as it is to feel; emotions and impressions of the sense of wonder are the soil in which feelings grow.

Scriptures from my culture relate that at the end of the creative periods the Gods saw all that had resulted and proclaimed it "very good." It is consistent with the Mormon cultural concepts of creation to believe it was very good and that it pleased the Gods because there was some relationship in the interactions between earth's organisms. The scriptures then say "I the lord stretched out the heavens and built the earth, my very handiwork; and all things therein are mine. . . . And if the properties are mine, then ye are stewards." [D&C 104:14, 56] This notion of stewardship, so far as I can determine, has a wider application and interpretation than just in a religious sense. I am not arrogant enough to believe that mankind was deliberately given the "purpose" of being a steward but I am practical enough to recognize that mankind's ability to control and greatly modify the environment, especially through synthetic means, demands some sort of stewardship mentality within the human mind.

Likewise, Henry David Thoreau seems to have grasped other meanings of stewardship. In his book *Walden*, he relates

> Near the end of March, 1845, I borrowed an axe and went to the woods by Walden Pond, nearest to where I intended to build my house, and began to cut down some tall, arrowy white pines, still in their youth, for timber. It is difficult to begin without borrowing, but perhaps it is the most generous course thus to permit your fellowmen to have an interest in your enterprise. The owner of the axe, as he released his hold onto it, said that it was the apple of his eye; but I returned it sharper than I received it.[6]

We are passengers on a borrowed earth. A simple form of stewardship is expressed in the lifestyles of two men I remember who used to live along the Yukon River in Alaska not many miles downriver from the boundary with the Yukon Territory. George McGregor, a prospector and trapper, was already very old when I heard of him. He has been dead now three or more decades, but for many years he lived alone in a log cabin he built at the foot of a peregrine falcon nesting crag. Every year the falcons migrated back from the south, probably Latin America, to nest on the rocks above his cabin. He did not disturb them, for he was a quiet man who blended serenely and unobtrusively into his surroundings and was a part of the land just as much as the falcons, the river, and the spruce trees. Once George saw a female falcon swoop out of the air and strike a marauding raven dead in midair over the river in front of his cabin, and his old eyes brightened when he told about it. He had never read *Walden*, but I am sure his internal landscape instinctively understood the meaning of stewardship.

In recent years another man built his cabin by a falcon cliff not far downriver from George's now crumbling cabin. This new man was loud, exploitive, cutting down excessive trees with a noisy power saw, and keeping a pack of howling sled dogs tied with short chains to their small, square sheds at the base of the cliff. He operated a large, creaking fish-wheel right in front of the rocks where the falcons bred and where the river runs deep and salmon swim up. He fervently tried to bring nature to his level with his rifle. No falcons returned to nest on the cliffs above his cabin. He too is now gone and one can only guess how long it will take for the scars to heal. And, as I passed in later years the mess he created along the serenity and solitude of the otherwise mighty river, my eyes moistened. The stewardship had been broken and violated.

An equally important variation of stewardship is reflected in the incident related by Barry Lopez, in his award winning book *Arctic Dreams*.[7] He tells of an Inuit, a native of Alaska, that in response to the question of what does he do when he visits a new place said, "I listen; that's all." By "I listen," he meant, "I listen to what the land is saying. I walk around in it and strain my senses in appreciation of it for a long time before I myself ever speak a word." Entering in such a respectful manner, he believed the land would open to him and they would then be one. I know what both Lopez and the Inuit refer to; I have been there and sensed the holiness of that union. As I sit in the visible landscape and ponder, I realize each leaf on the ground, each stone, each scree slope, each tree in the forest has a story to tell of how it came to be.

Most of the trails I have travelled have been in areas that, if not wilderness, certainly make one feel as though wilderness surrounds you. In reality, not too many people experience that feeling—but then not many probably want to. In fact, I suspect most people would not like true wilderness given the chance to be immersed in it, for although it stimulates the sense of wonder, and sometimes is beautiful, it can also be threatening. Let me relate three of the trails that for me were "spiritually inarticulate."

Living in the Aleutian Islands is like having the arctic fever celebrated by Farley Mowat. There is no known cure for the fever and no one can find the "bug" that causes it, but it is real. The fever drives one over and over again to those Aleutian tundra landscapes, if only for brief moments. I will probably never travel the Aleutian trail again. As I stood once below a cliff housing a cormorant colony, birds flying in and out of the cliff, and the incoming surf pounding at my very feet, I began to cry, for I was sensing what Ansel Adams did in Yosemite; earthly facts were changed into transcendental spiritual expressions. I felt intensely alive. I was on Agattu Island helping with the Aleutian Canada goose transplant. The goose had been nearly extirpated from the Aleutian chain when the arctic fox, an efficient predator, was unwisely introduced on the islands some 50 years ago to provide a fur trade for the native Aleuts.

It was 1972 and I was one of the few people to visit that island in the past several decades. I was about to leave and I knew that I would never return to this lovely, lonely, inspiring place of solitude. The smell of salt-drenched air differs in those islands from its smell on tropical beaches, perhaps because the air and water are so cold. I really don't know, but to my mind, no place else on earth smells like it. Home to the largest and darkest of all the peregrine falcons, rosy-finches and song sparrows. Nucleus of the sea otter's range. Former home of a giant, but now extinct, sea cow named for the first European to encounter it, Georg Wilhelm Steller. A chain of spectacular volcanos on which the sea breaks its back. It is a unique place and seen from a distance rising from the fog and mist generated seas, the islands are more "illusions," using Corey Ford's phrase, than Aleutians; they are magic. We stayed in a cabin built in the 1930s by Aleut fox fur hunters. It took some work to fix up. When the wind-driven rains were pounding against the walls and the roof so hard we could not work, we would stoke up the fire and listen to cassette tapes. Luckily the batteries lasted for the month I was there. One of the few tapes we had was the "Best of John Denver" and each time I hear it my mind travels again to that distant spot, especially still when he sings the song about getting old being a turn-on. Adjacent to Agattu, but separated by 90 miles and by a very rough riptide as waters rush back and forth from the North Pacific Ocean and the Bering Sea (one on the north and one on the south of the Aleutian arc), is Buldir Island. A tiny speck of lushly vegetated jutting volcanic rock 12 miles in circumference. Not visited since World War II when there was an outpost of a couple of soldiers, we were truly on virgin ground there as we trod its hillsides looking for geese. After that first visit I was privileged to go on Buldir before it became the stomping grounds for many goose biologists. I was among the first, however, and saw the deserted World War II water-cooled 30 caliber machine gun, all rusted and forgotten. An abandoned P-38 fighter aircraft that couldn't make it back to its base, probably Amchitka, belly landed in the tundra. A lucky pilot, for there is not much flat space available on that island sitting in a featureless ocean. Unclaimed by all, other than the weather, and forgotten to the world by all but a few. I walked on beaches few have trod since the Aleuts were slaughtered by the Russian sea otter hunters of the late 1700–early 1800s. My footprints in sands created from black lava remained only until tide. I often wonder how many foot prints have been erased from those sands. I am sure the number is not great and probably episodic. I feel that I have been on a piece of earth kept special and it was a spiritual experience.

My graduate student Sandy Boyce and I were in Argentina collecting blood samples of birds for his dissertation. It was 1984. We had rented a car (a tiny Italian tin can of a thing) and were heading north to the Bolivian border some 800 miles away. One of the last Argentine villages we visited before touching the Bolivian border was Cuesta de Azul Pampa, reachable only by a narrow, rut riddled dirt road winding up to 12,000 feet elevation. The bordering hillsides looked ancient, as though they had seen a lot of history. People doubtless once walked over most of the slopes but now they are not visited because of their uninviting character. No footprints remained there. The rain began before we left Azul Pampa and we slowly wound and clawed our way back down the muddy and puddled road. Rain had caused streams crossing the road to rise 2–3 feet. The force of the water on the steep gradient of streams forced boulders the size of basketballs to bounce along the stream bed like so many ping pong balls. We reached the last water crossing before entering the small valley below where we could get lodging for the night. The stream carried water reaching nearly to the bottom of the car doors. Besides the rumbling debris, the stream bed was strewn with jutting boulders and rocks fixed in place. We had little way of navigating these fixed objects now because of the water depth. If we didn't cross quickly we would not get across for a couple of days and no place to go back up the road that was now also impassable.

"What should we do, Boyce?"

"Let's go for it before it's too late," he said.

The car washed and bounced down the stream several yards and was about to go off the flat roadbed and on down the stream just as we reached the other side; gunning it, we made the last few feet. Rain-battered, muddy, and cold we reached a roadside hostel in San Salvador de Jujuy. That night in bed, covered by a worn, tattered but comfortably warm quilt I listened to the ethnically Incan music coming from the lobby below. Strains of "El Condor Pasa," "Canto al Altiplano," and "Mi Pueblo Azul," filtered up to the bedroom. My thoughts were not on the project nor the work still to be done. They were on landscape and family. I suspect when one is at peace within oneself the thoughts that come are those truly the most important. I fell asleep to the gentle patter of falling rain drops as they danced softly on the tin roof, dreaming good, peaceful dreams of landscapes.

The land from horizon to horizon beyond Almaty simulated the Basin and Range Province of the western United States. The flank of the Tien Shan Mountains jutting skyward behind Almaty, the capital of Kazakstan, approximated the Wasatch Mountains above Provo, Utah, that form the eastern boarder of the Great Basin. In fact the central Asian country of Kazakstan was itself a Great Basin metaphor; everything flowed inward just to sustain life, nothing flowed outward. It was only three months before the breakup of the Soviet Union in 1991 and I was in Kazakstan on a US/USSR environmental exchange program for the United States Fish and Wildlife Service. With two other state-side colleagues, a Soviet counterpart from Kazakstan, and a Russian interpreter, we were there to search for the enigmatic Altay falcon that theoretically breeds in the Altay Mountains and the companion mountain ranges that snake along the region and form the borders between Russia, Kazakstan, China and Mongolia. The sun was high, the skies bright, the air thin and cool as we wove our way along poorly defined jeep tracks through the hinterlands of the Tien Shan Maintains; animal hide yurts specked the land here and there. Horses roamed the meadowed hills. Although the lands had been occupied since long before the great Kahns, the inhabitants seemed to have peopled it sparsely enough to maintain its integrity.

We waded a shallow, rock strewn and frigid mountain river to get to a yurt opposite the track we were on to ask for information. A young Kazak or mongol woman, who had lived all her life as a nomad, emerged from the yurt to encounter what were perhaps her first western visitors. She may have been in her early 30s but the smooth, well-tended and bronzed facial skin belies age. She and the interpreter talked of things unknown to me. Suddenly her young son, injured on the hand, came crying for motherly comfort. Unabashed and unashamed she stopped the conversation to stoop, kiss her son on the forehead, wipe tears from his high-boned cheeks, utter some comforting words, and give him her complete attention. The look on her face was angelic. The empathy in her eyes was unmistakable. I'm sure she had never even seen, much less read,

Judeo-Christian writ but she epitomized the Christian tenet that unless you have charity you have nothing. Her poise and behavior were of someone at ease and peace with her internal landscape. Something about her presence, her actions, the outside landscape, and solitude touched me in such a way as to leave me in total accord. I never learned her name. I am sure I will never see her again but in fact she is vividly alive as indelible images in my mind. She was one who understood human stewardship and personhood and of how to preach a stewardship but use few words.

In these three experiences my internal landscape made the connection with the external landscape as the great philosopher Immanuel Kant did when he said, "Two things fill the mind with ever new and increasing admiration and awe, the more often and steadily we reflect upon them: the starry heavens above me and the moral law within me. . . . I see them before me and connect them immediately with the consciousness of my existence."[8] Like my memories of the Kazak woman, I pray that our dwelling places may be habitations of respect and stewardship. I pray that we may learn to give hugs that are lasting hugs—to make them part of a landscape stewardship, to love for the sake of simply loving. Love, like science, is at its best when driven by passion and emotion. To paraphrase David Orr's writings in *Earth in Mind*,[9] we are truly at our best when we create less dissonance between what we do for a living, how we think, and what we feel as creatures.

I have now come to the conclusion, after all the years of trying to leave a mark on this planet through my profession, that the only lasting mark I will make is to influence my children to be good and honorable people and to influence students to be good and honor their stewardships. The real quest is in trying to understand stewardship of all landscapes, find out how to live it, and then do it. To the reader I wish good luck with your lives and have memorable trails of your own.

CLAYTON M. WHITE*'s love of birds has taken him from the mountains of Africa to the coasts of Alaska. He is particularly interested in endangered species, and is currently studying the biological relationships of Peregrine falcons in the South Pacific and Australia. It is a task he describes as "the equivalent of tracing the genealogy of natives in the rain forest—it's impossible." Dr. White did graduate work at the University of Alaska, Fairbanks, and received a PhD in zoology from the University of Utah. Before joining BYU's faculty, he taught at the University of Kansas and Cornell University, and he belongs on a list of boards and committees as broad as the wingspan of an albatross. He's currently in demand as a consultant for both corporate and government agencies, and recently served as an expert witness for Alaska's 1989 Exxon Valdez oil spill case.*

Notes

1. Some of the material in this essay was taken from "Spiritual Trails I Have Travelled: The Inarticulate Speech of My Heart" by Clayton M. White in the book New Genesis: A Mormon Reader on Land and Community, edited by Terry Tempest Williams, William B. Smart, Gibbs M. Smith (Salt Lake City: Gibbs Smith, Publisher, 1998).
2. Simon Schama, Landscape and Memory (New York: Alfred A. Knopf, 1995).
3. Ansel Adams, On Our National Parks (Boston: Bulfinch Press, 1992).
4. Yi-Fu Tuan, "Surface phenomena and aesthetic experience." Annals Assoc. Amer. Geog. 79 (1989): 233–241.
5. Rachel Carson, *The Sense of Wonder* (New York: Harper & Row, 1956).
6. Henry David Thoreau, *Walden; or, Life in the Woods* (Boston: Ticknor and Fields, 1854).
7. Berry Lopez, Arctic Dreams, Imagination and Desire in a Northern Landscape (New York: Bantam Books, 1987).
8. Immanuel Kant, The Critique of Practical Reason (Chicago: Univ. Chicago Press, 1788) 1949 translation.
9. David W. Orr, Earth in Mind (Covelo: Island Press, 1994).

Questions

1. Both Allen Bergin ("Life and Testimony of an Academic Clinical Psychologist") and Clayton White have spiritual awakenings in Alaska. Do they grow out of similar experiences?
2. How does the metaphor of landscape function in this article? Does it make his argument stronger? Why or why not?
3. What do we learn from the spiritual trails White describes?
4. Who is the audience of this essay? What textual evidence do you have for your assertion?

From The Misadventures of a NAFTA Scientist

DOUGLAS HENDERSON

Douglas Hendersen is a quiet man, and his essay's origins confirm it. When Henderson presented a paper at a physics conference, he was obliged to provide a biographical history in order for a colleague to introduce him. In honor of his 60th birthday, conference organizers arranged to have his biography included with his published presentation. Henderson ended up revising and expanding the history until it became a personal essay. "It got longer than expected," he shrugs, "but they published it." It stands as the only narrative in the otherwise technical journal, Molecular Physics. *The editor later confided why he included it: "It made a cold winter day brighter." This excerpt follows Henderson's adventures through his mission and education.*

These memoirs were written with the encouragement of Farid Abraham. In October 1994 Luis Mier y Teran and Orest Pizio organized a conference at the Physics Department of the Universidad Autónoma Metropolitana (Iztapalapa campus) and the Institute of Chemistry of the Universidad Nacional Autónoma de México on the occasion of my sixtieth birthday. I had entertained Farid and John Barker at lunch for years with stories of my youth. He asked me to write up some of these stories for him to read at the beginning of the first day. This is the result.

I am grateful for the conference and this issue in commemoration of my birthday. I enjoyed the talks and articles, both personally and professionally. For me at least, science is both intellectually stimulating and an opportunity to make many good friends with whom I enjoy interacting. Some of these friends have participated in the conference or contributed to the issue or both. Many more would have done so if they could.

I am less certain about writing my memoirs, even briefly. The term memoirs brings to my mind those of the "villain" in the film *Kind Hearts and Coronets.* Although less colourful than his, my life has been interesting. Hopefully, I can share some of these experiences in a way that will be enjoyable.

I was born in Calgary, in Western Canada, in 1934. My parents were both from Scotland but had met in Calgary. I was born in the depths of the

Great Depression, which was worse in Canada than in the United States. The United States was fortunate to have F. D. Roosevelt as President. Canada had R. B. Bennett as Prime Minister. With good reason, he is almost forgotten. Although our family had difficulties, my father was hard working and always managed to provide for us. In 1939, my father, although old enough to avoid military service, joined the Canadian Army to help rid the world of Hitler. He was sent to Ontario for training. My mother and I moved to Toronto in 1940 so that we could be near him until he posted overseas. I started my education in Toronto. In 1942 my father was sent to England. My parents had always wanted to live in Vancouver. As a result, in 1943 my mother and I moved to Vancouver, where my mother still lives. I find it amusing to hear from my mother that her friends in Toronto strongly advised her not to move to Vancouver because of the possibility of a Japanese invasion. The offensive aim of the Japanese fleet had been crippled at Midway a year earlier. In 1943, the Japanese military was interested only in avoiding defeat. Invasion of the west coast of North America was the furthest thing from their minds.

I continued my education in Vancouver. The war ended in 1945. Many Canadian soldiers, particularly those who had served from 1939, were returned that year. In 1946 my father was still in England. The Canadian Army involved him in arranging the transportation of other soldiers back to Canada without much concern as to whether he wanted to return home. By 1946, my mother was indignant that my father was still overseas, seven years after enlisting and four years after being posted overseas, so she wrote to her Member of Parliament (MP). Our MP expressed outrage at this in the House of Commons and my father was promptly returned to Canada. On leaving the army, he joined the Canadian civil service, first in the Post Office, and then in the Canadian Immigration Service. During the course of his service as an immigration officer, my father managed to make himself the object of debate in the House of Commons for the second time. A sailor, claiming to be stateless, jumped ship on Vancouver and applied for entry into Canada. My father denied him entrance because he felt that he was a criminal. This became a *cause célèbre*. Outrage was expressed in the newspapers, women offered to marry the man to enhance his chances of entering Canada, and the issue was raised in the House of Commons. My father refused to budge. I am not sure whether the sailor was admitted into Canada. Perhaps he was because my mother says that my father's judgement was vindicated by subsequent events. There is a similar story in Hailey's novel *In High Places*. Very likely the story in the novel was inspired by father's experience. If this is the case it is the only instance of anyone in our family becoming a character in a novel.

Perhaps a few more words about my father's career are in order. He felt unrecognized in the civil service. He would routinely be placed very highly in the civil service examinations. At least once, he was first in all of Canada. However, he was passed over for promotion because he did not have a university education. Finally, he was recognized and was given fairly senior appointments, first in Berlin and then in Glasgow. Regrettably, I did not participate in these travels because I was a grown man by then. Later, I made up for this. My friend John Barker says that I am the only person he knows who has been everywhere twice. My father liked Berlin particularly, and said that he would have liked to retire there. When my father arrived in Glasgow to be the chief immigration officer, he found that the office manager had been keeping permanent files. Every time someone dropped in to inquire about going to Canada, the office manager would open a file that would never be discarded, even if that person never came back or went to Canada. When my father saw these files, he ordered them to be destroyed. Apparently the office manager was in tears as his beautiful files were thrown out. Another story concerns my father's reply to a friend's question whether Canada admitted immigrants without consideration of their country of origin. With his tongue in his cheek, my father replied that Canada did not practice any discrimination; however, it sent immigration officers only to certain countries. Very simple, no officers, no immigrants. This was quite true. In the early 1970s, Canada announced that it would admit a large number of people suffering from the attentions of Amin in Uganda. When the government was questioned about the location of the nearest Immigration Office, the very serious reply was given that there was one in Beirut. In fairness to the Canadian Government, I should point out that in the end an officer was sent to East Africa, and that the present immigration policies of Canada are more even. Let me briefly mention two additional stories. Once in a Berlin hotel, my father encountered L. B. Johnson, then Vice President. Bumptious as ever, Johnson bounded up to him and gave him a pen inscribed, "All the way with LBJ." In disgust, my father promptly threw the pen away. While in Glasgow, he turned down an invitation from Queen Elizabeth to have tea with her at a diplomatic reception because he thought it a waste of time. My mother was furious when she was told. Evidently, he was not impressed by the "rich and famous."

In Vancouver I continued school. Especially at high school, I specialized in doing the minimum required to pass and little more. My Spanish teacher called me, with some affection, I think, "muy perezoso." Little did she or I realize that later I would have occasion to make use of her lessons. Only in history did I excel. Despite my best efforts to just get by, I managed a B average. Perhaps one of the reasons why I was inattentive at school was that my father offered to match my savings for university, dollar for dollar. I went out and got an after school job and saved 35 dollars in the first week. My father had not counted on this. Thirty-five dollars was a large sum at the time. He kept his side of the bargain for the first year and then decided that enough was enough. Perhaps my less than inspiring high school record was in part due to having spent too much time working and saving, a misdirected emphasis, really. My bad habits caught up with me during Christmas of my senior year. My mathematics teacher gave me a D. I was so insulted that I changed my habits and applied myself the rest of the year and obtained As. However, she only gave me a B as the final grade. Life is hard!

While in high school, I worked at various jobs during the summers. Between my junior and senior years, I "went to sea." I worked on a boat that travelled up and down the coast of British Columbia. I still have my Seaman's Identity Card. After graduating from high school and before entering the University of British Columbia (UBC), a friend and I obtained jobs in northern British Columbia. We were hired to take an inventory of equipment at a mine. The name of the mining company was Western Uranium Cobalt Mines Limited. This was in the middle of the uranium boom in North America. Perhaps this was the reason for the choice of company name. In fact, there was no uranium or cobalt in the mine. The main mine, where I lived, produced copper. A second mine, located about 10 or 15 miles away produced tungsten. These mines had a history of being opened and closed over the years. The price of the stock in this company doubled shortly after I took this job. Shortly after I left to enter UBC, the price of the stock crashed. I have always felt that the stockholders had confidence in the company only if I was associated with it.

Shortly after we arrived at the mine, the mine manager would not allow us to take inventory. Very curious! Instead I was assigned to assist the mine engineer to survey the old workings of the mine, some dating back to the First World War. At least I learned about surveying. I put this skill to use in three summers during my career at UBC. The copper vein in the mine was inclined by at least 45 degrees. The working areas followed the vein, of course. The mine engineer was very sensible. He would stand at the bottom of an old working area, and have me climb a couple of hundred feet to the top with a long tape measure. I would have to climb the old working area using the support of old rotting timbers, one in two of which would give way. On my first day underground, the mine captain saw a loose piece of rock on the roof of the tunnel. He decided to break it loose. He was on the side closest to the surface whereas I was on the inner side. I had visions of being forever trapped in the mine. Fortunately, he knew what he was doing and no harm came. However, I learned to hate being underground. Men, and now women, who have, or choose, to make a career of being miners have my sympathy.

I had other adventures at this mine which would have caused my mother to have a stroke had she known. On the first weekend my friend and I went mountain climbing. The climb itself was easy and not dangerous. It was a little difficult only because of the snow. This mine had the shortest summer I have ever encountered. It snowed until early July and was snowing again by mid-August. When we reached the summit of the mountain, we found that, although the mountain had a fairly gradual slope on our side, there was a precipice on the other side; a little like Half Dome in Yosemite. Naturally, we went to the edge to have a look. Only after we had made our way along the edge of the precipice could we look back and see that we had been standing on a snow ledge, caused by the wind, which could easily have collapsed under our weight.

Once a month, the engineer and I travelled to the tungsten mine. Our purpose was to measure the volume of ore that had been removed during the month. In addition to their hourly salary, the miners were paid a bonus, based on our measurements. We were treated like royalty by the miners, particularly before we made our measurements. We would drive about 10 or 15 miles on dirt roads to the foot of a mountain. The mine was located at the very top of the mountain. How the original prospector found this site, I do not know. The customary method of ascending the mountain was to take a hair raising ride on a mine cable. I will describe the ride shortly. I had done this twice before during my short career as an inventory clerk and was not bothered by it. I suppose that now I would be terrified. The engineer was new and had not ridden the cable before; he was older and wiser than I and wanted to avoid the ride if possible. He insisted that we take the jeep on an old, poorly maintained, switch back road, which went up the mountain. Naturally we became stuck and the poor man had to endure my comments that we should have taken the cable while we (or rather he) worked to get the jeep free. We freed the jeep but gave up driving; we returned to the valley and took the cable.

The cable was used to transport large buckets of ore down from the mine. Gravity powered the system. Full buckets came down and empty buckets went up. In place of one of the buckets there was a platform, made from several two-by-fours, which was suspended by two large hooks which in turn were attached to the cable. This was used to transport food, mail, equipment, and people to the mine. One sat on the platform and held on to the hooks for dear life. It was a bit like a primitive ski lift except that there were no safety bars or safety belts and you were at least a couple of hundred feet above ground. The whole thing swayed considerably in the wind. The ride took about 30 minutes because the system had to stop as each bucket was loaded with ore. I am surprised that some safety inspector had not closed the system down or at least prohibited the transportation of men.

The mine itself was located on a ridge at the top of the mountain. It was above the timber line and very barren and must have been a ghastly place to stay. The ridge was subject to high winds. The ruins of a large tractor lay at the bottom of a canyon near by. It had been blown off the ridge by the wind. The bunk houses would have been blown off as well except that they were attached to the ground by large cables that crossed over their roofs. Periodically, the bunk house would rise with the wind and I would wonder if the cables would hold. They always did. I was always happy to leave and return to the other mine even if it meant a ride on the cable.

Finally September came and I left to enroll at UBC. My first class each morning was first year physics. The professor was G. M. Shrum, who was a legend in Canada. He was the Head of the Physics Department, and had, to put it mildly, a very strong personality. He had won at least two medals for valour in the First World War. During the Second World War, he had been the colonel of the officer training corps at UBC. The story told on campus was that it took three or so years after the end of the war before he adjusted to the fact that the students did not have to salute him. Whether this was true, I do not know. However, he was often called Colonel Shrum. In any case, he should have been an officer in the Prussian Army during the nineteenth century. Whatever else, he certainly got things done. At the end of the war, there were many barracks located in Vancouver. The City Council wanted to put these into use. While they debated the purpose to which they would be put, Shrum organized some students and had the barracks moved to the campus where they became classroom buildings. Shrum could not stand interruptions during his class. If a student arrived late, he would complain for half an hour about how much time this disruption wasted. Since his class was at 8:15 in the morning, many students were late. I was late once and he threatened to throw me in the pool in front of the library. He was big enough to have done it. Quickly we learned to skip class when late. After retiring from UBC, G. M. became the head of the BC Power Commission and built several dams. In the course of the construction of one dam, the use of a defoliant was thought necessary. There were protests about this; as a response, G. M. drank a glass of defoliant in front of the TV cameras. Whether or not he was right, the man had style. After this, he built Simon Fraser University and became its first Chancellor. He died in his eighties, "in harness," building a new court house in Vancouver.

Other physics professors whom I remember specifically are J. B. Warren and F. A. Kaempffer. In my second year, I attended Professor Warren's lectures on thermodynamics. During these lectures he mentioned that in contrast to solids and gases, there was no theory for liquids and suggested this as something for us to develop. The comment proved more influential than he or I realized at the time. I attended Professor Kaempffer's lectures on mechanics in my senior year. He had a gift for explaining, in public lectures, the most complex physical phenomena in simple intuitive terms. His classroom lectures were not always so simple. His derivations often involved elegant mathematics. However, sometimes his mathematics made things obscure, rather than clear, for the students. He wrote an interesting book on quantum mechanics. In reviewing the book, Coulson, the famous quantum scientist, said that the only reason that he knew the book was on quantum mechanics was from the title. I had an outstanding undergraduate education; one that was helpful in graduate school and throughout my life. It was an exciting place to study physics and mathematics.

In my first or second year, Henry Eyring came to UBC to lecture. I did not know of him but was told that he was a Mormon. Since I too was a Mormon, I decided to attend out of curiosity. Eyring was an engaging speaker. I believe that he could have made a good living as a stand up comedian, had he wished to. In any case as a result of his lecture and some favourable comments of Kaempffer about Eyring's book, I decided to enter graduate school at the University of Utah.

At the time, the Physics Department of the University of Utah was in transition and was something of a disappointment after my experience at UBC. I imagine that I annoyed people by making unfavourable comparisons. Let me say that Utah's Physics Department is now first rate. One pleasant part of my first year at Utah was that I met Michael Rochester, a fellow Canadian. He was at Utah beginning his doctoral studies in geophysics. We shared an office. Assigned problems play a larger role in US college education than is, or was, the case in Canada. Mike and I spent many hours working on these problems. In retrospect, it was a good experience. We have remained friends and, whenever possible, we hike together.

I debated about leaving but stayed, largely because of Eyring. There is a curious symmetry and asymmetry in our careers. We both had early and unpleasant experiences with mining. He was born in Mexico and I am now in Mexico. In any case, I obtained my PhD under Henry's direction. Unfortunately, he was no longer at the frontier of research. He was intellectually as keen as ever. I think he enjoyed being a sought-after speaker, and this took up much of his time. He still maintained a research program but usually either on eccentric topics or using out-of-date theories. He used to tell me that he was the world's greatest research director because he provided no direction. The student had to survive on his own. This was not quite true, but it was fairly close to the truth. Whether Henry's continued activity in research was a strength or weakness, others must judge. He was, at the time, interested in the theory of liquids. Because of the comment of Professor Warren, I worked on this problem. My thesis on liquids, using the out-of-date significant structure theory, was forgettable. But at least it was a start. After graduating, I gradually learned about the field. Frank Buff once introduced me before a talk, which I gave at the University of Rochester, as having worked on significant structure theory for my PhD research, but that, in spite of that beginning, I had made important contributions. What is clear is that Henry, with this enthusiasm and common sense attitudes to life, was an important influence on me. I was very sad when he died in unpleasant circumstances in 1981.

After going to Utah, but before starting my research, I went to South Africa for two years as a Mormon missionary. I was not enthused with my assignment to South Africa as I disliked the racial policies then in place there; however, I went. I travelled to South Africa by boat, taking a month to get there. I went by way of England and, while there, I was given a box containing some material to take to the mission headquarters in Capetown. When I arrived in Capetown, the bottom of the box fell out so I picked up the smaller boxes inside and carried them and my luggage to the customs inspection area. Earlier, I had filled out my customs declaration form. I had declared that I had three items of luggage. Because of the box breaking, I now had five items. The customs official said that this would not do. I offered to change the three to a five on the form. This apparently was not possible. I suggested that I should fill out a new form. He would have none of that. What to do? Then the customs officer had a stroke of genius. He tied a string loosely around the three small boxes. It was not sufficient to hold them together. However, with a look of great pride he said that I now had three items. I then cleared customs.

My first assignment was to the city of Benoni. Benoni is a biblical name meaning "child of my sorrow." When I learned this, I thought that this was not an encouraging omen. However, I spent 10 months there and enjoyed it. I made friends with whom I have remained in contact over the years. When I was assigned to Benoni, I was given a train ticket and told to change trains in Johannesburg. I was also told that I should not expect anyone to meet me in Johannesburg. This was fine. I was a big boy and could change trains by myself. The ordinary trains in South Africa are (or at least were) rather slow. I used to joke that if I became bored, I could go for a walk and then sit and wait for the train to catch up with me, an exaggeration, but only slight. On arriving in Johannesburg, I did what I was told, changed trains and went on to Benoni, about an hour to the East. However, the missionaries in Johannesburg, convinced that I was a poor lost soul who needed help, came to the station to meet me. This was kind of them. Not realizing that I had made a quick change of trains, they spent the day worrying about the "lost" missionary. It was sorted out by evening.

On arrival in Benoni, I asked the taxi driver to take me to 131 Ampthill Avenue. He replied something like, "you've got it," and drove me about 20 feet and said that I was there. I knocked on the door and my new landlady Miss Sargent opened the door. The hallway behind her was dark, and she was not a lady to pay attention to her appearance. Her hair was uncombed which gave her a wild appearance. She claimed that I had "a look of stark horror on my face." Miss Sargent and her boarding house were different, to say the least. One of the boarders used to come to the dinner table, get his plate, and scrape the food into the toilet. Miss Sargent claimed that he existed on alcohol and that his urine was pure alcohol. The rumour was that they had been engaged at one time. I think that she left her house to him when she died, as some months after she died, he wrote to me using that address.

Miss Sargent was an interesting character. She used to walk her pet duck on a leash. She was known in Benoni for making hats out of cereal boxes. I have several stories that I could tell about her but one will suffice. In her youth she had been an aspiring painter. One of her paintings was of Adam and Eve. She wanted her brother to pose in the nude; he refused. She obtained her model by knocking him out. When he regained consciousness, he was nude in a chair with his sister painting enthusiastically. She says that she debated as to whether Adam should have a navel. I saw the painting but cannot recall how she solved that problem.

After Benoni, I worked in Johannesburg and Capetown. I like Capetown better because there was a more tolerant attitude about race there. Apartheid was in full bloom then. Sharpville was only a few years off. During the time I was in South Africa, fifty people were on trial for treason. In South Africa, treason meant disagreeing with the government. Although, the name meant nothing to me then, Nelson Mandela was one of the defendants. The defendants were acquitted after two or more years. The judiciary was one of the few bright spots in South Africa. Eventually the government found a pretext to jail these people (and others). It was a curious but interesting time to be in South Africa. In South Africa, the term for whites was European and the term for non-whites was non-European. Once when I was in Capetown, a group of Americans visited the city. They used the commuter train to go somewhere. When they saw the signs at the train station they decided that, since they were not Europeans, they should use the non-European carriage. Naturally, this caused a stir. Such was the stupidity of apartheid. Other stupidities, included the fact that Japanese and Hong Kong business men, with whom South Africa had valuable trade relations, were given the title of honorary Europeans so that they could enjoy amenities, normally reserved for whites. Evidently, apartheid was fine as long as it did not conflict with business.

One South African man complained to me about some delays in building a hospital. He then said that such delays were the price of democracy. At the time, I thought that his comment was ridiculous. Blacks, Asians, and others were people too. But in a way he was right. There was enough latent democracy in South Africa to lead to genuine democracy three decades later.

When I returned to Utah, Henry asked me to speak to his class about South Africa. I forecast that South Africa could maintain its racial policies as long as it was surrounded by white controlled states such as Angola, Mozambique, and Rhodesia. However, I said that, when these states became ruled by the blacks, South Africa would not be able to survive as a racist state, but that majority rule would not be achieved before there was widespread bloodshed. I was half right. Majority rule in the adjoining states was one of the catalysts that led to the collapse of apartheid. On the other hand, I am happy that bloodshed was not necessary to bring democracy. The whites in South Africa were smarter than I realized. Also, I have always been amazed at the continued goodwill of the blacks and other races in South Africa towards the whites, although not always towards each other. I only hope that peace continues in South Africa.

It was in South Africa that I met my wife, Rose-Marie, who is originally from Capetown. I suppose that she has second thoughts from time to about the wisdom of marrying a "mad scientist." Once I said to Lesser Blum and his wife that a successful scientist must be a little crazy. By this I meant that to be successful as a scientist, one must be thinking constantly about one's research. In any case, Lesser's wife smiled but did not disagree. John Barker once said to me that it is asking a lot for a person to be both creative and normal. I will say more about these friends and colleagues later. But to return to my wife, despite any possible second thoughts (on her part, not mine), we have had a good life together and have three fine daughters and now four grandchildren of whom we are proud.

DOUGLAS HENDERSEN is a professor of chemistry, and known by many in his field as the "grandfather" of applying theory to the field of liquid surfaces. In addition to numerous scientific articles, he has also written a biography of his thesis advisor, Henry Eyring. Henderson says his interests haven't made him rich, but it has given him "a good life."

Questions

1. What is the organizational structure of this memoir?
2. Why does he include stories about his father and mother?
3. What textual evidence indicates a non-LDS audience?
4. Henderson says he wants his memoirs to be interesting and enjoyable. How does this affect the type of selection Kathryn Egan suggests in "Writing from Real Life: Why Writers Keep Journals"?

Living A Miracle

David L. and Delys Cowles

"Living a Miracle," originally published in Brigham Young Magazine, *is the story told in* Miracle Victory over the Flesh-Eating Bacteria, *David and Delys Cowles's book about David's recovery from* necrotizing fascitis *(or the "flesh-eating bacteria"). In contemplating writing about his experience, Cowles said, "I have hesitated to add another volume to the pile of existing books describing private and spiritual experiences in the most public and, I have often thought, undignified, and inappropriate ways." Indeed, some of the intensely personal things, he was "reluctant to commit . . . to paper." Despite all this, the Cowles have "felt a strong compulsion" to share their story, as they feel that the story is not just theirs, but belongs to the countless people who helped them through this experience. These people "are entitled to hear it all and to be honored for their contributions to it." Most of all, they decided to write this "as the influence and evidence of God's hand in all this are too strong for even a part-time skeptic to question." Her narrative appears in plain text, his is italicized.*

At Christmastime we were all worn out. Most English professors are. Between David and me, last fall semester we had taught five courses and more than 200 students in BYU's English Department. Finally, at three in the afternoon on December 22, 1994, we were ready with grades finished and family packed. The black duffel bag suitcases we bought when we directed the London Study Abroad program bulged with clothes, toys, and the inevitable books. Two years ago we looked like the Family Von Trapp in their traveling clothes. This year we looked like a family with warm California in its eyes. This year we were going to rest for a week at my parents' home in Southern California. David nicked his finger zipping up his bag, but it didn't bleed, so he ignored it. When I called my parents to tell them we would arrive late, my father, Merwin Waite, quietly told me his 94-year-old mother had just died, which meant we would be in California for her funeral. After a quick stop at BYU to turn in grades, we were off driving south on I-15. But the relaxing vacation in Hacienda Heights never really evolved.

The day before Christmas, David noticed his finger was slightly infected and asked for antiseptic and a bandage. That night he noticed some pain under his arm. Right after we opened presents on Sunday, Christmas morning, he broke out into chills, and his body began to shake. The next two days we were sure he had a terrible intestinal flu. By Tuesday morning his body ached so badly he could hardly stand the pain. We called his doctor in Provo, who said it sounded like the flu that was going around. Consequently, when it came time for Grandma's funeral, we felt we could leave David alone.

My grandmother had lived a long, full 94 years, so her funeral was a mix of grief and joy. As the oldest granddaughter, I stood at the pulpit and told about Waite women being strong.

Then the world turned surrealistic. As I sat down on the stand, my neighbor ran a note up to me: "Your husband has been taken to the hospital by ambulance." I asked my mother, June, to watch the children and rushed home. I called around, found the right emergency room, and then asked, "Is my husband okay?" They answered, "Yes." I drove quickly to the hospital, thinking David had probably overreacted and was just dehydrated. Instead, I found my husband on the edge of death.

EMERGENCY

Tuesday morning I felt sicker than I had ever been before. The body aches that accompanied this "flu" had become so painful, I could hardly stand to sit or lie or do anything. I kept taking hot baths, hoping for no good reason that this would reduce the pain somewhat. It never did, but at least filling up the bathtub helped distract me.

The pain continued with no significant change. Suddenly, I sensed within my mind the words, "You need an ambulance. Now." It wasn't an actual voice, but it was so insistent and forceful that I could not ignore it. Still, I hesitated. I'm not the sort of person who calls 911 for myself. If one of my children were in danger, I would call in an instant. But whether because of latent male machismo or just being too cheap to pay for an ambulance, I am the kind of person who would die sitting next to the telephone, wondering whether I was really sick enough to call for help.

Again the almost audible voice said, "You need an ambulance. Now!" I had had enough experience with that voice to obey it. I limped my way to the phone and dialed 911.

When a woman's voice answered, I repeated the words I had heard in my mind: "I need an ambulance. Now." The woman confirmed my address and promised to send paramedics. Then she tried valiantly to keep me on the line and conscious. "Sit up straight and keep talking," she said. "Put both feet on the floor." I did my best, but my body was becoming increasingly uncooperative. Finally, I just couldn't do what she asked any longer. "I'm going to hang up now," I said, as politely as I could. As

I reached to hang up the phone, I could hear her frantically trying to keep me on the line, but I was past caring.

I walked to the bedroom with excruciating slowness, leaning against the wall for support. With great effort I managed to exchange my robe for sweat pants and a T-shirt. Sensing that I was losing consciousness, I stumbled to unlock the front door, then literally crawled to the living room couch, collapsing in dizziness and pain.

A few minutes later two fire trucks and an ambulance pulled up outside the house, lights flashing wildly. A whole army of uniformed paramedics jumped out of each vehicle. Someone pounded on the door and called, "Paramedics."

"Come in," I called out, as loudly as I could. Apparently that wasn't very loud, because the knocking continued. Finally someone opened the door.

"I'm over here," I moaned.

Immediately, I was surrounded by people prodding, poking, and questioning me. While I tried to answer, one looked up from my left arm and said, "I can't get any blood pressure at all. Try the other arm." That one was equally unsuccessful. "Let's take him in," someone finally said. The paramedics strapped me to a gurney and hauled me out to the ambulance. Just before they put me in, an LDS neighbor rushed out of her house to see what was wrong. "Tell Delys," was all I could manage to say.

During the ride to the hospital, I first heard the set of questions medical personnel would ask me and Delys over and over again. "Are you a heavy smoker?" "No, I don't smoke." "Have you been drinking excessive amounts of alcohol recently?" "No, I don't drink." They would pause as if surprised, then ask suspiciously, "Are you sure?" Finally I said, "Of course I'm sure. I'm a Mormon." Even that didn't seem to satisfy them, but at least they quit asking for a while.

The next thing I remember is finding myself on a curtained-off cot in Emergency. An Asian man I would come to know as Dr. Shin was asking me the same questions everyone else had asked as he monitored my vital signs. He was obviously concerned about my condition but uncertain what my problem was. "You may find this uncomfortable, but we have to insert a tube through your nose." "What—" I started to say, but Dr. Shin had already begun worming the plastic tube into my left nostril. I gagged as it painfully passed through my nose and down my throat. After a few minutes I grew relatively accustomed to the tube, though I found it perpetually uncomfortable.

Dr. Shin and another physician discussed my symptoms while waiting for an X-ray machine to arrive. I apparently showed signs of heart attack, but some of my symptoms were inconsistent with that diagnosis. Finally another doctor told me he wanted to take a CAT scan. I was wheeled to another room, where my torso was exposed. Technicians moved me to a kind of tray that allowed my body to enter the unit. The CAT scan took about an hour.

As the technicians slid me out, someone noticed that a blackish-purple spot about four inches in diameter had formed on my side. It had not been there when I entered the machine. "Have you been kicked in that side?" someone asked me. No one had told me about the spot, so the question seemed absurd. "No," I said. "Why would they?" "Maybe you were drunk and didn't notice," someone else suggested. Here we go again, I thought.

I could see the physician speaking to Delys with considerable animation, but too softly for me to hear. Why don't they talk to me, I wondered. I guess I'll have to wait for Delys to tell me what the doctor said.

That was my last fully conscious thought for six days.

CRISIS

When I arrived at the hospital, I found David was not overreacting to the flu. The doctors were extremely concerned because he had almost no blood pressure, his kidneys had shut down, and no one could discover the source of his problem. David was still in a lot of pain, but they couldn't give him any pain medication until his blood pressure went up. They took him away for a CAT scan. Meanwhile, my mother arrived, and we waited together, dozing off in the hard chairs. We had stayed up late the night before preparing for Grandma's funeral.

Suddenly a concerned doctor asked me, "How did your husband get that big bruise on his side? Did someone kick him? Was he drunk last night?"

"I can promise you my husband does not drink alcohol." The doctors never seemed convinced. "And he did not have a bruise there when you took him into the CAT scan." Their concern obviously deepened.

Looking back on it, our being in the hospital at this very moment, with doctors examining his body constantly, helped save his life. The doctors quickly conferred with each other. Then they told me the dread news.

"We think this might be *necrotizing fascitis.* Have you heard of the flesh-eating bacteria?"

"I have, but I don't really pay attention to tabloid-type diseases."

"Well, this is probably what he has. It is an extremely aggressive bacteria and can spread as fast as an inch an hour. The bacteria and its toxins destroy the skin and soft tissue and shut down vital organs. Our only recourse is to take him into surgery right away and try to cut out the infected parts. I am going to open him up from wrist to hip, and he may end up looking like a shark bit him. Even so, this disease is so fast moving, he only has a five to ten percent chance of living."

I knew that "a five to ten percent chance of living" was the doctor's way of saying gently, "Your husband is probably going to die." But I also knew that he still had a chance, and I knew how to increase the odds. The doctors several times came to tell me how serious David's condition was and how little chance he had of living. But I am a pretty strong person, especially in a crisis. My calm confused them, and they asked if I understood the gravity of the situation.

I answered, "I do realize how serious this is. But I say a ten percent chance is worth going for. Let's go for life. Let's save him."

The nurse suggested we bring our children quickly before surgery so they could see their father, probably for the last time. My mother drove back to her home and gathered up our five children, who had just arrived from the family dinner after their great-grandmother's funeral. I secretly prayed that they would arrive before the surgeons took David away.

In the meantime, my father arrived with my sister's husband. They gave David a priesthood blessing. By this time, David was covered with tubes and surrounded by beeping machines. My father sat on a hard chair in the hall afterward; his face looked worried and starkly white. He realized that his oldest daughter, at the rather young age of 37, was likely to be a widow with five children and overwhelming responsibilities.

When the children arrived, they were in shock. They had spent the morning at a funeral, the first for most of them.

Then they came home to find that their fanatically healthy father might die. Emotions ran high. The nurse prepared them to see their father covered with tubes, and we went in to see him. I had decided not to tell David how serious the situation was because I wanted him to be in a positive mindset for the operation. We wished him well, squeezed his hand, then gathered out in the hall, where the nurse brought us apple juice and chairs so we wouldn't faint.

As the orderlies rolled David into surgery, my family moved to the waiting room. We knelt, and each of us offered a prayer for David's health. A nurse found crayons and paper for our two youngest, Steven and Marissa, and made arrangements so I could make long distance phone calls.

My daughter, Cristie, and I went into an unused office to phone friends. I called Leon and Beth Cowles, David's parents, in Portland, Ore.; Beth Hedengren, our neighbor and colleague in the English Department; Bruce Bryan, our bishop; and later Jay Fox, our department chair. I said, "I have something very serious to tell you. David has a rare disease called *necrotizing fascitis*. He has only a five to ten percent chance of living, and the next two hours in surgery will determine whether he lives or dies. But I believe in miracles and the power of prayer. Will you call everyone we know and ask them to pray for him?"

Within an hour nearly the entire English Department, our ward, other friends, and our extended family were actively praying for David. And David's parents gallantly worked to find plane tickets from Portland to Los Angeles the same week as the Rose Bowl.

The scary thing about waiting for surgery results is that you don't know which emotion to prepare for. I remember lying on the floor because I felt weak. Any minute someone could walk in and tell me my husband had died, or that he didn't really have this disease and would be fine. When the surgeons finally came, they had encouraging news. The disease had not progressed as far as they expected, so they did not have to cut much soft tissue. We all cheered and felt that the Lord had answered our prayers.

The surgeons told us they wanted to move David to another hospital four miles away when he stabilized. About midnight an ambulance arrived to take David, but his blood pressure was too low for them to move him. He was semi-conscious after the surgery, so I went in and talked to him. I held his hand and talked about simple things like the colors in the room and how proud I was of him. His blood pressure rose, and the ambulance took him away.

At the new hospital, the doctors (David had a team of about twelve different doctors) told me they were going to attack this bacteria on three fronts: first, antibiotic therapy, which would require a few days to take effect; next, surgery, cutting out all necrotized (or dead) and infected tissue; and third, a hyperbaric chamber. Only three hospitals in the Los Angeles area have a chamber like this. It looks like a long metal tube, about three feet in diameter. Inside, the atmospheric pressure increases to three or four times normal, and pure oxygen is pumped in. This forced oxygen into David's cells and helped his body fight the disease. He spent several hours each day in the chamber and would come out lobster red.

By now David looked terrible. He was so swollen the staff thought he weighed much more than he really did. Fortunately, we had taken off his wedding ring before the first surgery, and I wore it for several days next to my own. David had a tube going down his throat, one down his nose, one into a central catheter for all the IVs, and another into his arm for blood samples. He had electrodes all over his body and a clamp on his finger to monitor oxygen in his blood. The only place I could touch him was his left hand, so I held it a lot. Every time the doctors sliced his body, they left the wounds open and just wrapped them with gauze. "Continue to give him fluids," ordered his main doctor, Dr. Saketkhoo. "It's impossible to give him too much. His body is like a sieve—everything seeps out the open incisions."

David couldn't talk because of the tube down his mouth, but he could blink and squeeze my hand. He was semi-conscious, so I spoke to him.

"Do you want to know where you are?"

"Yes, desperately," his eyes told me.

"We are in a hospital in Whittier. Do you want to know what is wrong with you?" He looked quite confused. He nodded as vigorously as he could.

"You have an aggressive bacterial infection. I called your parents and told them, and they flew down here to see you."

David looked puzzled, as if saying, "Why are my parents here? Tell them not to go to all this trouble." I wanted David to fight for life and not give up, but I thought that if he knew that he was on the brink of dying, he would be shocked. Consequently, I tried to make all the visits from children, parents-in-law, and parents look like a normal thing concerned people do, not like a final goodbye march.

THE DARKEST HOURS

My memories of the next six days are vivid but detached and retain a certain surrealistic, fuzzy quality. I underwent major, life-saving surgery six times in those six days, so I constantly suffered from the effects of anaesthesia. And when that wore off, I was on high doses of morphine.

All my memories seem to be at night, though I believe this was because my room was always darkened. Outside, the busy desk for that section of the hospital made me believe I was in a back room at some sort of business establishment, perhaps a mail-order retailer. I remember people bringing mail and making other deliveries, but I never managed to connect what people said with any general sense of where I was or what was happening to me. I recall wondering with the paranoia that sometimes accompanies morphine whether I had been kidnaped. Perhaps I was being held here, drugged out of my mind, for some mysterious purpose. As nearly as I can recall, it never occurred to me that I was in a hospital.

I do retain several vivid memories from this period. I remember a doctor and nurse trying to adjust my bed, and having difficulties with a mechanism that I later learned kept squeezing and releasing my legs to keep the blood flowing through them. I remember Delys bringing my oldest children to see me. That memory, still rather vague, features Delys bending over me and repeating "Choose life, David. Choose life." I don't think I had the slightest idea what she was talking about. Her appearance somehow reminded me of a Fizzies commercial I hadn't thought of since I was a child, though now I have no idea what the connection might have been.

I also remember someone asking me if I knew where I was. I tried to answer, but could not because of the tube down my throat. I shook my head. "You're in a special medical facility," she said. "You've been moved here because you are very, very sick, and we have the facilities to take care of you." Sick, I thought. Imagine that. Then I lapsed back into unconsciousness.

The second day, Wednesday, was grim. I slept fitfully a while in the staff sleeping room. Dr. Shin, the surgeon, and my mother awoke me. There in the dimmed light of the room, Dr. Shin gave me his latest post-surgery prognosis. He said he did not have a good feeling about David's chances. His neck was so swollen that he worried the bacteria had spread there. Much of the skin on his arm was gone, and the bacteria seemed to have spread down his side. The surgeons were trying to anticipate where it would go next. They cut away anything that looked infected. They would probably have to amputate his arm and any other limb that became infected. Worse yet, his heart was acting strangely, and Dr. Shin feared that the bacteria might be there already. If so, he would certainly die.

Hope diminished. Although we celebrated earlier in the day when we reached the 24-hour mark, now I felt I should really face the idea of David dying. My parents brought the children again to say hello to David, but I hesitated taking them in because their father looked too swollen and sick—not a great sight to linger in your mind forever. I decided Steven, 8, and Marissa, 3, should stay in the waiting room. I didn't know whether 12-year-old Robby could handle it. He had been quite distressed the night before when he saw David on the verge of his first operation. I gave Robby the choice, and he decided to remain in the waiting room. Kathryn and Cristie, 15 and 17, came with me to talk to their father. All David could do was blink his eyes in partial recognition. It was very hard for us all.

That night we all went home to sleep. I slept on a hide-a-bed in the family room, because no one would sleep in the bed David had gotten sick in. We were afraid even to go in to change the sheets. We prayed as a family again, and we all tried to sleep. As I lay down after my long, heartfelt prayer, I used all my concentration to clear my spirit of a heavy darkness. Demons floated in my mind, and I had no peace. I heard Cristie locked in the bathroom, crying. But I couldn't move. It took all my energy to keep from sinking into the darkness assailing me. "Heavenly Father, please help me," I whispered over and over.

The next morning, I looked in my closet and noticed David's Christmas presents. I thought, "I wonder if I can take these back." My father and I sat down on the edge of the bed and talked. It sounded as if the doctors were going to amputate limbs wherever the bacteria spread. Even then, he would probably not live. I had just dressed my grandmother for burial two days before, and I couldn't figure out how I could even dress David for burial if he was severely cut up and missing limbs. Dad and I discussed life insurance, our finances, and how I would support the family.

But the timing seemed all wrong. David was only 40. In his teaching I have seen him influence many people to be more righteous and spiritual, more tolerant of others, more responsive to God's will. I've read students' notes to him, and I see the guidance he gives many who face intellectual-spiritual crises, as he did earlier in his life. I know the strong influence he has on his own sons and daughters. And on me, for heaven's sake. I remember bargaining with God: "If you need him, take him. But there are very few people who can do what David does here on earth. I know he can do much more to build thy kingdom."

I finally decided that if the Lord chose to let David die, I would let him go. But if he chose to spare him, I would do everything I could do to help him live.

Support from Home

Our family were not the only ones praying. Word spread quickly. My parents' ward and my Waite relatives knew David was sick because this all happened at the time of my grandmother's funeral. A high school friend who was a nurse at the hospital became our local informer; people called her for updates. My uncle passed on the news to my Waite relatives.

Back in Utah, our bishop spread the news. I originally caught him at his office in the middle of tithing settlement to tell him of our plight and ask for the prayers of the ward. Within minutes our entire ward was praying for our family. In several cases young children made sure their families never prayed without mentioning David.

Then on Wednesday night something quite magical happened. The fax machine at the nurses' station rolled off page after page of notes from our ward.

"Is this guy some kind of a celebrity or something?" the puzzled nurses asked.

"No, we just have a lot of people who love us," I said, with pride in my ward.

The next day, a FedEx messenger brought a large envelope full of letters for our children from their friends. Wow, it was comforting to receive support from so many people.

By this time our neighbor and colleague, Beth Hedengren, had called people who called other people until the whole English Department knew about my condition. The news shocked everyone, and the entire department began to pray for my recovery. One wrote me later that he told the Lord, "I will accept nothing less than Dave Cowles alive and back here teaching." On Wednesday morning—during the middle of the semester break—about 15 of my colleagues gathered in the department office and offered a prayer. Several members of this group began fasting at that time.

On Thursday, grades were due, so a lot of people showed up. By now the department office had become the central gathering point for sharing information and concern. That morning about thirty-five members of the English faculty and several colleagues from other departments gathered in the word processing center. After a long and moving prayer and many tears, the members of this group quietly dispersed to private places to pray again.

THE TURNING POINT

Thursday morning I went to the hospital, knowing I might have to let David go. But much to my surprise, when I got there Dr. Saketkhoo came to the waiting room to tell us David was doing better. He said David's body was stabilizing and that they had lowered his dosage of Dopamine, which helps raise blood pressure. His kidneys were beginning to work better. His blood looked good, and best of all, the bacteria did not seem to be in his heart or any other organ—only in the soft tissue under his skin. They had lanced and drained his badly swollen neck, and there was no sign of the bacteria there either.

I walked back to David's room, and when I got close, I could feel the full presence of his personality. He still had tubes everywhere, including down his throat to help him breathe, so he couldn't talk to me, but his eyes and hand-squeezes expressed much.

I asked David the question I had been mulling over for a day, even though I already knew the answer: "David, do you want to live?"

"*Are you crazy? Of course I do,*" his eyes told me. I could tell he had not considered death this whole time.

"Well, that's good, because you are going to live. I am proud of you for fighting off this infection so well."

David tried to move his right hand, but could not because it was wrapped up. He motioned with his left hand for a pen.

"I love you," he scrawled. I have a good husband.

"I love you," I replied.

Next he wrote "pillow," meaning, as he put it later, "Please find me a comfortable pillow like the one I have at home. This lousy hospital thing is driving me crazy."

The Right Arm

Thursday afternoon Dr. Shin, ready for the day's surgery, introduced me to Dr. Britto, a plastic surgeon. Dr. Shin told me he had asked Dr. Britto to join him in case they had to amputate David's right arm. This took me by surprise.

"But he is a pianist. Remember in your operation that he is a pianist."

"I thought he was an English professor."

"Well, playing the piano isn't his profession. It's his great love, though. He's composed many pieces. Remember he is a pianist."

I prayed hard during the operation that David would heal and that he would be able to keep his arm. After the operation the surgeons told us that after some discussion they had decided to leave his arm for today, but that they would reevaluate again tomorrow. More frightening, though, the bacteria was still spreading. Dr. Shin had expected it to go down his legs, but he saw a red streak across David's abdomen and traced the infection to his left side now. Dr. Britto said he had performed many operations, but the large amounts of dead jelly-like tissue they removed from David's abdomen had made him feel sick. Dr. Shin still only gave David a ten percent chance of living, but I could tell David was going to survive.

At home I discussed David's arm with the family. I felt funny praying for his arm at first. I felt as if I had already been offered a banquet with David staying alive, and now I was ungratefully asking for dessert. But my father reminded us that we should pray for the things we need. David needed his arm, and we prayed for it.

Three times the surgeons went in to amputate David's arm, and every time they decided it had enough healthy tissue to leave it. Even so, his arm had lost most of the skin and much of the underlying tissue. He was missing great clumps of skin and tissue over his entire torso; only about half the skin on his upper body remained. But his body was getting stronger and fighting the disease. The doctors took David off the respirator and lowered his morphine dose.

My first experience with complete and clear-headed consciousness took the medical staff by surprise. I suddenly awoke to find myself in a bed. A nurse was holding my right arm up in the air to change the dressing. I looked over at it and was horrified to see not my arm, but a shocking mess of blood, muscle, tissue—indeed, everything but skin. I remember formulating my question calmly and carefully: "What in the world happened to my arm?" I asked the nurse. She seemed shocked that I was alert enough to ask such a question. I wasn't supposed to see what had happened to me until I had been properly prepared. I didn't understand until later the panic my sudden awakening caused.

Nurses hurried off to fetch a doctor. The nurse holding my arm brought it down where I could not see it. "You've been very ill," she said. "Don't worry about anything. You're going to be all right."

"Oh," I said with relief. I thought, I'm going to be all right. I guess I can go back to sleep. But before I could, one of the nurses who had left returned to tell me about the hospital's counseling services. Did I want to see a psychiatrist? she asked frantically. Would I like a visit from the chaplain? The questions seemed unnecessary; I had already forgotten my arm as I slipped back into unconsciousness. "No," I answered. "Why should I want to see any of them?"

LOVE AND SUPPORT

By Friday the hospital was getting so many phone calls from Utah inquiring about my condition that the public relations department called Joyce Baggerly, the English Department's amazing secretary. For the next week Joyce left phone mail messages providing information on my condition, changed three times daily, including the weekend. For more than a month, she added daily updates. Hundreds of calls came in to the "David Cowles Hot Line," as it quickly came to be called, for the most up-to-date information available. Relatives and concerned friends in California also learned to check the department hot line. We sometimes joked that I even called in occasionally to see how I was doing that day.

At 3:00 every afternoon the department express-mailed me a box or large envelope with messages from colleagues and students. As Joyce put it in the department's history:

> *The envelope contains many different forms of love. Faxes have come from all over the United States, students have drawn booklets of their favorite subjects taught by David, extraordinary messages left on phone mail are put on ordinary phone message slips, books of cartoons (so far, 3 editions of Calvin & Hobbes), and several CDs and cassette tapes. Some faculty members come every morning to put their daily greetings in the envelope before they go to their offices: notes, letters, epistles, allegories, puns, jokes, or hand-drawn cartoons, and one even puts in a copy of* The Daily Universe.

These offerings were the high point of each day in the hospital. Many of my colleagues sent heartfelt letters that moved me deeply and helped sustain me through the most difficult times.

Many people, from on and off campus, contributed to the trust fund set up to help us with expenses. Periodically, I received door-sized sheets of paper that had been posted outside my office, filled with notes of care and concern from students, faculty, and friends. We received faxes and letters from friends, acquaintances, and even complete strangers from all over the United States. Members of the Whittier Stake found a place for my parents to stay, and LDS members from all over came to donate much-needed blood.

Prayers from members of my ward, from the Saints in California and elsewhere, and from many people who are not even Mormons helped sustain me during these months in the hospital. A Roman Catholic colleague sent me a note informing me that a mass would be held for me. Nurses, therapists, and even a few doctors in the hospital came in to say they were praying for me. One physical therapist generously brought me a blackberry milkshake I wasn't supposed to have. (She apparently knew that hospital food is what the starving children in third-world countries send back.) She told me her Bible study group had decided to pray for me daily. LDS wards from as far away as New York held special fasts on my behalf. And I learned that I was remembered in prayers offered in meetings of the First Presidency, the General Authorities, the BYU Board of Trustees, and others.

One morning after I had somehow survived a particularly horrendous day of crisis, Joyce talked with the head nurse of the Critical Care Unit to get information for the daily update. The nurse told her that it was yet another miracle day: "And I know you people believe in miracles. In fact, I would say that you people in Utah have kept this man alive with your prayers because he should be dead with what he's had."

There is no question in my mind that she was right. There is no way I should be alive today—let alone in possession of all my limbs and without serious permanent loss of function. I can't begin to count the number of hospital personnel—from doctors and nurses to cleaners and orderlies—who came into my room to see the "miracle man." I have no doubt that many generous and caring people did, indeed, pray me a miracle. I have been truly amazed—and deeply moved—at the tremendous outpouring of love and faith on my behalf.

I sometimes feel unworthy of all that love and faith, especially when I recognize that many, many people who have equally difficult trials may not receive the publicity and prayers I did. As one physician who appeared with me on a television interview joked privately, I had become the poster child for the disease of the month.

RECOVERY

Once the bacteria had run its course and my life was no longer threatened, I had to begin the long process of recovery. Part of recovery meant re-covering me with skin. The doctors predicted I would require at least five or six months of hospitalization and two years of therapy and surgery to regain my full strength and flexibility. I have always been a slow healer, so this news was quite disheartening. But as the prayers and support continue to bless me and my family, we find smaller, less obvious miracles everywhere. I left the hospital in less than two months. My body has healed at a rate that astounds many of those who saw me in those early, dark days. Though the process has been painful and sometimes frustrating, I expect to be fully healed and back in the classroom a year from the time I first got sick.

My parents reread some of my father's 1990 journal recently. My father had recorded a comment David made in a priesthood lesson about prayer—that we shouldn't pray that nothing bad will happen to us, but that we will have the kind of attitude that will turn whatever does happen into a blessing. I have seen very little discouragement from David in the past months. This gift to see the blessings in the trials has extended to our entire family. Last week I told some friends that when we arrived at the airport, we found our car in long-term parking with three flat tires. "Maybe after our experiences of the past months, I should rephrase that," I added. "I arrived at the car to find one fully inflated tire!"

David arrived home from the hospital eager to know whether his hand would work at all. He had already surprised the doctors just by moving his fingers, since they were sure they had nicked the major nerve. Though he couldn't even put on socks by himself, he hoped he would be able to play a few notes or a chord. He put his hands on the piano and we looked at each other hopefully. He then commenced to play beautifully, almost as if nothing had happened. He composed a new piece on the spot. Three miracles: he lives, he keeps his arm, and he can still play Beethoven sonatas.

I will lose very little that matters—a year of time, a bit of mobility—and I have had to endure some pain. Scars and skin grafts cover much of my body, though most of them are hidden beneath my clothing. I will probably never hit a killer tennis serve again, but I hope to play eventually. I have lost none of my facility and none of my enjoyment for playing the piano. Most important, I still have my family, whom I have come to love and appreciate even more than before.

And I love to laugh even more than before. Last week a physical therapist in Provo repeated what many people have said: "At least you still have your sense of humor." "That's terrible!" I replied. "I never had one before!"

Though I still can't always feel grateful for the experience, I wouldn't want to give back what it has taught me or lose the growth and insights it forced me to achieve. As promised in my father-in-law's blessing before we even knew how sick I was, I have gained understanding and sympathy for the suffering of others. I have an enhanced sense of what prayer can do, and I find myself praying for others much more than I did before. I often think with great emotion of the love, prayers, and concern of my friends and colleagues, and even of many people I will never meet. I feel God's presence in my life more than before, and I sense his love for me and for others. My voice is often softer, my perceptions and judgments gentler and much more positive.

And I find my prayers have mostly become prayers of thanks. The line from the hymn often echoes in my thoughts: "Oh, what shall I ask of thy providence more?"

DAVID L. COWLES *is an associate professor of English at BYU. He received his PhD from the University of Chicago in Victorian literature after receiving a BA and an MA from BYU.*
DELYS COWLES *holds a BA and an MA from BYU in English and is currently a part-time instructor in the English Department.*

Questions

1. Why does Delys Cowles mention her eulogy about "Waite women being strong"?
2. In this collaborative article, David Cowles is represented by italics and Delys Cowles by plain text. How does this device work? Does it make the story more interesting? Why do it?
3. Because David Cowles is one of the writers, it is obvious from the beginning that he survives. How, then, do the authors create suspense?
4. Why does the article end with a line from a hymn? How does it tie back to the rest of the story?

Grandpa's Place

EDWARD A. GEARY

Edward A. Geary didn't begin writing personal essays until he was teaching college in the late sixties. He first explored connections between Mormon culture and Victorian attitudes, but found the "flexibility of the [personal] essay appealing" when exploring his own heritage. Like much of Geary's writing, this narrative focuses on life in a small town and the formative influences of small-town life. Geary believes no individual is truly "cosmopolitan"—everyone is essentially small-town. "We always create smaller communities," he asserts. "Small-town communities just happen to be the ones that are already formed." "Grandpa's Place" was originally published in Goodbye to Poplarhaven: Recollections of a Utah Boyhood.

The oldest hath borne most: we that are young
Shall never see so much, nor live so long.
—Shakespeare, *King Lear*

When I was very small my grandfather used to take me on his knees and sing a nursery rhyme in his tuneless way:

Pace goes the lady
Pace goes the lady
Trot goes the gentleman
Trot goes the gentleman
Gallop goes the farmer
Gallop goes the farmer.

With each couplet he bounced his knees higher and faster until as the farmer I was charging along at a great rate, holding onto Grandpa's arms for dear life. I have since learned that in the original version of the rhyme it is the gentleman who gallops while the farmer proceeds at a hobble-trot on his old plowhorse. Grandpa must have modified the verse to fit his own sense of the relative dignity of the two stations, and I certainly would never have questioned the appropriateness of his version. Who would want to be a mere gentleman if he could be a farmer?

Grandpa was a farmer, "farmer and stockman," as he put it to indicate that he ran a hundred head of cattle on the range in addition to cultivating eighty acres or so. Grandpa himself rarely galloped, in my day, though he claimed to have had the fastest sleighing team in town when he was a young man. He usually left Old Nick, the saddle horse, in the pasture and drove the black Dodge sedan up into the foothills to check on the cattle. But I had seen enough of Pete McElprang and Miller Black and Frank Robbins to know that farmers could be dashing horsemen, and my chief aspiration was someday to be a farmer and stockman myself. No occupation was more esteemed in Poplarhaven, and while Grandpa engaged in many other activities during his life he never claimed any of them as a vocation. I suppose it is from those early influences that I gained the unreflective conviction that farming is the only real work. But though several of his descendants have remained attached to the land, Grandpa was the last real farmer in our family, the last to make a living at it. By the next generation most of the men in Poplarhaven were employed as wage earners and farmed only as a sideline. Even so, the farms were more often economic liabilities than assets. As Lynn Collard used to say about his job in the coal mines, "I can't afford to be laid off. I've got a wife and kids and farm to support."

Though Grandpa's acreage was not large by current standards, it represented a consolidation of several smaller farms, each with its own history. The home field lay at the northwest corner of the townsite. Grandpa had purchased this land from Levi Harmon at the time of his marriage to Grandma, and it was here that he built his house and barnyard. The first field, a mile away at the southwest corner of town, was brought into the family by Great-grandpa Geary through a series of trades with Samuel Rowley and Abinadi Porter in the 1880s. The middle field, half a mile farther away, was the oldest of all, having been part of Great-grandpa's original homestead. The level ground had appeared to be ideal farmland, but irrigation brought alkali salts to the surface, rendering the soil unfit for anything but rough pasture. Finally there was the farther field, out in the South Flats two miles from home, the ultimate range of my early childhood explorations. Grandpa had acquired it from his stepmother, Aunt Bell, who had been holding it in the hope that her runaway son, Joseph, might someday return.

Grandpa was born in 1878 and lived for his first five years in the rock house his father had built in Round Valley, near Morgan, Utah. I have described Great-grandpa Geary as a man of great physical strength and endurance. I can barely remember him as a silent visitor sitting in the front room, but even in his old age his frame was big and strong. He died at the age of eighty-seven, the result of going to work too soon after surgery. Grandpa, however, inherited his mother's small frame and was sickly as a boy. His childhood was lonely and difficult, especially after the death of his mother when he was eight years old, and of his brother Frederick two years later, but he talked of it in a matter-of-fact way as though one could expect nothing else. One night in his teens he attended a dance after a long day in the hayfield and returned home after midnight to find his father dressed and waiting. "If you can dance, you can work," Great-grandpa said, and work they did, through the remainder of the night and all the next day. With the demands of the farm, the threshing machine, and a contract to haul freight from the railroad at Price to the Ute Indian reservation, Grandpa was never able to complete a full term of school. However, he saved enough money from his work on the freight road to attend a business college in Salt Lake City for three months, acquiring, according to the letter of recommendation he brought home with him, "such a knowledge of Bookkeeping, though he did not complete the course, that he will make a good assistant bookkeeper."

On his twenty-first birthday, Grandpa received from his father a forty-acre farm and a team of horses. With this start on a livelihood, he began courting Lauretta Wakefield, but his plans were changed by two events, a call to serve a mission for the LDS Church, and, only days before he left for the mission field, Lauretta's death from rheumatic heart disease. After serving for two years in the Northern States Mission, he returned home, received another team of horses from his father (the first team had been sold to help finance the mission), married his deceased fiancee's younger sister Alice Grace, and settled down in Poplarhaven. In addition to farming, at one time or another he worked in a bank, operated a threshing machine, served as county road supervisor, constructed roads and reservoirs, operated a general store, sold insurance, took census, and was the local correspondent for the *Deseret News*. Besides these employments, he spent twenty years as a counselor to the ward bishop plus terms as town clerk, county commissioner, school board member, irrigation company board member and secretary, and organizer of a livestock show and of a community coal mine. The range of his activities was unusual but not unique. The civic well-being of small towns has traditionally depended on a small core of able and hardworking men and women who have the confidence to tackle jobs for which they have no specific training.

Grandpa and Grandma built a two-story house of local brick, which, by the time I came along, was shaded by tall trees and looked as though it had been there forever. Our place was just through the orchard from Grandpa's, and a well-worn path ran past the big pear tree that held the treehouse and the sweet cherry with the low-hanging branch on which I tried to chin myself each time I passed. None of the three children had wandered far from home. Aunt Fawn and Uncle Ray McCandless, after spending the early years of their marriage in the coal camps, returned to Poplarhaven to build a house across the road from Grandpa's. Uncle Merlin and Aunt Dora were the farthest away. They lived down in town, but hardly a day passed that Uncle Merlin didn't stop by for a few minutes. The whole family gathered formally at Grandpa's place on Thanksgiving and Christmas. Informally, the grandchildren congregated there daily, helping themselves to fresh bread and honey in Grandma's kitchen, playing with the marbles and blocks on the dining room floor, dressing up in the old clothes that were kept in an upstairs bedroom, enjoying a game of No Bears Are Out Tonight on summer evenings in the big yard.

Grandpa was a very early riser. The saying around town was that he had half a day's work done before most men got started. After tending the water and doing the morning chores, he would return to the house for breakfast, and sometimes, if I got up early enough, I could get there in time to share his grapefruit and tag along after him as he went on with his work. I can remember watching while he repaired harnesses and mended fence and gathered eggs. He took me with him when he went to the mill, or to Andrew Allen's blacksmith shop to get the plowshares sharpened, and, on one long, memorable day, across the mountains on a bull-buying expedition. On raw March days I played, thickly bundled, in the barn while Grandpa pitched manure in the reeking corral. When the manure spreader was full, I rode beside him on the seat as we hauled the load out to the fields. I liked best the moment when he engaged the lever that set the spreader mechanism in operation. The slatted floor moved slowly back, feeding the manure into the whirling tines that spread a brown path behind us on the still winter-bound earth.

Though not an inarticulate man (he was a frequent speaker at funerals), Grandpa had little use for idle conversation while he was working, and he liked to have me with him (I learned in later years) because I didn't chatter. We might go half a day without exchanging a dozen words, Grandpa only giving occasional succinct directions (so succinct at times that you had to know what he wanted beforehand in order to understand him) and swearing now and then at a recalcitrant piece of machinery or a cow that couldn't see an open gate. He had little patience with error and was capable of sharp rebukes, but he punished me physically only once, when I refused to divide a boiled egg with a younger cousin and instead smashed it in my hand. I remember three things from the incident, which must have occurred when I was four or five: the sensation of the mashed egg as it squeezed out between my fingers; the strong conviction that I was in the right (her brothers had eggs of their own, so why should I be the one to share?); and the hardness of Grandpa's hand as he paddled me. But that was the only time.

In the summer Grandpa worked outdoors early and late and fell asleep in his chair immediately after supper. After a two-hour nap he sleepily arose, scratched his bald head, wound the Regulator clock in the kitchen, and climbed the stairs to bed. On winter evenings he did the night chores in the early dark and then came inside, stamping his feet on the porch and pausing to warm his hands at the kitchen stove. Then, if he didn't have a meeting to go to or work to do at his oak drop-leaf desk in the corner of the dining room, he might tell us freight road stories.

He would tell of the time, on his first trip alone at age fourteen, when he was frightened by an owl as he lay in his bedroll, thinking it was someone demanding to know "Who's there? Who's there?" Or the time when an Indian rode into his camp and demanded cake when there was no cake, and so Grandpa had to mix up a substitute from breadcrumbs and sugar. Or he would tell of the winter trip when he nearly died of hypothermia before another teamster saw that he was falling into a stupor and forced him to get down from the wagon and run, hitting him with his whip when he tried to stop. Then there was the time when he developed a severe cold which infected his weak lungs so that he was unable to drive his outfit back from Fort Duchesne. A young drifter of questionable reputation, a man called "Six-shooter Bob," offered to drive the team with Grandpa lying in a makeshift bed under the wagon cover. On the way up Nine Mile Canyon they met another party of freighters who asked Six-shooter Bob whose team he was driving.

"Ed Geary's," he replied.

"Where's the kid?"

"Oh, he's damned sick in the wagon," Bob said. "Be dead by the time we get to Price."

"However," Grandpa would say, "I didn't die."

As a young child I regarded Grandpa's work as my play, but as I grew older and he expected me to take some responsibility for the work I found it less appealing and instead of seeking him out in the morning I would often try to avoid him. I remained fond of farming in theory, but I didn't much care for the dirt and chaff and heat of the actual labor. It annoyed me that Grandpa didn't consider that I might have other things planned for the day, that he began work too early in the morning and continued too late in the evening when I would have preferred to be out bumming with my friends. As a result of my changing attitude, Grandpa and I grew less close.

But there were still some memorable times. I can recall one day when we were harvesting grain in the middle field. I must have been about fifteen or sixteen. It was after the era of binding, shocking, hauling, and threshing. Lonnie Guymon performed all of those operations at once as he guided his big combine around the patch of oats in the one tillable corner of the field while Grandpa and I watched from our perches on the wagon. When the hopper was full, Lonnie pulled the combine out of the geometrical pattern of diminishing swaths and came bouncing across the furrows toward us. Grandpa and I held the burlap sacks up to the spout while they filled with oats then stacked them on the wagon. When the hopper was empty, the combine returned to its rounds, and we had nothing to do but sit on the full sacks and watch.

Grandpa was in a reflective mood that day. He told me about his first arrival in Poplarhaven. He could remember the long wagon trip from Arizona in minute detail: the swimming horse that almost upset the ferry-boat at Lee's Ferry, the old Danish woman who wandered away from camp and got lost in the Kaibab Forest, the pitcherful of honey that his father purchased at a ranch in Johnson Canyon. He pointed out the notch in the Blue Ridge from which they had caught their first sight of Poplarhaven. His father had stopped the wagons there while they viewed the cabins that were spread across the treeless flat. Grandpa remembered that his mother cried when his father told them that this was their new home. They lived in the wagon boxes until his father could build a one-room cabin, which was furnished, he remembered, with a Charter Oak cookstove, a wooden bedstead, a wash bench, a looking glass, a Woodbury clock, a rocking chair and four straight-backed chairs, a cradle, and a wheat bin in a corner. He remembered that his mother was never well after the birth of Maud Maryann and remarked that perhaps she would have lived if there had been a doctor. He recalled the death of Frederick, his closest playmate. His father had awakened him in the night to say that Fred was dying and to send him to fetch a neighbor woman to lay out the body. A few years later, as a boy of twelve, he had been in this very field, getting the horses to take his stepmother to the doctor in Price, when a man rode out from town to tell him not to bother, that she was already dead. He went on to talk of the long series of housekeepers and hired girls that passed through their home before his father finally married Aunt Bell, a witty and sensible English widow. "Her entry into our home made living conditions much better," Grandpa said.

Grandpa's heart failed in his last years, and he had to depend increasingly on others to do the work on the farm. But he continued to push himself for as long as he could. I can remember watching him stagger out to tend the water, shovel perched on his bony shoulder, and having horrific visions of him dying in the field before he could make it back to the house. It didn't occur to me then that that would have suited him better than a lingering death in bed. Finally he grew so weak that he had to stay in the house, often with an oxygen tube in his mouth.

I remember one day that summer when I was raking the hay into windrows. It had been a bad day, with several breakdowns of the machinery, and the job was still unfinished by late afternoon. I knew how Grandpa felt about getting the hay raked before it got too dry. (He was always suspicious of the side-delivery rake in any case, feeling that it knocked off more leaves than the old horse-drawn dump rake.) But I was tired and frustrated, and I had plans for the evening, so I drove the tractor in from the field as fast as it would go, jerked to a stop in the yard, and jumped off and started through the orchard for home. Before I had gone halfway up the path, I heard the creak of the gate and turned to look. It was Grandpa, shuffling painfully across the yard toward the tractor, going to finish the job.

EDWARD A. GEARY *is a professor of English, current director of the Charles Redd Center for Western Studies, and Associate Chair of the English Department. He is author of* Goodbye to Poplarhaven *(1985) and* The Proper Edge of the Sky *(1992). He is currently working on a family memoir about his grandmother.*

Questions

1. How do the Shakespeare quotation and the nursery rhyme at the beginning relate to the rest of the story?
2. This story is not told chronologically. It moves between three generations. How does this organization affect the story? Why not just tell the last story?
3. What kind of details in the text made the story more vivid?
4. How does the setting affect this story?

Self-Disclosure and Freshman Comp

Chris Crowe

"Self-disclosure and Freshman Comp," which originally appeared in BYU Today, *is Chris Crowe's personal reminiscence of his first year at BYU and his experience as an unprepared student in Freshman English. Crowe was on a football scholarship at the time and was taking the class with two of his teammates, who he describes as "real gorillas." This personal narrative tells what can go wrong as a student when you're not ready. The events Crowe recounts in this narrative, he says, are "all true, unfortunately."*

I haven't told anyone this before, but I figure it's time to come clean. Who knows, some day I might be a presidential candidate, a Supreme Court nominee or a BYU faculty candidate, and I figure it's better to get this thing out in the open now instead of then. Besides, I couldn't hide my secret even if I wanted to because it's right there on my official BYU transcripts, the very first class listed: ENGL 111: COMP & READING—C-.

And that's not the worst of it. From that humble and degrading beginning, I went on to become an English teacher.

I know what you're thinking: "Those who can do, those who can't . . ." but before you condemn me, at least let me tell my side of the story.

See, I didn't deserve that C-.

Like all the other freshmen in the fall of 1972, I showed up at the Richards PE Building one bright August morning to subject myself to the only officially sanctioned hazing ritual BYU has ever known—Walk-Through Registration.

After a couple hours of standing in line, and another hour trying to have a new registration packet made for me, I realized that the tentative class schedule I had planned the night before was becoming more tentative the longer I stood in line. It was then that I knew that I'd have to accept whatever class cards Fate dealt me.

One of the cards dealt me was English 111 taught on Mondays, Wednesdays and Fridays by a young graduate teaching assistant named Sister Olsen.

Sister Olsen was a dutiful TA. She taught us about rhetorical stance, dangling modifiers, commas, introductions, middles and conclusions—everything we would ever need to know to become skilled writers.

She also made us write essays. And I think it was my first one that set her against me, that jaded her opinion of my smooth and silky prose so badly that she was never again able to view my weekly masterpieces with any objectivity whatsoever.

Our first assignment was to write a "descriptive essay on some object in nature." Most of the students in class chose convenient objects to describe, with oranges being the most popular because they happened to be served in the Cannon Center on the day the assignment was given.

I wasn't too worried about the assignment. My high school essays had been good—at least that's what my teachers told me—and I didn't think I'd have much trouble cranking out a decent descriptive essay on a piece of nature. During the week when I should have been working on my paper, I concentrated instead on the four F's of freshman life: food, females, football and fun.

Around 10:00 the night before the paper was due, I decided it was time to get down to business. I stepped outside my room in Helaman Halls and grabbed the first bit of nature I saw—a bunch of tree leaves. I carried the leaves back up to my room, laid them on my desk and examined them for a few minutes. Then I pulled out a couple sheets of notebook paper and began composing my masterpiece.

Two paragraphs later, I was finished. I had said everything there was possible to say about those leaves. Unfortunately, two paragraphs were not enough. Sister Olsen insisted that our papers have at least six paragraphs, so I was stumped, temporarily.

After a few moments of meditation, inspiration struck—I'd use my sense of humor. My high school English teachers had always enjoyed my witty writing, probably because it was one of the few bright spots in their otherwise dreary job of correcting stacks of student essays. Anyway, I let my imagination run wild and set about describing that bunch of leaves.

I don't remember all of what I wrote, but I did say something about how those leaves burst their veins with pride each and every Arbor Day and how their cells slaved away over a hot photosynthetic stove every day so we could breathe fresh air. But the *coup de grace* of the paper still lingers in my memory. I wrote in some detail about how those humble leaves had a proud and noble heritage, indeed, a family tree that branched throughout history and had its roots in the Garden of Eden. The ancestors of those leaves played a vital role in the civilizing of humanity by providing a wardrobe for Adam and Eve.

I put my pen down and reread my essay. It was perfect. I copied it over in better handwriting, checked for spelling errors, and then, with a great feeling of satisfaction, tucked it away in my notebook for the next day's class.

I turned my paper in the next morning, confident that it would rise like cream to the top of Sister Olsen's stack of dreadfully dull essays about oranges, rocks, and grass.

She passed our papers back a week later. As soon as she handed me mine, I turned to the last page expecting to see a gleaming red 'A' along with a note from her praising my keen wit and smooth writing.

Where there should have been an 'A' was scrawled a 'D,' and her comments were less than glowing. Sister Olsen's reaction to my masterpiece showed, of course, her inexperience and lack of literary taste, but it also shocked me so deeply that her comment on that essay was tattooed forever on my memory. She wrote, "Two things are quite clear to me: One, you obviously didn't understand the assignment; and, two, you obviously don't have a sense of humor."

CHRIS CROWE*'s writing career began in the sixth grade after he read H. G. Wells's* War of the Worlds *and decided that he could write something just as good. Even though he never finished his post-apocalyptic novel, he has since published five books, a number of articles, and at one time had a regular column for the now-defunct* Latter-day Sentinel *newspaper. Crowe earned a BA in English and secondary teaching from BYU and then went to Arizona State University where he earned an MA and a EdD in English education. Over the last twenty years, Crowe has taught in Arizona (at his former high school), Hawaii, Japan, and he currently teaches creative writing, adolescent literature, and English for secondary education majors at BYU.*

Questions

1. What elements of Crowe's experience are similar to your own experience?
2. How does Crowe create irony?
3. How does the introduction set the tone of the article?

First Things First

LOUISE PLUMMER

Louise Plummer doesn't read the introductions to books and figures that most people don't either. So when her collection of "essays and oddities," Thoughts of a Grasshopper, *was published, she hid the introduction with the title "First Things First" hoping that people would read it. Since* Thoughts *contains some of Plummer's memoirs, she felt that it was necessary to explain to readers that memoirs are "not about fact, but impressions from the past" and that often "fiction and reality are blurred." Plummer has used this essay in her creative writing classes as a way to help students understand how to write about the past when memories have faded and details have gone. "You're going to have to fill some of that in," she tells students.*

In 1967 in Cambridge, Massachusetts, all our friends were having babies, but we weren't. We had no luck. And so we did what childless couples often do: we went to a pet store and bought a dog for Mother's Day. She was a Yorkshire terrier, six weeks old, as beautiful as any daughter could be, with deep brown eyes that could make you weep. We named her Emily. The cost was an extravagant two hundred fifty dollars, an amount that embarrassed us (we were students at the time), so we told our parents in long distance phone calls that she had been given to us by a vague "someone in the ward." Besides, Tom thought we could make up the money by breeding her and selling each of the offspring for the same two hundred fifty dollars. We could be rich, he said.

When Emily was old enough, we searched the greater Boston area for just the right mate for our daughter and found him in a kennel owned by Mrs. Iris Campbell, a squarely-built woman who bought her clothes from the Land's End catalogue. She reminded me of my mother. Her house was tidy, her living room dominated by an exquisite needlepoint rug festooned with wild roses connected with dark leafy vines. Only one dog was allowed in the house, her pet, a female Yorkie named Fiona, whose hair was fastidiously tied back from her eyes with a red grosgrain ribbon. She let us know what she thought of our intruding by yapping at us continuously from a safe distance. The rest of the dogs were housed outside in kennels kept as clean as Mrs. Campbell's house. It was here that Mrs.

Campbell introduced us to Emily's future husband, a small dog, only two and a half pounds, named Winnie. Our dog, we had explained to Mrs. Campbell already, was large for the breed, about eight pounds. She said we should aim for puppies that would grow to be no more than four pounds. "That's the perfect weight for Yorkies," she said. The petite Winnie and our buxom Emily would more than likely produce such a perfect product together. We were pleased and went home to wait.

When it came time for the conjugal visit, we washed and groomed Emily meticulously and tied her hair up in a swatch of narrow multicolored ribbons, which she pawed loose in the car.

Mrs. Campbell let us into her house. Tom held our Emily in his arms proudly.

"She's a good size to have lots of puppies," Mrs. Campbell said, stroking Emily. Her coloring was good too, she said. Tom and I gratefully soaked up these compliments for our daughter.

"Let's see her teeth," she said, spreading the dog's lips apart. "Oh my," she said in an altered voice. "Oh no." She spread the dog's mouth further apart and to the side to have a better look. "You can't breed this dog," she declared. "She has a bad bite!" It was a pronouncement like, "She has leprosy." Yorkies, she explained, should have an overbite, but "this dog," she gestured disgustedly with her hand, "this dog has an underbite." She stepped back from Tom and the dog as if the underbite might be catching. "It's not a trait I can allow to be passed on. As a breeder, I'm responsible for keeping the breed pure. The AKC could take my license if they found out I was breeding my dogs with inferior animals."

Tom's face fell with the phrase "inferior animals," and he held Emily a little closer, a little more protectively, as if he hoped she hadn't heard Mrs. Campbell's criticism of her.

"Where did you get this dog?" she asked.

We told her.

"It's too bad you didn't come to me," she said.

I felt crushed, and it must have shown on my face, because Mrs. Campbell's voice softened. "Of course, if you just want another pet, and if you promise not to sell any pups, then I might . . ."

"Yes," Tom and I said in unison. Suddenly we wanted to be grandparents more than we wanted to be rich. "Yes, that's all we want," I said.

"I really shouldn't . . . ," she hesitated.

"We promise," we said, eagerly.

And so Emily and Winnie were mated. But in those years, infertility ran in our family, and Emily, as it turned out, was even more barren than I was, because she never had puppies, while I, after a few more years, had four sons.

Some time after the first son was born, I told this story to dinner guests to show how parental we had felt about this dog, who was now no longer our daughter but merely a good pet. I took great pains to describe Tom's crestfallen face. I imitated the way he cradled the dog in his arms when Mrs. Campbell declared her unfit for breeding. I imitated Mrs. Campbell's firm voice when she announced that "this dog has a bad bite!"

From across the table, Tom interrupted my performance: "You weren't there," he said.

"What do you mean?" I asked.

"You weren't there when she announced that Emily had a bad bite. I went out alone with Emily."

"I was too there." I insisted. "I remember everything. I remember Fiona and the grosgrain ribbons and the needlepoint rug—"

"You were there the first time we went out," Tom said, "but I went alone with Emily the second time. You weren't there." His lips curled ever so slightly, ever so smugly—an irritating expression in a spouse. "You're deluded," he finished.

Well.

Our dinner guests turned their faces from Tom to me.

"I am not deluded," I said, my voice rising. "I remember the way you looked, the way Emily pawed the ribbons on her head—"

"Emily always pawed her ribbons loose. You've imagined it. You weren't there."

"I was."

"You weren't, and I can prove it."

No one was eating anymore.

"I know I was alone with Emily," Tom continued, "because she sat in the front seat and on the way home, she got so nervous, she threw up. If you'd been there, you'd have been sitting in the front seat, and she would have been in the back. She threw up in the front seat. You weren't there."

This new fact had a vaguely familiar ring about it. Suddenly I felt unsure. "But I remember it so vividly!"

"That, my dear," Tom's voice was kinder, "is because you live in a fictional world, and in your world, imagination is better than knowledge." Truth spoken by a triumphant husband quoting Einstein. I suppose we finished the dinner, but I never stopped muttering to myself.

That was the first time I became aware that for me the line between reality and fiction is blurred. My fiction is made up of autobiographical details, even though the events of the story are made up. For example, when I wrote my first novel, it took place in the house and neighborhood where I grew up in Salt Lake City, but the actual writing of the novel was done in Saint Paul, Minnesota. When I visited home after completing the novel, I sat on the front porch and had a confused few minutes as I looked up and down the street that I had so carefully described in my novel and wondered if I had invented the street or if it had invented me.

It works the same in reverse. My nonfiction (the true stories) are filled with little fictions. The story I told about breeding our dog, Emily, and thinking I was there is absolutely true, but I don't remember the woman's name. It wasn't Iris Campbell, in any case. She did keep a neat house, and she did have a wonderful Yorkshire terrier, a female, but it beats me what its name was. Probably not Fiona. My job is to tell a compelling story and the only way to do it is through "the divine details," as Nabokov phrased it, so that in my fiction, the divine details are often autobiographical, and in my nonfiction the divine details are imagined. And it is all true. That is why in this book essays are intermixed with fiction, with speeches, and with personal letters. It is all the same to me. My hope is that it is one joyful noise for you, the reader.

LOUISE PLUMMER *has written four books for young adults,* The Romantic Obsessions and Humiliations of Annie Sehlmeier, My Name is Sus5an Smith. The 5 Is Silent, *which won an ALA Best Book for Young Adults,* The Unlikely Romance of Kate Bjorkman, *and* Thoughts of a Grasshopper, *and is currently finishing her fifth book,* Hannah Ziebarth at Large. *Plummer received a BA in English and an MA in creative writing at the University of Minnesota. She currently teaches creative writing and introductory English classes at BYU.*

Questions

1. How does this essay affect the rest of the stories in the collection?
2. What does Plummer mean when she says, "for me, the line between reality and fiction is somewhat blurred"?
3. What power do the details have in the story of Emily?

A Song for One Still Voice

Bruce W. Jorgensen

"'A Song for One Still Voice' was the second fairly good short story I ever wrote," says Bruce Jorgensen. He wrote it as an entry for a short story contest sponsored by the Ensign, *which used to print fiction. Jorgensen actually began writing a different story, "Born of the Water," but the completed draft far exceeded the competition's word limit. However, at some point during the writing, he recalled an idea for a different story he'd attempted to write "nine years ago to the day." But the story had to incubate. "I tried to write it then," he explains, "but every time I wrote the first sentence I realized it didn't work." But this time, nine years later, Jorgensen finished the draft in one day. After cutting it down to meet the word count, he submitted "A Song for One Still Voice" to the* Ensign. *He won.*

He is awake, and knows the time. In its reliable way that he does not yet trust, his mind has waked him just before the alarm should go off. His side of their bed, in the small room, must be jammed close to the wall, so he leans across his sleeping wife to reach the nightstand and press down the button. He has set it early to have time to dress, get his shovel, and make his way through the block to the headgate, so he has maybe twenty minutes, and he half-wishes to wake her. With the children, there is little time when they are entirely alone, in quiet like this. But she was up till almost eleven settling the girls, and when he finally held her she turned, snuggled her backside against him, tucked his arm under hers, his hand spread on her chest, and mumbled into her pillow, "Let me go to sleep like this." He did, lay listening to random snapping and easing of joists, cyclic rumble and hush of heater, long past the time when his fingers told him she slept, till he turned over to find his separate sleep. He knows she still needs this placidity that he senses with his whole body. Touched, her skin would lie still as water without a breath of air moving on it.

But he slides out of the covers and scoots himself down his side, the lightstring from the ceiling brushing his scalp so the hair on his neck rises and he thinks for an instant: spider. Bugs are one problem of this old house; winter drives them in, and as spring swells into summer they will propagate madly. He has taught the girls to stomp on the slightest suspicion of a black widow.

Cold is another problem: their northwest corner room is farthest from the heater, which is central only in having been built into the wall between kitchen and living room so it blows both ways; to keep the girls' northeast corner room warm they must prop kitchen and bedroom doors at angles calculated to guide an optimal airflow. In winter, one of them will rise at least once each night to check and re-tuck blankets. Not quite twenty-six, he has begun to understand why some old people, his grandmother, brag of lasting out the winter. One night this past January he spent almost eight hours with a propane torch trying to thaw the water line; he'd come in for five minutes or so in every hour, sit at the kitchen table to drink hot chocolate, both hands on the mug, shoes off so warmed air would blow across his feet. Under the house, gloved hand gripping the pipe to feel when the water would start, he knew his first terror of the simple elemental world. And in this rented house, far more than in three years of apartments at school, he has felt on himself and on Lea the entire weight of their needs of shelter, heat, food, clothes.

He stands at the foot of the bed, thankful for carpet even if it is cool. And it is spring now, the worst of the cold past, and if there is no late frost, the lilacs may all bloom—first time in years if it happens, the old residents say. But the hawthorn came through anyway last year, and will again, a thick, monumental bouquet of red and green he is glad to have lived to see on a front lawn, even if not his own. A sort of stewardship. Just out that blinded window he could see the hawthorn if it were day, a few knots of bloom already open. He remembers coming into the room one afternoon last August to a moment's stunned joy at the pear-yellow light flooding through the drawn blind. He has been happier here this past year than anywhere or anytime else.

From the dresser mirror his clownish ghost shimmers back at him as he stoops with knees spread to hold his pants up while he reaches his shirt. He wonders if anything has been left on the floor between here and the door to trip him going out, but the way is clear, and he carries his shoes to the added-on porch that he and a colleague wired and plumbed for washer and dryer and he and his wife papered with yellow stripes—their first try and not a bad job. The door to the kitchen closed, he opens the back porch door and sits on the steps to pull on the heavy steeltoed shoes he bought years ago to work in the sheetrock plant, the summer before he met Lea. The stiff shoes pinch and bunch his toes.

Standing again to take his hat and gloves from the hooks below the back porch window, he remembers coming home early one afternoon last week, quiet to surprise them, walking through the house, then opening the door to the porch and seeing them blurred and pastelled through waterspotted glass and screen: sitting under the blossoming apple trees, petals strewn thick around them on the grass, the little girls calling to make it rain again, and she shaking a low branch to shower more on them. He stood and watched, drowned in delight that he could find no words for, hardly daring to go on out because his coming might be less to them than what they already had. Later he walked them to the corner and across the highway for soft ice cream.

Picking up the shovel he stood last night by the step, he crosses the yard to the southeast corner, climbs the fence at the solid post there, pulls his shovel through, and makes his way along the ditch that runs through his neighbor's deep back yard—a good man and kind to them, though Carl does not more than mildly like him yet and so feels undeserving of even shared surplus corn or broccoli.

He stumbles and almost falls over a short tree stump that he knows well enough to avoid, and chides himself again for not buying flashlight batteries. His shovel striking the ground has waked the dog, who comes dragging his chain from his house under a honeylocust, sniffing and starting to growl, then wagging his tail when he catches Carl's approved scent. Carl squats to stroke the dog and scratch his ears, trying to recall his name. He hasn't had a dog since high school, and it pleases him to make friends; he wouldn't mind just staying here and patting and talking to this one, but it is time to start the turn and he whispers, "Go back to sleep, boy, it's OK," and walks up through the driveway to the headgate in the cement ditch running north on the east side of the block. They don't have a dog because the fur makes Lea's asthma act up.

It takes only a minute to aim the water at his yard, a big stream so he doesn't need to seal the edges of the gate with mud—what runs on by won't matter. It is also simpler to walk back around the block, so he does that, his shovel balanced on his shoulder by his wrist crooked over its handle. He crosses the tracks he supposes they are on the wrong side of, though in Cedar the distinction hardly exists, and walks into the hard glare of mercury-vapor lamps along the highway that runs straight west to the interchange. He dislikes the lamps for the livid cast they give to skin, the tarry-looking shadows they throw around even pebbles, so he is glad to get past the big, blocky furniture store-warehouse, turn the corner, and walk in dark toward his house.

Out of the glare, he can look up at the stars, thick, clear, shining a steady, warm light. Living at home, he'd use his telescope on any night like this, could find his way from constellation to constellation, predict where, aimed carefully, the six-inch mirror would dazzle him with a nebula, a far galaxy like M31 in Andromeda, the jewelled globe of stars in Hercules toward which the whole solar system slowly spins. It felt good to know the sky, and he'd wonder what it was like to know it as God does, galaxies and even clusters of galaxies flung like seeds to the far fences of the universe. He'd read that a planet within the great Hercules cluster would be seared in the light of a thousand suns, and supposed that to be like the place where God dwells.

The sidewalk runs straight to the edge of his yard, stops for a foot-wide strip of bare red clay, then resumes as his own front walk angling up to the narrow concrete steps. In the backyard before the water, he has time to check his dams for watering the trees and flooding the small lawn. He really doesn't need all the water this second turn of the season—their garden is only half planted, peas, carrots, lettuce, thin grasslike spears of onion sets. He remembers last fall, when he came out from hanging several onion-stuffed nylons in the storage room and saw their cat leap three feet into the air to claw down the hummingbird that had darted at the hollyhocks all summer. He himself pounced on the cat to rescue the bird, got it in his hand, felt the shock of its unimaginably intense life, saw at its throat what he first thought was blood, then realized was the ruby, glowing in the dusk as if the bird bore the summer's whole harvest of light. Then, his hand stunned open, the bird flew away.

Kneeling in the grass to wedge a chunk of brick more firmly in the bank, he smells fresh mint growing along the ditch and bends closer to breathe it. He has seen Lea put a leaf to each nostril and inhale, an ecstasy of breath. They should learn to make mint tea.

Now the water arrives, a finger-size trickle swelling to fill the ditch and start spilling on the lawn. He stands, steps back near the house, and follows its spread by silver flickerings in the grass. The garden furrows were set right last time—he won't need to check them for an hour. He did not think he'd like gardening. His parents had a large garden and made him help weed it, a chore he escaped when he could. He still doesn't like weeding, but to have something grow by his own labor, something they can eat even if not at much less cost than buying, feels good. When the lawn is a still, blade-pricked sheet of dusky silver, he turns to go in.

He'll sleep on the couch near the bedroom door, and he steps into the bedroom to get a light blanket in case of cold. Coming back out he kneels by the bed to kiss Lea on her warm, pulsing temple, again half-wishing to wake her. The faint odor of the vinegar she rinsed her hair with last night reminds him how she came from the shower, blossoming from sharp spray. How she tangles sense and memory. There is no loneliness like the body, nor any delight. "Sleep," he whispers, content that she'll not know this riffle in the hidden stream of her ear. He will sleep without resetting the alarm, and see if his mind will wake him again in an hour.

But when he does wake again it is because one of his daughters has cried in her sleep. Guessing why, he takes a dry diaper with him, untwists her from her covers, changes her, for once without rousing her to open her eyes, and turns her warm, tumblesome body end for end so she lies as she should. When he stands and turns to check the older girl, he sees through the windows, taking both in at once, unbelievably, snow. The sight stuns him with delight and fear harmonized like a major fifth, and then he knows, barely trusting this, that it is some surprise of the light.

Stepping to the east window and bending to look out and up, he sees it is so: pale light pouring from a risen last-quarter moon and resting on bare clay, on weeds, on barely flowing water, on apple branches like silvery weightless snow. Looking at it, he is weightless, in free fall as if the earth has dropped from under him, or as if he is drawn up with the world's tidal bulge and loosed in the gravity of light, yearning farther out and from deeper within than in any prayer he has ever spoken. Undeserved, abounding, grace rings in his bones.

BRUCE W. JORGENSEN *has been a mainstay of BYU's creative writing program since 1975. Jorgensen completed his bachelor's at BYU, then moved on to Cornell University, where he finished his MA and PhD. Before BYU, he taught at Southern Utah State College in Cedar City, which he sometimes uses as the setting for his work. His poems, stories, reviews, and essays have appeared in such literary journals as* High Plains Literary Review *and* Carolina Quarterly, *as well as in almost every Mormon-related magazine or journal, including the* Ensign.

Questions

1. Most stories are told in the past tense. Why is this story told in the present tense? How does it affect the way you read the story?
2. What is the protagonist's relationship to Nature? How does this piece compare to Geary's "Grandpa's Place" or White's "The Power of Landscape and Place" in their understanding of land and/or nature?
3. How does Jorgensen make the images in this story so vivid? What do syntax and rhythm add to the effect of the imagery?
4. How does memory work in this story?

The Burial Pool

John Bennion

John Bennion based "The Burial Pool" (first published in Christmas for the World*) on a Utah legend he'd heard long ago ("I can't even remember where it came from," he says) about Goshute Indians who were sunk in a pool in the desert. He then combined this legend with an idea he had for a story about a pregnant woman because he saw a similarity between the situation of the woman and the situation of the people in the pool. When asked why he likes to write from a woman's perspective, Bennion answers, "I don't know why; a person who has been marginalized is interesting to me." Bennion has been reworking the novel he wrote for his PhD dissertation,* Court of Love, *with scenes from "The Burial Pool" and it will be published in 1999. He's learned a lot about revision working on this novel. From the original draft, his peer-review writing group had him cut it twenty percent, and then from that draft his editor had him cut it an additional thirty. John was initially apprehensive about the changes, but has since found that the revisions are actually "making [the novel] better."*

Alison dreamed that the Goshute woman stood next to her bed dressed in white doeskin. The woman's face was in darkness, and Alison panicked, rolling to her hands and knees, clutching at the blankets. Across the room Howard, dressed in his thermal underwear, loaded logs into the red mouth of the cookstove. "Can't you sleep either?" he said grinning.

"I was asleep until you started banging around," she said. "I dreamed that the angel of death had come." She sat on the edge of the bed. "But it was only you in your ghost suit."

Howard stood with his hands on his hips. "Is there something actually wrong?"

"No," she held her hands across her belly. "Except that you're using your fatherly voice on me."

"Then stop imagining that there is. You've been frightened ever since you've been pregnant." Three years earlier the nurse had brought that other child, blue-faced and cold, wrapped in a white blanket, and laid it across her belly in the hospital. The baby had a strong, square face and Alison had wondered ever since what it would have been like to live with such a powerful child.

"I can't help it," she said. She took his hand and placed it against her. "Feel. He's awake as well, awake and kicking."

He jerked away. "It's weird to feel something moving inside your stomach."

"Silly," she said and lay down again. He returned to his mattress near the door. When he couldn't sleep, he twitched and twisted, keeping them both awake.

Alison woke again shortly after dawn. The clouds had blown away in the night, leaving the flat bowl of the desert valley white with snow. The only dark was the lava ridge which extended north and south behind their cabin. With the field glasses she could see the blue tarp which covered the dig, two miles north at the base of the ridge, and next to it the salt pool and stream, from which rose a mist. Alison knew that despite the sun it was bitter outside, cold as January even though it was only November. As she moved toward the table, the wind breathed through the walls of the cabin and chilled her skin.

Howard gave her a bowl of Cream o' Wheat sprinkled with brown sugar. When she stirred, she brought up lumps, some an inch across. She flapped her spoon against the top of the mush.

"What's the matter?" asked Howard.

"I don't understand how you achieved such large clods."

"Dumplings," he said. "I cooked it that way on purpose." She pushed the bowl away.

Howard left to start the truck, which he ran every day for fifteen minutes in case they needed to drive her to town. She dressed and, swaying slightly from side to side, walked to the tractor. "Quack, quack," she said, but Howard was up on the haystack and couldn't hear. He was only half finished loading the wagon, so she leaned against the tractor to watch as he threw bales down, five or six at a time, and then clambered to the wagon to arrange them.

She felt the child kicking again—a son, she knew from the last ultrasound. "You are too active," she said. Her friend from Rockwood, who was into bees' pollen and higher states of consciousness, and who, for her sixtieth birthday, had changed her name from Mary to Aurora, suggested that Alison talk to the baby, give him a prebirth name. Howard suggested that Cletus the Fetus might be good. Even though she felt foolish, Alison did talk to the child, ignoring Howard's comments. For the past few weeks, without having any specific ailment she could point to, she had felt that the child's attachment to her had become uncertain. Perhaps the act of naming could hold him to her longer than the last one. "Adam," she called up to Howard. "Abraham, Aaron," she said.

"Eustace," said Howard, "Lawrence or Edgar. He shouldn't have a name which is less dignified than his father's."

"You don't have a dignified bone in your body," she said. "You don't have a dignified follicle." Howard's hair swirled at the front, a tangle of opposite-turning cowlicks.

He grunted, moving another bale. Despite her better sense, she was unsettled by the fact that no name would stick. "Have patience, my hasty one," she whispered. "You have three more months."

She slid behind the tractor wheel and pushed the button to warm the glowplug. The engine started easily and, with Howard perched behind, she drove toward the cattle, which had all turned to walk toward the sound of the tractor. The wind blew from the north, a penetrating cold. She drove in a wide circle through the fields and Howard threw the hay off the back. The cattle followed, some running up to the wagon and twisting their heads sideways, long tongues extended, to gather hay from the corners of the moving stack. She never understood why they didn't just wait for Howard to throw it down.

The lane below the cabin had turned white, outlined by gray which also showed white, a band of gravel which bisected the valley. Suddenly she cramped, a severe low pain, and bent forward ovcr the steering wheel. "Howard," she said, but he didn't hear. She stamped her foot down on the clutch. Her abdomen was so tight with pain that she thought she might pull a muscle. He threw off the last bale and walked up to the tractor.

"What's wrong?" he asked. She couldn't answer. "Can you get down?"

She shook her head. "Just let me sit here for a minute," she said finally.

He tried to take her hand; she didn't move to let him, so he stood, shifting from foot to foot in the cold. Finally the cramp faded, leaving a dull ache.

"Is it false labor?" he said.

"Not this hard," she said. "It shouldn't have happened."

"I'll finish, then we'll go in to the doctor. Do you want me to drive you back up?"

"I'm all right now." She drove the tractor homeward along the base of the ridge, passing the stream, so salty that not even halogeton or salt grass would grow near it. When she came to the pool, she stopped the tractor. She knew the dream woman had come to her imagination from the dig, as if the shrunken corpse that she had helped exhume had filled with life again. What was the connection between dream and life, mind and body?

The April before Howard had decided that they should sink logs for a small pier, because the mud along the shore of the pool was pale and stinky, unpleasant to wade through when they wanted to soak in the warm mineral water. But when he started to dig the holes, his shovel uncovered a human head, white with crystals of salt, shrunken but hardly decomposed, its teeth grinning, leathery eyes closed.

Alison and the two anthropologists sent out from the University of Utah had spent the summer spading and brushing the mud and crystals from the limbs and faces of the Goshutes. They had to use a plywood frame and a pump to keep the mud and water from filling their hole. Close to the first corpse, they found more—in all, three males and a female. Alison was most interested in the woman, who had a small child fastened across her belly with inch-wide bands of leather.

One anthropologist claimed that the corpses had originally been floating in the pool before silt carried up by the shifting water channel had covered them. He pointed to the thongs tied around the ankles of all four adult Goshutes. He thought that in the burial ceremony the Goshutes tied boulders to the ankles of the dead before dropping them into the mineral-laden water for preservation. The other anthropologist wasn't so sure. Alison agreed with the first, and she wondered what the Goshutes thought and felt when they stood on the bank and lowered their loved ones into the deep water. She knew that for Navajos heaven is earthward. Perhaps Goshutes were similar; they might have believed that passing down through the heavy water was part of being reborn into the next life. The woman's friends had hoped to bind her to her child through that difficult passage.

"Dear God," said Alison, putting the tractor back in gear, "bless me not to lose this one. Bless us to stay together." She steered around the pool and drove upward toward the cabin.

At the shed Alison cut off the engine and walked slowly into the cabin. She lay sideways on the bed, waiting for Howard. By the time he returned, she discovered that she had bled. "It's starting again," she said to him. "I'm going to lose this one too." Saying it opened a dark place inside and she found herself weeping. Howard helped her dress, then walked her out to the truck.

He drove slowly at first, but the truck continually slipped into the ruts, jolting her. She felt pain low in her belly and gripped the armrest. Howard pulled from their dirt lane onto the gravel road. "You should have called me." His face was white, frightened, and he drove too fast on the better road. She leaned across and put her head on his lap.

"I kept thinking you'd come in any minute." She turned on her back and reached upward between his arms to touch his face, which was still angry.

They drove up the long narrow valley, the last evidence of a river which had connected two parts of Lake Bonneville. From Howard's lap she could see a flat-topped butte, with huge boulders along its crown in a line, sentinels that seemed as tall and rectangular as those at Stonehenge. As they drove up around the flanks of the Simpson Mountains, she sat up and looked out at the hills below on the plane; they were rounded, knobby, so that they looked like the carcasses of huge prehistoric creatures, half sunk in mud. Finally, they crossed the pass into Rockwood Valley, down into the town.

Dr. Peterson, whose face was as broad and red as an old farmer's, wanted her to have another expensive ultrasound. Alison watched the monitor as he directed the gray, flat-bottomed instrument across her belly, which had been smeared with an amber gel. The child was curled, floating in what showed on the screen as shadows of flesh and liquid. She could see his arms and legs, his tiny penis, the coil of the umbilical cord. The image of the moving child had reassured her before, but now the tissues which were supposed to bind him to her seemed so tenuous.

"Your placenta is already starting to detach," he said, pointing to a cloud on the screen. "You should be in the hospital, but if you'll stay in bed and rest. . . ." He knew they couldn't afford that cost and she knew it was his way of frightening them into obedience. "If you can keep the baby until it's eight months along, it'll have a much better chance of surviving."

As soon as they were home, Howard made her lie down. The cabin was familiar after the doctor's office, filled with the smell of wood smoke and propane instead of antiseptic; the sight of her table and cookstove comforted her. She dozed but woke again when Howard came back in to cook. She ate sitting cross-legged on the bed—a bowl of potatoes and canned meat boiled in tomato sauce. "You believe in functional cooking, don't you?" she said.

The days through the bulk of November were like a tunnel, where she woke and dozed, keeping her body quiet. She believed that she was getting worse, that the placenta was continually loosening itself, getting ready so early that her child would die. But surprisingly, she didn't bleed again. Howard did his work and hers, seldom talking to her, moving quietly through the house: cooking, loading the fire, scrubbing the floor, fueling the generator. "You're too much of a slinker," she said to him one day. "Noise won't bother me. I'm bored out of my gourd." So he immediately made a symphony of banging pots with a wooden spoon. He sang old Rolling Stones songs to her while he boiled water in their canning kettle and started the wringer washer in the corner of their cabin. Later, she dozed to the rhythmic sound, willing the baby to stay. "Steady now," she said. "No need to be an early bird. Stay with me."

Several times she woke to the ticking of snow against the window. She sat on the bed watching the gray-white clouds sweep across the valley. With the binoculars she watched the water in the pool, blacker than the sky. Other days the clouds blew away and the bitter wind seemed to come through the wall to her bed. On those clear, cold days the sun made the snow burn with white light. Howard moved in his dark parka across the fields below her window. When he came in, he stamped his feet and banged his hands together. "Damn cold," he said. "The truck won't start today." He drained the oil and antifreeze and heated them in tin pans on the stove.

"Careful, you're going to burn us," she said. But by noon, he had the truck going.

The child seemed to grow larger every day, and she sat on the bed with her legs apart, her arms and hands limp. Her stomach bulged until she thought her skin would split. She no longer had the energy to change her clothing or wash her face and hair. Howard slept on his mattress, so that he wouldn't disturb her. He usually ate quickly, then left to work again.

Thanksgiving Day they ate canned quail, potatoes, sweetened carrots, and drank Coca-Cola. "When it's winter, it's hard to believe that things will grow again," she said. "It's easy to believe that everything will always be cold."

"You're beastly depressed," he said. "Think about something cheerful, like sleeping." She snapped her fingers in his face, and he went outside again. When she looked in the mirror, she found that her face had become pale and luminous, like the skin of a very old person.

The morning after another deep snow, she found blood again. Howard rushed out to start the truck. The wind blew against the cabin, making a low sound like an oboe. An hour later he came back in. "I can't figure out what's wrong," he said. "Maybe it's water in the gas. Maybe the timing chain has slipped. I don't know what to do."

She dozed, woke to a slight pain, dozed again. Finally, she sat up on the bed and looked out the window. Howard, dressed in his black parka, stood in front of the raised hood of the truck. Suddenly, he dropped to his knees. Soon he rose and chained the truck to the tractor, tied the wheel of the tractor straight and started it across the flat toward a patch of field which had already been blown clear. The wheels of the truck plowed sideways through the snow, until he jumped off the tractor and jerked open the door of the truck to straighten them. The tractor wasn't going straight and the truck missed the dry patch by fifty yards.

Alison got up slowly and, after dressing herself, stood in the doorway of the cabin. Somehow Howard had turned the tractor and truck and was crossing the patch of earth. Although the wheels raised dust as they dragged, the truck wouldn't start. Soon the truck was back on the snow where there was no traction. With the binoculars she saw Howard slumped inside the still-moving truck, his head forward on the wheel. "Please, God, no," she said. But then he opened the door and unhooked the chain. He drove the tractor back to where she stood.

"You should be inside lying down," he said. She heard the faint sound of another engine. Taking his shoulder, she turned him toward the far end of the valley, where the yellow plow crawled. He ran to the tractor and drove it toward the main road. Alison returned inside to sit at the table but soon the long yellow road-grader pulled up to the front of the their cabin, the door open, a small and swarthy man inside.

"*¿Que pasa?*" he said. "You need an ambulance?" She sat on the seat, while the driver stood beside her, steering. Howard crouched behind in the tool space. She looked down at the dig as they passed. The baby had been reattached to its mother with leather bands. "You can't beat death that easily," thought Alison. The driver, whose name she missed because of the noise in the cabin, apparently thought she was going to have her baby any minute: he kept the blade high and the speedometer at forty until they roared up to the doctor's office.

"I advise you not to go home," Dr. Peterson said later. "It's too risky to drive back and forth across bad roads in your condition. You need to use some sense. Stay in town."

Alison called her friend, Mary-Aurora, who came and drove them to her house. She owned a greenhouse, one section of which she kept going even in the winter. With Alison and Howard seated in her kitchen, she strode, self-assured as a goddess, back to that steamy building and returned with a tall poinsettia, which she gave to Howard. "We'll have a good time together," she said to Alison. "A woman's time without your husband."

He looked down into the exotic leaves. If a cow or a human couldn't eat a plant, Alison knew, Howard didn't see any use for it. But he walked to the door with the pot. "I'll come in every Sunday," he said. He walked down the street toward the house of a friend, who had agreed to drive him out and help start the truck.

Alison's bedroom was at the top of Aurora's white frame house, a pleasant room with a view of the mountains between the town and the deeper desert where Howard was. She stayed in bed night and day, talking to the child, whom Aurora had named Nicodemus because he was a waverer.

They had been friends for two years but were still unfamiliar with each other's deeper selves. Often, when they needed to talk, they instead found themselves issuing proclamations:

"You can will your body to heal itself," said Aurora.

"It's subject to powers beyond my control."

"You are majestic, an eternal being of power."

"We are transients, here a minute, then dead and buried."

"The earth is a garden."

"The earth is a cross on which we are sacrificed."

After these bold statements, they both became frightened and clung to each other on Alison's bed.

The first Sunday was warm. From her window she saw puddles melting in the roads. Although she watched the road until dark, Howard didn't have the sense to come before the roads froze again. Finally around ten, he drove up and pounded on the door. He lay his sleeping bag on the rug beside her bed and held her hand. He talked about how rough the early cold was for the cattle, the difficulty of breaking ice and hauling hay alone. She dozed until midnight, the pleasant rhythm of his voice recreating their valley for her. Shortly after light he was gone.

Although she was careful to keep herself still, she knew that resting hadn't prevented her bleeding a second time. Once the unnatural process of detachment started, she felt it would continue to its end. Aurora fussed over her, bringing dinner up and talking to her while she ate. She gave Alison positive things to read—*Walden* and New Age literature. She told Alison that depression could cause physical problems. Alison knew that her sadness was the natural fear of an impending death.

Contrary to both their expectations, toward Christmas Alison felt stronger again; she had a record of three weeks without bleeding. The doctor told her she should get some light exercise. She went on short walks, passing under the red and green lights on Main Street and the black-barked trees, their branches reaching up like fingers. She disliked the garish lights, but she enjoyed walking on the side streets, looking at the different kinds of houses. She walked with Howard one night, up onto the low ridge above town. They sat and watched the deer and elk come down to gnaw the hay stacks of the town farmers.

On Christmas Eve she and Aurora dressed themselves in heavy coats and built a fire outside in the barbecue. By the light of the flame Alison read the first part of Luke. They had finished and returned inside when Howard finally came—red faced from having to drive with the window open because the defroster had broken.

"You need a new truck," said Aurora.

"For once I agree with you," he said. "Maybe one of our prosperous friends will float us a loan."

"You don't have any prosperous friends," said Aurora. "You are such a pair. With that truck you're an accident waiting to happen. And

Alison—you spend all your time willing disaster. You believe in fate, don't you? Whatever will be, will be. You're like two pagans." She rose to bring some hot chocolate.

"How can I hold my head up anymore, knowing that?" said Howard.

"She's part right, you know." When Aurora came back, Alison turned to her. "I know we're jinxed," she said. "But we have kind friends." Aurora smiled at her and the three of them sat in a circle, their cups steaming.

Two days before New Year's Alison had another appointment with Dr. Peterson. He examined her carefully. "The placenta is firmly attached," he said.

"I'd like to go home then," she said

"We've about made it," he said. "You're eight months and a week."

"Yes," she said. "So I can go home for a while."

"You are a strong-willed woman," he said.

"Stubborn as a mule."

That Sunday she told Howard she was returning with him. It was evening before they started back. During the afternoon, clouds had blown in, covering Rockwood like a gray, inverted bowl. The street lights and Christmas lights were blurs of white, red, and green behind them as they started back across the desert. Snow beat into the windshield. Howard drove slowly so that they wouldn't slip off the road.

When they finally came to the mineral pool, Alison reached for Howard's hand. "Let's stop for a minute and look," she said. They walked out into the snow, and she watched the flakes spin in masses above them. The wind flapped the blue plastic, shrieked through the squat brush. "I want to have a warm soak," she said, walking back toward the truck.

"Don't be crazy," he said. She quickly slipped out of her clothes, leaving them in a dark heap on the seat.

"The snow is cold," she said, walking past him toward the pool.

"Alison," he said, touching her arm. "Use some sense. It's a blizzard out here."

"It's time for a celebration," she said. "We're all alive. What's the danger?"

"Cold," he said. The wind was freezing her so she stepped quickly down the bank into the warm water. She turned and floated on her back when it was deep enough. "We won," she called. "No one had to follow." Howard stood above her on the bank as she slipped backward through the water. The water was so thick with salt that it held her buoyant. Looking down at the pale curve of her belly, she kicked herself backward; she felt like a sleek water creature.

"Howard, I missed you, Howard." She floated, arms and legs motionless. He kicked off his boots and dropped his coat. When she glanced up again he had peeled down to his white thermals and was sidling down into the water. She watched his pale face come up to her. "It's all right," she said, touching his cheek. "Swimming is not strenuous at all. My belly keeps me up. And the water's not too hot for the baby."

"There's no fire in the cabin."

"So I'll sit in the truck while you build one."

"Thanks loads," he said. He touched her hand, her head, curved his arms around her. The storm whistled above them. Floating on her back, her hand in his hand, she watched the banks of snowflakes turning in the limitless depth above them. She felt disoriented, not knowing which way was up, which down, held between by the thick fluid. She imagined those other floaters, ankles bound, sunk upright in the deep water, waiting for passage back into the sun. She could leave the pool anytime she wanted, didn't have to remain as they had for year on year, century on century. She and her child had not been compelled to join them. The water was warm on her body and limbs, the air and melting flakes cold on her face and belly. Each sensation felt like a miracle.

"The snow's getting deeper," Howard said finally. "We need to get to the cabin." The bank was slick and he scrambled out on hands and knees. When he bent backward to help Alison, he slipped toward her, and she had to come out like a crab as well. He lifted her to her feet and they walked quickly through the snow, their palms and knees marked with black mud. "That was nice," said Alison. She laughed at Howard, who hobbled barefoot, carrying his bundle of clothing.

"I've been so lonely," he said. "I'm glad you're home."

She turned the heater on full and wiped herself clean with a newspaper she found on the floor. Then she slipped her dress back over her. Before they were halfway to the cabin she was warm again. Howard, who hadn't removed his wet underwear, shivered with cold, his teeth chattering. When they came to the cabin he left the truck running and rushed inside. Soon she saw a light, and then he stood naked in the door grinning.

"You are beautiful," she called, as she walked toward him. "He's kicking again. You should feel." She took his hand before he could step back, guiding his fingers over the curve of her belly. She looked up into his face as they both felt the bumping of a foot or fist knocking to get out.

JOHN BENNION *had writing in the back of his mind most of the time he was growing up, but it wasn't until a writing teacher at Utah State University praised a story he'd written that he felt like he had what it took to be a writer. He finished his degree at USU and then worked on a collection of stories for his MA at BYU while he taught English at a junior high school (an experience only made bearable, he says, because he was living on a ranch at the time). Bennion then received a PhD in literature and creative writing at the University of Houston. He has published one book, a collection of short stories called* Breeding Leah and Other Stories, *has had numerous short stories appear in* Dialogue, Sunstone, Ascent, *and* The Best of the West II, *among other places. He says of his writing, "My wife says that I'm a good writer after ten drafts. With me it's not an act of genius, it's hard labor."*

Questions

1. What does the burial pool symbolize in the story? Why does Alison swim in the pool?
2. What does the dialogue tell you about the relationship between the husband and wife?
3. Compare this story to Jorgensen's "A Song for One Still Voice." What is each couple's relationship with the land?
4. What is Alison's relationship to the Goshute woman?

Opening Day

Douglas Thayer

"Opening Day," Douglas Thayer says, is "a story about temptation." He wanted to write a story about the temptations facing returned missionaries (and all Latter-day Saints in general) that wasn't conventional, that showed temptations of a different sort. Basing the story in part on his own past experiences in which "hunting was the most powerful emotion I felt as a kid," Thayer shows the problems that can arise when someone "just gets too close [to temptation]." "Opening Day" is reprinted from Under the Cottonwoods and Other Mormon Stories.

Doc and my father got up at 4 o'clock to light the fire, heat water on the Coleman stoves for washing and get the breakfast started, then woke the rest of us. Standing outside of our white tent in the cool darkness, I buckled on my heavy cartridge belt and breathed in deep the smell of wood smoke and sagebrush. I looked down Blind Canyon and then turned to look up at the black silhouette of the ridge under the stars. I knew the bucks would already be out feeding in the draws. The ridge ran east and west, and we hunted the draws on the south and north slopes. I still felt the old excitement of the opening day of the deer hunt, an empty tight feeling as if my whole body were being squeezed. I still wanted to see the big mule-deer bucks jump out of the oak brush ahead of the line, shoot them as they ran. But then I hadn't expected to have absolute control over my emotions just because while I was on my mission in Germany I had decided to stop hunting. When I got married and had sons, I didn't want them to hunt, but I knew that it wouldn't be easy for me to stop killing birds and animals.

Bliss, Dean, and Ken stood by the fire, and Jerry washed in the pan of warm water on the end of the table. The light from the fire and the two Coleman lanterns glared off from their red hats, sweat shirts, and jackets. When they moved, the handles of their hunting knives, aluminum lids of their old GI belt canteens, and the shells in their full cartridge belts glinted.

When the rest of us had washed, Doc asked me to give the morning prayer and blessing on the food, said that we had to keep the returned missionaries busy. After we ate we got our rifles out of the cases in the tent, saddled Bliss's three horses, and put the lunches and the two walkie-talkies in the saddlebags. We turned off the lanterns, shoveled dirt on the fire, and we were ready, each of us carrying his rifle slung. My father, Doc, and Bliss, who were older and worked on the Union Pacific Railroad together, rode the horses, the rest of us following in single file across the sagebrush flat to the start of the trail at the base of the ridge. Every hundred yards we had to stop to rest, our breath white in the flashlight beams as we sat breathing hard.

I had been home from Germany four days, and while I was gone I had decided to quit hunting. Two years of knowing that I would probably be drafted and sent to Vietnam, hearing the older Germans talk about World War II, and every day preaching the gospel of Christ changed me. I felt guilty because of all the rabbits, pheasants, ducks, geese, and deer I had killed, which were beautiful and had a right to live. All things had been created spiritually before they were physically. Our family ate the meat, but we didn't need it. We weren't pioneers or Indians, and we were commanded to eat meat mostly in time of famine anyway, and then with thanksgiving. The deer herds had to be controlled, but I knew that I hunted because I liked to kill, not because I was a conservationist. A mule-deer buck was a beautiful animal, sleek and grey, powerful, had a being all its own. To kill was to deny the influence of the Holy Ghost, which I wanted to continue to develop.

I had started three letters to my father to tell him how I had changed, but I couldn't make them sound right, and I knew that I would have to wait until I got home to tell him. I had three older married sisters but no brothers, and my father and I had been very close. Even before I was old enough to buy a license for anything or even shoot, he took me hunting. He helped me make my bows and arrows, bought me a BB gun, my Browning .22, and my Winchester .270. For my birthdays and Christmases he always gave me something for hunting, although I had bought my own knife when I was eight. We built a walnut gun cabinet, a duck boat, and we cleaned and repaired the camping equipment together every year. Every month we read and talked about the stories in *Outdoor Life* and *Field and Stream*, which I saved.

We had even planned my mission so that I would have the deer hunt to look forward to when I got home. When I met my family at the Salt Lake airport, all my father could talk about driving home to Provo was the opening day Saturday and how wonderful it was having me home again to be with him in the deer camp. Upstairs in my room I found my .270, knife, full cartridge belt, and red hunting clothes laid out on my bed. My father had bought me a new red hat, cleaned and oiled my .270, and loaded three boxes of shells for me to use for target practicing. When I went back downstairs he took me out to see the new sets of antlers he had nailed to the back of the garage the two seasons I was away.

I knew then that I would have to hunt the opening day. I couldn't disappoint my father. We could have Friday night in camp together, and all day Saturday I would drive the draws, help clean the bucks if I had to, pack them on the horses, but I wouldn't kill a buck myself. I would shoot just to stop questions if a buck jumped up and a member of the camp was standing where he could see me, but I would miss. We always came home Saturday night to go to church on Sunday, and I would tell my father Sunday about my decision. I wouldn't hunt during the week or next Saturday, which was the last Saturday. My mother always said that my father should have been born an Indian two hundred years ago so that he could have hunted elk, wolves, buffalo, and grizzly bear, hunted every day.

Climbing up the trail I was the last in line. Ahead of me the flashlights lit up the high oak brush on both sides and the horses' hooves clicked against the rocks. Doc, Bliss, and my father stayed on the horses when we stopped to rest. Because we knew the ridge, organized our drives, and hunted hard, we always got bucks. A camp needed horses to haul the bucks off the high ridge, so we had little competition. Sitting on the edge of the trail, the sweat cooling on my back, I picked up little white pebbles, flipped them away, thought about Germany.

Although I had sold more Books of Mormon than any other elder in the mission and been assistant to President Wunderlich my last five months, I had baptized only two converts in two years. The younger Germans weren't interested in the gospel, and when the older Germans invited me and my companion in, they often talked about the war. They showed us pictures of their sons that we had killed, and they wanted to know why the American army hadn't joined the German army to fight the Russians. They showed us pictures of whole families of relatives burned alive or buried in the rubble during the great Allied bombing raids on Nuremberg, Hamburg, and Dresden. They called Hitler a madman and asked why the English and French governments didn't stop him before 1939. They wanted to know how there could be a God if he let such terrible things happen, and I told them that it wasn't God that caused wars but men. If all mankind would just live the gospel of Christ there wouldn't be any more wars. I wanted to get a doctorate in sociology so that I could teach at BYU and help people to live together in peace and harmony.

On the streets in the German towns, older men who had been invalided in the war wore yellow armbands with black circles, a lot of them amputees, but there were no beggars. My first fall in Germany, a German brother took me and my companion on a Saturday out to visit a small

German military cemetery near Offenbach. One of the caretakers raking leaves under the oak trees said that most of the soldiers had been killed fighting Americans. I picked up a handful of the leaves. In Utah in the fall I had followed wounded bucks by their blood trails on the leaves under the oak brush. In the places where they lay down, the blood soaked slowly into the pressed leaves.

The trail led onto a little flat, and above us the ridge was still black under the stars. In every direction were ridges, canyons, mountains, but they were still black and indistinct. Points of light flashed where hunters climbed other ridges, and in the bottom of Blind Canyon fires still burned. As a boy at night I dreamed about the ridge. Although a lot of big bucks hid in the short, steep, pine-filled draws on the north slope, I liked the south draws best because I could see the bucks running up through the oak brush, shoot for three and four hundred yards if I were on a good ledge. In my dreams I shot and shot, killed the running bucks, their antlers flashing in the sun like swords, rolled them back down the steep side of the draw. And I dreamed too that we jumped five and six bucks in one bunch, and it was like a battle with all of us shooting, but because we gang-hunted I wanted to fill all of the permits myself. I wanted to feel all of the thrill, cut the throats, the blood spreading out through the leaves, holler up to the others how big the bucks were, how many points on the antlers. If we shot too many bucks, on the way down Blind Canyon going home we always gave the smaller ones to other camps, didn't waste any. One opening day I shot three bucks, but they were all singles.

When we stopped on the trail again to rest, Jerry leaned forward to pour some dextrose tablets into my palm. "Quick energy, Troy," he said. "It takes a while for you returned missionaries to get back into shape." Chewing two, I sat and held my .270 between my legs, the barrel cold against the side of my neck, rubbed the stock with the flat of my hand. Up the trail one of the horses stomped.

A Winchester Model 70 mounted with a 3–9x variable scope, the .270 was a present from my father on my sixteenth birthday. The evening I got it, in the sitting position on my bed, left arm tight in the sling, I aimed at the pictures of bears, lions, and deer on my walls, and later out the windows at cars and people passing below on our street, centered the cross hairs. Then I broke the .270 down, oiled each metal part, reassembled it, broke it down again. And I kept filling the magazine with shells, worked the bolt over and over to flip them out on my bed. That night after I showered I got the .270 out of the case again to hold it against my body. I had a .22 pistol, .22 rifle, .22–250 varminter, two shotguns, but my .270 had always been my favorite gun. I had waited for it, knew that my father would give me a deer rifle too when I was sixteen, which was the first year I could buy a buck permit. I liked to take my .270 out of our gun cabinet just to hold it and work the action, wipe it clean with an oiled cloth.

I thought of my guns when I saw the filled-in shrapnel and bullet holes in the old stone German buildings that hadn't been destroyed. If the older German sisters talked long enough about the war, they always cried, and I never asked them about the concentration camps, the SS, or the Gestapo. On a street in Darmstadt after I was transferred from Offenbach, I saw a legless, armless blind man sitting on a padded box singing while another man played a guitar, but there was no cup or dish in front of them and they weren't begging. Some of the older Germans said that they were sorry for the young Americans in Vietnam and asked if my companion and I would have to go too. I knew that if I couldn't get a student deferment and go back to BYU to start my sophomore year, I would be drafted. It was impossible to get into the Utah National Guard. I would kill other men, shoot them in the jungle or running across the rice paddies, their blood turning the brown water near their bodies red. And I knew also by then that the excitement of killing a man must be a little like that of killing a buck.

When we got to the top of the ridge we sat and watched the band of white light grow over the east mountains, our red hats, sweat shirts, and jackets almost black in the half-light. Excited, my heart pounding hard even though I was rested, I pulled the cold shells from my belt to load the .270, heard around me shells clicking into magazines. "Good luck, son," my father said when we stood up, shook my hand. "I hope you nail a big one first thing." The others came over to shake my hand and tell me how good it was to have me back on the ridge again. Separating, we spread out along the top of the ridge to take the points we had drawn Friday night.

Ten minutes later, cradling the .270, I stood on my ledge in the half-light looking down into the pine-filled basin at the head of Sheep Draw on the north side of the ridge. Trembling a little, my mouth dry, I watched the clearings for movement. The light grew and the first shots came booming along the ridge. Then below me two does and a little two-point buck stepped out of the pines into a patch of brush. My body tight, blood pounding in my throat, I slowly raised the .270 and centered the cross hairs over the little buck's heart. I fought the desire to ease down into the sitting position, tighten into the sling, squeeze the trigger slowly. I wanted to hear the explosion, feel the .270 kick, see the little two-point hump and drop, feel that satisfaction again. The first season I carried the .270, I had killed a two-point at first light, had been unable to wait for the bigger buck I wanted. Fighting that feeling, I closed my eyes, opened them. Suddenly the three deer tensed, then crossed the clearing and slipped back into the pines as quiet and smooth as gliding birds. Glad I hadn't shot, I lowered the .270.

At 9 o'clock the camp met to drive Porcupine, the first draw on the west end of the south slope, where we always started. Jerry had passed up a small two-point, and Dean missed three shots at a big buck some hunters had pushed up from below. While Doc and Jerry tested the walkie-talkies again, I scoped the draw and the basin. Broken only by ledges and scattered pines, the leafless oak brush and scrub maple were like a smooth low-lying haze. But a dozen bucks could be hiding, waiting. You never knew. Each draw was a surprise. Everything would be quiet, not even a bird moving, then two or three bucks would be running in front of the line, running grey and beautiful, heads up, antlers gleaming in the sun, going for the top and the thick pines on the north slope, and then the shooting would start. It was as if you had waited all year for just that one moment because it was the best time out of the whole year.

I stopped the scope on a patch of scrub maple where I had killed a three-point the season before I left to go on my mission. To the left was the clearing where Jerry had killed the biggest buck ever killed on the ridge, a big eight-point with a forty-inch spread. He had the mounted head in his real estate office. I knew where all of the big bucks had been killed. We cut the legs off the bucks at the knee to load them on the horses, and sometimes I found legs from two and three seasons back. There was always a black stain on the ground where the entrails had lain the year before. In twenty-five years the camp had killed over a hundred and fifty bucks on the ridge.

"Okay," Doc said, "let's get the big ones. There's one down in there for you, Troy, a nice big four-point." The clear sky was dark blue, and now the warming sun brought out the dusty smell of brush and dead leaves. Lines of blue ridges and mountains extended to the horizon on every side.

Doc and my father stayed on the rim, and Jerry led the rest of us down into the draw to organize the drive, Bliss riding his horse. We formed the line, each of us a hundred yards apart across the bottom and up both sides, and started slowly back toward the top. Expecting to see a big buck jump up any minute, excited but controlling myself, I walked tense, stopped, checked the openings ahead on both sides, listened for deer running through the brush. Across the draw, Dean and Ken vanished, reappeared, stopped to throw rocks ahead of them, their red hunting clothes bright against the grey leafless brush. Jerry and Bliss were above me where I couldn't see them. I stopped to toe the fresh droppings with my boot, knelt on one knee to look at the fresh tracks in the deer trail I was on. Mouth dry, hands sweaty on the .270, I froze when Ken first jumped seven does and fawns, which I scoped until they vanished over the top, their white rear ends flashing. Shooting echoed from ridge to ridge, some of it coming in sharp bursts like machine-gun fire, and far down the draw four hunters stood together on a knoll. When I was a boy, the shooting from the other ridges always made me jealous.

I had just walked out onto a ledge at the bottom end of the basin topping the draw when Dean yelled, "Buck! Buck! Buck! He's in the bottom!" Dean shot twice, shot again. Warned, my heart pounding in my throat, I half raised the .270. Another rifle started. Then I saw the big buck moving through the high scrub maples, head down, going smooth like a cat, not making the big ten-foot bounding jumps. But when I jammed the .270 into my shoulder, got the cross hairs on him, he was already blundering, crashing into the brush. A round patch of blood widened behind the shoulder on the grey side, and his mouth dripped blood. Lung-shot. Hit again, he came crashing, rolling back down toward the bottom. He got up, shook his head. Hit again, he humped and dropped, lay in a clearing. The whooping started then, and Dean, Ken following him, jogged down through the brush, hollered for directions twice. They hollered up that he was a fat four-point, cut his throat, then got out their cameras to take colored slides before they cleaned him. Breathing deep, I tried to stop trembling.

"Aren't you coming down, Troy?" Bliss asked me when he came past leading his horse through the brush.

"No, I'll stay here. They don't need me."

"I shot but I think Dean got him, unless you did."

"No, I didn't."

"Too bad, looks like a nice buck. Jerry's going to stay put and watch for anything pushed up from the bottom by the other camps."

I sat down on the ledge, laid the .270 on my hat and ate a Hershey bar, rinsed my teeth and drank from my canteen. Dean, Ken, and Bliss bent over the buck. Watching two hawks circle out over the draw, I picked up a dead branch, broke off pieces and flipped them away.

Before I was sixteen and could shoot a buck, using my own knife I cut the throats of my father's bucks and other bucks I got to first. My father taught me how to clean a buck, cut around the genitals, up through the stomach and ribs, reach up into the chest and grab the severed wind pipe to pull everything out together without getting my hands bloody above the wrists. I always cut the heart away from the blue pile of entrails to hold up and see if it had been hit. Afterward my father poured water on my hands from his canteen and I wiped them clean with handfuls of dry leaves. Yet even with two or three of us shooting, hit several times, a buck still might not go down. A buck with both front legs shot off would still lunge forward, work his antlers through the low limbs, crawl to get away.

Following blood trails, I had found pieces of entrails snagged on the oak brush and splinters of bone lying on the leaves.

The limbless blind man made me think about the fantastic pain I caused by just squeezing the trigger of my .270 to send the hundred-and-fifty-grain slug at three thousand feet per second slamming into a buck. I saw him once more before President Wunderlich made me a zone leader and transferred me from Darmstadt to Heidelberg. He rode in a big rucksack on his friend's back, just his head showing, bobbing, as if he saw the passing people and into the store windows. His friend carried the guitar and the padded box. When I ate, dressed, showered, I wondered how he did those things. Lying in bed at night I tried to imagine what it would be like for him to be in bed, and I wanted to know if he was married. I knew then that I couldn't go on hunting and killing when I got home and still expect to feel the full influence of the Holy Ghost in my life, be spiritual, which had to be earned. Breaking off the last few pieces of the dead branch, I flipped them over the ledge. Then I got out my clean handkerchief and wiped off the scope and the .270.

Ken, Dean, and Bliss loaded the buck on the horse and we hunted the basin to the top of the ridge, where they hung the buck from the low limb of a big pine. In Middle Draw, the last drive we always made before lunch and the draw where I had killed the two-point when I was sixteen, Doc and my father both shot three-points as they came up out of the basin over the top. I didn't see either buck, but stood cradling the .270, counted the shots, felt empty, then heard Jerry hollering after he talked to Doc on the walkie-talkie. When we got to the top we helped drag the bucks over to the trail to hang them up. I broke sticks to prop open the stomachs so the bucks would cool faster. We always hung our bucks in the garage to cure for a week before we had them cut up for the freezer. Skinned, the heads cut off, they hung stiff and white upside down, the blunt front legs sticking out, spots of blood on the cement floor.

"Well, Troy," my father said when we all gathered to eat lunch on the ledge above Doc's draw, "I wish that you had been on the rim instead of me. Those two three-points came sneaking up through the brush ahead of you boys in the line just perfect. It couldn't have been prettier."

"No, I guess not," I said. Ken, Jerry, and Dean had black, dry deer blood on their red sweat shirts and blue Levis. You couldn't wash the smell of the blood from your hands unless you had hot soap and water, but you could get the blood out from under your fingernails with the point of a sharp hunting knife.

"Oh, we'll get Troy a nice buck today or next Saturday, don't worry about that," Doc said. Doc and Bliss had taken the bridles off the horses and poured some oats for them.

"Sure," Jerry said, unwrapping a piece of cake.

Eating my sandwich, I looked out over the draw toward the lines of blue ridges out past Blind Canyon. Doc had killed three bucks one opening day in the basin as they ran past him at seventy-five yards; after that everybody in camp called it Doc's Draw. Each line of ridges was a different shade of blue. All the shooting had stopped. I was glad that my father had Doc and Bliss to hunt with. They had worked on the Union Pacific together for thirty years. My father had never been on a mission. He had written me long letters about the duck, pheasant, and deer hunts and sent me the best colored slides he had taken. Every month he mailed me his copies of *Outdoor Life* and *Field and Stream.* When I was a boy and my mother made me turn off my bedroom light, I used a flashlight to reread my favorite hunting stories by.

After we ate lunch, the others got their red jackets from the saddlebags to use for pillows, pulled their red hats down over their eyes and lay back on the ledge to doze in the warm sun. Below me nothing moved in the draw. I picked up white chips of rock and flipped them over the ledge. Although I wouldn't hunt I planned to do a lot of backpacking, learn the names of all the Rocky Mountain flora and fauna, and at night study the stars. When I got married and had sons, I wanted them to see the real beauty, design, and completeness of Nature, which God had created. I wanted to be as close to my sons as my father had been to me, but without guns and killing. I wouldn't let them carry .22s or varmint rifles to kill the hawks, rabbits, rock chucks, and squirrels they saw, as my father had let me. I wanted them to understand the pioneers and Indians, but they didn't have to hunt to do that. We could start an arrowhead collection and visit all of the historical spots in the state.

A chipmunk came up over the face of the ledge, found a piece of bread. With the shooting stopped, it was very quiet. I flipped a chip of rock. I had read an article by one of the apostles who had visited the Mormon servicemen in Vietnam. He said that in one meeting the men came to the tent carrying their rifles. In the prayers they prayed for the Mormon boys killed the week before, prayed for the spirit of the Lord for themselves. After the testimony meeting some of the soldiers told the apostle that they had met him as missionaries in Europe nine months before when he was touring the missions. In the German magazines I saw pictures of American wounded being carried to helicopters on stretchers, medics running alongside with lifted plasma bottles. Wrapped in their ponchos the American dead lay in rows like packages, but the Viet Cong dead were never covered. I flipped another piece of rock and the chipmunk vanished back over the face of the ledge.

Before we dropped down into Doc's Draw, three hunters on horses from another camp came along the ridge trail. They wanted to know where we got the three nice bucks we had hanging up. "They don't organize and they don't know the country, so all they get are spikes and two-points," Doc said after they left. "They might as well stay in camp as come up on this ridge and ride around."

We jumped one bunch of six does and fawns at the lower end of Doc's Draw, and in the basin Ken, who was across from me, shot a big four-point. Hollering, he directed me to him in the thick brush. One antler dug through the dead leaves into the black dirt, the big buck lay on his side, the four points on each side of the antlers white-tipped, the blood bright red on the leaves. Standing there, I wondered if I had scared the buck out to Ken. I didn't pull his head downhill to cut his throat. He was still perfect, the eyes not yet glazed. He still seemed alive, still had that beautiful grey live symmetry as if he might suddenly jump and run. Bending, I ran my hand over the hard antlers, along the neck and onto the heavy shoulders. When Ken and Dean broke through the brush, I told them that I would go and show Bliss the best way to bring the horse down.

"Okay," Ken said. He leaned his rifle against a rock and got out his camera.

"Looks like you really busted a nice one, Ken," Dean said. "Good work."

"Finally."

Climbing up through the brush, I heard them talking. I had actually prayed for a big four-point like Ken's the first morning I had carried the new .270. My father beside me on the ledge overlooking the basin at the top of middle draw, I gripped the Winchester, whispered the prayer to myself, and I would have knelt down too if I had thought that it would do any good. But when in the first light I saw the little two-point standing in the patch of sagebrush with a doe, I moved into the sitting position, tightened into the sling, and killed him with a perfect heart shot, started then to run. When my father got down to me and the little buck, he put his rifle down and hugged me. I cleaned the buck, holding up his shattered heart in my hand to look for pieces of the slug. I had killed a lot of pheasants, ducks, geese, and rabbits before I was sixteen, but I had never felt like that. My father nailed the two-point's antlers over the garage door next to the biggest spread of antlers he had ever taken.

At 2 o'clock we crossed from the south slope of the ridge to the north to hunt the smaller steeper draws full of thick pines. It was cooler there than on the south slope. We jumped bucks, but they were hard to hit running through the pines, and they all got away over the top past Doc and my father. Because the bucks liked to hide in the pines, there was a lot of sign on the deer trails. I saw a beautiful little spike, but didn't even raise the .270 to put the scope on him, just watched him until he moved. It made me happy just to watch him. Other years I had found blood trails in the pines from the deer wounded lower on the ridge that sneaked up in the thick cover to die. The second year the scattered bones were white, with hair left only on the legs and skull.

In the next basin, ahead of the others, I sat down against a pine. I cut a Baby Ruth bar in sections with my knife, drank from my canteen, rinsed my teeth, the air cool against my face and throat. Taking off my heavy cartridge belt, I laid it across my knees, began to line the shells up in the loops so that they were all exactly even. I pulled one out and fingered it. The hundred-and-fifty-grain slug with the lead tip and core was built to explode on contact with bone or heavy muscle. In junior high school every fall I took some of my father's shells with me to class so that I could put my hand in my pocket and feel them. I took my hunting knife one day, but my home-room teacher picked it up and kept it in her desk until school was out in the afternoon. After my father gave me the .270 for my birthday, I loaded my empty brass on his reloading outfit. At night I poured three or four boxes of shells onto my bed just to run my fingers through them. Alone, I dressed in my red hat and shirt, wore my knife and full cartridge belt, cradled the .270 in my left arm to look at myself in the mirror.

Below me in the pines a small bird lit on a dead branch. Everything was in shadow. The German forests seemed always to be in shadow, as if the season were always winter but without snow. The .270 shell I had taken out of the belt was heavy in my palm. One Saturday afternoon a week before President Wunderlich called me to Frankfurt as his assistant, my companion and I rode our bicycles out into the woods near Heidelberg to an area where a German brother said there had been fighting. We walked through the trees until we came to the top of a hill dotted with shallow pits, which I knew must be old shell holes. Some of the pines looked as if they had been hit by lightning a long time ago. Scratching with a stick, my companion found an American hand-grenade pin and three empty rifle shells so corroded that he had to scrape them on a rock to tell if they were American or German. He offered me one of the shells, but I told him no. When we got back to our room he put his find in a little box to save and take home. Placing the .270 shell back in the belt loop, I took out my handkerchief and wiped off the scope and the rifle.

At 4 o'clock Jerry organized the drive for West Draw. It was the last drive before we went down the ridge to break camp and start the long trip out of Blind Canyon and back to Provo. The shooting from the other ridges had stopped again. The lines of ridges were darker blue now, some of the ledges white like patches of early snow. The Ute Indians buried their dead high in the canyons in the ledges, but I had never found one of the rock-piled graves. I had always wondered if the Indians had hunted the high ridges too or whether they found enough game lower down. As we stood together at the top of the draw, in the afternoon light the hats and sweat shirts seemed darker red. I was glad it was the last drive and we were going home.

Because Jerry wanted to take me out of the line and put me on a point above an opening in the pines called the bowl, Doc held out his walkie-talkie to me. The bowl was the best spot in the basin at the head of West Draw. "No," I said, "I'll go down in the pines and help make the drive. You take the bowl, Bliss; you haven't filled your permit yet."

"Now, Troy," Doc said, "you've hunted hard in that line all day without any luck, and this is your last chance until next Saturday, unless you and your dad get out during the week for a little afternoon hunting. We'd all like to see you get a nice buck."

"No. I don't want to do that."

"Go ahead, Troy," Jerry said. "We all got nice bucks the last two seasons. We're not sweating it."

"Oh no."

"Go on, son," my father said, and Doc put the walkie-talkie into my hand.

"Sure," Jerry said, gripping my shoulder.

Ten minutes later I climbed up to the ledge to the left and nearly to the top of the bowl and sat down. The oak brush was all knee high, stunted, and fallen leaves covered the rocks and bare spots. Because of the timber, none of the others could see me, so I wouldn't even have to shoot if a buck came up through the bowl. I had never killed a buck in West Draw. Sitting there, cradling the .270, I thought about Sunday morning and meeting everybody in church after two years away. I was anxious to tell about all the things that I had learned while I was in Germany on my mission, tell of my experiences, and I wanted to bear my testimony of the truthfulness of the gospel of Christ. I breathed in the cool air full of the smell of pines.

"You ready, Troy?"

I raised the walkie-talkie. "Yes."

"Keep your eyes open. There's an awful lot of tracks and droppings down here on these trails."

Picking up a handful of the wind-blown oak leaves caught in a crack in the ledge, I let them sift through my fingers. Perhaps my father and I could find something else we liked to do together. One of the reasons I wanted to get my doctorate in sociology and teach at BYU was so that I could live in Provo and raise my family there after I got married. Because my father had given me my .270 for my sixteenth birthday, I would always keep it, but I would get rid of my other guns and my eight-year collection of *Field and Stream* and *Outdoor Life*. I didn't want my sons to get started on them. "Keep your eyes open, Troy. Something moving out ahead." I reached down and clicked off the walkie-talkie. Nobody shot. Nothing moved. I waited. Then right at the bottom edge of the bowl a buck stepped out of the pines. Chest tightening, I slowly lifted the .270 to bring the scope to my eye. A nice three-point. Another buck stepped out, another three-point, moved up to the first. Heart slamming, I scoped them both, when two more moved out of the pines at the same place. They were both four-points, the last one a beautiful big buck with a wide heavy set of antlers.

Bent forward, breathing deep, the blood beginning to pound in my ears, I held the scope to my eye. They were beautiful. I just wanted to watch them, prayed nobody would make it to the edge of the pines in time for a shot. The bucks stopped to look back, started moving again, the big buck leading now. Slipping my arm into the sling, I got into the sitting position to steady my scope. The bucks were nervous but still walking. Beautiful. Biting my lower lip, I shifted the cross hairs back up to the big buck. The antlers were perfectly matched on each side. My pounding blood sounded like rushing water in my ears, louder and louder. Beautiful. I closed my eyes against the feeling, gripped harder, breathless.

The .270 slammed my shoulder, the explosion part of my feeling. Heart-shot, the big buck humped and went down. The other bucks ran now in high leaping bounds, instinct driving them toward the top and me. I shot over the leader, adjusted, got him through the back at seventy-five yards, and he went smashing down. I shot at the first three-point as he came level with me, missed twice. Kneeling, I crammed in more shells, cursed, slammed the bolt home, held the cross hairs on him, saw him come rolling back down the slope. Alone, the last buck was nearly to the top. I shot, missed, stood up, spun him around with a hit in the front leg, got him just as he topped the skyline. He came crashing end-over-end back down the steep slope into the bowl. I found the raised head of the back-shot buck in the scope, shot, and everything was quiet.

"Oh no, no, no," I said, "oh no." Grabbing the short oak brush with my free hand when I slipped, I angled across to the last buck. "No," I said, "no." I laid the .270 down to pull the buck around so that his head was down-hill, then cut his throat. I had to shoot the second buck again to kill him. Whooping and yelling, somebody was climbing toward me up through the brush. "Oh no," I said. I cut the big four-point's throat last, my knife and hands red with blood, his antlers thick at the base where I grabbed them with my sticky hands. "No, no." Still trembling, I knelt down by the big buck's head. His pooled blood started to trickle down through the oak leaves. "Oh, Jesus, Jesus," I whispered.

DOUG THAYER*'s novel* Summer Fire *is regarded by many people as the pioneering work in modern Mormon fiction. Thayer has also published another work of Mormon fiction,* Under the Cottonwoods and Other Mormon Stories, *and a collection of wilderness stories,* Mr. Wahlquist in Yellowstone. *Thayer received his BA in English from BYU and then received an MFA in creative writing from the prestigious Iowa Writers' Workshop.*

Questions

1. What is the central conflict in the story? How does hunting tie to Troy's relationship with his father?
2. What details does Thayer use to show that Troy is both a good hunter and a good missionary? Why is it important to the story for them to have this ethos?
3. How do the flashbacks to Germany work in the story?
4. What does the story say about the nature of temptations? Why does Thayer use hunting instead of smoking or drinking as the temptation in this story?

Nest

Lance Larsen

Based on a memory from his childhood when he found a pair of bird talons and then built a nest to put them in, "Nest" expresses what Lance Larsen calls "trying to understand experience by keeping a relic." While the impetus for the poem is based on his experience as a child, Larsen eventually changed what happens in the poem by letting the subject of the poem "incubate for a long time." After rewriting and revising the poem over a period of time, Larsen found that the original experience didn't make it into the poem and that the rest of the poem is "all made up." "Nest" was originally printed in the Paris Review.

The things I saved up there—mantis legs, cat fur,
porcupine quills tied with twine. I thought
this was religion. To climb through leaves

and pocked apples to the highest bough, to finger
what no one else wanted. Cicada husk,
dried fish tail. Not death, but what it left

behind. I touched tongue to rabbit skull, tasted
the eye holes. So many creeds, and only a crooked
wind and the sulfur glow of the railroad yards

to help do the sorting. Snake skin wrapping
my knuckles, the clink of wisdom teeth, my aunt's.
Worn down enough to make me think of food.

What it might mean to chew. And be chewed.
That divination. Then putting everything
back. Bone puzzle, flesh pieced against fur.

And swallowing as I climbed down—the creature
above and inside me now. Anything left over
circling like a hawk or accidental prayer.

And Also Much Cattle

Lance Larsen

Taking its title from Jonah 4:11, "And Also Much Cattle" started out as a poem about the cows Lance Larsen saw from the window of a time-share condo in Island Park, Idaho. In the first drafts of the poem, Jonah was a minor character, but as Larsen revised and expanded the poem, Jonah came out as a more important element. In this poem, reprinted from Salmagurdi, *Larsen says he is "re-imagin[ing] an experience."*

What did they look like—those cows God
took notice of in sparing Nineveh?
Bland-faced no doubt, eyes big as chestnuts.
Jonah must have loathed them. Jonah under
the gourd, Jonah in his cobbled-together
martyr's booth, sulking and praying
for plagues. Anything to teach Nineveh
a lesson. If not a cracked sky drumming
fire, then leprosy, or wells curdled
with blood. As for the cows, if Jonah
followed their grazing too long, he must
have pictured them fasting again—tricked
out in sackcloth, ashes brindling their sides.
Such cheap theatrics. Didn't real penitence
mean casting yourself into God's mouth,
and waking in the nave of His bowels?
Just you and an acidy soup of sin and rotting
fish. Those three days, they should have
clinched it for him—God's golden boy.
Now Jonah wondered. He tried shutting
his eyes, tried, but the drove wouldn't slow.
All those hooves and splattered flanks.
Cows whose only offering was a little snot
on the muzzle, maybe a cracked tongue.
Cows milling until their moos echoed
across the fatness of the afternoon
like untuned pleas deep inside a fish.

Throwing Papers

Lance Larsen

Lance Larsen says that "Throwing Papers" is "more straight autobiography" than what he usually includes in his writing. He says that writing autobiography presents different kinds of challenges than fiction, including having to "decide what to shape, how to shape it, what to include." "Throwing Papers" was originally published in Best of Writers at Work.

My feet carved an invisible path
of shortcuts until I knew every
geranium petal and rusted croquet hoop
and how to spell fifty-two names.
I was learning the mathematics
of adulthood, how to multiply myself
for Christmas tips and divide out
reprimands. And though I grew lighter
with each paper I threw, I felt
the same sky, the same bruised infinity
pressing down. And only peeling paint
and another story problem to help me
navigate my happiness. Do I wait
to collect from Old Lady Perkins
until after she buries her husband?
Do I tell the Colonel I scratched
his restored cherry Corvair? Yes,
and no. Whatever helped balance
the month. Compensations? A sweating
can of soda maybe, and the things
I found—women's nylons tied in a bow,
then John Sousa sheet music. And once,
stepping past a swing set, a goat head.
Fleshy, one-eared, it lay in the mums,
like a dimpled work boot. I rubbed
its jaw. Tried subtracting the gristled
windpipe, the necklace of ants.
Added fur to the leathered face.

Zeroes still blanked the eye sockets,
the tongue lolling like a pointer.
Across the street, in kitchens dressed
for the latest holiday, families
were lifting careful spoonfuls
of gravy. I was doing just enough
to keep them happy, a few hours
in the cold each week, cursory hellos,
all for three-and-a-half cents per paper
per day, per forever, collected myself.

LANCE LARSEN *got his first impetus to become a poet in a freshman English class at BYU when his teacher encouraged him to write. He later took a poetry class from poet Leslie Norris that further encouraged him to follow a career in writing. He began writing short fiction, essays, and poetry, but then settled on poetry when "it chose me." He earned a BA and MA in English from BYU, and then went to the University of Houston to earn a PhD in Literature and Creative Writing. He has been published in the* Paris Review, *the* Kenyon Review, *the* New Republic, *and* Shenandoah, *among other places. His first book of poetry,* Erasable Walls, *was released in May of 1998.*

Questions

1. In "Nest," what does the protagonist mean by "I thought / this was religion"? How does it relate to "Not death, but what it left / behind"?
2. In "And Also Much Cattle," Larsen alludes to the story of Jonah. How does this poem compare with Steve Walker's treatment of the Book of Jonah in "Jonah as Joke"?
3. What is the "mathematics of adulthood"?
4. How would you describe Larsen's style? What is the relationship between style and meaning?

To My Brother in His Casket

SUSAN ELIZABETH HOWE

Writing honestly about grief is something few people are willing to do. Even poet Susan Elizabeth Howe needed time. In May of 1981, her brother was killed while serving a mission in Kansas, two weeks after his twentieth birthday. In fact, only six months had passed since Howe's twenty-three year-old sister had died from a brain tumor, leaving behind a new baby. "I was really staggered by their deaths together," she says. With time, Howe was able to address her feelings poetically. Her poem was first published in The Literary Review.

Across the vast distance of the funeral
You are as luminous as the moon,
As graphic. I see on your face
How you rose over the hill, full
Of your future, into the path of the diesel.
You have been too clear, too insistent
To drop off now. You flew home
Across the night sky, new-scarred
Face, hands, silver
Twisted in your ring, the stone gone.
What if I were to touch you?

In Washington, in the Air and Space
Museum, is a small, darkening
Moon rock. Despite the blasted,
Broken quadrant where they found it,
A clean trajectory, cold relentless path
Brought it to my hand. Yet
My own fingers on that harsh, familiar
Surface didn't teach me
Why it had to come here, how it mattered,
Nor what it was that I had hoped to know.

Gringa

SUSAN ELIZABETH HOWE

In the summer of 1996, Mexico's Tarahumara Indians suffered from a severe drought in the Sierra Mountains. Susan Howe joined four other professors and a group of BYU students in a project to help the Tarahumaras by building water storage containers. Although Howe's poem "Gringa" contains pieces of her actual experience in Mexico, its narrative grew more from her anger over how little opportunity Tarahumara women enjoy as compared to the men. Although the wood carving represented in the poem is accurate, Howe invented the tension between the store owner and herself.

In the mountains of the mothers,
Mexico's *Sierra Madres*,
the sun sticks in my throat,
so I hope women will appear, cluck
me into their houses
for rest and something to drink.
But the *madres* I see, always at a distance,
babies lashed to their backs,
don't notice me, no words in their language
for *woman on her own.*
If I scatter their goats
these women will say, devil wind;
kick over the basket of corn,
they will shake their bright skirts
to frighten the burros.
I watch them across the valleys—colorful
wooden beads on the mountain's throat—
and stop at the one store
in the next Tarahuamara town.
Its sign—*Cokes en bolsa*—
must mean something watery.

But drought has broken in, left
dust on the vegetable tins, the barrel

of dried beans, the five stale packages
of gum. Winter-thick ponchos
for men, both overcoat and blanket,
range on pegs on the back wall,
their sticky-smelling wool enough
to block any current. Few goods
for women. Stacked out of reach,
bolts of fabric they can buy—
yellow, red, or green printed cotton.
Not to wear the traditional dress
will bring shame, so they
choose from what they find
and sew the printed cloth,
faded side next to the folded side.

From the cooler I slide a Coke
in its bottle of green glass.
Behind the counter, a stack
of white cowboy hats—clean—
under an eagle seizing a snake.
¿Cuántos pesos? I point first
at a hat, then at the wood carving.
Not for sale, the man says twice,
his English stiff for me.
Son para caballeros, for men.
But I take off the bottle cap
with my army knife,
put down a hundred pesos,
point again at the eagle and the snake.

Señor smiles with his lips
and hands it over,
then grabs my Coke, just two sips
gone, slaps it to the counter
on my money. The bolsa is a plastic bag.
He pours the drink in, fizz and foam,
ties the bag, a Coke balloon,
stabs it with a straw,
gringa not a word
he'd ever say. As I leave
he settles my account,
returns my empty bottle to its place.

Susan Elizabeth Howe *received her PhD in creative writing from the University of Denver and currently teaches classes in poetry, writing, and literature. Her first collection of poetry,* Stone Spirits, *won the Charles Redd Center Publication Prize in 1996. She is presently working on her second collection.*

Questions

1. How did the brother in "To My Brother in His Casket" die? What evidence do you find in the text?
2. Why the comparison with the moon rock? How does touching the rock both reflect back to the first stanza and move forward to the final questions?
3. In "Gringa," what factors come into play in the exchange between the storekeeper and the protagonist?
4. Why does Howe use the few Spanish phrases? How does it affect our reading?

Peaches

Leslie Norris

Although on a first reading it may not be apparent, Norris says this may be the most religious poem he's ever done. It is filled with Christian symbolism—Eden, the fall, the cross, resurrection—but it is still a poem that "looks forward" as much as it does back. Norris maintains that in reality, "we ourselves suffer the fall" and "grow aware of death." In the end, he says, "we desert our gardens deliberately, and we make a desert of them." "Peaches" is reprinted from Collected Poems.

In his life he has made seven gardens, two
from the untilled meadow, some in good heart
after the spades of other men. One, unkempt
inside its formal Georgian walls, he brought
to perfect order out of wilderness, its geometric
beds to flower, renewed its lawn, cut back
its gnarled espaliers and clipped their trimmed limbs
to the limestone. He remembers the rough bark
of those old varieties, pears mostly, and how
he hit the supporting nails into the mortar.

This is the first time he has grown a peach tree.
It is the third year of the small tree's bearing,
and already his black dog has cleared the lowest
bough of its green fruit, nibbled the flesh,
left a scatter of kernels about the grass. No matter,
there's plenty. He has posted a stout cross
beneath the branches, else a heavy harvest of peaches
pulls the whole bush down. Watching the early blossom
has been his pleasure, the frail brevity of blossom
blown in cold weather, then the incipient fruit.

He does not walk in the garden until evening,
the days too hot for his uncovered head. When shadows
spread from under the trees, he stands there,
near a dusty lilac, surprised by hot gusts

out of the desert. His roses are abundant now.
He has let them grow and mingle, throwing their trails
over and through the massed green of other shrubs.
Alba and gallica roses, damask roses, centifolia roses,
an old moss rose, a bed of hardy rugosa. Refreshed
by roses, he cherishes the garden air, his head filled

with generations of perfume. Far in his life,
he nods to the spent iris, remembering how in water
his yellow flags stood high, how as a child he took
in his father's garden bright vegetables from the soil,
and how in the autumn hedge blackberries glowed.
It is his way of life to desert his gardens.
The neighbour's evening lamps light up the peaches.
Fruit is ripening, orchards everywhere ripen.
He throws a fallen peach to his black dog.
The animals were not expelled from Eden.

Christmas in Utah

Leslie Norris

Every year Leslie Norris writes poems for Christmas, often as gifts for close friends. While living in another professor's house over the holidays, Norris spotted the Stellar's jay outside his window and thought it looked like a Christmas ornament. As the poem developed, Norris transferred Christmas images "to a Utah setting." The result demonstrates how things we normally may consider mundane can still hold significant meaning in our writing. This poem is reprinted from Collected Works.

In barns turned from the wind
the quarter-horses
twitch their laundered blankets.
Three Steller's Jays,
crests sharp as ice,
bejewel the pine tree.
Rough cold out of Idaho
bundles irrational tumbleweed
the length of Main Street.

Higher than snowpeaks,
shriller than the frost,
a brazen angel blows his silent trumpet.

Bridal Veil Falls, Early Winter

Leslie Norris

Norris describes this as a "philosophical poem," one in which he sought to "deliberately portray the position of the observer and commentator." Note how the commentator is standing at the side of the action rather than being a part of it, and then how he moves out of the action toward the end. Norris explains his intent was to explore "what happens to life after the summit." "Bridal Veil Falls, Early Winter" was originally published in Collected Works.

The season's freeze has locked the waterfall,
its wavering fluid, into a cold permanence.
The last arcs of free spray, crystalised
in mid-air, are scattered among the stones.
Here is a preserved droplet, a Victorian stopper,
which will not melt for months. Water is held,
as these lines hold under the bite of words.
The wind is the one sound, hissing
into the crevice over the quiet ice.

For seventy hardening seasons I've watched
the stopping of waterfalls. Some of the time
I knew and perhaps understood how water
changed in winter, what happened to molecules,
how the structures of elements could petrify
in a night from bounding liquid to
an obdurate smoothness. Not any longer.
All that's confusing now. I am content
to watch the world turn cold with its old grace.

Soon younger men will come, active, dressed
against ice, with crampons and pitons, coils
of nylon rope, looking up quite differently
from the river bed. They'll wear their red

windproofs on the pallor of the ice,
search for fingerhold and toehold, secure
their spiked boots, begin to climb.
It's grim work. At first one sees them progress
with a quick elegance, straight up, few overhangs.

But soon they must steady, take the ice axe
from its holster, with brisk hacks
of the blade cut steps out of the sliding
fall, blocks of cold spoil dropping
to the valley floor, skittering down.
They'll pull themselves up to the line
of sky above them, the canyon's edge.
What then? No axe will chop footholds
in that thin air. They won't fly, I can tell them.

LESLIE NORRIS *came to BYU a few years ago as a visiting professor of creative writing. To BYU's good fortune, he decided to stay. He is humanities professor of creative writing and earned a DipEd and MPhil at Southampton University, England. Originally from Wales, Norris is an internationally recognized poet with multiple publications. His* Collected Stories *and* Collected Poems *were published recently and he is currently working on a long autobiographical poem which will include his piece, "Peaches."*

Questions

1. In Norris's poetry, places are very important and they are filled with description. How does he use these descriptions to create narratives?
2. What allusions are made in "Peaches"?
3. What does Norris allude to in the last line of "Peaches"? How does it change the meaning of the poem?
4. In "Bridal Veil Falls, Early Winter," what kind of comparison is made between age and youth? What do the last two lines mean?

Listening to Others

In the academic community, listening to others often means reading their texts. And just as you can hear without really listening, you can read without really understanding. Close readings of texts can open up our understanding and our thinking in ways that a quick read never can. A large part of what we do at the university is analyzing texts. These texts are more than written documents. They include a variety of ways that people express themselves—art, film, articles, and oral accounts. Each genre has a different story to tell. The authors analyzing these texts attempt to explain both how and why the story is told.

In this section, we sample analyses of several types of texts. Some analyses come from fine arts like films and painting, such as Elouise Bell's "Reel Goddesses" and Jon Green's "Picasso's Visual Metaphors." Some look at various oral accounts. For example, Alan Wilkins and Michael P. Thompson analyze the meaning of rumors in a business while Jacqueline Thursby examines the place of "evil eye" stories in Basque narratives. Some are analyses of well-known texts like Steven Sondrup's look at the Psalm of Nephi or D. Kelly Ogden's study of biblical plants. Other analyses look at texts that we normally give little thought to, such as James Gordon's humorous look at legal writing or Danette Paul's study of scientific texts.

As you read these texts, you will want to evaluate how well the authors explain how the text they are examining tells its story. But more important, you will want to ask *why* the story is told. The answer to this question can only be found by listening carefully, reading closely.

An Open Letter to Students: On Having Faith and Thinking for Yourselves

C. TERRY WARNER

C. Terry Warner's "An Open Letter to Students: On Having Faith and Thinking for Yourselves" was published in The New Era *as an eye-opening insight into the apparent dichotomy between faith and reason in a time when many people believed that it was foolish for an intellectual to believe in God. Warner writes to his young LDS audience using persuasive examples from the scriptures and an overlying analogy comparing world view with a selective map which shows only certain features, but which is used as a guide nonetheless. He argues that those whose map includes only secular features cannot understand a faithful intellectual whose map is more complete.*

My dear friends,

Has it ever troubled you that many intelligent and highly educated people don't share your religious beliefs? Why do men who have spent their lives in learning often regard faith as a compromise of intellectual integrity because—or so they claim—it is not backed up by objective evidence? Why don't worldly knowledge and reason lead men to faith?

If you've discussed this problem with fellow believers, you may have received a frustrating response: "It gets you into trouble to think so much"; or, "What you need to do is exercise more faith."

Opposing pressures from these two kinds of people may have made it seem that only two choices were open to you: either become an "intellectual" and abandon religion or else turn off your brain. Faced with this dilemma, you may have become despondent and longed, perhaps even wept, for a solution. I'm writing this letter to suggest that there is another alternative besides unthinking belief and faithless reason and that it's a genuine and satisfying solution to the problem.

A Misconception of Knowledge

There only seems to be opposition between secular knowledge and faith when, as is usually the case, they are misunderstood. When the misunderstanding is cleared up—and I hope it will be in this letter—the appearance of antagonism between them vanishes.

According to the common misconception, human knowledge is a collection of facts that fit themselves together into the one true picture of reality. It is thought that this picture, though still incomplete in places, is generally accurate: additional facts, which it is the business of the natural and social sciences to discover, simply add more detail.

For most people, this erroneous view of knowledge goes hand in hand with an erroneous conception of faith. Because they think of science as objectively testing its theories against evidence and because they suppose that knowledge and faith are somehow opposites, they regard faith as an attitude of clinging to theological beliefs *in spite of* any evidence which might be found: an attitude of closing one's eyes to and stubbornly refusing to be swayed by the facts. They believe scientific knowledge to be unbiased and proven because obtained in the cold light of inquiry, and faith to be subjective and wishful because acquired in a search not for evidence but for the warm security of believing in divine beings and eternal rewards.

The temptation to think of faith in this faulty way will disappear when the foregoing idea of knowledge is seen to be in error. I'll try to indicate how it is in error and to sketch conceptions of knowledge and faith that are both tenable and compatible with each other. (Keep in mind that it is a *misconception* of science and knowledge that I am challenging, not science and knowledge themselves. Indeed, as you will see at the end of this letter, I believe our faculties for thinking about our world are God-given, and, when properly used, productive of much knowledge and much good.)

Maps

Up-to-date developments in the philosophy of science and the theory of knowledge are overwhelming against the foregoing erroneous conception of human knowledge. In order to express the general trend of these developments, which are highly technical, I shall use an analogy.

A person's knowledge is not like a *picture* of reality; instead, it is like a *map*. Think about maps for a moment. Maps of many different kind can accurately represent any given area. There are maps that show elevation; others, highways; still others, geological formation. Plant growth, population distribution, and political boundaries can be represented on maps. No map can show everything about the area it represents. Indeed, in order to be intelligible, a map must drastically simplify things; it must leave out all but what it means to represent. Maps are selective, then. Any one map represents or symbolizes only a fraction of the sector of reality to which it applies.

When cartographers make a map, how do they know what to represent on the map and what to ignore? The answer is found in the fact that they want to accomplish a certain purpose with their map: they include in it everything that will promote their purpose and excludes everything that's irrelevant. For example, they may want to make a map that enables motorists to travel most efficiently across the freeways and toll roads and elevations, hence they make no indication of fishing holes or lilac trees or shops that sell imported cheese. What they select for inclusion on a particular map depends on what they desire to accomplish with that map. Similar statements can be made about any person's system of knowledge or network of ideas. It is like a map in that it is selective; that is, only certain things are represented on it while others are left out. And it is like a map in that it represents those things that are most conducive to the person's desires and goals.

Some of the goals that shape people's individual "maps" or outlooks are those typical of their family and society; as they grows up under the influence of parents, teachers, and peers, learning their language and customs, they tend to adopt the prevailing ways of seeing the world as their own. But in addition to this social factor, their individual desires and goals also play an important part in the development of their "map" of reality. So powerful is this individual factor that two people having different desires and attitudes can grow up in the same environment and yet have strikingly different "maps," and therefore a person whose desires are different from those of his countrymen can end up (as did Abraham, Moses, and Joseph Smith) repudiating much of their way of seeing the world and can be thought by them to have peculiar ideas indeed.

"Maps" Influence the Way We See the World

Eskimos (an Eskimo told me) are able to discriminate nine kinds of snow. Koreans make sense of spoken sounds that are meaningless to me. Meteorologists can see a storm coming when certain kinds of clouds are on the horizon, but most people can see only the clouds. What Eskimos, Koreans, and meteorologists thus clearly perceive is in an important sense invisible to others. The trouble with the others is that, though they have perfectly good eyesight and hearing, their "maps" of reality—their networks of ideas—are deficient.

Think about hiking in the mountains with a map indicating that a certain creek, a clump of leafless trees, and a triangular lake are crucial spots along your homeward route. The map enables you to see the creek, the trees, and the lake as landmarks. Without it, they would have no more significance for your journey home than any other parts of the landscape; they would be visible as a creek, a tree, and a lake, but they would be invisible as landmarks. People see things only in the way that their "map," or network of ideas, represents them.

This is as true in matters of faith as anywhere else. Much that is invisible to those lacking the gospel "map" of reality is clearly perceived by men of faith. An associate of mine recently wrote:

> In the 89th Section of the Doctrine and Covenants . . . the Lord speaks of . . . "great treasures of knowledge, even hidden treasures". . . . As I pondered the meanings . . . of the phrase "even hidden treasures" it suddenly became apparent to me that I had received many treasures of knowledge that had been completely hidden from me during the time when my lifestyle kept me away from the Church. . . . [L]ike any seeker after hidden treasure one [desiring these spiritual treasures] must follow correctly the maps which point out the way. Faith that the maps are correct can only be established by the verification of the landmarks described on the maps. Those who do not possess the maps will certainly find no significance in the landmarks as they encounter them; but to those who have the gospel map, the landmarks are the fulfillment of the promise [of treasures of knowledge].

Without the gospel "map" we can encounter things of great spiritual significance without being able to recognize them as such. In one sense we will see them, but insofar as they are spiritual, they are invisible to us.

Alma and Korihor

Consider, as cases in point, Alma and the anti-Christ Korihor.

Korihor labored under the misconception that without divine help man can acquire full and "objective" knowledge of things; and, indeed, he professed to have such knowledge. Since he believed, he said, only in what he could perceive with his senses, he thought faith a figment of human fancy and denounced talk of prophecy and sin and Christ as either lunacy or lie. There is no evidence, he insisted, of God's existence.

In Korihor's eyes, everything in the world had a merely temporal significance, and it is precisely for this reason that he could recognize no landmarks or evidences of spiritual things. Whereas Alma, with his very different sort of "map," could discern sin and righteousness in men's acts, Korihor said he saw evidence of neither. For Alma a certain burning in one's bosom was an experience of the Lord's Spirit; Korihor, had he felt it, might have thought it some inexplicable surge of happiness or perhaps a sudden case of heartburn. Anything spiritual would inevitably be interpreted as merely temporal by Korihor, who therefore said he never saw evidence of God's existence. Alma, by contrast, saw such evidence on every hand, testifying, "all things denote there is a God; yea, even the earth, and all things that are upon the face of it . . . do witness that there is a Supreme Creator" (Alma 30:44).

Actually, my portrait of Korihor is simplistic. Because he had known something of the gospel and rejected it, spiritual evidence was not wholly inaccessible to him; the fact is not that he never noticed it, but that he always rationalized it away. (Someone wholly unacquainted with the gospel would have no occasion to rationalize such evidence away because he could not have taken notice of it in the first place.) This Korihor admitted during a moment of personal crisis. He had explained away all evidence that might discredit his atheistic "map" because he loved selfish and carnal gratification, which his "map" allowed him to justify, more than he loved the truth. In other words, he held onto his "map" because it helped him accomplish his purposes. He confessed: "And I have taught [these things] because they were pleasing unto the carnal mind; and I have taught them . . . insomuch that I verily believed that they were true" (Alma 30:53). Korihor could never have tried to justify his immoral conduct towards people, had he admitted their divine parentage.

Alma gloried in evidence that Korihor rationalized away. Because his heart was pure, he was receptive to the Lord's efforts to shape his outlook on the world. He had no need, as Korihor did, to rationalize away experiences that could provide evidence for his faith. The difference between Alma and Korihor was not a matter of objectivity and evidence, but of character.

Faith and Evidence

Now Alma, in bearing his witness, was not making the mistake of claiming that the existence of God can be proven. In the sense of the word *proof* that prevails in the scholarly world and that I am using in this letter, it can't be proven. Proof in this sense must be indisputable, so that every rational man (no matter what his "map") would be compelled to agree. Proof in religious matters, were it possible, would therefore have to be based *solely* on merely temporal evidence. Those limiting themselves to such evidence—individuals with an atheistic or agnostic "map"—would be powerless to discriminate facts that have a bearing on the question of God's existence from those that don't. They would be like people who, without a proper map, lose their way in the presence of many landmarks simply because they cannot recognize them as landmarks.

That principles of faith can't be proven does not mean that they can't be solidly based on evidence. In science, too, proof is impossible, and for reasons similar to those that make it impossible in religion; but scientific theories can be well confirmed by evidence. Such theories and "maps" of faith lead one to expect certain things to happen, and the more they do happen, the more one can justifiably put confidence in those theories and "maps." This is an exciting subject, raising important questions concerning bias and falsifiability in theory confirmation; but it's too complicated a subject to explore here. The main point is simply that just because the nonbeliever can't find evidence for God's existence, it does not follow that others, with more suitable "maps," can't find it either. Joseph Smith once revised Psalms 14:1 to read: "The fool hath said in his heart, there is no man that hath seen God. Because he showeth himself not unto us, therefore there is no God."

Faith, like science, is based on evidence. It is no more subjective and ignorant of evidence than secular knowledge is objective and unbiased about evidence. Having abandoned the idea that knowledge is like an objective picture, that it is in all respects to be contrasted with faith, we can see that faith and knowledge are similar in important ways. Instead of looking away from the facts of the real world, faith is one way, among many others, of looking at the world.

Thus our faith need be no less intellectual and well-founded than a scientist's belief about the temporal world, provided we are pure in heart, are honest and unrationalizing about the evidence we receive, and throw our energies into blessing others' lives. When we do this, we constantly encounter *and* recognize spiritual landmarks—"hidden treasures of knowledge"—that allow us with complete intellectual integrity to bear witness of the accuracy of the gospel "map" that we have personally verified. As the scripture says, "faith cometh not by signs"—again, you can't build faith on merely temporal evidence—"but signs follow those that believe" (D&C 63:9). (Indeed, as I understand it, faithfulness in heeding spiritual landmarks can ultimately lead us to a spiritual destination in which we may be privileged to behold spiritual things directly.)

Faith Can't Be Disproven by Nonbelievers

Each of us tends to find in our experience evidence for what we have always believed. We saw why this is so in discussing the way "maps" influence the way we see the world. Because they do, we tend to see just the kinds of things we already represent on our "map"—the kinds of things we have seen before. We thereby becomes more and more convinced that our "map" is a good one; for, relying on it as we must, we interpret the world on its terms and in so doing, systematically filter out evidence for opposing points of view.

It is for this reason that what you believe theologically can never be disproven by nonbelievers. To gather the facts that they would use against you, they must examine reality in terms of their own "map"; they have no choice. But in doing this, they filter out *in advance* any evidence that might support you and discredit them. The spiritual significance of temporal things escapes them. Therefore, their gathering of evidence is hopelessly prejudiced where spiritual things are concerned. In slightly technical language, we would say that in order to gather the evidence, they must assume as true the very "map" they want to prove true and thereby assume as false the "map" they want to prove false; this means that their argument is circular, that it "begs the question," that, in short, it is logically worthless. Nonbelievers cannot put faith to the test and therefore cannot discredit it. For the very same reason that merely temporal evidence can't serve to prove the existence of spiritual things, it can't be used to disprove it either.

Someone may object: "The defense you are giving of religious belief is going to backfire. According to you, the believer Alma says the atheist Korihor is wrong, and Korihor says Alma is wrong. There is no way to decide who is right. Each one simply believes what he wants."

When you see how this objection is based on a misunderstanding, you will have the knowledge versus faith problem solved. The objector would be right if Alma and Korihor were in fact accusing each other of being wrong. But it is not that simple. Korihor says that there *is* a temporal reality but that there is *no* spiritual reality. Alma says that there are both temporal *and* spiritual realities. So Korihor is denying the existence of something Alma believes in, but Alma isn't denying the existence of anything Korihor believes in. Whereas Korihor's position can be disproven by any spiritual experiences that Alma has, Alma's position can't be shown wrong by any temporal experiences that Korihor has. It follows that there is no way for Korihor to back up his claim that Alma is mistaken; but Alma can back up his claim that Korihor is mistaken simply by confirming the accuracy of his own "map"!

Alma's "map" *includes more* than Korihor's. This means that *just because Korihor's "map" of the temporal world helps him accomplish his purposes of deceiving others and aggrandizing himself, it does not follow that everything in the universe is represented on that map.* Just because a map indicating highway routes, gas stations, restaurants, and motels guides one successfully across the country, it does not follow that there are no fishing holes, imported cheese stores, or lilac trees. And just because scientists can use their "maps" or theories to build bridges, land on the moon, transplant hearts, and predict economic growth, it does not follow that nothing exists besides what is mentioned in those theories. This point should be written in ten-foot red letters. For all too often it is fallaciously supposed that just because a map seems to be accurate for a particular purpose, it is therefore a complete picture. Nothing, in my judgment, could be more philosophically naive. (If you've ever thought that Mormons have a narrower outlook on life than most people, you have reason to believe otherwise now.)

Some Conclusions Pertaining to your Life

1. If "intellectuals"—experts on certain secular subjects—reject your religious position, they have no good reasons for doing so. Hence, the fact that they are often nonbelievers should not cause you to doubt. For their purposes, their "maps" seem to have worked tolerably well. But, as we've seen, those "maps" are not pictures; there are "more things in heaven and earth . . . than are dreamt of in [the] philosophy" of nonbelievers, including things that only the faithful can discern.

2. It is good to learn all you can from academically trained nonbelievers in their respective professional areas, *where your purposes and theirs coincide*. But where your desires and purposes differ from theirs—where, for example, you are seeking eternal life and they are not—their "maps" will not help you. It would be unintelligent in the extreme to use an academician's "map" of society or of nature in your quest for eternal life just because it served him well in some secular project.

3. You can integrate a secular "map" into a gospel one, but not the other way around. This is because the latter represents more than the former. Many university students abandon faith because they think they've discovered intellectual problems in the gospel when, in fact, they have uncritically supposed that the viewpoints of their professors are "maps" of *all* of reality. What they in fact show by their discovery of such problems is the inadequacy of worldly "maps."

Indeed, I would go so far as to say that accepting the world's way of looking at reality is the problem of all so-called intellectuals who profess to find serious intellectual difficulties with the gospel. The power of the secular "maps" of reality is so insidious that the Lord, referring to them as the creeds and precepts and traditions of men, calls them "the very chains and shackles and fetters of hell" (D&C 123: 7-8). Those who accept them and see life in terms of it cannot perceive spiritual things:

> [A] light shall break forth among them that sit in darkness, and it shall be the fulness of my gospel;
>
> But they receive it not; for they perceive not the light, and they turn their hearts from me because of the *precepts of men*. (D&C 45: 28-29, italics added)

4. Intellectually speaking, you are in a powerful position. Yet strangely enough, you can't convince nonbelievers of this by reasoning with them. For they will interpret whatever you say in terms of their present "map" so that what they hear will be different from what you mean.

How, then, can you make an impact on others with your faith? Recall that people's "maps" are shaped (1) by social factors—their training and education in which the values and goals of their family and society are passed on to them—and (2) by individual factors—their own desires and goals. Many of the people on your campus have, in growing up, acquired a "map" of reality that is not well suited to their own goals in life. For example, some individuals may have learned that human beings are essentially animals, made up of physical bodies and nothing more, so that they act for selfish purposes; yet these same people may long for a society in which men and women treat one another selflessly. Their "map" of reality will not help them bring about their dreams. They will feel a vague dissatisfaction about life, as if something important were missing.

In my opinion, you can reach such people by capitalizing on the discrepancy between their desires and their inherited "map." For although they may think your religious ideas are peculiar in our supposedly enlightened age (remember, they have inherited a "map" in terms of which such things as revelation and ordinances appear foolish), *they cannot help but see, if they are honest, that you have achieved what they want in life*. You and your Latter-day Saint friends are, as a result of your purity, filled with love for each other and for nonmembers; to those standing on the outside, your group is a kind of inviting Camelot that exhibits what they long to enjoy. You with your gospel "map," your faith, are achieving their goals; while they, with their supposedly sophisticated view of life, is not. If they really wants what your life embodies, they will be persuaded to learn about your faith, try the gospel "map" on for size, and abandon their worldly way of looking at things. Reasoning won't budge them, but what you are, *if you are what you ought to be*, will call into question all they have been taught to believe about religion.

5. Finally, although the knowledge versus faith problem has dissolved, a new problem has arisen in its place. We have seen that if others want to acquire the gospel "map" of reality they must (1) undergo appropriate training and (2) purify the desires that have led them in the past to

overlook the gospel. (See Alma 12:11-12.) Only by these means can they gradually come to see reality more and more in the way the Lord sees it. Thus, the new problem is that of *changing and developing ourselves so that we can comprehend the things of God.* (Strangely, the solution to so-called intellectual difficulties with the gospel is not intellectual at all, but spiritual. Indeed, I would say that there are no intractable intellectual problems with the gospel; there are only "intellectuals" with problems with the gospel.)

I commend to you, as a solution to the new problem, two courses of action: (1) an earnest striving for a "mighty change of heart" according to the instructions to be found in the scriptures and the words of modern prophets; and (2) intense study of these inspired texts. Why these writings rather than others? Because they contain the core of the Lord's "map" of reality insofar as it can be adapted to our understanding. You should read, make notes on, and reread the scriptures and the conference reports, pleading with the Lord that your heart will be softened and that these writings will, line upon line, grow comprehensible to you.

If you do this, you will find that instead of running into dead ends of irreconcilability between knowledge and faith, your thinking will uncover more and more rich and thrilling connections between gospel truths and knowledge about our temporal world. Because your heart has become purified, you'll be able to use your mind to your heart's content. You'll realize, in short, that there is nothing to fear from the use of one's mind, but only from the use of a mind that is subservient to impure desires. For it is like any other faculty you have—benighted and even destructive unless sanctified by the power of God; but if so sanctified, glorious.

With a prayer that you may find excitement and peace in your studies.

—C. Terry Warner

C. TERRY WARNER *is a professor of philosophy and has served as Dean of the College of General Studies and as chair of the Department of Philosophy at Brigham Young University. He received his BA in history from BYU and then went to Yale University to earn an MA and a PhD in philosophy, which he studied because he has "always been concerned with the deepest questions." His work focuses on human behavior and alternatives to standard psychological theories.*

Questions

1. Answer for yourself Warner's initial question: Why don't worldly knowledge and reason lead to faith?
2. How is knowledge a "map"? How does the gospel provide a "map"?

3. How can maps help us understand our experience? How can they help to read and to write more effectively?
4. What happens when we substitute maps for the reality they represent? How do we resolve conflicts among our own maps of the world and between our maps and others'?

Growing Up: From Peter Rabbit to Rabbi Goldman

DENNIS JAY PACKARD

Dennis Packard was first attracted to philosophy "because of all the beauty of careful reasoning and logic." He says that philosophy is "a matter of poking your nose into other people's business." While serving as branch president in the MTC, Packard grew worried that young missionaries don't know how to read scripture very well. This concern led to the writing of "Growing Up: From Peter Rabbit to Rabbi Goldman" (first published in BYU Today*). He feels that scripture study is key to education at BYU because "if students can learn to read scriptures, they can read Plato." His article shows one person's route to becoming literate with the scriptures by going back to Jewish sources. Packard feels, as Nephi did, that "unless we understand the ways of the Jews, we can't understand the scriptures." His article shows how we can learn to do both.*

Most people learn how to study the scriptures from somebody else. A friend of mine, James Faulconer, an assistant professor of philosophy, learned from a rabbi. We met one day to talk about it.

I found his office on the fifth floor of the library, just behind the children's section. He hadn't arrived yet, and so I sat down at a study desk to wait. There was a stack of Peter Rabbit stories on the desk, about nine or ten of them. Someone must have read them all and, having finished with them, not bothered to check them out. I walked around, looked down the aisle for Jim, looked at the books in the stacks across from his office. They were oversized books, some about film, several about Dante. I was opening an old picture volume of *The Divine Comedy* when Jim walked up.

"I'm sorry I'm late," he whispered. He was dressed in a short-sleeved checked shirt, Levis rolled up two inches at the cuff, brown jogging shoes. In his shirt pocket were two pens and a credit card or a library card; once in his office, he took them out and set them on the desk—preliminaries, what he did before he started to work.

The office was a cubicle barely big enough for two desks and a small book shelf. There wasn't much to look at. Nothing on the walls but a bright blue magnetic coat hanger by the door, and two fluorescent light panels in the ceiling.

"How do you like your office?" I asked him.

"It's nice, quiet, no phones." He was still whispering. At his regular office he was interrupted all the time; here he could get work done. On Jim's desk was a box of Kleenex: the room was a little cold; I could hear the central air-conditioner going loudly. On one of the shelves were several books: *Being and Time*, *On Being a Christian*, *Plato's Dialogues*, *On the Bible*. The other shelves were empty.

Jim was working on a book about the individual and the community. This was his vacation, and he was trying to get as much writing done as possible. One of his first chapters was on Adam and Eve: "They finally see themselves as individuals," he said. "They see the difference between themselves and God. When they're cast out they see that they're supposed to be in community with each other and with God, but, at least in the beginning, they don't know really what that means."

Jim was talking with the help of his hands. He held them up, open in front of him. His short fingers extended out and then pulled in, as if he were coaxing thoughts out of the air. He continued, "All they know is, 'Well, now we see what it is to be individuals.' Separated from God, they see this difference. But that makes them more like God as well. Now that they're separated, now that they have a knowledge of good and evil and so on, they've got what it takes to be in community."

I asked about the rabbi who had started him studying Genesis. Jim sat back in his chair, his arms up with his hands folded behind his head, his feet dangling, not reaching the floor. He talked about the rabbi and told me, first of all, that they'd only made it through Chapter Three of Genesis.

The rabbi was Rabbi Goldman, Professor Goldman at Pennsylvania State University, where Jim had gone to school. Jim thought there was something in Genesis that would help him with his dissertation about community: "It seemed to me clear that a good deal of the Old Testament and especially of Genesis is this explanation of what it is to be Israel. And to be Israel is to be a community, to be the real community. To be the chosen people, I think, is to say, 'You are an example of what a community ought to be when you are what you are supposed to be.' "

He went to Rabbi Goldman and said, "Look, will you study the Old Testament with me next quarter?"

"Yes, sure. How much do you want to do?"

"Well, I was thinking we could do Genesis."

The Rabbi said, "Well, why don't we do Chapter One?"

"Oh, come on!" Jim said.

"No, I'm serious. Let's take the quarter and do Genesis Chapter One."

"I'll tell you what," said Jim. "Why don't we do as much as we can of Genesis?"

The rabbi said, "Well, okay," thinking, as Jim put it, that that would probably be Genesis Chapter One, maybe a little more.

The rabbi taught philosophy of science. He was a tall, thin fellow, who had a beard, always dressed nicely, and drove a sports car. The beard had seemed merely stylish: "I had no idea (that he was a rabbi) for a long time," Jim said. "I had this image in my mind of a rabbi—an old man, probably dressed in sort of seedy clothes—and this guy dressed in the latest styles and he drove a sports car. But he was the rabbi in the little town outside of State College. And an orthodox rabbi. You didn't call him on Friday afternoon, or bother him on the Sabbath. On the Sabbath he didn't use electric lights or answer the phone."

"Why?" I asked.

"It makes people work. So they just cut the power off to the house on Friday evening and restored it on Saturday afternoon. He had four children and the children from the very beginning were expected to live the Sabbath. It's a day of study. That is the way you observe the Sabbath. You go to the meetings with the congregation and then you study. There was nothing else to do."

Jim met with the rabbi twice a week at his office for lunch. "At the first meeting I was immediately embarrassed that he offered a blessing on his food when I was going to skip it and just eat. He put on his yarmelke, said his little prayer, and ate his lunch. The prayer was formal. It was in Hebrew, so I don't know what he said."

Was it aloud?

"Oh, yes. No qualms. He said his ritual blessing over the food, out loud, and then we ate."

And they talked: the rabbi said, "Did you bring your questions?" Jim had 10 or so questions on Genesis One.

"I had really worked hard to get those 10 questions. I was really proud of myself. You know, how many verses are there in that first chapter? There are 31 verses and I had 10 questions. I mean, I was impressed."

Jim handed the rabbi the questions and the rabbi looked them over. "*He* obviously wasn't very impressed. He said, 'Oh, well, okay.' Some of them were like 'What is this word in Hebrew?' and that sort of thing."

The rabbi took about 15 minutes and answered the 10 questions, and said, "Now, do you have any more?"

Jim said, "No," and thought, "Well, see, I was right—we really ought to go on to Chapter Two now."

But the rabbi said, "Well, I have some questions." And he started with verse one and he said, "What does this mean, 'in the beginning'?"

Jim said, "Well, you know, In the beginning—at the very start."

"Well, sure, but why is it important that we begin at the beginning? Why not later?"

For the rest of the hour they talked about that first verse: *In the beginning God created the heaven and the earth.* The Rabbi talked about why it was necessary to know that God created both the heaven and the earth; why we should know that it was the beginning, that there wasn't anything prior to him, that God was the most important, that we have a history that starts in the beginning so that nothing has been left out. "He really had this long discourse on that verse, on why we begin that way, and what it says, and what that means and why that's important. And he related that to Chapter Two: it begins, *Thus, the heavens and the earth were finished and all the host of them.* A lot of people want to take this first verse of Chapter Two and stick it in at the end of Chapter One. But Rabbi Goldman said, no!"

Jim was using his index finger for emphasis. He went on: "The people who divided these into chapters and verses weren't the original people, but they knew that was a natural division. Why? Because that's parallel to *In the beginning*. You get, *In the beginning was created*, and then the next chapter begins, *Thus, it was created*." Here Jim worked his hands like meat cleavers against the desk. "And there's another place, I don't remember where it is, that talks about 'in the beginning'. And so he'd show how this sets that off in certain ways. And I wish I had taken notes."

He put his hands down and continued, "The trouble was, I just hadn't gone there thinking that this was a real study." He hadn't taken the scriptures as seriously as the rabbi had. He had gone just like he would to a Sunday School class. No notes, just some scriptures. "You know, we'll talk about the scriptures for a while and we'll feel real good." Jim laughed a little.

The rabbi could talk about the scriptures like that for hours, and he did it from memory. "It took probably years of study to be able to do it," Jim said, "but he studies every Sabbath, all day long, eight to ten hours. He has a whole library of commentaries on the scriptures in his house and that's where they go. He and his wife will go in there and sit down at their desks and study the scriptures all day—look, read, get down the commentaries."

And his children?

"His children, as they get old enough to, do it. That's what they're expected to do. And if they're not old enough yet, they're expected to be quiet and leave everyone alone. They don't go out and play, though. Since the electricity is off they don't watch TV. They can do what they like, as long as they don't bother anybody and they're quiet. They can play in the house. He lets them play little traditional games and things, but nothing that we would consider inappropriate.

"I let my kids play basketball a little on the Sabbath," said Jim, "because I always think, Well, I make them study the scriptures for one hour every Sunday, and I always think, I'm really a progressive father: my kids read scripture for an hour, and then we talk about it for about an hour. We talk about whatever they've read. And about that time, they're tired and I'm tired and we quit.

"But this man was really diligent. He knew the stuff. He was talking to me, I got the feeling, as if I were one of his children: 'This is the obvious stuff. I'll just tell you this.' When my children ask me questions there are some answers that I can give right off the top of my head; it's not a problem and I don't even have to think about it. And it was obvious when I was talking to him that that was the kind of response I was getting: 'Well, Jim, let's see. I could tell you this and this and this. Everybody knows the following things . . .' But most of it was news to me," he said, shaking his head.

"The other thing that really impressed me," continued Jim—"and I never knew quite how to say this to Rabbi Goldman; I tried once and he gave me a really quizzical look, and so I didn't go much further—was how much of what he was saying to me was clearly true: it fit right into the kinds of things that are LDS doctrines, sometimes in ways I don't think he knew.

"Of course, it's a Jewish doctrine that the world was created from nothing, and he can get that out of that first verse. But that wasn't very important to him. What was important to him was that God was in the beginning, and that there isn't anything that isn't dependent upon him. And he would talk about marriage and its necessity. And he would go on and on about that sort of thing, and I really feel like I learned more about the gospel from him than I had learned in years previous to that.

"Maybe not about—what shall I call it—the schematic of the doctrines, but about what the doctrines mean. Doctrinal principles, the various principles you might list out, principles in the sense of general laws: that he didn't know much of. But then he didn't seem to care much about that. If someone had said to him, Well, what's the Jewish doctrine of this and that, he just didn't even care. He could say it, but he'd usually have to stop and think and say, 'Well, some Jews believe this, and some Jews believe that, and I believe such and such.'

"But it was obviously not very important to him. What was important was reading the scriptures and deciding what they mean, and that was central to everything that he wanted to talk about. I asked him about the tradition that there would be a savior from Joseph and a savior from Judah. I asked him, 'What about the savior from Joseph?' He said, 'Yes, let's talk about that.' And then he got out the scriptures. And I said, 'Yes, but other than the scriptures, what do people have to say?' And he said, 'Other than the scriptures what should people have to say? What do you mean, other than the scriptures?' He was loathe to talk about anything else."

Jim fell silent for a few seconds, and I thought about the rabbi and about his tradition of not talking about anything else. (In contrast, it seems we study scripture to be ready to receive more.) That was the problem with the Jews—they were willing to go with the old scriptures, the dead prophets, but never the new ones.

Then Jim said, "And I think that's one thing he was able to show me. There's plenty to talk about right there; you don't have to go anywhere else. You can just talk about the scriptures, and look at this passage, and look at that passage, and compare these and talk about what they mean. And in the end, frankly, it's just a lot more fruitful than the discussions we often get into.

"When you make the scriptures the focus, a couple of things happen. And one of them is that you really discover just how meaningful they are—something I didn't have any idea of when I was on my mission. If you think about the prophets in the Book of Mormon, Alma, for example—Alma, Ammon, all of them—what they do is expound the scriptures. Every single time."

Jim opened his Book of Mormon. "The way Ammon converts King Lamoni, for example, is to say, 'Well here, let me read you the scriptures.' And then he lays the scriptures out for him." Jim was bent over a verse in Alma. "It's significant that he does two things: he rehearses them, he repeats them to him; and he lays them out before him, he shows them to him, and I think that means more than just 'look at these.' It's like the rabbi did with me. He said, 'Okay, *In the beginning God created the heaven and the earth*, and that means that God is the founder . . .' and so on. Ammon explains it to Lamoni, and even though Lamoni is not the nicest guy in the world, he's converted like that, through reading the scriptures. And all of the other prophets in the Book of Mormon do the same thing: they convert people through reading and expounding scripture.

"The scriptures provide a check point," continued Jim. "If the scriptures are always at the center, you can go in all sorts of directions and always have something solid to come back to. If you go your own way with nothing to tether or anchor your ideas, you have no way to avoid apostasy."

We again talked about the first three chapters of Genesis. Jim pushed his glasses back up on the bridge of his nose—they kept slipping from where he liked them—and went on. "Rabbi Goldman called those chapters a childhood: it's something we can go through to gain a knowledge of good and evil; it's an experience that reflects our own childhood; it's something our own lives come to reflect as we study it and understand it. The need to be separated from parents, the need to work, the sorrow involved, all are part of the transition from childhood, a necessary thing, becoming like God.

"'If you weren't so literal about becoming like God,' the rabbi once said, 'I'd love it. You take it to a blasphemous point. But obviously, the point of these first chapters of Genesis is that Adam and Eve have to become like God. And that was the way they had to do it. Most Christian interpretations are offensive: that somehow God didn't know what was going on or was a trickster and got those people to do things which were terrible; that Adam and Eve ruined everything: life would be so much better if we just didn't have to have the world the way they made it. That's just stupid. Anybody who believes that hasn't read the book.

'It's a wonderful thing that that happened. Sure, God says the ground will be cursed and you'll have sorrow. But, yes, that's what it is to be human. You can't have a knowledge of good and evil and not have sorrow. You'd have to be an idiot to see evil and not feel sorrow. That's what it is to be a human being, that's what it is to grow up. And Adam and Eve here are growing up and becoming like God. Christians simply deny that they are made in the image of God when they talk about the fall and how terrible it was, because it made us like God.

'We Jews are caught up in this business about sorrow. World War II brought it home, though World War II was hardly the first instance. It's evidence that the Jews are the chosen people. We are like God. We will sorrow. We will sorrow for the whole world's sake. We are the people who will be punished for the entire world. God suffers for everyone. So will we. He doesn't have to suffer, only because we sin. Well, that's what happened in World War II: we didn't have to suffer, but because you sin, we suffer. If someone says to me, Well, why did God let it happen? I say, because we're the chosen people. He wants us to be like him. That is a terrible thing, in some respects, being like God. But if you are, you are. If you want to have it always sweetness and light, then you don't understand these chapters at all. You don't understand what it is to be like God.

'In the Jewish tradition we have those like Abraham and others who argue with God. The idea is that since they are like him, they have the right to ask questions, demand justification, and so on. It's not belligerent. It's the attitude, I'm willing to suffer, but since we're like each other I deserve some explanation. The problem with World War II and the death camps was not that there was suffering, but that there was no explanation. There should have been a prophet who demanded an explanation.'"

Jim paused, sat back in his chair and thought of Enoch talking to the Lord, asking, Why do the heavens weep? and then after finding out why, he refused to be comforted. Or Job, who says, I stand before God with my integrity. He knows who I am. I don't have anything to be ashamed of.

Jim continued, "The rabbi would say on several occasions, 'Well, the Mormons are more like Jews than any of the Christians that I know.' He was intrigued that a lot of our ideas and our doctrines are very much like Jewish notions and very unlike the Christian notions—ideas about marriage, about the nature of humans."

"Had he met other Mormons?"

"Yes. He said, Most of you act like a bunch of Protestants."

"That's damning."

"He thought that Catholics were generally better than Protestants. At least they have some strong sense of the truth, that this is to be done, that there is a tradition. But Protestants—he didn't have much good to say about Protestants—they just want to have it whatever way they want it. He did like Mormon doctrine, and I think he liked Mormon people. He just felt that we don't understand. I guess he would say that's evidence that there is something wrong with the Church: that very few Mormons understand their own beliefs or think about them or read the scriptures."

"Well," I wanted to know, "what would you say to him? The Church has only been here for so many years."

"He would say, 'So? Does that mean that Abraham and Moses didn't think about these things? In the beginning didn't men think about being Jews and what that meant? You don't think Enoch thought about these things?'"

"But those were the prophets."

Jim agreed. "Sure, and certainly President Kimball thinks about those kinds of things."

"Right. But what about the average person? How long does it take for a tradition to take hold?"

Jim didn't know quite what to say. "It didn't take long at all for a bad tradition to come in. Look what we have with Cain and Abel. The very first thing after the creation, we have apostasy. As soon as he finishes telling us about the creation, he tells us about murder, and the fall of man. The *real* fall comes in Chapter Four, not Chapter Three, with the people who decide not to pay any attention and follow Satan and not God. I guess someone could say, well, that's what happened in Chapter Three, too, but in Chapter Four it happened very differently. It's a different kind of succumbing to the temptations of Satan, a giving over to it."

There was silence for a while, and I realized that I had been sitting with my legs folded in my chair. "Do you want to get something to eat?" I asked.

"Yes, let's go get some lunch."

We walked out past the oversized books, past the Peter Rabbit stories. Jim was whispering again. We were in the library. People would be studying.

DENNIS JAY PACKARD *holds an associate's degree in music and a BA and PhD in philosophy from Stanford University. He has taught philosophy at both Carnegie-Mellon and BYU, where he focuses on logic and contemporary philosophy. He is also currently working on the philosophy of film and plans to offer a course in it soon. His work is varied and widespread, including studies in the philosophy of economics and linguistics, and he has produced a number of films on campus, some of which have been broadcast on PBS.*

Questions

1. What is the significance of the Peter Rabbit stories in this narrative?
2. How does the Rabbi Goldman's approach to reading the scriptures differ from how most people read?
3. How could the Rabbi Goldman's approach be used for other texts? Would some kind of texts bear this close scrutiny better than others?

Jonah as Joke: A Glance at God's Sense of Humor

STEVEN WALKER

Steven Walker believes that analyzing the humor in the Bible is "a way to get at some profound insights" and he has an orange crate full of his notes on this topic. His look at the Book of Jonah *was inspired by students of his who, when they studied the reluctant prophet's story in a Bible as Literature course, were "cracking up over Jonah." His article, "Jonah as Joke," which was presented at the Western Conference on Christianity and Literature, explores the amusing episodes and subtle meanings in the Old Testament book, and sets out to explore some important ideas, including spiritual insights, that can be had through humor. Walker's entertaining article works to bring out a balance between fun and seriousness and shows, as Walker believes, that "humor matters to God."*

When it comes to biblical humor, we miss the point. In fact, we mostly miss the humor. The Bible is the last place most modern readers would find a laugh. But the main reason we fail to find it there is that the Bible is the last place we'd look. Given how persistently humor smiles and chuckles and sometimes laughs right out loud in virtually every book of the Bible, it's astonishing how consistently we manage to overlook it. It's also unfortunate. Humor informs biblical texts. To miss the humor of the Bible is to miss not only much of its fun, but much of its meaning.

We are so bent on revering this literary text instead of enjoying it that we may have developed a cultural blind spot toward biblical humor. The problem is one of perspective; we view the Bible through sanctimonious glasses. Consider what a difference it would make, for example, if in place of Gregory Peck in our Cecil B. DeMille version of *David and Bathsheba* we cast Jerry Lewis.

Yet the Jerry Lewis version may better illuminate the biblical context. When in 1 Samuel 16:7 God directs the disappointed prophet to "Look not on [David's] countenance . . . for man looketh on the outward appearance, but the Lord looketh on the heart," Lewis's buck teeth, crossed eyes, and dopey grin drive home the point better than Gregory Peck's perfect features. And certainly Lewis would be more appropriate as the teenage David trying on the armor of that mighty Saul who "from his shoulders and upward . . . was higher than any of the people" (1 Samuel 9:2)—the Jerry Lewis David is easier to imagine with that oversize mail dragging on the ground, helmet down over his eyes, overweight spear clutched desperately in both hands.

Anyone who has seen Richard Pryor in *Holy Moses* or heard Bill Cosby's rendition of Noah will recognize that there can be as much insight as laughter in humorous readings of the Bible. Biblical humor is as much concerned with informing us as delighting us. That capacity of humor to illuminate biblical meaning is easiest to see in the funniest biblical character—not David, nor Cosby's Noah nor Pryor's Moses, nor (to mention but a few of the prime nominees) Peter nor Eve nor Samson nor Balaam nor Sarah nor Herod nor even Gideon. The funniest biblical character is Jonah.

And the book of *Jonah* is the funniest book of the Bible. Its structure is deliberately comic. On Michael Tueth's list of the five key comic elements in scripture, *Jonah* scores high in every category. The book features "the downfall of the serious"—it's harder to get much more serious than Jonah, with his endless groanings of "it is better for me to die than to live" (4:3, 4:8, 4:9). *Jonah* features the comic "element of surprise" in the prophet's flight, in the storm, in the whale, in the Ninevite conversion, in the withering gourd. *Jonah* "emphasizes the value of innocence and childlikeness" in its concern for those morally untutored Ninevites who "cannot discern between their right hand and their left hand" (4:11). The story "reverses previously held assumptions and values"; the whole point of the book is that God's love extends beyond the limits Hebrew prophets had imagined until *Jonah*. And, to complete its perfect alignment with Tueth's catalogue of the comic, *Jonah* "thrives" on "physical danger": "Harold Lloyd hanging from the clock, Abbot and Costello meeting Frankenstein, or even the fat man slipping on the banana peel" (Tueth 2) have nothing on Jonah going overboard or disappearing into the whale's gullet or venturing singlehanded into mighty Nineveh.

But it isn't only that *Jonah* fits abstract literary categories of the comic; the book is genuinely funny in its own right. Every scene in this story invites a smile—the picture of the recalcitrant prophet, for example, fresh from the belly of the whale, reeking of whale vomit, trailing seaweed and barnacles and old fishheads, bleached of all his color by gastric juices, his robe shrunk up to his knees and elbows by that interior humidity, disheveled and disgruntled, trudging into Nineveh muttering his message of doom in a language the Ninevites can't even understand.

Scenes that laughable dominate the book. The first chapter alone proposes enough ridiculous situations for a Marx Brothers movie. God calls Jonah to the Ninevite Mission at a time when there were no foreign missions. God says to go east; Jonah goes due west, as far as he can. God pulls out all stops to threaten Jonah with a "mighty tempest in the sea, so that the ship was like to be broken" (1:4); Jonah remains "fast asleep" (1:5). The heathen shipmaster, of all people, urges God's prophet to "call upon thy God" (1:6). God demands that Jonah be thrown into a watery grave, then rescues him. For the means of that gracious rescue, God devises the decidedly ungracious "belly of the fish" (1:17).

From its initial parody of the prophetic call to its concluding picture of those "much cattle" (4:11) penitently attired in sackcloth and ashes, *Jonah* is a funny book. And the funniness matters. As its pervasiveness suggests, the humor in *Jonah* is not incidental, not superficial decoration. The humor is not only fun, but functional. There is a moral to the *Jonah* joke.

To a Hebrew of the fifth century BC, the very premise of the story is absurd. *Jonah* is a midrashic tale, in the usual form of "imagine if." But in *Jonah*'s case the "imagine if" is unimaginable. The story's narrative situation is impossible for *Jonah*'s Hebrew audience; the tale is for the Israelite of the time an invitation to think about the unthinkable. God in those days just did not go around inviting heathen nations to repent. Even if He had, the hopeless heathens never would have repented. As Allen suggests, "The audience is asked to ponder a theological riddle: what would have happened if no less a den of foreign devils than Nineveh had repented?" (82).

The opening scene of the book sets the tone of that playing with biblical convention. The first thing we see in *Jonah* is a parody of the prophetic call. Prophetic convention dictated a certain shy reluctance in responding to the Lord's call; hesitance hallmarks responses to the call by such model prophets as Isaiah (6:5) and Jeremiah (1:6) and even Moses, who says demurely to the burning bush: "I am not eloquent. . . . I am slow of speech, and of a slow tongue" (Exodus 4:10). But *Jonah* carries that traditional reluctance to extremes that suggest parody. When the Lord calls Jonah, he refuses to answer at all. "Jonah's silence has the parodic impact of silence after the question 'Do you take this woman to be your lawfully wedded wife?' " (Miles 172).

Another indication that the humor of the book of *Jonah* is deliberate is that it is climactic; it gets funnier as it goes along. The closing statement of *Jonah* is not so much a statement as a punchline, its whimsicality underlined by its form as a question. And that concluding question is quietly hilarious: "And should not I," God wonders out loud to Jonah in that closing verse, "spare Nineveh, that great city, wherein are more than sixscore thousand persons that cannot discern between their right hand and their left hand; and *also* much cattle?"

That great exit line seems to me funny in at least five ways. The quantification is an insult to Jonah's accountant mentality, an early Hebrew equivalent of, "You want justice, I'll give you justice times one hundred twenty thousand"—"the quality of mercy is not strained," let alone the quantity. The reference to Jonah's relative sophistication, the implication that the prophet of the Lord ought to know better than "persons that cannot discern between their right hand and their left hand," hints that morally speaking "Jonah may not know his gourd from a hole in the ground" (Whitney 1). The reversal of Jonah's earlier "I told you so"—his insistent "was not this my saying, when I was yet in my country" (4:2)—turns the tables on Jonah with a "he who laughs last laughs best" twist.

The most obvious source of humor in that closing line is the animal reference. That anticlimactic apparent afterthought, "and also much cattle," is wonderfully prepared for by earlier jokes hinging upon creatures ranging from great whales to tiny worms. God as Trickster is not missing a trick. God's compassionate awareness extends to all creatures—not so much as a sparrow shall "fall on the ground without your Father" (Matthew 10:29). That "also much cattle" jibe suggests something very close to: "Jonah, I'd save the city despite—or even to spite—your petulance for the sake of its camels or even its cats, let alone its people. Especially," the text smiles between its understated lines, "when those camels are so penitently dressed in sackcloth and ashes." McIlrath suspects that the humor of the bestial imagery runs still deeper, that "the worm referred to in 4:4 may be a simile for Jonah himself," that "Jonah is the worm that the Lord brought to Ninevah to perform the smiting" (1).

The funniest thing about that divine last word at the conclusion of *Jonah* is the direct moral that it gives to the story, like David Letterman heightening the intensity of a joke by patiently explaining the punchline to Paul Shafer. There is strong implication here of gentle divine ribbing: "The reason you have too little compassion, Jonah, is that you have no sense of humor." There is also strong implication that that is what God would have us have—both the sense of humor and the compassion to which this book so warmly relates it. That anticlimactic closure focuses us back upon the second verse of this final chapter, where Jonah in his condemnation of God ironically vivifies the moral of the story: "I knew that thou art a gracious God, and merciful, slow to anger, and of great kindness, and repentest thee of the evil" (4:2).

That is the greatest joke of all in *Jonah*. What for Jonah is condemnation is for us—and for God—commendation. Jonah reprimands God for His unreliability. The omniscient and omnipotent Ruler of the Universe responds to Jonah's impertinent attempt to put Him in His divine place by gently allowing Jonah to put himself in his very human place with a smiling question about being humane: "Doest thou well to be angry?" (4:4). Jonah tells God how to be God; God shows Jonah how to be human. God invites Jonah out of his narrow theological certainties into life, into that risky and uncertain human life where things get unpredictable and as a result potentially funny.

The message of the book of *Jonah* is delivered with a divine smile that directly contrasts with Jonah's sullen message of doom to the Ninevites. That message is: live. The God of *Jonah*, much to His prophet's chagrin, transcends expectations. He urges us to expect the unexpected. Jonah reads that moral as "damned if you don't and damned if you do"; we are likelier to read it as God does: "blessed if you do, and blessed if you don't." Life with the God of *Jonah* is not far from the proverbial view of heaven—"better than we could ever imagine, and full of wonderful surprises." Those surprises are chancy business, like casting lots on a deck pitching in a storm so wild the dice don't have to be thrown. That undependability is an understandable threat to Jonah. But to us it is also a promise, a promise of fuller life, of God "come that ye might have life, and that ye might have it more abundantly" (John 10:10).

The laughter of the book of *Jonah* urges us in the direction of that abundance, in the direction of those wonderful surprises. The laughter urges us to find a way to laugh at ourselves, to laugh off our restrictive expectations, to laugh away our confining certitudes about our just desserts. The humor informs us that things may not be as bound by our expectations as we'd expect, that the "first [could] be last; and the last be first" (Matthew 19:30). "Among David's ancestors there may be a Ruth the Moabite, among the righteous a Job the Edomite; among the penitents a city of Nineveh" (Lacocque 94). "History would be more intelligible if God's word were the last word, final and unambiguous like a dogma or an unconditional decree. Yet, beyond justice and anger lies the mystery of compassion" (Lacocque 98)—and that compassion reveals itself in laughter.

The God of *Jonah* may be closer to us than we thought, closer even than we wanted. The point of His intersection with us is marked by laughter. Being "vomited out" by a great fish (2:10) is for Jonah trauma tinged with insult—"here's another fine mess you've gotten me into." For God the vomiting out is, like all of His acts in the book, an act of compassion. For the whale it's a relief—Jonah may have been "the worst case of indigestion he ever had" (Miller 1). For us, standing precariously between divine love and human selfishness, that incongruous juxtaposition of sublime possibilities and ridiculous actualities lies very close to laughter.

Robert Alter thinks

> The monotheistic revolution of biblical Israel . . . left little margin for neat and confident views about God . . . it repeatedly had to make sense of the intersection of incompatibles—the relative and the absolute, human imperfection and divine perfection, the brawling chaos of historical experience and God's promise to fulfill a design in history. The biblical outlook is informed, I think, by a sense of stubborn contradiction, of a profound and ineradicable untidiness in the nature of things. (154)

Jonah is an invitation to that ineradicably untidy biblical outlook. Like every other book of the Bible—where we even more thoroughly manage to overlook the humor—*Jonah* is an invitation to life. I think that invitation depends upon laughter because life does, and because that God who invented life loves the laughter.

STEVE WALKER *received a BA from BYU in English literature before he went to Harvard University to earn an MA and a PhD in English. He has taught at both of his Alma Maters and continues at BYU in the English Department where he teaches classes in Victorian and modern literature as well as Bible as literature courses.*

Questions

1. Do you agree with Walker's claim that we are reluctant to find humor in the scriptures? What might be the cause of this reluctance?
2. How can humor be used persuasively?
3. What are some of the humorous features of Jonah's tale? What insights do these humorous episodes provide?
4. How does Walker's interpretation of Jonah compare with Lance Larsen's poetic interpretation, "And Also Much Cattle"?

A Sampler of Biblical Plants

D. Kelly Ogden

D. Kelly Ogden says that "anything we can learn about the images that the prophets and the Savior used will help us understand what they taught." Ogden was asked by an editor for the Ensign *to write this article to help explain the symbolism of the plants in the Holy Land, and it was published in the August 1990* Ensign. *Ogden says that a study of the plants and general landscape of the Holy Land is helpful in order to see how the Savior used "the earth as a chalkboard to teach."*

The Holy Land has a rich variety of plant life, and plants figure prominently in the scriptures. The prophets used plants often as symbols in their teachings—in analogies, in prophecies, and in parables. In this sampler, some of the more important biblical plants are represented, with examples of how they are used in specific scriptural passages.

"Do men gather grapes of thorns, or figs of thistles?" (Matt. 7:16) There grew in the land of the Bible a formidable abundance of thistles and thorns. As sources of affliction and annoyance, they often served a symbolic role in the Savior's teachings and in those of his prophets. The parable of the four kinds of soil, for example, has seeds falling among thorns, which sprang up and choked the seeds (see Matt. 13:7). Those thorns represented worldly cares and pleasures and the deceitfulness of riches (see Matt. 13:22; Luke 8:14). Thorns seem never to symbolize anything good or positive. In short, "that which beareth thorns and briers is rejected, and is nigh unto cursing; whose end is to be burned" (Heb. 6:8).

While mocking Jesus, Roman soldiers wove thorns together in the shape of a crown and placed it on his head (see Matt. 27:29). The thorns, or thorn branches, could have been woven together only if flexible. The traditional candidate is *Ziziphus spina-christi,* otherwise called the Christ-thorn (*see colorplate 1, figure 1*). The etrog tree is also a producer of stout, tough thorns that could have been used.

"AS FOR MAN, HIS DAYS ARE AS GRASS" (PS. 103:15)
In the psalms and the writings of the prophet Isaiah, we see grass used as a symbol—a symbol that persists through the end of both Testaments:

> "As for man, his days are as grass: as a flower of the field, so he flourisheth.
>
> "For the wind passeth over it, and it is gone; and the place thereof shall know it no more." (Ps. 103:15–16)
>
> "All flesh is grass, and all the goodliness thereof is as the flower of the field:
>
> "The grass withereth, the flower fadeth: because the spirit of the Lord bloweth upon it: surely the people is grass.
>
> "The grass withereth, the flower fadeth: but the word of our God shall stand for ever." (Isa. 40:6–8)

Grass represented the transitoriness of man. With the heavy rains of wintertime, grass flourishes and spreads its velvety green carpet even over the barren wilderness, but with a blast of the transitional *khamsin* (the desert wind), it is gone. The blades are vivacious and vigorous one week—gone the next. So is the life of man.

With such a transitory life on earth, we can be comforted by the permanence of an unchangeable and never-ending Providence: "If God so clothed the grass of the field, which today is, and to morrow is cast into the oven, shall he not much more clothe you, O ye of little faith?" (Matt. 6:30).

The prophets also used grass symbolically in decrying the instability of riches and the emptiness of pursuing them:

> "The rich . . . is made low: because as the flower of the grass he shall pass away.
>
> "For the sun is no sooner risen with a burning heat, but it withereth the grass, and the flower thereof falleth, and the grace of the fashion of it perisheth: so also shall the rich man fade away in his ways." (James 1:10–11)

"HE WOULD FAIN HAVE FILLED HIS BELLY WITH THE HUSKS THAT THE SWINE DID EAT" (LUKE 15:16)
This line from the parable of the prodigal son refers to the carob, or locust tree. The Greek word *keratia*, which means "little horns" (apparently, from the shape of the fruit), is variously translated *husks* or *pods.* The carob tree, *caratonia siliqua,* produces leathery brown pods containing pea-like seeds or beans that are used today as a chocolate substitute (*see colorplate 2, figure 1*). The seeds are remarkably consistent in weight,

being used anciently to measure gem stones (the origin of our word *carat*). Carob pods were a staple fodder for cattle throughout eastern Mediterranean countries and were sometimes eaten by poor people. Some suppose that John the Baptist ate the pods of the carob tree, rather than locusts. Thus, the pods are called St. John's Bread.

"THEN ANSWERED AMOS, . . . I WAS AN HERDMAN, AND A GATHERER OF SYCOMORE FRUIT" (AMOS 7:14)

The Biblical sycomore tree (not the English/American sycamore) is known scientifically as *Ficus Sycomorus* (thus the spelling in the Bible). It is not found in the Near East more than 1,000 feet above sea level. In addition to his work as a sheep breeder, the prophet Amos was described as a cultivator or dresser of sycomores. Since the sycomore tree does not grow near Tekoa, Amos's hometown, which is more than 2,000 feet above sea level, the prophet's work with sycomore figs must have taken him to the oases in the Jordan Valley or into the lowlands of Judah.

Ficus sycomorus is a species of fig, or fig-mulberry, the fruit being like a fig and the leaf like the mulberry. The tree can grow to great size, sometimes attaining more than fifty feet in circumference, and is evergreen. Reproduction takes place only through the planting of cuttings, and the existence of the species, in Israel, at least, is totally dependent on cultivation. The fruit shoots forth on all parts of the stem, several figs on each leafless twig. The fruit is smaller than the regular fig and, though edible, is nearly tasteless. The fruit has to be pierced to ripen.

The Israelites prized the wood for construction. Beams made from the tree are light and impervious to rot for many years. When chopped down, the trunk will regenerate itself. David considered the sycomore valuable enough that he appointed a special overseer "over the olive trees and the sycomore trees that were in the low plains [the Shephelah]" (1 Chron. 27:28). Three times the Old Testament mentions that Solomon made cedars as plentiful as the sycomores of the Shephelah (See 1 Kgs. 10:27; 2 Chron. 1:15; 9:27).

"THEY FILLED A SPUNGE WITH VINEGAR, AND PUT IT UPON HYSSOP, AND PUT IT TO HIS MOUTH" (JOHN 19:29)

The hyssop (Heb. *ezov*; Arabic *za'atar*) is a small tree (though we would call it a shrub or a bush). It is used as a food, a spice, and a medicine, and the woody stem and branches are often used for kindling. Its appearance is neither imposing nor pretentious, and biblical writers often contrasted it to the lofty and mighty cedar: Solomon "spake of trees, from the cedar tree that is in Lebanon even unto the hyssop that springeth out of the wall" (1 Kgs. 4:33).

The cedar represented pride and haughtiness, whereas the hyssop symbolized modesty, humility, and purity. Leviticus 14 details its use in the cleansing process for a leper. A hyssop branch was used in applying the blood to the doorposts of Israelite houses in Egypt on the night that the angel of death passed over (see Ex. 12:22–23). Later, Moses used hyssop in sprinkling the blood of the testament on the scriptures and on the people (see Ex. 24:8; Heb. 9:19–20). David, aching to be cleansed, pleaded, "Purge me with hyssop, and I shall be clean" (Ps. 51:7).

The above title passage recalls the scene of a crucified Jesus still hanging on the cross and crying out that he was thirsty. Some soldiers attending him lifted a vinegar-filled sponge to his lips on a hyssop branch. The vinegar was a kind of cheap, sour wine commonly drunk by poorer people and soldiers. Use of the hyssop branch may have had some symbolic relation to the saving blood spread on the houses of Israel during that first Passover night, or to the blood of remission that Moses applied to the people. (Paul noted that the Mosaic practices were "patterns," "figures," "shadows," and "images" of things to come. See Heb. 9 and 10.) It may also be a symbol of humility involved in the fulfillment of a Messianic prophecy, "In my thirst they gave me vinegar to drink" (Ps. 69:21).

"The kingdom of heaven is like to a grain of mustard seed" (Matt. 13:31)

There is only partial consensus among botanists who have studied biblical plants about which member of the mustard family could be the plant or "tree" Jesus referred to. The most likely candidate is *Brassica nigra,* from whose seeds the condiment black mustard is derived (*see colorplate 2, figure 2*).

Jesus loved a contrast, even a hyperbolic contrast, to teach a lesson. He called the mustard seed "less than all the seeds that be in the earth" (see Mark 4:31). But he likened it to the kingdom of God, "which a man took, and cast into his garden; and it grew, and waxed a great tree; and the fowls of the air lodged in the branches of it" (Luke 13:19). Though the mustard seed is tiny, mustard plants can grow to a height of fifteen feet.

Thus, the seed can denote the strength and power inherent in even the smallest particle: "If ye have faith as a grain of mustard seed, ye shall say unto this mountain, Remove hence to yonder place; and it shall remove; and nothing shall be impossible unto you" (Matt. 17:20).

That the glorious kingdom of God would begin in such a small and obscure way was a very un-Jewish teaching—that the kingdom would be "the least" of all kingdoms was near heresy. Most Jews in the days of

Jesus expected the Messiah to come and champion their cause, overthrow the Romans (as Judas Maccabaeus had overthrown the Greeks), and reestablish a mighty kingdom with the Anointed One ruling as king. Jesus, however, implanted a different concept of greatness arising out of something small.

"I COME SEEKING FRUIT ON THIS FIG TREE, AND FIND NONE" (LUKE 13:7)

A practical lesson from nature was taught at the end of each winter season: the fig tree was a harbinger of hot weather, a signal of summertime (*see colorplate 1, figure* 2). Jesus observed, "When [the fig tree's] branch is yet tender, and putteth forth leaves, ye know that summer is nigh" (Matt. 24:32).

The fig tree and the vine together were tokens, or types, of prosperity and secure living. From the Old Testament, we have the following examples:

> "Judah and Israel dwelt safely, every man under his vine and under his fig tree, from Dan even to Beer-sheba." (1 Kgs. 4:25)
>
> "In that day, saith the Lord of hosts, shall ye call every man his neighbour under the vine and under the fig tree." (Zech. 3:10)

"Every man under his vine and under his fig tree" became a figurative, formulaic expression of living comfortably and securely. Just after Philip had encouraged his friend Nathanael to meet Jesus of Nazareth, the following conversation ensued:

> "Jesus saw Nathanael coming to him, and saith of him, Behold an Israelite indeed, in whom is no guile!
>
> "Nathanael saith unto him, Whence knowest thou me? Jesus answered and said unto him, Before that Philip called thee, when thou wast under the fig tree, I saw thee." (John 1:45–48)

The statement was not only literal—Nathanael probably *was* meditating under a fig tree—but may also have been figurative. Some rabbinical sources suggest that "under a fig tree" is the proper place for personal scripture study and that the phrase may be idiomatic, synonymous with "in search of truth." Thus, the reference to Nathanael being "under the fig tree" could also have meant that he was living comfortably and contentedly, having no reason to make any changes in his life. However, by meeting Jesus, the course of his life changed dramatically.

The most memorable encounter with a fig tree in the New Testament occurred during Jesus' walk one morning from Bethany to Jerusalem, during the last week of his earthly life. He became hungry, "and when he saw a fig tree in the way, he came to it, and found nothing thereon, but leaves only, and said unto it, Let no fruit grow on thee henceforward for ever. And presently the fig tree withered away" (Matt. 21:18–19). Mark added, "for the time of figs was not yet" (Mark 11:13). The New Testament contains no other instance of Jesus using his divine power to destroy, but he deemed the life of the fig tree a necessary teaching tool to illustrate, in an unforgettable way, the religious history of Israel.

Luke's gospel contains this related parable:

> "A certain man had a fig tree planted in his vineyard; and he came and sought fruit thereon, and found none.
>
> "Then said he unto the dresser of his vineyard, Behold these three years I come seeking fruit on this fig tree, and find none: cut it down; why cumbereth it the ground?
>
> "And he answering said unto him, Lord, let it alone this year also, till I shall dig about it, and dung it.
>
> "And if it bear fruit, well; and if not, then after that thou shalt cut it down." (Luke 13:6–9)

The fig tree was common in Jewish teaching as a symbol of the nation of Israel. Jesus, too, used the symbolism in this parable. The fig tree, or the people of Israel, had been planted in that part of God's vineyard, in the land of Israel. The Lord of the vineyard, through his earthly husbandmen, had watered and nourished the tree—he expected it to bear fruit.

When Jesus cursed the fig tree, it was Passover time in Jerusalem, half a year before figs would normally appear and ripen. He must have been referring to previous years' unfruitfulness. In the parable, the tree had produced a showy flush of leaves but was perennially barren and fruitless. For centuries, Judaism had been aggressive in maintaining the finer points of the law and the traditions, but it had neglected the weightier matters of justice, mercy, and faith. In the parable, the fig tree representing Israel was not cut down in that generation. But the warning was clear. If, after another season or generation of growth, it still bore no fruit, the Lord would remove it and scatter its pieces.

D. Kelly Ogden *is a professor of ancient scripture at BYU and has taught courses in Hebrew, Old and New Testament, Isaiah, the Bible as literature, history of the ancient Near East, biblical and modern geography of the Holy Land, Pearl of Great Price, Book of Mormon, and Doctrine and Covenants. He has also helped administer the study programs in the Holy Land for over fourteen years. His book,* Where Jesus Walked: The Land and Culture of New Testament Times, *continues the topics discussed in this article. Ogden is currently serving as president of the Chile Santiago East Mission.*

Questions

1. How does knowing something about the plants mentioned in the Bible help to understand the scriptural text?
2. How can researching context help with understanding all kinds of texts?
3. As a class project, find as much information as you can about the animals mentioned in the Bible. How does knowing something about these animals help to understand the scriptural text?

The Narrative Logic of I Nephi 7: A Textual Analysis

GRANT BOSWELL

At the same time that Grant Boswell was teaching a Book of Mormon class in the institute program, he was reading a book which looked at the New Testament using socio-rhetorical criticism. Applying this rhetorical perspective to the Book of Mormon, Boswell found that narrative, which, he says, "some may see as antithetical to logic," can indeed be analyzed logically as a persuasive text. In this article, he explores specifically how Book of Mormon narratives can function as persuasive texts.

The Book of Mormon announces itself as a rhetorical text. The title page declares that among its purposes is "the convincing of the Jew and the Gentile that Jesus is the Christ." Elsewhere we read of various other figures in the Book of Mormon engaged in the same rhetorical activity of persuading people to come to Christ. For example, Nephi writes "For we labored diligently to write, to persuade our children, and also our brethren, to believe in Christ, and to be reconciled in God" (2 Nephi 25:23). Jacob declares nearly the same intent in similar wording: "Wherefore we labored diligently among our people, that we might persuade them to come unto Christ, and partake of the goodness of God" (Jacob 1:7). And Alma gives up the judgment seat (Alma 4:18–19) because "as the preaching of the word had a great tendency to lead the people to do that which is just— yea, it had had more powerful effect upon the minds of the people than the sword, or anything else, which had happened to them—therefore Alma thought it was expedient that they should try the virtue of the word of God" (Alma 31:5).

There are many examples of persuasive discourses in the Book of Mormon. There are sermons such as Jacob's on the consequences of pride and marital infidelity (Jacob 2 & 3) and letters such as the one Captain Moroni wrote to persuade Pahoran to send aid (Alma 60). But there are also numerous stories that seemingly narrate events without any overt persuasive intent. When we think of persuasive discourse, we usually think of advancing some claim or assertion by means of appeals to reasoning (including facts, analogies, examples, and inferences), character, and emotional frames of mind. Stories however, seem to work differently from persuasive discourse, although they may include some of these elements. Stories have plots, settings, characters, actions, and motives rather than appeals to reasoning, character, and emotion. There is however, something very appealing about a good story. Notice how a congregation perks up when a speaker starts telling a story. What I want to investigate here is the persuasive force of a story that can be analyzed logically.

When we are analyzing the persuasive force of a text, we are concerned with two ways in which thought progresses through the text: syllogistic progression and qualitative progression (Robbins, *Exploring* 21-7). Kenneth Burke describes the two as forms. Syllogistic progressive form is the "form of the perfectly conducted argument, advancing step by step . . . . To go from A to E through stage B, C, and D is to obtain such form" (124). Qualitative progressive form differs from syllogistic progressive form in that qualitative progression is not anticipatory. Burke describes qualitative form thus:

> Such progressions are qualitative rather than syllogistic as they lack the pronounced anticipatory nature of the syllogistic progression. We are prepared less to demand a certain qualitative progression than to recognize its rightness after the event. We are put into a state of mind which another state of mind can appropriately follow. (125)

Syllogistic progressive form anticipates what will follow and creates a sense of fulfillment in the reader when the anticipated event occurs. The reader looks forward to what will follow with an expectation that it will follow. Qualitative progressive form creates a sense of fulfillment in the reader when the reader feels the appropriateness of the event in retrospect, looking back at what has already occurred with no expectation that it should occur.

Stories are more qualitative than syllogistic. That is, they advance, but the appropriateness of the next part of the story cannot be predicted easily (if it can, we say it is trite and hackneyed). Rather, events in stories progress qualitatively in that they seem appropriate retrospectively in light of what came before. As it happens, there is a pattern of inference that looks backwards. The American philosopher Charles Sanders Peirce identified an inferential pattern that he sometimes called "abduction" or "hypothesis" and sometimes "retroduction," literally a "leading backwards." He characterized this form of reasoning as being different from induction and deduction because it starts with a result and infers backwards to a probable cause. Peirce's famous example has to do with white beans:

> Someone observes the event or result that these beans are white.
> The person hypothesizes or abduces that if all the beans from a known bag are white, then it would follow as a reasonable hypothesis that these beans are from that bag. (Johansen 183)

This is what we would call guessing, but it is an inferential pattern as are induction and deduction.

Abduction then is the inference from effects back to cause when the cause is unknown or when there may be multiple causes. As Peirce described it, abduction takes the following form:

> The surprising fact, C, is observed;
> But if A were true, C would be a matter of course,
> Hence there is reason to suspect that A is true. (151)

As Peirce states, the conclusion of an abduction is a suspicion that something is true or probable, and he claims that hypothesis or abduction is very useful but not very reliable. In the above example, it would be a useful guess that the beans came from a known bag, but they may have come from any number of other places where white beans may be found. So while it is a good guess, it would have to be verified and secured through other means. Thus abduction is a form of hypothetical reasoning that needs to be verified in other ways.

One of the ways to strengthen the hypothetical conclusion of an abduction is to eliminate all other possibilities until you are left with the most likely explanation. For example, let's suppose you observe that Linda is pale; if she were sick, it would follow as a matter of course that she would be pale. But it is also possible that Linda is pale because she is frightened, surprised, in love, etc. To pin down the cause of the paleness would mean that all possibilities would have to be eliminated except the real cause. Another way to strengthen the conclusion of an abduction is to accumulate all other abductions until the cumulative effect of the string of abductions points to a single explanation. If Linda is pale, and is running a fever, and was recently exposed to someone who has come down with the flu, and has body aches, the cumulative result of all these abductive indications is that she is sick and that her paleness is one among many such indicators.

Narration works in both of these ways. Stories present us with various observable actions and characters from which we abduce various hypotheses until we eliminate possibilities and settle on the one motive or cause that appears most likely or until the cumulative sum of the inferences leads us as readers to a conclusion supported by all the abductions. As readers we understand actions as results of characters as causes. Thus we can look for narrative actions in a story and infer backwards to and hypothesize about characters as causes. In this sense reading is like detective work or the game of Clue; we observe clues and generate and verify hypotheses from them until we figure out who done it, where, with what instrument, and for what reasons.

Let's see how this plays out in the story of 1 Nephi 7. This is the story of Nephi and his brothers returning to Jerusalem to convince Ishmael to leave Jerusalem with his entire household and join Lehi's household in the wilderness. The beginning of the story informs us that Nephi and his brothers return to Jerusalem for the purpose of persuading Ishmael and his household to leave Jerusalem and follow them into the wilderness. Following Peirce's abductive form we could state the narrative inference thus:

> The fact of Nephi and the others' success is reported (verses four and five);
> But if Nephi and company were under an injunction from the Lord (which the narrative supplies in verse one), their actions would follow as a matter of course.
> Hence there is reason to suspect that they are complying with the Lord's commandment.

In the next sequence of the story line or plot, Laman, Lemuel and some of Ishmael's household rebel. In narrative terms some of the characters act, and thus conditions are right for us as readers to make the following abductive inference about the characters:

> The surprising rebellion is reported (act);
> But if Laman and Lemuel and others (characters) were not faithful in keeping the Lord's commandment, then their rebellion would follow as a matter of course.
> Hence there is reason to suspect that Laman and Lemuel and others are not faithful in keeping the Lord's commandment.

We as readers hypothesize abductively from the reported facts of the narrative. In each case there may be other explanations as to why certain actions occur, but the accumulation of narrative inferences will often lead the reader to a single conclusion, even though conclusions may vary with readers. So let me continue to lay out the other abductions from the remaining segments of the narrative.

The next segment also involves characters and their actions. This is where Nephi addresses his brothers directly, and the narrative inference can be stated thus:

> Nephi's rebuke of his brothers is narrated;
> If Nephi were trying to be faithful to the Lord's commandment, his rebuke would follow as a matter of course.
> Hence there is reason to suspect that Nephi is trying to be faithful to the Lord's commandment.

It is possible that Nephi simply enjoys telling his older brothers what to do or that he has usurped authority over them, and if either were the case his rebuke of their rebellion would also follow as a matter of course. In light of the other observable events in the narrative, however, these abductions seem unlikely. Nevertheless, Nephi is acutely aware that Laman and Lemuel, together with their posterity, may "read" the event differently (see Jacob 4: 3).

The next sequence in the narrative relates several incidents that can also be paired as characters in relation to their actions. Laman and Lemuel become angry and bind Nephi; Nephi exercises faith and the bands are loosed; Laman and Lemuel become angry again and attempt to lay hands on Nephi a second time; one of Ishmael's daughters intercedes on Nephi's behalf; Laman and Lemuel ask for forgiveness; and Nephi forgives his brothers. The abductive hypotheses from all of these incidents explain the actions as results or effects of the characters as cause in terms of the characters' faithfulness or faithlessness. The two incidents of Laman and Lemuel's anger and violent behavior are indications of their faithlessness; Nephi's prayer and subsequent delivery as well as his forgiveness indicate his faithfulness; and the daughter of Ishmael's intercession on Nephi's behalf is an indication of her faithfulness.

The narrative ending again exhibits actions as results of characters as causes. The entire party returns to Lehi's tent and offers sacrifice and thanks. These acts we understand abductively to be a sign of their thanks for having faithfully fulfilled the commandment the Lord had issued to them. The cumulative effect of all these narrative inferences is to strengthen the conclusion that if Lehi and his entire group are united in their faithfulness to the Lord's commandments, they will obtain his promised blessings; but if they are not united in their faithfulness, they will have contentions and problems. This is essentially the claim or assertion of the narrative, but it has been supported by a series of abductions based on the actions of certain characters. This is to say that the qualitative progressive form emphasizes a key premise in the narrative logic of the text: faithfulness to the Lord's commandments, which becomes the condition for obtaining promised rewards. Thus the logic of the narrative as it incrementally unfolds and is reinforced in each part of the story leads us to a conclusion about the benefit of faithful compliance to the Lord's commands. This is how the events in a narrative plot can proceed toward a conclusion, and an analysis at this level can help us determine "the persuasive effects of the parts, how they work together, in relation to the persuasive nature of the entire text" (Robbins, *Tapestry* 50–1).

GRANT BOSWELL, *an associate professor in the English Department, has been teaching at BYU since 1985. He received his PhD and MA from the University of Southern California and his BA from BYU. Boswell teaches classes in language, persuasive writing, rhetoric, and the history of critical theory.*

Works Cited

Burke, Kenneth. *Counter-Statement.* Berkeley: University of California Press, 1968.

Johansen, Jørgen Dines. *Dialogic Semiosis: An Essay on Signs and Meaning.* Bloomington, IN: Indiana University Press, 1993.

Peirce, Charles Sanders. *Philosophical Writings of Peirce.* Ed. Justus Buchler. New York: Dover Publictions, Inc., 1955.

Robbins, Vernon K. *The Tapestry of Early Christian Discourse: Rhetoric, Society, and Ideology.* New York: Routledge, 1996.

———. *Exploring the Texture of Texts: A Guide to Socio-Rhetorical Interpretation.* Valley Forge, PA: Trinity Press International, 1996.

Questions

1. What is "abduction"? How does abduction differ from induction and deduction?
2. How does abductive reasoning help to understand the structure of narratives?
3. How can abduction be used to understand other scriptural narratives? How can it be used to understand non-scriptural narratives?

The Psalm of Nephi: A Lyric Reading

STEVEN P. SONDRUP

According to Steven Sondrup, "Within scripture there are varying literary genres that require varied modes of reading and interpretation." Sondrup was inspired by an article by Ruth apRoberts that asserted that psalms were one of the most easily translatable forms of poetry, because of its emphasis on parallelism. Because of this, Sondrup was curious to see if the so-called "Psalm of Nephi" held up to this claim, as a translatable poem. His article was originally published in BYU Studies.

The Book of Mormon, like the Bible, is far from a generically unified work. Although the narratives, the epistles, the sermons, the exhortations, and the poems may well constitute a specialized encyclopedic form with a thoroughgoing figurative unity of the sort that Northrup Frye associates with the Bible, each section can profitably be read in terms of its own generic conventions in such a way that the understanding of the parts as well as the comprehension of the whole will be significantly enhanced.[1] The question of specific generic types within sacred writ is not simply an academic exercise in literary taxonomy, but rather a problem at the very heart of scriptural exegesis. One of the reasons, for example, that Isaiah appears particularly difficult to many readers may derive from the rather futile attempt to read the book as a simple linear narrative rather than as a collection of thematically related oracles. Much of the meaning of the Song of Solomon, moreover, depends directly on the generic assumptions that are initially made about the book.[2] Similarly, many passages from the Book of Mormon become more immediately and fully accessible when their study is guided by accurate generic inferences which facilitate interpretation in terms of appropriate conventions. To be sure, much can be said without any reference to the question of genre, but generic insights can heighten both the understanding and the appreciation of many passages. It might be argued that the use of generic concepts as a heuristic tool is tantamount to the inappropriate application of profane categories to the study of sacred texts and consequently in itself a violation of generic norms. The genre of sacred text, though, is very general, and sacred texts consist demonstrably of many more specific literary types involving various conventions and norms. Surely texts held to be religious in nature should be read with an eye to religious values while at the same time admitting of study in terms of appropriate generic practices which in turn add new levels and dimensions of meaning.[3]

Because by far the greatest portion of the Book of Mormon is narrative—though admittedly in several different ways—other literary modes embedded in the narrative flow are less obvious and consequently less easily identified and read in terms of their own unique generic conventions. One such passage occurs in the fourth chapter of 2 Nephi, verses 16 through 35, a passage that is often referred to as the "Psalm of Nephi," at least since Sidney Sperry provided this formulation in his commentary on the Book of Mormon.[4] The question to be discussed with reference to these verses is not whether they are a psalm in the biblical sense of the term but rather the nature and extent of their poetic qualities and some of the most central interpretive implications inextricably connected with their lyricism.

It may at first seem fatuous to argue for the presence of accomplished poetry in a volume identifying itself as a translation, particularly if one remembers Shelley's caveat that it is impossible to translate poetry[5] or Robert Frost's quip that poetry is what gets lost in translation. Although Shelley's and Frost's objection may well apply to the lyric mode they knew best—that based in formal terms on acoustical patterning like rhythm, rhyme, and alliteration and that which relies heavily on subtle connotations and associations of individual words—it does not necessarily apply in general.

Poetry can be viewed more broadly and taken to include all those utterances in which language artfully and significantly draws attention to itself by the intensification of its own linguistic and formal properties; poetry, thus, celebrates language as its medium of communication and as at least part of its raison d'être.[6] While rhythm, meter, alliteration, assonance, and rhyme are some of the ways most familiar to modern readers in which the poet can foreground his language, they are by no means the only possibilities at his disposal. In other epochs and in other cultures many different linguistic devices have been used. In the "Psalm of Nephi," just as in Hebrew poetry, an intricately patterned system of ideational parallels is the essence of lyricism. Logical, formal, or conceptual units are set parallel to one another rather than acoustic properties as is the case with rhythm, rhyme, alliteration, and assonance. Formal construction also survive, it should be noted, the process of translation far more readily than purely acoustic properties.[7]

This use of ideational parallelism in Hebrew poetry was first noticed by medieval Jewish biblical scholars and was given its technical name—*parallelismus membrorum*—during the eighteenth century by the Anglican bishop and scholar Robert Lowth. The basic principle is that "every verse must consist of at least two 'members,' the second of which must, more or less completely, satisfy the expectation raised by the first."[8] A third member may on occasion be present, but if there are more than three, it is usually possible using some rationale to group the members into twos or threes. Parallelism may exist, though, in many forms. The first and simplest is synonymous parallelism which occurs when the first member states an idea that is restated with variation by the second member.

> I am like a pelican of the wilderness;
> I have become like an owl of the ruins.
> [Psalm 102:7][9]

The second kind is antithetic parallelism in which the second member states the idea of the first but in negative or contrasting form:

> A time to weep,
> And a time to laugh.
> [Ecclesiastes 3:4]

The third kind involves a certain parallelism of form but continuous rather than balanced thought. It remains questionable, though, whether this synthetic or formal parallelism should be counted as parallelism at all. Further subordinate and specialized forms of parallelism also are attested, the most important, perhaps, being that known as introverted in which the first member is parallel to the fourth and the second to the third.

The Bible, though, is by no means the only example of parallelism being used as an organizing poetic principle: parallel structural arrangements of varied kinds play an important role in the poetry of many folk traditions as well as in works of highly divergent modern poets. Walt Whitman, for example, frequently uses parallelism as a structural device as in *Song of Myself.*

> I too am not a bit tamed. I too am untranslatable.
> I sound my barbaric yawp over the roofs of the world.[10]

Whitman is not alone in his interest in exploiting the poetic potential of formal parallelism: Charles Péguy, a French poet of the Third Republic, also makes extensive use of poetic parallelism, as does Augusto Frederico Schmidt, a Brazilian modernist who frequently drew on Péguy's stylistic innovations.[11] The poetry of Dylan Thomas abounds in parallelism of a particularly subtle and refined sort, as the first stanza of the poem "A Process in the Weather of the Heart" illustrates.

> A process in the weather of the heart
> Turns damp to dry; the golden shot
> Storms in the freezing tomb.
> A weather in the quarter of the veins
> Turns night to day; blood in their suns
> lights up the living worm.[12]

Modern poets not only have used parallelism as a particularly effective poetic device but have also on occasion sought to explain its importance. Gerard Manley Hopkins, for example, in an early essay which seeks to define the essence of poetic expression suggests that it is ultimately the use of parallelism on many levels that distinguishes poetry from other modes of discourse.

> But what the character of poetry is will be found best by looking at the structure of verse. The artificial part of poetry, perhaps we shall be right to say all artifice, reduces itself to the principle of parallelism. The structure of poetry is that of continuous parallelism, ranging from the technical so-called Parallelisms of Hebrew poetry and the antiphons of Church music up to the intricacy of Greek or Italian or English verse. . . . Now the force of this recurrence is to beget a recurrence or parallelism answering to it in the words or thought and, speaking roughly and rather for the tendency than the invariable result, the more marked parallelism in structure whether of elaboration or of emphasis begets more marked parallelism in the words and sense. And moreover parallelism in expression tends to beget or passes into parallelism in thought. This point reached we shall be able to see and account for the peculiarities of poetic diction.[13]

Against the background of this assessment of the importance of parallelism as well as that of its rich and venerable tradition extending at least from the Old Testament through Dylan Thomas, the arresting formal parallelism of the "Psalm of Nephi" invites particular attention. Although comparisons between this passage and other poems making use of parallelism—biblical psalms, for example—may help to isolate and identify the nature of the passage's lyric impact, the issue in question is emphatically not the proximity per se of Book of Mormon poetics to any other specific system but rather the inherent lyric qualities of the "Psalm of Nephi."

The basic characteristics of the parallelism of the "Psalm of Nephi" can easily be seen in what may well serve as the first of the four stanzas of the psalm.[14] The parallelism here is introverted or chiastic: the first member is antithetically parallel to the fourth, and the second synonymously to the third. In the first and the fourth members, the *soul* of the lyric I expresses two emotional effects—delight and grief respectively—and the source of the delight and grief are the antithetical poles in the individual's search for salvation, "the things of the Lord" and "mine iniquities." The parallelism of the second and third elements is somewhat more complex: the *heart* of the lyric I (in distinction to soul) engages in activities—pondering and exclaiming—which directly involve activities of the lyric I: "my *heart pondereth* continually upon the things which *I* have seen and heard" and "my *heart exclaimeth*: O wretched man that *I* am." The second element of the chiastic pair is itself a synonymously parallel couplet: "my heart exclaimeth" and "Yea my heart sorroweth." This sort of doubling of one element is found throughout the psalm and has the effect of conceptual reinforcement or expansion. The phrase in the middle of this stanza—"Nevertheless, notwithstanding the great goodness of the Lord in showing me his great and marvelous works"—is an introduction to the third member and the pivot at the center of the introverted parallelism. The lines of this stanza may be organized not only in this introverted parallelism but also in terms of a secondary synonymous couplet and triplet. The delight of the soul and the pondering of the heart are spiritual virtues that are extensions of one another whereas the heart's declaiming its wretchedness, the heart's sorrowing because of the flesh, and the soul's grieving because of iniquity are linked by their common concern with sin. It should be noted, moreover, that the soul, a relatively abstract notion, is appropriately concerned with abstractions—"the things of the Lord" and "mine iniquities," whereas the heart, a metaphorical but more concrete figure, deals with similarly concrete realities—"the things which I have seen and heard," "[the] wretched man that I am," and "my flesh." The verbs of each parallel structure—also function in a telling way: the soul in delighting and grieving is engaging in essentially emotional activities, while the heart in pondering and exclaiming is performing more or less physical actions. The spiritual nature of the soul is, thus, emphasized by its emotive properties, and the corporality of the heart is suggested by its tendency toward action. The second element of the inner chiastic pair, though, describes the heart sorrowing, an obviously emotional quality. Rather than a contradiction or an anomaly within the structure, this line is a synthesis of the two poles and provides a carefully wrought transition from the inner chiastic pair to the outer.

The lines constituting the second stanza of the psalm present a far more complex but basically similar organization. Three chiastic pairs surround a nucleus of two sets of six parallel members with each set further divisible into sets of parallel couplets. The outermost structure (1 / 23–25) is defined by the use of the first person singular pronoun I as the subject of the sentence. The second element of the pair consists of three parallel members all in the form of a rhetorical question: "Why should I yield to sin?" "They should I give way to temptations?" and "'Why am I angry?" While the lexical parallelism of this outer pair is synonymous, the grammatical parallelism is antithetic. The second pair (2–19) is defined by the use of the heart as the subject of the sentence: "my heart groaneth" and "my heart weeps." The parallelism is further established by the conceptual proximity of "groaning" and "weeping." As with the first pair, the second element of this pair is composed of multiple members (19–22) in the form of a question: here, though, two couplets replace the triplet of the first pair. The first of the two deals metaphorically with the afflictions of the heart and soul—the principal elements of the preceding stanza—while the second is concerned with the more concrete concepts of atrophying flesh and strength. In addition to this relatively obscure introverted parallelism, the last seven members (19–25)—the couplets and the concluding triplet—are all parallel to one another in terms of their rhetorically interrogative form and their implied antipathy toward that which would detract from a rich relationship with God. Similarly, the first two lines of the stanza (1–2), which were respectively the first elements of the two chiastic pairs, are synonymously parallel in describing what alienates man from God. The inner nucleus of the stanza (5–16) is introduced by a couplet announcing the subject of the next six lines: "Nevertheless, I know in whom I have trusted. / My God hath been my support" (3–4). This introductory couplet is in turn balanced by another couplet which is a kind of summary of the last six lines and the bridge to what follows: "If I have seen so great things, / If the Lord in his condescension unto the children of men hath visited me in so much mercy" (17–18). The first six of the twelve-line nucleus are all parallel in that they specifically detail how God has been a support and in that all have parallel structures beginning, "He hath" (5–10). The first two of the six (5–6) are linked by their description of God's protection from environmental dangers, "the wilderness" and "the waters of the great deep"; the second two (7–8) by detailing God's love for the righteous and the confounding of the enemies of righteousness; and the third (9–10) by the play on the antithesis of day and night. The second set of six lines (11–16) turns from the actions of God to those of man but can similarly be divided into three couplets. The

Behold, my *soul* delighteth in the things of the Lord; and

My *heart* pondereth continually upon the things which

I have seen and heard.

Nevertheless, notwithstanding the great goodness of the

Lord in showing me his great and marvelous work

My *heart* exclaimeth: O wretched man that *I* am!

Yea my *heart* sorroweth because of my flesh;

My *soul* grieveth because of mine iniquities.

first (11–12) portrays the ways in which the poetic voice has been raised to God; the second (13–14) discusses the ministrations of divine messengers; and the last (15–16) mentions the results of these ministrations. The parallelism of this last couplet, it must be admitted, is certainly not as marked as that of the others, but it is similar to the synthetic or formal parallelism common in Hebrew verse.

The third stanza is the simplest, yet, perhaps, the most elegant of the entire poem and parallels, moreover, as a stanza the first stanza of the psalm. The outer chiastic pair is defined by the awakening and rejoicing of the soul, while the inner pair is characterized by the rejoicing of the heart. The first member of the inner pair is supported by a subordinate couplet that expands the meaning of the line. The chiastic pairing of statements about the heart and the soul is, thus, the structural foundation of both stanzas and provides a formal parallelism of a new order.

This strophic parallelism is continued in the fourth stanza in that it generally reflects the structure of the second stanza. The outer chiastic shell around the conceptual nucleus of the second stanza is missing in the fourth, but the structural pattern of the nucleus itself still obtains. The stanza consists of two parts, each introduced by the parallel exclamatory expressions, "O Lord." As in the second stanza, the first part describes the

1 *I* am encompassed about, because of the temptations and the sins which do so easily beset me.

2 And when I desire to rejoice, my *heart* groaneth because of my sins;

3 Nevertheless, I know in whom I have trusted.

4 My God hath been my support;

5 He hath led me through mine afflictions in the wilderness;

6 And he hath preserved me upon the waters of the great deep.

7 He hath filled me with his love, even unto the consuming of my flesh.

8 He hath confounded mine enemies, unto the causing of them to quake before me.

9 Behold, he hath heard my cry by day, and

10 He hath given me knowledge by visions in the nighttime.

11 And by day, have I waxed bold in mighty prayer before him;

12 Yea, my voice have I sent up on high;

13 And angels have come down and ministered unto me.

14 And upon the wings of his Spirit hath my body been carried away upon exceeding high mountains.

15 And mine eyes have beheld great things, yea, even too great for man;

16 Therefore I was bidden that I should not write them.

17 O then, If I have seen so great things,

18 If the Lord in his condescension unto the children of men hath visited men in so much mercy,

19 Why should my *heart* weep and

20 my soul linger in the valley of sorrow, and

21 my flesh waste away, and

22 my strength slacken, because of mine afflictions?

23 And why should *I* yield to sin, because of my flesh?

24 Yea, why should *I* give way to temptations, that the evil one have place in my heart to destroy my peace and afflict my soul?

25 Why am *I* angry because of mine enemy?

actions of the Lord, albeit those for which the lyric I is praying, while in the second part the actions of the lyric I itself are evoked. In both sections the lines are even more intimately associated in conceptual couplets and triplets. In the first part, lines one and two are synonymously parallel, and line two forms an outer chiastic pair with line eleven, both centering on the escape from enemies. Line three and line ten form the inner chiastic pair in that they deal with the antithesis of sin and righteousness. Lines four and seven are related by the opening or not opening of gates and are supported by a subordinate pair, lines eight and nine, based on the image of walking the path of life. This image is taken up again in the couplet consisting of lines twelve and thirteen and enlarged in another subordinate couplet also based on the same image.

In the second part, lines sixteen, seventeen, and eighteen constitute a triplet defined by the trust of the lyric I in the Lord and expanded by a subordinate couplet evincing the curse upon those who trust in the arm of flesh, lines nineteen and twenty. Lines twenty-one and twenty-two form a parallel couplet in their description of the manner in which God will give liberally. The final three lines—twenty-three through twenty-five—are a triplet which enumerate the ways in which the lyric I will raise his voice to God. The second part is thus symmetrical in that the central couplet is surrounded by two triplets.[15]

The representation of this passage in poetic lines and stanzas rather than in the usual narrow, newspaper-like columns leads unavoidably to the insight that this passage is extraordinarily tightly structured in linguistic and conceptual terms and differs substantially from the surrounding narrative sections.[16] Its balanced ideational patterns are unlike the exhortations, the prayers, the epistles, and the epic narrative that constitute most of the Book of Mormon. This careful and obviously intentional structuring certainly seems to invite—if not to demand—interpretation on its own terms, and the terms that the passages seem to suggest are those that easily accommodate the arresting emphasis given to language as language, to formal structure as structure. The poet—a designation entirely appropriate for the author of this passage—seems intent upon drawing the careful reader's attention to the aesthetic fulfillment that intricate formal balance can provide and, in so doing, creates a text that is at least in part self-referential. Although debate continues on the definition of poetry and, indeed, whether a generic category as large as poetry can be defined in any meaningful way, many critics could agree that the extensive parallelism of the passage would warrant at least a tentative reading in terms of general poetic conventions.

A lyric convention which very significantly distinguishes a poetic reading of the passage from one determined by the norms and expectations of expository prose, for example, is the lyric practice of concentrating and symbolizing meaning. The delight of the soul in the things of the Lord is, thus, an animating and vivifying attitude rather than a prosaic report on psychic health; the grief because of iniquity is a soul-searing regret rather than a relatively passive evocation of guilt. And similarly, the final resolve to cry unto God eternally is heightened and amplified by the power of lyrical articulation to the level of an all-consuming passion. The joy in righteousness, the grief for sin, and the resolve to praise God are, moreover, all universalized and, within the poetic framework, all generally accessible. The text does not evince a historical time in the same sense as the ambient narrative with its specific temporal references, but rather evokes a heightened, eternal lyric present. The past events are only prior to the enduring poetic present and the future tenses suggest more a logical consequence than a chronological ordering. By recognizing the nontemporal lyric time, the reader engages the mind of the lyric I in a highly intimate yet universalizing way which is notably different from the reader's contact with the epic narrator.

In all verbal structures identified as literary, or more especially as lyric, meaning and value ultimately depend not on descriptive accuracy but rather on conformity with the postulates implied by the work itself. The poem does not literally describe nor does it directly assert: as poetry, the "Psalm of Nephi" cannot necessarily be taken to provide reliable information about Nephi's actions or attitudes.[17] The psalm rather evokes a lyric world responsive to its own internal rhythm and having only an indirect relationship with the world of externality. The inward striving for heightened reality must, perforce, take precedence over the outward motion toward empirical reality. In this rarified world of lyric intensity, truth becomes, at least in part, a question of poetic (poietic) coherence rather than referential veracity.

When the "Psalm of Nephi" is read with attention to its lyric qualities, it may be subsumed within the lyric genre and thus be in a position to enrich and to be enriched by other poems. Although it can be esteemed and valued in aesthetic isolation, its significance and appreciation expand when read in relation to and comparison with other works. Other poems may also conceivably emerge in new light as their poetic context is expanded to accommodate this poem.[18] It is true that in the sciences the discovery of a new example of a given species does not modify the characteristics of the species as a whole. Yet in matters of aesthetic concern, this is not the case: each new example necessarily not only extends and enlarges but also subtly and invariably changes the genre.[19]

A particularly good example of this kind of intertextual enrichment with regard to the "Psalm of Nephi" can be seen in its comparative juxtaposition to thematically similar Old Testament psalms. Psalm 51, which tradition holds was occasioned by Nathan the prophet's visit to David after David had sinned with Bathsheba, like the "Psalm of Nephi" expresses profound grief for sin and transgression and looks forward to God's righteousness. David's pleas to "create a clean heart, O God and renew a right spirit" (v. 10) evoke the sympathetic vibrations of Nephi's heart that sorrows because of his flesh and of his soul that grieves because of his iniquities but nonetheless knows in whom to trust and upon whom to rely. Although Nephi's sorrow for sin is certainly genuine and sincere, the gravity and immediacy of David's transgression emerges with harrowing power in contrast. David yearns for deliverance, so that his tongue can sing aloud of the righteousness of God (v. 14); yet in comparison, Nephi's resolve to lift his voice forever to the rock of his righteousness, to his everlasting God, is at once more ecstatic and more compelling. When Nephi exclaims, "May the gates of hell be shut continually before me, because that my heart is broken and my spirit is contrite!" he echoes David's assertion that "the sacrifices of God are a broken spirit: a broken and a contrite heart, O God, thou wilt not despise" (v. 17). And with this poetic echo comes some of the urgency and tragedy of David's penitence that shapes and colors the aesthetic impact of the line in such a subtle yet important way that it could be missed if the generic similarity of the two statements were not explicit.

Awake my *soul*! No longer droop in sin.

Rejoice, O my *heart*, and give place no more for the enemy of my soul.

Do not anger again because of mine enemies.

Do not slacken my strength because of mine afflictions.

Rejoice, O my *heart*, and cry unto the Lord, and say: O Lord, I will praise thee forever;

Yea my *soul* will rejoice in thee, my God, and the rock of my salvation.

O Lord, wilt thou redeem my soul?
Wilt thou deliver me out of the hands of mine enemies?
Wilt thou make me that I may shake at the appearance of sin?
May the gates of hell be shut continually before me,
    Because that my heart is broken and
        my spirit is contrite!
O Lord, wilt thou not shut the gates of thy righteousness before me.
    That I may walk the path of the low valley,
    That I may be strict in the plain road!
O Lord, wilt thou encircle me around in the robe of thy righteousness!
O Lord, wilt thou make a way for mine escape before mine enemies!
Wilt thou make my path straight before me!
Wilt thou not place a stumbling block in my way—
    But that thou wouldst clear my way before me,
    And hedge not up my way, but the ways of mine enemy.
O Lord, I have trusted in thee, and
I will trust in thee forever.
I will not put my trust in the arm of flesh;
    For I know that cursed is he that putteth his trust in the arm of flesh.
    Yea, cursed is he that putteth his trust in man or maketh flesh his arm.
Yea, I know that God will give liberally to him that asketh.
Yea, my God will give me, if I ask not amiss;
Therefore, I will lift up my voice unto thee:
Yea, I will cry unto thee, my God, the rock of my righteousness.
Behold, my voice shall forever ascend up unto thee, my rock and
  mine everlasting God, Amen.

Similarly, the avowal of the poet of the eighty-fourth psalm that "my soul longeth, yea, even fainteth for the courts of the LORD; my heart and my flesh crieth out for the living God" (v. 2) and Nephi's affirmation that "my soul delighteth in the things of the Lord and my heart pondereth continually upon things which I have seen and heard" mutually provide enriching and broadening interpretive contexts which potentially render the broadest meaning of both passages more accessible and more fully real.

Yet one further and more distant comparison may well serve to illustrate the point. In the thirty-first canto of "Purgatorio," Dante's weakness and shortcomings are brought fully and painfully to his mind. He stands conscience-stricken and penitent with his eyes cast toward the ground as Beatrice rehearses his transgressions; he is then told that the grief at hearing is not sufficient, so he must lift his eyes to behold and to experience even greater pain. Eventually the suffering is too great for Dante to endure; he collapses exclaiming: "*Tanta riconoscenza il cor mi morse / ch'io caddi vinto*" (So much recognition [i.e., self-recognition, self-condemnation] bit at my heart, that I fell overcome).[20] By means of a sensitivity to certain broadly shared generic conventions coupled with even the vaguest memory of Dante's penitential collapse at the sight of his weakness, the experience of hearing Nephi's heart exclaim, "O wretched man that I am," of seeing the poet come to an awareness of his own shortcomings to the extent that his heart groans and weeps, can be heightened, extended, and enriched and, more significantly, moved one step closer, perhaps, to full poetic universality. The two passages partake of the same traditions, and the lyric strength of one, consequently, poetically reinforces the other.

Neither the enrichment nor, indeed, the aesthetic fulfillment it produces in itself justifies the application of lyric conventions to the reading of the "Psalm of Nephi." Ultimately, the reason for reading this text as a poem is that the complex system of parallelisms suggests the author intended, at least in part, to call attention to language, his medium of expression, to write a text which was, at least to a degree, self-referential, and to celebrate the essence and power of the word as such: he intended his text should be read as a poem. By reading these words as they were intended to be read, by engaging the poetic mind, indeed the prophetic mind, on its own terms, the reader is warranted the most profound understanding of the meaning of the text and the richest appreciation of its significance.[21]

STEVEN SONDRUP *is a professor of comparative literature at BYU. He received his BA at BYU, and his MA and PhD at Harvard in comparative literature. Sondrup teaches classes in critical theory, and German, Italian, French, Scandinavian, Chinese, and Japanese literature. He has forthcoming books on European romanticism, contemporary Swedish poetry, and the translatability of culture.*

Notes:

[1]Northrop Frye, *Anatomy of Criticism* (Princeton, NJ.: Princeton University Press, 1957), pp. 315–16.

[2]See *The Anchor Bible: The Song of Songs,* ed. and trans., with commentary, Marvin H. Pope (New York: Doubleday, 1977), as an example of the problem of generic identification.

[3]See E. D. Hirsch, Jr., *Validity in Interpretation* (New Haven, Conn.: Yale University Press, 1967), pp. 68–126, for a detailed description of the importance of accurate generic definition in the process of interpretation. See also Hans Robert Jauss, *Literaturgeschichte als Provokation* (Frankfurt am Main: Suhrkamp Verlag, 1970), pp. 173–83.

[4]*Book of Mormon Compendium* (Salt Lake City: Bookcraft, 1968), pp. 152–53. Although Professor Sperry may be right in his unsubstantiated argument that "this is a true psalm in both form and ideas," he seems to have misunderstood the basic poetic structure of this passage, at least insofar as his arrangement of lines and stanzas allows inference. Reynolds and Sjodahl in George Reynolds and Janne M. Sjodahl, *Commentary on the Book of Mormon,* ed. Philip C. Reynolds, 7 vols. (Salt Lake City: Deseret News Press, 1955), 1:264–71, describe the passage as "A Song of Nephi" and call attention to some of its poetic qualities. The proximity of the passage to Hebrew poetry is also emphasized. At times the analysis is rather superficial, and many of the central lyric elements seem to have been misunderstood.

[5]"It were as wise to cast a violet into a crucible that you might discover the formal principle of its colour and odour as to seek to transfuse from one language to another the creations of a poet. The plant must spring again from its seed, or it will bear no flower—and this is the burthen of the curse of Babel." ("A Defense of Poetry," *The Complete Works of Percy Bysshe Shelley,* ed. Roger Ingpen and Walter E. Peck, 10 Vols. [New York: Gordian Press; London: Ernest Benn, 1965], 7:114.)

[6]This view of poetry is based on insights of the Prague School aestheticians and structuralist approaches to poetry. Jan Mukarovsky argues, for example, that "in poetic language foregrounding achieves maximum intensity to the extent of pushing communication into the background as the objective of expression and of being used for its own sake; it is not used in the services of communication, but in order to place in the foreground the act of expression, the act of speech itself" ("Standard Language and Poetic Language," *A Prague School Reader on Esthetics, Literary Structure, and Style,* ed. and trans. Paul L. Garvin [Washington, D.C.: Georgetown University Press, 1964], p. 19). Roman Jakobson makes a similar point: 'The set (Einstellung) toward the MESSAGE as such, focus on the message for its own sake, is the POETIC function of language. . . . Poetic function is not the sole function of verbal art but only its dominant, determining function, whereas in all other verbal activities it acts as a subsidiary, accessory constituent. This function, by promoting the palpability of signs, deepens the fundamental dichotomy of signs and objects." ("Closing Statement: Linguistics and Poetics," *Style in Language,* ed. Thomas Sebeok (Cambridge: Technology Press of Massachusetts Institute of Technology, 1960], p. 356.)

[7]See Ruth apRoberts, "Old Testament Poetry: The Translatable Structure," *PMLA* 92 (1977): 987–1004. Matthew Arnold was also aware of the translatable potential of Old Testament poetry:

> And the effect of Hebrew poetry can be preserved and transferred in a foreign language, as the effect of other great poetry cannot. The effect of Homer, the effect of Dante, is and must be in great measure lost in a translation, because their poetry is a poetry of metre, or of rhyme, or both; and the effect of these is not really transferable. A

man may make a good English poem with the matter and thoughts of Homer or Dante, may even try to reproduce their metre, or to reproduce their rhyme; but the metre and rhyme will be in truth his own, and the effect will be his, not the effect of Homer or Dante. Isaiah's, on the other hand, is a poetry, as is well known, of parallelism; it depends not on metre and rhyme, but on a balance of thought, conveyed by a corresponding balance of sentence; and the effect of this can be transferred to another language. ("Introduction to Isaiah of Jerusalem," *The Works of Matthew Arnold,* 15 vols. [New York: AMS Press, 1970], 11:333–34.)

[8]Theodore H. Robinson, *The Poetry of the Old Testament* (London: Duckworth, 1947) p. 21. See also Stanley Gevirtz, *Patterns in the Early Poetry of Israel* (Chicago: University of Chicago Press, 1963), and George Buchanan Gray, *The Forms of Hebrew Poetry* (1915; reprinted with a Prolegomenon by David Noel Freedman, New York: Ktav Publishing House, 1972). James Muilenburg provides a useful description of the value and limits of form criticism and *Gattungforschung* in "Form Criticism and Beyond," *Journal of Biblical Literature,* vol. 88, pt. 1 (March 1969), pp. 1–18. James L. Kugel's *The Idea of Biblical Poetry: Parallelism and Its History* (New Haven: Yale University Press, 1981) did not appear soon enough to be considered in this study.

[9]All biblical quotations are from the King James Version.

[10]Walt Whitman, "Song of Myself," stanza 52, *Leaves of Grass,* ed. Harold W. Blodgett and Sculley Bradley, vol. 9 of *The Collected Writings of Walt Whitman,* ed. Gay Wilson Allen and Sculley Bradley (New York: New York University Press, 1965), p. 89.

[11]See Joseph Barbier, *Le Vocabulaire la syntaxe et le style des poèmes réguliers de Charles Péguy* (Paris: Editions Berger-Levrault, 1957), especially pp. 434–56 for a discussion of Péguy's use of parallelism. See Jon M. Tolman, "A. E Schmidt and C. Péguy: A Comparative Stylistic Analysis," *Comparative Literature Studies* 11 (December 1974): 277–305, for a discussion of Schmidt's use of parallelism and Péguy's influence on him.

[12]*The Collected Poems of Dylan Thomas* (New York: New Directions, 1957), p. 6.

[13]"Poetic Diction," *The Journals and Papers of Gerard Manley Hopkins,* ed. Humphrey House and completed by Graham Storey (London: Oxford University Press, 1959), pp. 83–84. For a discussion of the import of parallelism in poetry from a linguistic point of view, see Roman Jakobson, "Grammatical Parallelism and Its Russian Facet," *Language* 42. (1966): 399-429. See also Paul Kiparsky, "The Role of Linguistics in a Theory of Poetry," *Daedalus* 102 (Summer 1973): 231-44.

[14]The stanza divisions used in this analysis are, of course, not in the printed text of the Book of Mormon, nor are they even suggested. They are, rather, divisions that the structure of the passage itself seems to dictate and have been used here to facilitate analysis. The line numbers refer to lines within the stanza. The terms *line* and *member* are used more or less synonymously. In the course of this discussion, several passages will be described as exhibiting introverted or chiastic parallelism. The term and concept of chiasmus have been widely discussed and have invited considerable speculation in certain circles; in the context of what follows, chiasmus is to be understood only in the sense of a rhetorical figure similar to *antimetabole* which has been used by writers—both religious and secular—since antiquity. The essential feature is an *abba* pattern in which the second part of the structure is balanced against the first but in reverse order as in the poetic line "Flowers are lovely, love is flowerlike." In the "Psalm of Nephi," it will be noted, chiastic structures are much more extended. (See the article on chiasmus in Alex Preminger, ed., *Princeton Encyclopedia of Poetry and Poetics,* enlarged ed. [Princeton: Princeton University Press, 1974], p. 116.)

[15]These embedded chiastic patterns could also well be considered in terms of the rhetorical principle associated with ring composition, a technique with a long and extensive history in which the final element in a series reflects or echoes the first in some way, the penultimate the second, and so on. This procedure was first investigated by W. A. A. van Otterlo in "Untersuchungen über Begriff, Anwendung und Entstehung der griechischen Ringkomposition," *Mededelingen der Nederlandsche Akademie van Wetenschappen, Afdeling Letterkunde*, NS 7, no. 3 (Amsterdam: Noord-Hollandsche Uitgevers Maatschappij, 1944); "Eine merkwürdige Kompositions form der alteren griechischen Literatur," *Mnemosyne*, 3d ser. 12 (1944); and "De Ringcompositie als Opbouwprincipe in de epische Gedichten van Homerus," *Verhandelingen der Koninklijke Nederlandsche Akademie van Wetenschappen, Afdeling Letterkunde*, NS 51, no. 11 (Amsterdam: Noord-Hollandsche Uitgevers Maatschappij, 1948). Cederic H. Whitman extends and amplifies this approach in *Homer and the Heroic Tradition* (Cambridge, Mass.: Harvard University Press, 1958). (See especially the detailed fold out chart at the back of the book. See also Julia Haig Gaisser, "A Structural Analysis of the Digressions in the *Iliad* and the *Odyssey*," *Harvard Studies in Classical Philosophy* 73 [1969]: 1–44.) This method of analysis has also been applied to literary traditions other than the ancient Greek (see David Buchan, *The Ballad and the Folk* [London: Routledge, 1972]; John D. Niles, "Ring-Composition in *La Chanson de Roland* and *La Chancun de Willame*," *Olifant* 1 [December 1973]: 4-12; John D. Niles, "Ring Composition and the Structure of *Beowulf*," *PMLA* 94 [1979]: 924-35.) Of particular interest in conjunction with the "Psalm of Nephi" is Michael Fishbane, "Composition and Structure in the Jacob Cycle (Gen. 25:19–35:22)," *Journal of Jewish Studies* 26 (1975): 15–38.

[16]The present arrangement in poetic lines and stanzas does not alone create, determine, or define per se the lyricism of the passage but rather makes more obvious the inherent lyric elements obscured by printing conventions. For an exchange of letters concerning the implications of typographical rearrangements, see the *TLS* of 4 February 1965, p. 87, for the beginning of the controversy which continues in the issues of 11 February 1965, p. 107, and 18 February 1965, p. 127, the latter touching on the question of biblical poetry. Finally, in a brief article in the issue of 25 February 1965, p. 147, an earlier (27 September 1928) letter of T. S. Eliot discussing the question is published. The question is also discussed by Hirsch, *Validity in Interpretation,* pp. 94–98. Jonathan Culler raises the issue with regard to the generic expectations that typographical rearrangements can imply (see *Structuralist Poetics* [Ithaca, N.Y.: Cornell University Press, 1975], pp. 161–62; see also Gérard Genette, *Figures II* [Paris: Seuil, 1969], pp. 150–51).

[17]Hans-Georg Gadamer argues convincingly that the essential difference between literary and nonliterary texts resides in their fundamentally different claims to veracity. "[D]er Unterschied zwischen einem literarischen Kunstwerk und irgendeinem anderen literarischen Text [ist) kein so grundsätzlicher. Gewiss besteht ein Unterschied zwischen der Sprache der dichterischen Prosa und der 'wissenschaftlichen' Prosa. Man kann diese Unterschiede gewiss auch vom Gesichtspunkt der literarischen Formung aus betrachten. Aber der wesentliche Unterschied solcher verschiedener 'Sprachen' liegt offenbar woanders, nämlich in der Verschiedenheit des Wahrheitsanspruches, der von ihnen erhoben wird." (*Wahrheit und Methode: Grundzage einer philosophischen Hermeneutik,* 3. erweiterte Auflage [Tübingen: J. C. B. Mohr (Paul Siebeck), 1972], p. 155.) It is, thus, questionable whether the "Psalm of Nephi" gives the reader any reliable information about Nephi's actions or attitudes. This view is contrary to that represented by Reynolds and Sjodahl and more recently by Steve Gilliland, " 'Awake My Soul!': Dealing Firmly with Depression," *Ensign* 8 (August 1978):37–41. (See also Frye, *Anatomy of Criticism,* pp. 74–76.) Gadamer's view of poetry, however, has not gained universal acceptance. Among

the opposing theories, for example, is that advanced by Kate Hamburgerin *Die Logik der Dichtung* (Stuttgart: Ernst Klett Verlag, 1957) in which lyric poetry is approached as "real utterance" (*Wirklichkeitsaussage*) having the same status as a historical narrative.

[18]T. S. Eliot advances this general argument in "Tradition and the Individual Talent," *Selected Essays,* new ed. (New York: Harcourt, Brace, and World, 1964), pp. 3–11. Though working within a very different framework, that of Russian formalism and semiotic theory, Julia Kristeva makes a similar point, ". . . tout texte se construit comme mosaique de citations, tout texte est absorption et transformation d'un autre texte. A la place de la notion d'intersubjectivité s'installe celle d'intertextualité, et le langage poétique se lit, au moins, comme double." (Σημειωτικη *Recherches pour une Sémanalyse* [Paris: Editions du Seuil, 1969], p. 146.)

[19]". . . toute oeuvre modifie l'ensemble des possibles, chaque nouvel exemple change l'espèce. . . . Plus exactement, nous ne reconnaissons à un texte le droit de figurer dans l'histoire de la littérature ou dans celle de la science, que pour autant qu'il apporte un changement à l'ideé qu'on se faisait jusqu'alors de l'une ou de l'autre activité. Les textes qui ne remplissent pas cette condition passent automatiquement dans une autre catégorie: celle de la littérature dite 'populaire,' 'de masse,' là; celle de l'exercice scolaire, ici." (Tzvetan Todorov, *Introduction à la littérature fantastique* [Paris: Scull, 1970], p. 10.)

[20]Dante *Purgatorio* 11.88–89. (The edition cited is that edited by Giorgio Petrocchi [Rome: A. Mondadori for the Società Dantesca Italiana, 1966–68].) The translation is my own. I side with Singleton against Grandgent in taking Dante's collapse to result from his contrition, the last stage of the sacrament of penance, rather than satisfaction. (See Charles S. Singleton, ed., *The Divine Comedy, Purgatorio, 2. Commentary,* Bollingen Series 80 (Princeton: Princeton University Press, 1973], p. 767.)

[21]To regard Nephi as a poet is entirely consistent with what is otherwise known about him. Hugh Nibley in *An Approach to the Book of Mormon*, 2d ed. (Salt Lake City: Deseret Book, 1964), pp. 220–21, notes that "in Lehi's day an inspired leader had to be a poet." Nephi, moreover, of all other figures in the Book of Mormon, seems most concerned with questions of language and is the most moved by the difficult yet lyrical mode of Isaiah.

Questions

1. How does understanding specific genres of sacred text help to interpret the scriptures? How can understanding genres of other secular texts help understand these texts as well?
2. What about a psalm makes it easier to translate than other poems?
3. What evidence does Sondrup use to argue that the Psalm of Nephi is translatable?
4. What are the implications of Sondrup's argument for readers of the Book of Mormon?

Logic in the Black Folk Sermon: The Sermons of C. L. Franklin

GARY LAYNE HATCH

Gary Hatch's "Logic in the Black Folk Sermon: The Sermons of C. L. Franklin" was first printed in Journal of Black Studies *and focuses on the rhetorical devices employed by preacher C. L. Franklin—father of singer Aretha Franklin—whose sermons in the fifties and sixties were so popular that they were released on blues labels and sold millions of copies. Franklin's preaching wasn't overt, but made implicit references to the civil rights movement. Hatch's article argues that the preaching tradition of African American culture, as exemplified by C. L. Franklin, holds a certain complex, poetic logic.*

In his rhetorical analysis of old-time Black preaching in Macon County, Georgia, William Harrison Pipes (1951) classifies and ranks the persuasive techniques used by various preachers. He concludes that the main persuasive strategy of these preachers is the emotional appeal. Pipes argues that folk preachers "excite the emotions of the audience" to help the audience "escape from an 'impossible world' " (p. 156). Pipes admits that the ethical appeal is also important for the Black folk preacher but argues that the logical appeal only appears in the sermons of "more highly-educated ministers" in "the less emotional points of the sermon" (p. 157). Pipes is not alone in assigning the emotional appeal predominance. Cowley (1966), in his study of Bahamian folk preaching, argues that the main strategy of the Black folk sermon is "to play upon the emotions of the hearers" (p. 16). Davis (1985) points out that the emotional element of Black folk sermons has traditionally presented a problem to some scholars. He notes that both Pipes and Cowley see the emotional nature of preaching as evidence of "a lack of sophistication and education" (p. 41). (Pipes sees education as the means of providing Black worshipers with a "normal" means of religious expression [1951, p. 158].)

One problem with Pipes's analysis is that he does not specify what criteria he uses to categorize persuasive strategies. Pipes gives plenty of examples of the emotional and ethical strategies of the sermons, but he does not tell how he isolated these examples. This flaw is particularly significant in his discussion of logic. Because Pipes does not outline what he means by logic, it is impossible to validate Pipes's claim that logical persuasion is largely absent from Black folk preaching. Pipes also talks about the presence of "inductive and deductive reasoning" in the sermons of more highly educated ministers, but he does not define these categories any further or cite any examples.

I will argue that the traditional definition of logic as inductive and deductive reasoning is much too confining for analyzing Black folk sermons. These sermons contain appeals to reason, but these appeals are not presented explicitly as a thesis with support or as claims backed by reasons and evidence. Nor does the preacher reason from individual instances to a general truth. The appeals to reason in Black folk sermons are embedded in the narratives, examples, comparisons, and biblical references chosen by the preacher. These narratives establish a series of relationships that appeal to the intellect and imagination as well as to the emotions. These relationships constitute a type of "poetic" logic in which reasoning is neither inductive nor deductive, but rather analogical, proceeding from one particular instance to another particular instance of the same relationship. I find this type of poetic logic in the sermons of Rev. C. L. Franklin, a preacher that is clearly within the tradition of "old-time religion" outlined by Pipes.

Clarence LaVaughn Franklin was born in Sunflower County, Mississippi, January 22, 1915. His stepfather, Henry Franklin, was a poor sharecropper. At the age of 12, Franklin joined the St. Peter's Rock Baptist Church; he began preaching at the age of 14. For a while, Franklin worked as a full-time circuit preacher in Mississippi, preaching at one of four different churches each Sunday. From his circuit in Mississippi, Franklin moved to the New Salem Baptist Church in Memphis, Tennessee, and then to the Friendship Baptist Church in Buffalo, New York. For the greatest part of his career, Franklin pastored the New Bethel Baptist Church in Detroit, Michigan, a church with a congregation numbering in the thousands.

In 1953, Franklin began recording sermons with Chess Recording Company. He recorded a total of 76 albums, many of which sold millions of copies. Franklin also had a successful radio ministry in Nashville. Through his record sales and radio ministry, Franklin's sermons reached millions of listeners. Franklin was a member of the Southern Christian Leadership Conference, and with Dr. Martin Luther King, helped organize the Detroit area Great Freedom March in June 1963. At this march, King first delivered his famous speech, "I Have a Dream."

Despite his family's difficult economic position, Franklin had numerous opportunities for education. After graduating from high school in Cleveland, Mississippi, Franklin finished a course of instruction at the Howe School of Religion, in Memphis. He received a BA from LeMoyne College and studied briefly at the University of Buffalo and at the Extension School of the University of Michigan. He received his divinity degree through the tutorship of Dr. R. B. Gayden. (For a more detailed account of Franklin's life, see Titon, 1987, pp. 86–105.)

Franklin's education had little effect, however, on the folk pulpit style he learned as a young man. Pipes (1951) characterizes this pulpit style in his study of preaching in Macon County, a style that Pipes argues is typical of Black preaching from slave times:

> The style of Macon County preaching is basically simple: short words which are familiar to the audience (with a long word thrown in occasionally for effect). Sentences are often elliptical (without complete subject and predicate). . . . Slang and Negro dialect (the language of the audience) form the level of expression. But the style is figurative, with the use of metaphor, based on the experiences of the audience or drawn from the Bible, taking the lead. The style is narrative—for the listener rather than the reader. (p. 157)

Franklin's style fits the model of Black preaching described by Pipes. Although Franklin does not use much slang in his sermons, his recorded sermons show that he does use traditional Black speech patterns. Franklin uses words his audience will understand and carefully defines any scholarly or unfamiliar terms he introduces to the audience. In "Ye Must Be Born Again," Franklin discusses the visit of Nicodemus to Christ by night. He is careful to define *Pharisee*, *Sadducee*, and *Sanhedrin* in terms that his audience will understand, comparing the Sanhedrin, for example, to the Supreme Court and calling Nicodemus a "court justice" (Franklin, 1989, p. 115). Franklin's sentences are often elliptical. Typically, after reading his scriptural text, Franklin will make a brief, elliptical statement that functions as a title or theme for his sermon. In "How Long Halt Ye between Two Opinions?" Franklin reads the text from 1 Kings 18:21 relating to Elijah and the priests of Baal and then says, "Israel in the throes of indecision. Israel in the throes of indecision" (Franklin, 1989, p. 71). In "Moses at the Red Sea," Franklin reads the text describing the children of Israel at the borders of the Red Sea, and he then says, "Facing a crisis with God. Facing a crisis with God" (p. 107). The largest number of elliptical sentences are found in the second half of each sermon, the half characterized by intoned chant'rag or "whooping." Consider this passage from "Without a Song":[1]

> O Lord.
> Everywhere,
> everywhere,
> ah everywhere
> (I don't believe you know what I mean,)
> oh everywhere,
> I said everywhere I go,
> every,
> yes
> ah everywhere,
> I said everywhere
> ohh!
> yes. (Titon, 1987)

Because this passage comes near the end of the sermon, where Franklin and his audience typically join in an enthusiastic emotional outpouring, it is not surprising that traditional syntax is ignored. Franklin's style is figurative. In "The Eagle Stirreth Her Nest," Franklin provides an extended comparison of God and an eagle. He also compares the members of the congregation to eaglets. In "Ye Must Be Born Again," Franklin compares the process of being born again to the metamorphosis of a tadpole into a frog. And in "Moses at the Red Sea," Franklin compares the Red Sea to adversity and the rod of Moses to the power of faith within each human being. He also compares Moses to Abraham Lincoln, Frederick Douglass, and George Washington Carver (1989, p. 107).

I will discuss figurative language at greater length later in this essay because the essential difference between my analysis and Pipes's analysis lies in how we each view figurative language. Pipes sees metaphor and comparison as an aspect of style, as a type of ornamentation. I see metaphor as an example of poetic logic, a type of concrete reasoning.

Franklin's sermons also fit the structure of the old-time sermons described by Pipes. According to Pipes, the sermon has four parts: the introduction, statement, discussion, and conclusion. The introduction often involves the reading of a scripture passage. The statement usually comes from the Bible. Pipes (1951) argues that the discussion "merely has the appearance of organization, for it is often a series of digressions aimed to arouse the emotions of the audience" (p. 157). He notes that "the more highly-educated minister" typically uses a more logical organization. The conclusion, according to Pipes is often absent when the emotional climax of the sermon is so intense as "to make articulate speech impossible" (p. 157).

Franklin typically begins by reading a passage from the scripture. He then makes a statement of his theme, usually in the form of a phrase taken from the passage or a phrase that refers to the passage. His discussion is divided into two parts: a spoken part and a part that involves intonation or whooping. He does not have a logical organization of the type imagined by Pipes, that is to say that he does not set forth a thesis and defend that thesis with reasons and evidence. Nor does he divide his sermon into logical parts. His sermons contain what Pipes might consider numerous digressions: narratives, comparisons, and examples that all relate in some way to the theme or subject set forth in the statement. In other words, Franklin's sermons are usually organized around a central image. Titon (1987) provides an example of how Franklin envisioned his own organization in the sermon "Without a Song":

> Singers
> Introduction
> Singing a distinguishing characteristic of man
> The effects that enslavement has upon oppressed peoples
> Israel should have sung
> The Negro sung in the night

The text of this sermon as it was performed shows that Franklin follows this organization of ideas. He begins by presenting his biblical text:

> By the rivers of Babylon, there we set down, yea, we wept when we remembered Zion. We hanged our harps upon the willows in the midst thereof, for they that carried us away captive required of us a song; and they that wasted us required of us mirth, saying, Sing us one of the songs of Zion. How shall we sing the Lord's song in a strange land? (Psalms 137:1–4; quoted in Franklin, 1989, p. 89)

The statement follows this text: "The subject that we're using tonight is, Without a song. Without a song" (1989, p. 89).

The discussion consists of a series of anecdotes and general observations. Franklin follows his outline, but he also includes a number of anecdotes and illustrations that are not part of his outline. He tells of the inhabitants of the West Indies who campaign for office through singing. He relates the story of Roland Hayes singing in front of the Nazis in Berlin. He tells the story of Mary, an old woman who is rejected by an English Methodist minister, and tells how the congregation comforts her by singing. "Without a Song" is organized in a topical and anecdotal fashion. Each "digression" or example relates back to the statement, "Without a song." I hope to show later that each example also has a logical progression that continues through both parts of the sermon to the emotional climax.

Pipes would most likely say that "Without a Song" lacks a conclusion because the sermon ends in an emotional climax.

Franklin does occasionally end in a spoken conclusion (in "How Long Halt Ye Between Two Opinions?" "Hannah, the Ideal Mother," "The Preacher Who Got Drunk," "A Bigot Meets Jesus," and "Meeting Jesus in the Dawn"). There is still a sense of closure, however, in the sermons that lack a spoken conclusion at the end of the intoned section. Pipes misses the fact that the emotional climax itself is a type of conclusion. In fact, the "calm to storm" format is one of the most common organizational patterns in Black folk preaching.

Because Franklin's sermons are so typical of what Pipes calls the old-time style of Black preaching, these sermons provide an opportunity for testing Pipes's claim that the logical appeal is largely absent from this style of preaching.

Consider "Without a Song" (Franklin, 1989). The scriptural passage describes the children of Israel captive in Babylon, far from their homeland. Their captors ask them to sing one of the songs of Zion. The psalmist asks, "How shall we sing the Lord's song in a strange land?" Franklin contextualizes the passage for his audience, describing how the children of Israel must have felt in this situation. Franklin takes the position that the children of Israel should have sung the songs of Zion in their captivity. He then moves to what might appear to be a series of digressions. First of all, Franklin discusses how it is natural for humans to want to sing and how humans can convey many messages through song. He gives the particular instance of the West Indians who campaign for office by singing. This example is not merely an illustration, however. Franklin mentions that the West Indians are under British rule. They are a people subject to a foreign government. They cannot get up on stage and speak, so they communicate their political views through music. Franklin's next story relates the visit of Black singer Roland Hayes to Berlin. Because Hayes is a Black man, the German audience refuses to be silent so that Hayes can sing. Hayes begins to sing above the noise of the audience, and his voice is so enthralling that the audience grows quiet and listens to him sing, "Lord, thou art my peace, thou art my peace." After his performance, many of the audience members rush to the stage and join in his song. Hayes is a Black man in a foreign land with an oppressive government. He wins their favor by singing one of the songs of Zion. Franklin then tells how the slaves sang for their White oppressors in the South. These illustrations are not mere digressions designed to hold the interest of the audience. Each story parallels the scriptural passage and establishes a set of correspondences that advance Franklin's argument:

Bible Text	*Illustration*	*Illustration*
Israel	Roland Hayes	African slaves
Babylon	Nazi Germany	slave owners
captivity	prejudice	slavery
did not sing	sang	sang

This matrix shows the relationships among Franklin's illustrations. Each column lists the essential components of each individual illustration. Each row shows the correspondences among the illustrations. Israel, Roland Hayes, and the African slaves represent those who are oppressed. Babylon, Nazi Germany, and the slave owners are the oppressors. Captivity, prejudice, and slavery are the types of oppression each group suffers. The final row indicates how each group responds to oppression.

Franklin's illustrations show how oppressed people should handle their oppression. The children of Israel are a negative example. Roland Hayes and the African slaves provide positive examples.

Franklin continues this argumentative strategy through the remainder of the sermon. His next story is about an old woman who goes to hear Charles Wesley preach. She is moved by his preaching and responds to his invitation for baptism. He rejects her because she is Black and tells her to go join a church for Black people. The other Black people, who are forced to remain outside during the sermon respond by singing:

> Oh Mary, don't weep, don't mourn;
> Pharaoh's army got drownded;
> Mary, don't weep, and then don't mourn.

In this case, Mary and the Black members of the congregation are oppressed by the White Christian church. The oppression takes the form of religious segregation. This story shows that the proper response to this segregation is singing a song of Zion. Mary and the Black Christians correspond to the children of Israel captive in Babylon. The White Christian church corresponds to Babylon. The verse from the spiritual also establishes a correspondence between Mary and the Children of Israel captive in Egypt and between the White church and Pharaoh's army.

Franklin continues the spoken part of the sermon with an extended discussion of the Black people in slavery. The slaves were prevented from wearing nice clothes, but they gained hope by singing, "I'm going to put on a long, white robe, one of these days." They could not ride in chariots, but they could sing "Swing low, sweet chariot, coming for to carry me home." They were not allowed to meet together for worship, so they had to meet secretly at night. They sang, "Steal away, steal away to Jesus. We ain't got long to stay here." With each example, Franklin shows how the slaves would sing one of the songs of Zion to give them hope in their oppressed condition. At the conclusion of the spoken part of the sermon, Franklin returns to the scriptural text, arguing that Israel should have sung the songs of Zion in Babylon because these songs would have helped Babylon to understand God's relationship with his people. Franklin then applies the text to his congregation, arguing that they should take the songs of Zion wherever they go and that they should not exclude themselves from others. In the intoned section of the sermon, Franklin repeats this theme and sings snatches from religious songs such as "Amazing Grace" and "On Jordan's Stormy Banks I Stand."

In "Without a Song," Franklin (1989) certainly appeals to the emotions of his audience. The story of Roland Hayes is designed to evoke feelings of pride and admiration just as the story of Mary calls forth feelings of pity. But the main function of these illustrations is to advance Franklin's logical argument that the members of his congregation should meet oppression and prejudice with songs that engender hope and understanding. This logical progression is not really deductive or inductive. It does not move vertically along the ladder of abstraction from general truths to specific instances or from specific instances to general truths. The logical progression in "Without a Song" is horizontal, from one specific instance to another. It is analogical. Each illustration provides a parallel instance of the same general truth that reverberates throughout the sermon. This type of reasoning is present in other sermons by Franklin. Consider "Dry Bones in the Valley" (Franklin, 1989). Franklin begins with his text:

> The hand of the Lord was upon me, and carried me out in the Spirit of the Lord, and set me down in the midst of the valley which was full of bones, and caused me to pass by them round about: and, behold, there were very many in the open valley; and, lo, they were very dry. And he said

> unto me, Son of man, can these bones live? And I answered, O Lord God, thou knoweth. And again he said unto me, Prophesy from these bones, and say unto them, O ye dry bones, hear the word of the Lord. (Ezekiel 37:1–4, quoted in Franklin, 1989, p. 80)

The controlling images in this sermon are Ezekiel as "son of man" and the valley of the bones. Franklin compares the valley to Babylon:

> So to Israel, we see in this vision, Babylon was a desolate place. Babylon represented a valley to Israel, a valley of depravity, a valley of disfranchisement, a valley of hopelessness, a valley of dry bones, a valley of lifelessness. (p. 81)

Franklin then compares the United States during the time of slavery to a valley:

> But to the Negro, when he embarked upon these shores, America to him was a valley: a valley of slave huts, a valley of slavery and oppression, a valley of sorrow. (p. 81)

The sermon also ties Babylon and Israel to African American slavery through the spiritual, "Ezekiel Saw the Wheel."

The valley of bones in Babylon is surrounded by a ring of "obstructing mountains": "Economic mountains, social and political mountains, religious mountains enclosed her in. And she was down here in the stagnant air of a valley in Babylon" (Franklin, 1989, p. 82). Franklin also compares this valley of the dry bones to life's problems:

> We know what the human problems are, we know men are mean, we know men are prejudiced, we know that men are narrow-minded, and we know they are selfish. We know men are unkind, ruthless, and cruel. We know men are murderers and sinful. But what we don't know is what to do about it! (p. 82)

As in "Without a Song," Franklin establishes a set of correspondences: Babylon, valley of dry bones, United States during slavery, life's problems.

The answer to each of these problems lies in the word of God preached by Ezekiel. Franklin says a number of things about Ezekiel. First of all, Franklin emphasizes Ezekiel's training:

> When we study his minute descriptions of the temple order and of the temple liturgy, when we read of his intimate knowledge of things directly or indirectly concerned with Judaism, we must conclude that he had formal training as a priest. (p. 80)

Franklin also stresses the importance of Ezekiel's role as a prophet or a preacher:

> You know, and the word *prophet* can be interchanged with the word *preacher*, for a prophet is a preacher, and a preacher ought to be a prophet. (p. 81)

The prophet is also one who receives visions. He has "sight, insight, and foresight" (p. 81). Franklin tells of Ezekiel's vision of the three wheels. According to Franklin, one wheel represents Israel. The wheel enclosing Israel's wheel represents Babylon, and the wheel enclosing both the other two wheels represents God's plan. Franklin's mentioning of this vision stresses Ezekiel's role as prophet and his knowledge of God's providence. But Franklin also stresses Ezekiel's role as "son of man," as a man limited in his vision and ability because he cannot answer the question, "Can these bones live?" Franklin equates Ezekiel's limitations as a "son of man" with human limitations in general:

> Son of man, you are a scholar, you are an educator. Son of man, you are a scientist: Can these bones live? Son of man, you are an engineer: Can these bones live? Son of man, you are a heart specialist; son of man, you are a geologist, you are a botanist, you are a specialist in various phases of the human body, you are a psychologist and psychiatrist, you know all about drives and reactions and responses and tendencies. I want to know with all of this knowledge can you tell me: Can these bones live? (p. 82)

Even though Ezekiel is a prophet/preacher and has received formal education, and even though he has had visions of the providence of God, he cannot comprehend how the valley of bones can live again. Franklin points out that the Lord even takes Ezekiel around the valley so that Ezekiel has a full understanding of Israel's problems, but Ezekiel, with his human limitations still cannot come up with a solution. The answer lies in preaching the word of the Lord to the bones.

The captivity of Israel in Babylon, slavery in the United States, and the obstacles faced by Franklin's congregation in the mid-1950s are all instances of the same problem—they each represent impossible situations that can be overcome only through the word of God:

> My Lord.
> "Tell those bones,
> "Hear my words."
> And that's my solution tonight,
> that's my answer tonight
> to every problem that we have:
> that is to hear God's words.
> Hear God's words.
> It's all right
> to go to the United Nations,
> it's all right
> to preach on international fellowship,
> it's all right
> to call on the scholars,
> to call on our businessmen,
> it's all right,
> but I tell you what you had better do:
> hear God's words,
> hear God's words. (Franklin, 1989, p. 87)

This passage shows the conflation of Israel's problems in Babylon with the problems faced by Franklin's congregation. It's all right to attempt to solve political problems through political means. In other words, it's all right for Ezekiel in his role as "son of man" to survey the valley of the dry bones to try to find a solution to the problem. But the only way out of an impossible situation is to hear the word of God.

"Dry Bones in the Valley" shows another instance of Franklin's use of analogical reasoning. He does not use Ezekiel's story merely as an example of his thesis; he presents the valley of the bones, slavery, and the problems of his congregation as parallel instances of the same problem. Again, the logical progression moves horizontally from one specific instance to the next.

The final sermon I will discuss is considered by many to be Franklin's greatest: "The Eagle Stirreth Her Nest" (Franklin, 1989). The controlling image in this sermon is the eagle. Franklin presumably begins by reading Deuteronomy 32:11–12 (the text is not included on the recording):

> As an eagle stirreth up her nest, fluttereth over her young, spreadeth abroad her wings, taketh them, beareth them on her wings: so the Lord alone did lead him, and there was no strange god with him.

Franklin states that the eagle symbolizes God and God's care and concern for his people. Franklin equates the nest with history and the eaglets with God's children. The stirring of the nest refers to God's changing people's circumstances to make them better:

> Some of the things that have gone on in your own experiences have merely been God stirring the nest of your circumstances. Now the Civil War, for example, and the struggle in connection with it, was merely the promptings of Providence to lash man to a point of being brotherly to all men. In fact, all of the wars that we have gone through, we have come out with new outlooks and new views and better people. (p. 47)

Early in the sermon, Franklin establishes a series of correspondences:

Eagle	God
Eaglets	God's children, human race
Nest	History, human circumstances
Stirring the nest	Adversity, changing human circumstances

The bulk of the spoken section of the sermon describes the attributes of the eagle that make it a fit symbol for God. Franklin points out that the eagle is regal, that the eagle is "king of the birds." This makes the eagle a fitting symbol for God because God is the king of kings. The second attribute of the eagle is strength. Franklin states that God is also strong. He compares God to a fortress or citadel that protects against the enemy. He also compares God to a leaning post that numerous people can lean on. The eagle's third attribute is swiftness. Franklin describes God's swiftness in freeing Daniel from the lion's den and in helping Peter to get out of prison. The eagle also has tremendous vision. The eagle can see a storm coming that is still far away. God has the same type of extraordinary sight:

> He can see every ditch that you have dug for me and guide me around them. God has extraordinary sight. He can look behind that smile on your face and see that frown in your heart. (p. 48)

In this section, Franklin is not merely enumerating God's attributes; he is also extending the system of correspondences he has already established:

Eagle	God	God	God	Citadel
Eaglets	God's children	Peter	Daniel	God's people
Stirring	Adversity	Jail	Lions	Enemy

Again, each column represents the narrative progression of a story or set of examples. Each row shows the correspondences between elements of each of these narratives. Through these correspondences, Franklin demonstrates that God has control over the circumstances of his people. He is able to deliver his people from their adverse circumstances whenever he sees fit. Franklin then addresses the issue of why God sometimes chooses not to deliver his people from adversity. He returns to the image of the eagle. He tells his audience that the eagle has an unusual way of building a nest. The eagle lines the nest with soft materials. After the eaglets are born, the eagle gradually removes the soft lining from the nest. The nest grows uncomfortable, so the eaglets want to leave the nest and learn to fly. Franklin compares this "stirring" of the nest to the adverse conditions humans frequently face:

> I believe that God has to do that for us sometimes. Things are going so well and we are so satisfied that we just lounge around and forget to pray. . . . God has to pull out a little of the plush around us, a little of the comfort around us, and let a few thorns of trial and tribulation stick through the nest to make us pray sometime. (p. 49)

Franklin then tells the story of the eagle that grew up in a chicken coop thinking it was a chicken. A man who knows about eagles comes to the farm, sees the eagle, and instructs the farmer to build a cage for the eagle. As the eagle grows larger, the farmer is to build bigger and bigger cages until the eagle becomes fully grown. At this point the cages would grow so uncomfortable that the eagle would want to fly with the other eagles and would leave the chicken coop. This story ends the spoken section of the sermon and continues into the intoned section. At first, this story may appear to be a digression, an afterthought on Franklin's part. But the story fits perfectly into the matrix of correspondences that Franklin has already established:

Eagle	Man who knows eagles	God
Eaglets	Eagle	God's people
Nest	Chicken coop	Comfort
Stirring	Cage	Adversity

Toward the end of the intoned section, Franklin adds one more set of correspondences based on the following passage:

> My soul
> is an eagle
> in the cage that the Lord
> has made for me. . . .
> my soul
> is caged in,
> in this old body,
> yes it is,
> and one of these days
> the man who made the cage
> will open the door
> and let my soul
> go. (Franklin, 1989, p. 53)

In this passage, God is the man who knows eagles and the man who made the cage. The eagle is Franklin's soul. The body is the cage. In accordance with the story, at some point, Franklin's soul will be set free from the body and will return to God.

"The Eagle Stirreth Her Nest" is more complex than the other two sermons I have discussed. In this sermon, Franklin's argument really has two parts. He has one matrix of correspondences to show that God has power to deliver his people from adversity. He has another matrix to show that God frequently does not deliver his people from adversity, so that they can experience growth. These two arguments are linked through the image of the eagle, the central image in the sermon. Part of the complexity of this sermon comes from the fact that Franklin uses the same image to describe both God and humans. The difference is one of degree: God is the grown eagle, and humans are eaglets. The double reference of this image implies that by relying on God and enduring adversity, humans can acquire some of the attributes of God and become like him.

Pipes's attempt to construct a hierarchy of persuasive strategies in Black folk preaching presents a number of difficulties. First of all, one must question the reasonableness of attempting to construct such a hierarchy in the first place. Pipes obviously favors the preaching style of educated ministers and the use of inductive and deductive reasoning. He uses his hierarchy to disparage old-time Black preaching. He sees this old-time style of preaching as the efforts of a frustrated and oppressed people to express itself. (The subtitle to Pipes's book is *A Study in American Frustration*.) His solution is to educate Blacks, to provide them with able leadership, and to extend to them all the opportunities of a democratic society (1951, pp. 158–161). Pipes predicts that once Blacks are removed from their frustrated condition, old-time Black preaching will disappear (1951, p. 158). One must admire Pipes's desire to improve social conditions in the Black community, but at the same time, one must reject his condescending attitude toward traditional Black folk preaching.

There is another problem with Pipes's hierarchy. He argues that Black folk preachers rely predominately on the emotional appeal because, in his analysis of the sermons, he has counted more instances of the emotional appeal than of the other appeals. He gives no consideration, however, to the degree of persuasive power that each instance carries. There could, for example, be only one instance of logical reasoning in a sermon, but that one instance could carry enormous persuasive power. It is difficult to see how one could measure the relative strength of a given strategy. This problem of intensity again calls into question the reasonableness of undertaking the task of ranking persuasive strategies in the first place.

The final problem I see with Pipes's study is that he does not specify the criteria he uses for his classification. Pipes's notion of logic is much too restrictive. The appeal to reason probably plays a much more significant role in Black folk sermons than Pipes imagines, but this appeal may often take the form of analogical rather than deductive or inductive reasoning. C. L. Franklin, a preacher in the old-time preaching tradition, uses systems of analogical reasoning that are often quite complex, systems that integrate logic, imagination, and emotion. I am not suggesting that the type of logical matrices Franklin establishes can be found in all Black folk sermons. There is the possibility that this type of reasoning is unique to Franklin. Some consider Franklin the master of the genre. He had more opportunities for education than some of his fellow preachers and admits that he consciously tried to make a logical appeal in his sermons (Titon, 1987, pp. 94–95). It would be useful, therefore, to test the sermons of other Black folk preachers for the presence of analogical reasoning—especially in those sermons studied by Pipes.

GARY LAYNE HATCH *received a BA* summa cum laude *from BYU and a PhD from Arizona State University with an emphasis in rhetoric and composition. He is an associate professor of English at Brigham Young University and has served as director of the English Composition office. He teaches graduate classes in rhetoric as well as a class in presidential campaign rhetoric, which he hopes will again be offered in the fall of 2000. Regarding that class, Hatch says, "I hope Jesse Jackson will run again so we'll have something interesting to talk about."*

Endnote

1. In his edition of selected sermons by Franklin, Jeff Todd Titon divides the sermon into two parts: a spoken part (represented in prose) and a chanted part (represented in poetry). Titon makes a line break whenever Franklin pauses for breath. The lines are indented to show musical pitch levels in Franklin's chant.

Bibliography

Crowley, D. J. (1966). *I could talk old-story good: Creativity in Bahamian folklore.* Berkeley: University of California Press.

Davis, G. L. (1985). *I got the word in me and I can sing it, you know.* Philadelphia: University of Pennsylvania Press.

Franklin, C. L. (1989). *Give me this mountain* (J. T. Titon, Ed.). Urbana: University of Illinois Press.

Pipes, W. H. (1951). *Say amen, brother! Old-time Negro preaching: A study in American frustration.* New York: William-Frederick.

Titon, J. T. (1987). Reverend C. L. Franklin: Black American preacher-poet. *Folklife Annual*, pp. 86–105.

Questions and Writing Assignment

1. How would you describe the structure of the black folk sermon? How is this structure "logos"?
2. How does the folk preacher also use emotional and ethical appeals?
3. What other kinds of texts may use analogical or "poetic" logic?
4. Write a sermon that follows a structure similar to the structures used by Franklin. How could this structure be adapted to an LDS audience?

Folklore, Ethics, and Conflicted Narratives

JACQUELINE THURSBY

While Jacqueline Thursby was working on her MA at Utah State, she had to come to a complete stop on a highway in Idaho to wait for a flock of sheep and their shepherds to pass. While she waited, she attempted to identify the language the shepherds were speaking, unsuccessfully. She found out they were Basques, and from that day has become intensely interested in studying Basque narratives. This particular article came out of her MA and PhD work on Basque Women's narratives. Yet in her work with Basque women, she has found that there are simply "some things that we do not build on" within ethnographic fieldwork. She found that her work often unearthed sensitive family issues, and has debated the inclusion of these items in her publications. In this article, she examines the differing narratives of three Basque-American sisters, and tries to sensitively approach the "bad blood" that surfaces as she examines the differences between the narratives.

In my research and collecting of Basque American women's narratives, I encountered three elderly sisters who have differing memories of several shared past events. In writing their narratives, subject to their approval before possible publication, there was no negotiation or compromise between them concerning their varying memories of past events. Each has constructed or invented her own narrative. In my dissertation collection of Basque American women's narratives, I omitted these conflicted stories. However, I believe that the variants should be collected and examined for folkloric elements, and that they should then be deposited in a folklore archive for possible use at another time.

Maurice Halbwachs states, "While the collective memory endures and draws strength from its base in a coherent body of people, it is individuals as group members who remember" (1980, 48). Shared histories and experiences, when retrieved and articulated for a researcher, can cause intense conflict and even estrangement between subjects. Though two of the sisters were usually not speaking to each other before I began my research with them, the third nearly separated herself from the other two because of conflicted memories inadvertently retrieved for my study. There is a question of ethics concerning whether or not to publish any of the information. I am using some of the material in a semi-fictional novel, but again, I am unsure as to whether or not it should be published until after their deaths. Like ideal medical practice, I believe that folklore should cause no harm. Again, Halbwachs reminds us that, "While these remembrances are mutually supportive to each other and common to all, individual members still vary in the intensity with which they experience them" (1980, 48).

> Memory's role in tradition bearers' accepting, rejecting, reshaping or even masking subject matter for depiction in folklore texts, and doing so in certain patterned and recurring ways, reveals how not only memory's passenger, (oral) history, but even the nature of remembering itself, is conditioned by cultural and personal restraints. (AFS News 26:1, 8)

One of the three sisters, Elena, came to America from the Basque Country in Northern Spain in the late 1930s, just after the Spanish Civil War. After marrying a Basque sheepherder in the United States, the couple settled in Idaho. They built a large home and invited her two younger sisters, Marya and Vera, to join them. At that time, the younger women lived with another sister in Guernica, in the Basque Country.

One example of differing memories among them arose in the recollections of the arrival of the two younger women in Shoshone, Idaho, in 1942. The oldest sister maintains that she and her husband were present at the arrival of the train, and that subsequent to meeting the young women, they all drove to a nearby town where the couple ran a boarding house for sheepherders (Elena 16 June 1990). The youngest sister, Vera, maintains that the husband was not present and that the oldest sister drove them to the boarding house where she lived and worked for several years (Vera 17 June 1993). The middle sister, Marya, maintains that though the couple was there to meet them, the home was not a boarding house. "It was just a private home" (Marya 21 April 1990).

It was not unusual for Basques to rent rooms to herders in California, Nevada, and Idaho. The sheepherders needed a place to stay, to receive mail, and to store their out-of-season gear. Many sheepherders worked in the United States for a few years, or even a decade, and then returned to the old country. Often they never had the opportunity to learn English, and the rooming houses, or even Basque hotels in larger cities, became social centers as well as familiar places of refuge in a foreign environment.

In one of the interview sessions with Marya, a widow but still active in helping to run her daughter's home, she told me about an incident that occurred during the time she was living in Elena's home. The boarding or rooming houses were nicknamed "marriage mills" because of the frequent pairing off and marriages that occurred between the herders and the young Basque female workers. Marya stated:

> One night there was a party for the sheepherders at Elena's house. Vera was invited, and Elena also invited some other girls from another boarding house. I had to leave. Elena said that I was ugly and the herders would never marry an ugly Basque girl. She said I had a bad nose. (Marya 17 June 1990)

Vera, the youngest sister, stated in an interview:

> Elena had a rooming house. She never said Marya was ugly. She had a party, but Marya didn't want anything to do with it. There has been bad blood between Marya and Elena for many years, and Marya left to work in a boarding house in Nampa. (17 July 1993)

This was not the first time the "bad blood" issue had been mentioned to me. I was first told in Boise by Alyse (3). I asked what the "bad blood" was about, and Vera answered that it was about control. Marya was an independent type, and Elena could not force her will upon her the way she wanted to (Vera 17 June 1993).

The conflicted memories of this incident revealed long remembered pain of exclusion. In Marya's version, Elena excluded her from the party by suggesting that she was too unattractive to interest any of the male guests as a possible marriage companion. Vera stated that Elena never said that Marya was ugly. The sheepherders were greatly respected by the Basque people; many established substantial wool-growing enterprises. Though disdained by outsiders, an industrious herder was considered a good catch for an immigrant Basque girl. As it all turned out, Marya married twice. Her first husband was a coal miner who died young; the second was an established rancher who raised sheep and cattle. Both of her husbands were Basque immigrants. Vera married a Basque sheepherder from Navarra and still lives in the house he built for her in Nevada. All three of the sisters are now widowed.

At a Jaialdi Festival (a Basque event usually held every five years in Boise, Idaho), in the summer of 1990, friends seated me at a specific table and then left to converse in Basque with people they had not seen for a long time. An elderly Basque woman leaned across a table towards me and said: "I hear you are collecting stories about us." This was Elena, the oldest of the three sisters.

I confirmed her statement and asked if she wanted to participate in the collection of narratives I was gathering.

"Yes, I do," she stated firmly. "I'll tell you my story now. You see that girl over there? That beauty? She is my granddaughter, but she didn't know it until a few years ago. She was adopted and raised by a couple in Idaho, a doctor and his wife—non-Basques and Protestants. Knowing nothing of her blood heritage, she decided that she would like to become a Catholic. The priest who was teaching her was a Basque. He encouraged her to search for her origins, and she learned that she had been born out-of-wedlock to a young Basque couple. They gave her up for adoption to the doctor. Eventually the search led to me, and I know I am her grandmother.

"I paid for a year of history and language study in the Basque Country for her, and now she spends her summers with me in central Idaho. The family at our ranch, my family, refuses to acknowledge her as one of us" (Elena 16 June 1990).

I made notes of the conversation when Elena leaned back in her chair to rest. We were soon joined by other relatives, and small talk about the festival and weather ensued. Elena had given me her home address and telephone number, and I was looking forward to interviewing both Elena and her granddaughter at a later date. It was a very hot afternoon, and I left my chair at the table to find something cool to drink. Elena offered to buy me some wine which I declined. She also invited me to have dinner with her later; I declined that also because I was unsure how long I would stay at the Jaialdi Celebration that day.

As I was walking towards the refreshment stand, a woman, a relative of Elena's who lived in Boise at the time, took me by the arm and said she wanted to tell me something about Elena. She said:

> She does not tell the truth all of the time. Also, she is the sister of Marya who has helped you a lot. There is bad blood between them. If you want to continue with Marya, and the other sister Vera, it would be best not to have anything to do with her. (Alyse 16 June 1990)

I have continued my research among the Basque American women, but I have never had the opportunity to go to central Idaho to visit further with Elena and her granddaughter. I have learned, in the course of the interviews with other women, that Elena, a widow, may leave her entire estate to the granddaughter. In the old Basque tradition, a complex primogeniture (which is still practiced occasionally in the United States as well as occasionally in the Basque Country in Northern Spain), the bulk of an estate is willed to the oldest living heir, male or female. Because of Elena's decision, a serious family rift has occurred. Elena had several children, now all adults, and the oldest is a son who has run the sheep business and ranch since before his father, Elena's husband, died. Elena, I was told, intends to ignore her oldest son and leave the estate to the "found" granddaughter. Basque American women from Southwestern Idaho, who wish to remain anonymous, have suggested that there is no proof that the girl is a biological relative of Elena's. The "bad blood" between Marya and Elena continues, and it has been reaffirmed by acquaintances of the sisters in several interviews. At this point, the oldest son and his family spend seasonal holiday celebrations with their Aunt Marya and her family; Elena is never invited. However, Elena lives near this same family in her own home at the Idaho ranch.

ANALYSIS

The narratives I have collected from Basque American women are frequently value-laden glimpses of very personal autobiographies. Roy Pascal wrote that "even if they [the subject] tell us what is not factually true, or only partly true, it is always true evidence of their personality" (1960, 1). The lore of the "bad blood" between the sisters, its origins, the continued oral transmission of the situation among people who are acquainted with the sisters, and the social arrangements made because of it, place the "bad blood" episode into the realm of folklore. In writing the information for presentation, publication, or even for family records, the researcher faces ethical choices. Is it appropriate to reveal informants' regret or pain for scholarly or family perusal and curiosity?

What about my own imposed values revealed by the inevitable selections I must make among vast collected materials? Discussion of language as an interactive phenomena subjectively appropriated by the researcher continues to be at the center of scholarly discussions of leading anthropologists, folklorists, and linguists (Clifford and Marcus, 1986; Dolby-Stahl, 1989; Duranti and Goodwin, 1992; Briggs, 1993; Linda Degh, 1995). Pascal calls autobiography a "shaping of the past'" (1960, 59). In collecting biographical information, or even folklore, the teller shapes a story for the researcher, and the researcher shapes the telling even further by determining what is included and what is excluded in his or her research report. Hidden agendas and political agendas can and do influence representation.

In interviewing these three sisters about their lived-experiences, it was evident that emotion often surrounded the original experiences and still colored the memories. That reality added psychological dimension to the analysis. One of the questions to ask concerns the importance of having only one version. After these interviews, Vera nearly broke off her lifelong relationship with Marya, according to Marya's daughter, when she was unable to convince her sister of her point of view about Marya's invitation to the party and the comment about Marya's looks. Another question: What is the psychological function of the transmitted story about the bad blood? My guess is that it somehow serves as a link to a cherished heritage. Is it their constructed evidence that there are still innate threads of "Basqueness" that go beyond North American acculturation and assimilation? The narratives were kept and valued enough by the informants to transmit to their families, mutual friends, and to the interviewer. The sisters each shaped their stories and assigned meaning to their experiences "by means of emphasis, juxtaposition, commentary, and omission" (Smith 1987: 45). Reflecting on the past incidents, two of the three expressed regret at the state of their relationships with one another. Yet, because of dimming recollections and determination to preserve personal dignity, the pain of estrangement remains for two of them and occasionally threatens the precarious position of the third sister caught between the others' so-called "bad-blood."

The struggle for power by the oldest sister continues to manifest itself in ambivalent complexities. The narrative she shared at the festival represented a benign giver. I was invited to share wine and food with her. Further, she has chosen to bestow her estate on the "found" granddaughter. Anthropologist Mary Douglas once wrote, "Goods are used for establishing social relations" (1980: 9). Folklorist Linda Degh stated that folklore is "a sensitive and immediate indicator of what we feel most deeply" (Degh and Vazsonyi, 1973: 8). One might wonder what need this oldest sister has in perpetuating inevitable disappointment and probable feelings of "bad blood" on into the next generation. An interesting aspect of the "bad blood," is that at the Jaialdi table, Elena and Marya made small talk about the day's events. An uninformed onlooker would discern no conflict in that polite conversation.

The woman at the Jaialdi, Alyse, who informed me first of the "bad blood" and suspected lying on the part of Elena, opened up an ethical and practical dilemma for my research. The question was, of course, should I pursue Elena and the granddaughter to see, possibly, how the grandmother was transmitting Basque culture and heritage to the girl? Or should I forego that in order to maintain my relationship with Marya and Vera and other individuals they had referred me to? Geographical logistics determined my response more than ethics; I moved to Ohio for a few years. My curiosity still remains, but I have not pursued further interviews with Elena.

My argument is that in writing collected stories for publication, family history, or archival repositories, each variant of collective memories, lore, or narratives can and should be recorded. This would accurately represent differing perspectives of the shared events. Reciprocal ethnography (Lawless 1992: 313), is a way of confirming representations of the subjects and it doubly confirms subjects' release of information. The collector's analysis of the collection can be viewed as "guessing at meaning" as Clifford Geertz suggested. Truth and authenticity may be interwoven with deliberate deceit from some informants, and the researcher may have a hidden political, social, cultural, or even economic agenda; I believe the reader will interact with these issues and either discard or value the information for his or her scholarly work and purposes. "Entextualization," a term used by Charles Briggs, is associated with "producing particular kinds of texts in the service of social and political agendas" (1993: 390). Folklore as a genre of social science, has been inclusive of all social and cultural groups during its infant one-hundred sixty (or so) year history. The study of intertextual comparisons between individuals or cultural groups willing to subject themselves to anthropological and folkloric scrutiny and analysis continues to be a key to informing students of the common ground and common human condition that link groups with even vastly differing characteristics. Tracing folkloric or vernacular anecdotes through generational or regional variants is an authentic method for historical scholarship. Comparing metadiscursive practices, and grasping the contrasts and similarities between myriad examples of rhetoric, behavior, and artifacts; that is, "things people say, things people do, and things people make" (Wilson, 1986:225), can only draw students and scholars closer to understanding that each one of us is, curiously, the other's Other.

JACQUELINE THURSBY *is currently an assistant professor at BYU. She received her bachelor's degree in English education at Idaho State, her master's at Utah State and a PhD at Bowling Green State University. She teaches classes such as English teaching procedures, introduction to folklore, women's folkore, women's culture, and literature, myth, and folkloristics. Thursby has published and presented at numerous conferences on English education as well as folklore. Her book,* Mother's Table, Father's Chair: Cultural Narratives of Basque American Women, *is to be published in Winter 1999, by Utah State University Press.*

Works Cited

Alyse. 16 June 1990. Personal Conversation. Boise, Idaho. "1997 Annual Meeting Call for Papers." *American Folklore Society News.* 1: 8.

Briggs, Charles L. 1993. "Metadiscursive Practices and Scholarly Authority in Folkloristics." *Journal of American Folklore* 106: 387–434.

Clifford, James, and George E. Marcus, eds. 1986. *Writing Culture: The Poetics and Politics of Ethnography*. Berkeley: University of California Press.

Degh, Linda, and Andrew Vazsonyi. 1973. *The Dialects of Legend*, Folklore Reprint Series 1, no. 6 (Bloomington, Indiana: Folklore Publications Group), 8.

Degh, Linda. 1995. *Narratives in Society: A Performer-Centered Study of Narration.* Helsinki: Suomalainen Tiedeakatemia Academia Scientiarum Fennica.

Dolby Stahl, Sandra. 1989. *Literary Folkloristics and the Personal Narrative.* Bloomington and Indianapolis: Indiana University Press.

Douglas, Mary. 1980. "Introduction." *The Collective Memory by Maurice Halbwachs.* New York: Harper & Row Publisher, Inc.

Duranti, Alessandro, and Charles Goodwin. 1992. *Rethinking Context: Language as an Interactive Phenomena.* Cambridge: Cambridge University Press.

Elena. 16 July 1990. Personal Conversation. Boise, Idaho.

Geertz, Clifford. 1973. *The Interpretation of Cultures.* New York: Basic Books, Inc.

Halbwachs, Maurice. 1980. *The Collective Memory.* New York: Harper & Row Publishers, Inc.

Lawless, Elaine. " 'I was afraid someone like you . . . an outsider . . . would misunderstand': Negotiating Interpretive Differences Between Ethnographers and Subjects." *Journal of American Folklore* 105: 301–314.

Marya. 21 April 1990. Tape-recorded Interview. Rupert, Idaho.

———. 17 June 1990. Personal Conversation, Boise, Idaho.

Pascal, Roy. 1960. *Design and Truth in Autobiography.* Cambridge, Mass.: Harvard University Press.

Vera. 17 June 1993. Tape Recorded Interview. Elko, Nevada.

Wilson, William A. "Documenting Folklore." In *Folk Groups and Folklore Genres: An Introduction.* Ed. Elliott Oring. Logan: Utah State University Press, 1986.

Questions

1. How can these three sisters give such different versions of the same event? Can you recall a time when you and a friend or family member remembered the same event quite differently?
2. Why do the differences among these sisters lead to conflict? In general, how can differing interpretations of texts and of our experience lead to conflict?
3. Is one version of the truth in this case necessarily the only correct one? Can we always determine the truth from recollected experience? Does finding the truth always matter?
4. What is the role of the folklorist in responding to the conflict caused by differing interpretations? What is the ethical response, getting involved or not getting involved?
5. What is "entextualization"? What implications can this principle have for how we read and write?

On Getting the Story Crooked (and Straight)

ALAN L. WILKINS AND
MICHAEL P. THOMPSON

Alan Wilkins and Michael Thompson share an interest in cultural change. As they have collected accounts of change within organizations, they have found that the stories they collected were extremely simplified—the stories were "straight" when the reality was much more "crooked." While they suggest a healthy skepticism of organizational narratives, they hope this does not turn into a complete cynicism; they simply encourage a "greater appreciation both of [narrative's] limitations and of its power." They suggest that narratives be treated as if they were haiku—one small facet of the truth that, when combined with multiple facets of the truth (or other narratives), can eventually "provide real understanding." Their article is reprinted from The Journal of Organizational Change Management*—a British journal—and it retains the original spelling and punctuation, which sometimes differs from Standard American English.*

Over the past year, we have been collecting accounts by change agents (external and internal) about culture change (Wilkins *et al.*, 1991). Our impression, especially in organisations where we have been personally involved as researchers or consultants, is that the stories, while persuasive, are too "straight"; they gloss over much of the messiness, the conflict and the detail of culture change.

In this article, we suggest some ways to remind us when the story is too straight. We will try to "get the story crooked" (Kellner, 1989, p. 3) in ways that can help us to acknowledge its constructedness. We will nevertheless suggest that getting the "whole story" of culture change is neither possible nor useful. We suggest how to acknowledge the incompleteness of stories about change while using them as temporary guides for the organisation's journey.

The Misuse of Stories about Culture Change

A colleague of ours recently received a request to "develop the same kind of video culture change process for our plant that you provided for the

Silver Creek plant". The request came from the manager of another plant in the company where they were both employed. Our colleague was amused and surprised! He was amazed that someone would think the wrenching cultural changes they had been through in the past three years were produced by videotape.

The plant had gone from last to first place in quality among the seven plants in its division. More importantly, it had achieved best-in-class, or best in the world, ratings (fewest repairs per 1,000 parts in the first year of service) in each of its seven product areas. People in and out of the plant were hailing the "dramatic culture changes" that produced these results.

Our colleague and the plant management team had produced a video describing some of their efforts to develop a "quality culture". The video was in large part a compilation of vignettes filmed over a two-year period where employees talked about what they were doing differently and how they felt about it. Apparently the internal auditors who evaluated the Silver Creek plant for a very rigorous and prestigious quality classification in the company had seen the video during their visit. They took a copy of the video with them to "tell the Silver Creek culture change story" wherever they went in the company.

The story, as heard by other plant managers, described the dramatically improved results and pointed to the video as the centrepiece of the change effort. According to the story, plant management had focused the attention of everyone in the plant on the abysmal quality numbers and asked for employee input. Then our colleague filmed various groups of employees who were enthusiastically supporting the programme. At first there were only a few really good employee efforts to chronicle, but as employees saw the videos of their cohorts in other parts of the plant they got on board and made their own improvements. Of course, plant executives involved their employees in the same statistical process control and continuous improvement training that other plants were receiving, but the real gains came from the employee enthusiasm fuelled by the videotaped "stories from the front line".

Our colleague was amused by the story because it missed not only the detail but the spirit of the change efforts. For example, the feeling of those involved in the change was that it had not started with a focus on quality at all, that it was much more political, and much less complete, than the story claimed. Management began the change with an effort to "improve the supervisory skills of supervisors". A cultural investigation, which the first author of this article helped management perform, led them to realise that they must first work on their own management skills and team relationships if they were to influence supervisors to behave differently.

Following six months of conflict-ridden struggles, they realised that they were responsible for much of the adversarial culture in the plant and they looked for a common goal that would unite them and help them develop pride of accomplishment among employees. Quality was the least controversial goal they could find.

In addition, there were myriad details about negotiating with the union; keeping division executives from knowing about their efforts and from meddling; the purchase of new equipment; the training in interpersonal problem solving, etc., that were critical aspects of what made the change possible. How could people be so gullible?

We have noted the enthusiasm of those who believed the initial story, waning in recent months. They were discouraged somewhat when they heard more about the complexity of the change and the degree to which the plant managers themselves had struggled to change personally. They have been further discouraged by news that the Silver Creek plant is not continuing to improve at the same rate that it did before.

As we have reflected on these experiences, we see a fascinating process through which responses to organisational narratives both fuel and scuttle organisational change efforts. It seems that stories of success provide assurance about outcomes and suggestions about how to go about changes. On the other hand, they also foster discouragement and even cynicism about the possibilities of change. And, in both cases, people rely more heavily on what are inevitably incomplete and even inaccurate accounts than seems reasonable.

Why are organisational leaders so susceptible to these narratives? How can we learn to think and talk more effectively about organisational changes? We live in a time of increasing international competition, rapid technological development, governmental deregulation and changing demographics. These and other factors have combined to present unprecedented challenges to change our organisations dramatically and continually. If leaders behave as true believers at one moment and cynics the next they are not likely to cope successfully with the chaotic world in which we live.

OUR PERSPECTIVE ON NARRATIVES

Narratives, or stories, are powerful tools for shaping action and reducing information overload. Stories are like maps in that they are tentative representations of what we think the real organisational "territory" looks like, but they are not the territory itself. Stories are, we believe, the primary tools with which organisational participants map their reality.

We need to provide a working definition of narrative. Any kind of organisational scheme expressed in story form is narrative (Polkinghome,

1988, p. 13). But we want to delimit the sense of this somewhat by drawing upon Jerome Bruner. Bruner says that all narratives have certain fundamental minimalist properties. They involve sequentiality. Events or mental states or observations in narrative are made over time, or within time. Narratives also involve some kind of agent or performer of actions, and those actions are expressed through a voice, a narrator or speaker (Bruner, 1990, pp. 46–9). Without narrative, Bruner says, it is impossible to make sense of our social experience, or to frame our expectations. Without narrative, there is no human past or future. We frame our experience in narratives.

The Power of Narratives

Research shows the power of stories in fostering belief in, recall of, and commitment to ideas presented in narrative form (Wilkins, 1983; see also Martin and Powers, 1983). Part of the power of stories, when compared with other means of making truth claims (e.g. logical support, statistics, statements of "fact"), is that when stories are full of vivid details and organisational significance they allow us to experience events vicariously and therefore to believe and remember what we hear. In addition, stories are often all we have to go on. That is, we don't usually experience more than a small part of the complex and diverse activities of the organisations to which we belong. A principal way we get a sense of what occurs and how things "really work" in organisations is through the stories we hear from others. As Weick and Browning (1986) point out:

> The sheer complexity of organizations and environments will put a premium on devices that store complexity in a compact, retrievable manner. And there will always be a premium on devices that reduce large inputs to small outputs (pp. 254–5).

They go on to argue that stories are the ideal devices of simplification. When we recognize the power of narratives in grappling with the problem of understanding and changing complex organisations, we see why executives and others might be "suckers" for a good story about organisational change. They probably have never been involved in such significant change and are a ready audience for stories about "successful" and "unsuccessful" experiences of others. That is especially true if the stories are performed persuasively by "eye-witnesses" (O'Barr, 1982, pp. 61–87).

NARRATIVES ORGANISE AND GUIDE ACTION

If stories are in many cases too powerful, then, why not just debunk stories and awaken organisational participants to the "truth"? Most of the interest in organisational culture in the past decade stems from the hope that when participants come to share a general view of the world, and some common ways of acting in that world, they will act more in concert and with greater competitive advantage than if they were motivated only by supervisors watching or by a rule manual. This argument contends that such concerted action is particularly critical when participants face challenges to innovate, to change, or to produce quality responses to a variety of different customers. Each of these situations makes commitment to the organisation and willingness to learn together more important than rigid rules and supervision or control. Stories become one of the primary means of passing on central ideas about the kind of company we are and common practices about how we do things together (Wilkins, 1984; Wilkins and Ouchi, 1983). They can give concrete examples of the big ideas of the organisation. They can at the same time illustrate the way things are done. Indeed, Burton Clark (1970) studied three distinctive small colleges and argued that the single most critical motivating factor in their distinctiveness was what he called an "organisational saga", a story of unique accomplishment about the institution which was passed on to succeeding generations. The saga operated to foster pride and commitment to the organisation and to encourage many stakeholders (alumni, students, faculty, external academics and administrators) to maintain and foster its success.

Thus, organisational narratives can become powerful motivating and directing guides to action in organisations. When believed and shared by some number of participants, narratives can provide enough general direction for a whole organisation to embark on new and otherwise improbable paths. They organise action through belief and commitment in a way that rational means of control and influence cannot. However, as noted earlier, stories can also lead to cycles of "true believerism" and cynicism.

NARRATIVES AS MAPS

Of course these cycles begin when we think and talk of stories as reality rather than as guides. We suggest that stories are best thought of as guides, as a kind of map.

What are maps good for? Maps reduce things to the essentials we need at the moment. If a map were as complex as the territory itself, it would be useless. Maps do not give all the details and that is exactly what makes them useful. If a map depicting the route from Seattle to San Diego left nothing out, it would have to be 1,256 miles long, and would be very difficult to fold and store in the glove compartment of the family car. Kenneth Burke says that a road map that can guide us across a continent owes its "great utility to its exceptional existential poverty" (Burke, 1966, p. 5).

We are struck by the utility of maps, even incorrect ones. For example, Columbus proposed that he could reach the Indies, the land of spices and gold, by sailing about 2,400 miles. The actual air distance between the Canary Islands and Japan, the route Columbus proposed to sail, is about 10,600 miles (Boorstin, 1983, p. 227).

When Columbus eventually sailed with support from Ferdinand and Isabella of Spain, his map and presentation were still both very "wrong" and very persuasive. But the map was accurate in many important respects, and it reflected a persuasive vision of possibilities. As the Renaissance historian, J. R. Hale observes, "Without a theory, mariners like Columbus and Magellan would not have sailed, and could not have found backers" (Noble, 1981, p. 66). The maps of the Renaissance explorers were not simply technical efforts. They were also rhetorical strategies that gave the most plausible face to an optimistic vision. Implicitly the Renaissance explorers were saying, "We concede that we're probably wrong about a lot of things, but we believe that we're *essentially* right, and we're going to find what we're looking for if we can get enough help to take the journey".

The maps that organisational members produce are a lot like that. To become paralysed by quibbles and technical details is probably not as useful as asking the question, "Can we agree that this is the best map we can construct now, and that if followed, it will lead us to our next, clarifying destination?"

When we think of narratives as maps of reality we realize that they are a construction, crafted for a particular purpose, and that they are not true. Especially when participants in organisations experience change and chaos in their "territory", they must become much more aware of the constructed nature of the narratives that guide their actions. Looking at them in this way allows us to see that people struggle to "get the story straight" in ways that inevitably make the map both more useful (because it is abstracted from reality to focus on a few of the many things that occurred) and at the same time more inaccurate (because they necessarily ignore other points of view, ways of thinking, aspects of the change, etc.).

Getting the Story Crooked

We can protect ourselves from "map-territory" confusion when we use a map (or story) by asking:

(1) What is outside the frame of the map (or story)?
(2) What is highlighted in the map (or story)?
(3) What aspects are ignored or downplayed within the map (or during the time frame of the story)?

We return to the stories referred to earlier about quality improvements in a machine tools company to illustrate what such questions might uncover.

OUTSIDE THE FRAME

The first author has been attempting for two years to write a case description of the change efforts at the Silver Creek plant. One of the barriers to approval to release the case has been a debate about when to begin the story. Union officials and some of the executives who were in the plant in the early 1980s believe that the turnaround began with the very awkward process of working out a relationship with each other. They didn't feel comfortable talking about anything but sports scores for the first several meetings with each other, so stereotyped and adversarial was their relationship. Together they developed an employee involvement (EI) programme that created groups of employees who would meet to focus on work-related improvements, make recommendations to management, and take action.

However, the new plant manager and several others believe relationships and performance in the plant were still abysmal when they arrived in 1985. The way they tell the story, real improvement did not occur until after their arrival. By contrast, the consultants, who arrived in 1987, tell the story about the changes that occurred following their arrival. Certainly, in this case, storytellers tend to see themselves at the middle of their stories and start their stories in ways that focus on their perspective and influence.

The end of the story is also problematic. Stories told of culture change at the plant often end with a list of significant improvements in the quality of the plant's products and with a much less adversarial relationship between plant and union officials. Indeed, these officials meet every Monday morning and collaboratively consider the status of plant performance and employee concerns. Plant output has continued to improve.

On the other hand, improvement is not as fast as many expected. Many, in and out of the plant, realise that Japanese competitors continue to improve at a faster rate and that greater changes must yet occur in the plant if they are to remain competitive. The current story being told by plant executives is one of "galloping expectations" by their bosses and some of the employees. They are not sure how they can keep up with the expectations that have been created.

HIGHLIGHTS INSIDE THE "MAP"

Different tellers focus on somewhat different aspects of the efforts to change the plant culture and performance. Some highlight the way that momentum for change was built by videotaping employees talking about their progress in making changes. Others detail the training of supervisors in more collaborative problem-solving behaviours. Many of the plant executives focus attention on the six months of painful personal and team changes they engaged in before they did anything with the rest of the plant. They also suggest how difficult it was to keep the division executives (their bosses) from meddling in the change efforts. They share with each other the "creative accounting" procedures they used to maintain change efforts while downplaying the financial commitment involved.

All of the versions we have heard about the change effort focus on the "planfulness" and good intentions of the people involved. The picture one gets from these stories is that most people knew all along what needed to be done and that finally the other people started listening to and working with them, resulting in eventual success. However, there were many other aspects of the organisation during this time frame that were not represented in any of the versions of the story about change.

WHAT IS NOT HIGHLIGHTED IN THE "MAP"

No versions of the story highlight the actions or point of view of division or corporate executives. Most of the employees in the plant would not agree with the sense of planfulness represented in the story as told by their union officials. Their day-to-day struggles to fight boredom, to try to understand what all of the excitement is about, do not get talked about much.

Most interesting to us, however, are the ways that people systematically decide what to leave out of the story. For example, plant executives do not want us to write about the belief of many of the employees, expressed to us in interviews and overheard by us in informal conversations, that during the late 1970s and early 1980s the attitude of executives seemed to be to "beg, borrow, steal—whatever you had to do—to get pieces out of the door, regardless of quality." Executives do not usually say so but they seem to be concerned about the negative publicity for them and the company if such an attitude were expressed.

Employees never mention that many of them were working five or eight hours during normal hours and then working overtime to make plant quotas. Many of them were worried that plant improvements would mean they would lose the extra income they had come to expect.

Union officials do not want any mention of the feeling by employees that most of the officials come from the ranks of the more educated skilled-trades people (electricians, maintenance people, etc.), represented an ethnic group and spoke Italian in their union meetings. Those who do not speak Italian feel left out and believe that the officials have led, and continue to foster to a lesser extent, resistance to improvement efforts.

TELLING CROOKED STORIES

So if there is so much that stories do not represent, including very critical and contradictory information, why not tell more crooked stories? Of course them are many reasons, not the least of which is that people want to keep the story straight in ways that make the most sense to them and that foster a point of view that will benefit them. Nevertheless, let us consider briefly what crooked stories might look like.

Crooked stories would have to include more attention to such things as: multiple perspectives, ambiguous beginnings and endings, unclear and complex causes, lack of endings (everything stays dynamic and in flux), and arguments over what should get into the story (see Martin and Meyerson, 1988). Certainly such stories would be "reflexive"— that is, they would call attention to themselves as merely a story that in spite of its crookedness still did not do justice to the complete "territory" of organisational change and behavior.

Most of the usefulness of the map, as we discussed earlier, comes from its "existential poverty." If it too closely duplicates the complexity and detail of the territory, it becomes overwhelmingly unhelpful for many purposes. We suggest the same is true for stories. Most of the time for most people the story will be constructed to enable understanding and appreciation of only part of the total complexity of the organisation.

As a result, we argue that our most important task as agents and students of change is to tell and listen to straight stories but retain "crooked ears".

GETTING THE STORY STRAIGHT

If we listen with "crooked ears", remembering the constructedness of stories, however, we can easily become cynics about any story. That is not our intent. In this regard, we see stories as being akin to Japanese *haiku*. *Haiku* are typically one-line phrases, crafted so as to highlight a particular relationship or bit of wisdom. The theory behind the poetry, we are told, is that truth is like a bright sun which is covered by a thick veil (of ignorance). Contemplating and apprehending the meaning of *haiku* is like piercing the veil with a sharp needle, thus allowing a sliver of light to come through. After apprehending the meaning of many *haiku* one comes to appreciate multiple facets of truth which in combination provide real understanding.

In a comparable way, stories about culture change may reveal facets which can, in combination with other facets, provide useful insights. We start with the premise that culture change is complex, is perceived differently by different participants and observers, and will inevitably be oversimplified by any story told to capture it. The solution is not to tell ever more complex stories but rather to train ourselves to think about stories as maps and *haiku* while remembering the limitations of stories as illustrated above.

Wanted: Better Producers and Consumers of Stories

In general, we believe that our narratives about cultural change are in danger of becoming too simple and too much believed. However, we hope that our efforts to encourage others to be more sceptical of organisational narratives do not lead to cynicism. There is no escape from narrative. We will continue to frame our organisational reality by telling stories about it. And if we treat the stories as maps and *haiku* we have much to gain. We are arguing not for the replacement of narrative, but for a greater appreciation both of its limitations and of its power.

We have seen organisations where participants get involved in building stories together and updating them on occasion. They take a more experimental approach to their efforts and are much less often prone to the true believer-cynic cycle we noted here (Wilkins, 1989). There are, nevertheless, times when they are willing to suspend disbelief and work together as if they believed that their current view of the world were the only possible one and that their tasks were extremely clear (see Dalton and Wilkins, 1990). Such vacillation between doubt and complexity, on the one hand, and passion and certainty, on the other, seems both ironic and critical for the times in which we live.

ALAN WILKINS *is currently the Academic Vice-President of BYU. He received a BA and MBA at BYU, and a PhD in organizational behavior at Stanford. He has taught classes at BYU such as organizational culture, Book of Mormon, and courses in organizational behavior in the MBA program.*

MICHAEL THOMPSON *is an associate professor in the Department of Organizational Leadership and Strategy. He received a BA in classics at BYU and an MA in technical communications and a PhD in rhetoric at Rennsselaer Polytechnic Institute. At BYU, he teaches primarily graduate classes, such as management communications and management philosophy and style. His current research centers on communication effectiveness and team effectiveness.*

References

Boorstin, D.J. (1983), *The Discoverers,* Random House, New York.

Booth, W.C. (1988), *The Company We Keep: An Ethics of Fiction,* University of California Press, Berkeley.

Bruner, J. (1990), *Acts of Meaning,* Harvard University Press, Cambridge.

Burke, K. (1966), *Language as a Symbolic Action,* University of California Press, Berkeley.

Clark, B. (1970), *The Distinctive College: Reed, Antioch and Swarthmore,* Hawthorne, New York.

Dalton, G. and Wilkins, A.L. (1990), "The Hurrier I Go the Behinder I Get: Lessons from Attempts to Improve Time to Market", Manuscript, Brigham Young University Marriott School of Management.

Kellner, H. (1989), *Language and Historical Representation: Getting the Story Crooked,* University of Wisconsin Press, Madison.

Martin, J. and Powers, M. (1983), "Organizational Stories: More Vivid and Persuasive than Quantitative Data", in Staw, B. (Ed.), *Psychological Foundations of Organizational Behavior,* Scott, Foresman, Glenview, Il, pp. 161–8.

Martin, J. and Meyerson, D. (1988), in Pondy, L., Boland, R. and Thomas, H. (Eds), *Managing Ambiguity and Change,* Wiley, New York, pp. 93–126.

Noble, J.W. (1981), *The Mapmakers,* Alfred Knopf, New York.

O'Barr, W.M. (1982), *Linguistic Evidence: Language, Power and Strategy in the Courtroom,* Academic Press, New York.

Polkinghorne, D.E. (1988), *Narrative Knowing and the Human Sciences,* State University of New York Press, Albany.

Weick, K.E. and Browning L.D. (1986), "Argument and Narration in Organizational Communication", *Journal of Management,* Vol. 12 No. 2, pp. 243–59.

Wilkins, A.L. (1983), "Organizational Stories as Symbols Which Control the Organization", in Pondy, L., Frost, P., Morgan, G. and Dandredge, T. (Eds), *Organizational Symbolism,* JAI Press, Greenwich, CT.

Wilkins, A.L. (1984), "The Creation of Company Cultures: The Role of Stories and Human Resource Systems", *Human Resource Management,* Vol. 23 No. 1, pp. 41–60.

Wilkins, A.L. and Ouchi, W.G. (1983), "Efficient Cultures: Exploring the Relationship Between Culture and Organizational Performance", *Administrative Science Quarterly,* Vol. 28, pp. 468–81.

Wilkins, A.L., Thompson, M. and Dyer, W.G. (1991), "A Consumer's Guide to Stories about Culture Change", in Gersick, C. (Ed.), *Frontiers in Human Resources,* UCLA Press, Los Angeles.

Questions

1. What are the differences between a "straight" and a "crooked" story?
2. Why are narratives particularly persuasive?
3. How can you get both the crooked and straight version of a story? What can be gained by getting both versions of a story?
4. In addition to organizational narratives, what other kinds of texts have crooked and straight interpretations?

Picasso's Visual Metaphors

JON D. GREEN

Jon Green has always been "fascinated by [Picasso's] strange ways," especially his way of "bringing together opposite things into a new unity." In "Picasso's Visual Metaphors" (first published in The Journal of Aesthetic Education*), Green shows how part of Picasso's genius rests in the way he effectively uses the principle of metaphor: a comparison between two inherently dissimilar things (for example, Picasso takes a bicycle seat and handlebars and makes them a bull's head). "All intelligence, all discovery," he says, "is based on Lehi's law of opposition . . . on the ability to put together two unrelated things." This ability to put together opposing things—the goal of metaphor—is a fundamental aspect of the connectedness that Green says is lacking from much thought. "The fun of learning," Green says, "is seeing the connectedness of things." He shows in this essay that Picasso not only understood this principle, but was a master of it.*

From the time I first saw a photograph of Picasso's *Bull's Head* (fig. 1), a remarkably realistic portrait made from a bicycle seat and handlebars, I was struck by its wry humor and the mongrel nature of its medium. Once I even made up a departmental exam tentatively likening Picasso's sculpture to literary metaphor (the question was later deleted by a more orthodox colleague). But it wasn't until I happened upon an article by V. C. Aldrich on "Visual Metaphor"[1] that my bloodhound instincts were aroused. His article began with an intriguing quote from Picasso himself: "My sculptures are plastic metaphors. It's the same principle in painting."[2] There it was! Picasso himself had verified my long-standing suspicion that there was such a thing as visual metaphor, and his *Bull's Head* was a prime instance. This article will explore the definition and function of visual metaphor in selected paintings and sculptures from Picasso's works. Before rushing headlong into the quicksand of inter-arts analogies, however, it would be wise at the outset to mention at least three potential problems and my tentative solutions.

First, the quotation Aldrich draws on comes from a widely used but largely discredited biography of Picasso by his former mistress, Françoise Gilot, and her art-journalist friend, Carlton Lake.[3] Dore Ashton excluded the Picasso quotations found in Gilot's biography from her own anthology of Picasso quotations, saying that "the mixture of possible

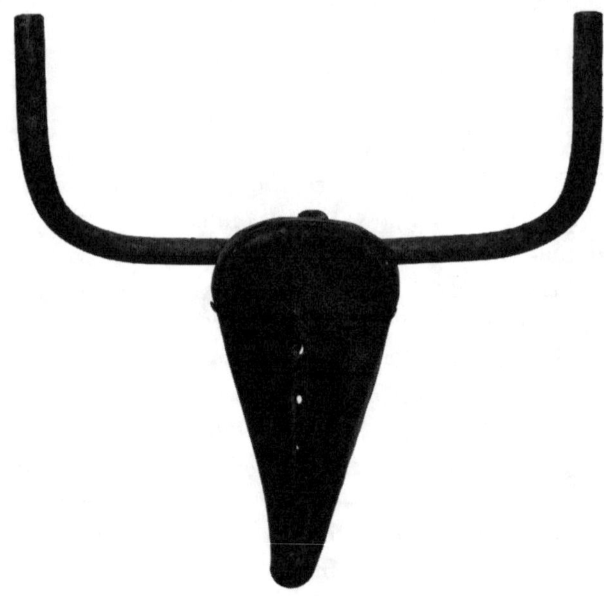

Figure 1. Picasso's *Bull's Head*

authentic statement and artful paraphrase seems to me to be of dubious value."[4] Nevertheless, there is a grain of truth even in a self-serving or distorted paraphrase. Even the forty-four distinguished artists who lodged the public protest and supported Picasso's unsuccessful libel suit did not dismiss everything in the book as patently false but merely as "factually unreliable." My position is to assume that what Gilot said Picasso said was generally true and to verify it by testing the ideas on the works themselves.

A second, less serious concern is Picasso's own doubt about the value of art criticism generally, perhaps because he of all artists has been most academically exploited. He warns, "Those trying to explain pictures are as a rule completely mistaken,"[5] because, he says later, "A painting, for me, speaks by itself; what good does it do, after all, to impart explanations?"[6] My answer to that is the same one Socrates gave concerning the "wisdom" of poets: "It is not by wisdom that the poets create their works, but by a certain instinctive inspiration, like soothsayers or prophets, who say many fine things, but understand nothing of what they say."[7] The same could be said of any artist, of course. Picasso's "native" language was not words but visual images—he knew how to draw before he could read or write.[8] That he resorted to defining his sculptural "collages" as visual metaphors says something about the tyranny of words in human communication, but it also betrays Picasso's insight into the possibility of deeper structures of common meaning beyond medium differences. His final word on the matter was, "Everyone wants to understand art. Why not try to understand the songs of a bird?"[9]

The third problem arises whenever an aesthetic principle associated primarily with one artistic medium is transferred directly to another: in this case, "metaphor," a central concept in speech and written literature, is used to define a special expressive domain of the visual arts. I am defining "metaphor" here in the general Aristotelian sense of giving one thing a name that belongs to something else because of some kind of similarity between them. The thing being described—Juliet, for example—is illuminated by comparison—e.g., to the sun. I. A. Richards clarified the relationship of the compared units by calling the idea or object (Romeo's love for Juliet) the "tenor" and the image by which the idea is conveyed (the sun) the "vehicle."[10] Within the area circumscribed by these two poles there exists a tension between the literal and the figurative, the meaning of the former poetically expanded by association with the latter. Because of the different manner in which the verbal and visual mediums render images—the former with greater individual imaginative latitude, the latter with more graphic immediacy—verbal metaphors tend to exploit the figurative pole, while visual metaphors gravitate toward the literal. For this reason, certain richly figurative images in literature become absurd when translated into actual images. For example, Nathaniel Hawthorne's short story "Dr. Heidigger's Experiment" was made into a fine short film, but there were certain verbal metaphors in the story which would not have worked had they been transferred directly into cinematic "language." How could any visual image convey the rich metaphorical associations in the story between the revived red rose and the long-dead Sylvia Ward without appearing absurd? "It [the red rose] was scarcely full blown; for some of its delicate red leaves curled modestly around its moist bosom."[11]

Visual Figures of Speech: Simile, Metaphor, Symbol

What does it mean to say that an art object is a visual metaphor? What, for example, would be an equivalent visual analogy to Shakespeare's "Juliet is the sun?" Perhaps a portrait of a radiant Juliet with a face resembling the form or color or position of the rising sun? Aldrich, for one, defines visual metaphor as a "fusion" or "interanimation" of two visual images (A and B), whose colors, forms, or positions cause us to link them visually into a single (though complex) metaphorical unit (C).[12] It is important to realize that metaphor is not simply a shorthand for simile but is more closely allied to the original meaning in Greek, to "carry across," hence to transfer meaning from one thing to another unlike it.

The inter-animation of A and B gives birth to a third thing, C, in which A and B are *aufgehoben* (transcended). "Thus though the realization of C may be logically dependent on A and B, and on some resemblance between them, yet to be aware of C is not to be aware simply of A and B or simply of their likeness."[13] Like a pebble in a pool, Shakespeare's metaphor, with great economy of means, sets loose in our minds a rich series of pregnant associations: by being compared to the sun, Juliet's image becomes the center of Romeo's personal universe, drawing him inexorably toward her radiant, gravitational center. For him she is the ultimate source of all light, love, and life.

Fairly clear and legitimate visual analogies to verbal figures of speech can be found in the visual arts. John M. Kennedy has noted several, including *oxymoron* (a man drawn with a halo and horns, for example), *persiflage* (a Disney rendition of the Crucifixion), *personification* (a depiction of a machine with human features), or even pictorial *puns* (use of a line element in a drawing in two incompatible ways).[14] Owen Barfield sets up a continuum of degrees of comparison among simile (A is like B), metaphor (A *is* B), and symbol (A is liquidated in the symbol B).[15]

It is not difficult to find visual correspondents to these more universal figures of speech. An example is Mary's close theological identification with Christ, a prevalent theme in Christian art. Van der Weyden's *Deposition* (fig. 2), for instance, depicts the dead Christ and the swooning Mary in virtually the same elegant semireclining position. The formal similarity of the visual pairing parallels the cause-and-effect relationship between the two holy personages, as if to say, "Mary suffers like Jesus in that his physical agony and death are played out again in her spiritual

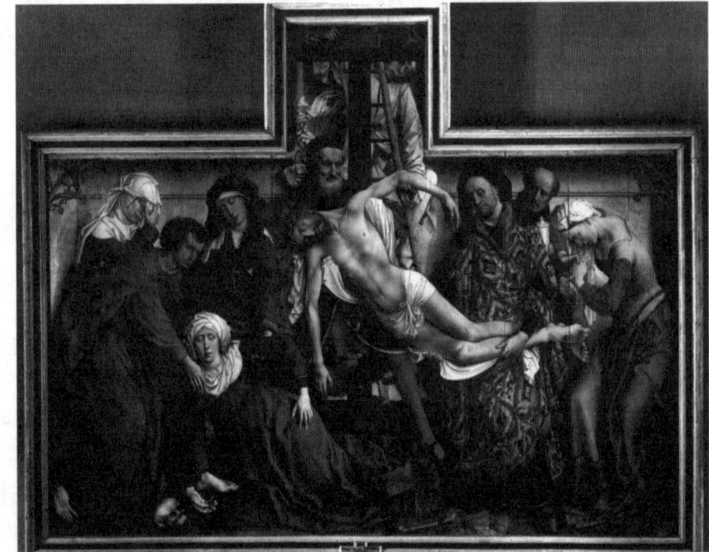

Figure 2. Van der Weyden's *Deposition*

anguish, amplified by the sorrowing figures supporting the two limp bodies." In such a highly charged religious context, the visual simile sets in motion mental associations as rich as those found in a Shakespearean sonnet.

Mary's portal on the west façade of Chartres Cathedral describes with simplified but highly symbolic visual forms the stages leading up to Christ's birth and blessing in the temple. Although the "story" is to be "read" from left to right and bottom to top (Annunciation, Visitation, Nativity, Adoration, and Presentation), the central portions of each level function as visual metaphors. Mary and the infant take up parallel reclining positions in the lowest level, suggestive of the visual simile noted earlier, but the encasement which encloses Mary and supports the Christchild creates a double (compound) metaphor: Mary, "entombed" after giving life to the Son, prefigures visually the Son's death, while the baby, positioned cocoon-like above her, anticipates the resurrection as well as his future sacrifice, an image made more obvious in the center of the next level, where the infant is placed upright on the altar of the temple. Finally, the child is sheltered between the knees of a crowned, haloed Mary in the center of the tympanum above, the two forms metaphorically "fused" in parallel positions as if on thrones, where the Christchild becomes the fruit emerging from the loins of the Queen Mother of Heaven, his physical birth anticipating both spiritual rebirth into the kingdom of God ("except a man be born again . . .") and his final victory over death as the "first-fruits of the resurrection." Again, the mental associations radiate out from the central metaphor: Christ's passion can be read in the patterns of the Virgin's own life. The whole, seen in toto, suggests the vertical movement from death to resurrection, earth to heaven, pain to epiphany.

The late fifteenth-century *Portinari Altarpiece* of Hugo van der Goes contains a symbol topically connected to the preceding simile and metaphor. The sharp leaves protruding from the foreground vase of irises (the German word is *Schwertlilien* = sword lilies) point to Mary's future vicarious suffering, suggesting the sword which pierced Christ's side while on the cross as well as Simeon's parenthetical warning to Mary in the temple: "Yea, a sword shall pierce through thy own soul also" (Luke 2:35). Moving from simile to metaphor to symbol creates an ever tighter connection between the things compared, until the distinctions are liquidated in symbol. The special evocative power of visual metaphor, however, derives from the tensions created by retaining an awareness of the contradiction between A and B as well as their fusion in C.

The subject matter of Picasso's *oeuvre* reads like the inventory of a very conservative museum: nudes, seated portraits, still lifes, bathers, and so forth. The complexity of his art is obviously not in the *what* but in the *how*. As he himself admitted in 1946, "It is not necessary to paint a man with a gun. An apple can be just as revolutionary."[16] Therefore, it is sometimes easy to overlook the subtle visual clues to metaphorical meaning in his two-dimensional works. Yet, given his acknowledged tendency to erotic fantasy, for example, a critic with even latent prurient interests can have a field day with certain periods devoted to the depiction of female figures: paintings full of visual puns connecting the human physiognomy to sexual organs; or evocative Freudian metaphors, such as psychosexual castration, which betray themselves in often savagely contorted facial grimaces.[17]

GUERNICA AS RESERVOIR OF VISUAL FIGURATIONS

The one work which harbors perhaps the richest trove of visual "figurations" (similes, metaphors, symbols, etc.) is Picasso's most powerful and most famous painting, *Guernica* (fig. 3). Once our sight is set on the possibility of visual metaphor, even a cursory exploration of this stunning work uncovers prodigious numbers of "metaphorical" connections. On the literal level, the light at the top of the canvas, for example, is an elliptical electric ceiling fixture, the "tenor" of the visual metaphor in Richards's terminology. Figuratively, however, as "vehicle" in the context of Picasso's allusions to classical and Christian iconography, it evokes wide-ranging associations that connect opposites in often paradoxical fashion. In one of the early stages of *Guernica*, this part of the picture was dominated by a flowering sunburst.[18] In the final version, this optimistic image of warmth and life-giving light gives way to a sterile, metallic "electric sun" bristling with threatening spikes which dominates the top center of the canvas "like some cyclopean eye."[19] It hovers over the scene of carnage but illuminates nothing, representing ironically "the coldness of an inefficient power," as Rudolf Arnheim writes, "a symbol of detached 'awareness,' of a world informed but not engaged."[20] Its elliptical shape

Figure 3. Picasso's *Guernica*

"echoes" the projectile shape of a bomb inserted into the gaping mouth of the horse, a symbol of the people, Picasso tells us.[21] As contiguous, parallel ellipses, the two forms "inform" of a significant, though paradoxical, metaphorical connection: the technological sources of beneficent power also contain the seeds of violent destruction, both ends achieved with equal efficiency. The Nazi saturation bombing quickly transformed a city into an inferno. Indeed, the "electric-sun" image easily translates into and eerily anticipates the first nuclear fireball eight years later. The threatening sterility of its form is subtly suggested by the black shadows its "rays" cast on the grey background behind, as though it were a foreign yet real object hovering over the canvas itself.

The actual illumination in the painting emanates from a more primitive and natural source of light, an oil (or kerosene) lamp placed at the apex of the pyramidal pattern in the center of the canvas. The lamp, though it exhibits a general likeness to the shape and content of the "electric sun," represents a quite different meaning. There is a dramatic shift from light as alien, destructive force to light as symbol of truth or, since the lamp is held aloft by a classicized nude thrusting her arm and "tragic-mask" head through the open window, as lamp of liberty. Below, another, analogous female figure lumbers anxiously upward toward the light, half kneeling, half running from the fiery destruction at the right. The downward-pointed spiked rays of the "electric sun" are inversely repeated in the spear-pointed flames of the conflagration devouring house and human on the extreme right. Thus, the destructive flames are linked iconographically to the central ambiguous metaphors of light as dual sources of life and destruction, truth and deception, culminating, on the left side of the canvas, in the bull's tail that suggests a wisp of smoke from an extinguished wick. The visual evolution of images from right to left marks the triumph of brutality and the spread of darkness. As an emblem of victimization, the screaming horse occupies a central position in the pyramid of light, an oblique but pictorially potent allusion to Christ.

In this new religious context, the abstracted light functions as a compound metaphor, both as aureole, suggesting the holiness of human life, and as abstracted crown of thorns. The allusion to Christ continues in the image of the gaping mouth as "the cry of sacrifice and martyrdom,"[22] the protruding spear as Centurion's lance, and the grieving woman and dead child on the left as "pietà" figures. The pyramid of light, buttressed by two adjacent side panels, recalls the traditional triptych form of a medieval altar, with the half-figures on either side acting as hinges.[23] It is, however, "a triptych submerged in a single panel"[24] in the manner of the Renaissance variant, the *sacre conversazione* (sacred conversation), as exemplified by Domenico Veneziano's *St. Lucy Altarpiece*. Picasso drastically alters Veneziano's reverential Renaissance tone by transforming this traditional scene of introspection into one of explosive violence. Yet it retains a deep sense of the sacred by contrasting the blatant contemporary profanation of human dignity with the sacred aura of medieval piety associated with the triptych form.

The headlong sweep of falling figures from left to right across the canvas in progressive stages of approaching death recalls the falling pattern of another favorite medieval theme, the Deposition, which is reminiscent of the overlapping stages of a time-lapse photograph. The visual analogy is significant, for the Deposition was designed to amplify the believer's sorrow over the suffering and death of Christ, the poignant calm after the storm. Here, Picasso expands the theme to embrace all suffering humanity, framed on each end by the two women of the side panels who represent the two extremes of human suffering: physical agony (death by fire) and bereavement (suffering for a loved one). The heads, alike as those on two coins, conduct a tragic dialogue with heaven. Their arms are flung out "in a symmetrical choreography"[25] at equal yet opposite angles (one reaching up, the other down), the bodies creating two triangular patterns pointing in opposite directions; one is suffering in mute (closed-mouth) agony, the other is hurling a Cassandra-like scream of cosmic proportions into the impassive face of the bull.

As Frank D. Russell suggests, the structural organization of *Guernica* combines in uneasy tension the competing values of classical restraint and romantic fervor. In a concatenation of overlapping, interlinking forms that break in and out of both triangle and triptych, classical (rectilinear) geometry attempts to hold burgeoning (curvilinear) living forms in check but buckles asunder in the process. Thus the prevailing structural metaphor depicts immanent cosmic disintegration. Certainly the total absence of any relieving color beyond black, white, and shades of grey bespeaks the absence of life, for life not only is curvilinear but also has color. The color harmonies of *Guernica* are only the incinerated remains of life—ash and dust, one of the most ubiquitous and dehumanizing metaphors of all. Thus, in *Guernica* we find *intrinsic* metaphorical connections marked by the similarity of forms which lead the mind to extrapolate deeper philosophical significance. This occurs by means of formal associations (through likeness)—as in the similar elliptical forms of the central light images—that link together such diverse objects as halos, crowns, suns, bombs, flames, and light fixtures into the central thematic conflicts of *Guernica*. *Extrinsic* metaphorical associations are established by allusions to formal conventions outside the painting itself, such as the classical pediment or pyramid, the medieval triptych, the cathedral façade, and the overlapping patterns of Christ's descent from the cross. In a manner reminiscent of Randall Jarrell's war poem, "The Death of the Ball-Turret Gunner,"[26] where death in the belly of a bomber is paradoxically likened to an abortive birth, Picasso exploits visual contrasts between light and dark, war and peace, truth and error, humanity and inhumanity, to generate some of his most potent and profound visual images.

As mentioned above, verbal metaphors set up mental oppositions between the figurative and the literal poles. Compared with similes, which may literally be true, metaphors are, literally speaking, false statements that nevertheless contain large amounts of "figurative" truth. Interestingly enough, these tensions between figurative and literal truth are the subject of many of Picasso's philosophical digressions on art. Eventually they precipitated his early Cubist experiments with collage, the technique that led to sculptural "combines" like his *Bull's Head.*

ILLUSION VS. REALITY

Picasso once said, "Art is not truth. Art is a lie that makes us realize truth."[27] For Picasso "truth" was almost synonymous with nature, with reality—"I work not after Nature but like Nature," he said.[28] But a mere four years after its birth in 1907–08, Cubism threatened to dissolve into abstract patterns totally divorced from reality. To counter this tendency, Picasso invented collage, i.e., the pasting of real objects onto paintings. Thus he set in motion a dynamic, often ambiguous tension between the real and the illusory (the real vs. the illusionistic is the visual equivalent of the literal/figurative tension in verbal metaphor). His first collage, *Still Life with Chair Caning* (fig. 4), poses the question "What is real?" by

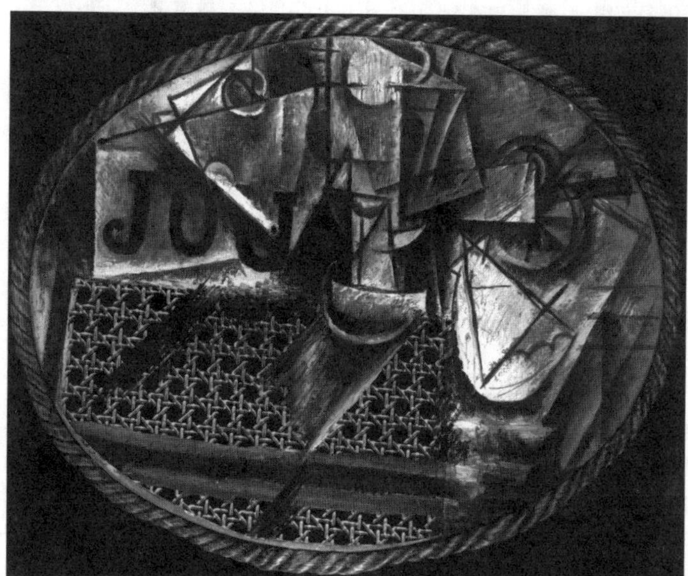

Figure 4. Picasso's *Still Life with Chair Caning*

creating a tantalizingly unresolvable visual puzzle. "The caning on the oil cloth looks as real as though it ought to be rough to the touch; yet it is fake, and smooth. The glass and the lemon look 'unreal' because their forms are Cubist; yet because they have been painted, they are 'real' aspects of the painting. The rope around the painting is 'real' as rope; but because it serves as frame, it suggests wood carving and therefore functions as illusion."[29] The puzzling effect of this unusual painting, which we might call a philosophical metaphor made visible, would be lost were it not for the curious interaction of reversed expectations between real and imitated objects. Where earlier artists had striven to "trick the eye" (*trompe l'oeil*), Picasso went beyond that to "a more profound likeness, more real than the real"[30] by tricking the mind, as it were, an effect he himself called *trompe l'ésprit*.[31]

Barfield's continuum from simile to metaphor to symbol curiously parallels the overall development of modern art out of the Renaissance *trompe l'oeil* tradition: increasingly successful attempts to make the aesthetic image look like the real thing led to the Cubist experiments with collage, combining unrelated real objects into new metaphorical relationships. The next logical step was taken by Marcel Duchamp in the creation of his "ready-mades," manufactured objects which stood for whatever the creative eye of the artist chose; an inverted urinal became a fountain; a metal bottle rack, a beautiful *objet d'art*. Warhol approached the absurd end of this line of development with his Campbell's soup cans, which he eventually simply bought off the grocery shelves and signed. The greatest potential for metaphorical illumination, however, seems to reside in those works caught between the poles of the illusionistic (figurative) and the real, namely, collages and combines. They seem to match most closely Picasso's "metaphorical" definition of art as a "bridge . . . reduced to a thread, a line, without anything left over; which [fulfills] its function of uniting two separated distances."[32]

To return to Picasso's original quotation, he said: "My sculptures are plastic metaphors. It's the same principle as in painting."[33] This was his reply to Françoise Gilot's question concerning the reason why he assembled ready-made objects instead of molding or carving his forms from the usual materials. Picasso's point, according to Aldrich, is that the resulting visual metaphor is not only more conspicuous when the parts possess an independent identity, but that the metaphor itself can move both ways between the poles of the illusory and the real. Picasso's *Goat*, for example, whose ribbed belly was fashioned from a wicker basket, illustrates "compound metaphor with a two-way thrust":[34] the wicker basket can be seen as the rib cage, or, conversely, the rib cage can become a wicker basket. As Picasso explained it, "I move from the basket back to the rib cage:

from the metaphor back to reality. I make you see reality because I used the metaphor."[35]

Bull's Head as Visual Metaphor

The way Picasso discovered his *Bull's Head* in a junk pile betrays the creative kind of seeing Albert Rothenberg has called "homospatial thinking," that is, the ability to conceive of "two or more discrete entities occupying the same 'space'. . . leading to the articulation of new identities."[36] Rothenberg concludes, after interviewing many types of artists, that metaphors, whether visual or verbal, naturally result from such thinking during the creative process. Picasso's account of his "discovery" in the junkyard parallels Rothenberg's profile quite closely: "One day I found in a pile of jumble an old bicycle saddle next to some rusted handlebars. In a flash they were associated in my mind. . . . The idea of this *Bull's Head* came without my thinking of it. . . . I had only to solder them together."[37] Each new viewer experiences Picasso's synthetic illumination in reverse when realizing that the bull's head was born of a marriage between two visually and functionally separated bicycle parts. The metaphorical "fusion" of parts works well, but there is also a material unity which results from Picasso's "bronzing." "What is wonderful about bronze," he says, "is that it can give the most incongruous objects such a unity that it's sometimes difficult to identify the elements that make them up. But it's also a danger: if you only see the bull's head and not the saddle and handlebars from which it's made, then the sculpture loses its interest."[38] Like an optical illusion, the *Bull's Head* would lose most of its charm if one were unable to flip into the bicycle mode at will. Further, it would cease to contain any metaphorical tension between the pair of real objects and the aesthetic image they together create.

The *Bull's Head* affects us in ways comparable to Picasso's painting *Still Life with Chair Caning*, mentioned earlier, by simply blurring the distinctions between reality and illusion. But once Picasso has linked the two bicycle parts into a visual metaphor, then unified and transformed the parts into the homogeneous form of a bronze sculpture, he anticipates a further stage by reversing the process. He imagines that someone might discover his discarded bull's head in a scrap heap and say: " 'Why there's something that would come in very handy for the handlebars of my bicycle.' And so a double metamorphosis would have been achieved."[39] Part of the value of Picasso's perverse kind of tampering with our normal expectations is to drain old images of their cliché-ridden contents and to invest worn-out metaphors with new life. Elaborating upon his answer to Françoise's question, he said: "The form of the metaphor may be worn-out or broken, but I take it, however down-at-the-heel it may have become, and use it in such an unexpected way that it arouses a new emotion in the mind."[40] This visual renewal is perhaps Picasso's most significant contribution to twentieth-century art. He is, indeed, "a contriver of glorious surprises."[41]

In discussing the stylistic range and pattern of development of Picasso's sculpture, Alan Bowness finally questions the "aesthetic status" of the *Bull's Head*, for, he asks, "Is it really more than a clever and surprising joke?"[42] As compound metaphor, the *Bull's Head* resonates humorously with the source of its two parts, namely the bicycle as bull or, conversely, the bull as bicycle, which, upon reflection, becomes even more ludicrous: the bull's ferocity is trivialized and the bicycle's spindly vulnerability is heroicized in comic associations extrapolated from the nucleus of the head itself. And yet, as Timothy Hilton rightly observed, "The emotional point is that Picasso had transformed his wholesome interest in racing cyclists into his own obsessions . . . had made a sort of fetish of death, a *momento mori*; for this is not a bull's head but a bull's skull."[43] As skull, however, the peripheral association of Picasso's hanging sculpture with mounted animal trophies creates an absurd contrast between the docile, seemingly innocuous *Bull's Head* and wild beasts of the jungle which "brave" man subdues and stuffs. In actuality, the bull can be associated as legitimately with the plow-pulling type as with the threatening beast simply by comparing the Indian and the African varieties. Picasso's unique stance toward the bull probably lies somewhere in between, in the man-animal confrontation of the Spanish *corrida de toros* (the bullfight). Part of the charm of this particular head is its docile innocence, this in stark contrast to Picasso's earlier renderings of bulls as threatening projections of brutality, fearsome symbols of man's two fundamental animal drives: to kill and to have sex.

Picasso's animal combines, while often initially humorous, upon reflection often give up deep secrets about art and its relation to reality. "Just as when he equates the motor-car with the ape's head, Picasso creates a modern version of the Minotaur," writes Roland Penrose. "The effects of these metamorphoses which begin as a joke are profound since they challenge our sense of reality. . . . The alliance of the grotesque with Picasso's ability to metamorphose objects at will is the key to the power of these composite inventions."[44] The cult of the animal in general and the myth and reality of bulls in particular are prime sources of some of Picasso's most compelling images. "The bull," according to Vincente Marrero, "is the supreme majesty of [Picasso's] art."[45] The most famous of his bull images is, of course, the impassive bull of *Guernica*, symbol of political tyranny. Most of Picasso's bull images of the thirties reflect this repellent truth of man's persistent inhumanity to man.

In light of these fearful precedents, the gentle humor of his *Bull's Head* can be viewed from several angles: as comic relief, if viewed against the fearful aspect of his other bull images, especially of the frightening *Skull of a Bull on a Table*, completed in 1942, one year before the *Bull's Head*;[46] as bitter sarcasm, if seen against the frightful specter of the Nazi holocaust (although it is uncertain whether Picasso, living in German-occupied Paris, was privy to its full horror as early as 1943); or as modern counterpart to the paleolithic cave paintings of Northern Spain (Altamira), linking Picasso's visual imagination to man's earliest attempts to come to terms with the mystery of life and death and the world of spirit. Picasso observed that "if it occurred to man to create his own image, it's because he discovered them all around him, almost formed, already within his grasp. He saw them in a bone, in the irregular surfaces of cavern walls, in a piece of wood. . . . One form might suggest a woman, another a bison, and still another the head of a demon."[47] When congratulated on the remarkable likeness of his *Bull's Head*, Picasso replied: "That's not enough. It should be possible to take a bit of wood and find that it's a bird."[48]

Finally, without wanting to read more into this ostensibly "little visual joke" than is warranted, might the *Bull's Head*, seen in all of these highly serious, even tragic contexts, harbor a deeper significance which rests on the cutting edge of the tragicomic? One of the funniest moments in Chaplin's silent film classic *The Gold Rush* occurs when the starving Charlie boils his own shoe and makes a feast of it. Chaplin said he got the idea from the tragic story of the Donner party, who resorted to cannibalism to survive. "In the creation of comedy," Chaplin wrote, "it is paradoxical that tragedy stimulates the spirit of ridicule, because ridicule, I suppose, is an attitude of defiance: we must laugh in the face of our helplessness against the forces of nature—or go insane."[49] In an age poised on the precipice of nuclear annihilation, the relieving humor of Picasso's visual metaphors is a therapeutic breath of fresh air.

JON D. GREEN, *associate professor of humanities at BYU, has been teaching for over twenty-five years. He received his bachelor's and master's degrees at BYU in humanities and German literature, and then completed a PhD in comparative arts at Syracuse University. His PhD work, looking at the relationship between music and literature, coincides well with his idea that "the fun of learning is seeing the connectedness of things." Green has published widely in the areas of interart analogies, comparative arts, and general education. His humanities textbook,* Coming to Your Senses: Writing about the Arts, *is recently going through its revised fourth edition with Simon and Schuster.*

Notes

1. Virgil C. Aldrich, "Visual Metaphor," *Journal of Aesthetic Education* 2, no. 1 (1968): 73–86.
2. Ibid., p. 73.
3. Françoise Gilot and Carlton Lake, *Life with Picasso* (New York: McGraw-Hill, 1964).
4. Dore Ashton, *Picasso on Art: A Selection of Views* (New York: Viking, 1972), p. xxvii.
5. Ibid., p. 23.
6. Ibid., p. 97
7. Plato, "Apology," in *Dialogues of Plato*, trans. Benjamin Jowett (Chicago: Encyclopaedia Britannica, 1952), p. 202.
8. Helen Kay, *Picasso's World of Children* (New York: Doubleday, n.d.), p. 23.
9. Ashton, *Picasso on Art*, p. 11.
10. I. A. Richards, *The Philosophy of Rhetoric* (New York: Oxford University Press, 1936).
11. Nathaniel Hawthorne, "Dr. Heidigger's Experiment," in *The Complete Works of Nathaniel Hawthorne*, vol. 1 (Cambridge: Riverside Press, 1883), p. 262.
12. Virgil C. Aldrich, "Form in the Visual Arts," *British Journal of Aesthetics* 11, no. 3 (Summer 1971): 222.
13. Ibid., p. 222.
14. John M. Kennedy, "Metaphor in Pictures: An Analysis with Examples" (Unpublished manuscript, University of Toronto, n.d.).
15. Owen Barfield, "Poetic Diction and Legal Fiction," in *The Importance of Language* (Englewood Cliffs, N.J.: Prentice-Hall, 1962), pp. 51–71.
16. Quoted by Harriet and Sidney Janis, *Picasso: The Recent Years 1939–1946* (New York: Doubleday, 1946), p. 1. See also Carla Gottlieb, "Picasso's Girl before a Mirror," *Journal of Aesthetics and Art Criticism* 24, no. 4 (Summer 1966): 509–18.
17. Robert Rosenblum, "Picasso and the Anatomy of Eroticism," in *Picasso in Perspective*, ed. Gert Schiff (Englewood Cliffs, N.J.: Prentice Hall, 1976), pp. 75–85.
18. Frank D. Russell, *Picasso's Guernica: The Labyrinth of Narrative and Vision* (Montclair, N.J.: Allanheld, Osmun, 1980), p. 102.
19. René Berger, *Discovery of Painting* (1958; New York: Viking, 1963), p. 345, quoted in Russell, *Guernica: The Labyrinth of Narrative and Vision*, p. 306, n. 90.
20. Rudolf Arnheim, *Picasso's Guernica* (Berkeley: University of California Press, 1962), p. 20.
21. Russell, *Guernica: The Labyrinth of Narrative and Vision*, p. 43.
22. Ibid., p. 15.
23. Berger, *Discovery of Painting*, p. 357.
24. Russell, *Guernica: The Labyrinth of Narrative and Vision*, p. 93.
25. Ibid., pp. 91–92.
26. Randall Jarrell, "The Death of the Ball-Turret Gunner," in *The Norton Anthology of Poetry*, ed. Arthur M. Eastman et al. (New York: Norton, 1970), p. 1097.
27. Ashton, *Picasso on Art*, p. 21.
28. Ibid., p. 19.
29. Lael Wertenbaker, *The World of Picasso* rev. ed. (New York: Time-Life Books, 1977), pp. 62–63.
30. Ashton, *Picasso on Art*, p. 18.
31. Gilot, *Life with Picasso*, p. 321. Picasso's *Still Life with Chair Caning* is a complex visual metaphor which explores the paradox of illusion and reality and whose philosophical equivalent would be something like "Art (the artificial) is real" or "Art (a

lie) is truth." Clive Bell came closest to realizing this philosophical-literary side of Picasso's genius when he wrote, "Picasso, the most visual of poets, is a literary painter. . . . It goes without saying that, in his visual art, it is not the ideas, but the connection of ideas that matters." Clive Bell, "Picasso's Poetry," in *Picasso in Perspective*, ed. Gert Schiff (Englewood Cliffs, N.J.: Prentice Hall, 1970), pp. 86–87.

32. Ashton, *Picasso on Art*, p. 65. Will Grohmann's brief philosophical analysis of Picasso's art in "Dialectic and Transcendence in Picasso's Work," in *A Picasso Anthology: Documents, Criticism, Reminiscences*, ed. Marilyn McCully (London: Thames and Hudson, 1981), pp. 186–88, provides an illuminating expansion of Picasso's metaphor by arguing that the essence of his artistic achievement comes from transcending antitheses: "The object swings between utter concrete reality (not imitation), at one extreme, and the role of a function of consciousness, at the other. The form oscillates between delineation and action always seeking to capture not the real world but the super-real or surreal world; as art is always a cipher for what transcends sensory perception" (pp. 187–88). Ulrich Weisstein provides a useful conceptual model for comparing collage and metaphor by locating collage in the center of an imaginary spectrum whose polar extremes are occupied by "raw nature/brute reality palmed off as art, on the one hand, and by art which claims to be nothing but art on the other." See Ulrich Weisstein, "Collage, Montage, and Related Terms: Their Literal and Figurative Use in the Application to Techniques and Forms in Various Arts," *Comparative Literature Studies* 15, no. 1 (March 1978): 124–39.
33. Gilot, *Life with Picasso*, p. 321.
34. Aldrich, "Visual Metaphor," p. 75.
35. Gilot, *Life with Picasso*, p. 322. The poetic relationship between metaphor and reality was most clearly explained by Phillip Wheelwright in Metaphor and Reality (Bloomington: Indiana University Press, 1962), especially chapter 4, as a semantic transformation brought about by the dual effect of an "outreaching movement" of what he termed "epiphor" (transfer of a concrete image over onto a vaguer one) and the "combining movement" of a "diaphor" (movement through certain particulars "producing new meaning by juxtaposition alone" p. 71). The legitimacy of transferring Wheelwright's notions of poetic metaphor to the domain of the nonverbal arts (music and the visual arts in particular) has been defended persuasively by Theodore M. Greene in "The Arts as Revelation and Cominunication: A Perspective on 'Metaphor and Reality,' " in *The Hidden Harmony: Essays in Honor of Phillip Wheelwright* (New York: Odyssey Press, 1966), pp. 23–40.
36. Albert Rothenberg, "Visual Art: Homospatial Thinking in the Creative Process," *Leonardo* 3, no. 1 (Winter 1980): 18.
37. Translated from Brassai, *Conversations avec Picasso* (Paris: 1964), and quoted by Alan Bowness, "Picasso's Sculpture," in *Picasso 1881–1973*, ed. Sir Roland Penrose and John Golding (London: Paul Elek, 1973), p. 146. However, the sequence of events in discovering the *Bull's Head* reverses the order of his creation of the *Goat*, where he began with the idea of making a goat and then cast about for objects which might be useful for his purpose. See Gilot, *Life with Picasso*, pp. 317–19. In general, Picasso's method of making visual metaphors seems to work in reverse direction from the usual pattern of creative verbal metaphors: the poet, moving from the familiar to the unfamiliar, might write, "Your hips are like porcelain vases," whereas Picasso might simply refashion an already existing vase into a woman's hip. The poet makes the hip into a vase; Picasso makes the vase into a hip.
38. Bowness, "Picasso's Sculpture," p. 146.
39. Herschel B. Chipp, *Theories of Modern Art: A Source Book by Artists and Critics* (Berkeley: University of California Press, 1971), p. 274.

40. Gilot, *Life with Picasso*, p. 322.
41. Kay, *Picasso's World,* p. 178.
42. Bowness, "Picasso's Sculpture," p. 146.
43. Timothy Hilton, *Picasso's Picasso's* (London: Arts Council of Great Britain, 1981), p. 79.
44. Roland Penrose, *Picasso: His Life and Work*, 3rd ed. (1958; Berkeley: University of California Press, 1981), p. 383.
45. Vincerite Marrero, *Picasso and the Bull*, trans. Anthony Kerrigan (Chicago: Henry Regnery, 1956), p. 90.
46. Marrero writes of this: "No artist has ever created anything more deeply horrible" (ibid., p. 78).
47. Ashton, *Picasso on Art*, p. 118.
48. Wertenbaker, *The World of Picasso*, p. 130.
49. Quoted in Stanley Kauffmann, "Chaplin's *The Gold Rush*," *Horizon* 15, no. 3 (Summer 1973): 42.

Questions

1. What is a "visual metaphor"? How are visual metaphors like verbal metaphors?

2. What problems does Green anticipate in understanding Picasso's art? How does he overcome these problems?

3. How does Green present the visual texts he is analysing? Why does he describe some visual texts and present others as photographs? How is Green's presentation of visual texts like using quotation, summary, or paraphrase to present verbal texts?

4. How can Green's analysis of Picasso be applied to other visual texts?

Reel Goddesses

Elouise Bell

Since she was five years old, Elouise Bell has felt compelled to fill blank paper. At one point in her career, she was writing nine columns a month for newspapers and journals. But deep in her heart she claims to be a film buff. "I grew up during a time when movies were it, *" she emphasizes. This interest, combined with what she describes as an impulse to ask about the changing images of women in American society, led to this essay. Bell believes writing is a tool for thinking, and often approaches topics through* freewriting, *a technique she claims often helps more than "planning it out." However, she admits that not every work created this way is a masterpiece. "Some of it isn't worth anything," she says, "but some means a great deal to me." This article was originally published in the book* Only When I Laugh.

Film and film images are as important to us today (though not consciously so) as religion was to many of our ancestors in past centuries. They are important because they shape the way we think, hence the way we feel, and thus the way we act. They are as powerfully formative as any religious ceremony.

Molly Haskill, the film critic, writes: "Whatever their roles . . . the women in the movies had a mystical, quasi-religious connection with the public. . . . They were real goddesses."

We in the Nineties may not idolize our film stars as American moviegoers of the Thirties and Forties did, but the power of the silver screen remains mystical. Whatever our backgrounds, I would guess that most of us have spent more hours paying attention to the messages of movies than to sermons and Sunday school lessons in church or synagogue. We may be hazy on our Apostles' Creed, our Articles of Faith, our catechism, but we are razor-sharp on the teachings of Hollywood. Biblical scriptures may be dim in our minds, but who doesn't know the following lines to live by:

"If you want anything, just whistle."
"This is bigger than both of us."
"I don't think we're in Kansas anymore, Toto."

"Come up and see me sometime." (And that even more memorable Mae West line, when an admiring ingenue said, "Goodness, those are wonderful pearls!"—"Goodness had nothing to do with it!")

"Ah, sweet mystery of life!" (Jeanette MacDonald rendition, Madeline Kahn rendition.)

. . . .

"You Jane, me Tarzan."

"If you want monogamy, marry a swan."

My premise here (certainly not original) is that what we see on film affects in a hundred ways our behavior and our concept of ourselves as women and men, whether any of us realize the full influence or not. Thinking from time to time about what Hollywood and TV are preaching can help us make more conscious life choices.

For purpose of analysis, I'd like to use the archetypal concept of the triple goddess as a way of looking at Hollywood's portrayal of women. Traditionally, the myths speak of Woman in three phases: Maiden, Mother, and Crone.

Films have always focused primarily on Maidens—young, beautiful, nubile—from the days when Mary Pickford dressed and performed as America's pinafored Sweetheart (even though she was married and an astute businesswoman at the time) to these days of Brooke Shields and Jodie Foster and Mariel Hemingway and the young women of the Brat Pack—Molly Ringwald, Ally Sheedy, the *Pretty-in-Pink, Sixteen Candles* starlets. There is a great deal to be said about Woman as Maiden, about the female role in romance. The essential point here is that the Maiden is young, beautiful, inexperienced (emotionally if not technically a virgin), and she gains her significance in terms of a relationship with a man. She is still Snow White, waiting for her Prince. And she becomes the model for a million daydreams.

Though Woman as Mother has not been a central role in Hollywood movies, it is exactly Woman as Mother who has changed the most in Hollywood's depiction. For decades, Mother meant Anne Revere or Fay Bainter or Spring Byington—sweet-faced, grey-haired, aproned—standing by a window, waiting and worrying. Just as no flesh-and-blood mother can live up to the Mother's Day hype, no real mother, sitting in the darkened theater watching the martyr parade go by, could avoid waves of guilt and self-condemnation. Today in movies, we have vastly more realistic Mothers, more fully human, fully female. Think of all the single mothers we have seen. Remember Sally Field in *Norma Rae,* a tough-talking, hard-working mother of three (each by a different father). Or Sally Field in *Places in the Heart,* the young widow saving the cotton crop. Or Sally Field in *Murphy's Romance,* the young divorcee finding romance with a sixty-year old who admits he's sixty (finally). And that's just Gidget grown up. What about Shirley MacLaine as the mother in *Terms of Endearment*, or Cher's wonderful role in *Mask*?

And what about Woman as Crone? Now wait: don't flinch at the word. Forget wrinkled, raddled, and rejected. In real life, it never has meant any of that, but for many years Hollywood focused on that perception of the mature woman. And we bought the Tinseltown doctrine that Geritol begins at thirty. Today, against great odds, we are shifting the spotlight to other, more realistic roles of that woman in her prime. (Let's all remember and keep quoting Gloria Steinem's great line at her fiftieth birthday party. Whenever anyone said to her, "You don't look fifty," she reminded them, "This is what fifty looks like." Well, maybe all Fifties don't look like Steinem, but we don't all look like Grandma Moses, either.)

Just what is the Crone? Go back to myth and legend. The Crone was a wise woman. One writer says, "The Crone was Wisdom herself . . . anciently dwelling in caves, walking the highways, standing at the crossroads, and making love on the vast seas."

Another historian speaks of Artemis as Crone, whose job was "To assist people who are no longer where they were and not yet where they hope to go." The Crone was also viewed as a seeker, a person in a time of introversion and spiritual search. More than anything else, the Crone was, and is, in the words of writer Vickie Noble, "A woman whole in herself."

This is what the fullness of mythology and history and anthropology says about the Crone. But what has Hollywood shown us? Two kinds of Crones, I think. First, the powerful Crones who are evil, menacing, in short, witches. Judith Anderson made a career out of Crones, highlighted by the controlling, devious, and deadly Mrs. Danvers in *Rebecca.* (She played a similar though smaller role as Memnot in *The Ten Commandments.*) Lining up behind Anderson are a whole host of mean housekeepers, governesses, school-teachers, prison matrons, nurses, and so forth. Again, as Anderson's Mrs. Danvers became mythic in its own right, Louise Fletcher's Big Nurse in *One Flew Over the Cuckoo's Nest* assumed archetypal dimensions. Cloris Leachman parodies these Crones in at least two roles—Nurse Diesel in *High Anxiety* and Frau Blücher in *Young Frankenstein.*

But powerful Crones are too fearsome for Hollywood generally. Film makers have preferred the ineffectual Crone, either sympathetic and powerless—the widow, the aged invalid—or silly and powerless—the sisters in *Arsenic and Old Lace* (reborn as the sisters guarding the Recipe in *The Waltons*), Joyce Grenfell as the daffy school-mistress hopelessly outwitted by the girls of St. Trinian's—you've seen them.

Despite the determination of script-writers and directors not to give powerful, positive Crones a central role in film, we in fact have had many memorable Crones. The reasons are several: first, even a small part for a powerful, autonomous woman stands out by comparison with weaker female characters. Mrs. Danvers haunts us; we have to stop and think to remember the nameless narrator (played by Joan Fontaine) in the same film. Whenever Maureen Stapleton shows up in a picture, even for a cameo role, she seems more alive, more real, more human than anyone else in the cast. Moreover, many film actresses have projected such strong, self-contained images that almost in spite of the scripts, they have given us mature, positive portraits.

Has Hepburn ever been anything but her own woman, even when cast as the Maiden (as in *Philadelphia Story*)? Hepburn turned every stereotyped "old maid" role into a three-dimensional character of dignity and power. (Think of *Rainmaker*, *Summertime*, *The African Queen*, *The Corn Is Green*, *Grace Quigley*.)

Think of women who seemed too powerful, somehow out of place, in Maiden roles, only to assume full stature after forty. Joanne Woodward, with a couple of exceptions (*Three Faces of Eve*, *The Long Hot Summer*), had to wait for her roles, and did one of her greatest turns as the "old maid" in *Rachel, Rachel*. Jane Alexander has come to prominence in her Crone roles—*Eleanor and Franklin*, *Dear Liar*, etc. Glenda Jackson made her mark on the American audience playing that quintessential Crone, Elizabeth R, and has become stronger and stronger as she leaves the farcical Maiden roles behind to do *Turtle Diary* and similar works. A look at the film *Julia* is revealing—Fonda is the Maiden in that picture and pretty much in the work she's doing even now; Redgrave, by contrast, has always been a Crone figure. (She was miscast, though regally, in Camelot. Can we doubt that she should have ended up running, or reforming, the Abbey at film's end?) The list of strong actresses who were almost never given roles to match their power until later in life goes on: Geraldine Page (think of all those neurotic Tenessee Williams roles), Kim Stanley, Julie Harris, Anne Bancroft, Colleen Dewhurst (whom Pauline Kael labels "that giant force of nature"). Was Simone Signoret ever as wonderful as a Maiden as she was as a Crone? (*Room at the Top*, *Ship of Fools*, *Madame Rosa*, *Le Chat*.) European directors seem to know better what to do with mature women, the likes of Melina Mercouri, Irene Papas, Anna Magnanni; it's America that has the obsession with youth.

Maybe, I keep thinking. Maybe when American women refuse any longer to buy into the youth cult, when we don't giggle or lie or hesitate about our ages, when we claim our own power, use it freely and confidently, to heal and to grow, maybe then we will get scripts and movies that do justice to the Crone, especially if, along with all these achievements, we have more women writing, directing, producing. And if we get films glorifying the American Crone (to paraphrase Ziegfeld in a way he would bellow about), then maybe we will celebrate the Crones in our own lives, beginning with ourselves.

I am not, I insist you note, advocating an eclipse of the Maiden's place in the sun. Tragedy, comedy, irony, and romance—each of these, but especially Romance, has a place for the Maiden. But each also has a place for the Crone. All I am calling for is a little affirmative action in films, a little readjustment of the imbalance. I dream of Things As They Can Be.

A final note to remind us of Things As They Are: Marilyn Monroe, proclaimed by many as the No. 1 Goddess, died more than twenty-five years ago. She is more acclaimed, more written and read about now than ever before. I think that tells us how our culture at the present wants its goddesses—on a pedestal and silent. Dead is no drawback.

ELOUISE BELL *is Professor Emeritus of English and former Associate Dean of General and Honors Education. This essay originally appeared in her collection* Only When I Laugh. *Other publications include essays, reviews, stories, and poems in periodicals such as* BYU Studies, Ensign, *and* Women's Studies Quarterly. *She currently shares a column with Tom Barberi in* The Salt Lake Tribune.

Questions

1. Do you agree with Bell's statement that film has become as important to many Americans as religion? What are some films that have shaped American values and perspectives?
2. What are the typical representations of women in film? What are some typical examples of these? What are some examples of women who don't fit the types?

Legal Writing

JAMES D. GORDON III

James Gordon has long been interested in humor and the law. He believes that humor helps to teach and finds that legal education is not only easy to poke fun at, but that legal education can be greatly enhanced through the addition of humor. "Legal Writing" is taken from his book Law School: A Survivor's Guide. *In this article, Gordon wanted to make fun of the way lawyers have traditionally written and encourage lawyers to be more concise.*

During your first year, you take a class called Legal Writing. The sole objective of this class is to make you write like real lawyers as little as possible. Lawyers write as if they were paid by the word, or maybe even as if they were born in a parallel universe. For example, here is the legal translation that has been offered for the simple everyday phrase, "I give you this orange."

> Know all men by these presents that I hereby give, grant, bargain, sell, release, convey, transfer, and quitclaim all my right, title, interest, benefit, and use whatever in, of, and concerning this chattel, known as an orange, or citrus orantium, together with all the appurtenances thereto of skin, pulp, pip, rind, seeds, and juice for his own use and behoof, to himself and his heirs in fee simple forever, free from all liens, encumbrances, easements, limitations, restraints, or conditions whatsoever, any and all prior deeds, transfers or other documents whatsoever, now or anywhere made to the contrary notwithstanding, with full power to bite, cut, suck, or otherwise eat the said orange or to give away the same, with or without its skin, pulp, pip, rind, seeds, or juice.[1]

This kind of supernatural incantation is designed to perpetuate the perceived mysticism of the law and its official high priests. However, legal writing teachers tell you that it is preferable to use concise language

[1]Plain Wayne [pseud.], Wis. Bar Bull., Feb. 1975, at 61.

and simple, everyday words. Benjamin Franklin said, "Never use a long word when a short one will do." Of course, he was a printer, and he had to set the type by hand. Naturally, he preferred "pay" over "remuneration."

Lawyers like to use "lawyerisms," like "aforementioned," "hereinafter," and "mortgagee." However, most people can't understand legalese. When the loan officer asked Archie Bunker if his home was encumbered, he replied, "No, it's stucco and wood." As Charles Beardsley said, "The writer who uses words unknown to his reader might as well bark."[2] So remember the words of the ditty:

> When promulgating your esoteric cogitations and articulating your superficial sentimentalities, beware of platitudinous ponderosity. Let your extemporaneous verbal evaporations and expatiations have lucidity and intelligibility without rodomontade or thespian bombast. Avoid innocuous vacuity, pompous propensity, and vaniloquent vapidity.

Lawyers do strange things to language. For instance, they add "-ize" to all sorts of words. They don't say "use"; they say "utilize." They also say "actualize," "initialize," and "prioritize." If you ask me, it's enough to make you "externalize" your breakfast. They should try harder to "laypersonize" their language.

Lawyers also write "said" a lot. For example, one complaint stated:

> "[B]eginning at a point on SAID railroad track about a half a mile or more north of a point opposite SAID curve in SAID highway, large quantities of highly volatile coal were unnecessarily thrown into the firebox of SAID locomotive and upon the fire contained therein, thereby preventing proper combustion of SAID coal, resulting in great clouds of dense smoke being emitted from the smokestack of SAID locomotive." . . . [Defendant] knew SAID smoke would "fall upon and cover SAID curve in SAID highway when SAID engine reached a point on SAID railroad tracks opposite SAID curve, unless SAID smoke was checked in the meantime."[3]

---

[2]*The Difference Between Writing and Yelping,* Cal. Law., Oct. 1989, at 136 (quoting an editorial in the *San Fransisco Chronicle* (1941)).

[3]Button v. Pennsylvania Ry. Co., 57 N.E.2d 444, 445 (Ind. App. 1944) (en banc) (emphasis added).

The judges who quoted this language, realizing that they had not yet used up their daily quota, then added another sentence containing eight more "saids." Said practice is supposedly invoked for precision, but said precision is illusory. Since the author referred to only one locomotive, "said" is unnecessary. If he had referred to two, "said" wouldn't tell you which one.[4] The real problem is that "the" doesn't sound important enough to lawyers, so they instead write said "saids."

Another sign of legal writing is verbosity. This problem has been around for centuries. In 1596 an English chancellor made an example of a wordy 120-page document by ordering that a hole be cut in it, the writer's head be stuffed in the hole, and the writer be led around and exhibited to all those attending court at Westminster Hall.[5]

One example of verbosity is the practice of using duplicative words, like "cease and desist," "null and void," "free and clear," "suffer and permit," "devise and bequeath," and "idiot and professor." This practice supposedly stems from periods in history when English lawyers had two languages to choose from: first, Celtic and Anglo-Saxon, then English and Latin, and later English and French. Who knows for sure whether this is true and correct? It sure creates a lot of redundancy and duplication.

A few judges have pursued the virtue of conciseness with a passion. For example, a taxpayer in the US Tax Court testified, "As God is my judge, I do not owe this tax." Judge Murdock replied, "He's not, I am; you do."[6] Another example is *Denny v. Radar Industries*.[7] Most of the opinion states, "The appellant has attempted to distinguish the factual situation in this case from that in [a prior case]. He didn't. We couldn't. Affirmed."

Another common booboo in legal writing is the mixed metaphor. This is a figure of speech that begins with one image and then, as slick as Elvis's hair grease, shifts to another. For example, a bar association committee reported that it had "smelled a rat and nipped it in the bud."[8] Donald Nixon complained, "People are using Watergate as a political football to bury my brother."[9] Even Jiminy Cricket told Pinocchio, "You buttered your bread—now sleep in it." Therefore, before using a mixed metaphor wedded to the very fabric of your argument, be sure to run it up the flagpole of microscopic scrutiny. Otherwise, the sacred cows will

---

[4]Richard C. Wydick, *Plain English for Lawyers,* 66 Cal. L. Rev. 727, 740 (1978).

[5]*Id.* at 727.

[6]Henry Weihofen, *Legal Writing Style* 41 (2d ed. 1980).

[7]184 N.W. 2d 289 (Mich. App. 1971).

[8]*See* Gyles Brandreth, *The Joy of Lex* 227 (1980) (quoting Boyle Roche).

[9]Gertrude Block, *Effective Legal Writing* 42 (2d ed. 1983).

come home to roost with a vengeance.[10] But I'm skating on hot water, so I'll move on.

Lawyers also use a lot of clichés. They say things like "The case is open and shut. Don't cut off your nose to spite your face." And "To think that you will escape the day of reckoning in the cold light of reason is the height of absurdity barking up the wrong tree." So bite the bullet and avoid old clichés like the plague. As Samuel Goldwyn said, "Let's have some new clichés."

Legal writing also often uses double negatives. The United States Supreme Court has truly refined this art, writing the world's first and only—believe it or not—QUADRUPLE negative:

> This is not to say, however, that the prima facie case may not be met by evidence supporting a finding that a lesser degree of segregated schooling in the core city area would not have resulted even if the board had not acted as it did.[11]

Government cryptographers have been trying to decipher this sentence for years. So far, they have been able to tell that it has something to do with schools.

In legal writing you are also introduced to the two computerized systems of legal research, Lexis and Westlaw. These systems permit you to find hundreds of cases merely by pushing a button. This allows you to avoid packing musty case reporters up and down the stairs of the library, which would interrupt your completely sedentary lifestyle. It's much better to exercise those finger muscles and let the rest of your body atrophy into a shapeless blob of protoplasm.

Lexis and Westlaw are very convenient, but they do have limitations. For example, suppose you want to find all the cases in which a lawyer called opposing counsel a "ferret face." Type in the query: counsel /s "ferret face." The computer will respond: "13,759 cases answer your query. Please narrow your search terms." So then you'll have to limit the search terms to "three-eyed ferret face," "banana-nosed ferret face," etc. As you can see, this can be a lot of frustrating work. That's one reason they call that little blinking thing on your computer screen "the cursor."

---

[10] Gyles Brandeth, *supra* note 8, at 227. Justice Stewart once wrote, "This case presents a double-barreled dilemma, which in all candor I think the Court's opinion has not succeeded in papering over." Sherbert v. Verner, 374 U.S. 398, 413 (1963) (Stewart, J., concurring).

[11] Keyes v. School Dist. No. 1, 413 U.S. 189, 211 (1973) (Brennan, J.).

The second half of your legal writing class is "moot court," a thrilling little death march in which you prepare a hundred-page document that is called, appropriately enough, a "brief."

The moot court problems are always fascinating hypotheticals addressing such stimulating issues as stagnant-water rights in sixteenth-century France. Although your professor tries to make the problem a balanced one, it turns out that your opponent has the law, the facts, and the policy arguments on his side—whereas all you have on your side is your ability to keep from laughing hysterically at your own arguments by sticking a pin into your palm. Never mind. The judges will tell you that the process is fair anyway, because having a really bad case reveals your mettle as an advocate. Then they will give the prize to your opponent.

Moot court gives you the privilege of getting in a heated argument with another student in front of a panel of judges composed of EXTREMELY experienced second- and third-year students who have never set foot inside a courthouse in their lives. After the argument, the judges give you helpful advice. The first judge says, "Don't wave your hands so much." The second judge says, "Use more hand motions." The third judge says, "All the hand motions were okay except when you punched your opponent in the eye. You should have punched him in the mouth."

The worst part of legal writing is having to learn the rules of legal citation. Literally thousands of subrules are set forth in a mutant mass of legalisms called the *Bluebook*. The operating principles of the *Bluebook* are: (1) Nature abhorreth a vacuum; and (2) Anything worth doing is worth overdoing. The first *Bluebook* was a simple booklet that showed how to cite the most commonly used sources. But because the *Bluebook* has insisted on having a rule for every situation imaginable, it has grown enormously (sort of like the Blob, but with a less appealing personality). So now the *Bluebook* describes how to cite such often-used sources as *Vanity Fair* and the Argentine provincial court of labor appeals. The twelfth edition fit in a person's pocket. The current (fifteenth) edition could have its own carrying case. The twentieth edition will undoubtedly arrive on a flatbed truck.

Under the prior *Bluebooks*, when citing books you had to give the initial of the author's first name, but for law review articles you didn't, which I guess was supposed to be some kind of stupid reward for writing books. You were never permitted to give the author's first name for articles, even though there are 4,000 law professors named "Smith." (I have a suspicion that the other law professors who share my surname have been really ticked off[12] at me because of this rule.) However, the newest edition of the *Bluebook* finally consented to giving the author's full name.

The *Bluebook* also contains the official "introductory signals," which lawyers use to introduce citations. The introductory signals have been attacked as

> an ultra vires imposition of a full-blown theory of stare decisis. . . . Use *no signal* when you've got the guts. Use *e.g.* when there are other examples you are too lazy to find or are skeptical of unearthing. Use *accord* when one court has cribbed from the other's opinion. Use *see* when the case is on all three's. Use *cf.* when you've wasted your time reading the case. Insert *but* in front of these last two when a frown instead of a smile is indicated.[13]

However, the *Bluebook* still leaves out some very useful signals, such as *read and weep* and *try to distinguish this one.* For contrary authority, it omits *disregard, ignore also,* and *for a bizarre view, see.*

The *Bluebook* has rules for everything. It permits legal writing teachers to penalize students for failing to grasp the subtle distinction between a period followed by an ellipsis and an ellipsis followed by a period. It has no fewer than 140 pages of mandatory abbreviations, which means that the space saved by abbreviations is purchased with the time wasted in looking them up. It dictates when numbers must be written as numerals and when they must be spelled out. Inexplicably, the rule is different for footnotes than it is for text, and the general rules are subject to six (6?) exceptions. The *Bluebook* is thick with thin things.

Despite all of this, the editors insist that the current edition of the *Bluebook* is "easier to use."[14] Easier than what? An F-16 fighter jet? Short of that, I'm not sure. But I am sure that studying the *Bluebook* is not likely to overload the pleasure sensors in your brain.

---

[12]From the German verb *aufticken.*

[13]Peter Lushing, Book Review, 67 Colum. L. Rev. 599, 601 (1967) (reviewing *A Uniform System of Citation* (11th ed. 1967)).

[14]*The Bluebook: A Uniform System of Citation* at v (15th ed. 1991).

JAMES D. GORDON III, *currently an Associate Academic Vice President at BYU, has taught at BYU's law school since 1984. He received his JD from the University of California, Berkeley in 1980. His interests in legal education, freedom of religion, and humor have prompted such articles as "How Not to Succeed in Law School" and "Free Exercise on the Mountaintop."*

Questions

1. According to Gordon, what is wrong with most legal writing? How many of these problems are unique to the legal community?
2. How does Gordon present to the reader the brief texts he is analyzing? How does he refer to the particular features of language he is analyzing?
3. How does Gordon use humor to expose poor legal writing?

Creating Chaos

Danette Paul

Danette Paul first became interested in chaos theory when two of her undergraduate students who were engineering majors recommended she read a book on the topic. Paul read the book Chaos: Making a New Science *by James Gleick and became more and more interested in how this theory had started and particularly how scientists sold the theory to other scientists and to the general public. When Paul spoke with the creator of the term "chaos theory," James A. Yorke, he said that other terms had been used for the phenomenon, but that "chaos theory" had stuck. He attributed a lot of the popularity of the theory to the simple fact that it had a catchy name. Paul's article was first published in* Penn State Research.

How did an obscure article in a 1960s atmospheric science journal become part of the plot of a 1990s box office hit?

In 1963, Edward Lorenz claimed that the extreme sensitivity of complex systems to initial conditions seemed to make long-term weather forecasting impossible, that is, that sensitivity to initial conditions created unpredictability. In 1993, Michael Crichton used this same notion of unpredictability, now known as chaos theory, to create a bio-technological disaster. The journey from scientific journal to *Jurassic Park* was long and complex, but clearly demonstrates society's fascination with this new science.

James Gleick's popular 1987 book, *Chaos: Making a New Science*, traces chaos theory from obscurity to its establishment as a new discipline, looking at the main American players in the scientific community and their important results. Gleick shapes his historical account into an argument: He contends that chaos theory is a revolutionary way of looking at and doing science. True or not, the scientists studying chaos theory often deliberately invoke the language of revolution. Having noticed this consistent use of language, Davida Charney, an associate professor in the Penn State English Department, and I determined to retrace chaos's journey from obscurity, looking at the rhetorical issues of creating a scientific revolution.

By rhetorical issues, we mean the strategies scientists use in their writing to convince others that their findings are not only valid but also important or, in this case, revolutionary. Along with writing style, these strategies include such things as the use of jargon and the coining of new terms, the use of citations, and the creation of a context for their work by shaping their own historical account of the field.

The introductions of journal articles offer a natural place for scientists to shape their story. Generally, scientists use a "create-a-research-space" pattern in these introductions, as documented by John Swales, a linguist who specializes in advanced writing. According to Swales, scientists use four standard rhetorical moves to create a context for their work. First, they demonstrate the interest or importance of the research topic. Second, they selectively review and summarize the previously published research literature. Third, they show that the research is not complete, that there is a gap in the previous research. And fourth, the current research is presented as a timely and appropriate "filler."

This model provides a useful pattern for established sciences; yet how do scientists doing "revolutionary" work tie their research to a non-existent past? When we analyzed the introductions to journal articles by two key chaos theory players, Mitchell J. Feigenbaum and James A. Yorke, we found that as the field became more established Feigenbaum and Yorke seemed to follow these standard rhetorical moves closely; in their early articles, however, they came up with a few moves of their own.

Perhaps the most interesting move in both articles is the first, in which writers usually attempt to demonstrate the scientific community's interest in their project by citing previous research. Both scientists in our study used an equation to create interest, but differed in how far they were willing to follow this unusual approach.

For example, in Yorke's earliest article with coauthor Li, "Period Three Implies Chaos," from 1975, they used the unusual first move, then returned to the conventional pattern. Since there was no established field, they found very little past research to draw from to show interest in their project. Of the seventeen articles they cited after the equation, six had not yet been published, and four were self-citations. So rather than demonstrate interest, they created it. The lure of Yorke's provocative title, which eventually gave the phenomenon its name, is reinforced by a mathematical puzzle: Li and Yorke presented what seemed to be a relatively simple differential equation, which, after several iterations, became chaotic. They then shifted to a traditional second move, establishing some ties to their community.

Feigenbaum had a different approach. He made no attempt to attach his research to an as-yet-insignificant past. In "Universal Behavior" (1983), he made a bold move. In almost a reversal of the Biblical account, he simply created chaos out of order, firmly attaching his article to the other side of the entire enterprise of western science since Newton.

"There exist in nature processes that can be described as complex or chaotic and processes that are simple or orderly," he wrote. In the first move of "Quantitative Universality" (1978), his best-known article, he set up a fictitious population as an example of a recursion equation and continued to use it throughout his introduction. Consequentially, his introduction looks like a long mathematical proof rather than a series of rhetorical moves. With the relentless logic of mathematics and without citations, he established his claim for a universal function. Feigenbaum's rhetorical message is clear. His research is something completely different from what had come before.

How well do these rhetorical moves work? From the perspective of a straight citation count, they both work very well. Li and Yorke's paper has been cited over 400 times and Feigenbaum's "Quantitative Universality" a whopping 1,100 times. (To give you an idea of how rare that count is, the average scientific paper is cited only once or twice per year and only two in 10,000 scientific papers are cited more than 500 times in their lifetimes.) Naturally, how the story is told is only one of many factors that account for the success of an article. To determine a reader's response to the individual rhetorical moves, we had 12 scientists from two large state universities read aloud and comment on various combinations of these two early articles and two more recent articles by the same authors.

For readers 20 years after the fact, Feigenbaum's brash approach seemed more appropriate. One reader of the article stated: "It reads like an announcement." Another commented: "You rarely see papers that are constructed of raw ideas." On the other hand, Li and Yorke's shift back to a traditional approach seems to backfire. For our readers, seeing the form they expected but little new information led many of them to classify the article as "simple," "generic," or containing "textbook information." Finally, even the claim made in Yorke's provocative title that "Period Three Implies Chaos" was challenged. One reader familiar with the article noted some problems with its content, explaining: "So [Yorke's claim] is [actually] 'Period Three Implies something,' but it's not 'Period Three Implies what-is-generally-taken-as-the-current-definition-of Chaos'."

Perhaps this comment explains our interest in the intricate negotiation between science and language in chaos theory. Even as theory changes and develops, language, with its fluctuating meaning is a constant. Yorke named the phenomenon "chaos" to attract attention to the new enterprise. And, despite the dethroning of Yorke's "Period Three" phenomenon, and despite some researchers who gruffly say, "We don't call it chaos theory," chaos it remains.

So in making that journey from journal articles to Jurassic monsters, our findings-to-date indicate that, along with presenting interesting science, how one tells the story does seem to matter. And a provocative name doesn't hurt.

DANETTE PAUL, *an assistant professor in the English Department, received her PhD from Pennsylvania State University in 1996, after receiving her MA and BA from BYU. She is currently associate coordinator of English Composition. Dr. Paul specializes in rhetoric, particularly, the rhetoric of science. She teaches such classes as rhetoric and composition and technical writing.*

Questions

1. Why are scientific articles about chaos theory an important set of texts to analyze?
2. What approach does Paul take to understand these texts? What does she mean by "rhetorical issues"? What particular features of language does Paul examine?
3. What does Paul's analysis reveal about how scientific articles are read and are written?
4. How could Paul's method be applied to texts other than scientific articles?

Creating Knowledge

Creating knowledge means research. For many of us, when we think of research, we think of scientists wearing white coats and peering into test tubes in a lab somewhere, discovering something very important. If we think of research as many of us did it in elementary school, we think of a couple of hours with some encyclopedia, finding the right answer to satisfy our teacher. At a university, research takes many different forms. It may be the results of an experiment conducted in a lab, of observation in the field, or of long hours in the library, but any researcher is looking for an answer—an answer to a question that hasn't been asked before—a mystery.

In the opening essay of this section, William Bradshaw argues that students should be sleuths like Sherlock Holmes, using intelligence, research, and logic to solve mysteries. Because most of us don't run into dead bodies or stolen jewels on a regular basis, we may wonder what sort of mysteries there are to be solved. One of the most exciting and compelling things about research is recognizing that there are mysteries all around us. Becoming educated means learning what questions need to be asked. In this section, the researchers look at areas that are very familiar to us, such as the Church, food, clothes, and drive-in theaters, and then ask new questions about them. For example, Alvin Benson examines from a geologist's perspective the familiar scriptural scene in 3 Nephi of upheavals and earthquakes. Philip Kunz asks us how age and cost are related in selecting ice cream, while Kirk Belnap asks why scones in Utah are different from scones in Britain. And Tyler and Heidi Jarvis ask if the odds are ever with you when you throw the dice.

This section allows you to sample the variety of research done at BYU. Each field at the university has different methods for finding evidence, and distinct methods of documenting that evidence (as you will see in the articles). In each field, different things count as proof, but all researchers share the fascination with mysteries and the desire to know. Once you know the tricks of the trade, you can search out your own mysteries.

I Would Be a Purveyor of Mysteries

WILLIAM S. BRADSHAW

Having taught classes ranging from zoology to religion to epistemology, William Bradshaw has always been interested not only in the subject matter of a particular class, but in how his students learn. In "I Would Be A Purveyor of Mysteries" (originally printed in Selected Essays*), Bradshaw talks about the moments in his life and in his students' lives when education has been more than just a hurdle to jump through and has become a wonderful experience in unveiling the mysteries of the world. Bradshaw also offers a variety of suggestions for students to become more fascinated with both their secular and spiritual educations. One suggestion that could be most useful to Freshman English students is the suggestion that "writing is a prerequisite to thinking." He says, "One thinks because one writes. I write—therefore I think."*

I was thirteen in 1950 when my seventh-grade class at Uintah School staged *A Midsummer Night's Dream*, and I can recall only a few of the particulars. Bob Williams, Dan Boone, and I edited the script. I had a crush on Helen Dean, who played Helena (or was it Hermia?), and my close friend Steve Watson was Bottom. I played Lysander—my first and last experience as a leading man. About the only recollection I have of the performance itself is that our parents seemed pleased. "Wasn't it well done? And Shakespeare at that!" But one incidental experience associated with that juvenile foray into dramatics, which should have been trivial, has since occupied a strangely permanent place in my memory.

We had been making a papier-mâché donkey's head with which Puck could work his mischief, and there was a lull in the afternoon's activities. Mr. McDonald went to the blackboard (was he just trying to keep us occupied?), wrote an unfamiliar phrase, and suggested we try to figure out what it meant. I've never forgotten it: "The anatomical juxtaposition of two orbicular muscles in a state of contraction." It might as well have been Chinese at first. We spent twenty or thirty minutes puzzling, consulting dictionaries, asking for hints, looking for clues. Then, for Janet

Smith, the light dawned—a kiss. (Janet was a very bright girl. I'm almost positive I proposed to her when we were in kindergarten.) A kiss! We groaned and blushed. I've never forgotten either the phrase or the fun. Even now, as I relive it again, I can almost taste that room, smell the glue and paint, see Janet's face and Jack McDonald's grin. I learned. And it occurred to me that if I could identify the critical element(s) in that experience and stimulate equivalent responses at BYU, others would learn too. I'd be a teacher.

I think I finally have it. Jack McDonald's triumph was that he set before us a mystery.

It's taken me a lot of years as a Latter-day Saint to appreciate mysteries. The earliest advice I received on the subject was simple and repeated: shun them. "Whence and whither the Ten Tribes? Is Judas a son of perdition? Where is the narrow neck of land? Will the real Three Nephites please stand!" Surely it was sound advice. Avoid the mysteries.

But at the same time that I was receiving this caution, I was standing up every Tuesday night at MIA with my Scout-aged buddies and uncomprehendingly mouthing the memorized lines for that year, "Seek not for riches but for wisdom, and behold, the mysteries of God shall be unfolded unto you, and then shall you be made rich. Behold, he that hath eternal life is rich" (D&C 6:7). H-m-m-m. Will the real mysteries please stand! And it's not an isolated injunction. "But unto him that keepeth my commandments I will give the mysteries of my kingdom, and the same shall be in him a well of living water, springing up unto everlasting life" (D&C 63:23). "And to them [who fear me and serve me in righteousness] will I reveal all mysteries, yea, all the hidden mysteries of my kingdom from days of old, and for ages to come" (D&C 76:7). And there are more, many more.

So there are mysteries (tenets—opinions held loosely, to quote Harold B. Lee—of which "thou shalt not talk" [D&C 19:31]), and there are mysteries (which are vital, which God knows, which he invites and requires us to know, and which remain hidden to those who don't pay the price, i.e., exercise the required faculties)—and the distinction is critical. Mysteries are not properly defined by the subject matter being addressed but by the epistemological techniques used in their solution. The eternal fate of Judas is a mystery of the first type because I do not have the wherewithal to investigate it satisfactorily, and the effort can only end in failure. The tools of the trade usually used to explicate this kind of mystery are well-meaning speculation, unintentional (probably) exaggeration, and passionate defense of personal bias in the absence of data. To abandon such cherished skills could mark the demise of the high priests quorum lesson hour as we now know it. The mysteries of godliness, on the other hand, are in a second, separate category because of the nature of the tasks and the attributes required for their investigation. These include desire (1 Nephi 2:16); search (1 Nephi 10:19); open ears, hearts, and minds (Mosiah 2:9); and inquiry (D&C 6:11), among others, and the effort can only end in learning. I met some of these conditions that afternoon at Uintah School, and that's why I remember what a kiss is, and that's why the occasion was such a satisfying experience. Mysteries can be beautiful.

Sadly, the number of sleuths in each year's entering class at BYU is small. Shown a picture of a man (whose craggy features include a hawk-like nose, sharp and piercing eyes, and a square, prominent chin; who wears an Inverness topcoat and a checked woolen cap with the flaps tied on top; who holds a smoldering pipe in one hand and a magnifying glass in the other) and given the question "True or false, is it Sherlock Holmes?" our freshmen would smile with recognition and eagerly darken space A on the machine-graded scoring sheets.

But they don't often act like the resident of No. 221 Baker Street. Sherlock was an investigator, "one given to observation or study by close examination and systematic inquiry." The investigator with his penchant to examine, interrogate, probe, scrutinize, and weigh the evidence seems such an appropriate paradigm for the university student. This is especially true for Latter-day Saints who, in a missionary context, maintain a special regard for the investigator as one making acquaintance with the restored gospel. But the learning strategies actually employed, from Freshman Orientation to Senior Seminar, usually reflect an approach to mysteries quite different from that manifested by Mr. Holmes. For example:

A Biology 100 lecture in the Joseph Smith Auditorium had just concluded, and my colleague Jim Barnes and I were headed down the aisle toward the door. Two young men in the class stopped us. "Could we ask you a question about the test?" (They'd taken the exam the day before.) "What was the right answer to the one about the sea urchin ribosomes, the frog tRNAs, and the human mRNAs?" The conversation lasted about four minutes. I asked the boys, John and Dave, to explain the reasoning they'd used in trying to solve the problem. Their responses demonstrated that they understood some concepts reasonably well; others essential to answering the question correctly were conspicuously absent. Then we disclosed the correct answer: human proteins only. There was an extended pause before one of the boys, with a perplexed look on his face, asked, "When were we supposed to have learned that?"

That question is significant. It reflects, I think, how that young man and a majority of his classmates view the teaching/learning process as they've experienced it from grade school to the university. The role of the system (teacher's lectures, textbooks, etc.) is clear: *provide the answers*. (The mysteries have already been solved.) The student's stewardship in such a scheme is also obvious: *remember those answers*. No wonder the uncertainty in the boy's countenance; he couldn't recall that the answer to that exam question had been provided earlier. During the last thirty seconds before we parted I asked, "Did you have to struggle and 'sweat' while trying to answer that question? Was it hard? Did you find it tough to put it all together while puzzling a circumstance you'd never encountered before?" They nodded! I grinned from ear to ear and shot up a clenched right fist in the professorial power salute. "Hooray! It worked! The question worked! Thanks for the compliment!" My guess is that they walked away from the building shaking their heads. A random approach to registering for classes can prove most unkind to the unsuspecting.

"When were we supposed to have learned that?" is not an uncommon complaint nor an infrequent misconception. That question is usually accompanied, moreover, by the plaintive "I really studied hard for this test" defense. I don't doubt it. The malingerers and manipulators aside, I believe the protestations about long hours in the library, multiple readings of text chapters, and a conscientious all-out effort to "learn the material." It's not easy to deal with the sense of injustice which arises when one challenges the notion that the laborer is worthy of his hire by suggesting that more than exertion is required for an A. But there might be a remedy.

If it were possible I'd send Moses, Elias, and Elijah to visit my two disconcerted Biology 100 students and all their fellows. What significance do the events of April 3, 1836, in Kirtland hold for a BYU teacher concerned about what goes on in the head of a sometimes reluctant student of biology faced with a theoretical proposition (of doubtful eternal moment) involving frog tRNAs?

Having led the children of Israel out of bondage in Egypt to the promised land, Moses consequently restored to Joseph and Oliver the priesthood keys for gathering the Saints in the latter days. If this concept were crafted into the usual multiple-choice question, the Church average would probably be in the mid-seventies—a strong pass. But what does gathering mean—really mean—in 1986 when the instructions are, "Don't move to Zion; stay home and make a Zion of Atlanta or Taipei or Quito"? What might gathering mean to one seated at her desk poring over the contents of a three-ring binder trying to extract "truth" from class notes made weeks before, or to one with legs propped up on the library table wading through page 63 of the text on his lap?

Isn't the essence of our legacy from Moses the spirit of making distinctions? Whether one were an Israelite walking out of Pharaoh's Egypt in 1300 BC, a newly baptized British Mormon walking up a ship's gangplank on the first leg of a journey to Utah in 1860, or a fourteen-year-old MIA Maid walking to seminary in Tokyo in 1986, the principle would still be the same: reject the error that's around you and espouse what's right. Make distinctions. The physical afflictions Jacob's family suffered as captives were immense, but the years in Egypt exacted an even more serious toll. Israel would sing, "Who is like unto thee, O Lord, among the gods? who is like thee, glorious in holiness, fearful in praises, doing wonders?" (Exodus 15:11). But the truth, ironically, is that they had acquired the same problem that Pharaoh had: neither could tell the difference between Jehovah and a metal calf.

The work of the second Kirtland visitor may be the most difficult to understand. There is some uncertainty about both his identity and the nature of his mission. He was probably Noah acting as Elias restoring the dispensation of the gospel of Abraham. The spirit which he returned to the earth appears to be one which facilitates the restoration of all things which were the special province of earlier prophets, perhaps through an awakening of missionary feelings. What is it that's held in common among the Eliases (who laid the preparatory groundwork for important persons and events to come after them), and Noah (who responded to the second commission to replenish the earth) and Abraham (through whose seed later generations would be blessed)?

Aren't they all concerned with *continuity*? Didn't Noah restore the keys and the spirit for the *transmission* of ideas and principles and learning? It's "genetics," isn't it—Mendel and Noah working on the mechanism for the high-fidelity *perpetuation*, respectively, of physical characteristics and spiritual character?

Finally, Elijah, who occupied a unique position between the living and the dead. He restored a spirit which promotes the reciprocal concern of fathers and children for each other across generations, and the priesthood authority which permits the eternal sealing of those family bonds. Sealing: the principle is mutual ownership—a bonding; the objective is possession.

All right. But what does this have to do with my freshman friends longing for the end of the semester and the completion of their general education requirement in biology? The proposition is that the principles over which Moses, Noah, and Elijah have stewardship are in the broadest sense keys of learning, and are as essential for genuine academic accomplishment at the university as they were for the further growth and development of the Church in the first years after its restoration.

So in my fantasy I envision a late-night cram session in a Deseret Towers bedroom with John and Dave frantically memorizing the names of the parts of a cell or the stages in embryonic development. With widened eyes and open mouths they turn from their desks to face the three unexpected celestial visitors whose advice will change not only their present study habits but their long-term view about what learning can be. In such a circumstance, I believe, the boys would hear the following prescriptions:

> I am not unacquainted with mysteries and have some advice for you: make distinctions. The path to virtue, like fitting the pieces of a puzzle, often lies in the ability to discern differences, sometimes quite subtle. With all your memorizing, stop frequently and generate your own right answers. Better an instrument disciplined to sort out and differentiate than one trained only to function as a recorder. At times your journey into learning may be as frightening to anticipate and as arduous to accomplish as was my trek to Sinai. One is sometimes required to walk some distance into the uncertain desert before its secrets turn to insights. And you must do it for yourself. No one else can truly carry you out of Egypt.
>
> Genuine education is not a dead-end process. You can proceed through your years at BYU as a hurdler if you wish, jumping over requirements which you view as obstacles on the way to a diploma. Don't. There is little of futurity and much of futility in such a program. You will have done a lot and have become nothing better, occupying a very poor position from which to benefit generations to come. There will be much in your life which, like the weather, cannot always be accurately forecast. One must prepare or perish. I know! If you act as you talk, you'll probably get your wish and find your "GE courses behind you," "your electives out of the way," and "your schooling over with." Such sentiments suggest termination, not continuation, education that is ephemeral not eternal. And you will find, when the rains fall and the flood comes, that they will not have served you well. This is not just advice about attitude, but a recommendation about tactics. If you cannot transmit what you have 'learned' to someone else (your roommates, your spouse, your children, your community, your company), you probably haven't learned at all. Don't remain the faceless social security number in the roll book, secure in your anonymity, fixed in your passive role,

> neither asking nor answering questions, reluctant to submit your ideas to scrutiny, refraining from discussion and debate, always a consumer and never a producer. Can enigma give way to understanding under such a strategy? It's not what you've done that's important, but what you are and what you'll leave to others.
>
> Seal it to yourself. Whatever principle of intelligence you suppose you have attained to at BYU which is not your own, to which you have not acquired title, will not rise with you in the life beyond graduation. It's not Professor Smith's class; it's *your* class. Ask not, 'What do you think I should study?' or 'Will this be on the exam?' but decide for yourself what property you want to have and hold. Acquisitions of the mind, heart, and spirit made at the university, like a BMW or 300 ZX, are repossessed when one defaults on the payment required for ownership. Seal it to yourself.

I suspect that one of the insights which John and Dave would retain from such a vision is that learning is not necessarily instantaneous, even though that may be the premise on which they usually operate. Much of what we are exposed to in school, especially at an early age, may give us that impression because it is self-evident (red hair is a hereditary trait), it is intuitive (April showers bring May flowers), or it is simply a matter of definition (animals which are born in water and later adopt a terrestrial lifestyle are amphibians). As a result we come to expect immediate comprehension; Sherlock Holmes is quite dispensable. "Did you *get it*? He *catches on* easily." It's as if learning were baseball, and the student's task were as simple as getting behind the plate with a reasonably good mitt. Fastballs are routine; beware the occasional curve. This model may serve us well at times because many subjects must be first approached with factual details and definitions. But this model does not always suffice. What do we do when life serves up the intellectual, emotional, or spiritual equivalent of a knuckleball?

Having failed to catch on, to actually achieve learning, we may make two bad assumptions. First, we question the subject matter: it's inherently overly difficult. Next, and worse, we question ourselves: "I can't do it." When we neglect to acknowledge candidly that there are mysteries (of intrinsic complexity, whose solutions require time, patience, and creative effort), we are inclined to decree ourselves inherently incapable. We lose interest and give up. This response is not a thoughtful appraisal of one's relative talent nor a justifiable decision to opt for one particular course or major instead of another, but indefensible self-desertion. By subscribing to the instant-learning fallacy one robs oneself not only of the potentially deep and long-lasting satisfaction which comes from dealing successfully with a significant problem, but also of one's most indispensable asset as a life-long student—self-confidence. If this assertion is true, its long-term implications for John and Dave and their BYU teachers are not trivial. Much more than an undergraduate diploma is at stake. There's also a hint here about where the pedagogical emphasis ought to be. As with baseball pitchers, the chief concern of most teachers is delivery: what do we throw, and when? Could it be that we ought to be paying more attention to the processing operations going on in those who are catching our strikes?

The disciples incurred the wrath of the Pharisees for yet another breach of tradition. They ate bread without washing their hands. In an attempt to help them understand, Jesus taught, "Not that which goeth into the mouth defileth a man; but that which cometh out of the mouth, this defileth a man" (Matthew 15:11). It seems to me that the corollary to that proposition must be that it is also only that which comes out of a person, not that which goes in, which cleanses, purifies, and exalts him or her. The import of this idea is immense for both student and teacher, although, as in Christ's day, implementing the principle may require overturning a widely held tradition to the contrary.

To our students education means listening (to lectures or tapes) or watching (movies or videotapes), and study means reading (books and class notes). It is further assumed that the mind somehow automatically catalogs, evaluates, and records "that which goeth in" so that (with a little bit of luck) it can be retrieved, unadulterated, on demand. But there is an insidious deception in this. Too often the student listens to a sequence of ideas spoken by a teacher (or written in a text) and mentally makes the casual judgment, "I understand that; it all makes sense; sure, that's the way it is." But there's a major difference between the ephemeral "understanding" one supposes he has of a notion expressed by another human being, and the genuine personal comprehension which is manifested by the articulation of the concept in one's own words. So the alternative is to talk and to write. "Not that which goes into the ear or eye, but that which cometh out of the mouth and the pen, this is the measure of learning." In my imagination I see the recalcitrant mystery applauding silence and blank pieces of paper.

When a student fails to understand what was said in class, what's her remedy? "Will you please repeat that?" ("Let me hear it again.") Does that fix things? Not very often. Is it possible that the injunction "Be ye doers of the word, and not hearers only" (James 1:22) is not simply a call to action and a condemnation of insentience, but a formulation of an educational axiom: to wit, you have to do something active (perform some meaningful operation) on what you hear or read before any legitimate learning takes place. Before the IBM PC as a word processor there was the mind, and only in the processing of "that which goeth in" is there realization of the student's expectation of understanding and retention.

I think nearly all of us picked up a bad notion in our early years. Go back with me to Uintah School for another brief recollection. It's the first day of school in September. It's fourth grade. After lunch Mrs. Blackburn gives each of us a piece of lined gray paper. "The theme for this essay, class, is 'What I Did during the Summer Vacation.' " But that's as far as I get, a title at the top of the page. I twist and squirm and chew the end of my pencil. More fidgeting. I'm not alone. "You don't seem to be getting very far. What's the matter?" "I can't think of anything to write, Mrs. Blackburn." Only ten years old, and already we've got it mixed up. The order of operations may appear self-evident: think it out, write it down; the text of the theme appears on a screen in the mind, the fingers simply copy the message. That must be right. After all there's *The Thinker* seated, bent over with his chin in his hand mentally preparing his fourth-grade essay for Mrs. Blackburn before he picks up his pencil to write. Wrong! Thinking doesn't precede writing. Writing is a prerequisite to thinking. One thinks because one writes. I write—therefore I think.

Acting as if fast and testimony meeting were designed for the benefit of the listening audience, many stand to issue historical reports, calls to repentance, favorite admonitions, and other helpful hints of various kinds to their listeners. Too much of too many such meetings thus fails. The real intent, I submit, is to permit the speaker to learn through the act of trying to articulate impressions which otherwise will remain vague and uncertain. Time runs out and we "also thank you who didn't get a chance for your unspoken testimonies." My guess is that the half-life of the unspoken testimony is very brief; that which is unuttered remains a mystery. Did Joseph have all the right questions worked out in his mind, ready to ask, before he left the house for the grove that morning? Would They have come in response to silent concerns had he failed to pray vocally? My hunch is no—on both counts.

Are personal histories of value to our descendants? Yes. Will children and grandchildren find inspiration in the expressions of trial and error, of faith and achievement from the past? Yes. Is that why we should write them—out of a realization of their benefit to future generations? No. Write and learn. Write and seal your own faith. Write for your own inspiration. Personal histories are intended first for their authors.

For nineteen or twenty-one years a young Latter-day Saint listens and watches and reads and as a result may make a modest commitment to

Christian precepts and lifestyle. Then in an interval one-tenth as long that commitment can take a giant step toward perpetuity. Why? Because of "that which cometh out." The missionary learns because he talks. "Declare my gospel and [as a consequence—cause and effect] learn of me" (D&C 32:1). Thus the mysteries of the kingdom yield to articulation.

As a teacher at BYU I would convert human tape recorders into investigators. I would advocate an intellectual gathering and sealing. I would promote a system of academic genetics based on talking and writing. I would be a purveyor of mysteries.

In *Casablanca* Bogart and Bergman fan the flames of romance to the strains of a great melody, and on request Sam plays it again. But you know, the lyrics are incorrect. "A kiss is [*not*] just a kiss." A kiss is the anatomical juxtaposition of two orbicular muscles in a state of contraction.

WILLIAM S. BRADSHAW *received his BA from Harvard University and his PhD from the University of Illinois. He has been teaching at BYU for over twenty years and has been described by students as the kind of professor that not only teaches facts, but changes lives.*

Questions and Suggestions for Writing

1. How do Bradshaw's metaphors for education ("mystery," "investigator," and "human tape recorder") reveal his assumptions about education?
2. How does Bradshaw use personal experiences to strengthen his argument? Are they effective?
3. How does he use the stories to create an interesting conclusion?
4. Write about your own experience with trying to solve a mystery.

Piecing Together the Original Manuscript

Royal Skousen

"Piecing Together the Original Manuscript," originally published in the May 1992 issue of BYU Today, *details Royal Skousen's findings from his intense study of the original handwritten copy of the Book of Mormon. After analyzing a previous attempt by the Foundation for Ancient Research and Mormon Studies (FARMS) to produce a critical text—a version of a book indicating the alterations made to it from one edition to the next—Skousen decided to tackle the project again. Though not all of the manuscript is extant, Skousen and his colleagues use what they have and take great pains to preserve the worn and weathered pieces. He says that when Oliver Cowdery copied the original manuscript for the printer, he made an average of three errors per manuscript page, and then the printer in turn made about the same number of mistakes. Most errors were minor, but some of them are significant and help to establish the original English-language text of the Book of Mormon.*

Since 1988 I have been working on a critical text of the Book of Mormon. The main purposes of this critical text project are to establish the original English language text of the Book of Mormon, to the extent that it can be discovered; and to determine the history of the text, in particular, the changes that the text has undergone, both editorial and accidental.

Sometimes people mistakenly think that a Book of Mormon critical text would be critical of the Book of Mormon. To the contrary, the critical text project has led to a number of important discoveries about the translation of the book, all of which provide evidence that the book is, as Joseph Smith testified, a revelation from the Lord.

A critical text has two parts: the text itself and an apparatus that describes significant textual variants. Typically, the apparatus is composed of notes at the bottom of the page, below the text itself. In fact, the term "critical" specifically means that alternative readings are provided so that readers themselves can evaluate the textual variants.

The Book of Mormon critical text project serves a number of purposes. First, the original English language text will help researchers in their study of the language of the Book of Mormon. For instance, there were a good many Hebrew-like expressions in the original text that were uncharacteristic of English; as a result, subsequent editing of the text into modern English has often eliminated these potential Hebraisms. As an example, in English we express a conditional statement by using *if* and optionally *then*, as in the sentence "if you come, (then) I will come." In Hebrew, this same idea would be expressed as "if you come and I will come." The original text of the Book of Mormon contains many examples of this Hebrew way of expressing a conditional statement. Consider, for instance, the famous passage from Moroni 10:4. In the original language, it read as follows: "and if you shall ask with a sincere heart with real intent having faith in Christ *and* he will manifest the truth of it unto you by the power of the Holy Ghost." Although this sentence is excellent Hebrew, it is rather difficult for English speakers to understand. Accordingly, the conjunction *and* was removed by later editing (in the 1837 Kirtland edition). But scholars are very much interested in studying such potential Hebraisms and similar language characteristics of the Book of Mormon.

A second purpose of the critical text project has been to find errors in the transmission of the text, especially between the two manuscripts of the Book of Mormon—the original manuscript and the printer's manuscript. The original manuscript was written down by Joseph Smith's scribes as Joseph dictated the Book of Mormon during the spring and early summer of 1829. The printer's manuscript is a copy of the original manuscript and was produced for the printer to set the type for the 1830 edition. One example of a transmission error occurs in Alma 51:7, which describes the recall election of Parhoron (apparently spelled that way originally). In the original manuscript this verse reads "and Parhoron retained the judgment seat which caused much rejoicing among the brethren of Parhoron and also *among* the people of liberty." When Oliver Cowdery copied this passage as he was producing the printer's manuscript, he accidentally wrote *many* instead of *among*. This error, a very natural one, probably occurred because *many* is orthographically similar to *among*. As the 1830 printer was preparing the printer's manuscript for typesetting, he couldn't make complete sense of the phrase "and also many the people of liberty," so he penciled in the word *of*, thus producing "and also many of the people of liberty," the reading in all printed editions of the Book of Mormon.

Another important purpose for this project is that it will provide a better understanding of the transmission of the Book of Mormon text. As a part of this project, we have been able to find support for what witnesses said about the translation process. In addition, we have been able to determine the kinds of problems the scribes had in writing down Joseph Smith's dictation as well as in preparing the printer's manuscript from the original manuscript. The critical text will also allow researchers to make a thorough analysis of the grammatical changes that have been made in the text over the years.

The first critical text of the Book of Mormon was published by the Foundation for Ancient Research and Mormon Studies (FARMS) during 1984–86. The three volumes of this critical text provide the complete text of the Book of Mormon plus selective notes on the history of the text. Nonetheless, this version is preliminary in many respects. It is based on a computerized version of the 1830 edition corrected to agree with microfilm versions of the printer's and original manuscripts. And its list of textual variants was determined by searching through various editions of the Book of Mormon. In 1988, at the annual meeting of the Deseret Language and Linguistics Society at BYU, I made a proposal for doing a computer-based critical text of the Book of Mormon. FARMS agreed to support this project; and John W. Welch, professor of law at BYU and, at that time, president of FARMS, arranged for access to photographs of the two manuscripts.

The first step of this project has been to create computerized versions of all the significant textual sources. This includes making facsimile transcripts of the two manuscripts. In a facsimile transcript we attempt to indicate in typescript precisely how the manuscript actually reads. We spell words as they are actually spelled in the manuscript. If words are crossed out, erased, or overwritten, we indicate the original as well as the corrected wording. The transcript also represents the exact placement of the words on each line or sometimes above the line in the case of insertions. In addition to making transcripts from the photographs of the manuscripts, we have also checked these transcripts against the actual physical manuscripts.

Besides the electronic versions of the two manuscripts, 17 significant editions of the Book of Mormon have also been electronically reproduced. All but one have been optically scanned by the Kurzweil scanner at the Humanities Research Center at BYU. Preliminary computerized collations (or comparisons) of these 17 editions have already been made. Ultimately, a complete collation of the editions as well as the manuscripts will allow us to make a detailed study of the textual history of the Book of Mormon. From this collation, a large database will be constructed that will allow us to look up any word or phrase and find its appearances in all the textual sources. The final stage of the project will then be to construct the critical text (including its apparatus) directly from this database. This project will probably take another three years to complete the task of producing the critical text.

One of the most significant accomplishments of the critical text project has been the conservation and photographing of the Wilford Wood fragments of the original manuscript. Wilford Wood, a furrier from Bountiful, Utah, was a collector of Mormon artifacts, and one of his most important acquisitions was Lewis Bidamon's remaining fragments from the original manuscript. In 1841 Joseph Smith placed this manuscript in the cornerstone of the Nauvoo House. In 1882 Lewis Bidamon, Emma Smith's second husband, removed the contents of the cornerstone and discovered that most of the original manuscript had been destroyed by water seepage. Over the next six years Bidamon handed out the larger and better preserved fragments of the manuscript. Most of these larger fragments are now housed in the LDS Church historical department in Salt Lake City, and account for about 25 percent of the text of the original manuscript. But Bidamon apparently kept for himself some of the smaller fragments. In 1937 Wilford Wood bought these fragments from Charles Bidamon, Lewis's son.

Last summer I arranged with the Wilford Wood family to conserve and photograph these fragments. As part of this work, I organized at BYU a professional team composed of Robert Espinosa, head of conservation at the Harold B. Lee Library; David Hawkinson, photographer for the Museum of Fine Arts; and myself as editor of the critical text project. On September 30, Richard Glade, representing the Wilford Wood Foundation, brought the fragments to the BYU library, and Robert Espinosa began the difficult task of separating the fragments, which were compressed together in a lump. Individual fragments, after being separated from the lump, were humidified, unfolded, and flattened. Robert Espinosa was assisted in this exacting work by Cathy Bell and Pamela Barrios, the two other conservators in the library's conservation lab. David Hawkinson then used various photographic techniques to reveal and document the very faint handwriting on the fragments. Black-and-white ultraviolet reflected photography proved to be the most successful in revealing the faded handwriting. In addition, Robert Espinosa identified the paper type for each fragment, excluding fragments smaller than half a square centimeter. In all he discovered four different kinds of paper for these fragments from the original manuscript. Finally, after encapsulating the fragments in mylar (polyester film), the conservators returned the fragments to the Wilford Wood family. This process took three weeks.

Using the ultraviolet photographs and the computerized scriptures, I have determined that the larger fragments come from six different places in the manuscript: 2 Nephi 5–9, 2 Nephi 23–25, 2 Nephi 33–Jacob 4, Jacob 5–Enos, Helaman 13–3 Nephi 4, and Ether 3–15. These fragments come from 29 leaves (or 58 pages) of the original manuscript. In all they account for perhaps 2–3 percent of the original text. And in each place the handwriting is Oliver Cowdery's.

Since the completion of the conservation, I have been working on identifying the smaller fragments. By means of a special computer database, I have been able to identify nearly all the fragments, except for the smallest ones plus a few larger illegible fragments that were badly damaged. For the most part I have been able to put together what are quite literally the "puzzle pieces" for these fragments. In addition, I have been working on the facsimile transcript for these reconstructions.

A number of significant findings have come from studying the Wilford Wood fragments. In particular, a few textual changes have been discovered. In producing the printer's manuscript from the original manuscript, Oliver Cowdery made, on the average, two or three changes per manuscript page. These changes are, for the most part, simple errors and do not significantly affect the text of the Book of Mormon. The errors frequently occur in groups, which seems to indicate tiring. Consider, for instance, a large fragment from 2 Nephi 7:1–8. In copying this part of the text Oliver Cowdery made six changes:

verse 2: wherefore when I *came* there was no man > *come*
I make *the* rivers a wilderness > *their*
they *dieth* because of thirst > *die*

verse 4: he *wakeneth* morning by morning > *waketh*
he *wakeneth* mine ear > *waketh*

verse 5: the Lord God hath *opened* mine ear > *appointed*

This passage is quoted from chapter 50 of the Book of Isaiah and in the language, of course, of the King James Version. Interestingly, each of the six original readings in this passage is identical with its corresponding reading in the King James Version. In other words, these six changes in the printer's manuscript move the Book of Mormon text further away from the King James text.

All these errors are accidental and introduce only minor changes. Still, two of them, *come* and *appointed*, do create difficult readings. In verse 2, the correct past tense form *came* was restored to the text in the 1837 edition of the Book of Mormon. Similarly, in verse 5, the correct verb form *opened* was restored in the 1840 edition, as well as later in the

1879 and all subsequent LDS editions of the Book of Mormon. In the other four examples, the changed form has remained in the text ever since its first appearance in the printer's manuscript.

Another interesting find from the Wilford Wood fragments is that we have the top outer corner for two leaves (from Jacob 6 through Enos 1). Page numbers appear here, namely from 111 through 114. Corresponding pages in the printer's manuscript are numbered from 107 through 111. Normally, each page in the original manuscript has a heading at the top of the page which briefly describes the page content. Such headings appear in the first half of 1 Nephi and in two extant portions of Alma and Helaman. But these headings are missing in the second half of 1 Nephi and in extant pages from the beginning of 2 Nephi. And they are also missing here in fragments from Jacob and Enos.

There is clear evidence in the original manuscript that Joseph Smith, as part of the translation process, could see the English spelling of names. Witnesses to the translation indicated that Joseph would sometimes spell out names so that the scribe could get them down correctly. Frequently, in the original manuscript, when a Book of Mormon name first occurs (or has not occurred for some time), that name is first written out in a more phonetic but incorrect spelling, then this incorrect spelling is crossed out and the correct spelling immediately follows. For instance, in Alma 33:15 Oliver Cowdery first spells the prophet Zenoch's name as *Zenock*, then he crosses out the whole name and rewrites it with a *ch* at the end rather than a *ck*, thus indicating that the correct spelling is *Zenoch* (as in *Enoch*). Similarly, in Helaman 1:15 Oliver ends *Coriantumr* with the spelling *-tummer*, then he crosses out the whole name and follows it with the correct spelling, which ends with *-tumr*, an impossible spelling for English. And in the Wilford Wood fragments, we find another example. In Ether 13:27, the place name *Gilgal* is first written by Oliver Cowdery with two *l*'s at the end of the word, then the second *l* is carefully crossed out. Since either spelling is theoretically possible, it appears that once more Oliver had to ask Joseph how to spell an unfamiliar name.

One group of fragments from the Wilford Wood collection form the gutters (that is, the inner fold) for a gathering of sheets from Ether. In the original lump, these fragments had been twisted into a roll. Attached to the roll was a piece of the original thread that had been used to hold the sheets of the gathering together. Reconstruction of these fragments demonstrates that originally there were at least four sheets in this gathering.

This gathering follows Oliver Cowdery's typical sequence for producing a gathering. The sheets were first ruled and then folded once, but only later—after Oliver had finished writing down the text—were the stab marks and the thread itself added to produce the sewn gathering. Evidence for this production sequence can be found from the center sheet of the Ether gathering. On the inner side of this sheet (unlike all other extant gatherings of either manuscript), Oliver Cowdery wrote all the way across the whole sheet. Words are written without break right across the gutters—and without smearing, thus showing that the gathering had not yet been sewn together.

Finally, the Wilford Wood fragments give strong evidence that for 72 pages the original manuscript rather than the printer's manuscript was used as the printer's copy for typesetting the 1830 edition. I first discovered this at the LDS Church historical department when I noticed a fragment from 3 Nephi 26–27 covered with printer's marks. Both the original and printer's manuscripts, when first written down, had very little punctuation. The Palmyra printer frequently added punctuation marks to his copy in order to help him typeset the 1830 edition. About a third of the pages in the printer's manuscript are covered with these printer's marks, mostly in pencil. The fact that a fragment from the original manuscript has these same pencil marks indicates that the original must have been used at least once as the printer's copy during the printing process.

Additional evidence for this use of the original manuscript can be found in the 1830 edition itself. For instance, in Mormon the name *Cumorah* is consistently misspelled as *Camorah*, yet the printer's manuscript (in an unknown scribe's hand) shows a clear *u* for the spelling of the first vowel of *Cumorah*. On the other hand, throughout both manuscripts Oliver Cowdery frequently makes his *a*'s like *u*'s and vice versa. This scribal characteristic of his could well serve as the source for the misspelled *Camorah*, but only if the manuscript source for Mormon in the 1830 edition is the original manuscript (and presumably in Oliver Cowdery's hand).

In April of last year, when I was able to work directly on the printer's manuscript at the RLDS Auditorium in Independence, Missouri, I discovered that for 72 pages of that manuscript, from Helaman 13 through Mormon, there is no sign that those pages were used as the printer's copy. Unlike surrounding gatherings of the printer's manuscript, the four gatherings for these 72 pages are not cut up nor are there any printer's marks. The threads that originally held these four gatherings together were removed only a few decades ago, and thus stains from those threads are clearly visible in the folds of these four gatherings. Since such stains do not appear on any of the other gatherings in the printer's manuscript, presumably their threads were removed soon after arriving at the Palmyra printer's shop, especially since so many of those sheets were cut up to facilitate the typesetting.

The Wilford Wood fragments provide important support for this extensive use of the original manuscript as the printer's copy. Large fragments from Helaman 13–15 clearly show the penciled printer's marks. Similar marks also appear on smaller fragments from the beginning of 3 Nephi. This evidence is important for establishing the degree to which the original manuscript was used as the printer's copy.

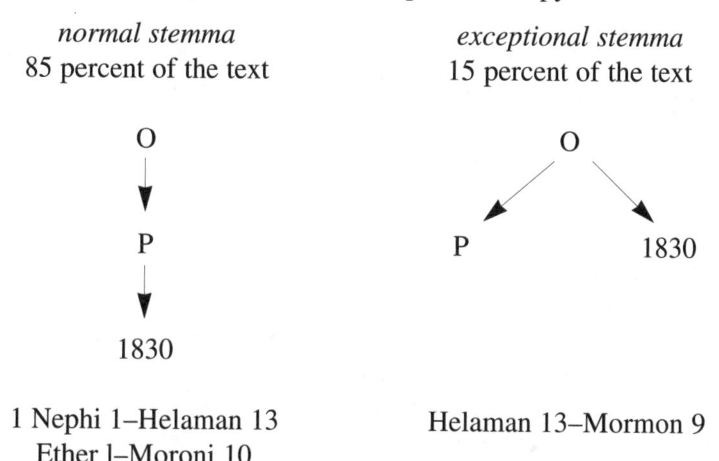

1 Nephi 1–Helaman 13
Ether l–Moroni 10

Helaman 13–Mormon 9

We may ask why the original manuscript was used for this purpose. One possible explanation is that those responsible for producing the printer's manuscript fell behind in their copy work. Oliver Cowdery, Martin Harris, and Hyrum Smith were not only responsible for making the copy, but also for overseeing its use at the printer's shop. Their responsibilities included proofing the typeset sheets (according to John Gilbert, one of the 1830 compositors). In order to meet the printer's demands for more copy, it was apparently decided to take in the original manuscript rather than having the press work stop. Presumably, these brethren no longer felt any great risk in using the original manuscript as the printer's copy, especially since they had already finished three-fourths of the typesetting without any problems of theft. In any event, they still attempted to catch up in their copy work and finally had Oliver Cowdery and another scribe (not yet identified) work together on the printer's manuscript. Apparently, Oliver had been able to complete the printer's manuscript up through 3 Nephi 19. The unknown scribe then continued the work from there while Oliver started on Ether. When this unknown scribe finally finished Mormon, he left the rest of the page blank. This nearly blank page is the last page of a short gathering of four sheets. Nowhere else in any of the manuscripts is there any page left partially blank; except for here, the scribe always begins the following book on the very next line. This hiatus at the end of Mormon strongly supports the hypothesis that in the printer's manuscript Ether was begun before the copying of Mormon was finished.

This partial use of the original manuscript as the printer's copy is very significant for the critical text project. For about 85 percent of the Book of Mormon, there is only one first-hand copy of the original manuscript; namely, the printer's manuscript. For this portion of the text, the 1830 edition is a copy of the printer's manuscript and is thus twice removed from the original manuscript. But for 15 percent of the text, from Helaman 13 to the end of Mormon, we have two first-hand copies of the original manuscript; namely, the printer's manuscript and the 1830 edition. We have relatively little of the original manuscript for this portion, but we can compare the two first-hand copies with each other. In most cases the printer's manuscript and the 1830 edition will agree, and we can be fairly confident that this common reading accurately reflects the reading of the original manuscript. In fact, consistency of the common reading can be tested, to some degree, by comparing it with what remains of the original manuscript. On the other hand, whenever the printer's manuscript and the 1830 edition disagree in these 72 pages, we can be fairly sure that one of the readings represents the original reading, but of course the problem here will be to determine which one is the right one. Nonetheless, we are delighted to be given two possibilities instead of just one.

These are some of the important findings from our work with the Wilford Wood fragments. I would like to express my thanks to the Wilford Wood family for their graciousness in allowing us access to these fragments. In addition, I am especially grateful for such colleagues as Robert Espinosa and David Hawkinson, who made it such a joy to work on the Wilford Wood fragments. I have also received a good deal of personal satisfaction in working on this project. My own professional work had led me to study a number of different academic areas without ever suspecting that these diverse fields would all come together in my work on the text of the Book of Mormon.

There has also been a spiritual dimension to this work. My own testimony of the Book of Mormon is not based on my work on the critical text, but rather on my own personal witness of some 15 years ago that this book records events which actually happened. Nonetheless, it has been a delight to have discovered evidence in the original manuscript to support what witnesses said about how Joseph Smith translated. The Book of Mormon is truly "a marvelous work and a wonder," and there is direct textual evidence that it is a revelation from the Lord.

ROYAL SKOUSEN *earned his BA in English at BYU and then received an MA and a PhD in linguistics from the University of Illinois. Before coming to BYU, he taught at the University of Texas. He has also taught in Finland as a Fulbright scholar and as a visiting professor at the University of California at San Diego. He is currently a professor of English at BYU, teaching English language courses and working almost full time on the Book of Mormon critical text project.*

Questions

1. How is Dr. Skousen's research project inter-disciplinary?
2. How was the evidence gathered?
3. Do historical studies argue for or against inspiration as the source of the Book of Mormon? Explain your answer.
4. What do textual variations reveal about the writing, translating, and printing processes? Do they have implications for revision in your own writing?

Black Mormons in the 1980s: Pioneers in a White Church[1]

CARDELL K. JACOBSON

In this article, which was orginally published in the Review of Religious Research, *Cardell Jacobson reviews the involvement of African-American blacks in the LDS church in light of the "streams" of religious "switching" that have traditionally occured in the United States. Traditionally upwardly-mobile people have joined religious congregations that correspond to their new-found economic status. Jacobson finds that African-Americans likely to join the LDS church generally fit this description, even though the LDS church is not generally considered to be a mainline church. Jacobson's research leads us to ask how as a church we can better help people from different economic and social backgrounds achieve full participation in the Church. As Jacobson notes, we don't always "do very well in keeping our working-class members active."*

Despite considerable desegregation of most societal institutions, Sunday mornings remain highly segregated as they have been for decades. For example, Roof and McKinney (1987) recently estimated that 85 percent of black Americans attend black denominations. As in earlier decades, others remain in segregated congregations within denominations.

The Church of Jesus Christ of Latter-day Saints, commonly known as the Mormon church or the LDS church, also never had many black members. Several factors contributed to the low numbers in the Mormon church. First, the LDS church was geographically isolated for much of its history in the inter-mountain west which has a very low proportion of blacks. The Church also did not proselyte among blacks and extended full priesthood rights to black members only in June of 1978. The lack of priesthood rights precluded participation in temple ordinances and some lay callings within the church.

Since the June 1978 announcement, church missionary work has been directed to predominantly black nations where it had not been previously and to all individuals within other nations. Since the LDS church does not keep membership records by race, the number of black converts to the LDS church is not known and is impossible to obtain. Nevertheless, the number is sizeable and growing. In 1988, Chandler (1988) estimated the worldwide black membership of the church as between 125,000 and 200,000. Sizeable numbers of black LDS members are located in both the North and the South, as well as in the West.

Almost nothing is known, however, about those blacks who have joined this previously predominantly white church. The purpose of this paper is to describe a sample of blacks in the United States who joined the LDS church. Later I shall offer some speculations about how they fit in the "streams" of religious switchers in the United States.

Sample and Data

The data presented below were coded from 224 oral history interviews conducted by the Charles Redd Center at Brigham Young University under the direction of Jessie L. Embry. All but one were converts to the LDS church and most joined after the 1978 change in priesthood policy. The oral histories were obtained from 1985 to 1988 by Alan Cherry, himself a black member of the LDS church. The interviews were obtained through a "snowball" technique in which the names of other black members were obtained through the first respondents. Cherry interviewed a diverse sample of converts, females as well as males, those who had been members for some time as well as new converts, etc. Except for a handful of unique cases, everyone responded positively to the opportunity to be interviewed. Thus, the response rate was well over ninety percent.

This same technique was used in various parts of the United States to obtain accounts of the experiences of black converts in all regions of the country. Thus, Cherry obtained interviews in the Far West (Northern and Southern California, Arizona, Hawaii), the Northeast and Near South (New York, Pennsylvania, Maryland, Washington, DC, and Virginia), the South (Georgia, Alabama, Mississippi, Louisiana, and North Carolina), and the Midwest (Illinois, Ohio, Michigan, Indiana, and Missouri). Between 30 and 40 interviews were obtained in each region. Fifty-six percent of the sample were female, 44 percent male.

The interviews were held in the homes of the respondents or their friends and, in a few cases, in church buildings. Cherry followed a consistent but very general outline of topics to be covered. The interviews ranged from one to three hours and were recorded. They were subsequently transcribed and sent to the interviewees for correction and/or clarification. The transcribed protocols range from 10 to 40 pages.

The sample has some important limitations. It is primarily a sample of active members of the church—those who joined the church and stayed. In general it does not reflect those who joined and later left the church or became inactive, though a few of them were included.

This paper is based on a content analysis of the transcripts. At least two coders read each transcript and recorded factual information such as age, number of marriages and number of children, where respondents grew up, education, and occupation. This information was relatively easy to obtain and intercoder reliability on these items was 95 percent or higher. More impressionistic observations, such as feelings about the priesthood announcement, reactions of other family members about their joining, and a variety of other topics were also coded. Intercoder reliability was lower on these items (about 85%), but these items are not generally discussed in this paper.

RESULTS

This sample is clearly religiously active. For example, where the information could be ascertained, 78 percent have had a patriarchal blessing and over 60 percent have been through the temple.[2] Both indicate high levels of church activity. Over 95 percent report reading the scriptures on a regular basis, either with their family or individually. Over eighty percent have family prayer. Information on payment of tithing could be coded in only 61 percent of the cases, but in those cases over ninety percent said they tithed on a regular basis. No doubt these questions elicited some socially acceptable answers instead of accurate answers. Neverthe-less, the overall religiosity of the sample appears to be very high.

The coders were able to identify an occupational or equivalent status for all but five of the 224 in the sample. Twenty-eight were students; fourteen were house-wives or homemakers. The most common occupation was that of teacher or teacher's aide (22). Ten were nurses. Others were managers at fast food places, worked in retail stores, and held a variety of other middle- and lower-middle-class occupations. Among the employed. 72 percent were engaged in white-collar occupations and 28 percent in blue-collar occupations.

The prestige scale of the (GSS) General Social Survey (see Davis and Smith, 1987) was used to code the occupational prestige of the black LDS sample. The average occupational prestige score of the LDS sample was substantially higher than that of the 1987 GSS sample of black Americans (46 compared to 32).

This sample is also better educated than the population of black Americans as a whole. This is shown in Table 1 where data from the LDS sample are compared to the Current Population Reports. Sixty-six percent of the black LDS sample had attended or graduated from college compared to 26.4 percent of the blacks in the Current Population Reports. On the other hand, 36.5 percent of the national sample had less than a high school education compared to less than 11 percent of the LDS sample.

The sample of blacks who joined the LDS church not only had higher educational levels than the black community as a whole, but they also had higher levels than the whites in the church (see Table 1), and the whites in the church have slightly higher levels of education than whites in the United States as a whole (Goodman and Heaton, 1986).

Table 1. Educational levels of the black and white LDS samples and national percentages.

Educational Level	Black LDS	US Blacks	White LDS	US Whites
Less than High School	1.1	18.3	15.9	12.0
Some High School	9.3	18.2		11.0
High School Graduate	13.7	37.1	35.3	39.2
Vocational Training	9.8	not given	not given	not given
Some College	33.9	15.7	26.8	17.2
College Graduate	32.2	10.7	22.1	20.5

Sources: White LDS sample data were collected in 1981 by Goodman and Heaton (1986). Black and White United States data are for the year 1987 and are from *Statistical Abstracts of the United States: 1989*, 109th edition, (US Bureau of Census, Washington, DC), p. 131.

Impressionistic indications of upward mobility were also garnered by the coders who were asked to estimate the social class of the LDS sample during childhood and at the time of the interviews. The ratings of the coders suggest that the respondents were somewhat socially mobile with most of the mobility occurring from the working class to lower middle-class. Table 2 is a cross tabulation of the coders' ratings of social class of the respondents during childhood and at the time of the interviews. Forty nine of the 108 who were judged to have grown up in the working class were rated by the coders as lower-middle class when they were interviewed; nine were judged to be either upper class or upper-middle class. Only two of those who grew up in poverty were thought still to be impoverished when they were interviewed whereas eleven were thought to be working class and four were thought to be lower-middle class. Two additional individuals were listed as being upper-class or upper-middle class. Most Americans have experienced some social mobility, however, and so these results may not be atypical.

Table 2. Coders' impression of the social class of the respondents during their childhood and at the time of the interview.

Social Class Growing Up	Social Class at Time of Interview: Poverty	Working	Lower-Middle	Upper-Middle	Upper	Total
Upper Class				1		1
Upper-Middle Class		1	4	5	1	11
Lower-Middle Class		4	37	5		46
Working Class	2	48	49	8	1	108
Poverty	2	11	4	1	1	19

$x^2 = 65.3$, df = 16, $p < .01$

Some educational mobility also occurred. Thirty-three of the 43 from lower-middle-class origins attended or graduated from college and 61 of the 98 working-class origins did as well. Eight of the 14 judged to have grown up in poverty also attended or graduated from college.

The family life of the black LDS sample appears to be more stable than that of the GSS sample. Most of the LDS respondents were married (49.5 percent) or remarried after being divorced (9.6 percent). The same figures for the GSS sample were 32.4 percent and 22.4 percent. Seventeen percent of the LDS sample were currently divorced or separated compared to 23.9 percent of the GSS sample.

The sample was also relatively young. The average age when they joined the church was 34. Over three-quarters of them were under 40; one third were under 25. The average age of the GSS sample was 45. Since the typical black convert joined between the ages of 25 and 40, most would have obtained their education (and attendant occupation status) before joining the church.

Finally, the converts had experienced considerable integration in other settings before joining the LDS church. Measures of contact and its favorableness are extremely difficult to obtain. Nevertheless, the oral histories indicate that nearly a quarter of the sample (53) had some military service and at least 16 grew up in military families. Obviously a lot of inter-racial contact would occur in such situations and might make some blacks feel comfortable about worshiping with whites. Attendance at desegregated schools and work with whites would also lead to more comfortableness.

The coders were asked to assess how much contact the respondents had with whites while growing up. The estimate was that most of the respondents had either some (17 percent) or frequent (53 percent) contact with whites. Almost 90 percent were judged to have had frequent contact with whites while an adult.

Furthermore, at least 22 individuals (ten percent) had been or were currently married to whites or mates of Hispanic origin. Again, these people would probably feel more comfortable than other blacks in attending a predominantly white church.

Discussion

The data reported here are limited. The sampling procedure probably resulted in more middle-class blacks in the sample than would be in the LDS church. Nevertheless, the respondents score high enough on the measures of education and occupational status to suggest that blacks who join the LDS church are not reflective of black Americans in general. A question naturally arises then as to how such a group would fit in the "streams" of religious switching in American society.

Religion in the United States has always been in a state of flux (Roof and McKinney, 1987), and the current religious scene is characterized by a high degree of religious switching. Switching, like religion itself, has been highly segregated in the past. Gradually, however, some integration occurred and some blacks have joined white churches. I have described a sample of blacks who joined a previously white church. How such switchers fit into the "streams" of religious movement is not clear.

Roof and McKinney (1987, chapter 5) note that three streams have existed in the "circulation of the saints." One stream is the "upward movement" that has usually resulted in gains for the liberal Protestants. But a reaction to the secular trends and accommodation of mainline faiths to the secular culture has produced a counter-stream. Roof and McKinney argue that this stream is usually composed of younger, less educated members who are often conservative on social issues such as abortion and gay rights. Their third stream is the general secular drift to non-affiliation.

The LDS church is clearly not a liberal church and is very conservative on abortion and gay rights. Its membership is mainstream or more liberal on the other scales developed by Roof and McKinney (1987, chapter 6), however. This includes the scales on civil liberties, racial justice, and women's rights. The members fall with the conservatives only on the moral issues.

Thus, the fit of the black Mormon sample into any of three streams is not obvious or clear. The attitudes of the sample towards social issues could not be ascertained from the oral histories. The educational, occupational, and marital characteristics, however, seem to describe what would have traditionally been part of the first stream. Interestingly, Heaton (1989) has found converts to the LDS church in Mexico to be upwardly mobile.

That Mormons are predominantly middle class may not be evident to all readers. Roof and McKinney (1987:110–111), have noted, however, that the social status of LDS church members in the United States has risen greatly over the past decades. While the LDS church scored near the bottom of their bottom rank in the mid-1940s, it was the highest of the middle rank (based on education, occupational prestige, family income, and perceived social class) by the 1980s. Only Unitarians, Jews, Episcopalians, Presbyterians, and the United Church of Christ ranked higher. (For corroborating data see Goodman and Heaton, 1986.) In the 1980s, the three major black denominations, Black Northern Baptists, Black Methodists, and Black Southern Baptists, on the other hand, ranked in the lower half of the bottom group of Roof and McKinney's (1987:112–113) classification.

For black switchers, the characteristics of the destination church may be especially important factors. In this light, membership in the LDS church could convey several positive benefits to black switchers which would assuage negative feelings about the church's previous (nearly) all-white composition and its priesthood ban. First, it is (now) an integrated church. Local congregations are based on geographical areas so that no official segregation occurs. Secondly, the LDS church has a middle-class core and lifestyle that would appeal to middle-class blacks or those who are socially mobile. Finally, doctrinal, biblical, and moral conservativeness combined with the middle class composition of the LDS church make an interesting attraction for middle-class blacks.

An additional factor which would distinguish the LDS church from the traditionally mainline churches as the destination church is the proselyting of the LDS church. Because of the missionary activity throughout the United States, blacks are perchance more likely to encounter the LDS church than other churches and receive requests to join.

If blacks who join the LDS church in the United States are part of the upward mobility stream that has existed among mainline Protestant denominations for a number of generations, the upward stream may be more fragmented than previously thought. Heretofore unnoticed subcurrents probably exist, especially within the black community and between black and white churches. Until these patterns are examined in several denominations, we cannot portray the full complexity of the streams, counter-streams, and eddies that comprise the religious currents of black and white society today.

CARDELL K. JACOBSON *became a sociologist of race and ethnic relations, he says, because of the racism he grew up with. Later experience living in North Carolina and Milwaukee, Wisconsin further heightened his interest in race relations. Jacobson received his BS in sociology from BYU and then went to the University of North Carolina at Chapel Hill where he received an MA and a PhD. He has been teaching at BYU since 1981 and has published widely on the sociology of race and ethnic relations and social psychology.*

Notes

1 This paper has benefitted from a critical reading by Tim B. Heaton anad Mary Lou McNamara. Principal coders were Mark Harris, Teresa Yancey, Trina Hope, Jon Davis, Donalda DeAdler, Tami Tank, Jeanne Husberg, Jenifer Kunz, Sheila Hewitt, and Jim Kanan. An earlier version was read at the annual meetings of the Society for the Scientific Study of Religion, Salt Lake City, October, 1989.

2 Mormons "in good standing" are encouraged to obtain a temple recommend and do proxy baptisms and "sealings" of couples and families together who have died. Patriarchal blessings are special promises and blessings given to individuals who seek them.

References

Chandler, Russell
1988 "Mormonism: A challenge for Blacks." Los Angeles Times (August 12).

Davis, James Allen and Tom W. Smith
1987 General Social Surveys, 1972–1987: Cumulative Codebook. Chicago: National Opinion Research Center.

Goodman, Kristen L. and Tim B. Heaton
1986 "LDS church members in the US and Canada: A demographic profile." AMCAP Journal 12:88–107.

Heaton, Tim B.
1989 "Religious influences on Mormon fertility: Cross-national comparisons." Review of Religious Research 30:401–411.

Roof, Wade Clark, and William McKinney
1987 American Mainline Religion: Its Changing Shape and Future. New Brunswick: Rutgers University Press.

Questions

1. What does the author mean by, "Sunday mornings remain highly segregated"? What figure of speech does the use of "Sunday morning" represent?
2. What does the author mean when he says, "the sample is not random"? Why is this statement important for understanding the data?
3. How do the water metaphors ("streams," "eddies") help to clarify the data in this article?
4. What do the results of this study (i.e., that predominantly upwardly mobile African Americans join the LDS church) imply for the future growth of the Church?

Gambling: A Lie and a Snare

TYLER J. AND HEIDI B. JARVIS

For the research reported here, Tyler and Heidi Jarvis talked to many people who said that they "believed that gambling was entertainment." The Jarvises claim that the public, however, misunderstands the odds, and thus doesn't fully understand the deceitful nature of gambling. In this article, they explicate the odds of gambling, including gambling at casinos and lotteries, and make a call for at least more extensive education on the truth about gambling, if not a call for its total eradication. For further information on this topic, you may visit their website: http://www.math.byu.edu/~jarvis/gambling.html.

The Lord's prophets have always been unequivocal in their opposition to gambling and lotteries. As President Joseph F. Smith said, "The Church does not approve of gambling but strongly condemns it as morally wrong, and classes also with this gambling, games of chance and lotteries of all kinds, and earnestly disapproves of any of its members engaging therein."[1] And President Kimball has said, "Filthy lucre is blood money; that which is obtained through theft and robbery. It is that obtained through gambling or the operation of gambling establishments."[2] Many negative consequences result from gambling, including greatly increased crime, the destruction of family and society, and the many problems that result from compulsive and pathological gamblers. Yet it is important to be aware of another issue as well, namely, that although most people believe they understand the risks involved, in fact they do not. And their confusion about risks, along with other misunderstandings and biases, makes it easy for gambling providers to manipulate and defraud them.

BACKGROUND

It is well established that crime rates rise substantially in areas where gambling is legalized. One striking example comes from Atlantic City, New Jersey, where according to the FBI, larceny increased by 467% in the first nine years after gambling was legalized there.[3] The state of Illinois, when debating whether to permit casino gambling in Chicago, estimated that increased costs in law enforcement would easily require more than all of the one hundred million dollars in expected tax revenue that gambling was supposed to bring the state.[4] And some estimates placed the increase in law enforcement costs at ten times that number—over one billion dollars annually.[5]

Not only does legalized gambling increase local crime, it is also destructive to individuals and families. Gambling is often addictive, and many people who gamble develop into problem or compulsive gamblers. The American Psychiatric Association's *Diagnostic and Statistical Manual of Mental Disorders* characterizes pathological gambling as a "chronic and progressive failure to resist impulses to gamble, a gambling behavior that compromises, disrupts, or damages personal, family, or vocational pursuits."[6] The number of compulsive gamblers and problem gamblers increases substantially when gambling is legalized. In 1974, when Nevada was the only state where gambling was permitted, the number of problem gamblers in the United States was much less than one percent of the country's population, whereas, in Nevada it exceeded 2.5%.[7] Currently, the number of compulsive gamblers is estimated at approximately 1% of the population in states where gambling is illegal, but close to 5% in states where gambling is legal.[8] And fully 10% of the entire population constitute problem gamblers.[9]

Compulsive and problem gambling lead to personal indebtedness and tend to destroy the gambler's family, emotionally as well as financially, as the family's income, belongings, and even groceries are sacrificed to the insatiable desire to win. Gamblers' debts frequently lead them to crime and other destructive behavior.[10] And this inflicts great costs, not only on the gambler and his or her family, but also on society as a whole. It is currently estimated that each problem gambler costs the state $52,000,[11] and in 1994, the state of Maryland put the cost of all compulsive gambling in that state at 1.5 billion dollars.[12] The national and global costs are huge, and this is only the financial cost of an immense problem that has many destructive aspects for society and our families.

Yet despite all of these facts, gambling is growing throughout the world. In the United States in the early 1970s, when the only legal gambling was in Nevada, the amount of money wagered legally was about 17.3 billion dollars. By 1993, however, that number had ballooned to 394.3 billion dollars,[13] far more than the amount spent on all other forms of entertainment combined.[14] In the United States, the average gambling expenditure per person was $200 during 1991, in Australia it was $400, and in Minnesota it was $500.[15] The problem is common in Europe, as well. Even Albania and Britain, the last European holdouts against state-run lotteries, finally succumbed to the temptation and instituted lotteries in 1993 and 1994, respectively.[16] This growth in gambling has made it seem more socially acceptable, to the point that even many members of the Church see nothing wrong with spending a little in the slot machines or buying a lottery ticket once in a while. It is another example of Satan's "deceiving the very elect" (Matt 24:24).

THE PROBLEM

Why is gambling becoming so popular in spite of its many destructive consequences? This is a difficult question which has been studied extensively, and for which there are few satisfactory answers. It seems that one of the biggest problems is simply misunderstanding. Although many people are aware of the moral and religious arguments against gambling, and some are also aware of the economic and social costs, there are three other issues which are less often discussed, and whose understanding is important. First, most of us do not understand just how bad the odds are; second, a variety of other misunderstandings interfere with our ability to use the odds; and third, casinos, lotteries, and other gambling providers manipulate these misunderstandings to entice and exploit gamblers. But by learning about the odds and examining the misunderstandings we can overcome all three of these problems. In fact, research shows that the more people learn, the less likely they are to gamble.[17] And it is important for us to be aware of these problems so we can add their strength to the more common arguments against gambling—to teach our children that gambling is not an innocent pastime, and to teach our legislators and the "honorable men of the earth who [are] blinded by the craftiness of men" (D&C 76:75) that gambling is not a legitimate way to raise revenue.

ODDS

Almost everyone has trouble understanding the huge and tiny numbers involved in gambling odds. But learning about these odds has convinced many people that gambling is not the harmless pastime they thought it was. As the Lord put it to his disciples, "The truth shall make you free" (John 8:32). In this way the Lord has given us "the word of knowledge, that all may be taught to be wise and to have knowledge" (D&C 46:18).

The main thing to understand is that the odds always favor the house. For example, the house's take on a slot machine is about 35%. This means that if you bet ten dollars, you can expect to walk away with only $6.50; if you bet $100, you can expect to keep only $65, and so forth. The more you play, the more you lose. Although some gamblers are ahead temporarily, in the long run the odds will prevail, and the gambler will lose. This simple principle explains why the casinos take in so much money.

The Foxwoods casino in Connecticut, for example, netted—and gamblers there lost—about $500 million in 1994.[18]

These odds become clearer when we think of a simpler example, like an unfair coin. If a coin were weighted to come up heads sixty-five percent of the time, no one would be willing to play a game where they were forced to bet on tails. In fact, the person who designed the game would be considered a cheat and a fraud. But this is essentially what happens in the casino and the lottery. Somehow when the rare win is called a "jackpot" and is accompanied by bells and lights, the odds become obscured in our minds and we suddenly think that this is a legitimate game we can win after all.

Of course, even with an unfair coin there will be rare occasions when the victim might be slightly ahead, but the chances of being very far ahead are tiny indeed. Take craps, for example, where the odds, though poor, are actually much better than the slot machine. Even so, if the gambler bets one dollar at a time, the odds of winning a thousand dollars before losing a thousand dollars are one in two trillion.[19] (That's a two with twelve zeros after it.) If every person in the entire world played this way until they had won or lost a thousand dollars, and then they did this over again three hundred times, only one of them would ever win, and only once of all three hundred times.

The odds for lotteries are even worse than casinos. The Minnesota State Lottery, for example, pays out only 60% of the money it takes in—substantially worse than slot machines or any other type of casino gambling. And the chances of winning the $5000 jackpot in the Minnesota scratch-off lottery are approximately one in 240,000. You are six times more likely to die from a lightning strike than to win this jackpot.[20] And bigger jackpots have still worse odds. The chances of winning the California Lotto Jackpot are approximately one in 18,000,000. If you have to drive ten miles to buy this ticket, you are three times more likely to be killed in an automobile accident on the way than to win the jackpot.[21] If all of the losers of this lottery were to stand in line, they would reach approximately 6800 miles, which is farther than the distance from Salt Lake City to Moscow, Russia. And to have a fifty-fifty chance of winning the jackpot of the British National Lottery, you would have to spend five pounds a week for the next 28,000 years.[22]

The worst odds are in the large multi-state lotteries like the Powerball, and they are almost non-existent. Chances of winning are worse than one in fifty-four million. To put this in perspective, if all of the losers for one drawing of this lottery were to line up, the line would stretch most of the way around the world. You are far more likely to be injured by a lightning strike this week than to win this jackpot.[23] And if you were to read aloud the names of the losing ticket holders for just one drawing, it would take about three-and-a-half years.

Many people change their attitudes and habits when they begin to understand these odds. And we have a duty not only to learn and apply these truths ourselves, but also to teach them to others. The Lord commands "Teach ye diligently . . . that you may be instructed more perfectly in theory, in principle, in doctrine, in the law of the gospel . . . that ye may be prepared in all things. Behold I sent you out to testify and warn the people, and it becometh every man who hath been warned to warn his neighbor" (D&C 88:78–81).

The fact that 25% of all United States citizens have a weekly lottery habit[24] shows that far too few people have been warned. In fact, research shows that most of us don't ask for the necessary information to figure the odds, nor do we know how to figure them even when we have that information.[25] Instead we estimate them based on various false perceptions and misunderstandings. For example, many people wonder, "But what if you're that one?" even though they would never bet on the much more likely chance that they would be struck by lightning this week. The problem is, the worse the odds are, the less likely you are to be that one, and these odds are so small as to be essentially zero. Or as Fran Lebowitz is reputed to have said, "As I figure it, you have the same chance of winning the lottery whether you play or not."

MISUNDERSTANDINGS, BIASES, AND MISTAKEN BELIEFS

Even when we know what the odds are, we still have many misunderstandings, false ideas, and other biases that interfere with our ability to understand how the odds apply to our situation. People often think they understand the odds, but mistakenly believe that they will be able to beat them in some way. The main problems seem to fall broadly into the following categories: 1. Misunderstanding: They misunderstand principles of probability. Many have a betting "system" which they incorrectly believe will help them beat the odds; 2. Availability error: They focus only on good, unusual, or easily remembered experiences, forgetting the bad, common, or less available ones; and 3. Luck: Some think they are "luckier" than the average person, or that they are more experienced. Unfortunately for the gambler, systems, luck, and experience are not relevant to most gambles, and only marginally relevant to the rest. But it is easy to become blinded by a desire to win, and by greed. As Isaiah says, they "are blind: they are all ignorant. . . . Yea, they are greedy . . . which can never have enough, and they are shepherds that cannot understand: they all look to their own way, every one for his gain, from his quarter" (Isaiah 56:10–11).

Misunderstanding of Probability: The Gambler's Fallacy. One of the easiest mistakes to make with gambling is thinking that past gambles influence future ones. This common mistake is sometimes called the "gambler's fallacy," and it often leads people to bet more money and to bet more often than they otherwise would. For example, many people know how to figure that there is only a one in sixteen chance that a fair coin will come up heads four times in a row.[1] But if the coin has already come up heads three times in a row, then the chances that it will do so a fourth time are the same as they would be if it had never been tossed before—one in two. However, it is easy to make the mistake of thinking that this coin has only a one in sixteen chance of coming up heads. It seems that the coin should make the average of past tosses "come out right." But in reality, the coin does not remember past tosses and feels no obligation to even out the number of heads and tails that have come up before. As we make more and more coin tosses, the ratio of heads to the total number of tosses will approach one half, but this does not mean that there will be exactly (nor even close to) the same number of heads as tails, nor does this mean that in the course of a few tosses things will come up anywhere near even. Misunderstanding this fact leads gamblers to believe they have more information than they really do, and can cause them to be more willing to gamble than they otherwise would.

Misunderstanding of Probability: Systems. Similar misunderstandings about numbers and odds are used to devise schemes and systems for picking lottery numbers, roulette numbers, or other gambles, and for deciding when and how much to bet. Most of the systems use impressive-sounding, but incorrect mathematics. One elaborate system depends on a faulty argument about distributing even and odd numbers. Other systems try to reproduce the techniques of lottery drawings, or figure odds from past numbers (the gambler's fallacy again). Although these systems sound impressive, surprisingly, none of them really improve a gambler's chances.[2] In fact, it is mathematically easier to show that by their very

[1]Simply multiply the odds of getting heads with each toss 1/2 x 1/2 x 1/2 x 1/2 = 1/16.

[2]There is one exception to this rule—strict card counting in Blackjack, which if done correctly does gives the card-counter a tiny advantage over the house (.05 to .2 percent advantage if done perfectly—which means that if you bet $100 per hour, you will win only 50 cents per hour); however, card counting can lead to immense losses if done incorrectly. Many casinos encourage people to try because they make a lot of money when you fail. The only people we know that have been able to master this system are professional mathematicians. Moreover, every card counter we know insists that it is too much work for too little benefit—they much prefer to make their money at an easy job, like solving problems in advanced mathematics or theoretical physics. (For the odds, see Willem A. Wagenaar's book: *Paradoxes of Gambling Behaviour,* London: Lawrence Erlbaum, 1988, p. 20.)

nature, all such systems must fail, than it is to devise a new one. These systems not only encourage gambling by making people falsely believe that their odds of winning are higher, but they also encourage gamblers to waste additional money buying the systems themselves.

Availability error. The second major problem which increases people's tendency to gamble, is called "availability error" by psychologists.[26] This is the common tendency we all have to focus only on good, unusual, or easily remembered experiences, forgetting the bad, common, or less available ones. For example, hearing that someone has won the lottery sticks in our mind more than hearing that someone has lost the same lottery. We remember winners more than losers, and mistakenly think that the chances match our memory. This explains why people put more money into slot machines that are in large groups, where they can hear and see signs that others are winning, rather than into lone machines, where they have no recent memory of someone's winning. And people consistently do this, despite the fact that the odds are just as bad for the group as for the lone machine. Memories of winners are simply more available for the large groups than the loners.

We may also think that if we know or have heard of a winner it must not be very hard to win. Many people have a story about how their Aunt Velda or their brother-in-law's boss's friend once won the jackpot in the lottery or a slot machine. But there are several things that are omitted from such stories. Most important is the fact that Aunt Velda lost thousands of dollars in the slot machines and lotteries both before and after winning her hundred-dollar "jackpot." Many so-called "jackpots" are really only small prizes that barely cover the cost of playing, and which serve to entice people to continue playing and losing more money. They take advantage of our tendency toward availability error and exploit our memory of the one "win" while encouraging us to forget the many losses.

Moreover, when we hear the story of our brother-in-law's boss' friend's win, we tend to assume that because we have heard of this person and have some connection to him or her, however remote, winning must be more likely than we had thought. But we never hear the story of our co-worker's Uncle Mack who lost a thousand dollars in the lottery. And if we wanted to hear all the stories of the times that our relatives' acquaintances' friends or our friends' acquaintance's relatives lost money while gambling, we would have no time for anything else. Indeed, by such a chain of associations you can hear the story of essentially every other person in the entire United States.[27]

Luck. The last in the list of problems is the gambler's mistaken belief in "luck." A disturbing result of the research of psychologist Willem Wagenaar shows that many people believe that chance and luck are different things.[28] This modern-day form of idol worship involves trusting a lucky number, a lucky rabbit's foot, or some other lucky thing to make them rich. Wagenaar and his associates found that people believed

> You should wait until luck happens, and in that sense it is much like chance. On the other hand you can lose your luck easily by using it unwisely. You can also fail to utilise it, when it happens, for instance by not even noticing that this is your lucky day, or lucky deck, or lucky dealer. In this sense, the utilisation of luck is more like a skill.[29]

Many also believe that luck is more important than skill and more than twice as important as chance in determining the outcome of a gamble.[30] In reality, most gambles are determined entirely by chance; none are influenced by luck, and only very few by skill. Yet greed makes us believe that there are moments when the universe or some cosmic force wants to make us richer.

This belief in luck indicates a failure of parents and schools to teach the basic truths and facts necessary to avoid fraud and deception. Gamblers' belief in luck and in the influence of skill in using their luck makes them susceptible to deception and manipulation by lotteries, casinos, racetracks and other gambling establishments, thus proving the Lord's words, "If thou serve their gods [in this case "luck"], it will surely be a snare unto thee" (Exodus 23:33).

MANIPULATION

Although gambling is trying to make itself over as a harmless form of entertainment for the whole family, and to tell legislators it is a legitimate industry, in reality it is a manipulative and destructive method for exploiting people's weaknesses and misunderstandings. Gambling providers, including state-run lotteries, manipulate people's misunderstandings about gambling to lead them to wager and lose more money.

Casinos have done extensive research into every conceivable technique they might apply to induce the gambler to stay longer and to bet more. One casino found that they could substantially increase the amount wagered in slot machines by blowing certain perfumes into the air around the machines.[31] They carefully track which colors of slot machines are most likely to attract players initially, and then which colors people prefer as they become more engaged, locating the different colored machines in such a way as to encourage people to gradually move into the center where they will stay longer. They also found that placing one or two machines with more generous odds than the rest in a large group of machines motivated people to search madly for the "good" machines by playing every machine they could. And similar principles in psychology have taught them to make each machine have many small payoffs, often less than was originally bet, in order to encourage players to continue trying for the big win, and to make them feel as if they were close. "It's like eating popcorn. It's very hard to stop playing," says one senior casino management consultant.[32]

Gambling chips themselves are a subtle manipulation to make gamblers feel like they are not losing actual money, and to make them feel more like it's just a game. One casino manager points out that the average person thinks of cash in terms of what it will buy, but the equivalent number of chips are just "betting units." And the same casinos have carefully studied the effect of the denomination of chips on how much a gambler bets, and now all dealers are instructed to give change in the smallest denomination possible, as those have been shown to be most likely to encourage more betting.[33]

Gambling establishments also try to make it easy for gamblers to play by offering check-cashing services, allowing them to post-date checks or buy back their checks if they happen to win, or neglecting to do credit checks to keep gamblers from going into substantial debt.[34] Casinos are in the business of making money, and will manipulate gamblers in order to do so.

Unfortunately, government lotteries are doing some of the same things. As Elder Dallin Oaks says, "That governments would tolerate gambling is regrettable; that governments would promote gambling is reprehensible."[35] But not only do governments promote gambling, they even sink to the same sorts of tricks that casinos use to manipulate the ignorance and misunderstandings of the gamblers. One especially reprehensible trick used by casinos in Nevada to exploit gamblers' misunderstanding was the "near miss" slot machine, which made the losing combinations appear to be close to a large jackpot, giving the illusion that the gambler had almost won. This trick was eventually banned by Nevada gambling authorities,[36] yet almost every lottery employs a similar trick. Namely, you would rarely think you were close to winning if you were supposed to pick a number between one and eighteen million, so instead lotteries have players choose many small numbers. They then give small prizes for partial matches, thereby strengthening the illusion that players are close to winning, and encouraging them to try again. In reality, their being close last time has absolutely nothing to do with how they will do in the future, but the lottery encourages them to think it does. State governments, whose duty is to protect citizens from exploitation and fraud, are actually taking part in them by promoting their own lotteries.

Conclusion

One of the main arguments used in favor of legalization of gambling and institution of lotteries is that the resulting tax revenue can be used for good purposes that otherwise would be underfunded—schools, for example. The most obvious flaw in this argument is that in many cases, the indirect costs of gambling to the state, such as increased crime and lost productivity, actually cost the state more than it gains in increased tax revenue. A second flaw in the argument is that funding worthy programs using gambling money creates perverse incentives and conflicts of interest for those causes. One example of this is the funding of public education with lottery revenues. Public educators' duty is to teach citizens, among other things, about mathematics, including probability. But if they had taught their students well, there would be no lottery revenues because no one would play. So we are rewarding them for failing to teach effectively.

But the most important flaw in the argument for legalized gambling is the simple fact that we cannot let good ends justify dishonest or immoral means to those ends. No legitimate government would legalize theft or fraud in order to increase tax revenues; why then do they permit gambling? The words of Joseph F. Smith are still relevant today: "The desire to get something of value for little or nothing is pernicious. Nor is [gambling] to be permitted or excused because the money so obtained is to be used for a good purpose."[37]

We know that gambling's philosophy of something-for-nothing undermines the framework of our society. But we also need to remember that gambling's something-for-nothing is a lie. Both the gamblers and the communities that vainly hope to benefit from it will find instead that gambling is nothing-for-something. President Heber J. Grant has said, "The Church has been and now is unalterably opposed to gambling in any form whatever. It is opposed to any game of chance, occupation, or so-called business, which takes money from the person . . . without giving value received in return."[38] Gambling gives nothing of value, but steals money and time, and corrupts the morals of our society. We have an obligation not only to avoid gambling ourselves, but also to teach the truth about gambling to others, especially our youth, and to use what we know to change attitudes, perceptions, and laws about gambling in our communities and nations.[3]

---

[3]More information about gambling and related topics can be found at the author's website <http://www.math.byu.edu/~jarvis/gambling.html>

TYLER J. JARVIS *is an assistant professor of mathematics at BYU. He received his BS and MS from BYU and his MA and PhD from Princeton in mathematics. Professor Jarvis teaches a variety of classes in the Mathematics Department at BYU, specializing in algebraic geometry.*

HEIDI B. JARVIS *received her BA and MA from BYU in English and her MLS (Master's in library and information sciences) from Rutgers University. The Jarvises have two children.*

References

[1] Quoted by Elder Dallin H. Oaks in *Ensign,* June 1987, p. 70.

[2] Spencer W. Kimball, "Keep Your Money Clean" in "Marriott School of Management: Quotes." Education for Eternity Collection (n.d.) http://cougar-net.byu.edu/tmcbucs/ fc/ee/ds_msm.htm (Accessed 19 July 1997).

[3] John Warren Kindt, "Gambling is Economically Harmful," in *Gambling,* Bruno Leone et al., eds. (San Diego, Ca: Greenhaven Press, 1995), p. 136.

[4] Ibid., p. 137.

[5] Ibid., pp. 139–142.

[6] Michael Marriott, "Compulsive Gambling: An Overview," in *Gambling,* Bruno Leone et al., eds. (San Diego, Ca: Greenhaven Press, 1995), p. 59.

[7] Henry R. Lesieur, "State Governments Should Provide Treatment for Compulsive Gamblers," in *Gambling,* Bruno Leone et al., eds. (San Diego, Ca: Greenhaven Press, 1995), pp. 72–73.

[8] John Warren Kindt, "Gambling is Economically Harmful," in *Gambling,* Bruno Leone et al., eds. (San Diego, Ca: Greenhaven Press, 1995), p. 134.

[9] Ibid.

[10] Valerie Lorenz, "Compulsive Gambling is a Serious Disease," in *Gambling,* Bruno Leone et al., eds. (San Diego, Ca: Greenhaven Press, 1995), p. 65; and Henry R. Lesieur, "State Governments Should Provide Treatment for Compulsive Gamblers," in *Gambling,* Bruno Leone et al., eds. (San Diego, Ca: Greenhaven Press, 1995), p. 75.

[11] John Warren Kindt, "Gambling is Economically Harmful," in *Gambling,* Bruno Leone et al., eds. (San Diego, Ca: Greenhaven Press, 1995), p. 142.

[12] Valerie Lorenz, "Compulsive Gambling is a Serious Disease," in *Gambling,* Bruno Leone et al., eds. (San Diego, Ca: Greenhaven Press, 1995), p. 67.

[13] The National Council on Problem Gambling, Inc. "The Federal Government Should Address Compulsive Gambling," in *Gambling,* Bruno Leone et al., eds. (San Diego, Ca: Greenhaven Press, 1995), p. 80.

[14] Gerri Hirshey, "Gambling is Entertainment," in *Gambling,* Bruno Leone et al., eds. (San Diego, Ca: Greenhaven Press, 1995), p. 52.

[15] The National Council on Problem Gambling, Inc. "The Federal Government Should Address Compulsive Gambling," in *Gambling,* Bruno Leone et al., eds. (San Diego, Ca: Greenhaven Press, 1995), p. 81.

[16] Richard McGowan, *State Lotteries and Legalized Gambling: Painless Revenue or Painful Mirage* (Westport, Connecticut: Praeger, 1994), p. 37.

[17] See Lamar E. Cooper, Sr, "Gambling Violates Biblical Principles," in *Gambling,* Bruno Leone et al., eds. (San Diego, Ca: Greenhaven Press, 1995), p. 26; and Reuven Brenner and Gabrielle A. Brenner, *Gambling and Speculation,* (New York: Cambridge University Press, 1990), p. 31.
[18] Jon Magnuson, "Critics of Indian Gaming are Wrong," in *Gambling,* Bruno Leone et al., eds. (San Diego, Ca: Greenhaven Press, 1995), p. 174.
[19] James Popkin, "Casino Tricks Encourage Heavy Gambling," in *Gambling,* Bruno Leone et al., eds. (San Diego, Ca: Greenhaven Press, 1995), p. 104.
[20] James Walsh, *True Odds* (Santa Monica, Ca: Merritt, 1996), p. 16.
[21] Michael Orkin, quoted in "FRONTLINE: California Lottery Odds." *FRONTLINE: Easy Money.* 1997. http://www.pbs.org/wgbh/pages/frontline/shows/gamble/odds/california.html (Accessed 19 July 1997).
[22] James Walsh, *True Odds* (Santa Monica, Ca: Merritt, 1996), p. 346.
[23] Les Krantz, *What the Odds Are* (New York: Harper Perennial, 1992).
[24] The Christian Science Monitor, "Gambling is Unethical," in *Gambling,* Bruno Leone et al., eds. (San Diego, Ca: Greenhaven Press, 1995), p. 21.
[25] Willem A. Wagenaar, *Paradoxes of Gambling Behaviour* (London: Lawrence Erlbaum, 1988), p. 71.
[26] See Daniel Kahneman, Paul Slovic, and Amos Tversky, eds. *Judgment Under Uncertainty: Heuristics and Biases* (New York: Cambridge University Press, 1982).
[27] John Allen Paulos, *Innumeracy: Mathematical Illiteracy and its Consequences* (New York: Vintage, 1990), pp. 38–39.
[28] Willem A. Wagenaar, *Paradoxes of Gambling Behaviour* (London: Lawrence Erlbaum, 1988), p. 93.
[29] Ibid.
[30] Ibid.
[31] James Popkin, "Casino Tricks Encourage Heavy Gambling," in *Gambling,* Bruno Leone et al., eds. (San Diego, Ca: Greenhaven Press, 1995), p. 103.
[32] Ibid., p. 106.
[33] Ibid., pp. 104–105.
[34] Henry R. Lesieur, "State Governments Should Provide Treatment for Compulsive Gamblers," in *Gambling,* Bruno Leone et al., eds. (San Diego, Ca: Greenhaven Press, 1995), p. 75.
[35] *Ensign,* June 1987, p. 75.
[36] James Popkin, "Casino Tricks Encourage Heavy Gambling," in *Gambling,* Bruno Leone et al., eds. (San Diego, Ca: Greenhaven Press, 1995), p. 106.
[37] *Gospel Doctrine,* p. 327.
[38] Quoted by Elder Dallin H. Oaks in *Ensign,* June 1987, p. 70.

Questions

1. Why do the authors provide moral, social, and numerical arguments against gambling? Which is most compelling?
2. How do the examples work in their argument?
3. Both this article and Kunz's article use statistics as evidence. Do they use them the same way?
4. What are the implications of this argument for you?

Geological Upheaval and Darkness in 3 Nephi 8–10

ALVIN K. BENSON

"Even as a teenager," Alvin K. Benson says, "I enjoyed reading the scriptures because it was fun to think about their content and try to understand their meaning." Benson has continued to try to understand the scriptures through the theoretical and empirical models he has learned as a scientist. "Geological Upheaval and Darkness in 3 Nephi 8–10" shows how an understanding of the phenomena of the natural world can lead to a greater understanding of the scriptures.

Prophets repeatedly warned the Nephites and Lamanites of judgments that would come at the time of Christ's crucifixion. Hundreds of years earlier, Zenos and Nephi had foreseen the great calamities that befell the Nephite nation in AD 34 (1 Nephi 12:4–6, 19:10–14; 2 Nephi 26:3–4). Some of Zenos' writings—which were preserved on the brass plates of Laban—prophesy of the destructions that would attend the Lord's death:

> The Lord God surely shall visit all the house of Israel at that day, some with his voice, because of their righteousness, unto their great joy and salvation, and others with the thunderings and the lightnings of his power, by tempest, by fire, and by smoke, and vapor of darkness, and by the opening of the earth, and by mountains which shall be carried up. . . . And the rocks of the earth must rend. (1 Nephi 19:11–12)

Furthermore, Zenos "spake concerning the three days of darkness, which would be a sign given of his [Christ's] death unto those who should inhabit the isles of the sea, more especially given unto those who are of the house of Israel" (1 Nephi 19:10). Apparently, portions of the house of Israel far removed from Jerusalem were destined to receive special signs as a witness of the Savior's death.

Nephi also foresaw in a vision the events which would occur among the Nephites when the Messiah died:

> And it came to pass that I saw a mist of darkness on the face of the land of promise; and I saw lightnings, and I heard thunderings, and earthquakes, and all manner of tumultuous noises; and I saw the earth and the rocks, that they rent; and I saw mountains tumbling into pieces; and I saw the plains of the earth, that they were broken up; and I saw many cities that they were sunk; and and I saw many that they were burned with fire; and I saw many that did tumble to the earth, because of the quaking thereof.
>
> And it came to pass after I saw these things, I saw the vapor of darkness, that it passed from off the face of the earth; and behold, I saw multitudes who had fallen because of the great and terrible judgments of the Lord. (1 Nephi 12:4–5)

Just forty years prior to the crucifixion of the Savior, another prophet of God, Samuel the Lamanite, also enumerated in glorious prophecy the calamities and destructions that would occur on the American continent at the time Christ would voluntarily give up his life:

> But behold, as I said unto you concerning another sign, a sign of his death, behold, in that day that he shall suffer death the sun shall be darkened and refuse to give his light unto you; and also the moon and the stars; and there shall be no light upon the face of this land, even from the time that he shall suffer death, for the space of three days, to the time that he shall rise again from the dead.
>
> Yea, at the time that he shall yield up the ghost there shall be thunderings and lightnings for the space of many hours, and the earth shall shake and tremble; and the rocks which are upon the face of this earth, which are both above the earth and beneath, which ye know at this time are solid, or the more part of it is one solid mass, shall be broken up;
>
> Yea, they shall be rent in twain, and shall ever after be found in seams and in cracks, and in broken fragments upon the face of the whole earth, yea, both above the earth and beneath.

> And behold, there shall be great tempests, and there shall be many mountains laid low, like unto a valley, and there shall be many places which are now called valleys which shall become mountains, whose height is great.
>
> And many highways shall be broken up, and many cities shall become desolate. (Hel. 14:20–24)

As the time of the Savior's death grew near and these prophecies began to be fulfilled, an underlying current of wickedness produced great instability in the Nephite society. The prevailing conditions included political unrest, terrorist activities, separation of society into classes, destruction of life and property, riots and wars, and political movements to overthrow righteous institutions (3 Nephi 6–7). Under these conditions, the more righteous Nephites were looking forward to seeing the signs associated with Christ's crucifixion (Hel. 14:20–28). But it had been thirty-three years since the birth of the Savior, and doubtings and disputations began to arise among the wicked despite the many signs that had been previously given (3 Nephi 8:1–4).

Geological Changes and Foreboding Darkness

As with all prophecies of the Lord, fulfillment of the Nephite prophecies came with total and unerring certainty. When the Master—hanging on the cross just outside Jerusalem—gave up his life, the American continent experienced great calamities. Speaking about the events recorded in 3 Nephi 8–10, Elder Bruce R. McConkie stated: "No single historic event in the whole Book of Mormon account is recorded in so great detail or such extended length as the fulfillment of the signs signifying that Jesus had been lifted up upon the cross and had voluntarily laid down his life for the world" (542).

For the Nephites, the subsequent disaster was ushered in by "a great storm, such an one as never had been known in all the land" (3 Nephi 8:5). That storm was so ferocious that thunder shook the ground, earthquakes rumbled, and lightning set cities on fire (8:6–8; 9:3). Other cities sank into the depths of the sea, and still others were buried in the earth (8:9–15; 9:4–10). The surface of the ground was generally broken up as open fissures developed and new hills and valleys were formed (8:12–13, 17). And people were carried away by the whirlwinds and never heard of again (v. 16). Intense cataclysmic events raged throughout the land.

Nephi summarizes the tremendous geological changes that occurred: "And thus the face of the whole earth became deformed, because of the tempests, and the thunderings, and the lightnings, and the quaking of the earth. And behold, the rocks were rent in twain; they were broken up upon the face of the whole earth, insomuch that they were found in broken fragments, and in seams and in cracks, upon all the face of the land" (3 Nephi 8:17–18). *Whole earth* is an interesting phrase. What does it mean? Does it mean that the catastrophic events experienced by the Nephites were global, or were they more localized phenomena? That phrase is used numerous times in describing the calamities (see vv. 6, 12, 17, and 18). If these tremendous geological changes and the ensuing three days of darkness had been global, we would expect to find accounts of them in the literature of other contemporary societies, such as the Romans, Greeks, Chinese, Persians. But since it is found only in Nephite writings, the phrase *whole earth* must mean the *whole land* of the Nephites. For example, this phrase is used there in a localized rather than global setting: "And they began to know that the Son of God must shortly appear; yea, in fine, all the people upon the face of the whole earth from the west to the east, both in the land north and in the land south, were so exceedingly astonished that they fell to the earth" (3 Nephi 1:17). This illustrates the point that the context and the audience for which a scripture is directed are very important in the interpretation of it.

The devastating events described in 3 Nephi lasted for about three hours and were followed by a foreboding darkness that the people could "feel":

> And it came to pass that when the thunderings, and the lightnings, and the storm, and the tempest, and the quakings of the earth did cease—for behold, they did last for about the space of three hours; and it was said by some that the time was greater; nevertheless, all these great and terrible things were done in about the space of three hours—and then behold, there was darkness upon the face of the land.
>
> And it came to pass that there was thick darkness upon all the face of the land, insomuch that the inhabitants thereof who had not fallen could feel the vapor of darkness. (3 Nephi 8:19–20)

The Americas were engulfed in darkness while the Lord's body lay in the tomb and his eternal spirit taught the righteous dead (1 Peter 3:18–20; D&C 138; see also McConkie 540). No glimmer of light could be seen for three days, and attempts to kindle fires with their "fine and exceedingly dry wood" were futile:

> And there could be no light, because of the darkness, neither candles, neither torches; neither could there be fire kindled with their fine and exceedingly dry wood, so that there could not be any light at all;
>
> And there was not any light seen, neither fire, nor glimmer, neither sun, nor the moon, nor the stars, for so great were the mists of darkness which were upon the face of the land.
>
> And it came to pass that it did last for the space of three days that there was no light seen. (3 Nephi 8:21–23)

How appropriate it is that at the Savior's birth *light* shone for a day and a night and a day (3 Nephi 1:19); whereas at his death, *darkness* prevailed among the Nephites for three days. It appears that the earth was symbolically manifesting its gloom over the death of its creator (9:15). As Professor Sidney B. Sperry pointed out, the darkness "may possibly be accounted for on the basis that the Spirit of Christ was withdrawn in part from the land (cf. D&C 84:45–46; 88:7–13)" (400).

GEOLOGICAL PHENOMENA: A POSSIBLE ANALYSIS OF THE EVENTS IN 3 NEPHI 8–10

Both Zenos and Nephi prophesied that the events described in 3 Nephi 8–10 would be accompanied by fire (1 Nephi 12:4; 19:11; 2 Nephi 26:6); and indeed 3 Nephi 9:11 states that the Lord "did send down fire." It is quite probable that this may refer to lightning accompanying volcanic activity triggered by the quaking earth (3 Nephi 8:17). Photos of erupting volcanoes, such as Mount Vesuvius in 1944 (Fodor 15) and Sakura-jima in 1987 (Kemp 40–41), show hundreds of lightning bolts in ash clouds above those volcanoes. The friction between fine volcanic ash particles in the atmosphere is very effective in generating severe lightning without any attending rain, leaving the ground and wood very dry. It is interesting that after hours of thunderstorm activity of unprecedented fury and violent earthquakes, the Nephites' wood was still referred to as being "exceedingly dry" (3 Nephi 8:21).

Furthermore, if volcanic eruptions lasted for several hours, as indicated in 3 Nephi 8, an enormous amount of ash would have been discharged into the atmosphere. The ash from a volcano can rise to great heights (many thousands of feet) and then spread out in the stratosphere to cover a large region with an impenetrable cloud of dust (Goldner and Vogel 37–43; Warren and Ferguson 42). Volcanic ash, smoke, and gases, along with dust and debris rising into the air from a large earthquake, could have produced the "vapor of darkness" spoken of in 3 Nephi 8:20 and 10:13. Professor Hugh Nibley also suggests that the vapor of darkness may have resulted from volcanic activity (267). Furthermore, volcanic ash and lava can be carried *up* to bury cities (Berger 57–61), and Nephi records that the earth was carried *up* on the city Moronihah (3 Nephi 8:10) and not down, as one would expect in a landslide.

Also, in 3 Nephi 10:13, an inference can be drawn that people died from suffocation from "the vapor of smoke and of darkness." Warren and Ferguson record that when the ash from a volcanic eruption "begins to fall back toward the earth, it is accompanied by many gases, including hydrochloric acid, hydrofluoric acid, carbonic acid, carbon dioxide, and ammonia. If the ash fall is heavy, people will naturally suffocate, not only from the ash content itself but also from these gases, which are lethal in large quantities" (42). In several modern cases, volcanic gases have collected in low spots after an eruption, killing people, animals, and vegetation (Montgomery 105–106; Macdonald 251–52, 257). The fate of a particular city would depend on its location relative to fault lines and volcanoes, and upon the direction of the wind carrying volcanic ash and gases. In the regions of the surviving Nephites, the concentration of volcanic gases may have been sufficient to prevent the ignition of fires but not high enough to suffocate people. Because most volcanic gases are heavier than air, they tend to hug the ground; hence, at ground level, concentrations could have been high enough to prevent ignition of the Nephites' dry tinder. However, in the more righteous cities, lethal concentrations may not have been present a few feet above the ground, allowing the more righteous to survive. As the period of darkness ended, Nephi records:

> And it came to pass that thus did the three days pass away. And it was in the morning, and the darkness dispersed from off the face of the land, and the earth did cease to tremble, and the rocks did cease to rend, and the dreadful groanings did cease, and all the tumultuous noises did pass away. (3 Nephi 10:9)

Since the verb *disperse* implies breaking up and scattering, the terminology in verse 9 could refer to the eventual dispersion of a volcanic ash cloud. That verse also indicates that the trembling of the earth continued throughout the three-day period of the Savior's entombment, suggesting continued volcanic activity and many aftershocks. Also, volcanic ash may have been coming forth all that time to sustain the thick darkness.

If volcanic eruptions were the source of the tremendous darkness, what initiated that activity? Modern models, examples, and descriptions of earthquake and volcanic activity provide many helpful insights. As an example, let us consider some of the recorded events associated with the Mount St. Helens volcanic eruption on 18 May 1980, which contain many descriptions similar to those in 3 Nephi 8–10.

Investigations suggest that an earthquake measuring 5.1 on the Richter scale may have triggered the eruption, and as the side of the mountain slid down and the top was blown away, the resulting shock wave blew down all the timber and vegetation within 15 miles. Some survivors referred to the noise and shaking as like being next to ground zero in an atomic bomb blast (Aylesworth 15–17; Berger 57–59). Visibility dropped to zero; and as the thick volcanic dust hid the sun, day became night as far away as 500 miles. Spokane, Washington, located just 250 miles east of the blast site, was in complete darkness at 3:00 PM. Bolts of lightning flashed from Mount St. Helens, sparking numerous forest fires, and the air was so full of smoke and pumice that people could not survive outside. Volcanic ash and gases irritated skin, eyes, and lungs, making breathing extremely difficult and fires impossible to ignite. Many earthquakes and/or aftershocks accompanied the eruption, and mud and debris flows changed the surrounding landscape for miles around (Goldner and Vogel 10–13, 27–29, 37–43; Aylesworth 15–17, 25–35; Berger 57–63; Fodor 11–15; Montgomery 99–102; Palmer 82–88; Rosenfeld 494–509). The similarities in these descriptions to the events in 3 Nephi 8–10 are striking: earthquake(s) (3 Nephi 8:6, 17–18), fire (9:11; 10:14), tumultuous noises (10:9), sharp lightning (8:7), darkness (8:19), suffocating vapors of smoke (10:13), aftershocks (10:9), and geological upheaval over large areas (8:17–18).

As with the Mount St. Helens catastrophe, the volcanic activity reported in the Nephite disaster most probably was initiated by earthquake activity. The main earthquake must have been gigantic since the "face of the whole earth became deformed. . . . And behold, the rocks were rent in twain; they were broken up upon the face of the whole earth" (3 Nephi 8:17–18), and "tumultuous noises" accompanied the quaking for three days (10:9). At appropriate locations on the earth, this quaking can trigger erupting volcanoes, showing that the ordering of events in 3 Nephi 8:6–7 would be correct: "There was terrible thunder, insomuch that it did shake the whole earth as if it was about to divide asunder. And there were exceedingly sharp lightnings." The first arrival of energy from an earthquake is the compressional wave that produces "noise," which could sound like "thunder." This energy is then followed by the arrival of shear and surface waves, which typically produce most of the shaking and damage along with more deafening noises. The "tumultuous noises" could be generated by the breaking of rock strata, the opening of cracks in the earth, the collapse of buildings, etc., followed by the noise of volcanic eruptions and associated lightning and thunder (Fodor 11–15).

Generally, earthquakes occur in well-defined belts or zones in the earth located at the junctions of lithospheric plates, which are large pieces of the earth's brittle crest. According to the theory of plate tectonics, as these plates move slowly over the surface of the earth, they either (a) collide with each other, (b) pull away from one another, or (c) slide over and beneath each, other creating subduction zones. These zones are characterized by (a) large-scale fault movement; (b) periodic, severe earthquakes; (c) volcanic activity; and (d) typically, a deep ocean trench (Montgomery 46–59).

One of the more active subduction zones of the world is located along the western coasts of Central and South America. The mountainous areas there extend oceanward to a long, linear ocean trench. This trench exceeds 20,000 feet in depth and is bordered along the shore by mountains over 22,000 feet high. This large elevation difference of over 40,000 feet is a likely site for large-scale fault development, allowing blocks of earth to slip oceanward (Montgomery 55–59; Baer 130). Such movement could occur during a large earthquake, which could explain the loss of the city of Moroni into the depths of the sea (3 Nephi 8:9).

It is common for areas that have frequent, severe earthquakes to have a high incidence of volcanic activity. Two devastating Guatemalan earthquakes (23 December 1586 and 29–30 September 1717) were accompanied by severe and violent eruptions of the volcano Fuego (Espinosa 87–90). Earthquake activity and active volcanoes are common along the west coast of South America and, particularly, Central America (Warren and Ferguson 40–45).

The earthquake activity described in 3 Nephi 8–10, including the main quake and the aftershocks, could well have occurred in three hours (3 Nephi 8:19) or lasted for three days (10:9–10). Many earthquakes in Guatemala, for example, have had a main shock followed by several aftershocks for as long as five weeks afterward (Espinosa 87–90). Similarly, the emission of volcanic dust and gas to sustain the darkness could easily have lasted for three days (3 Nephi 10:9).

Consequently, it is very feasible that a large earthquake and attendant volcanic activity could account for the geological catastrophes recorded in 3 Nephi 8–10, and it is also very feasible that this occurred along the west coast of Central and/or South America. Interestingly, as pointed out by Baer (131–32), the theory of plate tectonics describing subduction zones, etc. was not developed for well over a hundred years after Joseph Smith translated the Book of Mormon, and it is significant that this modern geophysical model of how the earth works supports the feasibility of the events described in 3 Nephi 8–10.

WHY THE DISASTER?

In the Book of Mormon the thick darkness lasted for "the space of three days," and there was "great mourning and howling and weeping among all the people continually; yea, great were the groanings of the people, because of the darkness and the great destruction which had come upon them" (3 Nephi 8:23). The Lord told the Nephites that all of these physical changes—geological upheaval and associated destruction—came as a just judgment upon the wicked: "It is because of their iniquity and abominations that they are fallen! . . . to hide their iniquities and their abominations from before my face, that the blood of the prophets and the saints shall not come any more unto me against them. . . . And many great destructions have I caused to come upon this land, and upon this people, because of their wickedness and their abominations" (3 Nephi 9:2, 5, 12). As the Lord describes why particular cities and their inhabitants were destroyed in 3 Nephi 9:2–12, he repeats the word *wickedness* eight times, *abominations* seven times, *iniquity* two times, and the phrase "that the blood of the prophets and the saints shall not come up any more unto me against them" five times. He leaves no suggestion as to the reason for the destruction: it was their own wickedness. The Lord also states that all these things were done "unto the fulfilling of the prophecies of many of the holy prophets" (3 Nephi 10:14).

In addition to destroying the wicked, the geological upheaval and associated devastation also served as a sign and witness to the remaining righteous people that the atonement, death, and resurrection of the Savior had taken place on the opposite side of the world. The Lord explained this to the surviving Nephites, as he declared his messiahship (3 Nephi 9:15) and extended an invitation for all to come unto him: "Behold, I have come unto the world to bring redemption unto the world, to save the world from sin. Therefore, whoso repenteth and cometh unto me as a little child, him will I receive, for of such is the kingdom of God. Behold, for such I have laid down my life and have taken it up again; therefore repent, come unto me ye ends of the earth, and be saved" (vv. 21–22). Although the remaining Nephites are referred to as "the more righteous" in a comparative sense to those who had been destroyed, they still needed to repent:

> O all ye that are spared because ye were more righteous than they, will ye not now return unto me, and repent of your sins, and be converted, that I may heal you?

> Yea, verily I say unto you, if ye will come unto me ye shall have eternal life. Behold, mine arm of mercy is extended towards you, and whosoever will come, him will I receive; and blessed are those who come unto me…
>
> And as many as have received me, to them have I given to become the sons of God; and even so will I to as many as shall believe on my name, for behold, by me redemption cometh, and in me is the law of Moses fulfilled. (3 Nephi 9:13–14, 17)

Thus, God uses his power to fulfill all of his purposes and promises; and even in times of great destruction, upheaval, darkness, and sorrow, the Savior will bring peace, joy, and great blessings into the lives of the "more righteous" through the gospel plan (10:10, 12, 18).

Conclusions

Both the scriptural prophecies concerning the birth of Christ and those which foretold the events associated with his death were fulfilled in unerring detail:

> And thus far were the scriptures fulfilled which had been spoken by the prophets. . . .
>
> And now, whoso readeth, let him understand; he that hath the scriptures, let him search them, and see and behold if all these deaths and destructions by fire, and by smoke, and by tempests, and by whirlwinds, and by the opening of the earth to receive them, and all these things are not unto the fulfilling of the prophecies of many of the holy prophets. (3 Nephi 10:11, 14)

The Lord "created the heavens and the earth, and all things that in them are" (9:15), and "though the heavens and the earth pass away" (D&C 1:38), all the prophecies and promises of the Lord will be fulfilled (Mormon 8:22). Chapters 8–10 of 3 Nephi clearly demonstrate that a nation cannot willfully sin and rebel against the Lord's commandments without upsetting the balance of nature and incurring the wrath of God through natural catastrophes which discipline his children and destroy the wicked (3 Nephi 9:5, 7–12). As pointed out by Elder Bruce R. McConkie, "It is perfectly clear that these destructions came as a just judgment upon the wicked, and that they are in similitude of the outpourings of wrath that shall come upon the whole world at the Second Coming" (McConkie 541).

The geological upheaval and physical changes described in 3 Nephi 8–10, which destroyed much of the Nephite nation, could easily have been caused by a gigantic earthquake with attendant storms, volcanic activity, and aftershocks of incredible proportions. The similarities in the descriptions of other documented catastrophes, such as the Mount St. Helens disaster in 1980, to the geological upheaval and darkness recorded in 3 Nephi 8–10 are striking. Most aspects of the geological changes in 3 Nephi can be accommodated by modern earthquake models through the theory of plate tectonics, and the very nature of earthquake and volcanic activity typical of South and Central America is consistent with the whole set of phenomena recorded in 3 Nephi 8–10. Modern geophysical and geological theories support the 3 Nephi events as realities and not—as some critics report—fabricated myths.

Although the geological changes in the earth were very spectacular and of such magnitude that "the face of the whole earth became deformed . . . [and] the rocks were rent in twain" (3 Nephi 8:17–18), they pointed to events of much greater importance. They were signs to signify that the greatest events in the history of this earth were now in place—the atonement, death, and resurrection of our Savior, Jesus Christ. Because of their vast importance, "no single historical event in the whole Book of Mormon account is recorded in so great detail or at such extended length as the fulfillment of the signs signifying that Jesus had been lifted up upon the cross and had voluntarily laid down his life for the world" (McConkie 542).

ALVIN K. BENSON *received both a bachelor's degree and a PhD from Brigham Young University in physics. Before he began teaching at BYU in 1986, he was a tenured professor at Indiana University. He had also spent nine years working as a research scientist for DuPont and Conoco, work which has since helped him to better teach his students about working in the private sector. Geophysics, physics, mathematics, and astronomy are all topics that he has taught either in the Indiana University System or at BYU.*

Bibliography

Aylesworth, Thomas G., and Virginia L. Aylesworth. *The Mount St. Helens Disaster.* New York: Franklin Watts, 1983.

Baer, James L. "The Third Nephi Disaster: A Geological View." *Dialogue* 19 (Spr. 1986): 129–132.

Berger, Melvin. *Disastrous Volcanoes.* New York: Franklin Watts, 1981.

Espinosa, A. F. "The Guatemalan Earthquake of February 4, 1976: A Preliminary Report." *United States Geological Survey Professional Paper 1002.* Washington: GPO, 1976.

Fodor, R. V. *Earth Afire! Volcanoes and Their Activity.* New York: William Morrow, 1981.

Goldner, Kathryn A., and Carole G. Vogel. *Why Mount St. Helens Blew Its Top.* Minneapolis: Dillion, 1981.

Kemp, Mark. "Power Surge." *Discover* 9 (Apr. 1988):40–42.

McConkie, Bruce R. *The Promised Messiah.* Salt Lake City: Deseret Book, 1981.

Macdonald, G. A. *Volcanoes.* Englewood Cliffs, NJ: Prentice-Hall, 1972.

Montgomery, Carla W. *Environmental Geology.* 3rd ed. Dubuque, IA: Wm. C. Brown, 1992.

Nibley, Hugh. *Since Cumorah.* Salt Lake City: Deseret Book, 1967.

Palmer, Leonard. *Mt. St. Helens: The Volcano Explodes.* Portland: Lee Enterprises and Northwest Illustrated, 1980.

Rosenfeld, Charles L. "Observations on the Mount St. Helens Eruptions." *American Scientist* 68 (Sep.–Oct. 1980):494–509.

Sperry, Sidney B. *Book of Mormon Compendium.* Salt Lake City: Bookcraft, 1968.

Warren, Bruce W., and Thomas S. Ferguson. *The Messiah in Ancient America.* Provo, UT: Book of Mormon Research Foundation, 1988.

Questions

1. How do the ideas in this article relate to Bradshaw's "I Would Be a Purveyor of Mysteries"?

2. How persuasive is Benson's evidence? Why?

3. How important to this argument is the fact that Benson is a physicist?

4. Is it appropriate to link science and religion in the way Benson does?

Feminism in the Light of the Gospel of Jesus Christ

B. KENT HARRISON AND
MARY STOVALL RICHARDS

B. Kent Harrison, a professor of physics and astronomy, has long been interested in women's issues. He said that this is partly because he has such "strong maternal ancestors." He started to become involved in the BYU Women's Conferences in the late 70s. In the mid-1980s he met Mary Stovall Richards, who was then chair of the BYU Women's Conference and director of the BYU Women's Research Institute. Their shared interest in trying to encourage "men and women to be fair with one another" led to this article. In its most basic form, Harrison and Richards argue, feminism echoes eternal truths of the gospel, which affirms the equal worth of all people, the equal right to and capacity for spirituality, and the evils of abuse. Their article was first published in BYU Studies.

> Perhaps it is no wonder that the women were first at the Cradle and last at the Cross. They had never known a man like this Man—there never has been such another. A prophet and teacher who never nagged at them, never flattered or coaxed or patronized; who never made arch jokes about them . . . who took their questions and arguments seriously; who never mapped out their sphere for them, never urged them to be feminine or jeered at them for being female; who had no axe to grind and no uneasy male dignity to defend.
>
> —Dorothy Sayers[1]

For some people, an unbridgeable gap stands between the gospel of Jesus Christ and feminism. To them, a Christian feminist or a Mormon feminist is an oxymoron,[2] a person who has not thought seriously about either the gospel or feminism. However, there are devoted Latter-day Saints, both women and men, who consider themselves feminists. They declare that, far from being antithetical to the gospel, their feminism arises from their testimony of Christ and commitment to him. Through their personal experience with his love, example, and teachings, they affirm the reality of Christ's devotion to every person as individually significant. Hence, the message of Christ's gospel ordains equality and fairness in all human relationships, including those between the sexes.

While even among feminists there are widely varying interpretations of the meaning of *feminism*,[3] we think most feminists would agree on a basic definition, with which we hope readers will concur: feminism advocates the equal treatment of women and men and states that discrimination, in particular against women, does exist and should be eliminated.[4] Far from promoting the reverse tyranny of women over men, such feminism simply affirms the equal importance of each individual, regardless of sex.[5] As scholars, we have tried to bring our academic interests to bear on issues of concern to our religious principles. Our purpose in this essay is to identify fundamental principles of the restored gospel of Jesus Christ that are consistent with this basic meaning of feminism and to draw certain practical conclusions that follow from those principles.

Valuing Others Equally and Divine Love

In affirming the equal value of men and women, feminism, as defined above, echoes eternal truth. The gospel of Jesus Christ teaches our eternal worth and supreme importance to God: "Remember the worth of souls is great in the sight of God" (D&C 18:10). As Moses 1:39 declares, "For behold, this is my work and my glory—to bring to pass the immortality and eternal life of man [and woman]." In fact, it is only through love that God governs, for "God is love" (1 John 4:8); he does not govern through coercion or manipulation. And it is God's supreme, all-encompassing love for us that draws us to him (D&C 121:41–46).

The scriptures show that this love encompasses all persons, who are equal before God regardless of gender, age, class, race, or nationality. Paul taught in his epistle to the Galatians that within the body of Christ, "There is neither Jew nor Greek, there is neither bond nor free, there is neither male nor female: for ye are all one in Christ Jesus" (Gal. 3:28). In the Western Hemisphere, Nephi explained the same doctrine: God is no respecter of persons. All persons "are privileged the one like unto the other, and none are forbidden" for "all are alike unto God"— "black and white, bond and free, male and female . . . Jew and Gentile" (2 Ne. 26:28, 33). In practical terms, this doctrine means, as Alma taught those Zoramites who were poor and had been turned out of the synagogues of the wealthy, that the Lord "imparteth his word by angels unto men, yea, not only men but women also. Now this is not all; little children do have words given unto them many times, which confound the wise and the learned" (Alma 32:23).

In his earthly ministry, the Savior exemplified concern for all persons. In fact, he flouted cultural and legal proscriptions regarding women's spiritual and social place in Jewish culture.[6] For example, although women were considered so spiritually inferior to men that they were not to read or study the scriptures and some rabbis would not even speak to a woman in public, Christ taught women the gospel. In his parables, he repeatedly paired female and male examples, such as juxtaposing the man who lost his sheep with the woman who misplaced her coin. By doing so, Christ not only couched his teachings in terms relevant to women's lives, but also underscored the eternal worth of women's souls.[7] Christ revealed himself as the Messiah to a woman (who was also an "unclean" Samaritan)—the first declaration by Christ of his identity that is recorded in the New Testament (John 4:25–26). Christ healed women and raised a woman from the dead (Matt. 15:22–28; Luke 8:49–56). Women were among his most devoted disciples, remaining at the cross and returning to the tomb to anoint his body (Luke 23:49; 24:1).

Further, while under Jewish law women were considered incompetent as legal witnesses, Christ chose to appear first after the Resurrection to a woman, whom he then charged to tell his apostles of the glorious event (John 20:11–17). Previously, he had sanctioned a woman's anointing him prior to his crucifixion (Mark 14:3–9; John 12:3–8), an act that, according to two Mormon authors, "may be seen as the prophetic recognition of Jesus as the Anointed."[8] Such actions by Christ appear to be deliberately chosen to contravene societal conventions that denied women's equality before God and full personhood. Christ desired to move his followers beyond their dehumanizing and constricting—but perhaps comfortably familiar—cultural mores to eternal truth.

Christ also ignored any sort of precedence that might be conveyed solely by categories, such as age or birth. Not only did he welcome and bless girls and boys during his ministries both in mortality and among the Nephites, but he specifically taught that all persons must become as little children to enter the kingdom of heaven (Mark 10:13–16; 3 Ne. 17:11–12, 21–24). Christ was quick to point out that pedigree, meaning descent from Abraham, would not save a person if he or she were unrighteous (John 8:33–39). Indeed, several Gentiles in the New Testament were especially blessed because of their righteousness: the centurion whose servant Christ healed, the Ethiopian whom Philip baptized, and Cornelius, who was baptized by Peter (Matt. 8:5–13; Acts 8:26–40; Acts 10). Prior to Cornelius's baptism, Peter had assumed that the gospel was mainly for the Jews or that it would be necessary for a Gentile to become a Jew before he or she could become a Christian. But after a marvelous vision, Peter learned that "God is no respecter of persons: but in every nation he that feareth him, and worketh righteousness, is accepted with him" (Acts 10:34–35).

Christ's emphasis on individuals, not categories of people,[9] is instructive to those seeking to follow him. In following his example, one should emulate the same equality of love as that shown by Christ for all humans, since any denigration of another's eternal worth or capacity is an affront to Christ's love. Christ's pattern is therefore not just prescriptive, but should be descriptive of behavior. President Howard W. Hunter counseled:

> We are at a time in the history of the world and the growth of the Church when we must think more of holy things and act more like the Savior would expect his disciples to act. We should at every opportunity ask ourselves, "What would Jesus do?" and then act more courageously upon the answer.[10]

Thus following Christ's example, we should be kind, considerate, loving. It is important to listen, as did Christ in his response to the Canaanite woman who wished her daughter healed. Despite her cultural status as a woman and a Gentile, Christ listened to her plea and forthwith granted her request (Matt. 15:21–28).[11]

Christ's and God's love has even more profound implications for all of humankind. *Lectures on Faith* explains that if God were a biased god, favoring certain persons over others, we "could not exercise faith in him. . . . [We] could not tell what [our] privileges were, nor how far [we] were authorized to exercise faith in him, or whether [we] were authorized to do it at all. All must be confusion."[12] Brigham Young University political scientist A. Don Sorensen affirms, "If inequality infected divine 1ove—if it singled out any person from others by excluding her from all concern or by not caring for her total welfare or by taking a weakened interest in her well-being—then love ceases to be perfect, and life cannot be full."[13]

In other words, if we could not trust God to love us equally, we could not depend on the efficacy of the plan of salvation—of faith, of repentance, of baptism, of keeping the commandments, or of the atonement in our lives, since if God were partial in his love toward certain of his children, he could choose those for whom these principles would work.[14] Others would simply be lost, eternally outside the circle of divine love and esteem. The gospel of Christ rejects such doctrines of election. Because we can trust the Lord implicitly, we know that we can come unto him with full confidence that we will be not be turned away but will be enfolded in his love. A favorite saying of Elder Marion D. Hanks is, "To believe in God is to know all the rules will be fair and that there will be wonderful surprises."[15]

EQUAL RIGHT TO SPIRITUAL OBSERVANCES

In response to God's love, which encompasses all humans, every able person has the agency and the capacity, both spiritually and intellectually, to understand and accept the gospel of Christ and to participate fully in its blessings. Those who die before the age of accountability or who lack sufficient mental or emotional development to achieve accountability are saved through the atonement of Christ (Mosiah 3:16; 15:25; D&C 137:10). The rest of humankind, however, are moral agents, individually responsible to God for their choices. Thus, it follows that women's conversions and spiritual lives must be immediate and individual, not derivative. To anchor their testimonies, women must have the witness of the Holy Ghost, must receive personal revelation and possess spiritual gifts, and become, in the words of President Spencer W. Kimball, "scholars of the scriptures."[16] Salvation is a matter for each person, male or female, who comes to Christ as an individual.

To come to Christ, one must be able to commune with God. All women, men, and children have an equal right to receive answers to their prayers. They have the right to revelation for themselves and for any area of stewardship they have. They may have spiritual gifts (D&C 46:7–33; 1 Cor. 12; and Moro. 10:8–30). Elder Dallin H. Oaks, using the scriptures just cited and other references, stated, "The gift of the Holy Ghost is conferred on both men and women. So are spiritual gifts. . . . The receipt of spiritual gifts is predicated upon faith, obedience, and personal righteousness."[17] Men and women have an equal right to attend the temple.[18] Both sexes may pray, speak, and give lessons in church. The youth of both sexes should be taught about the importance of chastity, preparation for marriage, education, service, missions, and the importance of mutual respect and partnership after marriage.

Both women and men have free agency to decide matters for themselves and the knowledge to enable them so to do. Nephi, speaking of "the children of men" notes that "because that they are redeemed from the fall they have become free forever, knowing good from evil; to act for themselves and not to be acted upon" (2 Ne. 2:26). Mormon, quoted by his son Moroni, says, "For behold, the Spirit of Christ is given to every man [woman], that he [she] may know good from evil; wherefore, I show you the way to judge" (Moro. 7:16).

Equal Spiritual Affinity of Both Genders

It is well to remember that the transgression in the Garden of Eden was the result of conscious decisions by both partners (Moses 5:10–11). Keeping both Adam's and Eve's decisions in mind precludes any tendency to adopt the view from some cultures that women are inferior or innately sinful because of Eve's transgression.[19] Furthermore, the principle of individual agency and accountability strikes at the diabolical[20] notion that one gender (either female or male) has less capacity or affinity for spirituality and thus must be manipulated, coaxed, or pushed by the other. While culture can cloud spiritual insight, the assumption that God would send half of humanity to earth with an inherently diminished ability to perceive spiritual matters undercuts God's equal love for all individuals and collides with a key component of the plan of salvation.

Throughout most of Christian history, women have been viewed as the lesser creation, the supposed inheritors of Eve's susceptible nature, who must be under subjection to men.[21] Since the nineteenth century, however, American men have been condemned as spiritually suspect as their workplace moved outside the home. Moralists argued that the world contaminated men and that women had to save them. Women, ensconced in the "sacred sanctuary" of the home, became guardians of their husbands' and sons' souls.[22]

Priesthood and Gender

In the twentieth century, some Latter-day Saints have greatly broadened this "environmental contamination" thesis to an "inherently deficient male" thesis (our terms). They argue, for example, that spiritually superior women do not "need" to hold the priesthood but defective men do. Such reasoning contradicts itself; according to this logic, those who qualify for godhood—who have all priesthood power (D&C 132:20)—must be the most spiritually impaired of all. This contention also denies the justice and mercy of the gospel by condemning half of humankind as innately flawed. If attempts to explain women's lack of ordination to priesthood have led to the castigation of the male, they have also led to the patronization of the female. The notion that for mortal women motherhood is the parallel to priesthood is equally spurious, since all women are not mothers; fatherhood, not priesthood, is the male counterpart to motherhood. Furthermore, motherhood and fatherhood are bestowed on the righteous and the wicked alike.

Perhaps the most helpful insight into the issue of priesthood and women has been given by President Gordon B. Hinckley, who, in a powerful address to the 1985 general women's meeting, refrained from citing dubious folk doctrines as reasons for not ordaining women to priesthood. Instead, he simply said:

> A few Latter-day Saint women are asking why they are not entitled to hold the priesthood. To that I can say that only the Lord, through revelation, could alter that situation. He has not done so, so it is profitless for us to speculate and worry about it.[23]

Partnership in Marriage

While we come to Christ as individuals, the paradox is that women and men who have endured to the end and overcome the world must be exalted jointly as wives and husbands, following the pattern of our heavenly parents (D&C 131:2). The scriptural promise of exaltation to husbands and wives contained in Doctrine and Covenants 132:19–20 is also a description of the current life of our heavenly parents, who are explicitly characterized as sharing "a fulness" (D&C 132:19):

> Then shall *they* be gods, because *they* have no end; therefore shall *they* be from everlasting to everlasting, because *they* continue; then shall *they* be above all, because all things are subject unto *them*. Then shall *they* be gods, because *they* have all power, and the angels are subject unto *them*. (D&C 132:20; italics added)

From this scripture, one may extrapolate that Heavenly Mother is a full and equal partner to Heavenly Father even though our knowledge of her is incomplete.[21] Additionally, General Authorities have repeatedly spoken of the eternal relationship between husbands and wives as that of "equal partners." President Spencer W. Kimball has noted:

> Marriage is a partnership. Each is given a part of the work of life to do. . . . When we speak of marriage as a partnership, let us speak of marriage as a *full* partnership. We do not want our LDS women to be *silent* partners or *limited* partners in the eternal assignment! Please be a *contributing* and *full* partner.[25]

This injunction has recently been reaffirmed by Elder Boyd K. Packer and President Howard W. Hunter in the 1994 general conferences and by the First Presidency and Council of Twelve's proclamation on the family in 1995.[26]

To specify the practical implications of full partnership, President Kimball remarked on another occasion:

> Our sisters do not wish to be indulged or to be treated condescendingly; they desire to be respected and revered as our sisters and our equals. . . . We will be judged, as the Savior said on several occasions, by whether or not we love one another and treat one another accordingly and by whether or not we are of one heart and one mind. We cannot be the Lord's if we are not one![27]

A similar statement is attributed to Elder Packer. When calling a stake president, he advised:

> I don't want you treating your wife like you do the stake. . . . In the stake when a decision is to be made, you will seek the opinion of your counselors and other concerned individuals. Then you will prayerfully reach a decision on that matter, and they will all rally round and support you because you are the president and you have the mantle of authority. In your family when there is a decision to be made that affects everyone, you and your wife together will seek whatever counsel you might need, and together you will prayerfully come to a unified decision. If you ever pull priesthood rank on her, you will have failed in your leadership.[28]

Peremptorily to *order* another person to obey, or especially to threaten her with harm or to wield tyranny in the home, exhibits unrighteous dominion or abuse (D&C 121:41–46). President Ezra Taft Benson spoke of "family government where a man and woman enter into a covenant with God" as a term equivalent to "patriarchal order."[29] This partnership will continue through the eternities, for, as noted above, both men and women may be exalted to godhood status (D&C 132:19–20).

Righteous Leadership

While we may guide, teach, and seek to persuade others, no person has the right to force another's action or even to attempt it. To so do is unrighteous dominion: "We have learned by sad experience that it is the nature and disposition of almost all men [women], as soon as they get a little authority, as they suppose, they will immediately begin to exercise unrighteous dominion" (D&C 121:39).[30] The neighboring verses often are taken to refer to men, as ordained priesthood holders:

> No power or influence can or ought to be maintained by virtue of the priesthood, only by persuasion, by long-suffering, by gentleness and meekness, and by love unfeigned; By kindness, and pure knowledge, which shall greatly enlarge the soul without hypocrisy, and without guile. (D&C 121:41–42)

Perhaps holders of the priesthood are specifically mentioned in this part of Doctrine and Covenants 121 because the authority of the priesthood is so easily misunderstood and wrongly transformed into authoritarianism.

Church leaders may appropriately assume, as a first approximation, that members make decisions about their lives correctly with the Spirit of the Lord. It is not one's place to force, control, or circumscribe another's thinking, but rather to allow every soul the freedom to search out his or her destiny. If, for example, a woman is working outside the home, she may be regarded as having made that decision prayerfully. It is not necessary to assume that she is going against the interests of her family. As Chieko N. Okazaki has reminded us,

> Not all situations are ideal. Not all women are mothers, and not all mothers have children at home. Furthermore, not all mothers can make the choice to be home with their children all of the time. Often circumstances constrain their choices. At other times, other responsibilities and opportunities require that difficult decisions be made.[31]

Where there are situations in the Church in which men have a larger voice or role than women—as in general priesthood administration and discipline—efforts to insure fairness are in order. Procedures and policies should be clear to everyone. In general stake and ward councils, both men's and women's advice may be sought and considered, as has been recently emphasized.[32]

In order to follow the Savior's example, all members should be as sensitive and believing to one sex as to the other, treating actions by both sexes equally and not regarding behavior by a member of one sex as permissible and the same behavior by the other sex as reprehensible. Statements by both sexes, for example, in marital disputes, generally should be given equal credibility. Accusations of abuse must be taken seriously and not be dismissed because of the alleged perpetrator's church calling or status in the community. Nor should victims be accused of culpability for another's abusive behavior ("What did you do to provoke him?").[33]

Elimination of Abuse

It should go without saying that abuse of anyone is wrong. Women are more at risk than men for physical abuse, rape, child sexual abuse, and sexual harassment, although abuse of both sexes and by both sexes does occur. Accordingly, a major concern for feminism is eradicating spouse and other types of physical, sexual, emotional, and verbal abuse. Such abuse has been soundly and repeatedly condemned by Church leaders in general conferences and elsewhere. Elder James E. Faust noted:

> Any form of physical or mental abuse to any woman is not worthy of any priesthood holder. President Gordon B. Hinckley has stated, "I feel likewise that it ill becomes any man who holds the priesthood of God to abuse his wife in any way, to demean or injure or take undue advantage of the woman who is the mother of his children, the companion of his life, and his companion for eternity if he has received that greater blessing." This, of course, means verbal as well as physical abuse.[34]

President Howard W. Hunter has stated categorically, "Any man who abuses or demeans his wife physically or spiritually is guilty of grievous sin and in need of sincere and serious repentance."[35] The *General Handbook of Instructions* makes it clear that such abuse may result in Church disciplinary action.[36] Similarly, proper conduct toward members of one's family, as well as payment of alimony and child support as required in divorce settlements, are appropriately reviewed in temple recommend interviews. As the apostle Paul taught, "But if any provide not for his own, and specially for those of his own house, he hath denied the faith, and is worse than an infidel" (1 Tim. 5:8).[37]

The attitudes of those men who presume superiority to women, however, may beget beliefs about shirking responsibilities or tolerating many sorts of abuse, including rape, where such men may believe that they know better than a woman what she wants. Wives may also abuse husbands (although such abuse happens more often verbally than physically). Such behavior is just as reprehensible as husbands' abuse of wives. *Any* abuse is destructive to the relationship and to the family and is demeaning to the individuals involved.

Overcoming Cultural Limitations

The restoration of the gospel reaffirmed these truths of our equality before God, even though we as a culture do not fully understand them even yet. Two months after the June 1978 revelation on blacks and the priesthood,

Elder Bruce R. McConkie, in a talk to religious educators, bravely admitted that he, and perhaps most of the Church, had not comprehended some scriptural passages: "Many of us never imagined or supposed that they [particularly 2 Nephi 26:33] had the extensive and broad meaning that they do have."[38] These scriptures speak not only of racial but of gender equality as well as an "equality of esteem" for all humankind.[39] To what extent have we discerned "the extensive and broad meaning" of this verse in relation to the equality of women and men?

To some, it may be reassuring to continue in accustomed cultural patterns, many of which are based on the assumptions of a fallen world, not on those of eternity. One may take great comfort in feeling like a favorite child if a culture has designated preferential status based on particular characteristics; yet, the logical extension of this belief is that those for whom life is differently situated in gender, class, or race are somehow less valiant or even defective in some fashion. We thus pass judgments on each other and ourselves with disastrous spiritual results.[40]

To the contrary, the gospel of Christ requires that we transcend erroneous cultural assumptions to view eternal truth. Recurrent in the Book of Mormon is the warning of the dangers of believing the false traditions of one's culture—the "traditions of [the] fathers, which are not correct" (Mosiah 1:5)—in preference to the full gospel (see also Alma 9:16; 17:9; Hel. 15:7). From a secular perspective, feminism also demands that we reexamine assumptions, particularly those traditions that inhibit our ability to see beyond gender stereotypes and that prescribe and proscribe one's development solely on the basis of sex. Such "assumed truth[s]," according to Lawrence W. Levine, "become so deeply ingrained, so taken for granted, that they do not seem like ideas at all but part of the natural order. Thus when someone comes along who both perceives and *treats* them as ideas, subject to the challenges all ideas should be exposed to, it is as if reason itself were being challenged."[41]

Although one may disagree, feminism argues that inequality is socially constructed and thus can be changed. While women have received the preponderance of the fallout from cultural systems designed to restrict their movement to narrow areas and to limit their access to social, political, and economic power, men too have suffered from narrow definitions of masculine behavior. As an important book on the history of fatherhood in the United States makes clear, men have indeed gained status and power from their role as family breadwinners,[42] but they have lost in their emotional development as nurturers. According to Robert Griswold, fathers "wedded themselves to a division of labor and a vision of the good life that made father-child closeness problematic. What men gained in the world of power they may have lost in the world of sentiment. Such was the trade-off at the heart of male breadwinning."[43] The stakes involved in a fundamental transformation of society along equity lines are high for both women and men. Feminism envisions a world in which both sexes are able to achieve full personhood as individuals rather than being rendered as stereotypes.

Gender-Inclusive Language

The weaknesses of language may also need to be overcome. Scholars have determined that using the generic *he* and *man* (one example of gender-exclusive language) affects perceptions—the way women and men read themselves and others into the text.[44] Gender-exclusive language builds needless cultural walls, whereas gender-inclusive expressions in contemporary discourse are appropriate and desirable, reflecting not only God's inclusive love for all his children, but also thc comprehensive nature of the gospel. Following Christ's example, both women and men should be included in classroom discussions, and illustrations from both women's and men's lives ought to be used in talks and lessons.[45] Many of Christ's parables draw lessons from the experiences of women. Moreover, scriptures that speak of "men" often refer to both sexes; that inclusiveness may be pointed out when these scriptures are used, or the scripture can be read to include women explicitly. To cite only one of numerous examples from recent general conferences, Elder Neal A. Maxwell emended 3 Nephi 27:27 to read, "What manner of men [and women] ought ye to be? Verily I say unto you, Even as I am."[46] By specifically including references to women, one not only reaffirms women's eternal identity and worth, but one also follows the pattern established by Christ in his mortal ministry.

Equality in Education

Brigham Young spoke extensively about the appropriateness of education for both sexes. Louisa Greene Richards, first editor of the *Woman's Exponent*, commented:

> President Young proves himself [the] most genuine, impartial and practical "Woman's Rights man" upon the American continent, as he has ever done; his counsels, instructions and advice to women being always directed toward their progress and advancement in usefulness and the possession of valuable knowledge.[47]

Karen Lynn, at the time director of the Honors Program at Brigham Young University, remarked, "No child of our Father in Heaven can afford, in all conscience, to ignore the responsibility of learning about the world and dealing with it."[48]

The importance of women's education has personal implications for the authors of this article. Neither of us ever considered not pursuing learning; such a course was simply unthinkable. For each of us, education is of great benefit directly, both personally and economically. That one of us is male and the other female is irrelevant to education's significance in our lives. Juliaetta Bateman Jensen, the maternal grandmother of the male author, wrote of her mother's education with Dr. Ellis Shipp to become a midwife. Her mother, Marinda Allen Bateman, saved the little five-dollar gold pieces she earned from delivering over seven hundred babies, and in later years some of that money helped finance the education of her last daughter, Juliaetta.[49] Juliaetta later earned normal, bachelor's, and master's degrees and taught English literature in the extension divisions at Brigham Young University and the University of Utah for thirty years. She founded the Browning Society in both Provo and in Salt Lake City. Her example influenced thousands of women, as well as her descendants, both male and female. Other Church members have similar stories.

EQUALITY IN EMPLOYMENT

Similarly, since all laborers are worthy of their hire (D&C 31:5), one should render to all workers according to their due (Mosiah 4:13) in the culture of the workplace. Such statements prescribe that all employees, whether women or men, should receive equal pay for equal work and should be treated fairly in hiring and promotion. On the surface, equality in employment is merely an economic issue, but it relates to Church matters if Latter-day Saint employers deny employment to women on the basis of marital or familial status, particularly on the belief that the woman is not following the prophet or that she is taking a job away from a man. Questions in job interviews about family situations are not only inappropriate, but illegal. Similarly, the gospel principle of equal opportunity for mortal experience would require that neither males nor females should be counseled categorically out of "nontraditional" occupations on the basis that such work is not "proper" for their sex or that such occupations for one gender or the other are somehow against Church policy.

Likewise, in employment, school, and church, supervisors, colleagues, and teachers can be of either sex. One may not assume that a leader's or colleague's ideas are bad or trivial just because of gender. Men and women have ideas of comparable quality; ideas can be good, no matter the sex of the originator. A woman's recommendations should not be denigrated because she is not a priesthood holder, nor should a man's suggestions be dismissed because he is a man or because he is not a bishop or a stake president. Respect for true ideas is appropriate independent of their source. Patronization is demeaning; every individual has as much right to be treated equally and to be heard as anyone else.

Conclusion

We are all children of God. The gospel, in which Christ was one with his father and with the Holy Ghost, clearly proscribes unequal, unrighteous treatment of anyone, by anyone. "Feminism," as defined and discussed here in the context of our own deeply felt beliefs, simply espouses fair and equal treatment for all of our heavenly parents' children as wonderful, holy, potentially divine beings.

B. Kent Harrison *is professor of physics and astronomy at BYU. He received his BA in physics at BYU and then his MA and PhD in physics at Princeton University. His primary interest has been gravitation theory. While publishing widely in physics, he has also recently co-edited a book entitled* Confronting Abuse: An LDS Perspective on Understanding and Healing Emotional, Physical, Sexual, Psychological, and Spiritual Abuse.

Mary Stovall Richards *is associate professor of history at BYU. She received a BA at BYU and an MA and PhD in American history at the University of Chicago. Among other classes, she teaches the history of the South and the history of the American family.*

Notes

[1]Dorothy Sayers, *Are Women Human?* (Grand Rapids, Mich.: William B. Eerdmans Publishing, 1971), 47, quoted in Kathryn H. Shirts, "Women in the Image of the Son: Being Female and Being Like Christ," in *Women Steadfast in Christ: Talks Selected from the 1991 Women's Conference Co-sponsored by Brigham Young University and the Relief Society,* ed. Dawn Hall Anderson and Marie Cornwall (Salt Lake City: Deseret Book, 1992), 97.

[2]Laurel Thatcher Ulrich has also, independently, used this term to describe Mormon feminism in her essay, "Border Crossings," *Dialogue: A Journal of Mormon Thought* 27 (Summer 1994): 1.

[3]*Feminism* is an umbrella term, encompassing many disparate approaches to defining and to solving the problem of gender inequality. A helpful analogy is the political party. The terms *Democrat* and *Republican* both contain a wide range of political philosophies so that, on certain issues (civil rights in the 1960s, for example), right-wing Democrats may be far more conservative than liberal or moderate Republicans. In other words, one can no more predict definitively someone's opinion on a specific question by knowing that she is a Democrat than by knowing he is a feminist.

[4]See Mary Stovall Richards, "Feminism," in *Encyclopedia of Mormonism*, ed. Daniel H. Ludlow, 5 vols. (New York: Macmillan, 1992), 2:506–7; and Elouise Bell, "The Implications of Feminism for BYU," *BYU Studies* 16 (Summer 1976): 527–39.

[5]The modern feminist movement, as a coalition of various individuals and groups, includes numerous points of view, some of which contradict gospel principles. Many persons, unfortunately, dismiss the entire movement because of its more radical elements and, in the process, fail to perceive many of its beneficial features.

[6]For an enlightening discussion of Jesus' break with the cultural taboos of his time, see Leonard Swidler, "Jesus Was a Feminist," *Catholic World* 212 (January 1971): 177–83; and the very excellent book from a Mormon perspective by Jeni Broberg Holzapfel and Richard Neitzel Holzapfel, *Sisters at the Well: Women and the Life and Teachings of Jesus* (Salt Lake City: Bookcraft, 1993).

[7]Luke 15:3–10; and Jolene Edmunds Rockwood, "Choosing the Good Part: Women from Christ to Paul," in *Women Steadfast in Christ*, ed. Anderson and Cornwall, 110; see also Holzapfel and Holzapfel, *Sisters at the Well,* chapter 7.

[8]Holzapfel and Holzapfel, *Sisters at the Well,* 139.

[9]For this point, see Holzapfel and Holzapfel, *Sisters at the Well,* 4.

[10]Howard W. Hunter, "Follow the Son of God," *Ensign* 24 (November 1994): 87.

[11]Holzapfel and Holzapfel, *Sisters at the Well,* 113–14.

[12]Larry E. Dahl and Charles D. Tate, Jr., eds., *The Lectures on Faith in Historical Perspective* (Provo, Utah: Religious Studies Center, Brigham Young University, 1990), 69, lecture 3, paragraph 23. Eugene England discusses the implications of this quote in "Are All Alike Unto God? Prejudice Against Blacks and Women in Popular Mormon Theology," *Sunstone* 14 (April 1990): 21.

[13]A. D. Sorensen, "No Respecter of Persons: Equality in the Kingdom," in *As Women of Faith: Talks Selected from the BYU Women's Conferences,* ed. Mary E. Stovall and Carol Cornwall Madsen (Salt Lake City: Deseret Book, 1989), 57.

[14]See England, "Are All Alike Unto God?" 21.

[15]Marion D. Hanks, "Equality of Esteem," in *As Women of Faith,* ed. Stovall and Madsen, 35.

[16]Spencer W. Kimball, "Privileges and Responsibilities of Sisters," *Ensign* 8 (November 1978): 102. See also Alma 19:9–10; Alma 32:23; Alma 56:47–48; Luke 2:36–38; and Joel 2:28. On spiritual gifts, see Dallin H. Oaks, "Spiritual Gifts," *Ensign* 16 (September 1986): 68–72; and Linda King Newell, "Gifts of the Spirit: Women's Share," in *Sisters in Spirit: Mormon Women in Historical and Cultural Perspective,* ed. Maureen Ursenbach Beecher and Lavina Fielding Anderson (Urbana and Chicago University of Illinois Press, 1987), 111–50.

[17]Oaks, "Spiritual Gifts," 69.

[18]President Howard W. Hunter has asked all Latter-day Saints "to look to the temple of the Lord as the great symbol of your membership [in the Church]." Howard W. Hunter, "Exceeding Great and Precious Promises," *Ensign* 24 (November 1994): 8. See also Carol Cornwall Madsen, "Mormon Women and the Temple: Toward a New Understanding," in *Sisters in Spirit,* ed. Beecher and Anderson, 80–110, for an important discussion of the historical significance of the temple to women.

[19]Jolene Edmunds Rockwood, "The Redemption of Eve," in *Sisters in Spirit,* ed. Beecher and Anderson, 3–36. See also "I Have a Question," *Ensign* 24 (February 1994): 63.

[20]"Diabolical" has been used deliberately since to demean, belittle, or to trivialize another and his or her eternal worth is to play on the devil's turf.

[21]For a discussion of the origins of this view, see Elaine Pagels, *Adam, Eve, and the Serpent* (New York: Random House, 1988).

[22]See James Wallace Milden, "The Sacred Sanctuary: Family Life in Nineteenth-Century America" (PhD diss., University of Maryland, 1974); Kirk Jeffrey Jr., "Family History: The Middle-Class American Family in the Urban Context,

1830–1870" (PhD diss., Stanford University, 1972); and Christopher Lasch, *Haven in a Heartless World: The Family Besieged* (New York: Basic Books, 1977), especially 168–69.

[23]Gordon B. Hinckley, "Ten Gifts from the Lord," *Ensign* 15 (November 1985): 86.

[24]See Linda P. Wilcox, "The Mormon Concept of a Mother in Heaven," in *Sisters in Spirit,* ed. Beecher and Anderson, 64–77.

[25]Spencer W. Kimball, *My Beloved Sisters* (Salt Lake City: Deseret Book, 1980), 31; italics in original.

[26]Boyd K. Packer, "The Father and the Family," *Ensign* 24 (May 1994): 21; Howard W. Hunter, "Being a Righteous Husband and Father," *Ensign* 24 (November 1994): 50; First Presidency and Council of the Twelve Apostles of The Church of Jesus Christ of Latter-day Saints, "The Family: A Proclamation to the World," September 23, 1995; printed in *Ensign* 25 (November 1995): 102.

[27]Spencer W. Kimball, "Our Sisters in the Church," *Ensign* 9 (November 1979): 49.

[28]Boyd K. Packer, quoted in Carlfred Broderick, *One Flesh, One Heart* (Salt Lake City: Deseret Book, 1986), 31–32.

[29]Ezra Taft Benson, "What I Hope You Will Teach Your Children about the Temple," *Ensign* 15 (August 1985): 9.

[30]This particular verse refers to both men and women, since a person of either sex may try to dominate another.

[31]Chieko N. Okazaki, "Rowing Your Boat," *Ensign* 24 (November 1994): 92–93.

[32]M. Russell Ballard, "Counseling with Our Councils," *Ensign* 24 (May 1994): 24.

[33]See B. Kent Harrison, "How Can I Help? Concepts and Cautions for Ecclesiastical Leaders and Others," in *Confronting Abuse,* ed. Anne L. Horton, B. Kent Harrison, and Barry L. Johnson (Salt Lake City: Deseret Book, 1993), 215–27; for the quote, see 217. For personal accounts of abused women, many of whom were not believed by ecclesiastical leaders, see the essays on domestic violence and sexual abuse in *Exponent II* 14, no. 1 (1987).

[34]James E. Faust, "The Highest Place of Honor," *Ensign* 18 (May 1988): 37; Gordon B. Hinckley, "Reach Out in Love and Kindness," *Ensign* 12 (November 1982): 77. See also, for example, Gordon B. Hinckley, "Our Solemn Responsibilities," *Ensign* 21 (November 1991): 51; H. Burke Peterson, "Unrighteous Dominion," *Ensign* 19 (July 1989): 6–11; the essays in Horton, Harrison, and Johnson, eds., *Confronting Abuse.*

[35]Howard W. Hunter, "Being a Righteous Husband and Father," *Ensign* 24 (November 1994): 51; see also Judy C. Olsen, "The Invisible Heartbreaker," *Ensign* 26 (June 1996): 22–27.

[36]"Members who abuse or are cruel to their spouses, children, or other family members violate the laws of both God and man. . . . Church members who abuse their family members are subject to discipline by the Church. Such members should not be called to positions in the Church and should not be allowed to hold or receive a temple recommend." "Abuse and Cruelty," *General Handbook of Instructions* (Salt Lake City: The Church of Jesus Christ of Latter-day Saints, 1989), 11–14.

[37]See Hunter, "Being a Righteous Husband and Father," 51; and also Doctrine and Covenants 75:28 and 83:4.

[38]Bruce R. McConkie, "All Are Alike unto God," in *Charge to Religious Educators,* 2d ed. (Salt Lake City: The Church of Jesus Christ of Latter-day Saints, 1982), 152.

[39]The term "equality of esteem" is quoted in Hanks, "Equality of Esteem," 30.

[40]Edward Gardiner has argued that imputing sin to innocent persons may be the reason for Mormon's severe castigation of infant baptism, as discussed in Moroni 8. See Edward Gardiner, "Spiritual Abuse," in *Confronting Abuse,* ed. Horton, Harrison, and Johnson, 170–71.

[41]Lawrence W. Levine, "Clio, Canons, and Culture," *Journal of American History* 80 (December 1993): 866; italics in original. Feminist scholars have argued that the definition of gender is one of these "assumed truths." Donald G. Matthews and Jane Sherron De Hart found in their study of support for and opposition to the Equal Rights Amendment in North Carolina that proponents and opponents differed on this basic definition: "What historians or anthropologists understand as historically produced and conditioned patterns of behavior and therefore malleable by human action may be understood by fundamentalists to be absolutely normative if thought to be similar to Biblical patterns." *Sex, Gender, and the Politics of the ERA: A State and the Nation* (New York: Oxford University Press, 1990), 178.

[42]The beginnings of industrialization in the early 1800s in the United States transformed the self-sufficient households of the previous centuries into units of consumption rather than production. Fathers increasingly left home for work, while mothers became the guardians of the "sacred sanctuary," as domestic moralists termed the home. What many twentieth-century persons have assumed was a timeless system of male breadwinner and domestic spouse is not quite two hundred years old and for much of that period has been true for white middle-class families only. Even then, there was significant variation across regions. Steven Mintz and Susan Kellogg summarize the literature on this development in *Domestic Revolutions: A Social History of American Family Life* (New York: Free Press, 1988), 49–51.

[43]Robert L. Griswold, *Fatherhood in America: A History* (New York: Basic Books, 1993), 33.

[44]See Barrie Thorne, Cheris Kramarae, and Nancy Henley, eds., *Language, Gender, and Society* (Rowley, Mass.: Newbury House, 1983).

[45]For a humorous, but pointed, examination of how gender can marginalize persons in an academic setting, see [Elouise Bell], "The Tables Turned: An Exercise in Consciousness-Raising," *Dialogue* 11 (Summer 1978): 113–18.

[46]Neal A. Maxwell, "Settle This in Your Hearts," *Ensign* 22 (November 1992): 65.

[47]Louisa Greene Richards, "Work for Women," *Woman's Exponent* 1 (April 15, 1873): 172, quoted in Carol Cornwall Madsen, "Voices in Print: *The Woman's Exponent,* 1872–1914," in *Women Steadfast in Christ,* ed. Anderson and Cornwall, 72.

[48]Karen Lynn, BYU *Daily Universe,* March 26, 1981, 4.

[49]Juliaetta Bateman Jensen, *Little Gold Pieces: The Story of My Mormon Mother's Life* (Salt Lake City: Stanway Printing, 1948), 88–98, 178–180.

Questions

1. Look carefully at the citations used by Harrison and Richards. What features do they have in common? How are these citations chosen to address their audience?
2. What role do definitions play in this argument?
3. What is the authors' most persuasive evidence?
4. How does this argument correspond to Bradshaw's article, "I Would Be a Purveyor of Mysteries"?

Why More Utah Mormons Should Become Democrats: Reflections on Partisan Politics

EUGENE ENGLAND

In this essay from Making Peace: Personal Essays, *Eugene England looks at how the American political system was built on the principle that opposing viewpoints would actually be better for the nation, with each viewpoint tempering and revising the other. England discusses this principle with regards to Utah politics, arguing that the overwhelming dominance of one political party over the other might be detrimental for the overall good of the people. He prefaces his discussion by recounting the time in Utah history when LDS church officials went door to door dividing Mormon Utahns evenly into Republicans and Democrats.*

Over one hundred years ago, in September 1891, there occurred in Huntsville, Utah, a strange incident. In this American town on a bright late summer morning with young cottonwoods and Lombardy poplars turning bright yellow along the streets and pockets of gold aspen and deep-red maples visible on the surrounding hills, Mormon church leaders went from door to door, assigning one family to be Democrats, the next to be Republicans. Thus were Mormons attempting to accommodate gentile political ways as a prerequisite for Utah statehood. David O. McKay, one of the most openly Republican of church presidents, confirmed this story of how his hometown of Huntsville had once been divided by alternate houses, while Joseph Nelson, head of the Saltair Corporation, reported that in his Salt Lake City ward his bishop stood and declared all the Saints on one side of the aisle Democrats and all those on the other Republicans.[1] In Rockville, in southern Utah, leaders divided the community down Main Street.[2] Whatever the mechanism, in the early 1890s Mormon leaders, from the First Presidency through stake presidents down to bishops and other local leaders, were energetically engaged in a remarkably paradoxical enterprise. They went about proving that the rank-and-file was independent of political influence from the church hierarchy by directing many Mormons, against their inclinations, to join the Republican party.

As everyone in Utah knew, a wholesale onslaught on Mormon beliefs had been led by the national Republican Party. Its initial platform had promised in the 1850s to eradicate what it termed the "twin relics of barbarism"—slavery and polygamy. In response, Mormons formed the anti-Republican People's Party and applications for statehood were denied as increasingly punitive measures were passed against Mormons by the Republican-controlled national government. But by 1891 church leaders had become convinced it must disband the Mormon party to avoid "carpetbaggers," Republican appointees from Washington who, as they did in the devastated South, exercised insensitive, tyrannous control that essentially disenfranchised the local people. Church leaders knew that if things were left to chance, most Mormons would become Democrats and in reaction gentiles would become Republicans, perpetuating the bitter political/religious division that had plagued Utah territory since the formation of the anti-Mormon liberal party in 1870.

The insight and intentions of the First Presidency are revealed in a letter written in May 1891 to John W. Young, who had long served as unofficial liaison to national Democratic party leaders. President Wilford Woodruff and his counselors George Q. Cannon and Joseph E Smith informed Young that the political field in Utah was "ripe ready to harvest," but that Mormons were anti-Republican in their sympathies and thus likely to "rush into the Democratic ranks." They believed it was "of the highest importance that this not be the case." Consider their reason, which helps explain their controversial and still sometimes maligned actions in directing people who naturally would be Democrats to become Republicans: "The more evenly balanced the parties become the safer it will be for us [Mormons] in the security of our liberties; and . . . our influence for good will be far greater than it possibly could be were either party overwhelmingly in the majority."[3]

That statement shows remarkable foresight. It demonstrates, I believe, greater understanding of the basic strength of our political system than that of anti-Mormons of that time, mostly Republicans, who were willing to use any means, however unconstitutional, to destroy Mormonism as supposedly un-American. And it shows better insight into the nature and value of political parties than that of many Mormons today, mostly Republicans, who believe that Truth resides with their party and who therefore seek overwhelming supremacy.

I believe things have come to such a pass that many Utah Mormons should choose to become Democrats—not because the Democratic platform is "truer," certainly not because its leaders and candidates are "better." Utah Mormons should become Democrats because for about twenty-five years Democrats have been a steadily dwindling minority in Utah, and thus Republicans are developing the attitudes and practices of one-party rule. Those attitudes and practices are more dangerous than the actual beliefs or programs of *either* party.

I believe some Utah Mormons should become Democrats for precisely the same reason the First Presidency encouraged some to become Republicans in 1891, which is well worth reading again: "The more evenly balanced the parties become the safer it will be for us in the security of our liberties; and . . . our influence for good will be greater than it possibly could be were either party overwhelmingly in the majority."

Some may think this is simply a partisan plea by a disgruntled Democrat. Not so! I am a lifelong Republican, a descendant of Wilkie and Dewey supporters. I voted twice for Nixon and twice for Reagan. I grew up hearing how my grandfather was kept in near starvation through the latter part of the Depression by anti-Mormon Democrats in Idaho. They swept in with Franklin D. Roosevelt and gave all the work painting state buildings to their incompetent cronies, who, as my grandfather said, besides depriving him of a living, "couldn't paint worth a tinker's dam." I often heard my father, a hard-pressed farmer in southeast Idaho, fulminate about Roosevelt's federal farm agents, many the sons of pork-barrel politicians. With no knowledge of local people and land conditions, they wasted money and tried to impose useless and destructive controls.

Despite all this I sincerely believe that I and other Utah Mormons should become Democrats—at least until the parties are nearly equal in strength again in the state. In fact, it might be good for church leaders to encourage some shifting. This would make clear to Mormons the fundamental Constitutional principle that American freedoms "are based on," separation of powers and prescribed checks and balances, strongly aided by the development of the two-party system. If those checks and the party system are kept strong and balanced, they create a *process* of government that is the surest guarantee of our liberties and of civil peace, much more sure than the particular content of any person's or party's ideas about what our government should do.

Political parties have generally had the opposite effect of that anticipated by the framers, who deplored partisan politics as too polarizing to society. Instead parties have reduced partisan polarization; they have helped keep politics in the United States mainly non-ideological, forcing partisans to compromise their demands, trade favors, unite with strange bedfellows to get *part* of what they wanted, and in turn help opponents get part of what they wantcd. This has provided a basis for cooperation among people of different religions, races, and sectional interests; it has tended to shrink volatile dogmatisms into manageable issues and has effectively translated what I think was the most profound and inspired insight of James Madison into reality.

In August 1786, just ten years after the Declaration of Independence and only five after the Articles of Confederation had been ratified, America's great experiment in creating a "new order of the ages" was failing so completely that George Washington wrote to John Jay, "What a triumph for the advocates of despotism to find that we are incapable of governing ourselves."[4] But at about this same time Madison, an intellectual and political leader from Virginia, set out to do something. He had been engaged in six months of intense study of books on history and government sent him from Paris by Thomas Jefferson. He now took time off from his studies to attend a convention at Annapolis on regulating trade among the states. There, together with two friends, the strong federalist Alexander Hamilton of New York and Governor Edmund Randolph of Virginia, he successfully led the delegates in making a unanimous call for another convention. It was to be held the next May in Philadelphia and to have a greatly expanded agenda, essentially to amend the Articles of Confederation.

In the meantime Madison wrote two papers and shared them with Washington, Randolph, and the rest of the Virginia delegation. When the new convention began on May 28, 1787, Randolph rose with a prepared sketch for a new Constitution. It was what became known as the Virginia Plan and was based on the papers by Madison. It moved the convention beyond its announced purpose and gave the edge to those favoring a strong national government.

By the second week, in a reconsideration of the means of selecting members to the proposed two-house Congress, a basic roadblock became visible. Some worried that states with small populations like Rhode Island would be "subject to faction," rent by the passions of large minorities, while others suspected that the large states like Massachusetts were so unwieldy as to be impervious to effective democratic government but inclined to anarchy and misrule. Madison turned these apparently mutually supportive arguments against each other. Drawing on his long study of republics and confederacies, he pointed out in an argument he later developed fully in *The Federalist*, letter 10, that all civilized societies are divided into numerous sects, factions, and interests; that whenever a majority is united by a common interest or passion, the rights of the minority are in danger; and that neither honesty, respect for character, nor conscience had succeeded in restraining the majority in past societies from infringing on the rights of the minority. In fact, he reminded his colleagues in a sentence that should burn with memory and caution for every Mormon, "Religion itself may become a motive to persecution and oppression."

What remedy then? It was brilliantly simple, original, and crucial in removing the roadblock to an acceptable Constitution: To *enlarge* the political sphere and thereby create a community with so many interests and parties that, in the first place, a majority would not be likely at the same moment to have a common interest different from that of the whole people, including minorities, and that, in the second place, in cases where the majority did have such an interest, they would not be able to unite in the pursuit of it.[5]

Madison thus provided delegates a way to believe that the evils they had seen flowing from an excess of democracy, rather than being increased in a national government and growing country, would actually be decreased as they counteracted each other. And as delegates acted on that faith to create our country, Madison became a prophet of how a pluralistic society can in fact work with unique success. The stability and internal peacefulness of our country have resulted from its governmental structure and what noted writer on education and on government Daniel Bell calls America's "constitutional culture," with its many checks and balances, including the two-party system.[6] Our system encourages the formation of shifting coalitions in ways that safeguard the liberties of all citizens, particularly minority groups, whose rights are always most at risk in any democratic society.

Two other moments stand out for me in that four-month process of compromise and shifting coalitions in the summer of 1787 that produced the document we honored much in the years approaching and including its bicentennial in 1987. Those moments are particularly important to my argument for political pluralism as an essential ingredient of national peace. They are the decision to give the war-making power to Congress, not the president, and the decision not to give either Congress or the president the power to impose what were called "sumptuary laws."

I begin with the second: In late August, as the Convention moved into its final stages, George Mason of Virginia moved to enable Congress to enact laws designed to regulate personal behavior on moral and religious grounds. He argued, in a way that sounds reasonable to most Mormons and conservative people generally, "No government can be maintained unless the manners [by which he meant private moral behavior] be *made* consonant to it."[7] After a few speeches in opposition, the Convention voted down the proposal, and, except for the unfortunate fourteen-year experiment with Prohibition of liquor from 1919 to 1933, our system has generally avoided wholesale infringement upon people's private morality.

Why would I, a teetotaling Mormon who believes that substance abuse and sexual promiscuity are among civilization's most destructive evils, want government to stay entirely away from trying to control those things—except as they directly victimize others? For two reasons: First, I want freedom of conscience in areas of personal faith and morality for myself, and I must therefore protect it for others. Second, I do not want to live in a society, like most of those in the world, driven by the conflict and violence that result from attempts to coerce personal faith and morals—conflict and violence such as were clearly produced under Prohibition and by the earlier attempt to control Mormon polygamy and which currently surrounds the abortion issue.

Daniel Bell's twofold explanation for the stability of our government for over 200 years is instructive. First, there is the unexpected stability in pluralism that Madison predicted, built on coalition-forming between interest groups and thus protection of the interests of potentially rebellious minorities. Second, we have reduced conflict by largely avoiding legislation in areas of personal morality. As Bell points out, for most people such areas are non-negotiable. They often involve deep personal convictions which cannot be adjusted or compromised, and when compliance is forced, that compulsion gives rise to deep resentments and eventually rebellion. The arena of law should be reserved for procedural matters and areas where we directly harm others or restrict their rights. These matters are generally clear and acceptable, or are at least negotiable, meaning we can compromise and live with the compromises. When we cannot compromise our consciences or we feel personally infringed upon, conflict is often the result.

Apostle Brigham Young, Jr., reflecting, I am confident, his father's view, confessed during the polygamy persecutions of 1884, "I am willing, in political matters, to . . . let the majority rule. . . . But in the things pertaining to conscience no man, no set of men . . . can control me before my God. . . . I am a free man in relation to these matters, not bowing to any majority nor to any party."[8]

Majority control over conscience was precisely what happened in polygamy, and Mormons should remember it well. As Daniel Bell pointed out to a BYU audience in the fall of 1986, "Cultural conservatives should be political liberals."[9] In other words, those, like Mormons, who want the freedom to practice their strong and unusual personal religious beliefs and ethics should be among the most active in promoting a system where *all* are free to do so, even those whose beliefs and actions are repugnant to them, as long as those beliefs and actions do not unavoidably and significantly infringe on the rights of others.

Mormons should also be among the most active opponents to anything like George Mason's sumptuary laws, such as Prohibition, to "blue laws" such as Sunday closing, etc.—that is, laws that try to control private morality or activities between consciously consenting adults, no matter how perverse. We should be against any governmental coercion upon teachers or curriculum, especially in areas of religious views, organic evolution, human sexuality, and partisan politics. We should even be against prescribed school prayer, including so-called "moments of silence," whenever, however subtly, those publicly mandated forms act to coerce young minds. Spiritual and moral coercion not only violate the most central value of the Constitution but the central values of the Mormon religion, the very ones that lead us to revere the Constitution.

Mormons belong to one of the few remaining religious bodies which still believes the US Constitution was inspired by God. The crucial scriptural passage is Doctrine and Covenants 101:77–80, a revelation to Joseph Smith in 1833. That was only forty years after ratification of the Constitution and not long before Madison died, the last surviving framer and certainly one of those to whom God refers in saying to the Prophet, "I established the Constitution of this land by the hands of wise men whom I raised up unto this very purpose" (v. 80).

Knowledgeable people may laugh at such a description of those fifty-five mortal men, most of them quite secular, very few of them pious, some dissolute. But after reading the story of their accomplishment in William Peters's excellent history, *A More Perfect Union* (1987), I cannot laugh. By devising the first government in history which allowed a group of people consciously to place themselves under the rule of law, these men proved to be extremely courageous and wise. At the same time they achieved a structure that promotes the most fundamental goal of many prophets through the ages, that individuals be able to assume moral responsibility for their own actions.

The revelation I have quoted says that the American Constitution and laws are acceptable to God *only* as they are "established and . . . maintained for the rights and protection of all flesh, according to just and holy principles" (D&C 101:77). These principles, as BYU professor Noel Reynolds points out,[10] are precisely what is meant by the rule of law. In the Lord's own words, "That every man may act in doctrine and principle pertaining to futurity, according to the moral agency which I have given unto him, that every man may be *accountable for his own sins in the day of judgment"* (v. 78; my emphasis). The framers wanted people to be free to pursue wealth and happiness and personal salvation in whatever form they chose and to do so with confidence that laws would apply consistently and equally to all, whatever their private goals. They could make both moral choices and legal contracts with reasonable ability to predict future consequences, confident there would be no intervention by the whims and arbitrary commands of rulers.

This system guarantees that all can be held morally responsible, both before the law where appropriate and always before their consciences and God; they are accountable for their actions and choices since they are free from compulsion. As Hugh Nibley has written: "The best of human laws leaves every man free to engage in his own pursuit of happiness, without presuming for a moment to tell him where that happiness lies; that is the very thing the laws of God can guarantee. At *best*, the political prize is negative."[11]

Mormons have trouble with this. Natural utopians, we tend to want more from the political system than it can give. We want a *positive* prize. Republicans in particular seem to want to legislate private morality, to use law to make people good, to force them not just to refrain from harming each other but to *be* good. Any such effort to do God's work, to use the power of the state to do what only churches and non-coercive social and cultural forces should do, once led the Republican party into one of the most outrageous intrusions upon human rights in American history, one that ranks with Jim Crow laws and our internment in concentration camps of US citizens of Japanese ancestry during World War II.

I mean, of course, the anti-polygamy crusade against Mormons. That crusade was doubly pernicious in that it not only violated a fundamental principle that government should not intrude into personal belief and morality, but it adopted unconstitutional means to serve that unconstitutional end. Perhaps most repugnant is that it employed two ancient enemies of the rule of law that the framers explicitly renounced: *ex post facto* laws, which make past actions criminal and thus remove predictability and moral responsibility,[12] and bills of attainder. The latter are declarations of guilt of specifically targeted individuals by legislative bodies rather than by fair trial in court.

Led by Republicans, the government passed, declared constitutional, and then brutally enforced a series of laws designed to coerce Mormons into conformity with Victorian America. The Morrill Act of 1862 forbade people from cohabitation in plural marriage; the Edmunds Act of 1882 imposed five-year sentences on polygamists and deprived them forever of the right to vote and hold office; and the infamous Utah Commission, appointed by Republican president Chester Arthur to enforce the

Edmunds Act, imposed a religious test oath by requiring that voters and office-seekers swear they had never practiced polygamy. In Idaho mere membership in the church was used as a test to disenfranchise *all* Mormons, polygamous or not.

In 1887 the Republican Congress moved directly to attack the organization behind the practice of polygamy. The Edmunds-Tucker Act disincorporated the church, confiscated most of its properties, disenfranchised all polygamists and all Utah women (Mormon or not), abolished the Perpetual Emigrating Fund that subsidized immigration from Europe, and took over the Mormon-dominated public school system. No wonder that James Henry Moyle, who witnessed this period as a young man, could write that reading the Republican-controlled *Salt Lake Tribune* for that time demonstrated that

> there was no fundamentally American political principle that [the crusaders] would not have sacrificed to achieve their ambition and determination to secure the political control of the Utah territory and the destruction of Mormonism. . . . Not a few of them placed no limit on the executive and judicial action which they would take to secure for the minority control of the majority and to deprive the majority of its most fundamental political rights.[13]

Moyle was an ardent, lifelong Democrat and devout Mormon. Though he eventually served as a mission president for the church, he suffered much humiliation under the cloud of anti-Democrat feeling that strangely developed among Mormons after the partitions of 1891. Mormons soon forgot their former evil treatment at the hands of Republicans, and Moyle was amazed and sorrowful that church leaders, in trying to prevent people from going overwhelmingly Democrat (which, in a moving passage of devotion to his leaders, Moyle says they were right to do), unintentionally made Utah Mormons overwhelmingly Republican. He regrets mainly the great confusions and personal tragedies these efforts produced, especially the tragedies that befell Mormon Democratic Party leaders B. H. Roberts and Moses Thatcher. He feels deeply the "great injustice to the Democratic Party that was perpetuated in the ingratitude and partisan excesses that followed." He concludes, in a lesson for Mormons and non-Mormons today, that it is futile for even great men "to be both political and ecclesiastical leaders at the same time in a government where political parties are controlling and voters divide on political lines. . . . In America politics and religion should never be entangled."[14]

My concern is that religion and politics are being entangled again in Mormonism, not among high-ranking leaders so much as among local leaders and in Mormon popular culture. It is no longer merely a joke that a good Mormon cannot be a Democrat, and Mormon Democrats are constantly on the defensive, seeming to feel a need to apologize for even *being* Democrats, whatever their particular views. The response church leaders feared in 1891 is also occurring, though now in the opposite direction: Non-Mormons and disaffected Mormons are gravitating to the Democratic Party, so that the political division is becoming a religious one.

One of the most troubling elements of this polarization is the growing Mormon tendency to find absolute or at least superior, even divine, truth in the Republican Party platform. At the practical level our system depends, I believe, on a difficult skill suited to that duality the framers called "the genius of our people." It is the ability to energetically pursue a program or idea in the political marketplace and then calmly to accept its defeat or modification through compromise and even to lend support to the "winners" in a genuinely united community. It is a skill based on recognition that the finest truth or law or program is never the creation of one person or partisan group but rather the result of the passionate conflict and combining of ideas and proposals in a democratic context.

I was somewhat pleased to see the Republican victories nationally in November 1994, because it seemed to me that many Democrats in Congress, like the Republicans in much of Utah, had during forty years of control begun to adopt the dangerous habits of one-party rule—cronyism, disregard of opposing points of view, failure to pursue new ideas—and I thought a shake-up and new lines of debate and coalition might help us find new solutions. But when the leader of House Republicans, Newt Gingrich, after the election announced he would "never compromise" with President Clinton, he revealed an ignorance of the basic strength of our political system that was breathtaking. When both Republicans and Democrats belittled Clinton's State of the Union address as too full of compromise, too much a combination of left and right, liberal and conservative ideas, I despaired that our political discourse had descended permanently into small-minded partisanship and resentment.

The kind of political skill and virtue I am trying to advocate is based on the notion articulated by Milton in *Areopagitica*, his great defense of freedom of the press and of expression. Milton's surprising idea is that virtue and truth are made pure and whole not by being cloistered and protected from exposure to contrary, even "evil," actions and ideas, but by the opposite: full engagement in a tempting world and a full marketplace of ideas to which we respond with reasoned criticism and rethinking and, yes, even changing our mind and compromising.

Three hundred years after Milton's essay, Walter Lippmann, writing in August 1939, just as liberty was under worldwide assault at the beginning of World War II, reminded us that our vaunted ideal of freedom of speech and political expression is not merely an abstract virtue or matter of simple neighborly toleration but an absolute practical necessity: "We must protect the right of our opponents to speak because we must hear what they have to say. . . . Because freedom of discussion improves our own opinions."[15] He points out that in our system we pay the opposition salaries out of the public treasury because like a good doctor who tells us unpleasant truths, an opponent can help us be more healthy.

Lippmann shows how dictatorships defeat themselves by liquidating or terrifying into silence the very voices that would help them avoid or correct inevitable errors. It is precisely such opposition and debate, especially concerning such a crucial matter as making war, which our Founding Fathers placed firmly in an open, contentious body like Congress, because they knew that there, rather than in the patriotic but narrow, cloistered vision of a single person like Oliver North or H. R. Haldeman, the best decisions would be made and most effectively changed if they needed to be. It is there where what Lippmann calls "the indispensable opposition" most effectively operates and where Reagan, as well as Nixon, should have turned to tell and hear the truth. As Lippmann concludes, "A good statesman, like any other sensible human being, always learns more from his opponents than from his fervent supporters. For his supporters will push him to disaster unless his opponents show him where the dangers lie."[16]

Good Democrats or good Republicans are not those who believe their party has all truth and who yearn for complete victory and one-party government control. They are rather those who seek the engagement, compromise, enlightening debate, checks on natural aggrandizement of power, etc., that the process of interparty dialogue makes possible. They are like Todd Britsch, who, while he was Dean of Humanities at BYU, said to me, "I do not feel good when I have power to implement my ideas without argument and opposition. I've learned that without strong rebuttal and rethinking they are likely not to be very good ideas—and may be very bad ones." Good Democrats and Republicans are those who realize that the political process is strongest when the parties are nearly equal in strength—and good Mormons, believers in our inspired Constitution and desirous of political peace and effectiveness, would work, or even change affiliations, to bring that about.

Let me illustrate the danger I feel in devotion to supposed one-party truth. In the spring 1987 run-off election for Brigham Young University student body officers, two students who had had some experience in negative campaigning in statewide elections used such methods to defeat a student they found objectionable simply because he was a "liberal Democrat." The candidate, who had led strongly in the primary and thus was likely to win, had been president of Response, a club that sponsored the Peace and Human Rights symposium held at BYU each year. He had participated in an on-campus anti-Contra demonstration and had signed a petition published in the *Daily Universe* calling for US–Soviet arms reduction.

The two students, according to a report in BYU's independent *Student Review*, "were committed to the perpetuation of a conservative political philosophy at BYU through the perpetuation of politically conservative [student] leaders."[17] Their campaign consisted of allegations about the candidate's financial management and criticism of his bringing to campus "leftist speakers." The candidate, and others, responded in a *Daily Universe* article with statements such as, Yes, he brought liberal speakers to campus—along with conservative and moderate speakers—as part of the function of the symposia to educate people to a range of views, and Yes, there was an $800 deficit listed on the Response account, but it was an accounting error and had been removed.

The two students printed a flyer which quoted only the admissions but not the explanations. When asked why they did this, they responded that to print the explanations as well would have limited the "rhetorical effectiveness" of their flyers.[18] These actions were probably the reason the candidate lost, and they reveal a profound and dangerous misunderstanding of our political process as well as Christian morality by some young Mormons.

Lest anyone think that such intolerance and misunderstanding of our system occurs only at BYU or among conservatives, let me tell about my alma mater, the University of Utah. Because the U was founded by Mormons and remained predominantly Mormon until well into this century, there was much church influence, and the increasing non-Mormon faculty at times felt somewhat beleaguered. In some departments there is probably still a Mormon clique that sometimes controls things unfairly. But when I was a student in the 1950s, I found in all the humanities and most of the social science departments an almost complete swing to the opposite condition. Nearly all teachers were non-Mormons or had left the faith, and I found in many classes and on most public occasions a subtle but unmistakable disdain for things Mormon.

Sometimes the disdain wasn't so subtle. Religiously pious themes and term papers by Mormon students were belittled among the faculty and graduate students. The "local culture" was openly stereotyped as ignorant, repressive, and prejudiced. A faculty member asserted at a public forum that it was inconsistent for a Mormon bishop to be a university professor because commitment to any particular set of beliefs precluded the necessary scholarly skepticism and objectivity. Which left unspoken the interesting question of what professors were to profess—apparently only criticism of religious or conservative beliefs or fostering of particular political and moral crusades. And that professing was done under what I believe is the most dangerous cloak for unexamined beliefs and assumptions, the aura of "objectivity."

In 1975 I found that things were getting worse. My visits to the U, and a stint teaching a class in the extension division, revealed that many professors thought of the university as a small island of light in the great darkness of Mormon country. Their mission was to disabuse the Mormon students of their conditioned naiveté and to belittle their church and culture—if in no other way than by simply not taking it seriously. Even though 70 percent of students were LDS, many professors and graduate assistants seemed to feel no obligation to respond to that reality in their teaching, the way their liberal convictions would have led them to respond in any university with predominantly black or Jewish students—by learning about and engaging in respectful dialogue with the ideas and art and literature and institutions and people of the local culture.

One of my former professors, in genuine sorrow, admitted that his department simply would not hire an active Mormon into a tenure-track position. It was extremely hard for me to believe that such blatant and illegal prejudice was possible at a modern state university, but as I looked more closely I could see he was right. They hadn't hired an active Mormon, despite excellent candidates, in twenty-five years and still haven't twenty years later. I also found that friends had similar experiences with other departments, one finding that he had been mistaken for a non-Mormon and invited to the separate non-Mormon party for candidates, where he was told frankly about their determination not to hire such intrinsically handicapped creatures.

Since anything a Mormon president or academic vice-president would do about this embarrassing and costly blot on Utah's fine higher education system would be immediately suspect, it seems to me that it is high time for non-Mormon leaders of stature in the administration and faculty to approach the question as an educational rather than a religious issue. They could set the example, showing respect for their Mormon colleagues and students by engaging openly in serious dialogue with them and their faith and culture. They could act on and vigorously promote the assumption that undergirds our Constitution, that all individuals and groups, ethnic or religious or whatever, are potentially equal in the value of their ideas and feelings and must be accorded equal opportunity to work and learn and teach, without being impeded by anything irrelevant to the matter at hand, whether race, sex, or their religion or lack of it.

There may be some still not convinced. Let me return to one of the two actions by the Constitutional Convention that I said were important to my argument that Mormons should become Democrats. Republicans have recently led the way in the massive erosion of a central constitutional principle, the restriction of war-making to Congress. They need some principled, even religiously passionate, opposition.

On August 6, 1787, the Committee on Detail distributed a printed draft of the proposed Constitution to the Convention which provided, "The legislature of the United States shall have the power . . . to make war." Pierce Butler of South Carolina suggested that the war power be given to the president, who, he said, "will not make war [except] when the Nation will support it." But he was the only delegate, then or ever, to suggest that the executive branch be given power to initiate war.

In fact, the danger of a powerful executive was perhaps the chief concern in forming a strong federal government in the first place. "It has been observed that in all countries," one delegate warned, when they were first deciding in May whether to have a one-person or three-person executive, "the executive power is in a constant course of increase."[19] John Rutledge of South Carolina said, "I am for vesting the executive power in a single person, though I am not for giving him the power of war and peace."[20]

During the August 6 review of the document, Madison moved to replace "make war" with "declare war" in the provision giving Congress that power, "leaving to the Executive the power to repel sudden attacks." And the discussion that followed makes clear that the general concern of the delegates was not to thus *narrow* the power of the Legislature but only to allow the Executive to respond quickly to direct invasion. George Mason of Virginia, the records of the Convention tell us, "was against giving the power of war to the Executive, because [he was] not [safely] to be trusted with it. . . . He was for clogging rather than facilitating war; but he was for facilitating peace."[21]

We have come to a condition, some 200 years later, where the president has effectively taken over the power of initiating war, with almost no opposition from Congress. This encroachment has reached such arrogance that President Johnson intentionally lied to the country and Congress in order to carry on the war in Vietnam, and President Reagan and his executive branch supporters continued the war they began in Nicaragua by secret and illegal means, even when polls consistently showed that a majority of Americans were against it and Congress had expressly forbidden such actions.

Congress is far from faultless. For forty years it has abrogated its Constitutional and morally sensible responsibility to debate carefully, decide cautiously, and then announce clearly to the world a declaration of war. Many Congressmen have violated the Constitution, it seems, out of a misguided loyalty to their president when he is of their same party. Such partisans fail to understand the basic constitutional principle of separation of powers, which means that to fulfill their oath of office they must oppose improper, unconstitutional actions by the president, especially infringement on the separation of powers, even when he is of their own party.

The fault is certainly shared equally by both parties, just as they share about equally the number of Imperial Presidents, beginning with Franklin Delano Roosevelt, who improperly took to themselves the war power. But right now Republicans seem most guilty, which is another reason I think more Mormons, who have particular reason to respect the Constitution and oppose war, should be Democrats.

Mormon Democrats might have had enough independence, as Republican presidents in recent years rushed us into wars, to point out that this country has not been subjected to "sudden attack," in the sense clearly intended by the framers, since Pearl Harbor. They might have asked why, given this fact, we have had a series of horribly costly wars in which tens of thousands of American soldiers and millions of our opponents have been killed and trillions of dollars wasted on massive destruction of both lives and the environment. They might have found impeachable offense in President Reagan's condoning of assassination, preemptive strikes, secret building of permanent bases in Honduras in violation of law and treaties, and his continued, arrogant disregard of the judgment of the World Court that we were to stop our unlawful interference in Nicaragua, a legitimate government which had committed no illegal or aggressive act against the United States.

Too many Mormon Congressmen have apparently become more Republican than legislators or Mormons. They seem more committed to the obsessive hawkishness of their party, which has allowed them to endorse violent efforts to overthrow governments we do not like, than to the teachings of Mormon prophets who categorically reject such acts. The Book of Mormom is quite clear on this, condemning all violence except defense against attacks within our borders (see Alma 24:17–19; 25:32–33; and 43:45–46). David O. McKay, speaking for the First Presidency at the beginning of World War II, outlined for modern nations the conditions under which such purely defensive war is justified, emphasizing carefully the limitations, especially this one: "Nor is war justified in an attempt to enforce a new order of government . . . however better the government . . . may be."[22]

The United States directly violated that prophetic principle in Vietnam, Grenada, Angola, Nicaragua, and the Gulf War. Yet most Mormons approved, apparently willing to accept this kind of argument from government and party leaders: "We're for peace in Nicaragua [or Angola or wherever], but you can't have peace without democracy." That is simply a way of saying we will use force to make other governments do as we want. Such an argument could have been used, just as rationally and probably more morally, to support intervention in South Africa for the disenfranchised black majority, but was not. Nor should it have been—in that case or in the others, where our intention only led to escalation and perpetuation of violence. In the meantime South Africa is achieving peace and reconciliation because of the self-sacrificing commitment of both white and black leaders to non-violence.

You can see how important it is for some Utah Mormons to become Democrats. First, it might produce some national leaders who could help stop the executive branch usurpation of power over war that right now most threatens our Constitution and our honor as a nation, our economy, and our lives. Second, it would produce a vital two-party system in Utah, one that could prevent a destructive Mormon/non-Mormon split and lead, through constructive dialogue and compromise rather than lazy ideology, to more innovative solutions to pressing state problems. Third, it might help us all to learn the basic lesson of our Constitution, that virtue and truth are the province of no single person or party—in fact, are best found in the process of civil debate, which includes listening because we want to, adjustment, compromise, and then honest and honorable acceptance of the results until new ones are created in the process.

The principle I am arguing for suggests that while Mormons in Utah should become Democrats, those in Democratic strongholds like Massachusetts and Chicago should become Republicans. Not only should qualified Mormons be hired in the humanities and social sciences at the University of Utah, more non-Mormons should be hired at BYU and invited to speak about challenging, controversial, "non-Mormon" subjects. I am suggesting that all military interference in other governments and lands should be renounced, even at the risk of communist or Islamic fundamentalist subversion there. That we should not only switch parties easily to help keep things balanced and the dialogue vital, but we should work against passage of laws about what are clearly private matters, even Sunday closing laws and imposed school prayer.

Is he saying (you might be asking yourself) that we should be less certain about the truth or virtue of our political positions, that we should be more willing to listen to opponents and change our minds, more passionate about the process of give and take in developing new truths than about which side we are on? Is he saying that anti-religious partisanship is as dangerous as religious partisanship, especially when mixed with politics or education?

And is he even saying that what he has said in this essay, despite his very best efforts to speak the truth, is surely a little and might be a lot wrong, that it ought to be argued with and modified?

Yes, you've got it. That's exactly what I'm saying.

EUGENE ENGLAND *recently retired from BYU after years of teaching Shakespeare, nineteenth-century American literature, and Mormon literature for the English Department. England received his BA from the University of Utah and his PhD from Stanford University. He was one of the founding editors of* Dialogue: A Journal for Mormon Thought *and spent a large part of his scholarly career dealing with issues pertinent to Latter-day Saints. Along with Richard Cracroft, he is one of the parents of Mormon literary scholarship.*

Notes

[1] J. D. Williams, "Separation of Church and State in Mormon Theory and Practice," *Dialogue: A Journal of Mormon Thought* 1 (Summer 1966) 37. See also Thomas G. Alexander, *Mormonism in Transition, A History of Latter-day Saints, 1890–1930* (Urbana: U. of Illinois, 1986); Gustive O. Larson, *The "Americanization" of Utah for Statehood* (San Marino, CA: Huntington Library, 1971); and Edward Leo Lyman, *Political Deliverance: The Mormon Quest for Utah Statehood* (Urbana: U. of Illinois, 1986).

[2] Williams.

[3] First Presidency to Joseph W. Young, 29 May 1891, archives, Historical Department, Church of Jesus Christ of Latter-day Saints, Salt Lake City, Utah.

[4] Quoted in William Peters, *A More Perfect Union* (New York: Crown, 1987) 1.

[5] Peters, 63.

[6] See Daniel Bell, "The End of American Exceptionalism," in *The Winding Passage: Essays and Sociological Journeys, 1960-80* (New York: Basic Books, 1980) esp. 264–71.

[7] Quoted in ibid., 160, my emphasis.

[8] Brigham Young, Jr., address given 22 June 1884, in *Journal of Discourses*, 26 vols. (Liverpool, Eng. F. D. Richards, 1854–86) 25: 191 (hereafter *JD*).

[9] Daniel Bell, "The Principles of Pluralism and Toleration," Brigham Young University Forum Assembly, 7 Oct. 1986.

[10] Noel B. Reynolds, "The Doctrine of an Inspired Constitution," in *"By the Hands of Wise Men": Essays on the US Constitution,* ed. Ray Hillam (Provo, UT: Brigham Young, 1979) 1–28.

[11] Quoted in ibid., 15.

[12] See *JD* 4:39 for Brigham Young's denouncement of this.

[13] James Henry Moyle, *Mormon Democrat: The Religious and Political Memoirs,* ed. Gene A. Sessians (Salt Lake: LDS Church Historical Department, 1975) 185–86.

[14] Moyle, 209.

[15] Walter Lippman, "The Indispensable Opposition," *The Atlantic Monthly*, Aug.

1939: 221.

[16] Lippman, 221.

[17] James Cromar, "When One Man Made a Difference," *Student Review*, May 1987: l, 16.

[18] Cromar,16.

[19] Peters, 57.

[20] Peters, 47.

[21] Quoted in Edwin B. Firmage and Francis D. Wormuth, *To Chain the Dogs of War* (Dallas: Southern Methodist U., 1986) 18.

[22] David O. McKay, in *One Hundred and Twelfth Annual Conference of the Church of Jesus Christ of Latter-day Saints* (Salt Lake: Deseret Book, 1942) 72.

Questions

1. Why does England state that he is a lifelong Republican?
2. What potential problems arise when one political party has an overwhelming majority?
3. Why does England believe that the process of dialogue and compromise, rather than "lazy ideology," is the best route to good government?
4. What is your response to Daniel Bell's statement that "cultural conservatives should be political liberals"?

Scones, Anyone?

R. Kirk Belnap

with Heidi Bay, Stephen Fairbanks,
David Lager, Jeana Yamamoto

When Kirk Belnap and a group of students in a linguistics and society class he was teaching discovered that different people had different ideas of what a "scone" is, they set out on a linguistic scavenger hunt to find the origin of the "Mormon scone" and along the way they learned something about language and culture. Belnap says, "People grow up thinking their own language community is the center of the world" when reality is something different. Belnap and his students discovered that wherever Mormons went in the West, they took with them not only their foodways, but an accompanying language. "You can draw an isogloss [a linguistic map] around Mormondom," he says. "Scones, Anyone?" was originally published in Proceedings of the Deseret Language and Linguistics Society.

Raymond Sokolov, food editor of *Natural History*, is not impressed by Utah's culinary offering. However, one item on the menu did arouse his curiosity, "Utah scones" (1985). Latter-day Saints from the Intermountain West are generally surprised to find that the fry bread near and dear to their heart—though none too good for it—is quite different from the scones eaten around the globe. For the rest of the English-speaking world scones are generally baked, biscuit-like, and often sweet. They are an essential ingredient of the British "cream tea" or "Devonshire tea." They are eaten with jam and heavy sweet cream, which one American described as being "sort of a cross between thick, cold, whipping cream and ice cream, but better." The denotation of the word *scone* is not the only difference one finds: outside North America *scone* rhymes with *gone* more often than *bone*.

How is it that we find this fried, leavened scone native to the shadows of the Rockies—but apparently nowhere else? This question caught the attention of a group of us in the Winter 1993 Honors "Language in Society" Seminar. In an exploratory query to LINGUIST, an electronic mail list, we asked subscribers familiar with scones of various sorts to tell us more. We soon had 68 responses (29 from the United States, 17 from the United Kingdom, 8 from Canada, 4 from Australia, the rest scattered across the world).

THE INTERNET

Most respondents from the US reported only the long "o" pronunciation (rhyming with *bone*). Canadian respondents favored the short "o." (To our surprise, we later discovered that isolated instances of the short "o" pronunciation for Mormon scones survive in the Intermountain West.) The question of pronunciation is far from settled in the UK. One Englishman noted:

> The pronunciation of this word is, in common lore, supposed to be a marker of a class or regional distinction. Nobody is really sure, but just about everybody knows it shows *something* and will defend their particular pronunciation. (Colin Phillips, email, 2 March 1993)

Another observed, "My mother says it with short, my father with long, and we used to argue in the school playground about it" (Richard Ogden, email, 3 March 1993). One respondent reported that a popular BBC television comedy devoted an episode to scones, strawberry jam, cream, and the pronunciation of scones. He concluded, "In general, rhyming scone with don is the 'best' i.e., higher class pronunciation (at least that's how I pronounce it!)" (Francis Bond, email, 3 March 1993).

Scottish perspectives illustrate how differently these pronunciations are evaluated. A Scottish respondent (from Fife and Lothian) mentions that he uses short "o" but noted that long "o" is "possible but upper-class/pretentious" (David Adger, email 2 March 1993). A number of people commented on short "o" being the Scottish pronunciation and long "o" belonging to England (particularly Southern England).

None of the UK respondents were familiar with scones as fried pieces of yeast-leavened dough (some reacted in revulsion to the notion). In fact, only the 12 respondents with some Utah or Mormon connection were familiar with this type of scone. Respondents who grew up with Mormon scones also had strong feelings about the legitimacy (if not primacy) of their scones. For example:

> I always assumed that my mother's folkways with scones were correct and that the local shop and my wife had some gussied up, yuppified version that might be an option for some people in England, but was some

> modern aberration—now I see I was too provincial in this. (Lyle Campbell, e-mail, 2 March 1993)

The LINGUIST survey strengthened our initial impression that the scones found in the Western United States are a Mormon phenomenon, but why?

Sokolov (1985) speculated that Mormon scones developed through post-exodus contact, that early Mormon settlers were influenced by one or both of the Southwestern fry breads: *sopaipillas* and *Navajo fry bread.* Even before we found his article we were leaning toward this explanation. Our study would probably have ended with this, but we came across a BYU student who recalled a scone vendor at a state fair in Indiana. As a result of this new lead we designed a small telephone survey to investigate the possibility of Mid-Western origins for Mormon scones.

Midwest Bakeries

For the telephone survey we chose to contact bakeries, assuming that people working in bakeries would be likely to know more about regional varieties of breads. We contacted bakeries in Omaha, Nebraska. No one was familiar with Mormon scones—and very few with any type of scone. One woman told us that her mother used to make something similar to the Mormon scones we described, but she did not remember them being called scones. She was from North Dakota so we contacted bakeries in Bismarck, Fargo, and Grand Forks, and struck out again. We did no better in Indiana. We found no one familiar with Mormon scones, but one person mentioned that they did sound similar to the local version of elephant ears, a fried dough rolled in sugar.

Cookbooks

One student took a different tack and searched over eighty cookbooks looking for recipes resembling the fried scone. These included historical and regional cookbooks, domestic and foreign. She found that frying bread dough is—or was—quite common.

US Varieties of Fried Bread

Our cookbook research and the reports of fried breads similar to Mormon scones in the telephone survey prompted us to consider the possibility that *scones* is merely one of many names found across the country for similar fry breads. We then turned to the treasure chest of information on US dialectal terms, the *Dictionary of American Regional English* (DARE). Unfortunately, only the first two volumes of DARE (vol. 1 A-C, vol. 2 D-H) have been published.

Baptist cakes, a term occurring in a New England cookbook, proved to be a crucial link. *Baptist cakes* are defined in DARE as "Raised bread-dough fried in deep fat" (Cassidy 1985: 150); all references were to New England (particularly Massachusetts and Connecticut). A DARE cookbook citation indicated that *Baptist cakes* are eaten with maple syrup; another mentioned that the name comes from the fact that they are immersed in deep fat. This entry also lists *fry bread 1, huffjuff,* and *holy poke.*

Morning glory and *spider bread* were suggested as other references under *fried bread* but, of course, are not included in the published volumes of DARE. *Morning glory* and *spider bread* apparently derive their names from the instrument used to cook them. *A Dictionary of American English* lists *morning glory* as a type of stove and *spider* as a type of "iron frying pan or skillet, sometimes provided with long legs" (Craigie & Hulbert 1944: 2191). *Spider* is used attributively "designating foods cooked in a spider" and gives the following citation: "**1920** LINCOLN *Mr. Pratt* 33 She'd been . . . giving 'em spider bread and dried apple pie for breakfast" (1944: 2191).

DARE lists two entries under *dough gods.* The first refers to a baking powder biscuit, usually cooked over an open fire. The second, native to the North and especially New England, refers to a raised dough that is fried. Related terms include *dough goddy, dough gob, doughboy,* and *doughbelly* (Cassidy 1985: 158–59). A single entry for Northern Maine mentions that *doughdab* is another name for a *dough god* (1985: 158). Speaking of *dough biscuits,* an informant from South-Eastern Wisconsin observed that:

> If bread was short and the housewife knew it would not be baked by mealtime, she used to cut off small biscuit-sized pieces of the dough, pat them flat, and fry them slowly on a greased griddle until lightly browned on both sides. These fried biscuits were served hot and buttered. (1985: 573)

Given that frying small chunks of bread dough was a common practice in many—if not all—regions of the country, there is no reason to assume that Mormon scones developed due to contact with Southwestern fry breads. Frying bread dough was clearly a common American practice. But the question still remains: How did scones come to refer to this common American fry bread?

ONE SOLUTION

A number of accounts of how Mormon scones came to be called *scones* are possible. The ingredients, method of preparation, and name might all have come from Europe with little or no change. It seems more likely, however, that scone-making evolved as immigrants adapted to the New World' s conditions, materials, and practices. But even if it is an importation one is still faced with the question as to why the name appears to survive only in the American West, that is, why do we not find other regions using *scone* for their fry bread?

The development of a name by association accounts for the origins of most, if not all, of the terms used for American fry breads. Some names reflect the means of cooking; for example, the origin of *Baptist cakes, spider bread,* and *morning glory.* Other names refer to the ingredients; for example, *dough bread, dough gobs,* and *dough biscuits.* A third method involves describing the shape of the finished product: *beaver tails, elephant ears,* and—perhaps—*scones. The Scottish National Dictionary* indicates that *scone* had come to mean "anything round, flat and soft resembling a *scone*" (Grant & Murison 1971: 62). *Scone* also referred to the "slap of the hand or any flat surface, a smack, spank" (Grant & Murison 1971: 62–63). As applied to Mormon scones, this could refer to the method of preparation in which the dough is punched down. But again, why were the early Latter-day Saints, and not others in the US, more apt to use the term scone?

The answer to this question may be found in the ethnic composition of the settlers of the Mormon West. Of all the states in the union Utah has the highest settlement rate by those of English ancestry. Utah also has the highest percentage of recent (predominantly 19th-century) British immigration. Di Paolo (1993) presented evidence of British dialect influence on the speech of Utah Mormons. Given that the largest and arguably most influential ethnic group in Utah in the nineteenth century was of English ancestry, the adoption of *scone*, the English generic word corresponding to American *biscuit*, to refer to an American fry bread should come as no surprise. As Di Paolo observed, "particular features of the English of English immigrants could have easily, but unconsciously, surfaced in the region as Mormon English" (1993: 347).

The idea that early Latter-day Saints came to call their fry bread *scones* due to the influence of English immigrants is not without parallel. Although *flatbread* (Norwegian *flatbrød, fladbrød*) is usually described as a thin, unleavened bread baked on the stove top, one informant from South Dakota described it as "fried bread dough" (Cassidy & Hall 1991: 467). Apparently, the name used to refer to a variety of

American fry bread may have been influenced more than once by the ethnic group that settled in large numbers in a given region. This, and other DARE references, also indicate the interchangeable nature of raising agents and methods of cooking.

CONCLUSION

Sokolov observed that "until some researcher makes a lucky strike in a Mormon woman's diary or a pioneer cookbook, we are never going to know for sure how it is that Navajos, Chicanos, and Mormons ended up eating similar fried breads" (1985: 83). Our research suggests that we can add Americans from all across the country to Sokolov's list. The fact that similar American fry breads are known by so many names suggests an American innovation. While we cannot conclusively account for the origins of Mormon scones, the method of preparation appears to derive from a well-established American tradition, suggesting continuity rather than a contact-induced development. As for the name *scones*, the fact that this common British term came to be used by the US speech community with the greatest post-colonial English ethnic concentration seems beyond coincidence.

R. KIRK BELNAP *is associate professor of Arabic. He received his bachelor's and master's degrees from BYU and earned a PhD from the University of Pennsylvania at Philadelphia. He has taught Arabic and religion courses both at the BYU–Provo campus and at the BYU Jerusalem center. The co-authors of this paper are BYU students who were enrolled in Belnap's honors linguistics course.*

References

Brown, N. I. 1939. *Recipes from Old Hundred: 200 years of New England Cooking*. New York: M. Barrows.

Cassidy, F. G. (ed.). 1985. *Dictionary of American Regional English*, vol. 1, A-C. Cambridge, Mass. & London, England: Belknap Press of Harvard University Press.

Cassidy, F. G. &. J. H. Hall (eds.). 1991. *Dictionary of American Regional English*, vol. 2, D–H. Cambridge, Mass. & London, England: Belknap Press of Harvard University Press.

Craigie, S. W. A. &. J. R. Hulbert (eds.). 1944. *A Dictionary of American English on Historical Principles*, vol. 4. Chicago, Univ. of Chicago Press.

Di Paolo, M. 1993. "Propredicate *do* in the English of the Intermountain West." *American Speech* 68(4): 339–56.

Grant, W. and D. D. Murison (eds.). 1971. *The Scottish National Dictionary*. Edinburgh: The Scottish National Dictionary Association.

Sokolov, R. (1985). "Everyman's Muffins." *Natural History*. 94:82–84. [Also printed in: Sokolov, R. 1991. *Why we eat what we eat: How the encounter between the New World and the Old changed the way everyone on the planet eats.* New York: Summit Books. pp. 169–172.]

Questions

1. How does Belnap catch the reader's attention in the opening lines? What type of appeal is he making?
2. What does Belnap use for evidence?
3. What are the implications of a "Mormon English"? What does that imply about language and communities?
4. Which of Belnap's answers to where the use of scones come from do you find the most compelling?

Ice Cream Preference: The Relationship of Cost and Quality

PHILLIP R. KUNZ

In his own English class at BYU, Phillip Kunz set out to show that the popular research on "sleepteaching"—listening to tapes of information to learn in one's sleep—was "a bunch of baloney." The paper he did on that topic showed he was right, and the impulse to debunk common misconceptions has never left him. This article, "Ice Cream Preference: The Relationship of Cost and Quality," is also the result of a similar sociological probe. Kunz set up an experiment with his students to determine whether expensive ice creams really were better than cheap ones. He says that "most people assume that higher cost equals a better product; that's why we need to do research." He published this article in Perceptual and Motor Skills.

This research assessed 12-year-old junior high school students from an across social class junior high and middle-class adults' discrimination of ice creams the local prices of which varied from $3 to $12 per gallon. The flavor—chocolate chip—corresponded with that used in an earlier study of college students (Kunz, 1983) as that flavor had been randomly selected from the flavors common to all three price ranges. Three brands of ice cream were selected, including the most expensive, the cheapest, and a randomly selected midpriced brand.

Forty-eight students in Grade 7 and 36 adults aged 39 to 75 years, tasted one scoop of each of the three ice creams placed into the three compartments of a paper plate. The rim of the plates next to each compartment was marked with I, II, and III, respectively. The subjects were also given a small piece of paper on which they were asked to assign a "high," "medium," and "low" to the ice cream that they judged would best fit that category as they tasted the ice cream.

Percents in the table show that the most frequent selections for "high" quality ice cream among the seventh grade students was actually the least

Price	Group	Liking of Ice Cream: Percent			N
		High	Medium	Low	
High	Jr. High	10.4	45.8	43.8	48
	University*	31.8	34.1	31.1	82
	Adults	44.4	38.9	16.7	36
Medium	Jr. High	39.6	22.9	37.5	48
	University	28.1	40.2	31.7	82
	Adults	44.4	5.6	50.0	36
Low	Jr. High	50.0	31.2	18.8	48
	University	39.0	22.0	39.0	82
	Adults	16.7	33.3	33.3	36

*University data from Kunz (1983, p. 720).

expensive ice cream, while that selected by the adults as "high" in quality was more often the highest priced ice cream. The percents from the earlier study of university students (Kunz, 1983) is also included in the table for comparison. As may be observed, their selections of "high" quality ice cream does not vary across the price range. As the price and quality may be treated as ranked data, gamma is presented for each age group. Gamma for the adult group was .264, indicating some positive correspondence between the cost and quality of the ice cream, while gamma for the university students was -.015, which shows no preference, and for students in Grade 7 gamma was -.400, showing a strong inverse relationship between the price of the ice cream and its judged quality.

This study shows a marked difference in the reported liking of ice cream by groups. Further study relating to possible learned tastes relating to age and cultural beliefs supporting the notion that high price means high quality seems warranted.

Reference

Kunz, P. R. Cultural influence on taste: a study of ice cream taste preference. *Perceptual and Motor Skills*, 1983, 56, 720.

PHILLIP KUNZ *received a BA and an MA in sociology from BYU and his PhD from the University of Michigan. After brief stints teaching at Michigan, Eastern Michigan, and Wyoming, he settled in as a professor of sociology at BYU, serving from 1990 to 1993 as president of the Louisiana LDS mission. His current work focuses on the family, divorce, and early Swiss conversion to the LDS church.*

Questions

1. What does Kunz mean when he states that the taste for more expensive ice cream is learned?
2. Does this research support or call into question the cultural belief that high price means high quality?
3. Compare this article to Belnap's "Scones, Anyone?" What counts as evidence in each case?

The Latest Fads to Increase Muscle Mass and Energy: A Look at What Some Athletes Are Using

BRUCE H. WOOLLEY

Bruce Woolley originally wrote this article in order to inform physicians of the various products and methods that athletes use to increase energy or recover from fatigue. Yet he admits that keeping tabs on products is a difficult thing to do, as the fads change so quickly. Woolley's interest in how athletes seek to maintain or improve their performance comes partially from his work with the Drug Abuse Treatment Program in LA County, as well as from his work for the NCAA and the US Olympic Committee. In this article, first published in Postgraduate Medicine, *Woolley asserts that "some of the substances used do have the desired effects, some appear to have little or no effect, and some have dangerous effects." Because of this inconsistency, Woolley hopes that physicians will "provide accurate data to athletes who seek their advice and provide positive changes in the attitudes and habits of their patients."*

Psychoactive substances have been used to alter mood and performance since the beginning of history. Ancient Greek athletes reportedly used stimulants to improve their performance as early as the third century BC.[1] Aztecs claimed that eating the myocardium from human sacrifice improved performance. They also used a cactus-based stimulant (probably aloe), the effects of which lasted up to 72 hours, to enhance long-distance running. In 1865, Dutch swimmers were reprimanded for using drugs containing caffeine; Belgian racers preferred sugar cubes dipped in ether. Brandy-cocaine mixtures were supposedly favored by boxers in the early 1900s.[2]

Over the centuries, the practice of taking drugs to enhance pleasure and performance has increased until it has reached pandemic proportions in contemporary cultures. Sports are no exception, since any propensity that pervades society will also pervade sports.

SUBSTANCE USE IN MODERN SPORTS

As the pressure to excel has increased, so has athletes' desire to enhance performance. Some athletes wonder if in the future their success will depend more on the chemistry laboratory than on their own abilities. In speaking at a world symposium on doping in sports, Doug Clement, MD, of the Canadian Track and Field Association, stated, "I wonder whether we're looking at the end of an era in sport . . . in terms of the integrity of sport, or its place as an important social value in our system. Are we looking at the sunset or are we looking at the sunrise?"[3]

Drug testing at the Olympics began in 1968, and since then numerous Olympic athletes have been caught taking substances ranging from alcohol to anabolic steroids (Table 1). For example, at the Seoul Olympic Games in September 1988, two Bulgarian weight lifters tested positive for diuretics, prompting the whole team to withdraw before testing. Also, two Hungarian weight lifters tested positive for anabolic steroids. Most recently, the finding of anabolic steroid use by Ben Johnson and the ensuing Canadian investigation focused the world's attention on the problem of substance use for enhancing performance.

Table 1. Categories of drugs and activities banned or restricted by International Olympic Committee

Banned	Stimulants
Anabolic steroids	**Restricted**
Agents banned for specific sports (e.g., beta blockers [rifle sports], sedatives [pentathalon])	Alcohol
Blood doping	Corticosteroids
Diuretics	Human chorionic gondatropin
Narcotics	Local anesthetics
Pharmacological, chemical, and physical manipulation of urine (eg., with probenecid [Benemid])	

In announcing a strict drug-testing program, F. Don Miller, the former executive director of the US Olympic Committee, stated, "This is the first step in our war against the use of drugs by our athletes, but not a war against our fine young men and women. We must wipe out this danger once and for all and obliterate the image of the 'chemical athlete' that is starting to shape itself in the public mind."[4]

On January 13, 1986, the National Collegiate Athletic Association (NCAA) approved mandatory drug testing for athletes. Testing is conducted at NCAA championship events, and as of August 1990, division IA football players are being randomly tested on campus. Athletes are requested annually to sign a waiver agreeing to submit to testing for substances banned by the NCAA (Table 2).

Table 2. Categories of drugs banned by National Collegiate Athletic Association

Anabolic steroids
Diuretics
Psychomotor and central nervous system stimulants
Street drugs
Substances banned for specific sports (e.g., beta blockers)

Substance use is not limited to Olympic and college athletes, however. A nationwide survey of anabolic steroid use among 3,403 high school seniors[5] showed that 225 (6.6%) had used steroids, 86 (38%) of them having begun by age 15 and over two thirds by age 16. Enhanced appearance was the only reason given for taking the agents by 61 of the students (27%). In a study of 2,113 male and female high school students,[6] 332 (15.7%) reported knowing someone who used steroids, and 732 (34.6%) felt that steroids were easy to obtain. Eighty-six (4.1%) of the students reported using steroids themselves, 15 (17.4%) for appearance alone. Twenty-one (24.4%) reported that they had obtained the agents from their coach, 30 (34.8%) from their physician, 39 (45.3%) from friends, and 23 (26.7%) from another source.

Properties of Commonly Abused Substances

Pharmacologic properties of performance-enhancing substances vary significantly but seem to follow a pattern, and it appears that certain of these properties render such drugs more susceptible to abuse. Although controversy exists as to what these properties are, the agents seem to have the following in common: potential for rapid development of tolerance, short duration of action, rapid onset of action, abrupt release at termination of action, anticholinergic action, production of pleasurable euphoria, and ritualistic administration.[7] The more of these properties that a drug possesses, it appears, the greater the potential for abuse. This may be especially applicable to athletes who are taking the agents to enhance performance.

Drugs used by athletes usually come from three general categories: street drugs (e.g., alcohol, tobacco, marijuana, cocaine), ergogenic drugs (e.g., central nervous system [CNS] stimulants, anabolic steroids, "designer" substances, nutritional supplements), and performance-continuance drugs (e.g., analgesics, anti-inflammatory agents). In this article, only selected ergogenic drugs and methods to increase oxygen capacity (e.g., blood doping) are discussed.

Ergogenic substances are thus named because they increase work output or energy. By taking them, athletes hope to enhance their performance by increasing lean muscle mass, strength, oxygen depth, oxygen capacity, and energy and by decreasing recovery time after exertion. Although the effects of ergogenic agents overlap, each is discussed under only one of these categories.

Literature on substance use by athletes is almost nonexistent. Much of the data in this article is drawn from my extensive interviews with high school, college, professional, and world-class athletes, so it is of necessity anecdotal. During interviews over many years, I have come to realize that the patterns of use are ever-changing and that keeping up with local or regional fads is impossible. However, any substance included in this article was described in at least 10 states and/or two countries.

AGENTS THAT INCREASE LEAN MUSCLE MASS AND STRENGTH

Although anabolic steroids are the agents most often thought of for increasing muscle mass, human growth hormone, cyproheptadine, ginseng, and amino acids have also been used for this purpose as well as to build strength.

ANABOLIC STEROIDS

Human or veterinary products of androgenic-anabolic steroidal hormones and synthetic testosterone-like drugs are used by bodybuilders and athletes in many sports to increase strength and muscle mass. Many nonathletes also use these substances to enhance appearance.

The American College of Sports Medicine stated in its original position paper on anabolic steroids that use of these agents neither helps nor hinders athletic performance. However, an oft-quoted literature search on the effects of anabolic steroids on strength, hypertrophy, and athletic performance[8] found that 14 (58%) of 24 well-documented studies showed significant enhancement. Dr Robert O. Voy, former director of Sports Science and Medicine of the US Olympic Committee, agreed, saying that about half of the well-conducted scientific studies published verify that steroids do increase strength slightly (e.g., by about 8 to 10 kg in the bench press) (oral communication, 1989).

The adverse effects of anabolic steroids are multiple but can be categorized into five general areas:

- Hepatic effects generally occur with use of oral or 17 alpha-alkylated agents. Side effects vary from fairly common (e.g., abnormal values on tests for liver injury and function, cholestatic jaundice) to very rare (hepatomas, peliosis hepatis).
- Endocrine effects occur because of decreased production of luteinizing hormone (LH), follicle-stimulating hormone (FSH), and testosterone, which leads to testicular atrophy and decreased sperm production. Acne, gynecomastia, altered glucose tolerance, and hyperinsulinism may occur in both sexes. In women, predominating effects include hoarseness, hirsutism, menstrual irregularities, enlarged clitoris, decreased breast size, and alopecia. The adverse effects in women are usually catastrophic and nonreversible.
- Cardiovascular effects include elevated blood pressure, increased low-density lipoprotein cholesterol levels, changes in triglyceride concentrations, decreased high-density lipoprotein cholesterol levels, and fluid and water retention.
- The major musculoskeletal adverse effect is epiphyseal closure.
- Behavioral effects may include excessive aggressiveness, changes in libido, psychotic symptoms, bipolar affective disorder, anxiety, and dependence.

Another significant adverse effect is now beginning to be more clearly described in the literature—the development of dependence in conjunction with psychosis (commonly called "roid rage" by athletes). Using criteria from the *Diagnostic and Statistical Manual of Mental Disorders*, Pope and Katz[9] evaluated 31 anabolic steroid users and reported that 3 (10%) had psychotic symptoms, 4 (13%) had "subthreshold" psychotic symptoms, 4 (13%) had manic episodes, and 5 (16%) had major depression. In another study,[10] these investigators reported that of 41 bodybuilders and football players using steroids, 9 (22%) displayed full affective syndrome and 5 (12%) displayed psychotic symptoms.

HUMAN GROWTH HORMONE

Human growth hormone is a lyophilized polypeptide hormone that in the past was extracted from pituitary glands of cadavers. The formulation includes FSH, LH, corticotropin (ACTH), thyrotropin, prolactin, and mannitol.

The Food and Drug Administration (FDA) recalled the product from the market in May 1985 because of enzymatic contamination. Four cases of Creutzfeldt-Jakob disease and some deaths had been reported. The FDA later released a hormone extract produced by recombinant DNA techniques, which contains an aminoterminal methionyl group not found in human growth hormone extracted from cadavers. No cases of Creutzfeldt-Jakob disease have been reported.

Antibodies to human growth hormone are produced in 30% to 40% of persons who take it. Adverse reactions may include unpredictable acromegaly, joint pain, osteoarthritis, a limitation of joint range and/or motion, soft-organ growth, and premature prostatic hypertrophy.

CYPROHEPTADINE

Cyproheptadine hydrochloride (Periactin) is popular with young athletes who do not want to take anabolic steroids to increase weight. This serotonin and histamine antagonist is purported to change the hypothalamic appetite set-point, producing increased appetite and weight gain (average, 1 lb/wk). It is also reported to stimulate the release of luteinizing hormone-releasing factor and, thus, the production of testosterone.[11]

A double-blind study was conducted on monkeys given cyproheptadine, methandrostenolone, or placebo. Those taking either of the two drugs gained weight over the control group. However, all groups gained strength.[12]

GINSENG

Ginseng is an herb classified by alternative healthcare providers as an "adaptogenic." These purveyors have convinced many athletes that ginseng helps them adapt to environmental and social stressors. It has been used in Oriental medicine to promote menstruation, combat infection, and enhance hormone production.

There are two species of ginseng. Both contain two 17 beta-hydroxylated steroids and are reported to produce direct stimulant effects on the CNS and hypertension with prolonged ingestion. However, some persons have paradoxical hypotension due to CNS depression caused by dammarenetriol glycosides.[13] Both species cause fluid and electrolyte imbalance, gynecomastia, and direct action on the heart and kidneys. Both contain triterpenoid saponins, which may be hemolytic.[14]

AMINO ACIDS

Because amino acids are highly nitrogenous compounds, their use may cause nitrogen retention. This retention is believed to enhance cellular protein formation and, thus, muscle growth. However, nitrogen retention is also a significant factor in kidney damage.

Half-truths extrapolated from the literature and presented to athletes have become a great source of confusion, debate, and misinformation. Physicians are often asked to authenticate the information. One of the major debates in the bodybuilding world concerning amino acids is between the supporters of free-form amino acids and the advocates of hydrolysate amino acids.

Free-form amino acids are single levoisomer crystalline compounds that are manufactured individually and then combined. Hydrolysate amino acids are derived from existing natural protein (e.g., casein), which is lysed by enzymatic action to provide amino acids in the same ratios as those found in protein. One article[15] recommended that amino acids be taken in a complete and balanced formulation, and some proponents believe that this balance can be obtained only through free-form combinations that provide for individual needs. Other proponents believe that the hydrolysate combination is more "natural" and better used by the body.

Another debate centers on the proper time to take amino acids. The popular recommendation at present is to take them with food. One article[15] stated that "supplemental amino acids alone don't stimulate the digestive enzymes required for the body to utilize the aminos. Take them preferably in the middle of the meal—to ensure that digestion is going full steam."

Methods that Increase Oxygen Depth and Opacity

Blood doping (i.e., induced erythrocythemia) is used to elevate the number of red blood cells in the circulatory system and thereby increase the oxygen-carrying capacity of blood. Athletes are interested in blood doping because it has been reported to improve endurance.[16] The use of methylating agents to improve oxygen delivery to the muscles and alkalis to increase the oxygen in the blood has also been tried.

BLOOD DOPING

Three methods have been used by athletes to induce this form of erythrocythemia. One is to have fresh red blood cells from a matched donor infused. Another is to have their own whole blood drawn and frozen until the blood volume has returned to normal and then have it reinfused.

In the third and most common method, 2 units of the athlete's blood is drawn and stored. The packed cells are reinfused 1 to 7 days before competition. Athletes believe that for the procedure to be effective, at least a 5-week interval must occur between removal and reinfusion of blood cells so that the erythrocyte level can return to normal.[17] Blood frozen at -80°C can be stored for up to 10 years with loss of only 10% to 15% of the red blood cells to processing and aging. Cells frozen at this temperature are not as fragile after reinfusion as are those stored under refrigeration for a shorter period.[16]

Studies show that blood doping undoubtedly improves performance in endurance events. In a study by Gledhill and associates,[16] infusion produced a 10% increase in hemoglobin, a 5% increase in oxygen uptake, and a 35% increase in treadmill running time. Williams and colleagues[17] evaluated performance in a 5-mile run after infusion of 920 mL of blood with control and placebo conditions and found that performance time was 49 seconds faster with blood doping. Goforth and coworkers[18] reported that when hematocrit was elevated by 10%, maximum oxygen uptake increased 11% and 3-mile run time improved by 23.7 seconds. Blood doping is banned by both the International Olympic Committee and the NCAA.

METHYLATING AGENTS

Improving oxygen delivery to the muscles has long been a goal of athletes and sports scientists. Theoretically, this could mean significant enhancement of athletic performance. Some scientists believe that the goal has been reached with the discovery of methylating agents. Their mechanism of action appears to be transmethyladon, and two such agents, trimethylglycine and dimethylglycine, are purported to be the biochemical catalysts that may improve oxygen delivery to the muscles.

Pangamic acid (which contains dimethylglycine) is sometimes called vitamin B15, but it meets none of the criteria of a vitamin. Introduced in 1943 as a methylating agent, it is purported to be obtained from the seeds of many fruits. In 1950, Russian investigators isolated a similar substance from the liver and called it dimethylglycine. In 1976, Butkin and Garkina reported that the addition of calcium gluconate greatly enhanced the methyl-releasing effects of dimethylglycine and that this combination keeps muscle tissue operating at peak efficiency for more extended periods because of aerobic oxidation.[19] At present, there are no restrictions on the use of methylating agents.

ALKALIS

Some athletic advisors and trainers believe that an easy way to increase oxygen-carrying capacity of the blood is to increase the pH of the serum. A popular formulation used by athletes is sodium bicarbonate (3.5 g), sodium citrate (5.0 g), and potassium citrate (1.5 g). It is taken with food for 2 days before competition and then for 2 days after competition to reduce the rebound phenomenon. Use of such agents is purported to increase oxygen depth and capacity, but improvement in muscle performance has not been reported.

AGENTS THAT INCREASE ENERGY

Some athletes expressed the belief during my interviews that stimulants allow them to perform at higher levels for longer periods. This belief may have gotten started because some bodybuilding magazines have alluded that stimulants, in some way, increase muscle efficiency and decrease fatigue. Other athletes believe that stimulants make them more aggressive. Actually, stimulants accelerate metabolism of glucose, glycogen, and fatty acids, which may result in decreased performance because the athlete "runs out of gas" more rapidly than would be expected. These drugs may cause dependence as well as hypertension, tachycardia, insomnia, loss of appetite, and, in rare instances, intracranial hemorrhage.[20]

The International Olympic Committee divides stimulants into the following groups:

- Psychomotor (local anesthetics; certain sympathomimetics; xanthines, e.g., caffeine)
- Sympathomimetic amines
- Direct CNS stimulants

LOCAL ANESTHETICS

Despite molecular differences, these psychomotor stimulants have similar properties and effects. They anesthetize by blocking sodium and potassium flow through nerve membranes (thus interfering with electrical conduction). Paradoxically, they may also increase CNS activity. They produce dependence.

Included in this group are cocaine, procaine hydrochloride (Novocaine), lidocaine hydrochloride (Xylocaine), and other synthetic anesthetics. Procaine is sometimes called "legal cocaine,"[21] but of these agents, only cocaine is currently banned by the International Olympic Committee and the NCAA. However, the executive committees of both governing organizations have expressed concern over these agents and have placed restrictions on their use.

SYMPATHOMIMETIC GROUP OF PSYCHOMOTOR STIMULANTS

This includes agents with the phenylethylamine chemical structure (e.g., amphetamine and its salts and similar psychoactive compounds).

XANTHINES

These consist of a number of alkaloids found in many beverages. Caffeine is the only substance in this group that is banned by the International Olympic Committee (above a urinary concentration of 12 μg/mL) and the NCAA (above a urinary concentration of 15 μg/mL).

Caffeine works by multiple mechanisms, the most apparent being CNS arousal. Caffeine sensitivity differs monumentally from individual to individual, but performance usually drops off above a urinary concentration of 5 μg/kg of body weight.

Adverse effects include jitters, powerful diuresis, dehydration, irritability, insomnia, and dry mouth. Heart disease, pancreatic cancer, and birth defects have been suspected but have not been definitively proven to be associated with high intake of caffeine.[22]

SYMPATHOMIMETIC AMINES

These agents mimic the effects of endogenous catecholamines (e.g., epinephrine, norepinephrine, dopa, dopamine, serotonin). Their effects are similar to those of psychomotor stimulants, and they produce glycogenolysis, liberation of free fatty acids from adipose tissue, increased cardiac output, and increased aggression. These agents are restricted by most international sports governing bodies. However, the NCAA has dropped the sympathomimetics from their list of banned drugs.

DIRECT CNS STIMULANTS

This is a miscellaneous group of drugs that are capable of stimulating the CNS. All are considered extremely dangerous because they may act as convulsants, producing cronic seizures and death. Agents in this category are generally included on lists of banned drugs.

Agents that Decrease Recovery Time After Exertion

These varied agents are used in an attempt to speed recovery after an injury, decrease edema after exercise, prevent cell-membrane damage, and achieve other ends that are, in many cases, beneficial only in theory.

OCTACOSANOL

Octacosanol is a 28-straight-carbon-chain alcohol expressed from wheat germ oil. Some athletes have used it to try to improve stamina, strength, and reaction time. Others believe it produces positive inotropic and chronotropic effects on cardiac function, enhances reproductive processes, and improves neurologic disorders and cholesterol elimination. Because no published data are available, all claims about this agent are, at present, conjecture.

GUARANA

Octacosanol is often combined with an herbal product from Brazil called guarana. It is commonly sold by health-food stores to increase energy. Guarana is prepared from the seeds of the Paullinia cupana tree. It contains 2.5% to 5% caffeine. One popular brand of the octacosanol-guarana combination is Boost.

GAMMA-ORYZANOL

This compound is one of four isomers of oryzanol. It is extracted from rice bran oil and is purported to stimulate the hypothalamic-pituitary-gonadal axis. However, athletes take this product as an antioxidant to neutralize the free radicals released during heavy exercise.

The concept of free radicals is not clearly understood, but many athletes believe that aerobic activity requires an extensive oxygen supply. Oxygen creates free radicals, which attach to and thereby damage cell membranes. Athletes believe that antioxidants compete with free radicals and prevent or eliminate cell damage, thus reducing recovery time after exertion. Many combine gamma-oryzanol with vitamin E.

PROTEOLYTIC ENZYMES

The inflammatory response is characterized by decreased tissue permeability and edema from accumulation of fibrin and other proteins in tissue spaces. This accumulation blocks the free flow of body fluids. Some athletes believe that proteolytic enzymes reverse these undesirable effects of protein deposition. Enzyme preparations commonly used by athletes include chymotrypsin, trypsin-chymotrypsin, and papain (obtained from Carica paya).

Rash, urticaria, pruritus, buccal tingling, menorrhagia, and metrorrhagia are among the reported adverse reactions to these compounds. Concomitant use of these agents with oral anticoagulants or during generalized or systemic infection is not advised. Data are lacking to establish the safety and efficacy of these compounds in pregnant or lactating women.

DIMETHYL SULFOXIDE

This agent has been used extensively in treating joint inflammation in animals. Physicians and trainers have used it as a performance-continuance drug in some athletes to speed recovery after an injury.

Dimethyl sulfoxide is cryopreservative and hygroscopic and forms nonpolar associations with water. It crosses physiologic membranes readily. In the body, it is rapidly metabolized. It is reduced to dimethyl sulfide and is oxidized to dimethyl sulfone.

Much of the drug is eliminated through the lungs and skin. Dimethyl sulfoxide cannot be detected in serum after 36 hours. However, dimethyl sulfone can be detected for up to 300 hours because of tissue binding. No matter what the route of administration, this agent must be considered a systemic drug because of its ability to cross tissue membranes.

For veterinary use, dimethyl sulfoxide is approved as a penetrant, local analgesic, anti-inflammatory, bacteriostatic, diuretic, and tranquilizer. Although some of these uses have been reported in the veterinary literature, most of them are not well documented in humans.[23] Recommended initial treatment is topical administration of a 50% concentration, which, if tolerated, may be increased to 70% or even 90%.

The most common side effect is a garliclike taste, which is perceived in the mouth within 45 seconds to 5 minutes after application and persists for 4 to 6 hours. A garliclike odor on the skin is another common complaint. Like most solvents, it produces a burning sensation and generates heat on application. High concentrations may produce blistering, burns, and generalized dermatitis. Also, severe allergic reactions (e.g., urticaria and angioedema) have occurred. Other reported adverse reactions include transient disturbance of color vision, lens opacities, photophobia, headache, nausea, diarrhea, dizziness, sedation, and burning on urination.[24, 25]

One article[26] concluded that dimethyl sulfoxide in high concentrations may diminish pain, muscle spasm, and swelling that accompany various acute inflammatory conditions and soft-tissue injuries. However, its safety has not been established, and preparations that have not been purified for human use may prove to be dangerous.

BEE POLLEN

Bee pollen has been purported to improve athletic and sexual performance; prevent allergy, infection, and cancer; prolong life; improve digestion; and improve weight gain and maintenance. However, the only published study on the effects of bee pollen on athletic performance[27] found no improvement.

NUTRITIONAL SUPPLEMENT

Nutritional supplements are not generally considered drugs of abuse, but some athletes consume excessive amounts in the belief that protein increases strength and builds muscle and that large amounts of vitamins B, C, and E promote athletic performance. However, the body does not store protein, and the energy used to digest it is more than it produces. In addition, according to physicians, vitamins B, C, and E do not improve endurance, muscle efficiency, or motor performance.

CONCLUSION

Today's athletes, from junior high school on, want to excel in competition. Efforts to reach their maximum potential may lead athletes to use substances that they see advertised or that their friends recommend.

Unfortunately, some of the substances that appear to enhance performance have adverse effects and are easily abused, and many of them have little of the desired effect.

Physicians are in a position to provide accurate data to athletes who seek their advice and to produce positive changes in the attitudes and habits of their patients. In answer to Doug Clement's question, a unified effort by physicians to combat substance abuse in athletics will help ensure that we are looking at the sunrise in modern sports competition.

BRUCE H. WOOLLEY, *a professor in the Department of Food Science and Nutrition, received his BA from the University of Utah and his PharmD from USC. Besides teaching at BYU, he has taught at UCLA and USC and has lectured or given presentations at over sixty universities. Woolley teaches such classes as sports nutrition, pharmacology, pharmacology of natural products, and Doctrine and Covenants.*

References

1. Hanley DF. Sports medicine and physiology. Philadelphia: WB Saunders, 1979

2. Drug abuse in sports: denial fuels the problem. Phys Sportsreed 1982; 10(4): 114–23

3. Clement D. Canada Report. In: Bellotti P, Benzi G, Ljungquist A. Proceedings of International Athletic Foundation World Symposium on Doping in Sports. Florence, Italy: International Athletic Foundation, 1987 May: 214–6

4. USOC's war on drugs. (Editorial) Swim World 1984; Feb: 60–3

5. Buckley WE, Yesalis CE 3d, Friedl KE, et al. Estimated prevalence of anabolic steroid use among male high school seniors. JAMA 1988; 260(23): 3441–5

6. McLain LG. The use of anabolic steroids in high school students. Am J Dis Child 1990; 144(1): 99–103

7. Woolley BH, Barnett DW. The use and misuse of drugs by athletes. Houston Med J 1986; 2(Mar): 29–35

8. Haupt HA, Rovere GD. Anabolic steroids: a review of the literature. Am J Sports Med 1984; 12(6): 469–84

9. Pope HG Jr, Katz DL. Bodybuilder's psychosis. (Letter) Lancet 1987; 1(8537): 863

10. Pope HG Jr, Katz DL. Affective and psychotic symptoms associated with anabolic steroid use. Am J Psychiatry 1988; 145(4): 487–90

11. Brooks GA, Fahey TD. Exercise physiology: human bioenergetics and its applications. New York: J Wiley, 1984

12. Richardson JH. A comparison of two drugs on strength increase in monkeys. J Sports Med Phys Fitness 1977; 17(3): 2514

13. Segel RK. Ginseng abuse syndrome? Problems with the panacea. JAMA 1979; 24(13): 1614–5

14. Claus EP. Pharmacognosy. Philadelphia: Lea & Febiger, 1961: 91–2

15. Colgan M. Amino acids: How much? What kind? Muscle Fitness Magazine 1989 Jun: 80–2, 202–4

16. Gledhill N, Buick FJ, Froese AB, et al. An optimal method of storing blood for blood boosting. (Abstr) Med Sci Sports Exerc 1978; 10(2): 40

17. Williams MH, Wesseldine S, Somma T, et al. The effect of induced erythrocythemia upon 5-mile treadmill run time. Med Sci Sports Exerc 1981; 13(3): 169–75

18. Goforth HW, Campbell NL, Hodgdon JA. Hematological parameters of trained distance runners following induced thrombocythemia. (Abstr) Med Sci Sports Exerc 1982; 14(2): 174

19. Check WA. Vitamin B15: whatever it is, it won't help. JAMA 1980; 243(24): 2473, 2480

20. Chandler JV, Blair SN. The effect of amphetamines on selected physiological components related to athletic success. Med Sci Sports Exerc 1980; 12(1): 65–9

21. Frederick L. Legal cocaine called deadly fad. Med World News 1982 Aug 16: 46, 51

22. DiPalma JR. Caffeine: AFP clinical pharmacology. No. 109. Am Fam Physician 1982; 25(3): 206–7

23. Wells J. An evaluation of the present indications of dimethyl sulfoxide (DMSO) in sports medicine. Athletic Training 1982 Spring: 26–9

24. Bristol T. DMSO: the responsible user's guide. Portland, OR: DMSO News Service, 1982

25. Scherbel AL. DMSO and its use in athletics. Sports Med Dig 1980; 2(4): 1–3

26. Abramowiecz M, ed. Dimethylsulfoxide (DMSO). Med Lett Drugs Ther 1980; 22: 94–5

27. Steben RE, Boudreaux P. The effects of pollen and protein extracts on selected blood factors and performance of athletes. J Sports Med Phys Fitness 1978; 18(3):221–6

Questions

1. Judging from the figurative language used in the quotes in the introduction, what tone is Woolley trying to create in this article?
2. What is the "chemical athlete"? Given this article, how great is the risk of chemical athletes in the future?
3. How do the examples in the introduction function in this article? Are they persuasive?
4. Take a paragraph of this article and translate it into less specialized language.

Communication Skills and Community Integration in Adults with Mild to Moderate Retardation

BONNIE BRINTON AND MARTIN FUJIKI

As speech-language pathologists, Bonnie Brinton and Martin Fujiki have always been concerned with how people communicate and behave. In their field of study, most researchers, therapists, and teachers work with the processes involved with how people speak, but Brinton and Fujiki focus more on what Brinton calls the "conversational level." It's one thing to teach people with a speech impediment of some sort to pronounce words, Brinton says, but it's something entirely different to teach them how to interact in a social setting where language use is required. In this article, which was originally published in Topics in Language Disorders, *Brinton and Fujiki look at the particular challenge facing adults with mild to moderate retardation who wish to communicate with other people. People with mental retardation, Brinton says, go through peaks and valleys in their lives. "The valley," she says, "is in language."*

For many years, segregation of individuals with mental retardation away from communities and into institutional settings was commonplace (Antonak, 1988). Beginning around the 1970s, however, many large institutions were virtually emptied in favor of community-based placement of these individuals. This movement away from placement in large residential institutions in favor of smaller, community-based facilities has been noted nationwide (Best-Sigford, Bruininks, Lakin, Hill, & Heal, 1982; Borthwick-Duffy, Eyman, & White, 1987). It is generally held that community-based placement is more conducive to developmental growth and independent functioning (Hemming, Lavender, & Pill, 1981).

Despite the trend away from institutional placement toward community-based residency, some individuals with retardation continue to reside in relatively large institutions. Many other individuals live in smaller institution-like facilities or in comparatively restricted community-based facilities. Moreover, many adults with retardation spend much of their work and leisure time in fairly confined settings. Although it is widely acknowledged that greater independence and fuller integration into communities of nondisabled persons is desirable, there are few definitive answers as to how this is best accomplished. Despite a good deal of work in this area, it is not entirely clear what variables determine how an individual with retardation becomes an accepted, valued, contributing member of a larger community (for a review of residential service issues, see Summers & Reese, 1986). The true integration of an individual within a community depends on many factors, some of which are intrinsic to the individual and some of which are determined by the community.

With regard to community factors, the place afforded an individual with retardation in a community will be influenced by social attitudes as well as by political and economic policies. For example, communities may or may not allocate resources to support individuals with certain physical, intellectual, or social needs.

With regard to individual factors, personal characteristics play an important role in the way a person with retardation fits into a community. Although no single characteristic is likely to be the sole basis for adaptation to community living, individual profiles determined by the combination and interaction of numerous characteristics are influential.

In an attempt to facilitate the integration of individuals with retardation into communities, efforts have been directed at examining community attitudes and policies. Efforts also have been directed at identifying those personal characteristics that are important to community adjustment.

One personal characteristic that has received little attention with regard to community adaptation is communicative ability (American Speech-Language-Hearing Association, Committee on Mental Retardation and Developmental Disabilities, 1989). Only limited information is available concerning the communicative functioning of individuals with mental retardation in relation to their ability to obtain and maintain placement within communities. By the same token, the communicative functioning of residents segregated in settings such as institutions and those living in less restricted community settings has not been compared systematically. Considering the importance of communication to social interaction, this lack of knowledge is of concern. The ability to communicate undoubtedly plays a major role in adaptation to, and acceptance by, a community consisting of persons with and without disabilities. Communicative skills are vital to initiating and maintaining personal relationships, exchanging information, negotiating misunderstandings, and directing the behavior of others. Communicative skills are also critical in following community rules and regulations and in making use of community resources.

Information about communicative skills and the association that they might have with community adaptation is central to service provision for adults with retardation. It is important to identify the communicative skills that will assist individuals in establishing and maintaining personal relationships within communities. It is also valuable to understand how communicative skills intertwine with other factors, such as maladaptive behaviors, that limit an individual's community adjustment. In addition, intervention programs must be planned to prepare youth and adults with retardation to employ communicative skills that will ease their transition from more structured situations (such as public schools) into more independent community settings (such as work settings).

A Preliminary Study

This article provides a general overview of some initial work examining specific communicative skills of persons with retardation at different levels of community integration. Two groups of individuals were considered: adults living in a relatively large institutional setting, and adults living in community-based settings. It was recognized that individuals within the group of community-based subjects undoubtedly experienced different levels of integration into (and ostracization from) their communities. By the same token, subjects in the institutionalized group experienced different levels of restriction within the institution. Nevertheless, as a group, community-based subjects could be assumed to be more integrated into, and more free to move within, their communities than institutionalized subjects.

The performance of community-based individuals was compared with that of a group of institutionalized individuals on a number of conversational tasks. In this way, the relationship between certain communicative characteristics and lifestyle options was explored. Because of space limitations, a detailed presentation of subjects, procedures, and results is not attempted here. Rather, specific tasks and results are summarized briefly, and trends evident across tasks are considered (see Brinton & Fujiki, 1991a, 1991b, for additional details).

Communicative skills probed in this project included aspects of conversational management that demonstrate responsiveness to the needs of a conversational partner as well as aspects that illustrate assertiveness to accomplish one's own goals in interaction (Fey, 1986). At the onset of the study, it was hypothesized that individuals who were functioning successfully in community placements would demonstrate conversational patterns that were responsive to conversational partners but not necessarily assertive in accomplishing their own ends. It was conjectured that a conversational style that appeared accommodating to listeners, and possibly reserved as well, would fit well within community placements. On the other hand, it was suspected that institutionalized subjects would demonstrate a greater level of assertiveness in conversation, possibly at the expense of responsiveness to their listeners. It was speculated that a lack of attention to a listener, coupled with an assertive manner in interaction, might be part of a pattern of maladaptive behavior that either contributed to or resulted from institutional placement.

PROCEDURES

Specific aspects of communicative ability in persons with mild to moderate retardation living in community settings were contrasted with those of persons in institutional settings. Subjects in the community group had lived in community residences and worked in community settings for more than 1 year without the occurrence of events or behaviors that jeopardized placement (50% of these subjects had some history of previous institutional placement). These subjects lived in group homes, semi-independent apartments, independent apartments, or family homes. Most were employed in supported work settings.

Subjects in the institutional group lived and worked in the institutional setting. These subjects either had been returned to the institution from a community placement within the past three years or were considered not ready for community placement during that time (almost all those considered not ready for placement in the past three years had been returned from a community setting to the institution at least five years previously). For all institutionalized subjects, the over-riding intervention objective was successful community placement and integration. In every case, however, the reported basis for institutionalization was the presence of various types of maladaptive behaviors. These behaviors included verbal aggression, physical aggression, noncompliance, destruction of property, elopement, and petty theft. Subjects with medical conditions that were considered difficult to manage in a community-based setting were excluded from the subject pool.

Twenty subjects were included in both the institutional and the community group for a sample of 40 persons. Subjects in the two groups were matched on a range of variables, including full-scale IQ from the Wechsler Adult Intelligence Scale-Revised (Wechsler, 1981; range of 50 to 76), unremarkable auditory and visual status, and structural language abilities as indicated by mean length of utterance (all subjects produced a mean length of utterance in morphemes greater than 4.0). All subjects were sampled from the age range of 20 to 42 years.

A 30-minute language sample was obtained from each subject. This session was structured as a job interview, with the investigator in the role of employer and the subject in the role of potential employee. The 30-minute interview was followed by a work activity consisting of a task in which the subject assisted the investigator in sorting items into gift bags. After the task was completed, an additional 15-minute language sample was elicited. Data from these samples and the direction-following task were used to study the conversational behaviors examined.

Two major parameters of communicative competence were examined: conversational responsiveness and conversational assertiveness (Fey, 1986). Consideration of patterns of assertiveness and responsiveness provided a means of examining communicative behaviors that were important in adapting to community living. Three aspects of responsiveness and three aspects of assertiveness were examined. Responsiveness measures included the ability to reply to question forms, to respond to clarification requests, and to contribute to topics initiated by a conversational partner. Assertiveness measures included the ability to ask questions, to initiate requests for clarification, and to introduce one's own topics in conversation. The following is a summary of the findings in each area.

PARAMETERS OF RESPONSIVENESS

Responding to questions. The ability of an individual to respond to questions is central to the concept of responsiveness. Although not all question forms require a reply, certain forms are powerful in obligating a listener to respond. For example, product and explanation questions that request specification of elements signaled by WH forms (who, what, where, how, why, and when) are extremely effective in eliciting responses of varying complexity. Question forms of varying complexity were used to examine responsiveness to bids that varied in terms of demand (Brinton & Fujiki, 1992).

During the job interview scenario, the investigator interjected a number of questions into the conversation. Two levels of questions were presented: simple and complex. Simple questions required the subject to name or specify an element that was of low complexity and high predictability (e.g., "What is your name?") (Garvey & Berninger, 1981). Complex questions required subjects to provide information of high complexity and low predictability (e.g., "What are some things you're really good at?"). Answering these questions required subjects to provide elaboration in addition to specifying a requested element. Responses were analyzed with guidelines based on Grice's (1975) notions of informativeness and truthfulness. Each response was evaluated according to how well it met the informational needs of the listener (informativeness) and according to its accuracy or plausibility (truthfulness).

It was hypothesized that the community-based subjects would respond to complex questions more appropriately than the institutionalized subjects. The community-based group, however, produced more responses that were informative and truthful to both the simple and the complex questions than the institutionalized group. The institutionalized subjects provided more answers that contained insufficient or excessive information and were contrary to known facts. Institutionalized subjects apparently experienced difficulty gearing their responses to the social context and the needs of their listener.

Responding to requests for clarification. Clarification requests are frequently used by listeners to indicate that a speaker's message was in some way unclear. Examples of clarification requests include "Huh?", "What?", and "I didn't understand that." The ability to revise a message in response to these requests is critical to the successful exchange of information in conversation. These requests can occur singly, or they can be repeated if the first attempt to repair is not successful. Responding to repeated requests for clarification of the same message demands that the speaker successively adapt a message until an understanding is reached. As such, the ability to provide repair in response to repeated clarification requests is a sensitive indicator of responsiveness (Brinton, Fujiki, Winkler, & Loeb, 1986; Brinton, Fujiki, & Sonnenberg, 1988).

In the current study, the investigator inserted 10 stacked clarification request sequences into the 30-minute conversational language sample described above. Each sequence consisted of three neutral clarification requests; the following is an example:

> Subject's original message
> *Investigator*: Huh? [upward intonation]
> Subject's response to clarification request [repair]
> *Investigator*: What? [upward intonation]
> Subject's response to second clarification request [repair]
> *Investigator*: What? [upward intonation]
> Subject's response to third clarification request [repair]
> *Investigator*: Oh, I see.

The sequences were distributed throughout the language sample in response to intelligible utterances of sufficient complexity that clarification requests would have ecological validity.

In responding to these sequences, subjects employed a number of repair strategies, including repetition of all or part of their original message, revision of the original message form, and addition of information to the original message. Although all subjects demonstrated the ability to repair, there was a relatively high proportion of inappropriate responses to the requests in both groups of subjects. This lack of responsiveness was not secondary to linguistic limitations of the subjects but seemed to reflect a lack of sensitivity to listener feedback (see Brinton & Fujiki, 1991b).

Although institutionalized subjects provided repair to the stacked requests as frequently as community-based subjects, subtle but important differences were observed in the repair strategies utilized by the two groups of subjects. Specifically, community-based subjects provided repair by supplementing their original messages with additional information more often than institutionalized subjects. Thus the community-based subjects demonstrated a greater sophistication in adapting their repairs to the perceived needs of their listener.

Making relevant contributions to topics introduced by a conversational partner. The term *topic* refers to the subject matter of a conversation, or what the conversation is about. Conversations tend to be organized as speakers introduce and develop topics. A topic is developed or maintained when speakers make contributions that are relevant to that topic. The ability to make contributions that are relevant to topics introduced by other speakers demonstrates responsiveness to the conversational goals and interests of others. The ability of subjects to make relevant contributions to topics introduced by the investigator was probed during a 15-minute dyadic conversational sample between the investigator and each subject. The investigator initiated six different topics with statements.

For example:

> Topic: Sports magazine. "I like sports. Football is my favorite, but here are all kinds of sports in these magazines." (The investigator then puts a sports magazine on the table.)

The investigator then paused to allow the subject the opportunity to collaborate on the introduced topic. The investigator's subsequent contributions to the topic maintenance sequence were limited to back-channel responses such as "Oh," "Uh-huh," or "OK."

Relevance in topic maintenance was examined by considering the topical sequences that followed the investigator's topic initiations. The parameters considered included the subject's contributions (utterances) that maintained the investigator's topic, the subject's contributions that shaded or shifted the investigator's topic by focusing on tangential (but related) content, and the subject's contributions that changed the investigator's topic completely. Further analysis also was employed to determine whether each topic change was appropriate or inappropriate for the situation.

Although individual variation within each group was notable, subjects in both groups usually maintained the topics introduced by the investigator. As subjects changed topics within the discussion, however, the groups differed. Subjects in the institutionalized group devoted more utterances to discussing inappropriate topics than community-based subjects. These individuals apparently had greater difficulty in limiting themselves to topics that were relevant and appropriate.

PARAMETERS OF ASSERTIVENESS

Asking Questions. Question forms may be used to obtain information from listeners, to introduce one's own topics, and to invite listener collaboration. Asking questions in a way that is appropriate for a given interactional setting is a primary indication of conversational assertiveness. The number and types of questions produced by subjects to request information in the interview with the investigator were examined.

During the 30- and 15-minute conversational samples, all naturally occurring questions were tallied. Questions produced by subjects were identified and coded into the following request categories: requests for information, including product and choice questions; requests for attention; social requests (e.g., "How are you?"); requests for clarification; and statements with confirmation tags (tag questions). Subjects' questions were then scored as to whether they were structurally and pragmatically appropriate for the interview situation. Structurally appropriate questions were syntactically well formed and intelligible. Questions were considered structurally inappropriate if they were syntactically ill formed or contained unintelligible elements. Pragmatically appropriate questions focused on job-related or contextually related information. These questions introduced new topics at the conclusion of previous topics or requested relevant information about current topics. Pragmatically inappropriate questions were socially unacceptable (e.g., "Why is your nose so big?"), disruptive, or irrelevant to the topic currently under discussion.

Institutionalized subjects produced a large number of questions in comparison to community subjects. The questions asked by both groups did not differ in structural appropriateness but did differ in terms of pragmatic appropriateness. Institutionalized subjects were more assertive in asking questions and were more inclined to ask pragmatically inappropriate questions compared with community-based subjects.

Requesting conversational repair. Requesting conversational repair demands that the listener recognize and signal trouble sources as they occur. To signal a trouble source, the listener must convey the need for repair (e.g., by producing a request for clarification such as "What?" or "I didn't understand"). As such, requesting conversational repair requires a level of assertiveness sufficient to allow a listener to provide the speaker with specific feedback. The ability of subjects to indicate the presence of various types of inadequate messages produced by an investigator was examined.

Each subject was asked to help the investigator fill gift bags with various combinations of colored pencils, paper clips, combs, and rubber bands. Subjects selected items in response to instructions such as "Give me a red pencil." The experimental task consisted of a set of 144 directions, 15 of which contained trouble sources. Directions containing trouble sources were distributed randomly. Three types of trouble sources were used: unintelligible words replacing key elements (e.g., "Give me the blue [bribit]"); ambiguous references containing insufficient information (e.g., "Give me a rubber band" when there were rubber bands of several different colors available); and compliance problems, in which an object that was unavailable was requested (e.g., "Give me a pink bottle" when no pink bottle was present).

The institutionalized and community-based groups did not differ in the frequency with which they requested clarification of the trouble sources. Both groups failed to request clarification on a relatively large number of directions with trouble sources, performing much like young children (e.g., Webber, Fey, & Disher, 1984). Although the subjects evidently had the linguistic ability to produce clarification requests, they frequently failed to do so. Either they did not recognize many of the trouble sources or they chose not to point out the trouble sources to the investigator. It was interesting to note that both groups of subjects requested information in response to unintelligible and compliance problem trouble sources more often than they did to ambiguous trouble sources.

Introducing and making relevant contributions to one's own topics in conversation. Speakers frequently accomplish their own goals in conversation by introducing topics that concern information they wish to discuss. Topic introduction may be followed by topic development through additional relevant contributions. The ability to introduce and develop topics of one's own choosing demonstrates a certain level of control over how conversations are structured, and therefore displays conversational assertiveness. The number of topics introduced by subjects and the manner in which they were developed were examined in the 15 minutes of interaction between each subject and the investigator. Subjects produced three different types of topic initiations: appropriate topic introductions, inappropriate topic introductions, and topic shadings. The total number of utterances that initiated and maintained appropriate, inappropriate, and shaded topics was calculated.

The groups did not differ in terms of utterances devoted to introducing and maintaining appropriate or shaded topics. However, they differed in the number of utterances devoted to inappropriate topics. Institutionalized subjects allotted more than 12 times as many utterances to inappropriate topics as the community-based subjects.

These findings suggest that institutionalized subjects discussed more topics that disrupted the interaction or contained inappropriate information compared to community-based subjects. Institutionalized subjects discussed topics with little awareness of or concern about how those topics would fit the social context of the conversation.

DISCUSSION

Five of the six studies described above supported the hypothesis that community-based individuals differ from institutionalized individuals in terms of their conversational profiles. As was cautioned previously, these results must be interpreted in light of the fact that there are many factors that influence lifestyle options for adults with retardation. It is safe to assume that there were a number of individual considerations that determined each person's institutional placement. By the same token, there were undoubtedly many reasons why community-based subjects lived and worked in their current settings. Even though subjects in the institutionalized group and community-based group were carefully matched for IQ and demonstrated similar structural linguistic skills, there was still considerable heterogeneity within each group. Considering the heterogeneity inherent in the population studied (and in virtually any population of adults with retardation), the differences between groups observed in this project are particularly interesting.

Table 1 illustrates how the conversational profiles of the two groups differed along the parameters of assertiveness and responsiveness. In Table 1, plus and minus signs are used to indicate the direction in which behaviors differed in some aspects. It is evident from Table 1 that the institutionalized group was more assertive and less responsive than the community-based group. This impression is vividly illustrated by the data on producing and responding to questions. Institutionalized subjects asked many more questions than community-based subjects. However, these same institutionalized subjects responded less appropriately to questions asked of them by the investigator. This tendency to be assertive but nonresponsive was also reflected in other behaviors. Subjects in the institutionalized group devoted more utterances to inappropriate topics compared with those in the community-based group. In addition, institutionalized subjects provided fewer repairs that contained added information for their listener.

Table 1. Patterns of conversational assertiveness and responsiveness in the institutionalized and community-based groups

Conversational feature	Institutionalized group	Community-based group
Assertiveness	+ asking questions + introducing topics	– asking questions – introducing topics
Responsiveness	– responding to questions – maintaining investigator's topics – responding to requests for repair	+ responding to questions + maintaining investigator's topics + responding to requests for repair

Community-based subjects demonstrated a conversational profile that was more responsive but less assertive to the conversational partner compared with the institutionalized group. This group asked fewer questions but responded more appropriately to the investigator's questions. The community-based subjects spent less time on inappropriate topics, and their conversational repair strategies included more attempts to evaluate their listener's needs.

The results of this project suggest that specific aspects of conversational management are related to social adaptation. Specifically, subjects who had histories of maladaptive behavior, difficulty in adjusting to community living, and institutionalization were assertive in accomplishing their own goals in conversation but paid relatively little attention to their listener's input. It is entirely possible that this conversational profile stemmed from, reflected, or contributed to a more general pattern of difficult social interaction.

Community-based subjects appeared more responsive to their listener in that they more readily adjusted their input to fit with the investigator's contributions and the nature of the exchange. In addition, these subjects were usually willing to let the investigator take the lead in interaction. A few of the community-based subjects were reticent in conversation, responding to the examiner's bids but initiating few assertive conversational acts of their own.

If the behaviors observed in this project are representative of the way in which subjects typically manage similar conversations, the results raise an important question. What is the source of the evident differences between institutionalized and community-based subjects? It is possible that the conversational profile demonstrated by the institutionalized group contributed to institutional placement. A high level of assertiveness coupled with limited responsiveness could be annoying at best, and at worst it might convey impressions of non-compliance or insolence. Perhaps an assertive, less responsive conversational style led listeners to expect a consistent pattern of aggressive behaviors as well. In addition, an assertive, less responsive pattern could interfere with verbal methods most commonly used by educational personnel to diffuse or manage aggressive behaviors in adults with retardation. The impressions created by assertive, less responsive styles might have exacerbated the perceived severity of overall maladaptive behaviors in the institutionalized subjects.

It is also possible that the institutional environment itself was instrumental in fostering the conversational patterns observed. It might have been the case that subjects learned to concentrate on their own goals despite the listener's input because of their experience living in an institution. All institutionalized subjects had occasional opportunities to observe challenging behaviors and to interact with aggressive peers. By the same token, their contact with the outside community was limited by the fact that they spent most of their time on the grounds of the institutional facility. It is possible that some subjects were more assertive and less responsive in an attempt to secure the investigator's attention or to sustain the interaction.

Although conversational patterns demonstrated by the community-based subjects showed some limitations, these subjects tended to be more accommodating to the investigator. Their less assertive, more responsive patterns appeared more compliant and cooperative. The fact that many community-based subjects were minimally assertive or even reticent in conversation probably did not jeopardize their community placement. From the perspective of many employers, supervisors, and support staff, it is likely that an individual who responds to bids in conversation but otherwise keeps fairly quiet would be viewed as far more socially adaptive than an individual who sometimes ignores a listener and talks a good deal.

The results of this study have important clinical implications. It seems clear that responsiveness to one's listener is a behavior that merits consideration in educational programs for many individuals with retardation.

The ability to make one's contributions in conversation fit the listener's needs, the social nature of the interaction, and the purpose of the conversation is a skill that will undoubtedly contribute to successful integration within communities. For those individuals with retardation who demonstrate maladaptive behaviors, maximizing responsiveness could be critical. Increased responsiveness could reduce impressions of noncompliance and might enhance techniques employed to manage aggressive behaviors when they occur.

The implications of this study with regard to conversational assertiveness in individuals with retardation are somewhat disturbing. A reduced degree of assertiveness (coupled with increased responsiveness) in conversation appeared to be associated with community adjustment. It may be the case that treatment geared toward increasing assertiveness in reticent individuals does not match the realities of community integration. The implied notion that assertiveness should be discouraged in individuals with retardation, however, is truly objectionable. Rather, coupling responsiveness with the level of assertiveness that fits an individual's personality appears reasonable. In addition, it may also be necessary to foster the acceptance of conversational assertiveness on the part of individuals who live and work with persons with retardation.

BONNIE BRINTON *and* MARTIN FUJIKI *met when they were working on PhD degrees in speech-language pathology at the University of Utah. They were married after they completed their degrees. Since then, they have written numerous scholarly papers together, team-taught classes together, and presented together at many scholarly conferences. Fujiki says jokingly of their sixteen-year collaboration, "We share a brain, which I guess makes us both half-brained." Brinton received her bachelor's degree from the University of Utah and her master's degree from San Jose State University. Fujiki received his bachelor's degree from the University of Idaho and his master's degree from the University of Utah.*

References

American Speech-Language-Hearing Association, Committee on Mental Retardation and Developmental Disabilities. (1989). *Deinstitutionalization: Its effect on the delivery of speech-language-hearing services for persons with mental retardation and developmental disabilities. ASHA,* 31, 84–87.

Antonak, R. F. (1988). A history of the provision of services to people who are mentally retarded. In S. N. Calculator & J. L. Bedrosian (Eds.), *Communication assessment and intervention for adults with mental retardation* (pp. 9–44). Boston: College-Hill.

Best-Sigford, B., Bruininks, R. H., Lakin, K. C., Hill, B. K., & Heal, L. W. (1982). Resident release patterns in a national sample of public residential facilities. *American Journal of Mental Deficiency,* 87, 130–140.

Borthwick-Duffy, S. A., Eyman, R. K., & White, J. F. (1987). Client characteristics and residential placement patterns. *American Journal of Mental Deficiency, 92,* 24–30.

Brinton, B., & Fujiki, M. (1991a). *Conversational skills of persons with mental retardation* (Innovation Grant Final Report, National Institute on Disability and Rehabilitation Research grant no. H133C90121). Available from B. Brinton, Brigham Young University.

Brinton, B., & Fujiki, M. (1991b). Responses to requests for conversational repair by adults with mental retardation. *Journal of Speech and Hearing Research, 34,* 1087–1095.

Brinton, B., & Fujiki, M. (1992). The ability of persons with mild and moderate mental retardation to respond to questions in conversation. Unpublished manuscript.

Brinton, B., Fujiki, M., & Sonnenberg, E. (1988). Responses to requests for clarification by linguistically normal and language-impaired children in conversation. *Journal of Speech and Hearing Disorders, 53,* 383–391.

Brinton, B., Fujiki, M., Winkler, E., & Loeb, D. (1986). Responses to requests for clarification in linguistically normal and language-impaired children. *Journal of Speech and Hearing Disorders, 51,* 370–378.

Fey, M. E. (1986). *Language intervention with young children.* San Diego: College-Hill.

Garvey, C., & Berninger, G. (1981). Timing and turn taking in children's conversations. *Discourse Processes, 4,* 2757.

Grice. H. P. (1975). Logic and conversation. In P. Cole & J. L. Morgan (Eds.), *Syntax and semantics: Speech acts, Vol 3* (pp. 41–58). New York: Academic Press.

Hemming, H., Lavender, T., & Pill, R. (1981). Quality of life of mentally retarded adults transferred from large institutions to new small units. *American Journal of Mental Deficiency, 86,* 157–169.

Summers, J. A., & Reese, R. M. (1986). Residential services. In J. A. Summers (Ed.), *The right to grow up* (pp. 119–148). Baltimore: Brookes.

Webber, S. A., Fey, M. E., & Disher, L. M. (1984). *What's a grizic? Clinical sampling of children's contingent query behavior.* Paper presented at the American Speech-Language-Hearing Association Convention, San Francisco, CA, November 1984.

Wechsler, D. (1981). *Wechsler Adult Intelligence Scale Revised.* Cleveland: Psychological Corporation

Questions

1. In the last paragraph of the section titled "A Primary Study," what do the hypotheses indicate about the authors' assumptions about community and language?
2. How do the researchers collect their data? How does it differ from or complement Belnap's methods for researching about community and language in "Scones, Anyone?"?
3. How persuasive are the authors' methods? Why do they point out potential flaws with their own experiment?
4. Why, according to the last paragraph, are the implications of this study "somewhat disturbing"?

First Impressions of the Nurse and Nursing Care

SANDRA MANGUM
WITH CAROLYN GARRISON, CHARLENE LIND,
AND H. GILL HILTON

Sandra Mangum has become somewhat concerned with nurses' uniforms, particularly with how patients perceive nurses in different uniforms. She heard of a project that Charlene Lind had participated in that determined how people perceived female lawyers according to their neckwear. Seeing this study inspired her to go forward with her nurses' uniforms project, as she had finally found a method to conduct her study. As administrators, nurses, and patients each have a stake in the uniform of the nurse, this study attempts to represent each of their opinions. This article was originally published in the Journal of Nursing Care Quality.

To evaluate the effects of the first impression of the nurse and nursing care, nurses and administrators need to focus on the recipient of that care: the patient. This focus provides the opportunity to examine the effect that appearance has on the patient's perception of professionalism.

Clothing is a form of nonverbal communication that reflects confidence in ability and judgment, personal behavior, and sense of professional image.[1,2] Expectations about the dress of individuals are often based on their role in society and on membership in various organizations.[3] In first encounters, people use physical appearance as well as gender, age, and race to form impressions of each other.[4] Thus if people have stereotyped expectations of dress for certain groups, they may be confused by deviations in appearance of those who do not fit their mental model.[5]

Kaler and colleagues provide an explanation for the power of first impression observations.[6] When incoming personal information is complex, the existence of information processing schema permits a reduction in the processing load. Researchers have determined that stereotypical expectations bias the processing and interpretation of information in the direction of confirming those expectations, whether the expectations are positive or negative.[7–9] The expectations about an individual's dress seem to be based not only on his or her role in society but also on the type of organization to which he or she belongs.[3]

Thus patients' initial perceptions of competence and professionalism and their satisfaction with nursing care are often based on a first impression. The way nurses dress symbolizes role identity, function, authority, and their professional image of commitment and accountability.[10,11] In addition, dress makes a statement to patients about the nurse that may influence the nurse-patient relationship, which is an integral part of providing care. Nonverbal visual signals are interpreted by the patient, affecting his or her opinion of nurses and their abilities.[12]

HISTORICAL PERSPECTIVE

The nursing uniform tradition originated with Theodor and Friedericke Fliedner in Germany. They believed that a standard uniform attire was necessary because the nurse had to have a respectable and competent outward appearance as both an individual and a member of a respected occupational group.[13]

As Florence Nightingale reformed hospitals in England, women from higher social classes were recruited into the profession. It was important for the emerging professional nurse to wear a uniform to be distinguished from the "pauper nurses" of earlier years. By 1888, descriptions and pictures in the popular press were pervasively positive and fulfilled an important function not only for the nursing world but for the patient as well. These stylized and idealized images represented attempts "to portray a model of behavior, expectations and performance to which all nurses could aspire and subscribe. They also formed the basis for the criteria by which nurses and nursing might be judged."[14 (p.19)]

Changes in uniform styles since the Florence Nightingale era followed general trends in women's fashion and had a traditional look until the 1970s, when dress codes changed to allow for variation from traditional dress. Nurses have chosen to wear white pants with colored tops, all colors of print uniforms, and colored scrub uniforms. Tennis shoes and other types of nonuniform attire began to appear as the norm. The professional nurse, in many instances, became unidentifiable by uniform. Even the name pin might not include the full name of the nurse or the identifying credential RN.[10,15,16]

Nurses have stated that they do not see the need for a traditional dress code because it is more important to be recognized for what they know, not how they dress.[17] This view is directly opposite to patients' need to identify and relate to their caregiver as someone who is competent and professional. Patients have expressed confusion when they are unable to identify a nurse from a hospital ancillary worker, such as a certified nursing assistant, respiratory therapist, dietitian, or housekeeper.[10]

How do patients relate to a more casual appearance of the nurse? Does this casual appearance contribute to a professional image or detract from it? Are patients' perceptions different from nurses' and administrators'? These questions provided the impetus for a study first reported in *Image.*[18] A volunteer sample of patients (n=100), nurses (n=30), and administrators (n=15) was surveyed at a large regional medical center in the western intermountain area. Since that study, 22 replications have been completed in nearly all areas of the United States. A summary of data analysis from these replications is discussed in this article.

Subjects

Volunteer samples of patients (n=1,180), nurses (n=918), and administrators (n=332) were interviewed primarily in medical-surgical and obstetrical units. One sample included psychiatric patients, and another included outpatients in an ambulatory care antenatal and postpartum clinic (Table 1).

Patient ages ranged from 10 to older than 80 years. Eighty-seven percent of patients were white. The highest percentage of patients (37 percent)

Table 1. Replication by location

		Number of respondents			
Location by State	**Number of replications**	**Patients**	**Nurses**	**Administrators**	**Type of unit**
Arizona	1	57	54	19	Psychiatric
California	4	130	119	53	Med-surg*
Conn.	1	100	30	19	Med-surg
Florida	1	30	30	15	Med-surg
Hawaii	1	20	17	17	Obstetrical
Indiana	2	35	78	8	Med-surg
Iowa	1	111	27	3	Outpatient OB clinic
Kentucky	2	79	93	25	Med-surg
Michigan	1	45	29	15	Med-surg
Missouri	3	273	137	43	Med-surg
New York	3	171	221	101	Med-surg
Penn.	1	29	27	5	Med-surg
Wisconsin	1	70	56	9	Med-surg
Total	22	1180	918	332	

*Medical-surgical

lived in towns with populations of 50,000 to 100,000, with the next highest population being less than 5,000 (19 percent). Patients in occupations classified as professional/technical, clerical and sales, service, machine trades, benchwork, and construction constituted 43 percent of the sample.

Eighty-nine percent of nurses were between 20 and 49 years of age. A large majority of the nurses were female (96 percent) and white (95 percent). Nurses' educational background included diploma (13 percent), licensed practical nurse (11 percent), and associate (37 percent), baccalaureate (35 percent), and master's (4 percent) degrees. About 30 percent of the nurses had worked 5 years or less. The highest percentage of nurses (33 percent) had worked 11 to 20 years. Most worked on medical-surgical units in acute care hospitals (Table 1).

The majority of hospital administrators were 30 to 49 years of age. Seventy-three percent of the administrators were women, and 94 percent were white. Sixty-nine percent of the administrators were middle managers and had their undergraduate education in nursing.

INSTRUMENT

The Nurse Image Scale was used to collect the data.[19] This instrument consists of a Likert type rating scale of professional image traits from 5 (highest) to 1 (lowest). These descriptors were compiled from a literature search of adjectives used to describe a nurse. The following ten most often used traits were selected for the study: confident, competent, attentive, efficient, approachable, caring, professional, reliable, cooperative, and empathetic.[20]

An overall Nurse Image Scale score was determined from means of the ten professional image traits. Data were analyzed to determine whether there were significant differences in the respondents' ratings of the nurse in each of the uniforms. Coefficient α reliability of the instrument used in this study was computed to be .9676 from the combined samples. This was based on data from the ten attributes.

All the studies used the original nine pictures of a female nurse in different uniforms (*see colorplate 3*); these were considered representative of current professional dress:

1. a dark blue plaid skirt with a light blue blouse and a Navy blue sweater vest, a white laboratory coat, and Navy blue pumps
2. a white dress uniform, no cap, and white nurse's shoes
3. white pants with a maroon top, no cap, and white nurse's shoes
4. a white dress uniform, no cap, a stethoscope draped around the nurse's neck, and white nurse's shoes
5. a white pant uniform with a cap and white nurse's shoes

6. maroon designer scrubs, no cap, and white nurse's shoes
7. a white dress uniform with a cap and white nurse's shoes
8. a white pant uniform, no cap, a stethoscope draped around the nurse's neck, and white nurse's shoes
9. a white pant uniform, no cap, and white nurse's shoes

The photographs were taken by a professional photographer. Care was taken to ensure that the nurse adopted the same stance and facial expression for each picture.

Procedure

Data were gathered first by presentation of the demographic questionnaire to the subjects. The interviewer then showed the nine pictures in random order. Respondents were asked to rate the ten professional image traits of the nurse in each picture. They were then asked to sort through the pictures to determine the nurse they would most and least like to care for them. The same procedure was followed when nurses and administrators were interviewed. The data from each study were sent to the investigators for data entry and analysis of each sample. The entire data set was then analyzed, and comparisons were made.

Data analysis was performed using the SAS program. Using the uniform mean as the dependent variable, an analysis of variance was performed for each uniform. If significant differences were found among the three groups, Fisher's LSD was used to determine which groups were different.

Results

Comparison of Uniforms

When the ratings of uniforms by all respondents (n=2,494) were compared with every other uniform using Fisher's LSD, some interesting groupings appeared. As can be seen in Table 2, the white pant uniform with stethoscope was rated significantly higher than other uniforms. The white pant uniform with cap, dress with cap, pants suit, and dress with stethoscope scored closely in a second place grouping. The white dress uniform and street clothes with laboratory

Table 2. Comparison of scores for nine uniforms by all respondents (n=2,494)

Uniform	Mean score*
Pants/scope	3.94[a]
Pants/cap	3.77[b]
Dresss/cap	3.77[b]
Pants	3.75[b]
Dress/scope	3.75[b]
Street/ lab coat	3.62[c]
Dress	3.69[c]
Colored scrubs	3.30[d]
White pants/ colored top	3.26[d]

*Means that do not have the same letter are significantly different at the p=.05 level.

coat ranked third. Colored designer scrubs and white pants with colored top scored lowest.

The ratings of uniforms by all respondents in both the original and the multi-site study showed similar results. Patients in the original study rated the dress with cap highest, with pant uniform with cap and pant uniform with stethoscope in second and third places, respectively. All three groups in the original study rated the nurse in street clothes, colored designer scrubs, and white pants with colored top lowest. Nurses' and administra-tors' scores were similar but lower than the patients' scores in both studies.[18]

In the multi-site study, the most highly rated uniform was the white pant uniform with stethoscope. Scores for the pant uniform, dress with stethoscope, and dress were not significantly different among groups. The same three uniforms—street clothes with laboratory coat, colored designer scrubs, and white pants with colored top—were rated lowest. All three groups most preferred the nurse with pant uniform to care for them and least preferred the nurse in colored scrubs, street clothes with laboratory coat, and pants with colored top.

COMPARISON OF GROUPS

There were significant differences among the groups of respondents for some uniforms (Table 3). All three groups rated the pant uniform with stethoscope highest, although the administrators' rating was significantly lower than patients' and nurses'. Patients rated the pant uniform with cap

Table 3. Comparison of the mean scores of nine uniforms as rated by patients, nurses, and administrators*

Uniform	Patients (*n*=1,173)	Nurses (*n*=898)	Administrators (*n*=332)	*p*
Pants/scope	4.04[a]	3.86[a]	3.77[b]	.0086
Pants/cap	3.91[a]	3.61[b]	3.70[b]	.0002
Dress/cap	3.86[a]	3.64[b]	3.77[ab]	.0072
Pants	3.83[a]	3.68[a]	3.68[a]	.0464
Dress/scope	3.81[a]	3.71[a]	3.68[a]	.2072
Dress	3.65[a]	3.60[a]	3.57[a]	.7332
Street/labcoat	3.65[a]	3.52[a]	3.62[a]	.5716
Colored scrubs	3.22[a]	3.48[b]	3.14[b]	.0190
White pants/ colored top	3.24[a]	3.35[b]	3.08[c]	.0323

*Means in the same row that do not have the same letter are significantly different at the p=.05 level. These p values for the f test are from analysis of variance of group differences.

significantly higher than nurses and administrators. The scores of patients, nurses, and administrators for the pant uniform, dress with stethoscope, dress, and street clothes with laboratory coat were not significantly different. Patients rated colored designer scrubs significantly lower than nurses. Administrators rated that uniform significantly lower than nurses and patients.

When asked to choose the nurse they would most and least like to care for them, patients, nurses, and administrators agreed that the nurse with pants suit and stethoscope was most preferred. Least preferred by patients and administrators was the nurse in colored scrubs; nurses least preferred the nurse in street clothes and laboratory coat (Table 4).

Table 4. Percentage preferences of patients', nurses', and administrators' most and least preferred uniforms*

Uniform	Patients	Nurses	Administrators	Total
Most preferred				
Pants/scope	22.0[a]	25.1[a]	22.9[a]	23.2
Dress/scope	12.6[b]	15.9[b]	14.7[b]	14.0
Street/lab coat	16.2[b]	10.6[cd]	14.7[b]	14.1
Dress/cap	13.9[b]	9.1[c]	15.0[b]	12.4
Colored scrubs	6.6[c]	14.9[c]	5.7[c]	9.4
Pants/cap	12.9[b]	4.9[de]	8.0[bc]	9.4
Pants	7.7[cd]	6.6[de]	10.1[bc]	7.7
Pants/ colored top	5.8[cd]	9.2[d]	3.8[c]	6.7
Dress	2.4[d]	3.8[c]	4.8[c]	3.2
Least preferred				
Colored scrubs	36.3[a]	15.8[b]	35.8[a]	29.0
Street/lab coat	19.5[b]	34.1[a]	21.8[b]	25.0
Pants/ colored top	18.2[b]	17.0[b]	17.7[b]	17.7
Dress/cap	7.5[c]	13.4[b]	7.9[c]	9.7
Dress/scope	5.6[cde]	5.3[cd]	4.8[c]	5.4
Dress	6.1[cd]	3.8[cd]	4.8[c]	5.1
Pants/cap	1.9[cd]	6.7[cd]	6.0[c]	4.8
Pants	1.9[e]	2.6[cd]	1.0[c]	2.1
Pants/scope	1.7[e]	1.4[d]	0.3[c]	1.4

*Values in the same column that do not have the same letter are significantly different at the p=0.05 level.

DISCUSSION

The patient's first impression is a powerful determinant of his or her opinion and anticipated satisfaction or dissatisfaction with care because the nurse is judged primarily by what he or she wears at the bedside. Many comments in the literature support the patient's point of view. According to Smith, "Nurses should consider image and professional polish as the competitive edge one needs to gain a client, solicit cooperation, or elicit a listening ear."[21(p.28)] The mandate that nurses have a respectable and competent outward appearance, both as individuals and as members of a respected profession, and 100 years of nurses appearing in traditional dress have had a strong impact on the public.

The study also points out that the stethoscope, a relatively new nurse symbol, carries an element of nurse identification the plain pant uniform and dress do not and may be replacing the cap as the key professional nurse symbol. The results of both studies leave no doubt as to which uniforms are least preferred: those that are more casual and generic and do not portray a clear professional identity.

Nurses should be encouraged to consider the importance of patients' opinions and perceptions of professional image and the fact that how they dress makes a statement about how they are perceived as professionals. The current literature is replete with articles about the need to differentiate professional nurses from other members of the health care team, although suggestions for professional image building efforts have not focused on uniform choice as an important way to accomplish that goal.[15–17] Patients' first impressions do set the stage for immediate recognition of the nurse as a person with unique skills and knowledge. Nurses can then be accepted as the personification of that image as they provide care.

Nurses should consider the past and the Fliedners' and Florence Nightingale's purpose in establishing the uniform as a symbol of professionalism and dedication to set the nurse apart from other health care workers of the time. Perhaps we have come full circle and now need to reestablish a traditional image by which a professional nurse can be easily identified and his or her anticipated care accepted as representative of professionalism and commitment.

SANDRA MANGUM, *a clinical professor in the College of Nursing at BYU, received a BS in nursing and a BA in music and French at BYU and an MN at the University of Washington. She has been teaching at BYU since 1969.* DR. CAROLYN GARRISON *is an assistant professor in the Department of Clothing and Textiles at BYU.* DR. CHARLENE LIND *is an associate professor in the Department of Clothing and Textiles at BYU.* DR. H. GILL HILTON *is a professor in the Department of Statistics at BYU.*

References

1. Molloy, J.T. *The Woman's Dress for Success Book.* Chicago: Follett. 1977.
2. Pante, R. *Dressing To Win.* New York: Doubleday, 1984.
3. Davis, L.L. "Clothing and Human Behavior: A Review." *Home Economics Research Journal* 12 (1984): 325-338.
4. Horn, M.J., and Gurel, L.M. *The Second Skin.* 3d ed. Boston: Houghton Mifflin, 1981.
5. Bickman, L. "The Social Power of a Uniform." *Journal of Applied Social Psychology* 1 (1974): 47–61.
6. Kaler, S., et al. "Stereotypes of Professional Roles." *Image* 21 (1989): 85–89.
7. Hamilton, D.L. "Analysis of Stereotyping." In *Advances in Experimental Social Psychology,* edited by L. Berkowitz. New York: Academic Press, 1979.
8. Bem, S.L. "The Making of Images: A Psychological Perspective." *American Nurses Association Journal* 161 (1983): 39–48.
9. Kalisch, P.A., and Kalisch, B.J. *The Changing Image of the Nurse.* Menlo Park, CA: Addison-Wesley, 1987.
10. Hughes, E., and Proulx, J. "You Are What You Wear." *Hospitals* 53 (1979): 113–118.
11. Little, D. "The 'Strip Tease' of Nurse Symbols or Nurse Dress Code: No Code." *Imprint* 31 (1983): 49–52.
12. Hinshaw, A.S., and Atwood, J.R. "A Patient Satisfaction Instrument: Precision by Replication." *Nursing Research* 31 (1982): 170–191.
13. Poplin, I.S. "Nursing Uniforms: Romantic Idea, Functional Attire, or Instrument of Social Change?" *Nursing History Review* 2 (1994): 153–167.
14. Davies, C., ed. *Rewriting Nursing History.* Totowa, NJ: Barnes & Noble, 1980.
15. Carpenito, L. "A Nurse Is a Nurse Is a Nurse." *Florida Nurse* 43 (1995): 1–3.
16. Holleran, C. "Was It a Nurse? Why the Confusion?" *International Nursing Review* 38 (1991): 62.
17. Zimmerman, P. "Dressing the Part." *Journal of Emergency Nursing* 22 (1996): 267–268.
18. Mangum, S., et al. "Perceptions of Nurses' Uniforms." *Image* 23 (1991): 127–130.
19. Mangum, S., and Bown, B. *Nurse Image Scale.* Provo, UT: S. Mangum and B. Bown. Unpublished.
20. Bown, B., et al. "A Pilot Study of Nurse Uniform Preference." Provo, UT: Brigham Young University Department of Home Economics, 1988.
21. Smith, B.A. "Marketing a Profitable Nursing Image: Recognizing Image Is Power." *Imprint* 33 (1986): 27–31.

Questions

1. Nurses have argued that "what they know is more important than what they wear." While this statement is true, how does this article complicate the issue?
2. What seem to be the reasons that the white pants with stethoscope outfit is preferred?
3. How might this study relate to other professions whose members wear a uniform?
4. Do the arguments for professional uniforms have any bearing on arguments for school dress codes?

The Demise of the Drive-In Theater: A Small Town Landscape Feature Slowly Disappears

RICHARD H. JACKSON
AND J. MATTHEW SHUMWAY

"Geographers," Richard H. Jackson says, "are always looking at the landscape and asking 'why?'" As a geographer and former city planner, Jackson asked himself why the drive-in, once a dominant feature of the American cultural landscape, has disappeared in recent years. As he found out through his research, the decline of drive-ins corresponds with the "decrease in community contact" characteristic of comtemporary America. "Americans are becoming more and more isolated," Jackson says, "as people spend more time alone or with family than with members of the community." The demise of the drive-in marks the move from community to private life as more and more people watch movies on their home entertainment systems rather than participating in community activities such as attending the drive-in. As Americans become more "idiosyncratic rather than community-oriented," Jackson says, it results in the "homogenization and impersonalization of America." Jackson's article was originally published in Small Town.

For many young Americans, the drive-in theater is already a feature of their parents' and grandparents' nostalgic reminiscing. Yet, for those who grew up in small towns in the decades of the 1950s and 1960s, the drive-in theater, in many ways, symbolized their life and times. The drive-in combined the new freedom provided by mass automobile ownership achieved after World War II with the hey-day of the golden age of Hollywood. The drive-in allowed residents of small town and suburban America to combine entertainment, friends, families and their ubiquitous cars.

Invented nearly 60 years ago, the first drive-in opened for business in Camden, New Jersey, on June 6, 1933. Handicapped by the Great

Depression and World War II, drive-ins were still a novelty when World War II ended. Following the war, their numbers exploded, increasing tenfold by 1955 when over 4,000 drive-ins dotted the landscape. At their peak in 1960, there were nearly 5,000, but today we are witnessing the disappearance of this unique American and small town landscape feature as less than 1,000 are estimated to be in operation in 1993. In the lifetime of many Americans, the drive-in theater has gone from novelty to institution and landmark—only to fade into nostalgic recollections. The story of the rise and fall of the drive-in theater parallels the dramatic change in technology, transportation and social mores in America in the post-World War II era. Analysis of the causes of its original widespread adoption and its subsequent precipitous decline illustrates how small town America has been impacted by the changes in the broader American society in the last half century.

A Brief History of the Drive-In Industry

Invented by an out-of-work businessman, Richard M. Hollingshead, Jr., the first Drive-In Theatre (Hollingshead's spelling) was designed to appeal to what he thought was a neglected market: those people who wanted to enjoy their automobiles and movies at the same time.[1] The importance of Hollingshead's invention was not lost on contemporary observers. Within a few weeks of opening, the national news magazine *Literary Digest* reported that "A coliseum for movie-minded motorists has just been completed at Camden, New Jersey. In this novel experiment, the audience drives into the theater and watches the show from their automobiles, which are in effect private boxes." The *Literary Digest* described the layout of Hollingshead's theater and concluded that "either because of the novelty or the convenience, the Drive-In Theater has proved very popular."[2]

The author of this first report on drive-ins was guarded about the potential of the genre, however, stating that, "Time alone will tell whether unfavorable weather conditions, which take up a rather sizable part of the year in some sections of the country, will prove too great a handicap to this type of theater. Its success will also depend upon whether or not the public will be willing to exchange the intimacy of an indoor theater for the convenience of an outdoor one."[3]

Such reservations were not evident to the observers of the rapid growth in number and popularity of drive-ins following World War II. Commenting on the future, they confidently predicted that, "the drive-ins seem here to stay—and to grow. They may not represent the sophisticated urbanite's idea of a glamorous evening, but they have captured the fancy—and the steady trade—of millions.[4]

The importance of the drive-ins as a part of the American landscape was early recognized. One author, in a flight of fancy, even compared them to the cathedrals of Europe:

> Motoring through much of the countryside of Europe, the imposing outline of a great cathedral ahead or the graceful spires of a smaller church usually are the first indication that you are approaching a town. Driving through America—and especially Southern and Western sections—a less romantic symbol is often the advent-courier of the town to come; it is the great, blank, precise rectangle of the drive-in movie theater.[5]

Concentrated in suburban and small town America, the giant screens of the drive-ins were often the highest feature in the landscape, dwarfing even the grain silos of the Midwest. Examination of the rapid diffusion of drive-ins suggests that the reasons for their rapid acceptance and equally rapid demise are intricately related to the complex social and technological forces affecting America during the past half century.

The thousands of new theaters served the sprawling, automobile-oriented suburbs whose residents no longer went downtown for entertainment. They also served small town and rural residents for whom the combination of cheap automobiles and big-screen Hollywood productions provided a new and attractive type of weekend entertainment. Admission was inexpensive, allowing even large families to bring their children along and save the hassle and price of a babysitter. The drive-in was casual. Families didn' t have to dress up (kids were often brought in their pajamas) and could bring a picnic dinner from home and eat it in the car or at facilities provided by the management.[6] Moviegoers could freely talk, smoke, drink or engage in other types of behavior that would interfere with patrons at a regular indoor theater.

At the same time, fear of inappropriate behavior dogged the drive-in industry, with many observers maintaining that they were "passion pits; magnets for teenagers or Lotharios preying on innocent young girls, and a general threat to community morals."[7] Other concerns centered on purported traffic congestion during the patrons' arrival and departure, light and noise nuisance to neighbors and the opportunity for children outside the theaters to observe inappropriate behavior by screen actors. Such fears led many communities to prohibit drive-ins through zoning or other ordinances designed to protect the community from the perceived social threats posed by the theaters.

Numerous lawsuits and changing social standards combined to defuse most of the early laws that restricted the locations of drive-ins. But, as the theaters began to decline in attractiveness in the 1960s, many owners began showing pornographic films. This resulted in the enactment of new laws designed to discourage them. Courts struck down such ordinances when they were so broad as to essentially prohibit showing R- or X-rated movies, but did allow cities to craft narrow regulations designed to protect children and unwilling adults from exposure to images on drive-in screens.[8]

Concern for the reputation of drive-ins led the owners' association to publish a manual for profitable operation that included the following admonition:

> One of the most important managerial tasks falling under the general heading of proper supervision is that of preventing breaches in good conduct. In this regard a special officer or night watchman should be assigned to patrol the lot after 10 p.m., looking casually into every car without disturbing the occupants. He should go from the front ramp to the back ramp and back again, never stopping, so as to prevent any sort of misconduct.[9]

Growth and Expansion: The Golden Fifties

In spite of the caveat of concern lest the drive-ins become a concentration of immorality, drive-ins expanded dramatically. Contemporary reports concluded that some 75 percent of their patrons were individuals who had not attended movies before. Given that the drive-ins always suffered from showing second rate or out-of-date movies, observers in the 1950s concluded that there was something unique about the drive-in experience that prompted people to attend. One article explained why numerous kinds of people saw movies there:

> • Drive-ins gave benefits to married couples who had one or more young children and who could not afford or obtain babysitters.
> • The elderly, infirm or physically handicapped people unable to or unwilling to cope with crowds, standing in line or other inconveniences of attending a theater in the center of the city or town found these theaters attractive.
> • Families willing to take a long automobile ride after a hard day's work, but unwilling to dress up and go into

town for recreation after a day's work made up a large segment of the audience.

• Drive-ins attracted health-conscious people. Customer surveys of drive-in patrons revealed that, "surprising numbers of people look upon drive-ins as healthful out of door recreation." Others felt that the privacy of their own cars protected their children from the spread of germs associated with infectious diseases such as the flu, measles and whooping cough.[10]

Enthusiasm for the drive-in is reflected in numerous contemporary references in the 1950s and 1960s. In October of 1950, a survey indicated that the average drive-in had space for 447 cars, with each car averaging 2.34 adults and 0.94 children for a total of 3.28 individuals per vehicle. By the calculations found in the media, three million people were attending the 2,100 theaters each showing—assuming full attendance.[11]

Once the drive-ins became accepted as an important part of a new automobile-oriented society, their role is mentioned in periodicals and newspapers on a regular basis in the 1950s, 1960s and 1970s. Most of the references at the national level related to either the growing importance of drive-ins, their growing scale and diversity of attractions or the advantages of the drive-in versus the old enclosed theater. The significance of the drive-in to the American society is epitomized by the *New York Times Magazine* report in 1957 that the first drive-in had opened in Europe. Located near Rome, it had space for 750 cars and 250 motor scooters. Complete with Coca Cola, popcorn, ice cream, hot dogs and hamburgers (alongside pasta dishes and espresso), the transplant was called the Metro Drive-In Cine.[12] Unlike the later diffusion of another automobile-spawned phenomenon, the fast food drive-in restaurant, the drive-in theater apparently failed to catch on in Europe and disappeared from the scene.

THE SMALL TOWN AND THE DRIVE-IN

The small towns of America and drive-ins were largely synonymous during the theaters' hey-day. The first drive-in in Camden, New Jersey, was in a, then, small community. During the period of greatest expansion at around 1950, some 60 percent were located in towns with fewer than 10,000 people. Forty percent of all of the drive-ins at that point stood in towns with fewer than 5,000 people. The last peak for drive-ins occurred in 1980 when there were approximately 3,500, of which 30 percent were found in towns under 5,000, and 51 percent were located in towns of 10,000 or less. From 1950 to 1970, approximately three-fourths of all of the drive-in movie theaters were in communities of 20,000 or less.

The factors that made rural and small town America the focus of drive-in theaters centered on the availability of land at low cost and the need for alternative forms of entertainment. The existence of so many drive-in theaters in small towns should not be remarkable when we consider that the greatest cost for such a facility was the expense of the acreage on which to park the viewers' automobiles. Even where drive-ins were located near large urban areas, such as around Chicago or New York City, their need for large spaces dictated that the owners actually construct them in small towns.

One of the largest drive-in theaters in the United States was the All-Weather Drive-In in Copiague, New York. It had space for 2,500 automobiles and also featured an indoor theater that seated 1,500 people and showed the same bill as the outdoor portion of the complex.[13] Other super drive-ins near urban areas provided a wide variety of attractions intended to satisfy the needs of families on the go. They included swimming pools, full service gas stations, playgrounds, Ferris wheels, laundromats, lakes, cafeterias and a number of other facilities. For most Americans, however, the drive-in with which they were familiar was the one found in small town America.

The small town drive-in theater was often a barebones facility. The screen was apt to be supported by exposed steel girders or wood trusses on one side, with the white, flat surface to project the picture upon covering the other (*see colorplate 4*). Parking for patrons might be covered with asphalt, but was just as likely to be gravel or grass. The facilities rarely included much more than the cafeteria to buy drinks, popcorn, hamburgers and ice cream.

The Spud Drive-In Theatre, Driggs, Idaho.

For small town America and their rural service areas, the drive-in provided entertainment. The entertainment brought to town the wonders of Hollywood in a setting that could be shared with the family. All of the factors that caused drive-ins to flourish were intensified in small towns. The lack of alternative competing entertainment forms, the necessity of working long hours on farms or in small businesses and the importance of family life combined to make the drive-in a center of small town entertainment. For the majority of families in the 1950s, 1960s and the early 1970s, attending the drive-in was as much of a ritual as attending church on Sunday. For teenagers experiencing the new-found freedom of driving and dating without parental supervision, the drive-ins were the place to be on Saturday night with friends of both sexes.

The actual landscape characteristics of the drive-in in small towns were as varied as the communities themselves. Some incorporated local distinctive products in their advertising, as did the Spud Drive-In Theater in Driggs, Idaho. But, whatever the name, form or appearance, for the small town residents and for the rural people who came to town on Friday and Saturday to attend, they represented one of the most important landscape features and entertainment forms in rural America for three decades.

THE DISAPPEARANCE OF THE DRIVE-IN FROM SMALL TOWN AMERICA

During the 1980s, the number of drive-ins fell precipitously. At the beginning of the decade the number stood at 3,469, but, at the end, only 1,014 survived. That barely equaled the number found in 1947 at the beginning of the postwar automobile boom. The reasons for the abrupt decline of the drive-in industry are varied, but some seem to be more important than others.

Traditionally, it has been assumed that the advent of television destroyed the drive-in industry. In fact, it seems to provide the same amenities as a drive-in. Television is convenient, since viewers need not dress up or leave home and parents do not require babysitters. Once families purchased the television, it was cheap to watch, and the presence of the kitchen and the bedroom made it possible to have refreshments or send sleepy children off to bed.

Examination of the growth in home television sets, however, does not support the conclusion that this phenomenon caused the demise of the drive-in industry. The drive-ins' peak growth years are almost identical with the peak growth years for televisions. Drive-ins peaked at nearly 5,000 in 1960, the same time that the number of homes with televisions neared 90 percent.

One reason for the rapid growth in both drive-ins and home televisions is that they did not necessarily compete with or substitute for one

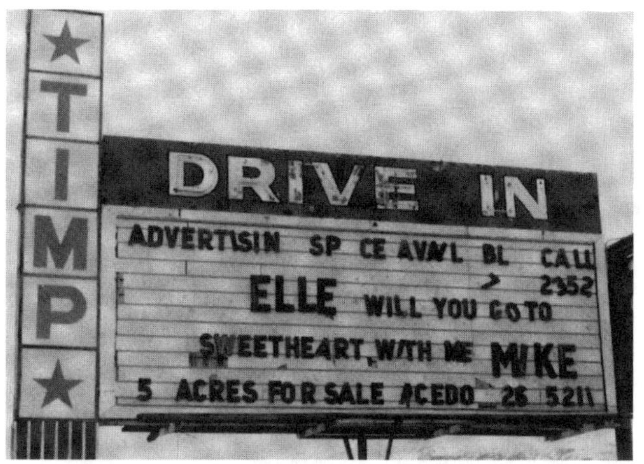

The Timp Drive In, in Orem, Utah, advertises the sale of the drive-in property.

another. Also, home television still had the disadvantage of lack of choice for the viewer. Particularly in the early years of television, persons could pick up only a limited number of channels and few major movies appeared on the tube. For the average American, the drive-in was still the place to go to see a movie production.

Statistically, the one factor that most closely corresponds to the decline in drive-in numbers is the advent of cable television and the video cassette recorder (VCR). Both provided the viewer with greater options including full-length feature movies. These two technological changes meant that the old advantages of the drive-in theater were largely gone. In 1980, only 2.4 percent of American households utilized VCR machines, but by 1992, nearly 70 percent of all homes had at least one videotape recorder. At the same time, the proliferation of cable television and the wide variety of programming that it provides gives viewers ever greater opportunities to see feature-length movies on pay channels.

For the owners of the drive-ins the biggest threat to their continued operation has been the cost of land. Since the facilities utilize anywhere from 10 to 30 acres, the drive-ins have been faced with strong competition from higher rent uses. As cities have expanded outward with suburban sprawl in the 1970s and 1980s, the drive-in theaters that once lay on the rural fringe have been surrounded by residential or commercial activities. It is difficult to justify maintaining the land for seasonal or limited daily use as a drive-in when land prices have increased so dramatically. Consequently, in many areas, suburban housing or retail, commercial or business activities have replaced the drive-in. Some idea of the pressure on land owners to sell their drive-ins is given by the case of the Morris Plains Drive-In in New Jersey. The land cost the owners $10,750 to acquire in 1947. They sold the acreage in 1981 for $1.25 million.[14] The

Drive-ins and swap meets have become nearly synonymous.

continued escalation in either land values or property taxes have ultimately forced many owners to look to alternative forms of land use.

Another broad category of factors affecting the decline in numbers of drive-ins involves the movies they show. Initially, the theaters were not known for their high quality movies, but so long as patrons had no option, this was not a handicap. In the words of one observer, "Drive-ins were always noted for their screen fare of blood, breasts and beasts."[15] The difficulty of obtaining good quality films intensified in the late 1970s, and, in the 1980s, as the film industry began making fewer films, each aimed at obtaining large box office revenues, and scaled down their production of low-grade, B movies.[16] Ironically, the lack of low-priced popular movies has been accentuated by the lack of good family films. A survey of drive-in users in 1983 indicated that 72 percent of patrons were young married couples with two or more children and this trend especially affected them.[17]

Other reasons speeding the decline involve environmental issues. The theaters operate for limited seasons outside of the sunbelt, they lack air conditioning for hot, muggy nights and they must cope with the effects of daylight savings time. That often pushes showtime back too late to show movies for children. Tied to these issues are rain, bugs (the days of spraying the entire audience with DDT are long past) and the perennial problems of technology which prevent many theaters from profitably changing to in-car radio broadcast sound, 3-D or air conditioning to attract customers. A final issue has been the rise in insurance costs associated with the proliferation of lawyers and lawsuits. The concern for injury to patrons on drive-in-related amenities such as playgrounds, swimming pools or ponds have forced some owners out of business.

A technological change that has impacted drive-ins since 1980 is the rise of the multiplex theater. While drive-ins can only operate at night, a multiplex can run day and night. Historically, drive-ins with only one screen always faced the problem of whether their offerings would be attractive, but a multiple screen indoor complex allows theaters to flexibly respond to public demand by showing an individual film in as many of their theaters as ticket purchases warrant. When owners converted their drive-in theater, which had held 1,800 cars, into an eleven-screen indoor theater complex, the resulting Long Island, New York, multiplex was able to serve as many potential customers in any day as the old drive-in could at its maximum—and could do so day and night and throughout the year.[18]

A final factor some people believe caused the decline of drive-ins grew out of changing sexual mores of the 1960s. The sexual revolution made it unnecessary to go to a drive-in to experience either the titillation of questionable movies or to escape from parents. The widespread adoption of a more lenient and tolerant view of sexual behavior made many of the functions of the drive-in obsolete.

The Future of the Drive-In

The drive-in will probably never disappear completely. In places it has remained successful, particularly in the sun belt where it can be operated for more days out of the year. It is also a successful adjunct to many small towns that are attempting to develop their tourism industry. For such small towns, the experience of attending a drive-in is an attraction for many visiting families. For the children who did not experience the drive-in era, attending a movie in an automobile and sitting in the evening air watching a movie is a unique and attractive experience.

For those of us old enough to remember when drive-ins were a staple part of summer activity, the experience is an integral part of our youth. For many middle-aged Americans, the drive-in has come to symbolize those halcyon days of our youth when summers were not times of riot and violence, but endless days of sheer pleasure. Even the unending work of hauling hay, hoeing corn or cotton, or other rural activities of small town and rural America seem much less unpleasant when remembered in combination with the experience of the drive-in. The drive-in has come to symbolize not only those remembered summer days when all seemed well in America, but they also recall our own youth when the future seemed faraway and filled with potential.

For communities that have managed to retain their drive-in theaters, they provide an important opportunity to capitalize on the nostalgia movement which sees yesterday characterized by a kinder, better lifestyle. Communities with drive-ins have the opportunity to recall for Americans the life which they perceived as characterizing small town America in the decades from the 1950s to the 1970s. Rural communities and small towns may wish to try to encourage the remaining drive-in theaters to remain in business. This may involve changing zoning ordinances to allow use of the space for nonmovie activities (such as swap meets) or it may involve allowing them to provide a multiple-use complex. In some locations, drive-ins have managed to maintain their traditional role in spite of rising land costs and their engulfment by suburbia by allowing them to provide retail activity on the street portion of the property. Communities that actively seek to maintain the drive-in as a part of their culture and geography will find that it is not only rewarding financially, but helps to maintain a part of our collective past that is important and relevant.

RICHARD H. JACKSON *has a BS and an MS in geography from BYU and a PhD in geography from Clark University in Worcester, Massachusetts. Other than teaching, Jackson has used his skills as a geographer during the eight years he spent on the Orem City Council and as a consultant for city planners of small towns.*

J. MATTHEW SHUMWAY *is a former student of Richard H. Jackson. He received a BS and an MS in geography at BYU and then completed a PhD in geography at the University of Indiana. He currently teaches in the BYU Geography Department.*

Endnotes

1. David Bruce Reddick, "Movies Under the Stars: A History of the Drive-In Theatre Industry, 1933–1983," Michigan State University: Unpublished PhD dissertation, 1984, pp. 1–3.
2. *Literary Digest*, July 22, 1933, p. 19.
3. *Literary Digest*, July 22, 1933, p. 19.
4. Marguerite Cullman, "Double Feature: Movies and Moonlight," *New York Times Magazine*, October 1, 1950, p. 22.
5. Cullman, p. 22.
6. Lewis Beale and John Stanley, *San Francisco Examiner and Chronicle*, June 5, 1983, as quoted in *Landscape*, Summer, 1983, p. 22.
7. Lewis Beale, "50 Years Ago, On a Screen Far Away…," *Calendar*, June 5, 1983, p. 5.
8. *Erznoznik v. City of Jacksonville*, 422 US 205 (1974).
9. Cullman, p. 22.
10. Cullman, p. 22. See also "Drive-Ins," *Time Magazine*, July 14, 1941.
11. Cullman, p. 22.
12. "Drive-in Cine," *New York Times Magazine*, September 29, 1957, p. 32.
13. "The Colossal Drive-In," *Newsweek*, July 22, 1957, p. 85.
14. Barbara Bradley, "That's All Folks at Drive-in Movies as Land Values Upstage Profits," *Christian Science Monitor*, December 10, 1982, p. 11.
15. Joan Liftin, "Films Alfresco," *American Film*, July–August, 1986, p. 42.
16. Bradley, p. 11.
17. Louis Sahagun, "Drive-In's Future Dims Across the US," *Los Angeles Times*, August 22, 1983, p. 3.
18. Bradley, p. 11.

Questions

1. What factors influenced the decline of drive-in theaters? How are these factors influencing other aspects of small town life?
2. Technological progress is generally seen as positive. How does this research complicate this view of technology?
3. In what other ways has America's love affair with the car changed our landscape?
4. According to the authors, how are drive-ins a part of our collective past?

Preserving or "Pickling" the Constitution

RICHARD DAVIS

As Richard Davis has discussed the idea of "preserving" the Constitution with his students, he finds that they want to somehow follow the Constitution as if they were still living in the late eighteenth century. As this is not possible, Davis asserts that we need to "be like the framers of the Constitution—bold and futuristic." Davis is interested in how the Constitution is relevant today, how it applies to current problems, and believes that the framers left much of the language of the Constitution open and ambiguous to provide space for the change that necessarily comes with each new era and its problems. His article was first published in Brigham Young Magazine.

Recently, I listened to a speech by a member of Congress. At one point, he emphatically, exclaimed that he wanted the American voters to send more members to Congress who "love the Constitution."

This statement would be unremarkable for most Latter-day Saints in the United States since we often hear politicians from the right-hand side of the ideological spectrum assert their love for the Constitution, accompanied by a mournful cry that others in political life in the middle or on the left of the political spectrum do not share their view. But those on the political right would have been shocked by the source of this statement. In fact, they would positively assert that this particular congressman is one of those undermining the Constitution.

This member is well known as a liberal Democrat; according to many political conservatives, he would be termed a socialist. He supports active government involvement in social welfare programs, and in fact would argue we have not gone far enough in that direction. He supports a more active role of government in protecting labor, offering universal health care, and increasing government spending for the poor.

Moreover, his personal appearance hardly fits the conservative's stereotype of the Constitution lover, as he sports a full beard and shoulder length hair. With those views and that physical appearance, how could he love the Constitution? How could he support the election of more politicians who love the Constitution?

PRESERVING WHAT?

On the first day of class each semester, I ask my students why they are taking a course in American politics. Invariably, some students respond along the lines of needing to learn more about American government so they can help "preserve the Constitution." After hearing this answer repeatedly, I have been tempted to ask them what they mean by "preserving the Constitution."

Subsequent class discussion over the course of the semester usually reveals the source of their assertion, however. Although generalizations are dangerous, a pattern of beliefs does emerge from these encounters.

These students believe dangerous forces today are undermining the Constitution, that the Constitution has been subverted by socialistic government policies inimical to the interests of the United States. The range of these policies stretches from governmental social programs (Social Security, medical care, welfare programs) to the graduated income tax. Some of those in this philosophical camp see danger in the 14th and 16th amendments—the 14th because of its subsequent use as a basis for the expansion of civil rights and the 16th because it provided the revenue base for federal government growth. If they had their way, they would eliminate most, if not all, of the federal governmental programs of the past 60 years because, in their view, these programs are not Constitutional.

I sometimes find myself wondering how these students and this member of Congress (as well as others who share his view) can both have such firm, but contradictory views of the Constitution? How can they both seek the preservation of a single document they view so differently?

CHANGE AND THE CONSTITUTION

The United States' Constitution is one of the briefest in the world. Vague statements like "necessary and proper" or "supreme law of the Land" pepper the document. This brevity and vagueness is the result of two problems the framers faced. One was the existence of fundamental disagreements among themselves over the structure and powers of the new government. They resolved many of their disputes by parsing their words.

The second problem was predicting the future. While they were some of the best and brightest of their day, they were not prophets. Greater specificity, may have helped settle some of the subsequent Constitutional debates over our history, but it also would have bound future generations to provisions no longer applicable in a different age they could not foretell.

The wisdom of the framers' penchant for future adaptability became apparent almost immediately: They even saw the folly of some of their handiwork, when actually implemented, during their own generation. For example, they had envisioned the second top vote-getter in a presidential election as the occupant of the vice presidency. But in application, the plan was a mistake. After George Washington's two terms, the second top vote-getter became the candidate of the opposition party. That person's role as vice president in the administration of his competitor became quite awkward, so through the Twelfth Amendment (ratified in 1804), the plan was abandoned in favor of the current system.

Change did not always come by Constitutional amendment. Even though the framers had not specified it in the Constitution, George Washington felt two terms should be the limit for presidential office. That interpretation of presidential tenure was adhered to for over 100 years until Theodore Roosevelt ran for a third (although not consecutive) term. After Franklin Roosevelt successfully won a third and then a fourth term, the tradition was formalized in the 22nd Amendment. But the interpretation alone had worked well for most of our history.

Presidential term of office was not the only interpretive adjustment in the framers' own generation. George Washington, as the new president, took the Constitution literally when it stated that the president should seek the "advice and consent" of the Senate on the ratification of treaties. He went to the Senate personally and sought their advice on negotiation of a treaty on Indian lands. The Senate debated the issue throughout the day and finally postponed consideration. Washington was so frustrated that he stormed out of the chamber, vowing never to seek their advice again.[1] Subsequently, the interpretation of that provision has focused on the "consent" requirement rather than "advice."

Despite the history of Constitutional adjustment in interpretation, there are still many, such as the students mentioned previously, who view the Constitution as in danger because the framers' original intent has not been upheld. They read the brief document that is the Constitution and see nothing about social welfare programs, graduated income tax, or health care and conclude that these activities do not fit under the role of a government created by the Constitution.

Obviously, what these advocates are really seeking is not to preserve the Constitution, but their interpretation of it. However, their interpretation does not preserve the Constitution. Rather, it pickles it. It pickles it by retaining the context of the Constitution's framing—the political, social, and economic conditions of an earlier age—while discarding one of the most important principles upon which it was framed—adaptability to changing times.

That is not to say there are not significant Constitutional principles. But those principles must be viewed in accordance with the needs and demands of the current generation. For example, the member of Congress mentioned above was not supporting principles of limited government no matter what the common consent. Rather, he was advocating the principles expressed through the Constitution as viewed by most 20th century Americans. For example, through that interpretation of the Constitution, the rights of minorities could be safeguarded. These provisions guarantee his right to express opinions in opposition to those of the government, his right to run for political office, and even his right to dress differently.

The Consequences of "Pickling" the Constitution

"Pickling" the Constitution requires Americans to revert to a "horse-and-buggy" age the framers knew but that we have long since abandoned. That was an age far different from our own—economically, socially, and politically. Preserving the framers' world view would return us to that age.

Economically, the nation would revert to a laissez-faire approach to economic activity, regional versus national or global economic markets, and a fractured economic regulatory structure (adopted on a state-by-state basis solely) that would harm the expansion of American business in an era of increasing global economic competition. If we seek to undo government's regulatory role over business, then we return to an age of "consumer beware" when consumer protection was a dream and worker safety standards were nonexistent.

Socially, preserving a pinched view of the Constitution's applicability to the changing needs of our day would reverse gains in racial relations, recognition of minorities, and the political and economic gains of women.

Without the broadened view of the Constitution advocated by the Supreme Court during the past 70 years in the areas of civil rights and civil liberties, our social fabric would be unwound by continued racial strife and minority struggles for a political voice. Civil rights legislation in the last 40 years has benefitted from interpreting the Constitution to incorporate racial and ethnic groups excluded in the framers' day.

Not until the early 1920s were First Amendment guarantees applied to the states. The First Amendment says nothing about states guaranteeing individual rights. Only with an expansive interpretation of the Constitution that limits state governments' powers to curtail our freedoms have the rights of Americans been made more secure in the areas of free exercise of religion, freedom of speech, and a free press.

Likewise, much of the protection for religious freedom in the United States has emerged in this century. For example, if the First Amendment's religious establishment clause were not applied to the states, the rise of the LDS Church would have been far more problematic. In the framers' day, majority denominations received state sanction, and the persecution of religious minorities was common. Returning to that earlier era of restricting the First Amendment only to the national government would allow greater state control over religious life.

And the political system as we know it would be fundamentally altered. Over the past 200 years our nation's political system has expanded the right of political participation to include previously excluded groups. The framers drew up a document that in practical terms restricted mass participation to those individuals possessing the education and property stake supposedly requisite for intelligent policy choices.

Thankfully, over 200 years we have decidedly rejected that restrictive view of a democratic society. Increasingly, although not without struggle, we have extended the suffrage to those directly affected by policy decisions. These include the propertyless, African Americans, Native Americans, and women. Whereas in the framers' time, the majority of those directly affected by policy decisions suffered exclusion from policy decisions, today they possess political power.

ADAPTATION—A CARDINAL CONSTITUTIONAL PRINCIPLE

The principles of the Constitution, not the context of its founding, should be preserved. The context of its founding includes the biases of the framers that most Americans have now rejected. Although some of the best educated and most enlightened men of their time, most of the framers reflected the prejudices of their age. Some strongly advocated the continuance of slavery. All seemingly rejected a political role for women. Most viewed with suspicion the ability of the common people to make rational decisions.

But wisely, the framers acknowledged that change would be necessary for their handiwork to endure beyond their own generation. Two aspects of the Constitution provided the vehicle for future change.

One is the amendment process inserted in the Constitution itself. With its two-thirds majority requirement in Congress and three-fourths approval of the states, the amending provision hardly facilitated rapid change. The addition of 17 amendments beyond the Bill of Rights in over 200 years is mute witness to that fact. But the framers sought to assure that those alterations actually appended to the document were those certain to stand the test of time. With one exception (alcohol prohibition), they have succeeded.

The other is the vague nature of the wording of the Constitution. Many of the powers and relationships of our founding document are ill-defined and offer little guidance for the future.

A fitting example is the military power of the president. In recent years the Congress has struggled to determine the appropriate balance of power over war-making between the president and the Congress in a nuclear age. The Constitution itself has been of little assistance.

However, that vagueness has been one of the Constitution's great blessings. Rather than tie the hands of future generations, the framers left a document of extraordinary flexibility.

Under this same document, the United States has emerged from a third-rate world power with limited global influence to the sole superpower with greater influence on international, political, and economic relations than any other single nation.

Also under this same document, most 19th-century presidents could interpret narrowly the powers of the presidency while most 20th-century presidents have employed a broad interpretation to meet public demands for more presidential leadership in public policy.

One of the most endearing, and enduring, qualities of the Constitution is its ability to sustain varying government policies and even ideologies under its umbrella. Many similar written documents of other systems have been too time bound—reflecting too closely the particular idiosyncracies of an age.

Ours is a living Constitution because the framers inserted flexibility of interpretation—adaptability for the future—as a cardinal element. They could not have predicted how social trends would have altered the nation as they knew it. Successive waves of immigrants, the upending of existing social class structures inherited from the British, and the demands for participation by those previously excluded have tested our political system. The greatest strain was a civil war that pitted citizens against one another over slavery and regional self determination—the problems the framers were incapable of resolving.

They also could not have imagined the technological innovations of telephones, telegraphs, and television. Satellite, cable, and information superhighways would have been impossible to comprehend, much less foretell.

But to have left a legacy of adaptability was worth far more to us than any specific provisions of power relationships doomed to rapid obsolescence. The framers did not bind future generations to more than abstract principles, which meant we were not bound to reject their work in order to make government work in our day.

A More Perfect Constitution

The Constitution in its original form was not a perfect document. Nor is it one today. Nor will it ever be because those of us who apply it are still attempting to form that "more perfect union" of which the framers dreamed.

Periodically, we need to review the Constitution's provisions to determine if they are appropriate for our age. For example, the framers sought to create an institution that would have the effect of checking public passions. George Washington told Thomas Jefferson that the relationship of the Senate to legislation was like that of a saucer to coffee in a cup, i.e., to cool it.[2]

But taken from another perspective, large segments of the American public have paid a heavy price for this strategy. This has occurred because the requirement of statewide election has restricted the policy role of minorities. Through American history, most candidates from racial and ethnic minorities simply could not win statewide elections. For example, while African Americans constitute 12 percent of the population, only a single member of the Senate today is from that racial group. With the exception of the brief period of Reconstruction following the Civil War, only two African Americans have served in the US Senate during over 200 years of American history. Not until 1992 was a Native American elected to the Senate. Hispanics, Italian Americans, and Asian Americans similarly have been under-represented in the Senate.

This may seem like a minor problem for Latter-day Saints since we have not experienced it, although we did come close. When Utah became a state in 1896, Latter-day Saints were highly over represented in the United States Senate in comparison with the percent of LDS Church members in the population. Today, Latter-day Saints are still somewhat over represented in the Senate. LDS Church population as a percentage of the United States' population has been less than 2 percent, while Utah's senators, constituting 2 percent of the Senate membership, have almost always been members of the LDS Church.

However, if Utah Territory had been merged into several neighboring states, as had been originally suggested by opponents of the LDS Church to dilute its political power, the result would have been long-term minority status. Until the Church acquired widespread social acceptance, the chances of winning statewide elections would have been remote.

Perhaps the Constitution need not be amended to correct this under representation since there is evidence in recent years of public acceptance of racial, ethnic, and religious minority candidates as statewide elected officials. But over our 200-year history, this acceptance has come only of late.

The Constitution says nothing about how state legislative districts are to be drawn. That remained a state responsibility. But gross disparities between districts within states began to arise, creating inequities in the value of an individual's vote in different parts of the same state. Powerful rural interests in some state legislatures were unwilling to dilute their own political control by readjusting urban districts to reflect population growth. It took two Supreme Court decisions in the early 1960s to assure equal power, called "one man, one vote," for all voters.[3]

I do not believe the framers necessarily intended for minorities to be excluded from elective office forever. Nor do I believe the framers envisioned the state legislatures creating unequal voting districts. However, as the nation became more diverse and African Americans and Native Americans were accorded full rights of citizenship, and as the nation's cities gained population, that was the effect of some of the framers' choices. The changes in our social and political landscape require us periodically to look anew at the Constitution that governs our land. We cannot be bound to the framers' worldview, however idyllic it may seem. They did not face the problems we do today, and since we can only speculate on how they would have handled them, resorting to a debate over their intentions seems fruitless.

The framers could not have envisioned all possible problems. But they made provision for subsequent change by amendment or, more commonly, by new interpretation.

Preserving the Constitution means cherishing what was the most salient original intent of the framers—that future generations adjust the document to their own needs rather than attempting to retrogress to an earlier bygone era. Retired Supreme Court Justice William Brennan once remarked that "the genius of the Constitution rests not in any static meaning it might have in a world that is dead and gone, but in the adaptability of its great principles to cope with current problems and current needs."[4]

Rather than wanting us to copy their 18th-century prejudices, the framers would probably be most pleased if we adopted their innovativeness, creativity, and pragmatism in addressing the problems of our own day. As they devised a government fit for a nation of sparse population, much land, little government role, and low technology, so we must frame a government for a nation with a rapidly expanding population, greater human interaction, significant government role socially and economically, and high technology. Moreover, they dwelt in a world where the United States was a third-rate military power and a minor player in world politics. We face the reality of the United States as the global superpower, with a military and economic role in the world far surpassing any other single nation.

Our task is far more complex than theirs. As these challenges have beset us as a people, each succeeding generation has become framers of the Constitution in a new era. It is the task of our generation to frame the

Constitution for our age and needs. Only by becoming framer-like—incorporating their boldness and energy—can we continue to preserve the Constitution for the 21st century.

RICHARD DAVIS, *an associate professor of political science at BYU, received a BA in political science and an MA in communications at BYU. He then received another MA in political science and a PhD at Syracuse University. He primarily teaches classes in American politics and media and politics. Much of his research focuses on the effects of the Internet and the media on politics, on which he has published books titled* New Media in American Politics *and* The Web of Politics: the Internet and American Political Power.

Notes

1. Richard Allan Baker, *The Senate of the United States: A Bicentennial History* (Malabar, Fla.: Robert E. Krieger Publishing Co., 1988), 21.
2. Quoted in Richard F. Fenno, Jr., *The United States Senate: A Bicameral Perspective* (Washington: American Enterprise Institute, 1982), 5.
3. See *Baker v. Carr*, 396 US 186 (1962) and *Wesberry v. Sanders*, 376 US 1 (1964)
4. Speech at Georgetown University, Oct. 12, 1985.

Questions and Activity

1. What are the implications of the play on words in the title "Preserving or 'Pickling' the Constitution"?
2. How does Davis's statement that the congressman with a beard and long hair does not fit the stereotype of a lover of the constitution relate to Mangum's "First Impressions of the Nurse and Nursing Care"?
3. What does Davis mean when he says, "They resolved many of their disputes by parsing their words"?
4. Interpretation plays a large part in our understanding of the Constitution. How is this an advantage and a disadvantage?
5. As a class, consider amendments that you would like to see in the Constitution (including removing existing passages). Write your amendments in a way that preserves the Constitutional principles outlined in this essay and then write a justification for your amendment.

Wealth and Poverty

RICHARD E. JOHNSON

In "Wealth and Poverty" (first printed in BYU Today) Richard Johnson unabashedly makes a moral argument, indicting materialistic excess in the face of desperate want. Ultimately the article seeks to instill a heightened sensitivity to economic injustice by creating a moral obligation in its audience. In the process, Johnson challenges many narrow-minded and naive attitudes frequently expressed by his students.

I regularly teach a course at BYU on Current Social Problems. As students in the class become exposed to the extent and seriousness of problems facing our nation today, many conclude that the Millennium must be just around the corner because America seems to be plagued by unprecedented evil.

I am troubled by several aspects of their reasoning. First, it seems rather narrow-minded for American students to evaluate the state of humankind and the fate of the planet almost solely on the basis of America's social problems. Circumstances in the rest of the world just might also play a role in the timing of the Millennium. Second, the criteria used to judge the "badness" of American society strike me as rather limited. Almost every indictment I hear of the nation's moral climate is based on observations about sex, drugs, street crime, and/or violence. I wonder why wealth and poverty almost never come to mind in evaluations of human societies. Finally, the view that "everything must be worse here and now" rings of parochialism and historical ignorance.

Judging the relative seriousness of social problems or the extent of sin across time and place is difficult if not impossible. That is not my purpose here. Nevertheless, it seems safe to conclude that the overall pattern of "always worse" almost never applies (compare Hunter, 1993). Scriptures and secular history alike abound with awful accounts of massive brutality, perversion, suffering, and indifference. I believe modern America faces serious social and moral problems. However, I seriously question the notion that unprecedented evils especially in the forms of sex, drugs, street crime, and violence is a documented fact.

I claim no special right or ability to judge the moral condition of modern America, but I believe that moral self-assessment is an obligation that is vital to the quality of life of any individual or group. We should all benefit from reflecting on the underlying values and morality of all social systems to which we belong. Surely, we will not all reach the same conclusions. We will probably not even begin with the same definitions or premises. I freely admit to applying a very personal and subjective "moral measuring rod" to American society, one that is based on LDS scriptures and my interpretation of their meaning. I know I cannot be objective, and I know I may be wrong. In many ways, I hope I am wrong.

It seems to me that if we are serious about contemplating the moral state of contemporary American society, we must begin by broadening or revising the usual measures of morality. It is possible that the traditional sins of sex, drugs, crime, and violence may not even be the most appropriate markers as we search for signs of "unprecedented evil." While such behaviors are certainly proscribed in the scriptures, the most powerful and consistent scriptural warnings given to those who live in the "last days" (particularly as found in the Book of Mormon) center around a single set of interwoven evils—the sins of materialism, consumerism, worldly vanity or pride, and socioeconomic inequality. These traits and conditions are unequivocally condenmed throughout LDS scriptures. Moreover, they are generally described as the root from which the more "traditional sins" take nourishment, and as the ultimate cause of both personal and social destruction. (See, for example, as a beginning list: 1 Nephi 22:23; 2 Nephi 9:30,51, 26:20,31, 28:12–13; Jacob 2:13–19,21; Mosiah 4:16–18, 21–23; Alma 1:26–32, 4:6–15, 5:53–56, 16:15–16,21, 31:24–30, 34:28–29,40, 60:32; Helaman 3:33–36, 4:11–12, 6:17, 7:20–21, 12:1–3, 13:21–22, 27–28; 3 Nephi 6:10–15, 24:5, 26:19; 4 Nephi 1:3,24–26,43; Mormon 8:35-41; Doctrine and Covenants 6:7, 11:7, 38:26, 49:19–20, 52:40, 56:16–19, 59:17–20, 70:14, 78: 5–6, 82:17–19, 104:14–18, 105:3, 117:4, 121:34–37; Moses 7:18; Matthew 6:24, 19:21–24, 25:31–46; Mark 4:19, 10:21–25, 12:38–44; Luke 1:53, 3:10–13, 6:20, 24, 8:14, 12:15–21, 14:11–13, 16:13–15, 19-31, 18:22–25, 21:1–4; Acts 2:44–45, 4:32–35; 2 Corinthians 8:13–15; Galatians 2:10; 1 Timothy 3:3-8, 6:5-10, 17–19; 2 Timothy 3:1–2; Titus 1:7; James 1:27, 2:1–9, 5:1–6; 1 John 2:15–17, 3:17.)

In view of these repeated scriptural pronouncements, it seems that the most appropriate measure of any group's moral climate may be the extent to which that group is characterized by selfish, prideful striving for the "lifestyles of the rich and famous." The consequences of that individualistic and hedonistic materialism—inequality, suffering, and neglect—then become additional indicators of evil in their own right. I choose these as my measures of sinfulness here. Judging from the reactions of my students (who are typically "active LDS" from relatively comfortable socioeconomic backgrounds), these are not commonly employed measures of immorality or evil. Some students simply cannot believe that any legal and socially acceptable behaviors may in truth be as immoral as are many traditionally-condemned crimes. Others are shocked by the suggestion that morality could have anything to do with either the seeking or obtaining of a high standard of living, or with the presence of grossly unequal standards of living. Still others agree that a "high" standard of material comfort in the midst of poverty may in fact be a form of selfishness or oppression, but then are usually quick to define "high" as well above their own level.

These responses are not at all surprising. "Getting rich" and "getting ahead" (of others) have been ingrained in most Americans' minds not merely as morally neutral cultural goals, but as highly valued and righteous pursuits. It is certainly understandable that mainstream American Mormons and typical BYU students are more inclined to condemn the behavior of "traditional sinners" (thieves, addicts, prostitutes, etc.) than to condemn the behavior of materialistic consumers of legal goods obtained by legal means. After all, traditional sinners are clearly self-indulgent, satisfying their whims and appetites for comfort or pleasure through sexual, chemical, or violent means. And innocent others clearly suffer because of their self-indulgence.

We law-abiding high-living consumers, on the other hand, satisfy our self-indulgent whims and appetites for comfort or pleasure through clearly superior means—we buy ever-larger houses and fill them with ever-more goodies. "And where is the harm in that?" we ask, not seeking or wanting an answer. We deny the obvious truth that there is always a more Christian use for money that is spent self-indulgently. We even have the audacity to tell ourselves and others that we "earn" or "deserve" the goodies that give us comfort and pleasure. We seem to have little difficulty divorcing wealth, materialism, and self-indulgent consumption from serious contemplation of Christian morality.

I am frankly confused and troubled by the connection between morality and economic inequality that I see in our holy writings. I often fear, for example, that my "modest" American lifestyle may represent a sinfully "high" level of comfort and convenience, given what I know about inequality and destitution in America and throughout the world. I fear too that our traditional definitions of morality—our divisions of the world into the "good guys" and the "bad guys"—are based on convenience and rationalization as much as upon empirical reality or revealed truth.

Whether or not materialism, poverty, and inequality are the best measures of a society's level of immorality, the fact is that these conditions are flourishing in America today. In particular, there is firm empirical evidence of two important trends. First, the distribution of income and wealth in America is growing more unequal. Second, increasing numbers of American children are growing up in poverty and neglect.

While various studies define terms differently and employ a variety of measures of income, it is safe to conclude that since 1980 in America, the rich are getting richer and the poor are getting poorer (Nasar, 1992c; Phillips, 1990; Barlett and Steele, 1992; Dentzer, 1994). The Census Bureau reports that the richest one-fifth of American households received almost twelve times the income of the same number of the poorest households in 1990 (46.6 percent versus 3.9 percent). The comparable rich-to-poor-fifths ratio was 10.5 in 1980 (44.1 percent versus 4.2 percent) (U.S. Bureau of the Census, 1991). By yet another measure, the average real income (adjusted for inflation) of the bottom fifth of American workers declined 10 percent from 1980 to 1990, while the real income of the top one percent jumped 122 percent during the same period (reported in Coleman and Cressey, 1993:142).

This growing income inequality is occurring fastest among the very rich and the very poor, and it has not been slowed by the structure of taxation. For example, the after-tax real income (adjusted for inflation) of the bottom one-tenth of American families dropped from $3528 to $3157 (in 1987 dollars) between 1977 and 1988. The after-tax real income of the top one-tenth rose from $174,498 to $303,900 during that same period. In other words, the poor lost 11 percent of their spendable income while the wealthy increased theirs by 74 percent (Zuckerman, 1988; see also Nasar, 1992a).

As troubling as they may be, statistics on income inequality hide two even more disturbing truths. First, abstract numbers fail to capture the human misery that poverty often entails. Income inequality represents more than mere differences in the sizes of the piles of "goodies" that families can afford. For millions of families at the bottom of the distribution—even in affluent America—we are talking about malnutrition, little or no access to health care or education, homelessness, and bleak and utter hopelessness.

Income statistics also mask that fact that wealth—total assets, genuine access to goods and services—is much more unequally distributed than is annual income. While the top one-fifth of U.S. households receive a bit over 45% of the income each year, the top one-tenth own about 70% of the wealth (Institute for Social Research, 1987:3-5). Moreover, the proportion of the total wealth controlled by the top one half of one percent (the very rich) increased by 38% from the 1960s to the 1980s (Joint Economic Committee of the United States Congress, 1986). Meanwhile, the bottom 20 percent of the population owned -0.4 percent (more debts than assets) of the wealth in the 1980s (Kerbo, 1991:40).

The "very rich" top one-half of one percent fared even better during the 1980s. In a report released by the Economic Policy Institute, ecnnomist Edward Wolff shows that their average net wealth increased from $8.5 million in 1983 to $10.7 million in 1989, a rise of 26 percent over six years. Put another way, the top one-half of one percent accumulated 55 percent of all the increase in net wealth in the United States between 1983 and 1989. The rest of the increase went to those almost as wealthy. The net wealth of the bottom 80 percent of Americans, by contrast, went down by an average of 6 percent over the same period. Wolff concludes that by 1989, the concentration of American wealth was more extreme than at any time since 1929 (Wolff, 1992; see also U.S. News and World Report, 1992; Wolff, 1993). And there is no indication that this trend is reversing in the 1990s (Dentzer, 1994).

While the wealthy control ever-larger shares of the "American pie," poverty and homelessness among our children are becoming increasingly widespread. Official poverty in the United States is measured in a rather arbitrary manner, and its validity has been debated by experts since its inception around 1960. Any poverty statistics are therefore subject to varied interpretations, but this is not the place to discuss measurement details. I will simply use the official figures, noting that the poverty line has been adjusted over the years to supposedly reflect changes in the cost of living, but that most experts (including the developer of the original poverty line) believe that more accurate adjustments would show even more persons in poverty today compared to the past (Orshansky, 1993; Schwarz and Volgy, 1992).

The percent of Americans in poverty declined substantially during the 1960s, remained stable through most of the 1970s, then jumped significantly during the recession years of the early 1980s. For the past decade, the rate has hovered around 13 to 14 percent poor, rising to 14.5 in 1992. In raw numbers, there were 37 million officially poor Americans of all ages in 1992 (1992 poverty statistics from the US Bureau of the Census are summarized in a non-technical fashion in Newsweek, 1993:44). Meanwhile, the poverty rate among America's children has consistently increased. The percent of children (defined as under age 18) in poverty rose from 15 percent in 1970 to 18 percent in 1980 to 22 percent in 1992—almost one of every four. In raw numbers, about 14 million of America's children are now living in poverty, compared to about 11 million in 1980 (U.S. Bureau of the Ceusus, 1993: 469; Newsweek, 1994: 44).

Since 1980, while the wealthy have succeeded in vastly increasing their already abundant resources, more and more children in this country have fallen into or been born into poverty. Ironically, many disadvantaged infants escape tbe struggle. America's infant mortality rate is higher than virtually every other modern industrialized nation, primarily because of very high death rates among infants born to poor families (Haub and Yanagishita, 1991; National Center for Health Statistics, 1992).

Most poor infants, of course, grow to become poor children. Tbey are often also hungry and sick children, even in affluent America. A study released by the Food Research and Action Center in 1994, for example, estimated that 5.5 million American children are malnourished (reported in Shapiro et al., 1994:59). As many as 30 million Americans of all ages suffer chronic hunger (Sivard, 1991:48). Even more—between 35 and 40 million—have no public or private medical insurance coverage, including 15 percent of all American children (US Bureau of the Census, 1993: 116). While rates of immunization for childhood diseases in the United States are lower than those in most industrial nations, the cost of giving a child all of the recommended immunizations rose more than 1000 percent from 1977 to 1992 (Roberts, 1994; Rosenthal, 1993).

Education is presumed by many to be a readily available means of escape from poverty, but poverty in America is highly correlated with adult illiteracy and lack of education, as well as severely reduced educational opportunities for children (Kozol, 1985, 1991; Manski, 1992). And for homeless children, of course, adequate education is virtually impossible.

Although almost everyone agrees that the number of homeless Americans has increased over the past decade, there is wide disagreement over the precise meaning or extent of homelessness. Reasonable estimates range from well under one million to well over three million (Coleman and Cressey, 1993:146–147). The profile of the homeless has changed along with their numbers. The "traditional homeless" (alcoholics, addicts, traumatized war veterans, unemployables) are being joined in increasing numbers by the "new homeless"—single mothers with children, working poor, throwaway teenagers, and deinstitutionalized mental patients. Probably between one-fourth and one-third of today's homeless are in family units. And children may comprise more than 15 percent of all homeless Americans (Blau, 1992; Wright, 1988). Millions of other poor and not-so-poor families are just "one bad day" from homelessness. That bad day could be marked by a fire, the death of a breadwinner, a divorce, an illness or accident, or the closing of a factory.

In sum, rising numbers of Americans, millions of them children, suffer needless death or face lives of poverty, hunger, inadequate education and health care, and homelessness. All of this occurs in the midst of wealth almost unimaginable to the vast majority of the planet's past or present inhabitants; all of this occurs while the rich get richer. How can these circumstances not be considered a moral indictment? How can Americans face these facts without a sense of shame?

Why have these trends occurred? At the risk of tremendous oversimplification, let me offer a "short list" of seven possible contributing factors. Each may or may not have anything to do with the moral quality of American society.

(1) There has been a prolonged and general decline in America's "smokestack industries." Basic manufacturing plants, which often paid relatively high union wages for unskilled or semi-skilled labor, have been closing in the face of increased international competition and a global transition into hi-tech industries. Almost all markets are now worldwide. Operations in other countries benefit from cheaper labor and more recently built—and therefore more modern and efficient—facilities. Indeed, most of America's urban "underclass" areas today were once healthy communities sustained by factories which are now closed and have not been replaced. Displaced American workers are often untrained for newer hi-tech jobs, which are located in different areas and do not pay well even when they are obtained (Reich, 1987, Wilson, 1987).

(2) Within American industry, conditions have allowed salaries and wages to become increasingly unequal. Simply put, the bargaining position of American workers has been eroded by the availability of cheap foreign labor, the increasing availability of American female labor, and the failure of labor unions to gain a strong foothold in newer, hi-tech industries. Unions (or non-union workers) rarely succeed in obtaining higher wages when others will do the same work for less. Nowadays, those "others" include desperate workers all over the world. Successful labor movements also require strong feelings of discontent among workers. Meanwhile, discontent has been diffused in America in part through a tremendous increase in tim number of dual-income families. A single low income, which would be very aggravating if it were the sole means of family support, does not seem so bad when pooled with another low income.

Corporate leaders in the United States are not inclined to share the wealth. Given the American value of getting all you can for yourself, it should be no surprise that the top executives of U.S. corporations often make more than one hundred times the income of their factory workers. The ratio between chief executive and factory worker, which averaged 93 to 1 in one American study in 1988 (up from 29 to 1 in 1979 and 12 to 1 in 1960), is many times lower in many very successful capitalist countries (Phillips, 1990; Reicb, 1991). More recent news is no more encouraging. "From 1989 through mid-1993, earnings fell for most American workers, yet the drop was sharpest for those at the lower end of the income scale.

New surveys show that the average corporate CEO earns 149 times the pay of the average factory worker, while nearly 18 percent of full-time workers don't make enough to keep a family of four out of poverty" (Dentzer 1994:53).

(3) There has been a slowing or stagnation in the growth of available wealth relative to the size of the population in America. An ever-growing economic pie could be divided very unevenly without anyone being left with too small a piece to subsist. But an increasingly unequal division of a finite pie must eventually leave some with only crumbs. Real median household income (controlling for the effects of inflation) doubled from 1950 to the early 1970s in the United States, but has fluctuated around the same level for the past two decades (Gill et al., 1992:428). Real average weekly earnings increased over 60 percent from 1950 to the early 1970s, but declined almost 20 percent from the early 1970s to 1990 (Gill et al., 1992:428). While median income for female workers did rise about 40 percent from 1970 to 1990 (due to the women's movement and more women devoting more of their energies to employment outside of the home), real median income for male workers declined slightly over the same period (US Bureau of the Census, 1993:466). The net result is that the only type of American household that has been able to continue advancing economically over the past twenty years is the intact, two-worker household (U.S. Bureau of the Census, 1993:465). A return to an era of ever-increasing living standards seems neither likely nor ecologically viable. Current national and world economic conditions suggest that there is only one way to reasonably expect those who now receive only crumbs from the American pie to be able to "scrape up enough" for a home, food, education, and health care—others must take a smaller share.

(4) Our nation has witnessed a substantial increase in some population categories that have always been at high risk of being poor. One of the fastest growing categories of the poor is members of single-mother families. Members of single-mother families have always been at higher-than-average risk of poverty, but the sheer number of single-mother families has grown dramatically in recent years, due primarily to increases in divorce and out-of-wedlock births. In 1970, 11 percent of American children lived with a mother and no father. By 1991, the figure had risen to 23 percent (U.S. Bureau of the Census, 1992:55). While the poverty rate for female-headed families has not changed much, such families comprised 23 percent of all poor families in 1959 and 53 percent of all poor families in 1990 (Sullivan and Thompson, 1994:171).

Another category of Americans which has always been disproportionately poor is members of racial and ethnic minority groups, and some of those groups have also increased in size substantially over the past few decades, one observer noted in 1988, for example, that "there are now 3.3 million more Americans below the poverty line than in 1980 . . . nearly 2 million are Hispanic. The number of Hispanics is increasing five times faster than the total population; half comes from migration" (Samuelson, 1988:49).

(5) Sexism and racism persist in America and prevent members of high risk groups (like female-headed families and racial and ethnic minorities) from escaping or avoiding poverty at the same rate that others do. Gender, race, and ethnicity would not be important factors in predicting poverty rates in a society free from prejudice and discrimination. In spite of what many of my fellow white males seem to believe, research continues to show that equally qualified minorities and women are not afforded the same opportunities for employment and income that white males are afforded. Progress toward equal socioeconomic opportunity remains slow in numerous areas, particularly for certain racial and ethnic groups. By every measure of destitution and disadvantage mentioned earlier (poverty, infant mortality, hunger, inadequate education, and inadequate health care), blacks, Hispanics, and Native Americans continue to experience rates much higher than—and usually more than double—rates for whites (see Coleman and Cressey, 1993: chapters 6,7,10; Eitzen and Baca Zinn, 1994: chapters 2, 6, 7, 8; Sullivan and Thompson, 1994: chapters 5, 6, 7).

(6) The unavailability of affordable child care or parental leave programs makes employment almost impossible for poor single mothers and very difficult for poor two-parent families. Among all industrial nations in the world, the United States ranks at or near the bottom in efforts to accommodate the needs of working parents. It is difficult to find another society that penalizes its members economically for having children as much as ours does, or that so neglects the needs of children of working parents (Smolowe, 1992; Shanker, 1990; Baca Zinn and Eitzen, 1993: 178-179; Lubeck and Garrett, 1988; Creighton, 1993).

(7) Finally, and I believe most relevant to the moral questions that guide this analysis, public attitudes and policies regarding the poor have contributed immeasurably to recent increases in inequality and deprivation. Frankly, I am continually amazed at the strength and harshness of the anti-poor attitudes exhibited by some of my students, and at their stubborn unwillingness to reconsider their stereotypes on the basis of clear contradictory evidence. Anti-poor attitudes come in a wide variety of hues, but the predominant theme is that the poor have determined their own lot in life because they are lazy, stupid, and/or satisfied with the way they live—that they "deserve" to be poor.

From a Christian point of view, neglect of the poor appears to be inexcusable for any reason. From an empirical perspective, there is no evidence that the poor as a group are any more "deserving" of their plight than is anyone else. Numerous studies show that the poor as a group have the same goals, desires, work ethic, and work habits of the non-poor as a group. The Institute for Social Research at the University of Michigan has summarized findings relative to this matter over the years in their ISR Newsletter publication. A sampling of conclusions from that source includes the following: Accumulation of wealth "is strongly influenced by chance: having the right parents or the right genes or being in the right place at the right time." Hard work and frugality "are as easily found among the poor as among the rich" (1987:4). "We found no significant effects of motives on families' economic outcomes" (1985:3). "The temporarily poor are quite similar to the population as a whole. There appears to be virtually no attribute that distinguishes them from the rest of society. Few of us are completely immune to such misfortunes as personal illness, adverse local or national economic conditions, the death of a spouse, or the breakup of a marriage. . . . On the other hand, the 2 percent who were persistently poor differ in many demographic characteristics from both the temporarily poor and the population at large, although there is little evidence that personality traits such as motivation, orientation toward the future, and sense of control affect the economic status of the persistently poor." Rather, the persistently poor are different in that they are "affected by severely restricted labor market opportunities" [based on their age, race, and marital statusl (1984:3–4).

In short, poor Americans are poor primarily because they were born poor, have few opportunities to escape poverty, have characteristics that are socially devalued (including race, gender, and age), or have "landed" in an unfavorable economic setting—not because they decide to be lazy. It makes just as much sense to blame more than a small fraction of current poverty on individual laziness as it does to cite laziness as the cause of the Great Depression of the 1930s. (For related data and similar conclusions, see also Garfinkel and Haveman, 1977; Nasar, 1992b; Jaynes, 1989; Ryan, 1976; Katz, 1989.)

Certainly, some poor folks should heed the traditional advice to "get a job." However, full-time jobs are often very difficult to obtain. And even if obtained, full-time employment hardly amounts to a guarantee of escape from poverty or access to adequate housing, education, or health care. A staggering 40 percent of all year-round, full-time workers in the United States earn less than it takes to lift a family of four out of poverty (Schwarz and Volgy, 1992). Moreover, approximately half of all poor Americans are too old or too young to work, and most of the rest already work or would need substantial child care assistance to make work feasible (US Bureau of the Census, 1992:15,457).

Empirical data and Christian teachings notwithstanding, it is fashionable in the United States to vilify, stigmatize, and neglect the disadvantaged and destitute. The lessons of the Great Depression and World War II—that hardships are shared by all and best overcome through common effort—have been relentlessly overwhelmed in succeeding decades by a tide of individualistic materialism and affluence. As a people, Americans seem to have become increasingly motivated by individualistic consumption over the past few decades, climaxing in its open acceptance as a way of life in the 1980s. Changes in public policies reflect this trend, as those who influence such policies have increasingly shaped them to suit their own self-interests at the expense of others. The less privileged and powerful (who may be just as uninterested in the common good but merely less able to translate their desires into results) are being left behind. A huge number of the stragglers are children, who are not only being neglected, but are being taught that taking all you can for yourself and neglecting others is an appropriate way to live.

I almost hesitate to support my claim of self-interested and neglectful public policies by mentioning specifics, as some readers will immediately lose sight of the larger purpose of this analysis and become obsessed with political and partisan issues. I know this to be true from responses to my previous writing on this topic (Johnson, 1990), but rising inequality and destitution simply cannot be understood without looking at government programs and policies.

Beginning with tax policies, political rhetoric would have us believe that the US tax structure is "progressive," taking a larger proportion of the incomes of those who have more. This is hardly the case. Describing changes that occurred in the decade from 1980 to 1990, one analyst concluded, "The overall tax burden—federal, state, and local—ceased being progressive, so rich and poor now give about the same percentage of their income to tax collectors. All uf these shifts were unprecedented in the post-World War II era" (Taylor, 1990:12). A more recent and extensive study by Barlett and Steele (1994) shows that major changes in federal income and Social Security taxes since the 1950s, and especially those enacted during the 1980s, were mostly "regressive," taking a larger share from those who already had less. The combined federal income tax and Social Security tax rate for millionaires, for example, dropped from 48% in 1953 to 27% in 1991, while the same rate for middle-income families rose from 11% to 18%. Even taking into account the slightly more progressive tax revisions of 1993, the authors conclude that the net changes over the past fifty years clearly favor the wealthy at the expense of the poor and the middle class.

The other side of the budget coin is govermnent spending, which brings us to yet another pernicious public stereotype regarding the poor. There is widespread belief, at least among my students, that public spendlug on the poor is a major government expense and a significant cause of budget deficits. Furthermore, the poor's willingness to "take something for nothing" is cited as proof of their degeneracy. Not a few students ask, "Why should I work hard just so others can receive a handout?" That is certainly a valid public policy question, and asking it should not necessarily call into question one's morality. The problem is that it is misdirected. Vastly greater sums of public money are doled out to the non-poor in "wealthfare" than to the poor via welfare. The difference is that the price of benefits to the poor includes public humiliation and loss of self-respect, while the rest of us take our handouts with clear consciences and unsullied reputations.

"Wealthfare" abounds in the United States, including direct subsidies and credit to numerous businesses and corporations, tax deductions for which only the non-poor qualify, reduced-tax forms of income available almost solely to the more affluent, non-taxed employer-paid medical insurance premiums, social security payments to the wealthy far above the amount they contributed, free medical care based on age and regardless of financial need, and many more (see Peterson, 1988).

As one example, the federal government spends more on health care for the richest 10 percent of elderly Medicare beneficiaries than it does for all job training, Head Start, and Women, Infants and Children nutrition subsidy programs for the poor combined (Waldman, 1992). An extensive and detailed analysis of data from the Congressional Budget Office by Howe and Longman (1992) reveals numerous similar comparisons. The cost to the federal government of the home-mortgage tax deduction benefit was $37 billion in 1991, of which approximately $30 billion went directly to households with incomes over $50,000 a year. Meanwhile, till housing programs for the poor totaled about $7 billion. In 1991 over $55 billion in Social Security payments went to households with incomes over $50,000 a year. "For that much money the government could have provided every American with cradle-to-grave insurance against poverty—including the one American child in twenty who lived in a household reporting a cash income during 1991 of less than $5,000" (Howe and Longman, 1992:89).

Combining all forms of tax expenditures and direct outlays, Howe and Longman calculate that in 1991 the average government benefit to households with incomes below $10,000 was $5,690, while the average benefit to households with incomes over $100,000 was $9,280 (1992:93). Overall, one half (over $400 billion) of all entitlements went to households with incomes above $30,000, and one quarter (over $200 billion) went to households with incomes over $50,000 (1992:93). Clearly, more than enough public money is being sent to individuals to eliminate poverty, which the Children's Defense Fund (1989) estimates would take about one percent of our gross national product, or $57 billion, based on 1987 figures.

Just as most of the money distributed to individuals by our government goes to the non-poor, most of the poor receive little or no assistance. "Just under half of families below the poverty line receive food stamps or AFDC, and only 36 percent get housing subsidies" (Waldman, 1992:57). "Quite simply, if the federal government wanted to flatten the nation's income distribution, it would do better to mail all its checks to random addresses. The problem is that poverty programs don't target the poor" (Howe and Longman, 1992:90).

During the 1980s virtually all government programs that benefited the poor were slashed, many by more than 50%, while Social Security and Medicare benefits, which primarily go to the non-poor, were increased. Howe and Longman point out that "From 1980 to 1991, in constant dollars, the average federal benefit received by households with incomes under $10,000 declined by seven percent.... During those same eleven years, among households with incomes over $200,000 the real value of average benefits received . . . fully doubled" (1992:9192). Waldman notes that "according to a U.S. Census Bureau study, tile portion of the [government benefits] pie going to the poor has been shrinking in the past 25 years, while the slice going to the rest of the country has grown" (1992:57).

When housing policies are examined, it should be no surprise to recall that perhaps half a million American children are sleeping on the streets or in shelters this very night. Three-fourths of the federal housing budget for the poor was cut between 1981 and 1988. Many of the remaining funds were lost to speculators and crooks through the HUD and Savings & Loan scandals. Many low-income housing projects that became infested with crack gangs were simply allowed to deteriorate during the 1980s. (See Ifill, 1990; Morganthau, 1988. Budget figures are available in US Bureau of the Census, Statistical Abstract of the United States, various years.)

More and more Americans simply have no place to go if they lose their current residence. Almost no new low-cost housing is being built privately or publicly. The number of federally subsidized units of low-income housing, for example, averaged 170,000 per year between 1976 and 1982. In 1988, only 23,000 units were built (Ifill, 1990:106). Mean-while, old low-cost housing units are being lost to commercial development, public works, gentrification, and blight at the literal rate of millions per year. Others are being priced out of the low-income housing market. By 1990, more than half of all tenants were paying rent that exceeded the federal government's definition of affordable housing (not more than 30 percent of household income). More than 25 percent of all renters paid more than half their income for rent. For decades, rent has risen substantially faster than renters' incomes (Gilderbloom, 1991).

Of course, it is even more difficult to buy a home than to merely rent housing. The net result is that the demand for low-income housing (the number of families who cannot afford more than $250—in 1988 dollars—per month for housing) exceeded the national supply of low-income units in 1987. By 2003, the gap between supply and demand will reach ten million if recent trends continue (Morganthau, 1988; see also Eitzen and Baca Zinn, 1994:139). It is not simply a matter of the poor being "choosey" about accommodations; it is increasingly becoming a matter of having no choice.

So where have these attitudes and policies brought us? Inequality and deprivation flourish. The public vilifies the poor for being lazy leeches. Tax policies are disproportionately more burdensome to the poor. Government spending withers for the needy and becomes more generous to the affluent. Our society is virtually abandoning millions of poor children, relegating them to lives of stunted physical, intellectual, emotional, and moral development. A 1994 report by the Carnegie Corporation on the state of America's children describes the situation as a "pattern of neglect" of our "most vulnerable" citizens (reported in Roberts, 1994). Our attitudes and policies have fostered the growth of a national disgrace and a human tragedy.

So what can be done? Happily—yet sadly—the resources needed to save America's poor—adults as well as children—are readily available, all at affordable cost. The price tag would amount to relatively small sacrifices of time and slight reductions in the consumption of unnecessary goods and services for the rest of us. Inaction in the face of the current situation invites moral censure on each of us individually. It also invites social self-destruction. Because of our selfish and short-sighted yearning for immediate materialistic self-indulgence, mainstream America is nurturing the growth of a sub-population within society that will have little or no ability or desire to participate in conventional social or economic life. The prospects for a productive economy in years to come are thereby reduced. The prospects for flourishing drug and crime problems are thereby increased.

Everyone's quality of life will eventually be threatened by the current neglect of our impoverished children. Responding to a joint research report by the Labor and Commerce departments issued in June of 1994, US Labor Secretary Robert B. Reich warns, "A society divided between the haves and the have-nots or the well-educated and the poorly educated cannot be a stable society over time." The report itself concludes that "A healthy society cannot long continue along the path the US is moving" and that one consequence of these trends is "a large, growing population for whom illegal activity is more attractive than legitimate work" (reported in Manegold, 1994:A10).

"Doing nothing" is justified by some on the grounds that everyone simply has what she or he has earned. That conclusion, of course, fails morally and logically. Scriptures state clearly that the obligation to assist the poor remains intact whether or not the poor are judged to be "deserving." And how can anyone reasonably view the growing millions of poor infants and children as undeserving of help, regardless of one's opinion of their parents?

Moreover, empirical studies show that when the disadvantaged—children and adults alike—are given real opportunities to succeed, the vast majority work hard and take advantage of those opportunities. Many efforts have been found to be very successful in helping members of our society escape poverty (Schorr, 1988). Programs and opportunities can be provided publicly or privately. On the private side, for example, there is the case of Mr. Eugene Lang, who lowered the high school dropout rate in his old New York City neighborhood (which had become a rundown, poor area since he left) from over 50% to about 10% by promising to fund a college education for every law-abiding, successful high school graduate (Seligmann, 1990; Lapinski, 1986). The missing ingredient in the lives of Mr. Lang's recipients was not a desire or willingness to work. It was hope. Most college students I meet have long taken for granted that college was an expectation or at least a realistic option for them. Are they—we—to be particularly admired for simply following the most reasonable path to socioeconomic success, while others "fail" because they see no realistic chance of even being allowed to step on that path?

Looking at public programs, there is no longer any reasonable dissent to the conclusion that comprehensive and well-run federal Head Start programs for poor pre-school children are a tremendous success. (And neither is there reasonable dissent to the conclusion that not all versions of Head Start are comprehensive and well-run.) Graduates of intensive Head Start programs do better in school, stay in school longer, and get in trouble less than their fellow disadvantaged non-Head Start classmates. Moreover, intensive Head Start is generally cost-effective, saving more in future unemployment, welfare, and criminal justice expenses than it costs to provide the program (Zigler and Muenchow, 1992; Schorr, 1988:192;

Lee et al., 1990; Besharov, 1992; Berrueta-Clement et al., 1984). While there appears to be a need for follow-up programs to sustain the benefits of some versions of Head Start, results are so favorable that Head Start is one program that generally receives bipartisan praise in Congress. Still, funding is inadequate to cover more than two-thirds of all eligible children.

I have absolutely no particular political agenda in mind as I cite examples of programs aimed at reducing tbe ill effects of poverty. If true Christianity prevailed in our nation, there would be neither economic disadvantage nor the need for government programs to address it. All would be taken care of through private acts of sincere charity. But economic injustice and suffering persist, and something must be done. To me, the options for action include public as well as private efforts.

Unfortunately, there is a mind set among some members of the LDS subculture that if I do not completely rule out *all* public programs as possible means to deal with poverty and inequality, I must be an evil or misguided "socialist" whose moral ponderings—the real issue here—may therefore be dismissed offhandedly. This is not the place for a long discussion of the meaning of "socialism," but I must admit that the notion that it is "socialism" and "of the devil" for citizens of a democratic nation to voluntarily address human needs through taxation and government programs strikes me as patently absurd. If that were so, perhaps we have the devil to thank for public libraries, highways, police and fire departments, and American aid to postwar Europe, to name a few. If we choose to irrationally recoil from the label "socialism," we can simply refrain from using it, as we do with reference to Social Security and Medicare, for example. And if we believe that public funding of a basic "safety net" of minimal standards of decency in health, education, shelter, and opportullity are impossible to provide in a setting of political democracy and religious freedom, we can ignore the existence of most Western European nations.

Finally, if we believe that any curtailing or criticism of free-reign capitalism somehow violates the laws of heaven, we must discard numerous sermons of early LDS prophets (many conveniently collected by Nibley, 1989a, 1989b), significantly abridge or alter both the Doctrine and Covenants and the Book of Mormon, and reject outright such "radical" and "socialist" suggestions as the following:

> But since all capitalistic systems are founded upon the institution of private property, inheritance and the profit motive, great inequalities of ownership and income inevitably result. . . . Among the more plausible suggestions offered to correct existing abuses without adversely

> affecting the productive system, is to coutinue the socialization of our service institutions through a system of progressive taxation based upon ability to pay . . . taking the bulk of their [captains of industry] profits to finance free education, free libraries, free public parks and recreation centers, unemployment insurance, old age benefits, sickness and accident insurance, and perhaps eventually free medical aid and hospital service. . . . The average family may not have much more money, if any, to spend under such a system than now. But . . . then the meagre family income can be devoted entirely to the necessities of life, plus some of the comforts now enjoyed by the higher income classes. To finance all of this, of course, will necessitate huge sums of money And it will also require a carefully worked out tax system so that every one will contribute according to his financial ability. Inheritance and estate taxes will become progressively higher, until the present system of permitting large forttunes to be passed on from generation to generation will become extinct. And incidentally, the so-called idle rich who have been living off the earnings of past generations will be no more (source to be identified below).

The above "plan" for equalizing living standards and life chances for Americans may or may not be politically or economically desirable or possible. Some economists, for example, tell me that providing such a social "safety net" of basic human rights (shelter, food, access to medical care, education) would not be an "efficient" system, that it would remove incentive for work and advancement. Their argument seems to be that the presence of suffering and deprivation is useful, because others will therefore try harder to avoid joining the sufferers. I resist accepting such a pessimistic and self-fulfilling view of humanity. Of course people will act selfishly if they are socialized in a system within which selfishness is routinely assumed and rewarded. I can, on the other hand, imagine good people acting in the best long-term interests of their community, even at immediate personal expense. I can also imagine a generous social safety net acting to increase rather than decrease entrepreneurial incentive and enterprise, by reducing the awful cost of failure that looms over prospective entrepreneurs in a "safety net-free" setting (namely, jeopardizing the health, education, and safety of one's children).

But I digress. The point here is not to recommend any particular plan (including the one quoted above), and I am not doing so. The point is simply to note that even such a seemingly radical plan as the one cited above cannot be written off as un-Christian or anti-Mormon simply because it involves taxing and spending. It is perfectly cousistent (as are countless other private and public approaches) with the gospel of Jesus Christ. Its source, it turns out, is the LDS Melchizedek Priesthood Study Guide for the year 1939, copyright by Heber J. Grant (Grant, 1938). I cite it only to reject the notion that the eternal principle of "free agency" somehow translates into an economic system of "free capitalism." They are not the same. Such an equation strikes me as terribly ironic and potentially terribly tragic. Of course we can question the wisdom of specific government programs, or in general prefer private to public efforts. Those are not basic moral issues. But when the public nature of a program is used as an excuse to do nothing or to selfishly cling to one's wealth while others suffer, wickedness has entered the picture.

I do not anticipate much repenting being called for as the result of our political party affiliations or specific policy preferences. However, I can easily imagine a hereafter in which most of the regretting, repenting, and pain experienced by contemporary middle- and upper-class "active" American Mormons is due to the sin of keeping too much for themselves while so many others have so little. I believe it to be the great unrecognized sin of our LDS subculture (myself included), if not the chief cause of problems in our nation and throughout the world (compare Benson, 1989).

To be sure, some "hoarding" of personal resources seems necessary these days, primarily because of the very fact that our society chooses not to provide even a minimal safety net for many of its members who might happen to encounter difficult circumstances. My children or grandchildren may be denied important opportunities in the future (such as shelter, education, or health) if I am too generous with my resources today. I do not know how much are we justified in keeping to meet our present or future needs, or how much are we keeping unjustifiably to simply satisfy our wants. Unfortunately, we do not seem to have given any pat dollars-and-cents answers. "Keeping versus giving" is a wrenching moral and financial dilemma with which each of us must struggle continually and individually.

I would like to believe that my material living standard is not a moral issue, as long as I behave as a "good person" in other ways. It would be sublimely comfortable aud convenient. But it is also wishful fantasy. The evidence is simply too clear that most or all the evil and suffering in our land can be traced to the hedonistic pursuit of material comforts aud pleasure, and to the tremendous socioeconomic inequality that follows. Thanks primarily to glitzy and glamorous portrayals in American advertising and entertainment, selfish values are embraced throughout our socioeconomic hierarchy. No one group has a corner on the market of greed. Though the rich (them? us?) have greater opportunity to display their selfishness, the poor who long to win the lottery and live the opulent "American dream" lifestyle portrayed in the mass media have values no nobler than the "fat cats" they both condemn and envy.

On the other hand, it is not impossible for recipients of high incomes to live modest lifestyles and use the money truly to benefit others rather than indulge themselves. However, as the scriptures repeatedly remind us, a high income represents a temptation that very few can withstand. Moreover, the definition of "modest" can easily be stretched beyond all recognition. A major point from the parable of the widow's mite seems to be that the Lord's judgment over the use of money is based not on how much we give away, but on how much we keep for ourselves.

As a nation, we may not be in the most self-serving of times, and we may even be heading into a period of reduced selfishness. (Indeed, I sometimes sense—perhaps wishfully—a bit of a "de-greeding" in the 1990s compared to the 1980s.) Whatever the short-term direction may be, I hope we have not already reached the level of individualistic materialism that jeopardizes the very foundations of a democratic society. Republican democracy, after all, requires a certain degree of public wisdom and public virtue. America was built upon the pillar of self-restraint as well as the pillar of personal freedom, on a presumption of community responsibility as well as individual responsibility. Indeed, community responsibility is the heart and soul of everyone's personal responsibility. Thomas Jefferson and James Madison warned that republican democracy could only survive in a society of relative equals in which the public good, not individual interests, remained the supreme objective (cited in Dennis, 1990:57 and in Bellah et al., 1985:30–31). Jefferson observed that if people forgot themselves "in the sole faculty of making money," the future of the republic would become bleak (in Bellah et al. 1985:31).

I do not mean to paint a hapless or hopeless portrait of America. There is much to be admired as well as questioned in our history and traditions. Still, we cannot deny the fact that most of our lifestyles are far from modest, especially by world standards. Even those of us who may feel comfortably unselfish within the context of American society must face the fact that all people everywhere are our sisters and brothers. And while our nation's present and future may be significantly troubled by these matters, problems of poverty and inequality arotmd the world make our national situation seem almost trivial by comparison. Of course, the typical American has limited political or logistical ability to ease the world's suffering. Still, it is the global scene, not just the national one, that represents a more fitting context for speculating about "unprecedented evil" or the "signs of the last days."

Whether or not we are witnessing signs of the earth's final days, we are certainly witnessing global trends and events unprecedented in world history. Hundreds of millions of people have been freed in recent years from political oppression, from the "oppression" of Nature's harshness, and from virtual isolation from the affluent and technologically advanced portions of the world. The materialistic "good life" exemplified by the American middle class, unknown to or beyond the wildest dreams of the majority of humankind for millennia, is rapidly becoming a global aspiration.

Could not the great and unprecedented evil that seems to be predicted for the last days refer to the dual evils of insatiable materialism and unspeakable inequality? While perhaps never enjoyable for its own sake, it is comparatively easy to "do without" economically under conditions of universal destitution, ignorance of alternatives, or political totalitarianism. Indeed, throughout history only a relative few have been afforded the "opportunity" to engage in selfish economic consumption and oppression. Now, for the first time ever, the test seems to be underway on a truly massive scale. There may even be more people alive today exercising substantial economic agency—facing real choices between personal luxury and Christian charity—than in all previous centuries combined. How will they handle their opportunity to engage in direct or indirect oppression, their choice to indulge or divulge? How are we handling ours?

It is no longer possible to believe or pretend that material acquisitiveness can be morally neutral. Never before has it been so clear that the earth's capacity to sustain life is limited. Never before could we expect humankind to realize that a high standard of living must be purchased at the cost of depletion of finite resources and pollution of a fragile environment. While the earth can still sustain life for all of its current inhabitants at a healthy but simple living standard, it most probably cannot sustain life for all at the wasteful and destructive living standard of middle-class America (Durning, 1990). And even if it could for now, what about the extra billions that will be added in the next few decades?

The inescapable conclusion is that when one person lives a life of luxury in a nation or a world of limited and finite resources, others are forced to have less. Many, in fact, have so much less that they will lose all brightness of hope, suffer, and die, but only after watching their loved ones suffer and die. Increasingly, the dying—and the injustice—are becoming more difficult to ignore. Modern communications systems continue to shrink the world, bringing into greater light and clearer focus the awful juxtaposition of unprecedented abundance and unprecedented suffering.

The rich have run out of excuses. What happens when the poor run out of patience? Is literal global war a necessary part of our future? If so, it is reasonable to predict that it will involve an attack by "have-not" nations on the "haves" of the world, rather than a confrontation between superpower "haves" with differing political ideologies. After all, the have-nots would have nothing to lose in a global conflagration, by definition.

We must become more willing to sacrifice and share. Whether we do so out of obedience to God, out of genuine charity, out of earthly fear, or in view of long-term economic and political self-interest, the time has come to share or face the consequences. How long can we ignore the scriptural description of socioeconomic inequality as evil? How long will we be guided by the "traditions of our fathers" instead of the Savior of humanity? How long will LDS church members join mainstream America in not only condoning, but admiring and pursuing, worldly self-aggrandizement? Might not the great lesson for the last days be that in order for peace to prevail or for Zion "with no poor among them" to be established, that there must also be no rich among them?

> Then said Jesus unto his disciples, Verily I say unto you, That a rich man shall hardly enter into the kingdom of heaven. (Matthew 19:23)

> But it is not given that one man should possess that which is above another, wherefore the world lieth in sin. (D&C 49:20)

RICHARD E. JOHNSON, *professor of sociology at BYU, received a BS in sociology from BYU and an MS and PhD from the University of Washington. He has published several articles on adolescent crime and delinquency. Students have described him as very approachable and willing to talk one-on-one with them about the issues they are concerned with.*

References

Baca Zinn, Maxine, and D. Stanley Eitzen. 1993. *Diversity in Families.* 3rd ed. New York: Harper Collins.

Barlett, Donald L., and James B. Steele. 1992. *America: What Went Wrong?* Kansas City: Andrews and McMeel.

Bellah, Robert N., Richard Madsen, William M. Sullivan, Ann Swidler, and Steven M. Tipton. 1985. *Habits of the Heart: Individualism and Commitment in American Life.* New York: Harper & Row.

Benson, Ezra Taft. 1989. "Beware of Pride." *Ensign* (May): 4–7.

Berrueta-Clement, John R., with others. 1984. *Changed Lives: The Effects of the Perry Preschool Program on Youths Through Age 19.* Ypsilanti, Michigan: High/Scope.

Besharov, Douglas J. 1992. "A New Start for Head Start." *The American Enterprise* (March/April): 52–57.

Blau, Joseph. 1992. *The Visible Poor: Homelessness in the United States.* New York: Oxford University Press.

Children's Defense Fund. 1989. *A Vision for America's Future.* Washington, DC: Children's Defense Fund.

Coleman, James William, and Donald R. Cressey. 1993. *Social Problems.* 5th ed. New York: HarperCollins.

Creighton, Linda L. 1993. "Kids Taking Care of Kids." *US News and World Report* (December 20): 26–33.

Dennis, James L. 1990. "For the Common Good: Reclaiming our Ethical Tradition." *Trial* (September): 55–62.

Dentzer, Susan. 1994. "Bridging the Bitter Incomes Divide." *US News and World Report* (May 30): 53.

Durning, Alan. 1990. "How Much is Enough?" *World Watch* (November-December): 12–19.

Garfinkel, Irwin, and Robert Haveman. 1977. *Earnings Capacity, Poverty, and Inequality.* New York: Academic Press.

Gilderbloom, John I. 1991. "Housing in America: It's Time for a New Strategy." *USA TODAY* (magazine) 120 (November):30–32.

Gill, Richard T., Nathan Glazer, and Stephan A, Thernstrom. 1992. *Our Changing Population.* Englewood Cliffs, New Jersey: Prentice Hall.

Grant, Heber J. (copyright). 1938. *Priesthood and Church Welfare: A Study Course for the Quorums of the Melchizedek Priesthood for the Year 1939.* Salt Lake City: Deseret Book.

Haub, Carl, and Machiko Yanagishita. 1991. "Infant Mortality: Who's Number One?" *Population Today* (March 19): 6.

Howe, Neil, and Phillip Longman. 1992. "The Next New Deal." *The Atlantic Monthly* (April): 88–99.

Hunter, Howard W. 1993. "An Anchor to the Souls of Men." *Ensign* (October):70–73.

Ifill, Gwen. 1990. "No Place to Call Home." In The 1990 World Book Yearbook: Annual Supplement to the World Book Encyclopedia. Chicago: Scott Fetzer Co., pp. 97–105.

Institute for Social Research. 1984. "Poverty Turnover High." *ISR Newsletter* (Winter 1983–84): 3–5. Ann Arbor: University of Michigan.

Institute for Social Research. 1985. "Economic Mobility." *ISR Newsletter* (Autumn):3. Ann Arbor: University of Michigan.

Institute for Social Research. 1987. "Wealth in America." *ISR Newsletter* (Winter 1986–87): 3–5. Ann Arbor: University of Michigan.

Jaynes, Gerald. 1989. *A Common Destiny: Blacks and American Society.* Washington, DC: National Academy Press.

Johnson, Richard E. 1990. "Socioeconomic Inequality: The Haves and the Have-nots." *BYU Today* (September):47–58.

Joint Economic Committee of the United States Congress. 1986. *Poverty, Income Distribution, the Family, and Public Policy: a Study.* Washington, DC: Government Printing Office.

Katz, Michael B. 1989. *The Undeserving Poor.* New York: Pantheon.

Kerbo, Harold R. 1991. *Social Stratification and Inequality: Class Conflict in Historical and Comparative Perspective.* 2nd ed. New York: McGraw-Hill.

Kozol, Jonathan. 1985. *Illiterate America.* Garden City, New York: Anchor Press/ Doubleday.

Kozol, Jonathan. 1991. *Savage Inequalities: Children in America's Schools.* New York: Crown.

Lapinski, Susan. 1986. "Now, They Have a Dream." *Parade Magazine* (September 7): 8, 11.

Lee, Valerie E., J. Brooks-Gunn, Elizabeth Schnur, and Fong-Ruey Liaw. 1990. "Are Head Start Effects Sustained? A Longitudinal Follow-Up Comparison of Disadvantaged Children Attending Head Start, No Preschool, and Other Preschool Programs." *Child Development* (61): 495–507.

Lubeck, Sail, and Patricia Garrett. 1988. "Child Care 2000: Policy Options for the Future." *Social Policy* (Spring): 31–37.

Manegold, Catherine S. 1994. "Study Warns of Growing Underclass of the Unskilled." *New York Times* (June 3): AI0.

Manski, Charles F. 1992. "Income and Higher Education." *Focus* (Winter 1992–1993): 14–19, Madison: University of Wisconsin.

Morganthau, Tom. 1988. "The Housing Crunch." *Newsweek* (January 4):18–20.

Nasar, Sylvia. 1992a. "The 1980s: A Very Good Time for the Very Rich." *New York Times* (March 5): A1.

Nasar, Sylvia. 1992b. "Those Born Wealthy or Poor Usually Stay So, Studies Say." *New York Times* (May 18): A1.

Nasar, Sylvia. 1992c. "The Rich Get Richer, but the Question Is by How Much." *New York Times* (July 20): C1.

National Center for Health Statistics. 1992. *Health, United States, 1991.* Hyattsville, Maryland: Public Health Service.

Newsweek. 1993. "America's Poor Showing." (October 18): 44.

Nibley, Hugh. 1989a. *Approaching Zion.* Salt Lake City, Utah: Deseret Book, and Provo, Utah: Foundation for Ancient Research and Mormon Studies.

Nibley, Hugh. 1989b. "What is Zion?: A Distant View." *Sunstone* (April): 20–32.

Orshansky, Mollie. 1993. "Measuring Poverty." *Public Welfare* (Winter): 27–28.

Peterson, Peter. 1988. "Get the Rich off the Dole." *Time* (October 31): 66–68.

Phillips, Kevin. 1990. *The Politics of Rich and Poor.* New York: Random House.

Reich, Robert B. 1987. "The Future of Work." *Harper's Magazine* (April): 26, 28, 30–31.

Reich, Robert B. 1991. *The Work of Nations: Preparing Ourselves for 21st Century Capitalism.* New York: A. A. Knopf.

Roberts, Steven B. 1994. "Neglecting Children—and Parents." *US News and World Report* (April 15): 10–11.

Rosenthal, Elisabeth. 1993. "Debate Fails to Explain Vaccine Costs." *New York Times* (March 15): A8.

Ryan, William. 1976. *Blaming the Victim.* New York: Random House.

Samuelson, Robert J. 1988. "An Economic Missile Gap." *Newsweek* (September 19): 49.

Schorr, Lisbeth B. 1988. *Within Our Reach: Breaking the Cycle of Disadvantage.* New York: Anchor Press/Doubleday.

Schwarz, John E., and Thomas J. Volgy. 1992. *The Forgotten Americans.* New York: W. W. Norton.

Seligmann, Jean. 1990. "Chance of a Lifetime." *Newsweek Special Issue,* Vol. 115, No. 27 (Summer): 68–72.

Shanker, Albert. 1990. "The Family Medical Leave Act." *New York Times* (June 24): E7.

Shapiro, Laura, with others. 1994. "How Hungry is America?" *Newsweek* (March14): 58–59.

Sivard, Ruth Leger. 1991. *World Military and Social Expenditures 1991.* Washington, DC: World Priorities.

Stoolowe, Jill. 1992. "Where Children Come First." *Time* (November 9): 58.

Sullivan, Thomas J., and Kenrick S. Thompson. 1994. *An Introduction to Social Problems.* 3rd ed. New York: Macmillan.

Taylor, Paul. 1990. "A Nicer Way of Saying 'Soak the Rich'." *The Washington Post National Weekly Edition* (February 26–March 4): 12.

US Bureau of the Census. 1991. "Money Income of Households, Families, and Persons in the United States: 1990." *Current Population Reports,* Series P-60, No. 174 (August): 6. Washington, DC: Government Printing Office.

US Bureau of the Census. 1992. *Statistical Abstract of the United States 1992.* Washington, DC: Government Printing Office.

US Bureau of the Census. 1993. Statistical Abstract of the United States 1993. Washington, DC: Government Printing Office.

US News and World Report. 1992. "The Rich are Still Getting Richer." (November 9): 16.

Waldman, Steven. 1992. "Benefits 'R' Us." *Newsweek* (August 11): 56–58.

Wilson, William Julius. 1987. *The Truly Disadvantaged: The Inner City, the Underclass, and Public Policy.* Chicago: University of Chicago Press.

Wolff, Edward. 1992. *The Rich Get Increasingly Richer.* Washington, DC: Economic Policy Institute.

Wolff, Edward. 1993. *Poverty and Prosperity in the USA in the Late Twentieth Century.* New York: St. Martin's Press.

Wright, James D. 1988. "The Worthy and Unworthy Homeless." *Society* (July–August): 64–69.

Zigler, Edward, aud Susan Muenchow. 1992. *Head Start: The Inside Story of America's Most Successful Educational Experiment.* New York: Basic Books.

Zuckerman, Mortimer B. 1988. "Dreams, Myths and Reality." *US News and World Report* (July 25): 68.

Questions

1. Does capitalism inevitably lead to economic inequality? What changes could be made to our current system to alleviate inequality? Is welfare the only answer? Is equality always good?
2. Are the dangers of sustained economic inequality only moral? How does Johnson appeal to morality as well as self-interest?
3. Are economic rights as important as political rights? Can the two be reasonably separated? Does the apparent futility of achieving ideal economic justice remove a personal responsibility to work towards it?
4. Do the poor "deserve" the position they're in? Do you "deserve" the position you're in? How much of our advantages, opportunities, and luxuries are a direct result of our personal efforts?
5. How does Johnson tailor his argument to his audience? Is this manipulative? How well does Johnson achieve his purposes? Do you feel any differently about poverty, morality, materialism, socialism, etc.?

Canada–US Economic Relations: The Role of the Provinces and the States

EARL H. FRY

Earl H. Fry's initial interest in Canadian studies came because he married a Canadian. His interest expanded as he worked at British Columbia University and taught Canadian economic issues. While teaching, Fry says he has been surprised at students' (and Americans') ignorance of the sizeable trade that occurs between Canada and the United States. When he asks students who America's biggest trading partner is, they generally say Japan, when in reality it's Canada. "In fact," says Fry, "[Japan]'s not even close." In this article, first published in Business in the Contemporary World *in 1990 (prior to the passage of the North American Free Trade Agreement), Fry looks at what happens when subnational governments—particularly those of states and provinces—become involved in international trade. Fry argues that in this day of increasing international trade, provincial and state governments need to work with Ottowa and Washington, DC, to remove barriers such as tariffs, subsidies, and procurement and investment restrictions that will put North America at a disadvantage in the global economy.*

The United States and Canada are, respectively, the world's largest and eighth largest economies, with a combined gross national product (GNP) of approximately $6 trillion in 1990. They trade more with each other than with any other nation, with three-quarters of Canadian exports destined for US markets and one-fifth of American exports for Canadian markets. They also rank as the world's number one and number two host nations for foreign direct investment, and are the favorite foreign investment sites for their respective business communities.[1]

If the more than $200 billion in annual trans-border trade in goods and services is to continue to grow, the Canada–US Free Trade Agreement (FTA) must be faithfully implemented by the end of the 1990s and workable solutions found to such nagging problems as trade-distorting subsidies and dispute-settlement procedures and mechanisms. Such solutions will depend not only on the goodwill of leaders in Ottawa and Washington, but also in the capitals of the 50 American states and the 10 Canadian provinces.[2]

This paper examines the growing importance of state and provincial governments in the international economy and the role these subnational units are playing in the evolution of US–Canada economic relations in the new FTA era.

STATES AND PROVINCES AS INTERNATIONAL ECONOMIC ACTORS

The FTA binds Canada in an economic relationship with a nation whose population and economy are approximately 10 times larger. Indeed, the United States has one state, California, which surpasses Canada both in population and economic production. On the other hand, Canada has one province, Ontario, which during the 1980s was a larger recipient of US exports than Japan.

To illustrate the economic prowess of these subnational actors, consider the following. If one were to rank the 25 leading nations in the world by GNP, one could insert 10 states and 2 provinces; among the top 50 nations, 33 states and 4 provinces; and among the top 75 nations, all 50 states and 9 of the 10 provinces. California, with its 29 million people, produces more agricultural goods than over 90 percent of the world's nation-states. It also enters the 1990s with a $700 billion annual gross state product and would rank as the eighth largest country globally. New York is not far behind with its top 10 ranking, and Texas alone has twice the production base of neighboring Mexico.

Furthermore, the annual budgets of states and provinces such as California, New York, and Ontario are surpassed by only a handful of national governments around the world. To put this purchasing power in perspective, California's budget is four times greater than that of the Philippines, a nation with 56 million people. At the municipal level, New York City's annual budget is also twice as large as that of the Philippines, and the four-county greater Los Angeles metropolitan area, with an annual production of goods and services approaching $300 billion, ranks as the 12th largest economic power in the world, ahead of India, Australia, and Switzerland.

Because of the need to cater to local constituencies, and in view of the diversity among subnational units in such nations as Canada and the United States (which rank as the second and fourth largest globally in land mass), pressure intensifies for the development of subnational industrial policies which protect and enhance the economic interests of local constituencies. At times, these policies may even differ from those of national capitals.[3]

To illustrate this point, one should keep in mind that economic development prospects differ dramatically from one subnational government to the next. In Canada, Ontario alone is responsible for 40 percent of Canada's gross national product and manufacturing exports. Ontario and its eastern neighbor, Quebec, jointly account for over 60 percent of the nation's population and productivity, and more than 55 percent of all exports. Moreover, Ontario consistently maintains an unemployment rate far below the national average, whereas the four Atlantic provinces of New Brunswick, Nova Scotia, Prince Edward Island, and Newfoundland suffer from chronically high unemployment rates. The Western provinces of British Columbia, Alberta, Saskatchewan, and Manitoba have traditionally endured boom-and-bust cycles associated with resource-dependent economies.

In the United States, the per capita income in Connecticut is more than twice as great as that of Mississippi.[4] Several of the Western states are also predominantly owned by the federal government, with federal ownership ranging from 30 percent in Montana to 86 percent in Nevada. A former governor of Montana once described the five "human resource" problems of states in his region: (1) out-migration of working people, (2) a resulting small return on heavy educational investments, (3) a burdensome per capita tax load attributable to sparse populations and vast spaces, much of which are owned by the federal government, (4) a "colonial" status imposed by out-of-state control of an almost purely extractive economy, and (5) the commercial disadvantage of being far away from major markets.[5]

During a substantial portion of the 1980s, the economic development rate of the Atlantic and Pacific Coast states tripled that of the interior states, prompting one US senator to warn that the nation was sliding toward "two Americas: flourishing, urban coastlines and a declining rural heartland."[6] In particular, those states which are heavily dependent on agriculture, resource extraction, and traditional industries suffered significant economic upheavals during the past decade. In 1987, for example, the United States created almost 3 million net new jobs, most of which were "bicoastal" employment opportunities, but Dallas, Texas, lost 39,000 jobs and several Mountain and Plains states experienced a new outflow of workers.[7] During all or part of the 1980s, 11 states, mostly from the interior, actually lost population.

Within states, 30 US counties had jobless rates above 25 percent in 1988, and 100 had rates above 15 percent. Far too often a vicious cycle occurs in these high-unemployment areas. A lack of jobs reduces the tax base; a shrinking tax base hurts schools and other community services;

and problems with the educational system diminish the chances of attracting new industries and jobs.[8]

Thus, in view of the wide variety of economic profiles present at the subnational level, it should not be surprising that decisions rendered in the foreign economic policy realm may be viewed differently by subnational governments within the same nation. In the case of the FTA, members of the US Congress voted overwhelmingly in favor of the pact. Near the end of the negotiating process, however, a group of 21 senators, mostly from the Western states, signed a petition asking for major changes in the accord because they perceived that Canada would have a noticeable advantage in trans-border trade in natural resources. In Canada, provincial representatives were consulted on a monthly basis during the negotiating process, and their influence on Ottawa's final proposals on such issues as subsidies, government procurement, and investment restrictions was far greater than the influence wielded by their state counterparts on Washington's final set of proposals.[9] Without any doubt, the capacity of US and Canadian subnational governments to influence future international commerce across the 49th parallel, whether positively or negatively, should not be underestimated.

THE ECONOMIC POLICIES OF THE STATES AND PROVINCES

REVERSE INVESTMENT PROGRAMS

In 1970, four American states had opened offices overseas for the purpose of attracting foreign investment and enhancing trade and tourism opportunities. By 1990, 41 states had opened more than 120 offices abroad. During the two intervening decades, the number of states having international trade and development programs increased from 15 to 49.

By contrast, 7 of the 10 Canadian provinces have opened more than 50 offices abroad, a far higher number than the US states on a relative basis. Many of their expenditures on overseas activities are not in the public domain, but it is generally accepted that the Canadian provinces are more actively involved than most of the American states. Indeed, in the mid-1980s, the province of Alberta sponsored more international trade missions annually than the 13 US Western states combined.[10] Alberta and Quebec have also created separate Departments of International Trade.[11]

Foreign direct investment is responsible for more than 6 million jobs in North America, and the states and provinces have been willing to spend hundreds of millions dollars annually in incentive packages to attract this investment. When Volkswagen announced in the mid-1970s that it was searching for a plant location in the United States, 35 states expressed a strong interest. Pennsylvania finally landed the VW facility, but because of the intense bidding war among the states, officials in Harrisburg had to offer an incentive package worth more than $70 million to the German-based transnational corporation. Ironically, although it will continue to collect benefits from the incentive package into the 21st century, VW closed its Pennsylvania assembly plant after only a decade.

Thirty-nine states also entered the bidding war for Nissan Motor Company's proposed truck assembly plant. Tennessee won the contest with an incentive package valued at $66 million. In another instance, the taxpayers of Kentucky will provide $325 million in incentives to Toyota over a 20-year period to entice that Japanese firm to construct a new automobile assembly plant in Georgetown.[12]

Often in concert with Ottawa, Canadian provincial governments have also provided hundreds of millions of dollars in incentives to US and Asian automakers for the establishment of assembly plants. Recently, the Alberta government also offered to provide Alberta-Pacific Forest Industries, a subsidiary of Mitsubishi, with a $250 million loan guarantee and $65 million in infrastructure development grants for a $1.1 billion project in rural Alberta.[13]

Many subnational governments are fond of telling overseas investors about the particular advantages to be found within their areas of jurisdiction. Kentucky has touted itself in Canadian newspapers as "Canada's 11th province," and New York proclaims to domestic and foreign investors alike that "the ninth economic power in the free world isn't a country," and that it has established a special hotline to service potential investors.[14] Ontario has purchased space in European magazines, claiming it enjoys the "strategic location in North America."[15] California has done the same, using the slogan, "one of the world's leading economic powers doesn't have its own currency, army, or Olympic team."[16] Ontario, Quebec, and British Columbia officials have also directed investment missions abroad proclaiming their provinces as the gateway to the American market by virtue of the new FTA.

EXPORT PROMOTION

Almost all states and provinces now provide significant export assistance to small- and medium-sized firms. For example, the American states spent $62 million in staffing and maintaining their trade departments in 1988, almost double the 1984 expenditures. This figure, however, may be less than the combined spending of just four Canadian provinces: Ontario, Quebec, Alberta, and British Columbia.[17] Twenty-seven states have also passed legislation to implement some form of export financing. Twenty-two of these programs were operational in 1988 with over $32 million allocated for financing purposes, most commonly for loan guarantees to commercial banks willing to issue credit to exporting companies. The California Export Finance Office (CEFO) has emerged as a leader in providing financial support to smaller enterprises, and from its inception in 1985 through November 1989, CEFO guaranteed 190 working-capital loans valued at $36.5 million and supporting $174 million in new export sales.[18]

COOPERATION AND COMPETITION

To enhance cooperative ties and facilitate economic linkages, certain subnational governments have strengthened relations with their counterparts in other nations. This is particularly the case between the United States and Canada. Eleven New England governors and Eastern Canadian premiers have met annually since 1973 and have established a broad range of institutional agreements. For example, at the 1990 annual meeting of this group held in Connecticut, the leaders spent time on the regional ramifications of the Canada–US Free Trade Agreement and solutions to the acid rain problem. Governors from eight states and premiers from two provinces have agreed on a charter to protect water rights in the Great Lakes.[19] Representatives of Alaska, British Columbia, and the Yukon also meet on a regular basis, as do officials of several other provinces and border states. Tourism is also an area where cooperation among subnational units is not unusual. This is a multi-billion dollar industry with record numbers of foreign visitors coming to North America in the latter part of the 1980s. The state of Washington and the province of British Columbia have agreed to set aside $75,000 each for joint advertising campaigns. The New England governors and Eastern Canadian premiers also work together to entice residents from North America and abroad to visit their region. These regional contacts may also lead to special trans-border economic arrangements, as illustrated by the Quebec government's agreement with New York and some of the New England states to export more than $30 billion worth of electricity over the next two decades.

On the other hand, economic competition among state and provincial governments is at times very intense, and beggar-thy-neighbor tactics are not uncommon. For example, Indiana business development officers spend time in Michigan, Missouri's governor meets with business representatives in Illinois, North Dakota officials host receptions for businesses in Manitoba, and Ottawa works with various provincial governments to entice firms to locate in Canada instead of in neighboring US border states.[20] A classic instance of cross-border competition occurred several years ago when an incentive package worth almost $70 million was pieced together by Ontario and Ottawa in order to entice Ford to locate a new plant in Ontario instead of Ohio.[21] During the FTA negotiations, some of the most bitter disputes involved arguments among bordering states and provinces which shared similar natural resource bases. This included major disagreements over the treatment in the FTA of potatoes, corn, wheat, raspberries, oil, natural gas, timber, and fish.

Subnational Industrial Policies

State and provincial governments are clearly in the process of developing their own industrial policies and this will certainly have an impact on future trade and investment activity across the 49th parallel. In the United States, two dozen states are now directly involved in the venture capital game, committing in excess of $300 million for projects over the past few years. State agencies also provide low-interest loans, help in securing private financing, and technical managerial assistance. As an illustration, the Connecticut Product Development Corporation has invested more than $12 million in approximately 60 small businesses. The state receives a 5 percent royalty on products sold by the companies backed by the venture capital.[22] Recently, the Connecticut state government also entered into a controversial agreement to purchase 47 percent of the equity in Colt's Manufacturing Company, a major supplier of automatic weapons. Pennsylvania's Ben Franklin Partnership has provided over $80 million for state-based technology projects, and the Massachusetts Technology Development Corporation has distributed more than $10 million in seed money.[23] Several states have also set up industrial parks, enterprise zones, business incubators, and greenhouse projects to spur on economic development, with the latter program geared to the construction of special buildings to house new high-technology businesses.

In general, state governments are also much more involved than ever before in regulating businesses, whether domestic or foreign. A Conference Board study of 253 of the largest corporations in the United States reveals that 75 percent now engage in lobbying efforts in one or more states, and nearly one-half of the companies which employ state-government relations specialists have hired them since 1975. This seems to be an astute decision because at least seven times as many business-related laws are being passed by state legislatures as by the US Congress.

As for Canada, most provincial governments are much more active than their state counterparts in regulating businesses. Provincial governments also own hundreds of Crown corporations and are integrally involved in most facets of the economy.[24] In addition, they provide about $2 billion (Canadian) annually to support agricultural programs.[25] In general, provincial governments are also much more deeply in debt than their counterparts in the United States, and they view trade, reverse direct investment, and tourism as indispensable revenue sources.

Quebec, for example, is one of a handful of provinces which sponsors an investor-immigrant program, Under the provisions of this program, a prospective immigrant will be given preference if he or she is willing to bring at least $700,000 (Canadian) in net capital and invest at least $500,000 (Canadian) for three years or more. This investment must be made through a stockbroker and targeted at Quebec-based businesses with assets of less than $25 million (Canadian). Quebec's Solidarity Fund and the Caisse de Depot et Placement are also used to promote economic development in the province.[26] This organization, established in 1965, administers the funds from 11 Quebec public-pension and insurance plans. It is one of North America's largest financial institutions with assets exceeding $30 billion (Canadian), and has participated in the capitalization of hundreds of Quebec companies. Provinces such as Quebec also provide incentives to foreign investors, often in conjunction with local governments and with federal government agencies such as the Department of Regional and Industrial Expansion (DRIE). Moreover, in an effort to maintain its francophone culture, the Quebec government provides cash bonuses, income-tax cuts, interest-free loans for homes, and other inducements to families willing to have more than two children. Quebec also has its own immigration agents who work hand in hand with federal immigration officials to screen potential immigrants to the province on the basis of their knowledge of French.

SUBNATIONAL GOVERNMENTS AND THE FTA: THE ISSUE OF SUBSIDIES

THE CANADIAN DIMENSION

Under Chapter 19 of the Canada–US Free Trade Agreement, the two North American neighbors have from five to seven years to define what constitutes a subsidy and then to determine how such subsidies will be treated under the bilateral accord. Both sides are in general agreement that the policies of subnational governments such as state, provincial, and municipal governments must be included in the overall subsidy discussions.

Without any doubt, Canadian subnational governments are providing significant financial assistance to their business communities, and many of the complaints received by the Office of the US Trade Representative against Canadian subsidy practices in the 1980s zeroed in on the provincial govemments rather than on Ottawa. Indeed, the protectionist policies of Canadian provinces are legendary, with more than 300 major barriers estimated to be in place.[27] Ironically, some Canadians who supported the FTA hoped that it might pave the way not only for freer trade in North America, but also for freer trade within Canada. For instance, because of onerous provincial restrictions on beer, Canadian brewing companies actually enjoy freer access to US markets than to neighboring provincial markets. In addition, Prince Edward Island limits the purchase of waterfront property to its own residents, British Columbia gives preference to local contractors for bridges and roadwork, Ontario bars Quebec milk, and in 1985 the Quebec government ordered the town of Aylmer to rip the Ontario-made bricks out of a completed sidewalk and then replace them with Quebec-made bricks.[28]

Unfortunately, the FTA will only have a modest direct effect on interprovincial trade and on restrictive provincial economic policies. In the area of government procurement, the FTA will open up for Canadian suppliers approximately $3 billion in new US federal government contracts and for US suppliers almost $500 million in Canadian government contracts. However, these new liberalized standards do not apply to state, provincial, and local governments.[29] At the multilateral level, a 1987 General Agreement on Tariffs and Trade (GATT) decision tackled for the first time protectionism at the subnational level by condemning the discriminatory liquor laws of the provinces, but this decision only touches the surface of Canada's deeply entrenched parochial economic policies. Indeed, unless substantial progress is made in dismantling provincial barriers over the next couple of years, it is possible that trade will be freer within the post-1992 European Community, composed of 12 nation-states and 320 million people, than in the single country of Canada with its 26 million inhabitants.

THE US DIMENSION

On the other hand, far too many members of the US business community, and far too many trade officials in Washington, DC, who are accustomed to pointing accusing fingers at other nations, seem to forget about the subsidy policies being pursued by their own subnational governments. A National Governors Association report suggests that the states spent $20 billion on financial assistance to businesses in the year 1981, including incentives designed to attract new businesses or retain existing ones, but excluding public investment in human resources, universities, research institutions, and physical infrastructure.[30] Nor does this estimate include county and city spending. If this figure is roughly accurate and if 1981 were fairly typical of the entire decade, then state governments alone may have provided around $200 billion in financial assistance to the business sector during the 1980s.

A large part of this subnational government support has come in the form of tax-exempt bonds. The Public Services Association (PSA) in the United States calculates that $687 billion in all types of long-term tax-exempt bonds were issued by state and local governments between 1984 and 1988. If these bonds had been taxable, the PSA estimates the additional interest costs until the year 2000 would have been $284 billion.[31] Using a similar formula for calculating interest savings for businesses, $220 billion worth of tax-exempt industrial development bonds were issued by subnational governments between 1979 and 1989, leading to savings in interest charges of $103 billion. If private-exempt entity bonds which assist private hospitals, educational facilities, and similar organizations are included, an additional $63 billion in savings would be added to the equation.[32] These figures do not include "taxable" state and local issuances which are subject to federal taxation but often exempted from both state and local taxes.[33]

Growing exposure to the international economy has also prompted far too many state and local governments to adopt protectionist policies designed to help marginally competitive local industries to survive. Forty-six states maintain some form of Buy-American or Buy-State provisions for state and local government procurement, an increase of one-third since the late 1970s. These provisions restrict or eliminate foreign firms from bidding on more than $20 billion in government contracts annually. More than two-thirds of the state legislatures have also enacted anti-takeover statutes, and the very stringent Pennsylvania law signed in April 1990 may become the new model for most states. This law forces corporate raiders to surrender short-term profits from takeover attempts, clamps down on the raiders' corporate voting rights, and establishes special protection for labor contracts when corporations change ownership.[34] Frequently, these state-level protectionist policies have been used as the last line of defense for US-owned companies resisting unfriendly takeover bids by Canadian and other foreign corporations.[35]

RESOLVING THE SUBSIDIES ISSUE

In their subsidy negotiations which will hopefully move into high gear once the Uruguay Round has been concluded, both US and Canadian officials must take a hard look in their own backyards and determine which subnational policies are acceptable and which may violate both the spirit and the letter of the FTA. Currently, the US International Trade Commission and the Department of Commerce distinguish between "generally available" government programs and those available only to specific enterprises; or in other words, "to one company or industry, a limited group of companies or industries, or companies or industries located within a limited region or regions within a country." For the moment, the latter would constitute a harmful subsidy.[36]

In his insightful work on subsidies, Gary Hufbauer suggests the development in the United States and Canada of a "green list" of acceptable domestic subsidies, a list which would include the following: (a) generally available subsidies involving health benefits, worker training, utilities, roads, and broad tax incentives; (b) adjustment subsidies which are paid strictly for the purpose of downsizing an industry (such as retraining allowances and pension benefits); (c) regional subsidies which solely compensate for demonstrated cost differentials of establishing facilities in a depressed region; and (d) research subsidies, so long as the research findings are released freely into the general body of scientific knowledge or can be licensed by firms of foreign nationality on the same basis as domestic firms.[37] Yet even under such a framework of liberalized subsidies many questions would remain concerning the acceptability of targeted business attraction, business retention, venture capital, technology development, enterprise zone, and related programs.

Subnationalism and the FTA: Concluding Observations

This article has focused on some of the troubling by-products of state and provincial activism in the domestic and international economies. At this juncture, it is important to point out that many subnational activities are positive forces for change, representing a grassroots effort to familiarize people with the challenges and opportunities in a rapidly evolving global economy. For example, the National Governors Association is prodding its members to push for the reinstatement of foreign-language proficiency as a requirement for college admission, the restoration of geography as a core subject in school curricula, the introduction of foreign-language training at the elementary school level, and state-sponsored courses in international commerce for local business communities. These and other related measures should help prepare the citizenry on both sides of the 49th parallel for a truly internationalized economy.

The FTA is also a proper response to the exigencies of globalization, and trade continues to increase between the two North American neighbors. In Canada, however, the FTA is off to a rocky start. It has been blamed for every societal ill, whether real or imaginary, and a plurality of Canadians still disapprove of the accord. In the United States, most Americans have little knowledge about the FTA or what is transpiring in US–Canada economic relations, in spite of their friendly perception of Canada in general.

Future prospects for the FTA have been further complicated by the failure of the Meech Lake constitutional discussions and the possibility that Quebec will distance itself from the rest of Canada. On the other hand, America's current negotiations with Mexico for a free-trade agreement may eventually lead to a North American Free Trade Area, and

George Bush has suggested an even broader trade zone covering both Central and South America.

Yet in spite of the FTA, numerous trade restrictions still exist between the United States and Canada at the state and provincial levels. These include non-tariff trade barriers, trade-distorting subsidies, government procurement limitations, and investment restraints. With increased competition from across the Pacific and the Atlantic, it would seem prudent for the North American economies to rationalize and eliminate the remaining subnational-level trade constraints. The FTA must be improved, and if the barriers highlighted in this article are to be dismantled, provincial and state governments must be willing to join with Ottawa and Washington in a new set of trade negotiations.

EARL H. FRY *is a professor of political science and director of Canadian Studies at BYU. He has done extensive work on the economic activities of subnational governments, particularly the American states and the Canadian provinces. Fry's most recent publications are* The Expanding Role of State and Local Governments in US Foreign Affairs *and* Canada's Unity Crisis: Implications for US–Canadian Economic Relations. *He teaches classes on US foreign policy, international political economy, international relations of North America, and Canadian government.*

Notes

1. Based on asset value, US individual and corporate investors account for about 70 percent of all FDI in Canada, whereas Canadians are the fourth largest investors in the United States after the British, the Japanese, and the Dutch. At the end of 1989, Canadians accounted for $31.5 billion in cumulative FDI in the United States.
2. At the 1988 annual conference of the provincial premiers, these subnational government leaders demanded "a strong provincial role" in the management of Canada–US free trade, the definition of subsidies, the development of common trade remedy laws, and the determination of dispute-settlement mechanisms. The National Government Association has also requested that the Office of the US Trade Representative consult with the states on any bilateral economic issue which impacts upon the economic well-being of the states. See the *Globe and Mail,* August 20, 1988, pp. A1–A2.
3. Canada has a much more decentralized system than the United States and federalism is a far more prominent feature of Canada's political structure. As Peter Leslie observes in *Federal State, National Economy* (Toronto: University of Toronto Press, 1987), p. ix, "[i]n Canada, the most fundmental political relationships, defining the character of Canadian society, are bound up in the structure of the federal system. It shapes them, and they shape it."
4. The 1987 per capita income in Connecticut was $20,980, compared with that of Mississippi, $10,204.
5. These comments were made by former Governor Forrest Anderson. See Jerry Hagstrom, *Beyond Reagan* (New York: W. W. Norton, 1988), pp. 76–77.

6. This statement was made by Senator David Durenberger at the 1988 Minnesota Republican nominating convention. See the *St. Paul Pioneer Press Dispatch,* June 18, 1988, p. 6A.
7. In 1987, 8 of the 10 most robust economies were found in coastal states, and the other 2, Arizona and Nevada, depended on California for much of their growth. See *Inc.,* October 1987, pp. 76–77.
8. See the *Wall Street Journal,* April 21, 1988, p. 1.
9. This conclusion is derived from the author's interviews with representatives of the US and Canadian FTA negotiating teams and with provincial and state officials who interacted with their national teams. The large provinces established special FTA task forces and produced some very sophisticated papers on the economic and social impact which dimensions of the FTA would have on their constituents. These papers were discussed with Simon Reisman and his FTA team and viewpoints were exchanged on a regular basis.

   In contrast, few state representatives followed the FTA negotiations closely, and meetings between officials of the National Governors Association and the Office of the US Trade Representative were held on a very infrequent and ad hoc basis. On the other hand, state representatives were able to make their positions known through the US Congress, whereas strict party discipline, reliance on executive federalism, and an anachronistic Senate made Canada's Parliament a poor conduit for the expression of provincial concerns. Nevertheless, the articulation of state concerns in the House of Representatives and the Senate was far less effective than the consultative mechanism worked out by Canada's Trade Negotiator's Office and the provincial governments.
10. This conclusion is based on a survey conducted by the author in 1986. See Earl H. Fry, "The Economic Competitiveness of the Western States and Provinces: The International Dimension," *The American Review of Canadian Studies,* no. 16, Autumn 1986, pp. 301–312. Since that time, however, the states have become much more active in sponsoring international missions and it is doubtful that the same results would be found in 1990.
11. Some of the provincial export-related programs are listed in Department of External Affairs, International Trade, *Provincial Trade-Related Assistance Programs,* April 1989.
12. *Wall Street Journal,* June 9, 1987, p. 33.
13. *World*Watch,* March 1990, pp. 7–8. This project has been bitterly criticized by environmental groups. It may be canceled or significantly revised.
14. *New York Times,* October 13, 1980, p. D3
15. *The Economist,* February 25, 1984, p. 40.
16. Ibid., July 15, 1989. California's advertisement was a three-page insert attached to the cover page of the magazine.
17. When the costs of maintaining foreign offices for trade purposes are included, it is more than likely that these four provinces spend more on trade promotion than the 50 states. See, for example, Douglas Brown's discussion of Alberta in "Canada's Provinces in the International Economy: A Survey of the Field," a paper presented at the Dartmouth Conference on Comparative Federalism, June 22–25, 1989. Also consult Ivan Bernier and Andre Binette, *Les provinces canadiennes et le commerce international* (Quebec City: Centre québecois de rélations internationales, 1988), pp. 65–73, and *Provincial Trade-Related Assistance Programs.*
18. California World Trade Commission, *Newsletter,* Winter 1989–90.

19. The Great Lakes Charter was signed in February 1985 by the governors of New York, Pennsylvania, Ohio, Michigan, Indiana, Illinois, Wisconsin and Minnesota, and the premiers of Ontario and Quebec.
20. *Wall Street Journal,* February 14, 1983, pp. 1, 11, and December 28, 1983, pp. 1, 13.
21. See Earl H. Fry, *Financial Invasion of the USA*. (New York: McGraw-Hill, 1980), p. 146.
22. *Christian Science Monitor,* November 20, 1984, p. 37.
23. *Wall Street Journal,* November 9, 1987, p. 27.
24. It is extremely difficult to place a dollar figure on the direct and indirect subsidies provided by the provincial governments. In 1984, Statistics Canada reported that perhaps $4 billion (Canadian) in indirect subsidies were provided by these subnational governments, a 100 percent increase from 1980. See Bernier and Binette, op. cit., p. 63. Also, consult pp. 64–73 for a look at provincial programs which assist local exporters.
25. *Globe and Mail,* May 16, 1989, p. A6.
26. Quebec's Solidarity Fund began in 1984 with a $10 million (Canadian) provincial government loan and $6 million raised from union members. In 1990, it ranked as Quebec's single largest source of venture capital with $294 million in assets and 85,000 shareholders.
27. *Financial Post,* September 13,1989, p. 10. These barriers include restrictions on government purchases from sources outside a province, industrial subsidies that favor local suppliers, and regulations that discriminate against out-of-province goods and services.
28. See the *Ottawa Citizen,* February 3, 1988, editorial page.
29. Debra Steger, *A Concise Guide to the Canada–US Free Trade Agreement* (Toronto: Carswell, 1988), pp. 37–41.
30. John DeWitt, *Shifting Responsibilities: Federalism in Economic Development* (Washington, DC: National Governors Association, 1987), pp. 69–70, and Roger Wilson, *Economic Development in the States: State Business Incentives and Economic Growth: Are They Effective? A Review of the Literature* (Lexington, KY: Council of State Governments, 1989), p. 3.
31. Public Securities Association, Facts on Tax-Exempt and Taxable Municipal Bonds, May 1989, p. 1.
32. These savings were calculated by using the PSA's computation of a 2.65 percentage point differential in 1988 between Moody's average A-rated tax-exempt municipal bonds (7.59 percent) and taxable A-rated corporate bonds (10.24 percent) and assuming the life of the bonds would be at least 12 years. In the mid-1980s, the average maturity for small-issue industrial development bonds was about 14 years and for other industrial development bonds about 20 years.
33. In 1988, almost $3 billion in long-term taxable state and local issuances were recorded with over $200 million going for industrial development and economic development purposes. See Public Securities Association, p. 9.
34. *International Herald Tribune,* April 28, 1990, p. 16.
35. This anti-takeover strategy was used by Federated Department Stores against Canadian-based Campeau, Farmers Group Insurance against British based BAT Industries, and Koppers against British based Beazer PLC.
36. Quoted in Andrew Anderson and Alan Rugman, "Subsidies in the US Steel Industry: A New Conceptual Framework and Literature Review," Working paper No. 14 (Toronto: Ontario Centre for International Business, October 1989).
37. Gary Haufber, "A View of the Forest," in *Subsidies and Countervailing Measures,* World Bank Discussion Paper No. 55, ed. Bela Balassa (Washington, DC: The World Bank, 1989), p. 16.

Questions

1. What are the implications of some states having budgets as large as or larger than some countries?
2. Given the date of this article (1990), how accurate is the information?
3. What are the potential problems of states or provinces pursuing their own interests?
4. Should the trade situation remain as it is? Or should action (i.e., new regulations) be considered?

The Quest for Relevance: Roles for Academia and Industry in Japan and the US

TAKUTO YAMADA AND ROBERT H. TODD

In this article, first published in the Journal in Engineering Education *in October 1997, Takuto Yamada and Robert H. Todd examine the interrelationship between higher education and industry in both the US and Japan. The authors address the questions of how to make higher education in engineering more relevant and how to make graduates more ready to enter the workforce. They assert that "engineering education in the US is strengthening its relationship with industry and increasing relevancy" while "Japanese industry and academia appear not to be headed in a collaborative direction and are even more detached from one another than in the US." With this article, Todd and Yamada hope to "further motivate US educators to collaborate with industry and continue to integrate greater relevancy into engineering education."*

While US industry is making headway in worldwide markets, much remains to be done. Some have proposed that improving the relevance of engineering education can have a marked influence on the future success of US manufacturing. Some in academia have heard industries' cries for help to improve relevancy in engineering education and have responded with various solutions. Is this the situation in Japan? What is the state of engineering education in Japan? Where is it headed and how does the US compare? We found that industry–academia relationships like those being strengthened in the US are minimal in Japan. Surprisingly, Japanese industry and academia appear not to be headed in a collaborative direction and are even more detached from one another than in the United States. This paper presents some differences in the way Japan and the US view their roles for academia and industry and their interrelationships. Our objective is to further motivate US educators to collaborate with industry and continue to integrate greater relevancy into engineering education.

I. Introduction: The Problem

American academia has been the envy of the world in engineering research for decades. In recent years, however, US engineering schools have been criticized for not preparing graduates adequately for engineering practice. Some have observed that a lack of interaction between industry and academia has resulted in a divergence of goals for graduates' educational preparation. Others have suggested that academia's failure to emphasize industrially important goals has reduced the ability of US manufacturing enterprises to compete with foreign enterprises in such areas as customer satisfaction, quality, cost, and time to market–subjects not typically emphasized in academia. Some believe that the competitiveness of industry in the US can be greatly enhanced through a quest for relevance: the pursuit in academia—particularly in undergraduate engineering education—to better prepare graduates for the practice of engineering by having students learn more of the skills and aptitudes required by industry.

This quest for relevance is exemplified in calls for increased relevancy of higher education in general, with greater industry-academia collaboration, more emphasis on teaching by faculty, and a customer-supplier relationship with employers of graduates.

Todd et al. list weaknesses (see Table 1) of US engineering graduates as seen by industry.[1]

- Technical arrogance
- No understanding of manufacturing processes
- A desire for complicated and "high-tech" solutions
- Lack of design capability or creativity
- Lack of appreciation for considering alternatives
- No knowledge of value engineering
- Lack of appreciation for variation
- All wanting to be analysts
- Poor perception of the overall engineering process
- Narrow view of engineering and related disciplines
- Wanting not to get their hands dirty
- Consider manufacturing work as boring
- No understanding of the quality process
- Weak communication skills
- Little skill or experience working in teams
- Taught primarily to work as individuals

Table 1. Industrial perceptions of weaknesses in new US engineering graduates.

These weaknesses may be symptoms of a larger problem. As reported in a survey as part of a Mechanical Engineering Curriculum Development Project by The American Society of Mechanical Engineers, some industries evaluated new graduate mechanical engineers as "OK or marginally prepared"[2] in skills necessary for effective industry practice. As long ago as 1989, MIT conducted an important study on US industrial productivity and concluded that "America does indeed have a serious productivity problem."[3] This study places the blame for inadequate productivity and quality of the workforce squarely on the "institutions that educate Americans for work."[4]

Fortunately, more and more educators are becoming aware of this problem and are taking steps to improve. One approach has been to form symbiotic partnerships between industry and academia through senior capstone projects.[1,5,6] A particularly exemplary institution is Harvey Mudd College[7] where industry-academia projects known as Engineering Clinics have been conducted for more than 30 years. Another approach has been an emphasis throughout undergraduate curricula on the Product Realization Process (PRP).[2] Nevertheless, there is much more that can and must be done.

How does Japanese engineering education fare by comparison?

A. INDUSTRY–ACADEMIA RELATIONS IN JAPAN

Since World War II, no other country has captured an equal amount of attention as Japan. In 1993, Japan became the world's largest[8] manufacturing economy. While the US has a higher Gross Domestic Product (GDP), Japan has a higher gross domestic product per capita: in 1993 at $33,903 compared to $25,009 for the US.[9] Further, and surprisingly to some, Japan is America's second largest export market after Canada.[10] The strength of the Japanese economy and its rapid rate of increase are important reasons to learn more about engineering education in Japan.

One of the authors traveled to Japan recently to visit with several leading industries and universities to discuss and observe the state of industry-academia relationships in Japan. Surprisingly, industry-academia partnerships are minimal in Japan. Japanese industry and academia appear to be even more detached than in the United States, suggesting that new Japanese engineering graduates may have some of the same problems observed in the US. Even more surprisingly, higher education in Japan appears not to be a major contributor, at least in a direct sense, to the success of Japanese industry.

These preliminary observations prompted us to investigate further how Japan is dealing with increased global competition through its educational system and industry.

In this paper we will attempt to demonstrate, by comparison, that engineering education in the United States is strengthening its relationships with industry and increasing relevancy. In Japan, however, engineering education does not appear to be moving in this same direction.

As we discuss these events, some questions that will be addressed are:

• What is the state of undergraduate engineering education in Japan and where is it headed?

• Is engineering education in Japan addressing the problems of relevancy? If so, how?

• Where are we headed in the US in relation to Japan?

Answers to these questions should provide encouragement and perspective to those working to improve the relevancy of undergraduate engineering education in the US and also to the stake holders in US industry.

In the past, there have been studies of education and specifically of engineering education in both Japan and the US. However, there have not been any to date which examine engineering education, industry, and their interrelationships. In 1983, Lawrence P. Graysonn[11,12,13] published an excellent, in-depth, three-part series on engineering education in Japan. Since his examination, many aspects of the socioeconomic system in Japan have changed. With the help of past studies,[13,14] together with our first hand findings in Japan, the underlying purpose of this paper is to further persuade US engineering educators to continue integrating greater industrial relevancy into undergraduate engineering education. It appears that current efforts to improve engineering education in the US combined with the situation in Japan may prove a window of opportunity for US industry in the near future.

B. BENCHMARK ASSUMPTIONS OF ENGINEERING EDUCATION

In the United States, some have proposed that many of our present problems in industry can be traced to engineering education, where many of the skills and attitudes for engineering practice are acquired. Some believe that better preparation of graduates can result in significant advantages upon entering industry. In the US, we seem to be rediscovering the importance of relevance in engineering education as we prepare students for engineering practice. The ASME[2] report found 56 "best practices" of engineers as perceived by industry. Table 2 lists the Top 20 "Best Practices" for experienced and new BS level mechanical engineers as perceived by industry and academia. The fact that industry and academia agree on the items of this list is, in itself, a positive step forward.

Further, the report suggested that "industry must provide clear customer requirements (expectations or educational outcomes) and academe

1. Teams/Teamwork
2. Communication
3. Design for Manufacture
4. CAD Systems
5. Professional Ethics
6. Creative Thinking
7. Design for Performance
8. Design for Reliability
9. Design for Safety
10. Concurrent Engineering
11. Sketching/Drawing
12. Design for Cost
13. Application of Statistics
14. Reliability
15. Geometric Tolerancing
16. Value Engineering
17. Design Reviews
18. Manufacturing Processes
19. Systems Perspective
20. Design for Assembly

Table 2. Industry and academe's top twenty "Best Practices" for new BS-level engineers.

must develop curricula that meet these requirements (i.e., prepare graduates)."

C. BACKGROUND

After WW II, US and Japanese engineering moved in different directions. While Japan was starting almost from scratch to develop its economy and catch up with the West in manufacturing, the US was concentrating on defense and the space program motivated by the Cold War. Consequently, while the focus in engineering in the US was largely on defense, in Japan, the focus was largely on the commercial products industry. In the US, this initiated a paradigm shift in engineering education toward engineering science and away from industrial practice and manufacturing. Reinforcing this trend, government-sponsored research in higher education encouraged more "basic and applied scientific research."[16] Evaluation and promotion of engineering faculty emphasized quantity and quality of research papers, and engineering program accreditation became activity based. In short, many believe engineering education became less relevant to the needs of the consumer products industry and manufacturing.

Meanwhile, in Japan, the economy was experiencing unprecedented growth fueled by industrial advances relating to quality management and favorable economic conditions. As Japanese industry refined manufacturing methods, the quality gap between US and Japanese commercial products widened, as did the trade deficit. Eventually, competition from Japan combined with a changing global socioeconomic scene triggered major changes in US industry.

Congruence of industry and academe's top 20 best practices suggests that we know what we should be teaching. The fact that new graduates are seen only as marginally prepared shows that we are falling short of some of our most important goals.

Presently, the US is concentrating on improving industrial competitiveness, and industry is seeking a stronger voice in academia. Engineering accreditation is heading towards an outcomes-based approach, and more practice is beginning to be integrated with theory. The pendulum in engineering education seems to be swinging toward more relevance for meeting the needs of US industry.

However, what is the situation in Japan?

II. Engineering Education in Japan

The success of Japanese industry has intrigued both industrial and academic observers worldwide. The typically high scores of Japanese students on international mathematics tests and the success of its industry have led many to believe the two are linked and that the educational system in Japan is exceptional. However, a correlation of test scores with industrial success may not necessarily indicate the effectiveness of an educational system. Often, these tests only measure a narrow range of student abilities. Japanese education must be more carefully examined within the context of its culture and society.

Although education has helped Japan "catch up" to the rest of the world technologically and economically, education in Japan is now facing some key challenges to further progress—especially in higher education. An article in *Tokyo Business Today* recently reported that, "Japan may be respected abroad for its primary education system, but its universities are a shambles. . . . Its vaunted science and engineering departments resemble those in Third World countries."[17]

Surprisingly, the quality of education for engineering practice is seen as deficient. We found that Japanese engineering education seems to have many of the same problems as in the US, but to an even greater extent. It also has some additional challenges due to its unique structure and its place in Japanese culture.

A. EDUCATION AS AN ECONOMIC TOOL: THE CATCH UP EDUCATION SYSTEM

To understand today's state of engineering education in Japan, it is important to understand a little of the Japanese educational system and its establishment. The most significant change in the educational system of Japan occurred during the American occupation of Japan after WW II.

At this time, the Japanese recognized the value of an educated and skilled workforce, so they looked to the West as a model.[18] Today, Japanese primary education is similar to the US, but with a much stronger emphasis on the college entrance examination. Although the general organization is similar, there are some key differences in its internal structure that will be discussed further.

In 1960, The Economic Counsel, which spearheaded the economic initiative to double the national income of Japan declared: "Economic competition among nations is a technical competition, and technical competition has become an educational competition." Academia, which was controlled by the Ministry of Education, followed the government's lead by increasing science and technology faculty,"[19] emphasizing science and mathematics[20] in government policies throughout all levels of education,[21] and prolonging the school week to 5.5 days. Consequently, Japanese students in primary education attend 240 days of school a year compared to 180 days in the US.[22] It is no wonder Japanese students are known for doing well in mathematics and science; however, are these skills sufficient for success in engineering practice?

From its establishment, education was used as an instrument to meet economic goals in Japan. This is not necessarily a harmful purpose for education, but for Japan it seems to have been taken to an extreme. Education became subservient to the narrow goals of the government, which interacted closely with industry. Consequently, education's purpose and operation were defined within a limited scope. Teruhisa Horio, a well-known critic of education in Japan confirms this: "those who control education in Japan have paid scant attention to the idea that education should be organized from the perspective of human development."[23] This use of education as an economic tool was effective in developing a "catch up" economy, but unfortunately, it has also produced a "catch up" form of education that emphasizes convention, strict conformity, and collection of facts over innovation. This form of education is now seen as an impediment to further improvements. The main difficulty in Japanese undergraduate engineering education appears to stem from the examination system.

B. COLLEGE ENTRANCE EXAMINATIONS

The College Entrance Examinations (CEE) are administered only twice each year—once for national universities and once for private universities. Since the examination is the only consideration for college entrance, the focus in lower education has become examination-oriented.[24] One's whole future hinges upon the CEE. With little social mobility, virtually no chance to return to college later in life, and emphasis in society and industry on credentials (where one attended college), the importance of the CEE is magnified. Due to the severe competitive nature of these exams, they are known as "examination hell." Students who enter the most prestigious universities, which require the highest test scores, are reported to study five hours every day for at least the three previous years.[25] Some students acquire help of supplementary schools called "Juku" (private educational organizations run by individuals or corporadons to help students "cram" for the CEE). In 1995, 62.7% of lower secondary students[26] enrolled in Juku. These private schooling services, which grew with the importance of the CEE, have become an integral and important part of education in Japan today.

Often, these supplementary schooling services make a great difference in determining which university a student attends. Because many students attend at least a year of outside schooling in order to qualify for their university of choice, the educational system can practically be thought as a 6–3–3–1–4 year system.

Typically, examinations are taken in the US to get through school. In Japan, exams are taken to get into school. Therefore, in Japan it is hard to get into college, but relatively easy to graduate—nearly the opposite of the US. This has a strong but opposite effect upon the quality of education in primary and higher education. Nicholas J. Haiducek, an educational advisor to a large corporation in Tokyo, explains that "the demand for excellence, so prevalent from kindergarten through senior high school, stops at the university doorstep."[27]

The CEE is the one aspect of Japanese education that affects the quality of undergraduate engineering education most profoundly. The CEE causes the role of primary education to be a time of preparation for the CEE. The role of higher education, however, tends to be a selection mechanism for companies. These narrowly defined roles may thwart reaching the potential of an effective and relevant undergraduate education.

The main difficulty with the CEE, as seen recently by both insiders and outsiders, is that it promotes rote and uniform learning over independent thought. In fact, some even view it as actively suppressing independent and creative thought. Ouchi Tsutomu, in his retirement speech from the faculty of Economics at the University of Tokyo, the pinnate of prestige in Japan, declared, "Today's students . . . are thoroughly deficient when it comes to thinking critically about problems other than those they have been tutored to respond to on entrance examinations."[28] Though harsh, his evaluation is typical of thoughtful educators in Japan and other outside observers. While the CEE system is effective in developing stu-dents who can learn vast amounts of "testable" information, it falls short in fostering creativity and analytical skills that are more difficult to test—skills that are essential in engineering.

Many of the weaknesses of Japanese and American engineers, such as those in Table 1, cannot be easily measured by examination. As a result, the emphasis on rote memorization over other kinds of learning has brought the effectiveness of Japan's education system into question. Evidently, from the perspective of industry, the definition of a quality graduate is markedly different in Japan and the US. In the US, a "good" graduate, among other characteristics, is defined as one who will be immediately useful to the company, has graduated with high marks, and has relevant work experience. In Japan, a "good" graduate is one who is flexible, fits in well with the company (trainable), and has proven their potential in the harsh entrance examination by attending a prestigious university. As a result, in Japan, "good" primary schools are thought of as those that successfully prepare students ultimately for the entrance exam. Also, "good" universities are those that lead to famous companies and government service. The difference is the emphasis on credentials versus relevant acquired skills for engineering practice.

Hence, the CEE system indirectly fosters irrelevance to engineering practice in engineering education. Broadly speaking, this encourages university students to put off serious study and training until after graduation, making college a break from study.

CURRICULUM

The curriculum is an important factor in determining what kinds of skills and aptitudes are taught in higher education. In the US, the curriculum of engineering education is shaped by the engineering accreditation criteria of the Accreditation Board for Engineering and Technology (ABET) which represents 22 professional engineering societies.[29]

In Japan, by contrast, the curriculum is determined by the Ministry of Education without any direct link to the engineering profession. This has rendered the curriculum rigid, uniform, and often outdated and irrelevant to the needs of industry. One computer student's confession at Tokyo Denki University was surprising. He felt that the US was so far ahead of

Japan in his area of study that he had to study the journals on his own to be current because the curriculum at the university was almost backward and out of date.[30] As an explanation, Dr. Dore and Dr. Sako say, "The school and university system . . . keeps industry very much at arms' length . . . engineering faculties have fewer links with industry than their counterparts in this country, [Britain, and we add the US]" and, "The feeling that . . . scholarship should not be corrupted by those who live in the world of the profit motive is a strong one."[31] Does this sound familiar?

During the US occupation of Japan, university boards of trustees were suggested, but "Japanese academicians and students fiercely resisted . . . board of trustee governance . . . on the grounds that business-dominated boards of trustees would attempt to impose right-wing agendas on universities."[32]

While academia's reluctance to work with industry is understandable, it can unfortunately lead to technological obsolescence and irrelevance in education. However, this detached role of the university is seen by some as justified in part because they feel the role of the university is to teach the fundamentals—not applications. In engineering, however, helping students learn how to apply fundamentals to practice is what our profession is all about. Consider the words of this anonymous poem:

> Today a professor in a garden relaxing
> Like Plato of old in the academe shade
> Spoke out in a manner I never had heard him
> And this is one of the things that he said.
> Suppose that we state as a tenet of wisdom
> That knowledge is not for delight of the mind.
> Nor an end in itself, but a packet of treasure
> To hold and employ for the good of mankind.
> A torch or a candle is barren of meaning
> Except it give light to men as they climb,
> And thesis and tomes are but impotent jumble
> Unless they are tools in the building of time.
> We scholars toil on with the zeal of a miner
> For nuggets and nuggets and one nugget more,
> But scholars are needed to study the uses
> Of all the great mass of data and lore.
> And truly our tireless and endless researches
> Need yoking with man's daily problems and strife,
> For truth and beauty and virtue have value
> Confirmed by their uses in practical life.[33]
>
> (Anonymous)

Eventually, as the rate of technical obsolescence increases, the gap between academia and industry is sure to widen—especially without input from industry.

Ironically, in Japan, in the past, the cooperation between government and academia has been a major force in the development of the Japanese education system. Government cooperated with industry to produce a large pool of scientists and engineers to close the knowledge gap with the West as quickly as possible.[34] Grayson explains that the economic success of Japan was possible because of the "clear economic policy that has guided government actions."[35] He describes the many programs where the Ministry of Education "acted in harmony" with the government's economic goals.

Recently, however, education in Japan has become somewhat detached from economic pursuits and has become like a creature with its own motivations. It seems that educators and those making educational policies have taken to an extreme their position of avoiding interaction with industry.

D. PROFESSORS IN JAPANESE UNIVERSITIES

Even more than in the US, professors in Japan are very highly respected. The detached and independent role of higher education in Japan is best embodied in the professor. In most of academia worldwide, professors are mainly rewarded according to output of scholarly research. Teaching tends to be de-emphasized. To improve the relevancy of engineering education, we believe that teaching, or more fundamentally, student learning needs to be emphasized. Some universities in the US are starting to progress in this area. Generally in western schools, student–teacher interactions are encouraged and expected. Further, in US education, some are realizing that it is important not only to ask questions, but to learn how to ask the right questions. Two-way interaction between the student and the teacher stimulates learning for all parties.

In Japan, however, whether owing to cultural differences in the highly respected, almost aristocratic view of the professor, or to the fact that active learning is less "positively motivated," education is generally "one way." The result is minimal interaction between students and teachers. Professors lecture and students listen without question or discussion, thus stifling meaningful interaction.

According to Po S. Chung, there are no systems such as student evaluations to check the professor. As a possible explanation, he says, "In a society like Japan in which the teaching profession is extremely well respected, such assessment would be regarded . . . as showing great disrespect for the professors."[36] This also suggests a reason for the hesitation of students to interact with the professor. Interestingly, there is no teaching assistant form of grading or involvement by the student with the professor until in the final year of college. At this point, however, the student does interact closely with a professor to write a thesis for graduation. Otherwise, there are serious impediments to student learning in Japanese undergraduate engineering education.

This passive transmission of knowledge in higher education is also reflected in student evaluation. As a general role, according to two engineering professors at Musashi Institute of Technology, all students are passed.[37] Why is this so? Again, since industry does not expect immediately useful graduates, industry is not concerned with the performance of students in college. Rather, it is concerned with the prestige of the university which is based on the number of research papers published and not necessarily in preparing graduates for practice. As a result, Japanese engineering professors do not expect as much from their students as in the US.

Each year, the Ministry of Education evaluates the productivity of the professor solely based on the number of presentations and research papers written. This method of gauging faculty performance is similar to that in many US institutions, although to a greater degree. The more respected the papers they publish, the more the professor is respected, and the more their institution is respected. The more the institution is respected, the greater the demand for students seeking degrees. The greater the demand for these institutions, the harder and more selective the entrance examinations need to be. Also, the more respected the institution becomes, the more companies want to hire its graduates, further increasing demand. The harder these examinations become, the greater the pressures on prospective students. The greater the pressure to perform on the CEE, the more emphasis put on rote learning and the less emphasis on creativity and critical thinking.

Ironically, by bearing the major responsibility in Japan of training their workers for engineering practice after undergraduate schooling, industry has, in effect, robbed higher education (students and professors) of the motivation to prepare their students with practice capability.

E. RESEARCH AT JAPANESE UNIVERSITIES

In Japan, not only is teaching undervalued, but relevant research is also. Even though US university-based, basic research has been productive, it has often been seen as lacking relevancy. On the other hand, having no clear direction, university research in Japan suffers even more from what might be called a "dream syndrome," where the research objectives of universities are detached and even farther from that of industry than in the

US. Professors seem to choose research topics according to their own whims—these topics having little to do with real application. Although government–industry research in Japan is very active, industry–academia partnerships are very rare. In explaining why few cooperative studies with industry have been successful in manufacturing engineering in Japan, the first author has observed that, "In general, professors will research into too dreamful theme[s] and engineers from industry request too practical solutions."[38] This lack of relevance suggests the incompatibility between two seemingly different worlds. Where the US problem in research has been largely due to academia's focus on theory and science without teaching students how to apply it to real, open-ended problems most often encountered in industry, Japan's problem seems to be due to the reluctance of academia to work with industry. As a result, Japanese industry has relied on its own research efforts and university-based research remains largely irrelevant to the needs of industry.

F. STUDENTS AT JAPANESE UNIVERSITIES

As predicted, when shown the list of weaknesses of new US graduates, professors and those in industry in Japan conceded that this list also pertains to their own graduates. They added that the problem may exist to an even greater degree in Japan, because of the image of universities as more of a selecting mechanism for companies than a place to gain competencies for engineering practice.

Another challenge facing engineering education in Japan stems from ongoing socioeconomic changes. A trend in Japan of students opting to study subjects other than science and engineering has caused concern in academia. Engineering's attractiveness is being overshadowed by jobs in areas like banking and service, where there is higher pay and relatively easier studies in college.[39] Engineering as a profession is increasingly seen as *kiken, kitanal,* and *kitsui* (dangerous, dirty, and strenuous). The new generation of graduates do not see the company as such an important part of their lives. William Tabb, an economist, notes that the elders of Japan fear that the new generation will not be loyal to the old ways of living and no longer "slave away their lives for the good of the company."[40]

Incompatibility between the catch-up form of education that may have outlasted its usefulness, and the new more western-minded generation of students calls for marked change in Japanese engineering education.

G. FUTURE DIRECTIONS IN US AND JAPANESE ENGINEERING EDUCATION

The Japanese have a philosophy that can also be applied to the emerging view of the customer–supplier relationship between industry and academia in the United States "the next process is the customer." Who is listening to the needs of industry? Broadly speaking, it seems that engineering educators in Japan are not listening. We struggled to see a customer–supplier relationship between industry and academia comparable to that between Japanese industry and their consumers.

In the US there is encouraging evidence that academia is beginning to listen to the needs of industry. There are three points that support this.

First, new capstone-type courses in progressive institutions show that academia is listening and responding to the needs of industry. Many of these courses involve the use of industry projects. Further, the initiation of an Advances in Capstone Education Conference[41] is also encouraging, for it shows that engineering educators are concerned about their role in improving engineering education.

Second, funding from the government in efforts to improve educational relevance from The National Science Foundation (NSF) is increasingly more common. This is shown in the sponsorship by NSF of the aforementioned conference and of a large number of projects and several university consortia to improve undergraduate engineering education.

Third, ABET is heading toward outcomes-based accreditation. In two years, ABET plans to integrate outcomes oriented accreditation versus activity oriented.[42] In addition, US industry is encouraging relevance through programs like the Boeing's Outstanding Educator Award. Boeing has set a standard to encourage academic relevance. This award is presented to educators who "turn undergraduates into well-grounded engineers" and encourage students to develop attributes for success in engineering practice.[43] Not by chance did virtually all of the attributes Boeing listed as those needed to succeed as practicing engineers coincide with the top 20 best practices mentioned earlier.

We have painted a grave picture of Japanese engineering education. Japanese engineering education is unmistakably headed towards a crisis—if not already in it. However, there is evidence that some measures are being taken to improve the situation.

Government is calling for a more flexible structure of education that fosters creativity. Recently, a white paper report by the Prime Minister's Office (1995) pointed out that Japan has depended primarily on foreign nations for creative activities to generate knowledge and technology for innovative new products. From now on, Japan needs to foster creative activity by "institutional encouragement of such activity and remove any institutional impediments to it."[44]

In response to its past failed efforts at reform, the report says, "from now on the necessary improvements should be initiated under the nation's own initiative and with the understanding that failure to do so will greatly impair stable growth in the future."[44] The report concludes that Japan has not been successful at creating new knowledge and technology, but that "it is now important that Japan should find new breakthroughs and create new markets."[44]

III. INDUSTRY IN JAPAN

Japanese industry, has been the envy of the world for the past two decades. It has caught up and, many believe, surpassed the United States in manufacturing. However, recent socioeconomic changes have brought the continued economic success of Japan into question.

The prolonged recession and rising yen have dramatically changed the economy in Japan and continue to do so. By contrast, in the US, we are enjoying a period of sustained economic growth. These economic changes affect the way industry operates in both of our countries. Japanese industry is going through a period of restructuring. For example, the practices of lifetime employment and seniority-based compensation, the hallmarks of Japanese industry, are being changed to meet a new global market.

A. LIFETIME EMPLOYMENT

If the CEE is central to the education system in Japan, the practice of lifetime employment can be seen as central to the success of industry in Japan. This practice has allowed industry to invest in employee training, a seniority based pay system, job rotation, and selective hiring from prestigious institutions. The lifetime employment system, although it has encouraged a lack of preparation in higher education, has enabled excellent on-the-job training to take place. In contrast, US engineering graduates are increasingly expected to come with adequate training and to be immediately useful. This expectation is seldom voiced in Japanese companies.[45]

However, with changing socioeconomic conditions, lifetime employment is being challenged. As Tabb noted, the new generation of workers are not as motivated to put their company first and sacrifice for it as past generations did. Workers expect to have specific and interesting jobs and not be moved around with job rotation. If they are not satisfied, they are not afraid to change jobs. In many ways, employment practices are becoming more like those in the West.

The pressure of the appreciating yen also threatens lifetime employment in Japan. The most immediate consequence is what economists call the "hollowing-out" of Japan: "a shrinkage of the manufacturing sector as a result of a decline in exports due to a strong yen, a substitution of imports for domestic production, and a substitution of foreign investment for domestic investment."[46] Due to high costs of operation in Japan, industry is shifting manufacturing abroad at a stunning rate.

As the quality of foreign manufacturing increases, it is becoming more feasible to manufacture outside the country. Norio Ohga, chairman of the Sony Corporation states, "In Japan today, manufacturing just doesn't pay. . . . Since we have obligations to our shareholders, we've got no choice but to move manufacturing overseas. This may be an acceptable solution for a single company, but what does it mean for the country?"[47] Does this sound familiar? Industry seems to be responding to the appreciation of the yen in many different ways, but overseas production seems inevitable.

B. Future Directions of Industry's Role in Education

In a survey by Jetro[46] conducted in May 1995, Japanese companies expected to raise the overseas production rate from an average of 8.7% to 30.9% of total production. This may have serious consequences for engineering in Japan. Increasing overseas production will lead to fewer Japanese workers in their own companies. Having fewer workers in manufacturing means less Japanese technical expertise and demand for engineers. What does this mean for engineering education?

Industry will either need to seek a stronger voice in academia, as is starting to occur in the US, or continue to carry the burden of training employees. However, academia may be very slow to respond to the needs of industry, particularly in Japan. The failures of past reforms have only shown the tremendous inertia of the Japanese educational system. Not even a Prime Minister could overcome this inertia. Furthermore, industry seems to perpetuate the present system through its current practices of training on the job and not expecting adequately prepared graduates, a tradition of lifetime employment, and selective hiring practices based on credentials.

If industry in Japan does not pressure academia to prepare graduates more adequately, then students will continue to take their studies less seriously. Also, without more industrial influence, research will continue to be irrelevant to the needs of industry, and professors will continue to undervalue teaching.

What seems to be necessary in Japan is a crisis situation, similar to the one in industrial America in the mid-eighties, to influence industry to exert pressure on education to change. Will the current pressures on industry in Japan initiate this reformation in education? Will this reformation include a shift in engineering education toward industrial relevance? These questions will be answered as Japan deals with their current challenges.

IV. Conclusion

Many have suggested importation of the Japanese educational model to improve the US situation. We believe, however, that this is not the best solution. The Japanese education system is burdened with a rigid, creativity-suppressing examination system which has profoundly affected the quality of higher education. This system has produced weaknesses similar to those observed in US engineering graduates, but to a greater extent.

The strength of Japanese engineering education has been the combination of a strong but unbalanced primary education and extensive continuous training on the job. However, the very system that has enabled it to succeed is being questioned. Unfortunately, higher education in Japan seems to contribute little to the engineer and is the weak link in education. Can Japan afford to ignore this situation with increasing economic pressures on industry worldwide? Probably not. Japan will need to mobilize its education system just as it did after the war in an effort to catch up economically with the West.

Apparently, industry is going through changes, but academia has been reluctant and slow to respond.

Given this situation, one would expect academia to respond with some solutions. Apparently, engineering educators in Japan have not conceived of working with industry to increase relevance in higher education. Evidently, they see no motivation for change.

These problems are ripe for change in Japan, but the outlook is not encouraging. On the whole, industry in Japan is not calling on educators and educational policy makers to improve higher education. In addition, the rigid education system seems to perpetuate itself. Challenging times await.

However, Japan has always been capable of adaptation and change. As Japanese industry restructures, there will be a chance for US industry to catch up in areas like customer satisfaction, quality, cost, and quickness to market. At this decisive time, if engineering educators and stake holders in the US industry take advantage of this opportunity by continuing to increase the relevance of engineering education, the US will certainly have an advantage in the long run.

In the US, we have already started to make headway. Indeed, American engineering educators can learn from the long-term vision of Japanese industry. The Japanese invested in new technologies to produce growth for the long range in the automobile, electronics, and semiconductor manufacturing industries, and in human resources through the practices of lifetime employment and extensive on-the-job training. Similarly, continued investment in the quest for educational relevance in undergraduate engineering education will bring rewards in greater productivity and competitiveness for the United States.

TAKUTO YAMADA *is currently working at John Deere Worldwide Construction Equipment Division in Dubuque, Iowa as a mechanical engineer. He graduated in 1997 from Brigham Young University with a degree in mechanical engineering. He wrote this paper in collaberation with Professor Todd while he was an undergraduate research assistant.*

ROBERT H. TODD, *currently a professor in the Mechanical Engineering Department and past chair of the Department of Manufacturing Engineering and Engineering Technology at BYU, received his PhD from Stanford in 1971. He teaches several courses in manufacturing processes, process machine development, manufacturing systems, and engineering design.*

Acknowledgments

The research and travel association with this effort were sponsored by the Air Force Office of Scientific Research, Air Force Material Command, USAF, under grant number F49620-95-1-0052, US–Japan Center of Utah. The authors gratefully acknowledge this support. The US government is authorized to reproduce and distribute reprints for government purposes notwithstanding any copyright notation thereon. The views and conclusions contained herein are those of the authors and should not be interpreted as necessarily representing the official policies or endorsements, either expressed or implied, of the Air Force Office of Scientific Research or the US government.

References

1. Todd, Robert H., Carl D. Sorensen, Spencer P. Magleby, "Designing a Senior Capstone course to Satisfy Industrial Customers," *Journal of Engineering Education,* vol. 82, no 2. April 1993, pp. 92–100.

2. American Society of Mechanical Engineers, "Mechanical Engineering Curriculum Development Initiative: Integrating the Product Realization Process (PRP) into the Undergraduate Curriculum," American Society of Mechanical Engineers, New York, December 1995, pp. C2–C5.

3. Dertouzos, Lester, Solow, The MIT Commission on Industrial Productivity, *Made in America: Regaining the Productive Edge,* The MIT Press, Cambridge, Massachusetts, 1989, p. 166.

4. Ibid., p. 81.

5. Sharpe, William N., Jr., and Andrew F. Conn, "An Industry-Sponsored Capstone Design Course," *1993 Frontiers in Education Conference Proceedings,* ASEE 1993, pp. 493–496.

6. Dutson, Alan J., Robert H. Todd, Spencer P. Magleby, Carl D. Sorensen, "A Review of Literature on Teaching Engineering Design Through Project-Oriented Capstone Courses," *Journal of Engineering Education,* vol. 86, no. 1, 1997, pp. 17–28.

7. Bright, Anthony, "Teaching and Learning in the Engineering Clinic Program at Harvey Mudd College," *Proceedings, Advances in Capstone Education August 3–5 1994: Fostering Industrial Relations,* Provo, UT 1994, pp. 113–116.

8. Fingleton, Eamonn, "Don't Let Up on Japan," *New York Times,* April 9, 1994.

9. US Department of Commerce, 1993, and Economic Planning Agency, Japan, 1993.

10. Jetro, *White Paper on Science and Technology,* 1993, Science and Technology Agency.

11. Grayson, Lawrence P., "Japan's Intellectual Challenge: The Strategy," *Engineering Education,* December 1983, pp. 139–147.

12. Grayson, Lawrence P., "Japan's Intellectual Challenge: The System," *Engineering Education,* January 1984, pp. 211–220.

13. Grayson, Lawrence P., "Japan's Intellectual Challenge: The Future," *Engineering Education,* February 1984, pp. 296–304.

14. National Council on Educational Reform, *First Report on Educational Reform* (Tokyo, June 26, 1985); *Second Report on Educational Reform* (Tokyo, April 23, 1986); *Third Report on Educational Reform,* (Tokyo, April 1, 1987). Also see Amano Ikuo, "The Dilemma of Japanese Education Today," *The Japan Foundation Newsletter* vol. 8, no. 5, March 1986, pp. 1–9.

15. US Department of Education, *Japanese Education Today*, Washington DC, 1987.

16. Dertouzos et al., *op. cit.* ref. 3, p.78.

17. Uchida, Michio, Ishii, Yohei, "The University in Decline," *Tokyo Business,* Jan./Feb. 1993, pp. 52–56.

18. US Department of Education, *Japanese Education Today,* Washington DC, 1987.

19. Shimahara, Nobuo K., *Adaptation and Education in Japan,* Praeger, New York, 1979, p.133.

20. Ibid., p. 137.

21. Grayson, *op.cit.,* ref. 11, p. 139.

22. Anderson, R.S., *Education in Japan: A Century of Modern Development,* HEW, 1975, p. 108.

23. Horio, Teruhisa, *Educational Thought and Ideology in Modern Japan,* University of Tokyo Press, 1988, p. viii.

24. Shimahara, Nobuo K., *op. cit.*, ref. 18, p. 85.

25. Rholen, Thomas P., *Japan's High Schools,* University of California Press, Los Angeles, 1983, p. 87.

26. The Tokai Bank Ltd., Expenditure on Education for Children, *Cram School Enrollment, (1984–1995),* 1995.

27. Haiducek, Nicholas J., *Japanese Education: Made in the USA,* Praeger, New York, 1991, p. 40.

28. Horio, Teruhisa, *Educational Thought and Ideology in Modern Japan,* University of Tokyo Press, 1989, p. 13.

29. ABET, "What is ABET?" http://www.abet.ba.md.us/ABET.html, May 10, 1996.

30. Personal conversation with student at Tokyo Denki University, November 15, 1995.

31. Dore, Ronald P. and Mari Sako, *How the Japanese Learn to Work,* Routledge, New York, 1989, p. xii.

32. Ellington, Lucien, *Education in the Japanese Life-Cycle: Implications for the United States,* The Edwin Mellen Press, Wales, 1992, p. 141.

33. Packer, Boyd K., "The Snow White-Birds." Address given at Brigham Young University's Annual University Conference, August 29, 1995.

34. Grayson, Lawrence P. *op. cit.,* ref. 11, p. 140.

35. Grayson, Lawrence P. *op.cit.,* ref.11, p. 139.

36. Chung, Po S., "Engineering Education Systems in Japanese Universities," *Comparative Education Review,* August 1986, p. 425.

37. Conversation with Masaru Hoshiya and Nozawa Kazunori, Professors, Mechanical Engineering Department, Musashi Institute of Technology, November 15, 1995.

38. Yamada, Takuro, "An Approach to Educate Useful Production Engineers." *Proceedings, Manufacturing Education for the 21st Century Conference,* San Diego, March 13–15, 1996, p. 49.

39. Conversation with Takashi Matsumura, Associate Professor, Mechanical Engineering Department, Tokyo Denki University, November 14, 1995.

40. Tabb, William K., *The Postwar Japanese System,* Oxford University Press, New York, 1995, p. 304.

41. Brigham Young University College of Engineering and Technology, *Proceedings, Advances in Capstone Education August 3–5 1994: Fostering Industrial Relations,* Provo, UT, 1994.

42. ABET, Engineering Criteria 2000, *Engineering Accreditation Commission,* http://www.abet.ba.md.us/EAC/eac2000.html, May 10, 1996.

43. The Boeing Company, Poster of Outstanding Educator Award, Seattle, Washington, 1996.

44. Science and Technology Agency, "White Paper on Science and Technology—1995: Fifty Years of Postwar Science and Technology in Japan," *Prime Minister's Office, Japan,* July 1995.

45. Dore et al., *op. cit.,* ref. 31, p. 77.

46. Jetro, "Diverse Measures to Counter the Appreciation of the Yen and a Higher Rate of Overseas Production," http://www.jetro.go.jp/WHITEPAPER/tra1-5.html, May 10, 1996.

47. Takai, Madoka, "Vanishing Point Ahead: Industry Begins to Disappear," *Tokyo Business,* August 1995, pp. 8–11.

Questions

1. What does the customer/supplier metaphor—used here to describe the relationship between industry and the university—reveal about the authors' assumptions about at least one of the purposes of education?
2. Why is the comparison between Japanese and US industry useful?
3. What counts as evidence in this article and how is that evidence collected?
4. What do the authors mean by "relevance"? Do they demonstrate that relevance is necessary for successful education? Are there any reasons for creating a curriculum that is not "relevant" according to the authors' definition?

Going Forth to Serve

At the entrance of BYU is written the phrase: Enter to Learn, Go Forth to Serve. The "Enter to Learn" is easy to understand. We come to a university to learn. What exactly is meant by "Go Forth to Serve" is a little less clear. Everyone in the Church serves in one way or another—teaching a lesson, cleaning a yard, giving food to the hungry. A college degree isn't a requirement for opening your heart. So what is the relationship between learning and serving, especially academic learning? Naturally, anything we learn helps us to think through problems more clearly, to have more understanding of others, to listen to others carefully, and to bring additional knowledge to any discussion or process—improving our capacity to serve. But is there any way to serve in the academic community? Can we add to the conversation in meaningful and productive ways?

In this section, the articles by John Tanner and Madison Sowell discuss how education—and a BYU education in particular—can enrich the "real world" and provide service opportunities. The other articles present three ways in which to give academic service. The most traditional method is joining the academic conversation by collaboration with colleagues both from inside and outside BYU. For example, artists Gary Burton, Joseph Ostraff, and Brian Christensen created a collaborative art project built around a quote by Paul Tillich, which Ed Cutler critiques. Thomas Plummer and John Murphy debate the lessons learned from the character Ophelia in Shakespeare's *Hamlet.* Another method of serving is using research to improve the world around us. For example, Kate Kirkham's research helps businesses to value diversity in the workplace and Paul Cox's research helps to save Samoan rainforests. The final method is service learning. Suzanne Lundquist explains service learning and discusses her students' experiences in Mexico. These articles give you an opportunity to explore ways in which you can go forth and serve.

The Real World

JOHN SEARS TANNER

When John Tanner received his acceptance letter to Berkeley's graduate school, he also received another letter telling him candidly that the graduates of their program—one of the best in the nation—were not getting jobs upon graduating. Having decided to pursue graduate work in literature instead of law, he went into graduate school aware of the risk he was taking and with a desire to justify his own decision. While in school, and especially during his summer work in a brick yard, Tanner meditated upon his decision to study literature. Little by little, he sought to justify the study of literature, and liberal arts as a whole, in the light of the dearth of job opportunities in the seventies. Would he use his degree to "sell shoes and drive taxis," as it was rumored? Was literature worth it when other training could get him a more secure job in the "real world"? In the following article, originally published in College English, *Tanner defends the study of liberal arts, saying that literature is not just a form of escapism, but is a tool that allows us to deal with the true complexities of human existence.*

Recently I spent about an hour being interviewed by a man who repeatedly invoked a phrase that both rankled and intrigued me. "Unlike teaching writing in college," he said, "doing consulting for our firm will require you to interface constantly with the real world of business and industry"; or again, "Our PhD consultants report that it is two or three times more strenuous teaching writing to professional adults in the real world than it is instructing unskilled kids in the college classroom." Real world? The phrase always enters conversations thick with assumptions about the negligible value of competing realities. Anyone wishing to distinguish one's own occupation as more "relevant" or "practical" (other question-begging terms) than another's is likely to appropriate the label "real world" to his or her own sphere of interest and action, thus denying equal ontological footing to other, quite dissimilar realities. What is seen as the real world varies according to one's vantage.

As a student I frequently heard "real world" used to differentiate the nonacademic from the academic realm. This usage implies that the university forms an enclave of unreality, an ethereal ivory tower floating above a more mundane landscape where, presumably, real people do things that really matter. So prevalent is this stereotype that even those within the academy partially accept it, characterizing university disciplines according to their relative interest to those on the outside. Thus students see an accounting major as better preparation for the "real world" than the detached rigor imposed by a mathematics major; the experimental physicist looks slightly askance at the pure speculation of a theoretical colleague, seeming so abstracted from the "real world."

Outside university portals, the extramural world is similarly stratified into varying levels of reality; ironically, not all the landscape outside the ivory tower is equally real. Business executives regard the produce-or-perish marketplace they inhabit as the "real world," unlike the over-protected environment of government bureaucrats; while for their part, artisans see all desk jobs as slightly unreal, compared to the "real world" where durable goods are made and tangible services rendered.

In general, as our society uses "real world," any activity failing to satisfy directly our material needs may be suspect as less than real. By contrast, the more nearly work comes to moving earth usefully from one place to another, the more undisputedly it belongs to the "real world." Paradigmatic of "real world" labor would be such actions as constructing a house, farming a field, fixing a toilet. This view of reality . . . is also akin to a long line of more philosophical affirmations of the priority of the sensory world over our speculations about it. . . . However, it is in the spirit of Samuel Johnson that our society employs the tag "real world." Johnson's kicking of a rock to refute Berkeley's idealism well expresses a gut-level feeling we all share about what, after all, is real and unreal.

Philosophers like Berkeley, however, remind us that the assumptions about reality built into the casual cliché "real world" may be turned completely on their heads, and that the reality of any perception of the world ought not simply to be taken for granted. According to Plato, for example, the real circle is not any shape that ever has or can exist in even our best representations, which merely approximate a perfectly round ideal form residing in our minds—and, for Plato, in a realm of ideal forms. (Can you imagine how Plato's Socrates would have badgered someone using such a presumptuous, unexamined locution as "real world"?) Likewise, looking at a piece of wax through Descartes's eyes, we recall that the true wax cannot be apprehended by any sense perception it may leave on our taste, touch, or smell, for all these are merely accidents of temperature; all change when solid wax melts and burns. To the Cartesian mind, the real wax is, rather, that tasteless, odorless, colorless substance which persists through whatever changes we may induce in the laboratory.

These inversions of our ordinary notions of reality disclose some of the controversies buried below the surface of the loose label "real world." Neither the materialist's nor the idealist's view of reality will ever (I hope) crowd out the other completely, for there will always be someone in the academy eager to speculate about the imperfections of circle-drawings, as well as someone ready to go out in a field and kick his foot against a rock.

In my years as a student, I have bounced back and forth between environments where either mental or material realities alternatively laid claim to greater ontological truth. In common with many who have worked their way through school, I spent my undergraduate mornings discussing Donne or Kierkegaard, or Marx, and my afternoons cleaning ovens in a student housing project or hauling away frozen debris from a construction site. Likewise, I began graduate studies by attending school all day and working (and sleeping) as a watchman all night. Similarly, during summer vacations I regularly did work unrelated to my studies—from bucking bales of hay to barking for a bumper car ride, from collating computer print-outs to cooking as a short-order chef. In order to put myself through school, I had to become an amphibian of sorts, capable of surviving contrasting philosophical ecosystems. The challenge of survival often prompted reflection about the relationship between the divergent worlds real in my workplace and in my lecture hall.

A couple of years ago, I spent the summer employed in a Utah brickyard. The work was hot, dirty, and heavy. One night on a graveyard shift, between two and four in the morning, I found myself inside a deep vat, so narrow that I could not square my shoulders to its sides, wiping off spent hydraulic fluid with rags—and, in the process, with my clothes, face, and hair. Another night I shoveled broken bricks, dust, and oil out of sump underneath a dangerous, deafening banding machine. Scraping and digging until I had finally excavated a pit well over my head, I scooped the greasy, sodden waste onto the floor above, then shoveled it again into a wheelbarrow which I dragged outside, dumping the contents while the sweat cooled on my back and face in the welcome silence of the cool mountain air.

Work in the brickyard, like much labor in the "real world," entailed a great deal of routine, which employed my hands and back but left my mind largely unoccupied. Since my days of working after high school as a grocery bagger, it has been my custom to use free mental time for focused reflection. That summer in the brickyard, I set about reviewing and memorizing Milton in preparation for my doctoral exams. One morning while sweeping brickdust off the factory floor, I found myself remembering Satan's heroic boast in *Paradise Lost:* "The mind is its own place, and can make a Heaven of Hell or a Hell of Heaven." As an undergraduate, I had often thought of those lines in connection with my part-time work, discovering in them a justification for liberal education and a vindication for a difficult decision to do graduate study in English despite the grim prospects for subsequent employment in the field. Whatever I eventually have to do in order to earn a living, I had often reasoned (attempting to reassure myself), I will be the richer for having learned as much as I can about our literature. For my actual environment will be the one within my mind, whatever external conditions I endure. "The mind is its own place," I mused again. I am not confined to this pushbroom; I can turn my Hells into Heavens.

No sooner had Milton's poetry set in motion this familiar, comfortable, indeed self-serving sequence of reflections than I found myself stopped short by a new realization born of a deeper understanding of the poem. I saw more clearly than ever before that Satan's boast is preposterous, a mixture of gross self-deception and ironic truth. He cannot turn Hell into Heaven by thinking it so, though he can convert Heaven into Hell by force of his own tormented mind. For all its seeming appeal, Satan's proud stoicism is thoroughly undercut in the poem. Could my defense of the liberal arts be equally suspect?

I saw quickly that it was indeed inadequate, and was so for the same reasons that Satan's position is untenable. Satan's posture towards Hell, as mine towards my workplace, involves an utter denial of external reality, a spirit of *contemptus mundi* (highly parodic otherworldliness in Satan's case), a denigration of creation. For Satan, the created world exists only as something to be denied, and he denies the world by attempting to subsume it into his own head and thus to shape it according to the arbitrary fiat of his own will. In his pretension to Godlike power to make the world over merely by renaming it (Hell is Heaven, Heaven Hell), Satan cuts himself off from the possibility of ever learning from a universe outside himself. He is, as Milton so imaginatively portrays, like a sailor passing beyond the Cape of Hope (i.e., in despair), one who cannot be well-pleased by the grateful smell of the Sabean odors from the spicy shore of Araby the blest, nor delay, nor slack his course (*Paradise Lost,* IV, 158 ff.). Satan cannot profit from the physical universe; he has severed himself from it, preferring instead the world of his own mind, his own wretched mind: "Which way I fly is Hell; myself am Hell." Satan is an escapist damned never to escape himself, displaying in painful clarity the perils of positive thinking engaged in by an absolutely wilful being.

So my thoughts, prompted by the predicament of Milton's Satan, led me to see the escapism implicit in an apology for liberal education generated from Satan's rhetoric. If knowledge of the liberal arts provides nothing more than a pleasant escape from present drudgery—the implication of my reasoning that the mind is its own place, having the power to release me from the humdrum of merely pushing a broom into a free-ranging gambol with great ideas—then how could I defend my studies as more valuable than the radio headsets or girlie magazines others use to distract themselves from the tedium? These diversions, too, free the mind from boredom induced by menial tasks. To argue for the value of the study of the humanities on the grounds that it gives one something to take one's mind off routine work is to permit no distinction between *Romeo and Juliet* and *Hustler*. Such a defense of the liberal arts concedes as much irrelevance to them as their most philistine detractor could desire.

As soon as I had formulated the problem clearly, however, I recognized that the error lay in my reasoning and not in my experience of the worth of the humanities. Humanistic knowledge frees the mind for flights of speculation, to be sure, but education in the liberal arts can and ought not merely detach one from the "real world" so much as allow one greater vantages from which to view the world as it really is, in all its variety. *Romeo and Juliet* is a more valuable object of attention than *Hustler* because it has more—immensely more—to say about love and the human condition. Shakespeare provides a better prism than does pornography through which to see the spectrum of our human complexity.

This fresh formulation of my old argument in behalf of the value of liberal education clearly represented a deeper, more tenable justification. But was it true? Did my reasoning conform to my experience that summer in the brickyard? Did the humanities illuminate the factory? Gratefully, I remembered recent moments which confirmed the power of education to reveal inconspicuous brickyard realities. I recalled many thoughts and several conversations with fellow workers about the alienating, dehumanizing pressures within the factory; and these observations were deepened, and in some sense enabled, by my reading of Dickens, Carlyle, Marx, Thoreau, Veblen, and the like. Without an acquaintance with the nineteenth-century writers who described acutely the industrial revolution, I suspect that much of what I felt in that huge brick factory would have remained indistinct and inarticulate.

I recollected another instance when years of paying attention to aesthetic matters rewarded me with an unforgettable moment of vision in the factory. Resting during a breakdown on the conveyor belt one evening, I glanced across the machinery, through a maze of huge crossbeam girders, at my foreman unwedging some jammed bricks. For a few thrilling seconds I did not see Neldon Hansen straining on a sixteen-inch crescent wrench, but beheld a curved human figure amid the angular lines of machines. He was framed by steel structures as though in a picture, like

Charlie Chaplin strapped on a giant gear in *Modern Times,* an image of some of the great conflicts of our age. And I wondered how to interpret the symbol revealed in this epiphany: does his contorted posture display the crushing tyranny of machine over man? Or do his curves witness to a distinctly human flexibility allowing us the suppleness to adapt when our rigid inventions run amok?

These experiences enabled by philosophy, history, literature, art, and movies constitute, surely, realities about the "real world" (albeit of a different order from the useful knowledge of operating a kiln, running a bander, driving a fork lift). The "real world" to which my interviewer referred intersects many realities; it cannot be reduced to a single dimension. No province hastily designated as the "real world" is well-served by ignorance of, or lack of sympathy towards, very different conceptions of reality. What I knew about the humanities enriched my experience in the brickyard, and conversely, what I lived in the brickyard brought to life ideas and images garnered from the classroom. Without either, I would be the poorer.

Yet, as I leaned against my broom in the factory that day, doubts still persisted. Some irrepressible voice inside of me urged, "Only this is real: this concrete, this steel, these solid bricks—and this paycheck for which I endure it all." I felt the urge to kick my foot against the nearest brick and exclaim, "Thus I refute all this super-subtle speculation! What does a fancy liberal arts education have to say, really, about the fine art of shoveling broken bricks? Can Milton truly help me better understand my present task of sweeping a factory floor?"

Then came the culminating insight: Milton had indeed taught me something about sweeping, something very profound, that very hour. Through a poem written in an age and about a supernatural realm seemingly so remote from my present circumstances, I had been reminded about what truly happens when a human being does something so simple as sweep or shovel. Confronted with routine work, the mind can and will range; humans cannot be confined to the boundaries of their immediate sensations. Consequently, every one of my fellow laborers (whom I surveyed in a glance) inhabits a unique world, even while we share a common one. We are created like Satan, with minds that are their own place, and like Hamlet, "with such large discourse, looking before and after." Human "capability and godlike reason" are part of our glory, and one of our burdens. Since each human being lives in a world of both mind and matter, each perforce must arbitrate between imagination and sensation. None is exclusively what she does or what he thinks, none lives in a single "real world." For the real world is not a universe but a multiverse.

John Sears Tanner, *professor of English, received his BA from BYU in 1974 and his PhD from the University of California, Berkeley in 1980. Before his recent appointment as chair of the English Department, he served as Associate Academic Vice President. Tanner specializes in Milton and seventeenth-century English literature as well as in philosophical and religious approaches to literature. Before coming to BYU, Tanner also taught at Florida State and in Brazil as a Fulbright Lecturer. Tanner has published extensively, including a book on Kirkegaard and Milton. He also wrote the text for "Bless Our Fast We Pray" in the* LDS Hymnal.

Questions and Writing Activity

1. What is "real" about the "real world"? How does the "real world" differ from the academic world?
2. What is the relationship between theoretical knowledge and practical knowledge?
3. Write a personal essay in which you describe some "brickyard" realities that you have endured. How do your experiences compare with Tanner's? What have you learned through your practical experiences that can enhance your academic training?

Diagnosing and Treating the Ophelia Syndrome

THOMAS G. PLUMMER

Originally presented as a lecture for college juniors and seniors, "Diagnosing and Treating the Ophelia Syndrome" was published in BYU Today *in January 1981 and has been published as part of a pamphlet given to incoming freshmen at BYU. In this article, Thomas G. Plummer laments the existence of the "Ophelia Syndrome," a condition wherein students (Ophelia) do not think for themselves, but rather have a teacher (Polonius) feed them information as one would feed a baby. Plummer claims that universities are particularly susceptible to such a syndrome and that both students and professors are implicated when it occurs. After explicating the problems underlying the Ophelia Syndrome, Plummer discusses six possible treatments, things that he himself wishes he had done while an undergraduate.*

In *Hamlet* (Act 1, Scene 3) Laertes warns his sister, Ophelia, to avoid falling in love with Hamlet, whose advances, Laertes claims, are prompted by fleeting, youthful lust. He cautions her against Hamlet's "unmastered importunity" and counsels her "that best safety lies in fear."[1]

Then her father, Polonius, begins to meddle. He knows, he tells Ophelia, that she has responded to Hamlet's attention, and then informs her that "she does not understand [herself] so clearly." He asks if she believes Hamlet's affections are genuine, to which Ophelia responds, "I do not know, my lord, what I should think." Polonius answers, "I'll teach you. Think yourself a baby."

In this scene Shakespeare has given us the essence of what I call the "Ophelia Syndrome." It requires two players, a Polonius and an Ophelia. It is condensed into these two lines: "I do now know, my lord, what I should think," and, "I'll teach you. Think yourself a baby." Ophelia does not know what she should think, and Polonius, reducing her to the stature of a baby, presumes to tell her. Polonius pontificates. He purports to know answers when he has none. He claims to have truth when he himself obscures it. He feigns expertise by virtue of his authority. But his real interest is power: he clamors to be a parent to other adults and exhorts them to become children to his word. Ophelia is less than naive. She is chronically ignorant, chronically dependent, and chronically submissive. She is an adult who chooses to be a baby, one who does not know her own opinions and who would not express them to an authority if she did.

S. I. Hayakawa describes symptoms of the Ophelia Syndrome in his essay "What Does It Mean To Be Creative?":

> Most people don't know the answer to the question, "How are you? How do you feel?" The reason why they don't know is that they are so busy feeling what they are supposed to, that they never get down to examining their own deepest feelings. "How did you like the play?" "Oh, it was a fine play. It was well reviewed in *The New Yorker*." With authority figures like drama critics and book reviewers and teachers and professors telling us what to think and how to feel, many of us are busy playing roles, fulfilling other people's expectations. As Republicans, we think what other Republicans think. As Catholics, we think what other Catholics think. And so on. Not many of us ask ourselves, "How do I feel? What do I think?"—and wait for an answer.[2]

Charles Schulz characterized the Ophelia Syndrome more succinctly in this "Peanuts" cartoon:

PEANUTS reprinted by permission of United Feature Syndicate, Inc.

Psychologist Carl Jung describes this dependence on others for one's thought in the context of his discussion of "individuation."[3] Individuation is the process of learning to integrate the diverse parts of the Self into a coherent whole. It is a psychological "growing up." It means to discover those aspects of the Self that distinguish one person from another. Failure to achieve individuation leaves people dependent on other, stronger personalities for their identity. They fail to understand their uniqueness.[4]

I have a friend who is fond of saying, "If we both think the same way, one of us is unnecessary." The clone, the chameleon personality, is the Ophelia Syndrome in another form. One reading of Ophelia's suicide later in *Hamlet* suggests that because she has no thoughts of her own, because she has listened only to the contradictory voices of the men around her—Laertes, Polonius, and Hamlet—she reaches a breaking point. They have all used her: "She is only valued for the roles that further other people's plots. Treated as a helpless child, she finally becomes one."[5] Her childishness is just a step along the regression to suicide, a natural—if not logical—solution to her dependence on conflicting authorities.

The Ophelia Syndrome manifests itself in universities. The Ophelia (substitute a male name if you choose) writes copious notes in every class and memorizes them for examinations.[6] The Polonius writes examination questions that address just what was covered in the textbook or lectures. The Ophelia wants to know exactly what the topic for a paper should be. The Polonius prescribes it. The Ophelia wants to be a parrot, because it feels safe. The Polonius enjoys making parrot cages. In the end, the Ophelia becomes the clone of the Polonius, and one of them is unnecessary. I worry often that universities may be rendering their most serious students, those who have been "good" all their lives, vulnerable to the Ophelia Syndrome rather than motivating them to individuation.

And so what? Is it such a bad thing to emulate teachers? What if you are a student of biochemistry or German grammar? Then you have to memorize information and take notes from instructors who know more, because the basic material is factual. There is no other way. And this is a temporary condition of many areas of study. But eventually every discipline enters into the unknown, the uncertain, the theoretical, the hypothetical, where teachers can no longer tell students with certainty what they should think. It is only an illusion, a wish of the Ophelias and the Poloniuses that literary texts have just one interpretation or that the exact sciences be exact. At its best, even science is a creative art. Hayakawa quotes his good friend Alfred Korzybski as saying,

> Creative scientists know very well from observation of themselves that all creative work starts as a feeling, inclination, suspicion, intuition, hunch, or some other nonverbal affective state, which only at a later date, after a sort of nursing, takes the shape of verbal expression worked out later in a rationalized, coherent . . . theory.[7]

Most of us have metaphors—either subconsciously or consciously—of our student experience. I asked several of my students about theirs. One said he thinks of himself as a computer with insufficient memory. He is able to enter information but cannot recall it. One said he is a sieve. A lot of stuff goes right on through, but important pieces stay lodged. One said she feels like a pedestrian in front of a steamroller, and the driver will not give her any hints about how to get out of the way. Another described his metaphor as a tennis match in which he must anticipate his instructor's response to each shot. Another thought of herself as a dog jumping through a hoop. Another described himself as a mouse in a maze with no directional signs and no exits. Another felt like a child in a candy store where you can choose only one or two pieces to take home. Those metaphors describe people at various stages along the way from Ophelia to individuation.

Talk is cheap. It's one thing to say, "Learn to think for yourself," and it's quite another to do it. A recent *Fortune* magazine article described the plight of middle managers in American corporations. Driven by chief executive officers at the top for greater profits and productivity, many are working 70 or 80 hours a week and sometimes more. The article reports that the corporate byword for urging these people on is "think smarter." But since no one really knows what that means or how to think smarter, they just work longer. And people are burning out.[8]

Learning to think while still in college has its advantages. It may mean shorter working hours later on. It may mean not having a mid-life crisis because you chose to study what you wanted rather than something someone else wanted you to study. It may mean becoming your own person. It may, purely and simply, mean a much happier life. I want to suggest things you can do—six things I wish I had done—to treat the Ophelia Syndrome.

TREATMENT 1: SEEK OUT AND LEARN FROM GREAT TEACHERS, REGARDLESS OF WHAT THEY TEACH

How do you find them? First of all, they have a reputation among students. They are known to set people on fire, to inspire them. They are known to be challenging, fair, and tough. They refuse to be a Polonius, they refuse to make you a baby, and they refuse to do your thinking for you. They join you as a partner in a learning and research enterprise. I recently heard a nationally-televised interview with violinist Itzhak Perlman and his teacher, Dorothy Delay, at the Juilliard School of Music. Perlman, now 45, was sent to Juilliard as a gifted child prodigy. He was angry to have been sent to New York, far from his friends and family in Israel, and he was furious to live in the Juilliard student hotel, an environment that he considered unseemly.

The interviewer asked him how he had liked his teacher.

"I hated her," he replied.

Ms. Delay, a gentle woman with an air of complete calm, smiled into the camera.

"I hated her," he repeated.

"Why?" the interviewer asked.

"She would never tell me what to do," said Perlman. "She would stop me in the middle of a scale and say, 'Now Itzhak, what is your concept of a C-sharp?' It made me furious. She refused to tell me what to do. But," he went on, "I began to think as I played. My playing became an engaging intellectual exercise in which I understood every note and why I played it the way I did, because I had thought about it myself."

In that same spirit, Wayne Booth in his book, *The Vocation of a Teacher,* asserts that regardless of whether a teacher lectures or runs discussions, the "teacher has failed if students leave the classroom assuming that the task of thinking through to the next step lies entirely with the teacher."[9] To this point, Booth adds three more principles that will help teachers and students avoid the Polonius role. Addressing instructors, he writes,

> 1. You gotta get them talking to each other, not just to you or to the air.
> 2. You gotta get them talking about the subject, not just having a bull session in which nobody really listens to anybody else. This means insisting on at least the following rule in every discussion. Whether I call on you or you speak up spontaneously, please address the previous speaker, or give a reason for changing subject.
> 3. You gotta find ways to prevent yourself from relapsing into a badly prepared lecturette, disguised as a discussion. Informal lectures are usually worse than prepared ones.[10]

Treatment 2: Dare to Know and Trust Yourself[11]

Perhaps it goes without saying that you cannot know what to think if you do not know who you are. People go about self-discovery in various ways, and I can only share my own experience. I did not begin a truly honest search for my "self" until I was 40 years old. Then it became an obsession. I took personality tests. I reread old letters I had written and received. I began keeping a journal. I wish I had done it all 20 years before.

I now keep track of myself and my thinking through writing. I write letters and keep copies of what I write. I have had two sons on missions, and I make sure that I say things to them not only that I want to say but also want to remember. Second, I keep a journal—sporadically but frequently. I never take more than five or ten minutes to write in it, and when I write, I write intensively. I write to find my own voice, my own thoughts. I do not worry about who may read it later. It is for me. I write about my subconscious as well as my conscious self, because I believe that dreams do much of my thinking for me. Here is a dream from November 15, 1987:

Louise and I were driving through a sparsely populated, desolate area. The car engine faltered and quit. Luckily, just across the road was a Chevron station. I knew the repair work was minor and pushed the car into the station. It was ready later in the day.

The service station attendant pushed a credit card bill toward me and said, "Sign here." I signed. "How much was the repair?" I asked.

"$963," he replied.

"$963? What cost $963?" I was incredulous.

"Well, the repair work, and we put in a new dashboard."

"A new dashboard? How come a new dashboard?"

"The old one was scratched up," he replied.

"Why didn't you ask me before you did that?" I was now screaming. "I won't pay."

"You've signed the bill," he said. "You have to pay." His voice was gravely, firm.

He was right. I'd signed the bill. I had to pay.

"Just let me see the bill again," I asked. "I won't destroy it. I'm not a cheater."

Reluctantly he let me take it. I could tell he didn't trust me. Other mechanics surrounded me and stared, sober faced, menacing. Heavy, burly faces. I looked at the bill. $963. It will take months and months to pay off.

As I look back through this journal, I rediscover myself. There are notes about my son's crisis with his mission president, a painful chapter, and my efforts to play diplomat. There is a love note from my wife, notes on a line from Blake's poem "London," reflections on a painting in our dining room, a list of highlights from 25 years of marriage, a greedy wish list for ourselves, plans for a trip to Tokyo, a red horse chestnut blossom from a BYU tree, and a poem in reference to William Carlos Williams:

The chocolate hazelnut torte
At the Market Street Broiler
After a bowl of clam chowder
Makes more of a difference
Than that red wheelbarrow

There is a tribute to shrimp scampi, eaten at dinner at Sundance on May 5, 1989, with Elizabeth and Daryl Pedersen:

> Hail shrimp scampi, a flourish of trumpets!
> Shrimp beats the hell out of tea and crumpets!
> Shrimp and pasta and garlic butter,
> Divine crustaceans, you set me aflutter.

The point is this: As I write my life, I learn my thoughts, whether good or ill, conscious or subconscious. They are my thoughts and as I come to recognize them I become less and less vulnerable to the Ophelia Syndrome through which others once dictated my life to me.

You can also increase your confidence in your own judgment if you take courses that teach you how to ask good questions, how to define the terms of your position, how to employ strategies of rhetoric and logical argumentation, and how to employ critical theory. Such courses may be elementary philosophy classes, advanced literature classes, or math classes. One of my colleagues once quipped, "If a course isn't about method, it isn't about much of anything." I believe that.

As you come to know yourself and gain confidence in critical skills, you must also learn to play your hunches, to follow your intuition. You truly are the only one who knows what you think and feel, and you, consequently, are the only one who knows what feelings and ideas you must follow through on.

Treatment 3: Learn to Live with Uncertainty

To put it differently, surrender the need for absolute truth. The English poet John Keats wrote a landmark letter to his brothers, George and Thomas Keats, on December 22, 1817. It has become known as the letter on "Negative Capability." In part it reads,

> . . . it struck me what quality went to form a Man [or Woman] of Achievement, especially in Literature, and which Shakespeare possessed so enormously—I mean Negative Capability, that is, when a man is capable of being in uncertainties, mysteries, doubts, without any irritable reaching after fact and reason.

I do not want to do Keats an injustice by oversimplifying a magnificent statement, but I believe he is saying essentially this: The world is a complex place, and absolute truth is elusive; the greatness in Shakespeare may be attributed to the fact that he didn't feel inclined to explain what he could not, but only to portray the human condition as he saw it.

This concept drives a stake into the heart of the notion that Polonius has the answers. Overcoming the Ophelia Syndrome, becoming an independent thinker, includes giving up romantic notions of the world as a place where everything can be explained. It includes giving up the need to be fooled into thinking that Polonius does indeed have the answers when he does not. I wish he did. I wish I did. I wish any or all of my colleagues did. We do not. We can only join with students and others in the pursuit of answers, and even then we must remain ultimately in some degree of uncertainty.

The corollary to this is that to treat the Ophelia Syndrome, one must develop a healthy distrust of authorities and experts. Experts disagree more often than they agree. Those who pose as authorities are as likely to be a Polonius trying to turn Ophelia into a baby as they are to have a real handle on what they are talking about. Is there a solution? I can think of two: First, for every important opinion you hear, get a second opinion. Second, in the words of the Lord in the ninth section of the Doctrine and Covenants, study it out in your own heart.

When I was in graduate school, I took a seminar on Heinrich von Kleist from Bernhard Blume, one of the grand old men of German scholarship. One day we were to discuss a paper by a classmate, Ken Tigar, on Kleist's play, *Der zerbrochene Krug.* The paper seemed sound enough to the rest of us. Tigar's argument was based on a description written by Professor Walter Muschg, the great Kleist scholar at the University of Basel, of a plate with figures engraved on it. Professor Blume came to class with a large volume under his arm. He opened it to a picture of the plate that Muschg had described and passed it around.

"Well," he asked, "what do you see?"

No one saw anything.

"Does the woman look pregnant to you?" he asked.

Ken's face blanched.

Professor Blume continued, "No. But Muschg says she is pregnant, and Mr. Tigar's paper rests on that premise."

Ken stammered, "I just thought Muschg would be right."

Professor Blume shut the book and said, "Let that be a lesson to you. Never trust anyone. You must examine the source yourself."

TREATMENT 4: PRACTICE DIALECTICAL THINKING

By dialectical thinking, I mean thinking in alternatives and, if possible, in opposites. If you hear one solution to a problem, look for an alternative solution. If you write a draft from one point of view, write a revision from another point of view. If you formulate an argument on a point, try to formulate a counterargument. I have one student who writes his journal entries in dialogues. The speakers argue with each other. He is thinking dialectically. If you see things from a male point of view, think about them from a female point of view for a change. Psychologist Lawrence Kohlberg defines morality as the ability to see an issue from other people's points of view. He cites E. M. Forster's observation that most of the trouble in the world is due to our "inability to imagine the innerness of other lives."[12]

And this is where your peers come in. They represent alternative points of view. Their ideas are as important—if not more important—than your instructor's. The most memorable hours of my graduate education were not spent in the classroom. Some were spent with classmates in the café across the street after class. That is where Vicki Rippere, my classmate from Barnard, introduced me to critical theory. Some were spent in the graduate students' room on the third floor of Boylston Hall. That is where Bodo Reichenbach and Mark Lowry debated hotly for two hours about whether Faust was a moral man.

You may have to please Polonius by writing acceptable papers for him, but your peers will teach you how to escape his power as you wrestle with them.

Treatment 5: Foster Idle Thinking

I asked a friend of mine, a neurologist, how he thinks. He said, "If I have to tell a patient something hard, and I don't know how to do it, I sit in my office and daydream or fantasize about something that has nothing to do with the problem. When I'm through, I know what I have to say." This is a strategy for thinking by disengaging with the subject.

My wife, a fiction writer, gets her best ideas by taking long, hot baths. She doesn't try to think in the tub. She just soaks. Ideas float in of their own volition. Other people may take hikes, play basketball, or ride bikes. Still others may read novels or magazines. Idle thinking frees the mind for creative ideas. Hayakawa suggests that the creative person "is able to entertain and play with ideas that the average person may regard as silly, mistaken, or downright dangerous."

One of my students asked me if I thought television was bad for the mind. He said his father was always arguing that students in his day did more thinking than students today. I may have answered "yes" unequivocally to that question ten years ago. Now I am not so sure. If television is a means of retreating totally from thinking, then of course it is bad. But it may be as entertaining and pleasant as a hike or a long bath. The answer is no longer so clear-cut for me.

TREATMENT 6: PLAN TO STEP OUT OF BOUNDS

By "out of bounds," I mean out of the limits that Polonius may have prescribed for you. Independent thinking means to question the presumed bounds of thinking, reading, writing, or learning in general. A colleague at BYU once told me that years ago as a student, in a moment of boredom and desperation, he wrote a final examination in a form of a rhymed poem. He got an "A."

My own best experience with this was two years ago. It was a Saturday night, the last night of final examinations, 7 to 10 PM. I dutifully carried prepared tests to my class on "Reader-Response Theory," a course for advanced undergraduate and graduate humanities students. As I walked through the door, Holly Lavenstein, a gutsy student now enrolled in a graduate program in film making in Chicago, met me. She looked me straight in the eye and said, "We don't want to write an examination."

Now Holly didn't threaten me at all, but the better part of honesty told me that the written exam I had under my arm was an exercise in futility. The students had already written three papers, a weekly journal, and complete reading notes. What more did I need to grade them?

"Well, we have to have a final," I said. My voice lacked conviction.

"Yes, but not that one," she replied, pointing to the stack I was cradling. "If you'll step out in the hall for five minutes, we'll give you an alternative proposal."

Obediently I stepped back into the hall of the Maeser Building and sat on the steps. There was a lot of talking going on behind the door, and I could tell the tone was earnest, the atmosphere heated. In about five minutes, Holly poked her head out and motioned me in.

"We want a group oral examination," she said.

"And how's that supposed to work?" I asked.

"You just sit and watch," she said, "and we'll talk about what we learned in the course. I will lead the discussion. You don't have to do anything."

"OK," I said. "On two conditions: First, everyone has to talk; and, second, everyone gets the same grade as the lowest performer on the exam."

Those were two of the finest hours of my entire career. The conversation was lively and challenging. The class became united. People who hadn't said five words all semester were talking like crazy. Of course the group would have killed them if they hadn't. They talked reasonably, they argued, they screamed and hollered at each other.

When three hours had passed, Holly turned to me and said, "Well, how did we do?"

"'A'!" I said. "The best 'A' I ever gave."

The point here, however, is not that grade. The point is that this class, as a group, realized that their learning experience was more important than the grade, and they were willing to put all of their grades on the line to prove it. Sometimes escaping the Ophelia Syndrome means taking that kind of risk.

Treating the Ophelia Syndrome has its price. Only you can decide whether taking control of your education, whether using college as a time to achieve individuation, is worth it:

1. It may take time. A student in my class said, "I don't have time to learn to think in college." He said it sincerely. I inferred from what he said that getting out of college on a fast track was important to him. He wanted to be shown the hoops and jump through them. One of the costs of thinking is time. It means enrolling in courses not relevant to your major or minor because you want to take some great teacher outside your field. Or it may mean investing more time in discussions with classmates than you want to spare. Thinking takes times.

2. It means tolerating confusion about insoluble problems rather than finding "safety" in the arms of a Polonius who offers you a security blanket.

3. It means possibly getting lower grades than you'd like while you take a challenging teacher or try something out of the ordinary on an assignment.

4. It may mean going against the advice of people you love. One student noted in my class that it was hard to grow up as a good child and then study something that worries or frightens your parents. At the end of Act I, Scene 3, Ophelia submits to Polonius: "I shall obey, my lord."

To all of this I can only ask, which is the greater price to pay: "To think or not to think"?

THOMAS G. PLUMMER *is a professor of Germanic and Slavic languages at BYU. He received his BA from the University of Utah and his MA and PhD from Harvard University. Besides teaching at BYU, Plummer has also taught at Northeastern University and the University of Minnesota. Among the classes he teaches at BYU are German literature, memoirs and imagination (an Honors course), and humanities film theory and criticism.*

Notes

1. I am indebted to Kimberly Halladay, a BYU student, whose paper, "Ophelia Oppressed" (English 252, Spring 1990), led me to coin the term, the "Ophelia Syndrome." Dr. Clyde Parker and Dr. Jane Lawson introduced me to theories of cognitive development from which I distilled several ideas into the Ophelia Syndrome.

2. S. I. Hayakawa, "What Does It Mean to Be Creative?" *Through the Communication Barrier,* ed. Arthur Chandler (New York: Harper & Row, 1979), 104–5.

3. Halladay's paper applies to Jung's idea of Ophelia.

4. Carl G. Jung, *Archetypes and the Collective Unconscious* (New York: Pantheon Books, 1959). Discussed in Wilfred L. Guerin et al., *A Handbook of Critical Approaches to Literature,* 2d ed. (New York: Harper & Row), 178–83.

5. David Leverenz, "The Woman in Hamlet: An Interpersonal View," *Signs: Journal of Women in Culture and Society* 4 (1978): 302–03.

6. Erich Fromm, "Learning," *To Have or To Be* (New York: Harper & Row), 17–19.

7. Hayakawa, 105.

8. "Is Your Company Asking Too Much?" *Fortune,* March 12, 1990: 39–46.

9. Wayne C. Booth, "What Little I Think I Know About Teaching," *The Vocation of a Teacher* (Chicago: University of Chicago Press, 1988), 214.

10. Booth, 215.

11. I became familiar with the general idea of dialectical learning in an article by William G. Perry, Jr., "Cognitive and Ethical Growth: The Making of Meaning," *The Modern American College,* eds. Arthur W. Chickering et al. (San Francisco: Jossey-Bass, 1981), 76–116.

12. Lawrence Kohlberg, "A Cognitive Developmental Approach to Moral Education," *Humanist* 32, no. 6 (1972): 15.

Questions

1. What is the Ophelia Syndrome? How does it manifest itself in college classrooms?
2. According to Plummer, what is the proper intellectual relationship between a student and teacher?
3. Do you see in yourself any symptoms of the Ophelia Syndrome? How can this malady be treated?

Defending Polonius: A Response to Plummer's "Ophelia Syndrome"

John J. Murphy

When John Murphy was asked to discuss Thomas Plummer's article "Diagnosing and Treating the Ophelia Syndrome" with Honors freshmen students, he felt uncomfortable because he disagreed with many of the assumptions Plummer makes in his article. He was subsequently invited by a colleague to write a response to Plummer's article, and the following is the result of that invitation.

While I was pleased to be invited to spend time with some Honors freshmen during their orientation, the prospect of discussing Tom Plummer's "Diagnosing and Treating the Ophelia Syndrome" delayed a ready response. Plummer's lecture makes several worthy points: that students should learn to think in college, that they should learn to be discriminating about what authority articulates as truth, that life is a process of self-discovery, and so on. But Plummer makes other assumptions about the process of teaching and learning that are misleading if not dangerous. Since one of his "treatments" emphasizes thinking in alternatives, I will begin with an alternate reading of the *Hamlet* scene that inspires his title and then address, in my own order, some of his other "treatments."

"It is only an illusion, a wish of the Ophelias and the Poloniuses that literary texts have just one interpretation," writes Plummer subsequent to condemning both Ophelia and her father—one for being "worse than naive" and the other for "pontificat[ing]." In the first place, meddlesome age is confirmed by hot youth in its opinion of Hamlet's affections, for Laertes too mistrusts Hamlet's intentions toward Ophelia as well as the quality of the tendered affection. When Polonius asks his daughter if she trusts Hamlet's "tenders" toward her, she replies that she doesn't know what to think. Polonius is asking her for an opinion she does not have. He doesn't then exactly answer, as Plummer says, "I'll teach you. Think yourself a baby . . . ." He swears by the Virgin in his consternation:

"Marry, I will teach you [an opinion]: think yourself a baby / That you have ta'en these tenders for true pay, / Which are not sterling." Because you have been fooled, he is saying, "consider yourself a baby." He expects a daughter of his to value her uniqueness, to "tender [her]self more dearly." He realizes that a chamberlain's daughter has no chance of marriage to a prince. Polonius might be considered the teacher who seems on the surface a maxim-ridden fool—and might even approach the fool in essence—but one who expects his or her students to be wiser and more discriminating than they are, realizes their vulnerability to be duped, and preaches defense: "Set your entreatments at a higher rate." The situation is more complex than Plummer presents it, as is the individuation-authority discussion he uses to introduce it. Plummer talks about the "temporary condition" of learning the basic material of any discipline, although he seems to restrict such periods to biochemistry or German grammar and make them unrealistically brief. He tells us that he himself didn't "begin a truly honest search for my 'self' until I was 40 years old. Then it became an obsession." This implies that his temporary period was not brief, since he seems to separate this uncertain and theoretical stage of disciplined learning from the discovery of one's own uniqueness. Such phases of learning and teaching should not be divided from "self" search, but neither should one's discipline become a conscious exercise in self-discovery.

I don't worry about the "most serious students, those who have been 'good' all of their lives," as candidates for the Ophelia Syndrome of never discovering their uniqueness or exercising their ability to think independently. I worry about the bright but slipshod students (frequently in Honors) who fail to read carefully or take careful notes. The latter become candidates for what I'll call here the "Muschg" Syndrome (Muschg was a critic misused by one of Plummer's classmates), when students carelessly glean, say, a Henry James novel rather than scrutinize it and either raid the library for a handy meaning or argue for the meaning they have arrived at independently of anything but themselves, or of exploring the author's full text, expressed intention, or background. We must qualify Plummer's assertions that the ideas of student peers are as valuable or more valuable than those of their professors by limiting those peers to the careful note takers and scrutinizers of texts who have challenged their professors to really share their insights. Otherwise classes might be "talking like crazy." So Plummer should not apologize for taking so long to focus on his "self," for it merely bears out the popular view that, except in rare cases of genius, people shouldn't publish books before they're 40.

I have a personal theory that formal education becomes unhealthy when it is consciously directed toward "individuation," the discovery of the uniqueness of self. Every discipline, even the softer ones like my own has become, has a body of knowledge "out there," that is, away from our own emoting. It used to be our responsibility to read in each period of English literature, for example, to make sure we had firsthand experience with the range of our discipline. It used to be required that we know at least the history of the West to understand ourselves in our culture. (The recent popular discovery that our world is not limited to the West shouldn't excuse us from anything; it should merely add to our responsibility.) Then, too, educated people seem to have a responsibility to give what has become denigrated as elite art a fighting chance to become part of their lives. What Plummer terms as "idle thinking" can relate to exploring such art; he says such thinking "frees the mind," but let's say it enriches the mind by freeing it from self and propelling it toward a world beyond self.

The more worlds we discover and penetrate without a conscious intention to appreciate ourselves, the greater our self-knowledge will become. Conscious concern about ourselves will minimize not only our knowledge of what is out there but, in the end, stifle our own soul knowledge. Literature courses frequently occasion complaints from students required to read this disliked poet or that disliked novelist, and some courses are tailored according to student likes (after all, one doesn't want one's class canceled in this age of electives). Consider the ridiculousness of an anatomy course omitting the spine or a history of France omitting the Revolution for similar reasons. Knowing the self, the infinity within, is learning as much as possible about the infinity without, even when the learning is painful.

Plummer reveals bravery in discarding the exam he concluded would be "an exercise in futility" when he was confronted by gutsy students who wanted an oral exam instead, but this implies that the exam was not what it should have been, was not the kind that led students out of the precise focus every good class must have, the temporary condition of becoming conversant with the discipline, and into the area of uncertainty and speculation. Teachers must emphasize the discipline in order to encourage responsible exploration of the unknown, that which is beyond the firm grasp of the teachers themselves. Walt Whitman points us towards roads into the unknown in "Song of Myself," but only after teaching us through minute detail about the road he traveled and what he learned from those before him and accompanying him. But we must be careful not to construe as a great teacher the perhaps dynamic individual more interested in having us follow her/his road than launching us on ours, and we must realize, too, that parents and authority figures can contribute to as well as discourage the individual journey each of us is expected to make as a responsible adult. There need be no generation gap, unless, like Ophelia, the child is too immature for that journey.

Finally, let me make an observation as a Gentile in this Mormon world and apply the spirit of Plummer's lecture to religious life. Higher education of the denominational variety must offer the temporary condition of discipline in religion on as high an intellectual level as other disciplines, and it must do so with the intention of pointing the faithful in the direction of "the unknown, the uncertain, the theoretical, the hypothetical, where teachers can no longer tell students with certainty what they should think." Plummer quotes S. I. Hayakawa's criticism of herd thinking: "As Republicans, we think what other Republicans think. As Catholics, we think what other Catholics think. . . . not many of us ask ourselves, 'How do I feel? What do I think?'—and wait for an answer." While I believe both these sample groups demonstrate more public diversity than is exhibited in the BYU community, as a Catholic I must acknowledge my responsibility to know what the church teaches and why and what is central and peripheral to my belief before disciplining my conscience according to the church, challenging the church to be faithful to the gospel, or following my conscience instead of the church. Because as intellectuals we have to make well-informed decisions in this area as well as in the arts, humanities, and various sciences, the quality and duration of the gestation period are strategic.

Risking incoherence, I want to balance the scene from Shakespeare with one from Willa Cather. In *Shadows on the Rock,* the motherly teenager Cecile Auclair expresses her fear to old Bishop Laval that the waif child Jacques she has befriended will not appreciate the discipline of the Brother's school in Montreal the old man plans to enroll him in. "I don't think he would be happy in school," she says. But the Bishop thoughtfully responds, "Schools are not meant to make boys happy, Cecile, but to teach them to do without happiness." This is an old-fashioned philosophy of education we probably reject but must continue to ponder. According to it, individuation is limited by reality and freedom by the responsibility of the roles all of us, not only Ophelia, must accept as participants in other people's plots.

JOHN J. MURPHY *received his BA and MA from St. John's University, New York, and has also studied at Harvard, Oregon, Stanford, and Notre Dame. Before coming to BYU in 1984, he taught at Merrimack College, Massachussetts and the College of St. Teresa.*

Questions

1. What problems does Murphy see with Plummer's argument? Do you wholeheartedly accept either Murphy's or Plummer's views?

2. What are Murphy's views on education? How do these compare with Plummer's?

Legends of Entelechy

GARY BARTON
JOSEPH EVAN OSTRAFF
BRIAN DEAN CHRISTENSEN
ED CUTLER

Three members of the BYU visual arts faculty—Gary Barton, Joseph Evan Ostraff, and Brian Dean Christensen—came up with a concept for an art show which would include, paradoxically, the ideas of "legend" and "entelechy." Their purpose was to play the concept of "an unverified story" off the concept of "a vital force of self-fulfillment" to see what questions would arise about how one person's truth can be another person's legend and how legends can become part of the vital force of entelechy. Each of the artists decided to tell, in one way or another, a legend which tries to get at what Paul Tillich calls "the ultimate reality . . . in the flux of transitoriness and finitude." The text for each of the pieces of art is written by the artist and was included with the art show. Following the artists is a critical essay by Ed Cutler of the BYU English Department in which he discusses how to approach the art and offers a critical reading of the three pieces.

It is the awareness of the deceptive character of the surface of everything we encounter which drives one to discover what is below the surface. But soon we realize that even if we break through the surface of a thing or person or event, new deceptions arise. So we try to dig further through what lies deepest below the surface—to the truly real which cannot deceive us. We search for an ultimate reality, for something lasting in the flux of transitoriness and finitude."

—From an essay by Paul Tillich

Legend: 1. a. An unverified story handed down from earlier times, especially of one popularly believed to be historical. b. A body or collection of such stories. c. A romanticized or popularized myth of modern times. 2. One that inspires legends or legendary fame.

Entelechy: 1. In the philosophy of Aristotle, the condition of a thing whose essence is fully realized; actuality. 2. In some philosophical systems, a vital force that directs an organism toward self-fulfillment.

Colorplates

Biblical Plants

Figure 1. Christ-thorn (*top*)
Figure 2. Fig tree (*bottom*)

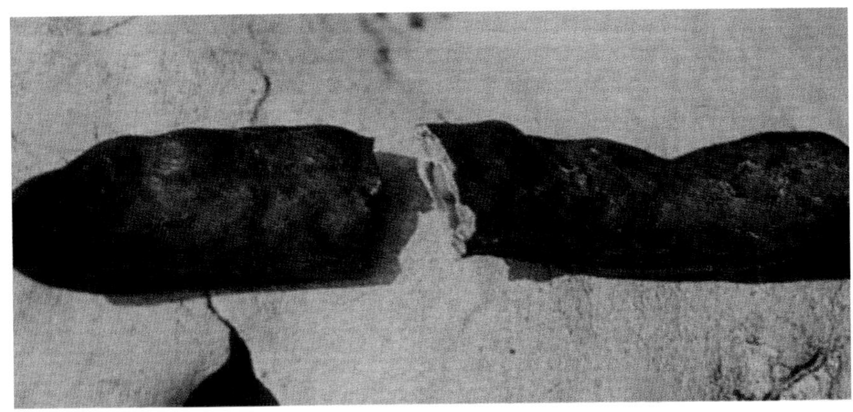

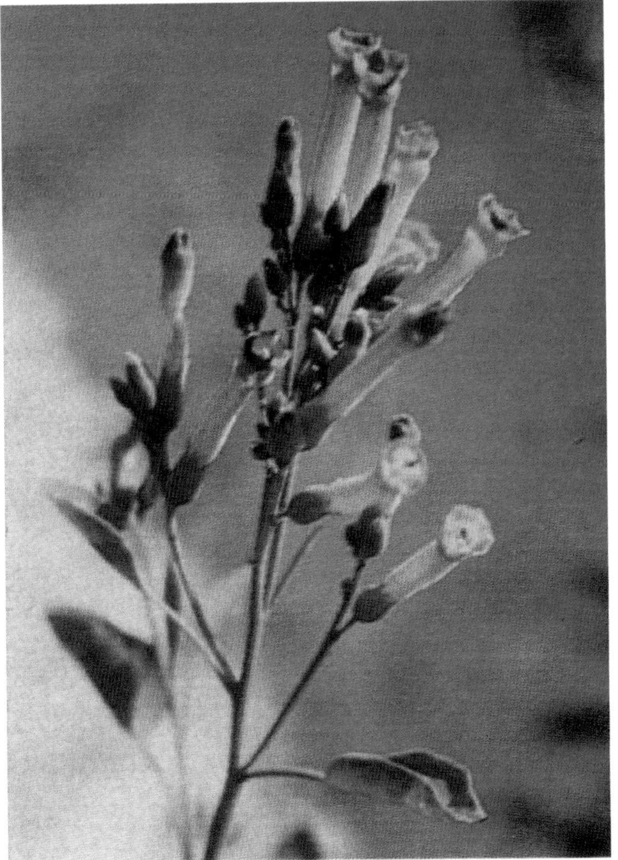

Figure 1.
Carob bean
(*above*)
Figure 2.
Mustard plant
(*left*)

Nursing Care

The nine pictures used in the nursing care study.

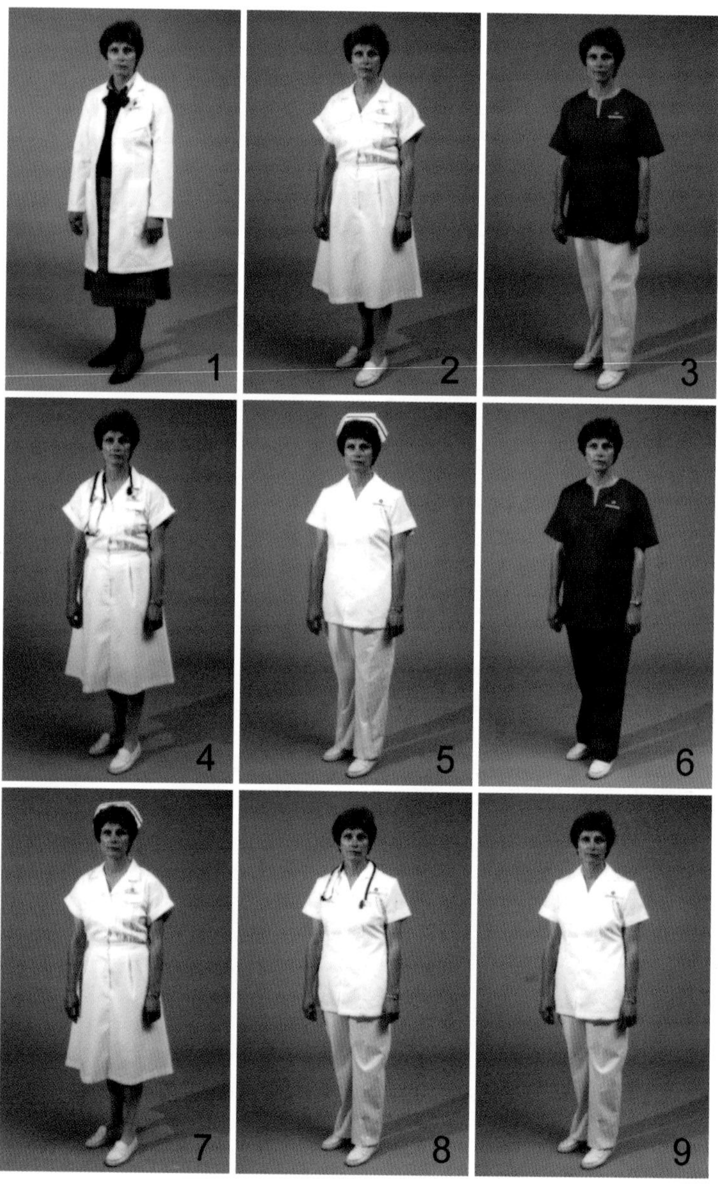

Drive-In Theater

The Pioneer Twin Drive-In, Provo, Utah (*top*)
The Art City Drive-In, Springville, Utah (*bottom*).

3 Back

Gary Barton

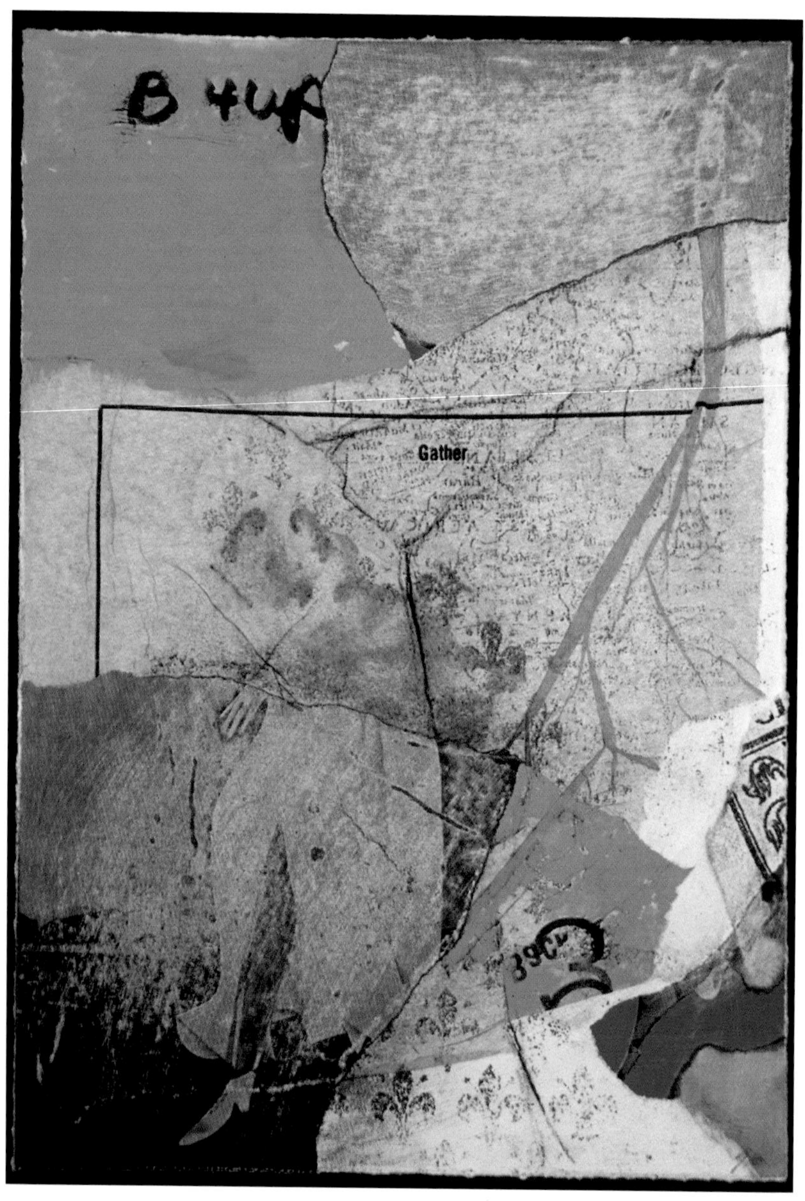

Colorplate 5

Kupesi ‘O Tonga (Patterns of Tonga)

JOSEPH EVAN OSTRAFF

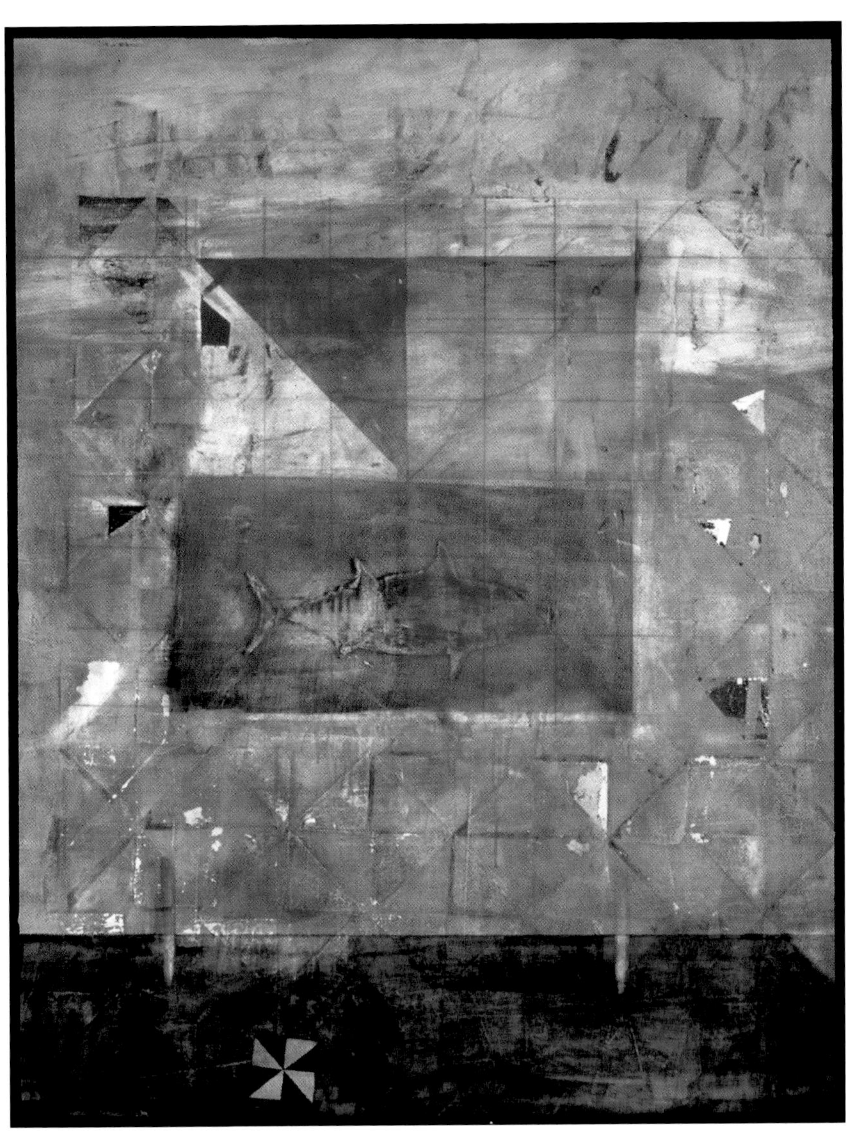

Colorplate 6

Veiled Door

BRIAN DEAN CHRISTENSEN

Colorplate 7

3 Back

Gary Barton

Colorplate 5

In the museum, I stood surrounded by some of the early paintings of Jean Dubuffet, a prominent postwar artist. I moved through the room examining each piece. The work had an ungainly child-like quality. It was rough, and by some interpretations crude—a notable contrast to much of the popular art of the previous centuries which I had seen earlier in the day. Interested but struggling to remember historical interpretations of these works, I found myself contemplating their purpose and their creator's motivations and intentions. I also considered the possible factors that brought this artist and his works to a level of such esteem in the art world.

In the room there was also a man with two children. As they walked from painting to painting, one of the children, a young girl around six or seven years of age, declared at each stop, "I could do that!"

Gary Barton *received his BFA in printmaking at BYU and his MFA in studio art at Ohio State, where he was a University Fellow. He calls his return to BYU as a professor a "fortunate event" as he is back in the environment that nurtured him in the early days of his art career.*

Kupesi 'O Tonga (Patterns of Tonga)

JOSEPH EVAN OSTRAFF

Colorplate 6

An old man named Hiko rowed out in his hand-carved canoe from the bay which framed his ancestral village of Ha'ano on the island of Kauvai. Calling fish was a gift passed from father to son for many generations. Legend has it that a king in Samoa gave one of Hiko's ancestors the gift of two atu (skipjack tuna). They were brought back to Ha'ano alive to grow and proliferate in the bay. A moray eel was called on to guard the atu. Since then this family has had a gift of calling in the atu. On this day we were three miles away in Faleloa when word came that Hiko had called the fish and they had come. The boats came to our village loaded to the rails with atu, thousands of fish freshly netted from the bay or collected by hand from the beach where the most obedient atu had jumped. Some people talked about the profit to be gained. Others listened in disappointment; they knew it was tapu, or forbidden, to profit from fish called in by Hiko. People from the village ran to the beach and began to eat raw fish; there was a frenzy of excitement. As a family, my wife, children, and I ate fish called in by Hiko. A woman turned to me and asked if I believed.

JOSEPH OSTRAFF *received his BFA from BYU in 1982 and his MFA from the University of Washington in 1984. Ostraff has had his works exhibited extensively throughout the United States.*

Veiled Door

Brian Dean Christensen

Colorplate 7

When I was a young boy my father worked in a dental lab on Olive Street across from Balboa Park in San Diego. The building was a pink Art Deco dinosaur with a bullnose corner in glass brick, a round window, and a flat roofed upper floor with a bent pipe railing like the deck of a ship. It was like a bastion of the old navy town days, right in the middle of the 1970s. My dad worked on the upper floor with three other dental technicians. The old oak work benches were polished and darkened with use and carving wax and gleaming chrome arm drills were bolted to them. I loved to watch the technicians melt gold in the crucible and let go the spring arm of the centrifuge as it spun wildly in its well as it slammed the hot metal in the mold.

I was fascinated by one of the lab men, although I seldom had the courage to speak to him. His name was Jonathan Johnson but everyone called him Johnny. He was still doing crown and bridge work into his nineties and I had known him only as a fixture of the lab as long as I could remember. Johnny used to give me hard candy and, most impressive to me, old street car tokens and skeleton keys from a cigar box which he kept in his cupboard. I would peek at him through the dusty round window as he would ease his bony old figure outside for a smoke.

When Johnny died, his odds and ends were distributed to the other technicians. So I came into a small inheritance which to me was a treasure chest: Johnny's cigar box full of keys. Skeleton keys, padlock keys, car keys, house keys—the keys of a lifetime, physical question marks. I would spend hours sorting through the old man's keys, wondering what doors Johnny had passed through.

Brian Dean Christensen *received his BFA from BYU in 1990 and his MFA from Washington University in 1993. Christensen's artwork has been exhibited throughout the United States in a variety of settings.*

Legends of Entelechy: A Critical Essay

Ed Cutler

I. Visual Art and Critical Response

How does one approach the "Legends of Entelechy" exhibition? What, if anything, do the visual works of these three artists have in common? Do the brief narratives accompanying each work (part of the original exhibition) provide insight into the meaning of the individual works? Do they help us find connections between the works? What is the significance of the quotation from the philosopher Paul Tillich and the opening definitions (also part of the original exhibition) of the terms "legend" and "entelechy"? One might even begin by asking if there needs to be any "significance." Perhaps visual art just is what it is, and should simply be seen and appreciated, not interpreted and deeply analyzed. The quotation from Tillich, moreover, suggests that interpretation itself is at best a problematic activity: "even if we break through the surface of a thing . . . new deceptions arise." Is any attempt to get at the "truly real" nature of a thing or person or event bound to be frustrated by the "flux of transitoriness and finitude"? If so, does criticism and interpretation play a meaningful role in the experience of visual arts?

Even if the critic or analyst fails to pin down the "ultimate reality" of an object, critical interpretation the response of an individual viewer is nonetheless a vital dimension of visual art. In approaching "Legends of Entelechy," I suggest that the goal of criticism and analysis should not so much be to "explain" the visual objects, but to interact with them, to explore one's reactions and to seek out possible connections. While no critic will offer the one and only way to understand and evaluate works of visual art, critical response nonetheless completes the process of artistic display. Will individual interpretations and responses differ? Most likely. Can a critic find a significance in the exhibition that the artists may not have intended? Certainly. But these subjective ambiguities should not be understood as shortcomings of critical response to a visual exhibition like "Legends of Entelechy." If Barton, Ostraff, and Christensen had intended to express a fixed meaning, they would have been more careful to assert one. Yet they choose to frame the exhibition loosely, around some philosophical concepts, personal narratives and visual works, offering something more like a constellation of stars that invites completion on the part of the viewer, rather than a formal argument that tries to secure a given meaning.

II. A Critical Reading of "Legends of Entelechy"

Three distinct but interconnected elements make up the exhibition: the works themselves, their accompanying narratives, and the introduction. What is the significance of the terms "legend" and "entelechy" in this exhibition? According to the definition provided, a "legend" is an "unverified story." The attraction of any legend may in fact be that it remains unverified. It is "believed to be historical," but not confirmed so. The uncertainty of a legend's claim to truth, to being a story of a real event, stands in contrast to the meaning of "entelechy," which identifies "the condition of a thing whose essence is fully realized, [or] actuality." Is a legend a "fully realized" story? The definition implies it is not. Rather, a legend hints at an actuality that cannot be independently verified. The drive towards verification, towards confirming the actuality of our stories and understanding the essence of our world, is a manifestation of the entelechial impulse in humanity. We seek to know "the answer" to all that appears on the surface of things, the quotation by Tillich asserts. But Tillich goes on to indicate the difficulty of fulfilling the entelechial quest for knowledge. Can we ever really come to a full knowledge of the past? Of the natural world? Ourselves? "We search for an ultimate reality, for something lasting in the flux of transitoriness and finitude," but do we finally arrive there? Do stories and art offer us the actuality of things, or is entelechy itself haunted by indeterminate legends, by possible meanings which cannot be verified or fully expressed? The artists' juxtaposition of the two terms "legend" and "entelechy" indirectly expresses this tension between ultimate reality and ultimate uncertainty.

The narratives and visuals by each artist play upon this theme of uncertainty in representation. Joe Ostraff's story of Hiko the fish caller refers directly to a Polynesian legend. Can one really call in fish? The old woman asks if he "believed." In this moment, the tension between entelechy and legend, between actuality and myth, is laid bare. From a scientific perspective, it would be difficult to imagine the tuna were actually called in by the old man, even if this is believed in Faleloa. Yet this legend is experienced as "actuality" in the short narrative. The painting further suggests the important interconnection of natural phenomena and cultural experience as well. At the center of the geometric patterns is an image of a tuna. The layering of the Polynesian patterns with the organic referent of the fish provides a lens that allows us to see how another may see. The legend of Hiko's ancestor is itself an organizing cultural frame that explains an event in the natural world—the arrival of the tuna—to the people of Faleloa. Science provides a different frame of understanding, of course, an explanation that would almost certainly reject the belief in fish calling. But is scientific explanation, driven by human entelechy to get at the reality of things, really the last word? Ostraff demonstrates that belief persists even in the face of rational explanation, and that this capacity is importantly bound up in any culture's way of seeing. If a more rationalistic and scientific culture provides a different frame for seeing and knowing the world, the perpetuation of legends such as the fish caller indicate that there are other ways of knowing and experiencing "reality." The painting and narrative together push the question: might not the scientific frame simply be a frame for knowledge, not the frame?

Gary Barton's "3 Back" plays upon the difficulty of determining meaning and significance in the face of shifting perspectives. In his narrative, he is studying Dubuffet's "ungainly child-like" paintings in a museum. While he struggles to recall the various interpretations of this artist from his earlier art training, a child moves from painting to painting, declaring "I could do that!" This moment brings up the tension between perception and actuality that is indicated throughout the exhibition. Barton knew that there was something "official" to be known about the paintings, an explanation of their significance, an "actuality" behind the ungainly paintings of Dubuffet. But was his way of knowing them really more legitimate than that of the young girl? Perhaps Dubuffet would have welcomed the spontaneity of the child's response over the pretension of an academic one. If so, the simple faith that sustains a legend would take precedence over the explanatory rigor that underlies entelechy. Barton's painting might itself be accused of having an "ungainly" quality; it meets the eye as a fragmented, random collage. One sees only a slightly discernable human form, lines that resemble cracks (possibly road lines from a map) unintelligible inscriptions, even a straight line with a right angle that intersects the painting just above center. What does it mean? Perhaps the better question is, why doesn't it mean? Codes that normally provide us with meaning are broken down here; the lines of a map transform themselves into sheerly organic cracks. The letters fail to signify anything, yet are still recognizable as letters. In such distortions of referential signs, "3 Back" seems to undermine the entelechial quest for certainty, offering instead a mixture of references that disintegrate. Perhaps taking inspiration from Dubuffet, Barton creates an "open" work that cannot be reduced to a given formal meaning.

Brian Christensen's "Veiled Door" explores the passageways between meaning and uncertainty. In the narrative, the keys from Johnny's cigar box open up more questions than answers. They stand, in Christensen's words, as "physical question marks." Both Ostraff and Barton make use of layering to convey multiple senses of meaning and frames of reference, but Christensen's three dimensional work provides a sense of inside/outside. The block appears in the form of a treasure chest, but where one would expect to find a lock is instead the image of a key. This subtle inversion is significant, given that the meaning of the keys themselves is "locked" in Christensen's narrative; they serve as the traces of the old man's life, but the keys do not reveal who he was and what doors he had passed through in his life. The obscure shape above the block is also suggestive of larger thematic issues in the "Legends of Entelechy" exhibition. A translucent form appears held fast by three metallic braces. What is the translucent form? Air? Water? A cloud? Could such a thing be strapped down? Whatever its inspiration, the image is certainly surreal, providing a vivid but unreal sensation of impossible enclosure. The attempt to bind the mystery of the natural world, to control or explain it, is evoked in this peculiar image. Yet the keys in the narrative fail to unlock the mysteries which they betoken. What promised access fails to provide entry—we are left, as with Barton's "3 Back" and Ostraff's "Kupesi 'O Tonga" with a meditation upon the boundaries of meaning making, rather than with clear meaning itself.

What then is the lesson of "Legends of Entelechy"? To answer this is tricky, because the artists' paradoxical goal appears to have been calling into question the possibility of ultimate interpretation. One sees in each work and their accompanying narratives a desire to preserve a sense of ambiguity, mystery, and uncertainty. If the works themselves are not legends, they rely upon the same qualities that sustain legends: belief in the face of the unknown. Each work resists a complete decoding and interpretation, I would argue, in order to preserve the possibility of belief. In a sense, the exhibition is exploring one of the unique problems of our contemporary age. As science and technology continue to unmask all of the former mysteries that were once the province of faith and legend, and as the world continues to shrink and become "known," we lose by degrees the very sense of mystery and the unknown that are the prerequisites of faith. Although the entelechial desire to know all things in their fullest sense, to unmask all mystery, is a necessary step in the pursuit of truth, so also is the faith born of perspective and limitation. The domination of nature and the liquidation of the unknown, is in a sense also the domination of ourselves by ourselves, should every mystery eventually be explained. What the exhibition offers is a paradox at the center of meaning-making, a "legend of entelechy." It does not deny the quest for knowledge, but it does not deny the unknown, either. In our day, the pendulum has swung toward the rationalistic and scientific, toward an intense integration of knowledge and information. As a corrective, "Legends of Entelechy" offers a "dis-integrating" form of art, one in which signs do not easily translate and images resist full explanation. This frustrating space in which certainty breaks down, the space of the legend, is vital, however, in order to preserve faith and humility in the otherwise actual world.

EDWARD S. CUTLER *is an assistant professor in the English Department. Cutler received his BA in English and Korean and MA in English from BYU and his PhD in literature from the University of California at San Diego. He specializes in American literature and Modernism and teaches classes in 19th- and 20th-century American literature and world civilization.*

Managing in a Diverse Workforce: From Incident to "ism"

KATE KIRKHAM

"I am an applied behavioral scientist," says Kate Kirkham. By this, she means that she always seeks to apply the theories that she uses in academics to the workplace. Through most of her academic career, Kirkham has studied the implications and problems that arise due to diversity in the work environment. In this article, she seeks to apply diversity theory to help team leaders and corporate managers better understand possible diversity problems at individual, group, and corporate levels in a business. The tricky part is to determine if an incident is simply a problem at the individual level or if it pervades the entire business. Kirkham asserts that if the incident does indicate signs of racism, sexism, or another "ism," then one group is being favored at the expense of another, and managers must take some sort of concerted action. Kirkham's article was originally published in The Diversity Factor: Capturing the Competitive Advantage of a Changing Workforce.

How does a manager know if a difficult exchange between two employees who differ from each other by gender or race is an "isolated incident" or evidence of sexism and racism in the work environment? What can a manager do to accurately identify problems, coach others, or redress systemic inequities? Managers (and other employees, as well) who want to contribute to effective work relationships in a diverse workforce must address these questions. Often, a manager's own race or gender affects the answers and actions.

Managers receive a variety of descriptions about problems from their co-workers and employees. Some people suggest that personality differences are the primary factors in any exchange: "that's just the way he/she is." Others imply that a complainant is trying to "make a racial issue" out of an unpleasant incident, or that his or her "oversensitive" or "strident" behavior results from "baggage" carried into the workplace.

There are those employees who will take the manager aside and confidentially suggest that "after all, there is a perfectly logical explanation" for the particular incident. And finally, there may be people who point to racism or sexism as the source of problems.

How can a manager sort through the collection of perceptions and "facts"?

Two assumptions affect the answers to this question. First, the workplace is not "neutral ground"; and second, employees who are competent in other arenas are not necessarily competent in race and gender issues.

Workplace Dynamics

The reporting relationships, business practices, policies, and even the physical structure of any workplace are based on the cumulative experiences of organization—the people who have made up the workforce over time, the larger culture they have created, and the total context in which the organization operates.

If all the supervisors in a company have always been men, a woman appointed to a supervisory position faces a situation where her performance is evaluated in a far larger context than her own individual behavior. Such evaluations are simultaneously conscious and unconscious, intended and unintentional. Often, even individuals' traits are evaluated on the shared norms or beliefs of the dominant employee group—beliefs about what constitutes "masculinity" or "femininity," for example, or shared norms about the value of long work days, or about assertive or aggressive behavior.

So the workplace is not a totally objective setting. The manager who attempts to figure out the dynamics of differences between employees must understand that the environment itself colors the ways employees relate to each other and to their management. Some managers say that understanding this actually complicates their worklife. The white manager who begins to realize the extent that attitudes about race impact behavior—or the male manager who recognizes the complications of sexism in his employee group—may be reluctant to explore further. Yet failure to do so means that many problems will "recycle" without resolution.

Getting Good Advice

All of us have people we trust, to whom we look for advice. In the workplace, these relationships have endured the test of problem-solving on difficult business issues.

However, the fact that a person has a track-record of giving competent advice on business matters does not guarantee that same competence when the focus is on race and gender. For example, a white manager may have often turned to a white colleague for advice on fiscal matters. Trusting that relationship, the manager now raises an issue involving a conflict between a white employee and a black employee. Unfortunately, the colleague may have no expertise in areas of employee diversity.

Constructing a Framework

In order to contribute to the creation of a workplace that confronts race and gender problems **and** values diversity, a manager must analyze issues at the individual, group, and organizational levels. A fourth level is societal. This discussion, however, focuses only on the first three.

Finding solutions to many workplace problems requires insight into these levels. However, it is *crucial* to analyze these three levels when the issues concern race and gender. As one of my colleagues said, "When it comes to race and gender, sometimes people who are ordinarily good thinkers become 'stupid'!" Such poor thinking is evident, for example, when a manager who needs to understand complex problems in the workplace only looks for blatant examples of individual prejudice in employee behavior.

Structural Levels

At the individual level, each person is seen primarily for his or her own unique characteristics—attitudes, assumptions, mannerisms, workstyle and personality. This level includes the interpersonal relationships we build one-on-one with others, based on mutuality of interests, similarity of attitudes, and the like.

The group level is the site of our identity as a man or woman and as a member of a racial or cultural group. This level has four important dimensions:

• Group level identity can exist whether or not the individual sees it as a primary factor in interactions in the workplace. A senior white manager, for example, may not think of herself as "white"—but others may see her "white" group identity as an important part of their experiences with her in the workplace. So even though, individually, she is known for her sense of humor, she is also one more white manager at the senior level.

• "Group" does not necessarily mean an actual, numerical group within the workplace. For example, whether or not there are other Asians present, an individual Asian manager can feel and be experienced as a member of an "Asian" group.

• Individuals also belong to groups on the basis of self-identification. Someone who does not "look" like a person of color to others may identify quite strongly as a "Latino," "First American," or "African

American." Thus the group level includes how people identify themselves as well as how others see them.

• Group identity impacts work relationships and organizational dynamics not only because of actual behaviors, but also because of perceived possible experiences. This is tricky business. For example, at the end of the day, a white male manager may not feel that he is a part of the dominant power structure in the organization. In fact, on some days the white manager may feel quite powerless. Yet, in the perception of employees of other racial groups, he is seen as likely to have more access to other white managers, or less likely to experience negative interactions on the basis of his race. These are all forms of power, or options, that are connected to the likely experiences a white person may have.

The basis of these perceptions is the pattern of repeated experiences of that group's members in the organization—not on stereotypes. Stereotypes do exist at the group level, but the aspect of perceived possible experiences is different from stereotypes attributed to all members of a group because of bias.

The organization or institutional level incorporates the entire culture of the organization, and analysis requires attention to policies, business practices, customs, and norms of behavior. Managers attempting to get a full picture of the issues must look at their roles and responsibilities within this total framework. In addition, each organization—as well as each member of the organization—is influenced by the larger society in which we operate. Employees bring to the workplace the individual expectations, biases, and prejudices developed through the socialization processes of family, school, and community.

NEGATIVE EXPRESSIONS OF STRUCTURAL LEVELS

Each level has both positive and negative implications. At the individual level, the negative experience of difference results in prejudice. Any two people can be prejudiced towards one another. All relationships have the possibility of some degree of prejudice. I may have negative feelings about people who have different physical abilities. Prejudice is not the prerogative of any one person, nor is it directed at only one group.

At the group level, prejudice is translated into the way people behave in concert with others. Collective prejudice is expressed in some form of discrimination. Yes, it is individuals who carry out discrimination. But discrimination results from more than individual action—it is the patterns, stereotypes, and conditions that are generated by more than one person's behavior. The resulting negative experiences are more potent than one individual can cause. Collective prejudice or discrimination determines what neighborhoods people can live in, what schools they may attend, what jobs they are considered eligible to apply for. Discrimination determines who gets to do what in our society. Discrimination assigns value to the color of skin, or to gender, and is the primary reason that some people's "difference" is experienced in a negative or life-threatening way.

The "isms" identify this negative experience of difference at the organizational level. Racism, sexism, homophobia, and other discriminatory patterns operate through pervasive and pernicious mechanisms that the larger systems control: what is valued, who has authority, how one ought to look, how budgets are allocated, who gets what opportunities in the largest context. The "isms" are the phenomena that underlie the fact that almost all CEOs, managing boards, presidents and other top management in our corporations are white men. The "isms" require some form of power to perpetuate the complexity of beliefs, behaviors, and values that oppress others based on their race or gender.

Interaction Between Levels

One way to understand the levels is to think about who we are in relationship to each level. An individual can often discern when the person he or she is working with is exhibiting some form of prejudice. Individuals can also collect evidence of collective prejudice, or discrimination: they can see what's going on around them regarding education or housing in society, and, within the organization, explore to see who gets what positions or training opportunities.

It is harder to see the way the "isms" operate. Obviously, some individuals have direct experience of racism and sexism. But others, particularly the traditional majority group members in the US workforce, have difficulty seeing the "big picture": the workplace patterns based on race, sex, or cultural identity. Therefore, they do not recognize that these patterns create barriers which prevent some employees from thriving in the organization. These patterns also benefit others, based on membership in the dominant group.

The interaction of the three levels adds to the complexity of the issues a manager must confront. In organizations where individual employees exhibit blatant prejudice, the patterns of the "ism" may be easier to see. Ironically, however, in such organizations, these systemic patterns may receive less attention because the individual bigoted acts require more dramatic attention in the day-to-day relationships.

In organizations where most employees are not personally prejudiced and do not intentionally discriminate, the subtle forms of sexism and racism may be harder to identify. Where the majority of the workforce is well-meaning (or their attitudes well-hidden), the search for understanding of the deeply embedded patterns of "isms" may be very frustrating. Some majority group members will regard any discussion of racism and sexism in work practices as a personal attack, rather than an attempt to see what is really there.

Racism and sexism (and other "isms") are far more subtle than the overt joke or derogatory comment. The existence of an "ism" means that the norms, values, practices, and way of doing work favor one group at the expense of another. It isn't just that difference exists, it is the cost of that difference that matters. An "ism" is always attached to some form of organizational power used to enforce the oppression of others.

When new employees join an organization, they receive an orientation to help them "get up to speed" as quickly as possible. This is just as important in diversity work as in every other aspect of corporate life. A new employee needs to know what "isms" are operating in the culture of the organization. Unfortunately, if the organizational analysis has stopped at the individual level, there may be no awareness that work processes may support one group and subordinate another. A manager may decide, "I'm not prejudiced." But if that manager fails to go further into the "isms" of the culture, he or she cannot give new employees an adequate understanding of the environment of the organization. Saying "I'm not prejudiced" is an opening, not a closing, statement on diversity.

DIVERSITY RECYCLING: INTENT VERSUS OUTCOME

Learning to observe the three different levels involved in the dynamics of racism/sexism and diversity is a skill all managers can learn, just as they learn other skills. Further, managers must learn to see that their intent not to be prejudiced or discriminatory may be different from the actual result of their behavior.

For example, a manager may decide that all employees in a certain salary grade are not eligible for educational benefits, based on the amount of funds available in a fiscal year. This decision may have no element of bias or prejudice. However, if all employees in that salary grade are women or people of color, the decision results in an outcome that provides educational benefits disproportionately to whites or to men. Therefore, the policy has race or gender outcomes that are different from the original intent.

Intent and outcome are factors at each level. Personal intent and behavior may or may not match. As a member of a group, I may demonstrate attitudes and behaviors of which I am not aware, and my work practices may result in discrimination and subordination that I did not intend. Organizationally, the structures determining policies and practices may actually prevent me from proceeding in a manner consonant with my good intentions.

Therefore, managers must work hard to develop insight into what they intend and also develop greater ability to listen to others who describe the results of the managers' behavior. The workplace is not neutral ground, and my behavior may demonstrate insensitivity, discrimination or failure to see how I collude with the racism and sexism that operate in a given work unit. I am not required to abandon my intent. But if I am to be successful, I need to make it clear that I am open to dialogue and welcome feedback when my intent diverges from the outcome expected. The ability to make sure intent lines up with outcome is another skill to be learned, practiced, and internalized. It cannot be relegated to an "interesting experience" in a workshop, but must become second nature—just like any other managerial ability.

From Theory to Practice

Understanding the concept of individual, group and organizational levels—and recognizing how they play out in a given setting has no value unless managers commit themselves to action. What does the manager do if, for example, there is a difficult exchange between a supervisor and an employee who are different from each other by gender or race?

First, the manager should ask a series of questions:

- What do I know about the ability of these individuals to work with each other?
- Are these individuals who are generally not biased? Do they have effective interpersonal skills in most situations?
- Is the problem that the supervisor lacks skills in supervising someone who is different from him (if the supervisor is a man)?
- If the supervisor is a woman, does the problem exist because women have not had positions of authority in the organization prior to this? Are her contributions questioned more closely than if she were a man?

In some way, each level may be involved in both the diagnosis of the problem and the action to resolve it. However, the action must be carefully targeted to the level which requires the most attention. It is counterproductive to counsel white women or people of color to "develop more interpersonal effectiveness" when the real problem is the racist or sexist attitudes and behaviors of their supervisors or co-workers.

For example, one black woman was criticized by her supervisor for "always having a chip on her shoulder." She was written up as distant, hostile, not a team player. If the supervisor had been paying attention to the group and organizational levels, the supervisor would have learned that this employee was never included in lunch dates with co-workers and that, organizationally, she knew that no black woman had ever been promoted from her position to the next level. She needed the job and was determined to stick it out. But her determination could not carry her through to responding pleasantly to those who excluded her, or to maintaining an optimistic attitude about her chances for success in the face of overwhelming evidence to the contrary.

Managers must consistently be alert to the dynamics at each level. Do men in the organization share a perception that some women co-workers are "too aggressive?" What role do white employees play in the turnover of black employees? Managers need to pay attention to the behavior of individuals, the patterns of groups, and the race or gender implications of any policy and practice.

In general, the more powerful a particular "ism," the more leadership it takes to work against it. At the individual or group level, some problems may be delegated. For example, if the issue is the absence of a certain group in the workplace, the manager can ask others to learn how to recruit more representatively. If the problem is inter-group cooperation, the manager can develop some strategies which create natural arenas where cooperative behavior will develop.

But if the problem is the core beliefs about the abilities of others based on race and gender, and these core beliefs undergird the entire corporate culture, the problem cannot be delegated. The manager cannot delegate his or her role in creating a different workplace climate to human resources or Affirmative Action personnel.

The manager's own visible commitment to continue learning across all three levels sends a powerful message that individual incidents will be addressed and that systemic "isms" will be challenged.

KATE KIRKHAM, *an associate professor in the Department of Organizational Leadership and Strategy, has taught at BYU since 1979. She received her PhD from Union Graduate School in 1979 after receiving her MA in human resources and development from George Washington University and a BA in sociology from the University of Utah. At BYU, she teaches introduction to organizational behavior in the MBA program and teaches small group dynamics, and diversity and difference in organizations—the latter a class she developed herself.*

Questions

1. What do conflicts arise in the workplace? What are some of the advantages and disadvantages of conflict? How does conflict manifest itself at different levels of the organization?

2. How should managers and workers deal with conflict?
3. How do race, gender, or other differences complicate the management of conflict in the workplace?
4. What model of negotiation does Kirkham articulate? How could this model be applied in contexts other than the workplace?

Dealing with Opposition to the Church

Rex C. Reeve, Jr.

As Rex C. Reeve, Jr. studied and taught Mosiah 25–29 in the Seminary and Institute program, he began to see how, in those chapters, both the government and the church suffered from internal as well as external attack. In this article from The Book of Mormon: Alma, the Testimony of the Word, *Reeve has developed several scriptural-based solutions to deal with external and internal opposition as they apply to the Church.*

About 120 BC, king Mosiah gathered the people of Zarahemla together to hear accounts of the afflictions and bondage suffered by the people of Limhi and the people of Alma in the land of Nephi (Mosiah 5:1–6). Those hearing the stories wept because of the suffering of their brethren, but were filled with joy and thanksgiving when they learned that deliverance from bondage came through the power and goodness of God (Mosiah 25:7–10).

From the time of his conversion, Alma the Elder labored faithfully to reestablish the Church among his followers in the land of Nephi and in the city of Helam for more than 25 years. After Alma's arrival in Zarahemla, Mosiah, who was both king and prophet, gave Alma authority to ordain priests and teachers and to administer the true church of God throughout the land. Under Alma's able leadership and with an outpouring of the spirit of the Lord, the Church grew and propsered, eventually having seven churches in the land of Zarahemla. We might call them wards, or even stakes, but they were all part of the true church of God (Mosiah 25: 19–24).

When doctrinal and procedural questions arose in the Church, Alma the Elder received guidance through revelation. From time to time, the members were admonished to have faith in Christ, to properly repent of their sins, and to become clean and pure before the Lord (see Alma 5:15, 21, 32–33).

In Alma 1–4, the Church, then under the leadership of Alma the Younger, faced new internal and external problems. These problems eventually caused Alma to resign from his position as chief judge, allowing him time to administer the affairs of the Church and to travel among all the people of Nephi, bearing testimony against the wicked (Alma 4: 16-19). The purpose of this paper is to identify both the internal and external problems faced by the Church; to see how Alma the Younger instructed Church members to deal with both problems; and to see how Church members should react to similar problems.

External Opposition to the Church

In Alma 1:2-33, a large and powerful man named Nehor established a church of his own. In sharp contrast to the true doctrines of Christ, he taught "that every priest and teacher tought to become popular; and they ought not to labor with their hands, but that they ought to be supported by the people. And he also testified unto the people that all mankind should be saved at the last day . . . for the Lord had created all men, and had also redeemed all men; and, in the end, all men should have eternal life" (Alma 1:3-4). Through his powerful teaching of these false doctrines, Nehor gained many followers who gave him money and who no longer felt obligated to follow the strict commandments of God.

Under Nephite religious law, all people were free to believe whatever they desired (see Alma 1:17). The law protected the right of personal belief and even allowed individuals to teach those beliefs as long as others were not forced or injured. An important teaching of the Church was and always will be to eliminate religious intolerance and bigotry. The true saints of God respected Nehor's right to believe and teach as he pleased, but they armed themselves with the word of God so they would not be deceived.

In Nephite society, all were required to obey the civil laws of the land or face the prescribed punishment. Nehor violated the civil law by killing Gideon, and old and greatly respected man of God (Alma 1:9). In his position as chief judge, Alma was required to judge Nehor according to those crimes he had committed. The law required those guilty of murder to be put to death. In the process of judgement, Alma said, "Behold, this is the first time that priestcraft has been introduced among this people. And behold, though art not only guilty of priestcraft, but hast endeavored to enforce it by the sword; and were priestcraft to be enforced among this people it would prove their entire destruction" (Alma 1:12).

Many years earlier, Nephi had warned his people against the evils of priestcraft, which he defined as "men preach[ing] and set[ting] themselves up for a light unto the world, that they may get gain and praise of the world; but they seek not the welfare of Zion" (2 Nephi 26:29).
In our day, Elder Bruce R. McConkie has amplified this definition:

> Priesthood and priestcraft are two opposites; one is of God, the other of the devil. When ministers claim but do not possess the priesthood, when they set themselves up as a light to their congregations, but do not preach the pure and full gospel; when their interest is in gaining personal popularity and financial gain, rather than in caring for the poor and ministering to the wants and needs of their fellow men—they are engaged, in a greater or lesser degree, in the practice of priestcrafts. (593)

Nehor was put to death for his crimes, but this did not end priestcraft. Many people became worldly and, following Nehor's example, preached false doctrines for riches and honor (Alma 1:16). Those who did not belong to the Church began to persecute the members of the Church of God (Alma 1:19). This external persecution was a war of ridicule against church doctrines and beliefs: "Yea, they did persecute them, and afflict them with all manner of words, and this because of their humility; because they were not proud in their own eyes, and because they did impart the word of God, one with another without money and without price" (Alma 1:20).

External persecution was either a blessing or a curse, depending on how the members responded to it. When members followed the laws of the Church and the counsel of their leaders, they became stronger in their faith and were blessed both individually and as a church. When members refused to follow this counsel, they brought many trials and afflictions upon themselves and the whole Church. If they did not repent, their membership was taken away.

The leaders' counsel for reacting to this opposition was simple, yet when followed, had a profound influence for good: "Now there was a strict law among the people of the Church, that there should not any man, belonging to the church, arise and persecute those that did not belong to the Church (Alma 1:21). The members were expected to turn the other cheek, or to return good for evil. They were expected to be living examples of the teaching of Christ and to love their enemies. When some members violated this instruction and fought openly with their enemies, even with their fists, it caused much affliction and trial for the Church. Guilty members who would not repent and leave nonmembers alone were removed from the Church (Alma 1:23–24).

In addition, members were to be united and show love and respect for each other. They were to forgive and support one another, especially in times of persecution. The "strict law among the people of the Church" included the stipulation that "there should be no persecution among themselves" (Alma 1:21).

These members who stood fast in the faith remained "immovable in keeping the commandments of God" (Alma 1:25). They were true followers of Christ at all times, in all places and in all things (see Mosiah 18:9). The humble, sincere, and obedient individuals were living examples of the truthfulness of the gospel, which withstood all persecution.

Faithful members meekly suffered the persecutions heaped upon them (Alma 1:25). They had faith in their leaders and in the Lord. They did not take matters into their own hands; if wrongs needed to be corrected, the leaders took appropriate action. They saw persecution as an opportunity to grow and a challenging time to apply the teachings of Christ.

Still, members took time to sustain one another. When the priests left their labors to teach the word of God, the people would come to listen to their words. When the priests had completed teaching, all would return to their work (Alma 1:26). Even in times of persecution, members were to continue in their daily labors and their family duties, along with attending meetings and doing the work of the Church.

The priest would not elevate himself, understanding that the teacher was no better than the learner. All were considered equal; all labored according to their strength (Alma 1:26). All imparted of their substance, according to that which they had, to those in need. The people were instructed to be neat and clean in their dress, yet they were not to wear costly apparel in order to appear better than others (Alma 1:27).

Members were basically taught not to react to the persecution, but to focus on being good members of the Church: keeping the commandments, attending to their church duties and continuing to take care for the needy. If further action did need to be taken the Church leaders would be responsible to see that it was done, such as Alma dealing with Nehor. Being patient and Christlike in a difficult situation would be an example to others and would open the eyes of some nonmembers who were sincerely seeking after the truth.

External Opposition to the Modern Church

Since 1830, the modern Church has faced various types of external persecution, and the counsel to church members has been exactly the same as in the time of Alma. And when members have followed this counsel, they have been individually blessed and the Church itself has grown and prospered.

During the past few years, there has been a widespread effort by groups outside of the Church to criticize the doctrines and ordinances of the Church. One example of this is the film *The Godmakers,* which has been shown in many places around the world. In a letter dated 1 December

1983, the First Presidency carefully taught members of the Church how to respond to external opposition. Their instructions have a familiar sound and are in harmony with Alma's instruction to his people in similar circumstances.

> We are pleased that in recent months there has been a growing interest in the Church on the part of the media. . . . Much of what has been presented has been accurate and favorable to the Church.
>
> However, some of it has been inaccurate and parts of it highly critical of the Church. These include films which pretend to represent the position of the church on matters of doctrine and belittle the ordinances of the gospel, including the most sacred temple ordinances.
>
> We wish to point out that this opposition may be in itself an opportunity . . . These criticisms create . . . an interest in the Church . . . We have evidence to indicate that in areas where opposition has been particularly intense, the growth of the Church has actually been hastened rather than retarded.

The First Presidency continued and recommended the following:

> 1. Do not "challenge" or "enter into debates" with those who criticize the Church. Meet every situation "without resentment and without malice."
> 2. Prepare with "prayer" and "humility," to be guided by inspiration, and take every opportunity to explain the doctrines and practices of the Church in a "positive" Christian-like manner.
> 3. In the proper forum, "point out the high standards expected of members of the Church." Stress positive values such as "temperance . . . morality . . . fidelity in marriage [and] . . . worthy citizenship." Discuss the "dedication and faithfulness of members . . .taking care of [members] who are in need, in service to others, in missionary work, in the payment of tithes [and] in keeping their covenants and obligations."
> 4. "Above all . . . bear testimony of the restoration of the gospel, that Jesus is the Christ, the Son of God, the only

> begotten of the Father. And that "There is none other name under heaven, given among men whereby we must be saved.'"
>
> 5. Even if opposition seems hard, members should "renew . . . faithfulness to the principles of the gospel . . . take upon [them]selves the armor of righteousness" and the Church will be blessed and prosper (First Presidency letter 1 December 1983).

In summary, members both in Book of Mormon times and today are taught to react positively to persecution, to look at it as a blessing and an opportunity to demonstrate and to teach the doctrine and blessings of the gospel. They are counseled to seek the guidance of the Holy Ghost and to increase faith and obedience to the commandments of the Lord. The assurance is given that when the membrs do their part in facing persecution the kingdom of the Lord will continue to roll forth until it fills the whole earth.

Internal Opposition to the Church

By following the counsel of their leaders and humbly serving one another, the Church in Alma's day enjoyed a period of peace and prosperity, despite the persecutions the members suffered. Because of the steadiness of the Church, they accumulated flocks, herds, grain, gold, silver, 'fine-twined linen," and "precious things" (Alma 1:29). Though they were prosperous they were generous to all and did not lust after riches, but took care of the poor and needy— whether they were members of the Church or not (Alma 1:30). Because of this, "they did prosper and become far more wealthy than those who did not belong to their church. For those who did not belong to their church did indulge themselves in sorceries, and in idolatry or idleness, and in babblings, and in envyings and strife . . . and all manner of wickedness" (Alma 1:31-32). For the people of Alma, it was a time of prosperity and happiness in the midst of a world of wickedness and sorrow (Alma 1:28-33).

As is typical in the Book of Mormon, the members of the Church were not able to keep the commandments of God for long in the face of such prosperity. The paradox lies in their becoming prosperous because of righteousness, industry, hard work, and generosity, and then permitting that same prosperity to lead them to pride, contentions, and other serious sins. A cycle can be seen:

1. They followed their leaders and kept the commandments of God.
2. Because of their obedience and industry they were blessed with prosperity and many riches (Alma 1:29; 4:6).
3. Some began to be proud because of their riches even to wearing very costly apparel and thinking they were better than others (Alma 4:6).

4. Some began to set their hearts on riches and the vain things of the world (Alma 4:8).

5. Some began to be scornful toward one another (Alma 4:8).

6. Some began to persecute those who did not believe as they believed (Alma 4:8).

7. There began to be envyings, strife, malice, persecutions and great contentions among the members of the Church (Alma 4:9).

8. Many members of the Church became more prideful than those who did not belong to the Church of God (Alma 4:9).

9. Many members of the Church turned their backs and would not help the needy, the naked, the sick, and the afflicted (Alma 4:12).

10. Those members of the Church who remained faithful and who continued to be humble followers of God had to endure greater and greater afflictions and persecution from both members and nonmembers of the Church (Alma 4:15).

Wickedness from within creates many serious problems for the Church. When members are contentious and do not keep the commandments of the Lord, the Holy Ghost withdraws and leaves them without guidance. They do not accomplish the mission of the Church to perfect the saints, not do they proclaim the gospel; therefore, the Church does not grow and prosper. In Alma's time, the contention and wickedness within the Church was most likely a great stumbling block for nonmembers who were seeking for truth and would have like to be baptized. Alma was concerned because he knew that wickedness both in and out of the Church would soon bring destruction to all the people (Alma 4:10-11).

In combatting internal wickedness, Alma the Younger could look to an experience his father had dealing with the same problem. When Alma the Elder was the leader of the Church, many of the younger generation did not believe the traditions of their fathers and would not become members of the Church. This was a serious problem, but the greater problem was that many of the Church members followed the nonmembers in committing many serious sins (Mosiah 26: 1-6). To solve the problem, the Lord instructed Alma the Elder in the following points:

1. When there was sin in the Church it was necessary, even required, that the leaders of the Church admonish, instruct or confront the guilty members. Leaders could not just ignore the sin. It was imperative that they do something about the problem (Mosiah 26:6).

2. Alma the Elder had been a priest of king Noah in his young life, and from his own experience learned that repentance works. Repentance cleansed his sin so that he was now worthy of eternal life (Mosiah 26: 15-20). This same repentance was available to each member.

3. Alma the Elder was taught that it was Christ who would perform the Atonement and take upon himself the sins of the world. Christ would freely forgive sins of any person who was received into the Church by faith, repentance, and proper baptism (Mosiah 26: 22-23).

4. Alma the Elder was told that those who sincerely sought forgiveness must confess their sins before Church leaders and before the Lord (Mosiah 26:29).

5. If they expected to be forgiven of their own sins, members must forgive their neighbors' trespasses, especially when their neighbors say they have repented (Mosiah 26:31).

6. Those who would properly repent could be forgiven and could still be numbered among the Church of God (Mosiah 26:35).

7. Those who would not repent were excommunicated from the Church and their names were blotted out (Mosiah 26:36).

Alma the Younger knew that the basic solution to the problem of sin within the Church was for the members to either sincerely repent or to be removed from the Church. In either case, the Church would become clean again. He also knew that bringing people to repentance would require all his time and effort, so he resigned as chief judge to devote himself to the duties of the high priesthood. The only way to stir the people up to repentance was to bear "pure testimony" against them according to the spirit of revelation and prophecy (Alma 4:19-20). Alma spent the rest of his life laboring to bring people to repentance and regulating the affairs of the Church.

Internal Opposition in the Modern Church

In our day the Lord has established his Church. He is desirous that there be no iniquity in the Church and that the members be clean and pure before him. He said this is "the only true and living church upon the face of the whole earth, with which I, the Lord, am well pleased, speaking unto the Church collectively and not individually—For I the Lord cannot look upon sin with the least degree of allowance" (D&C 1:30–31). On another occasion he said, "Purge ye out the iniquity which is among you; sanctify yourselves before me" (D&C 43:11). He said, "Behold, I, the Lord, have looked upon you, and have seen abominations in the Church that profess my name. But blessed are they who are faithful and endure" (D&C 50:4–5). His command is, "Wherefore, let the Church repent of their sins, and I the Lord, will own them; otherwise they shall be cut off" (D&C 63:63).

Certain officers in the Church have the responsibility to be judges in the Church. They are to see that there is no iniquity in the church. They are to counsel members and use church discipline when serious transgressions have occurred. Just as in Book of Mormon times, there are still only two ways to cleanse the Church: (1) Members can sincerely repent, or (2) they can be excommunicated. Either way the Church will become clean before the Lord.

CONCLUSION

Simple principles govern how members should deal with outside and inside opposition to the Church. The principles taught and used in the Book of Mormon still govern what is taught and used in our day. When the Church is being attacked by those outside the Church who would destroy its doctrines and beliefs, members should not retaliate. Members should live good lives, be steadfast and immovable in keeping the commandments, and be patient in their affliction. They should take opportunities to positively teach the doctrines of the Church. When the Church is attacked internally by sins in the lives of its members, there are two ways to restore the Church to an acceptable and clean condition. The members guilty of sin can sincerely repent and live in harmony with Church standards. If they will not repent on their own, Church leaders are expected to continue to teach with the spirit and encourage them to repent. Members who will not respond and who continue to commit serious sins must be removed from the Church.

REX C. REEVE, JR., *an associate professor in ancient scripture, has been teaching at BYU since 1981. Besides teaching ancient scripture at BYU, Reeve has taught in the Seminary and Institute program for BYU. He received his EdD in education administration from BYU.*

Bibliography

Letter from the First Presidency, 1 Dec 1983.

McConkie, Bruce R. *Mormon Doctrine.* 2nd ed. Salt Lake City: Bookcraft, 1966.

Questions

1. What are some of the causes of external opposition to the Church,both now and in ancient times? How should members of the Church respond to external opposition?
2. Why do conflicts sometimes arise within the Church? How should members of the Church respond to these conflicts?
3. Do members of the Church always need to agree on everything? How should members of the Church deal with differences of opinion that are not related to doctrine? What kinds of issues can members of the Church disagree about and still be faithful to the Church?

Conflict

Paul Cox

This story, taken directly from Paul Cox's book Nafanua: Saving the Samoan Rain Forest, *chronicles the difficult and precarious process that Cox had to follow in order to help save a particular area of the Samoan rain forest. As Cox went through the frightening and intimidating negotiation process with Samoan chiefs, he found that "it is scary to step to the edge of the light, but if the path is right, you will be helped." Cox makes it a point in this story to "portray Samoan people as more than the cutout cartoon characters that have typified most caricatures of indigenous people" as a way to help readers understand the Samoan people in an intimate way.*

> Every age, every culture, every custom and tradition has its own character, its own weakness, and its own strength, its beauties and ugliness; accepts certain sufferings as matters of course, puts up patiently with certain evils. Human life is reduced to real suffering, to hell, only when two ages, two cultures and religions overlap. . . . Now there are times when a whole generation is caught in this way between two ages, two modes of life, with the consequence that it loses all power to understand itself.
>
> Herman Hesse, *Steppenwolf*

After carefully adjusting the formal lavalava and red *Pandanus* lei that Lamositele had sent me for the occasion, I picked up my long, slender kava root and walked along the beach to the north side of the village, where a tiny and rustic *fale* on crooked stilts served as the gathering point for the chiefs. The poles were decorated with red hibiscus flowers and pink torch ginger, while the stilts were adorned with coconut fronds. I could see about twenty large men packed inside, each stripped to the waist. Among them were both men holding the title of Fuiono: Fuiono Senio, short, handsome, but aggressive in demeanor, and tall slender Fuiono Mase'ese'e, who seemed possessed of ineffable grace and dignity. As I looked inside and saw all of the paramount chiefs of the village there, I had a heightened sense of being from a different culture and even a different time. Indeed, I was the only man present not to hold chiefly rank. I climbed the notches in the coconut trunk ladder, stepped inside, and sat down on the mat. I heard someone murmuring in the back, "What's Koki doing here? Doesn't he know this is a chiefs' meeting?"

The men's bodies glistened with scented coconut oil. A few more red *Pandanus* leis like the one Lilo had given me, while Fuiono Mase'ese'e wore one made of tiny red *nonu* fruit, which he occasionally nibbled on. He looked formidable, inscrutable, and very Polynesian, like a statue from Easter Island. He began speaking in the loud, clear voice characteristic of high orators:

Ia, ia susu maia lau susuga Koki, o le ali'i saienisi mai le atunu'u tele o Amerika!	Highest welcome, Koki, the scientist from the great country of America!

I responded by reciting the village *fa'alupega,* the list of paramount chiefs of Falealupo village:

Ia, ia afio lava le pa'ia maualuga o le maota nei,	*Highest greetings to the sanctity of those assembled,*
Aua ua afio mai le pa'ia maualuga o Au'va'a ma Aiga	*Because of the sacredness of the presence of high chief Auva'a and his family.*
Ua afio mai le Ma'opu o Nafanua	*The presence of the Glory of Nafanua*
Ua afio mai le pa'ia o le Matua a Lamositele	*The presence of the Majesty of Lamositele.*
Ua susu mai Alo o Losina	*The Sons of Losina are here.*
Ua maliu mai le paia o le Toa'fa ma le fetalaiga a Silia La'ei,	*The sacredness of the Four Orators and of the orator Silia La'ei is present,*
Ma le mamalu o le Tapua'iga.	*And the dignity of their Assistants.*

The men smiled, surprised that I could speak their esoteric rhetoric. Calls of "*Malo!*" ("Well done!") were heard throughout the *fale.* But despite their praise, I knew that the real test of my knowledge still remained ahead. In contrast to the precisely articulated chiefly Samoan with which he greeted me, Fuiono Mase'ese'e now switched to colloquial language with "k" sounds substituted for the "t," to tell a humorous story. Everyone laughed, and the jesting continued for some time, with everyone joining in the fun. After my entrance, the men ceased to pay any attention to me, and I became just part of the group, sitting in the hut and listening to Fuiono's story. For years I had longed to be so accepted in Samoan society that my presence, my foreignness, would no longer be noticed. In that little hut that morning, I glimpsed what it might be like to finally blend in, to have a clearly demarcated place in Samoan society.

In America and similar Western societies, wariness characterizes relationships between men. Although relative differences in physical, political, or financial power are seldom articulated, they are never ignored. A subtle accounting for differences in power creates a difference that makes it particularly difficult for men to form close bonds with coworkers after reaching adulthood. In such societies, which embrace egalitarianism in theory, but in fact defer to the strong, the rich, or the educated, a polite but detached demeanor proves prudent in most social settings—at least until one figures out for certain whose star is rising and whose is on the wane.

Such social ambiguity does not exist in Samoan society, which is perhaps why Western hierarchies appear so mysterious to many Samoans. In Samoa, one's position in the male echelon is always crystal clear: during kava ceremonies, the cup is passed from the highest chief to the lowest in strict order of rank. There is no point in jockeying for position, because status is strictly determined by one's chiefly title. The resultant hierarchy, frozen in the *fa'alupega,* can never change. Perhaps as a result of this immutability of social status, envy plays no significant role in chiefly councils. The Falealupo chiefs regard Fuiono's right to speak first as inalienable, and do not question it. Although such social stratification is foreign to American culture, steeped as we are in the cult of egalitarianism, Samoan stratification provides the comfort of always knowing where one is to sit, when one is to speak, and what one should say. And the Samoan social system produces in all a deep feeling of inclusion. Here, as a foreigner and an untitled man of Falealupo, sitting in a little hut, I felt as if I had been invited to fly in the corporate jet or join the executives playing from the professional tee at Pebble Beach.

Our period of relaxation ended when a messenger arrived, summoning us to the large meeting house where the investiture ceremony was to occur. Each chief took his kava stick as he left the hut, and together, we joined the stately procession to the investiture ceremony. As a group we entered the large, decorated *fale* and were given fragrant leis made from *moso'oi (Cananga odorata)* flowers. We shook hands with the four or five chiefs representing the families of those who were to receive the titles. The two chiefs-to-be were sitting on either end of the *fale,* gaily dressed in fine mats, beads, and paper currency folded in their hair. When the entrance rhetoric was complete, a young man dragged a mat before our group. As the mat arrived in front of each chief, he ceremonially placed his kava stick on it, a symbol of his respect for the families of those who would become chiefs. The young man paused in front of me, but I motioned him on. "You're supposed to throw your kava stick on the mat," the chief sitting next to me whispered.

"I know what I'm doing," I whispered back.

"All of the kava from the Falealupo districts has been received," the orator representing the prospective chiefs' families intoned. "Is there any other kava remaining?"

I slapped the mat in front of me and the young man dragged the mat around again. I placed my kava stick on it, making certain that the long stem faced toward the end of the hut.

"This kava is the respect from the distant country of America," I said in Samoan. "As a professor from the United States, I too, honor the candidates who wish to become chiefs."

There was a murmur of approval and broad smiles of surprise from the visiting chiefs. Lilo had taught me this little piece well.

The kava ceremony progressed through all of its fine intricacies. At the climax, the large tapa ribbons tying the fine mats around the candidates' waists were removed, much like unwrapping a Christmas present. Each was ceremonially served a cup of kava. As each partook, he became a chief, forever with a new name, title, and responsibility.

Lunch was served on banana leaves placed on woven trays. The high chiefs were served the *tuala,* the ribs of the pigs, while the orators were presented the *alaga,* or flanks. In addition, all were served taro and *palusami.* Conversation ceased while the chiefs quickly ate, a form of respect: no one can eat until the chiefs have finished. The chiefs then placed their considerable leftovers in baskets, which were carried by members of their families. As soon as the meal was removed, hot Samoan cocoa was served.

After a few minutes of conversation, Fuiono Mase'ese'e cleared his throat and addressed the gathering, "I understand that our visitor from overseas, Koki, has something he wishes to say to the village council. Koki, the time is now yours."

I slid slightly forward on the mat, and closed my eyes. In Samoan rhetoric, form matters far more than substance, and it is important to begin with composure. The orator who is most eloquent and persuasive will likely rule the day, regardless of the merits of his argument. I knew the rules of the game—to the chiefs, I must speak persuasively, without fear, without hesitation.

I began speaking slowly and loudly, and in the precise intonation and cadence that Aumalosi taught me so many years before: *"E vae ane la le paia fa'atafafa o le maota lenei, ou te tau pa'i malu atu ai i lo outou paia . . ."* "With due respect to the great sanctity of this house, I gently speak, because we are in the presence of the sacredness of Auva'a and Aiga. We are in the presence of the glory of Nafanua. We are in the presence of the majesty of Lamositele. The sons of Losina are here. We are in the presence of the Four Orators and their assistants. May the waters be calm, and may you be appeased because I have abused the sanctity of this gathering. I have no *agatonu* with you. But I praise God because we are one in Christ. Even though we are of different color, and speak a different language, it is because of His love that we are able to greet each other on this beautiful morning."

"I thank each of you because you have accepted me and my family, as well as my research associates, in Falealupo. It is a source of great pride to me that I am able to be one part of the untitled men in this village. You have accepted me as an untitled man, and I have in my possession a fine mat named 'testimony,' which evidences that I am a true member of Falealupo village."

"In this morning gathering, I remember the words of Princess Leutogi Tupa'itea when she said that she had been saved in the crotch of a *Callophyllum* tree. Just as that woman was saved by the rain forest, today the rain forest continues to protect our lives."

"Two days ago, I saw the terrible destruction caused by the loggers. I know that you are not happy with that situation because the forest is precious to you. I have heard that you have for many years refused logging companies, but now have accepted their offer only because you need money to build a new school."

"Therefore, I gently approach your sanctity and sacredness with my humble opinion. I scratch the roots of the *fau* tree and beg your indulgence. Could I pay for your school so that you can save your rain forest? I have no other objective than the preservation of the rain forest. I do not wish to control your land nor to make decisions concerning your forest. I am merely proposing a covenant: I will raise money to pay for your school if you will protect your rain forest. I believe the forest is sacred because it was created by God's holy hand. We must find a way to save it.

"Thank you very much for the opportunity to visit you in clear skies and in health. I pray that God will cause the orbit of the moon to be high above the heads of the high chiefs. May God also bless the orators that their whisks may never fall nor their staffs ever break. May my voice continue to live. May our morning be blessed."

There was a moment of silence after my speech, and then the chiefs, along with the villagers assembled outside the hut, burst into applause. Fuiono Senio exclaimed *"O ia o le suli Nafanua"*—"He is the heir of Nafanua." Fuiono Mase'ese'e addressed me with a short, formal reply:

"Thank you for your kind words. We all appreciate your excellent speech. As you know, anything involving land is very difficult in our culture, so we will need time to consider your proposal. Many thanks again for coming."

Fuiono motioned for me to leave, so I got up, shook all of the chiefs' hands, and left.

"That was very impressive, Koki. Everyone was amazed at how well you speak," Lilo said afterward.

"I didn't think you were coming," I said.

"I sat under the breadfruit trees behind the hut so I could listen in. I was very proud of you."

"But do you think the village will accept my offer?"

"I don't know. Anything involving customary land in Samoa is hard to predict. There will be much suspicion of your motives. We'll just have to see."

The next three days seemed to last forever. Apparently the chiefs felt that it was not appropriate to discuss my proposal immediately following the investiture ceremony honoring Foa'imea and Foa'imea, the two men who had been granted identical titles, so they decided to postpone public discussion until they could assemble the entire village. The meeting was to include all of the chiefs, but I was very conspicuously not invited.

I walked to Vaotupua in the southern part of the village to visit healer Lemau's husband, Seumanutafa Siaosi. Seumanutafa, usually jovial and full of merriment, was uncharacteristically withdrawn.

"I'm sorry, I really can't predict what will happen. Land issues are complex in Samoa, and Samoans are filled with suspicion. In the old days, the Germans gave some of the chiefs cigarettes, and had them make a mark on a piece of paper. Without realizing it, the chiefs signed away vast tracts of land for only a plug of tobacco. So even though everyone in the village respects you, those memories are still very painful."

"But don't you trust me? Can't you go plead my case?"

"I trust you, but I'm in trouble with the village council over another matter, and can't attend.

That day Bill, Dixie, and Thomas had driven around the island to count flying foxes, so I did my botanical work alone. I avoided the part of the forest that was being logged—it was just too upsetting to see again now—and collected medicinal plants in the littoral forest by the sea instead. But I could not forget the scene of devastation that I had witnessed. And I knew that hour by hour, more and more of the rain forest was disappearing.

That night I sat at the water's edge, and the waves swept over me. Why not let the waves carry me out? Perhaps I could disappear into forgetfulness of what had happened here, forgetfulness of how I had tried but almost certainly failed. Not far from where I sat was the westernmost point of Savaii—'O le Fafa—the connection point in legend between this world and Pulotu, the undersea world of spirits. Lilo had told me that Nafanua arose from the sea at the same spot.

"Lilo," I asked later that night, "Something that Fuiono Senio said at the chiefs' meeting puzzles me. Fuiono Senio called me the *'Suli o Nafanua.'* What did he mean?" I had always found Fuiono rather intimidating: he struck me as the most aggressive member of the chiefs' council.

Lilo gave me a long, sideward glance. "Perhaps you should ask Lamositele tonight after dinner."

That night, sitting with Lamositele and Silia Tusi, an extremely brilliant orator, I posed my question again. The two looked at each other. Lamositele spoke first. "What Fuiono means is that you are animated by the Spirit of Nafanua."

"Why did he say that?" I asked.

Silia then spoke. "Koki, that is not a simple question. I must first help you understand who Nafanua was and what she stood for. And that will require some time to explain."

"I would be very interested."

Silia explained that Nafanua's father, Saveasi'uleo, was the god of both the sea and the underworld, and appeared as a combination of man and moray eel. Nafanua's mother, Tilafaiga, was one of a pair of Siamese twins, and her liaison with Saveasi'uleo resulted in a pregnancy. Saveasi'uleo routinely destroyed all of his offspring, eating them alive. Knowing Saveasi'uleo's viciousness, Nafanua's mother successfully concealed her pregnancy and childbirth, and hid the placenta deep in the ground. The child was thus named *"Nana Fanua"*—"Hidden in the Earth."

But as a child, Nafanua once strayed too close to the beach. Suddenly the evil sea god rushed at her from the sea. Before he could seize her, however, her uncle Ulufanuasese'e surfed along the tops of the waves to decoy the monster beneath. Looking at Saveasi'uleo in ridicule, Ulufanuasese'e said: "Look what has become of you! Would you even kill and eat your own brother? We will separate: you stay in Pulotu and I will stay on the land. But we will meet again at the end of time and our lineage." Saveasi'uleo slid back beneath the waves, but demanded the presence of his daughter in Pulotu. There she remained under her father's tutelage and studied the art of destruction, but she also carried with her the knowledge of the rain forest and the healing power of the plants.

On land in Falealupo, oppression reigned. The people were made slaves on their own land, forced even to climb coconut trees upside down. One day a man named Tai'i called out in desperation: "Is there no one to save us?" Deep within the ocean, his words found an audience.

Saveasi'uleo commanded his daughter Nafanua: "Go up and free the people. Destroy the oppressors utterly with three war clubs: *Fa'auliulito, Ulimasao,* and *Tafesilafa'i.*"

Nafanua looked on the earth with compassion, however, and took only two of the war clubs, leaving behind *Fa'auliulito,* lest the entire world be turned forever to ash. Nafanua swam toward the portal of the underworld, to the place of her birth, Falealupo.

Nafanua surprised the village with the ferocity of her solitary war against their oppressors. No one suspected that such a mighty warrior could be a woman until one day in Faia'ai village, the people were stunned to see her breasts. Chiefs came throughout Samoa to pay her homage. Nafanua sought to establish for the first time a central government for all of Samoa headquartered in Falealupo and redistributed all of the chiefs' titles. But to the villagers of Falealupo came some special charges, or *tofi.* "Auva'a" became a sitting monarch, and the priest of Nafanua. The rest of the high chiefs became her *aiga,* or family. One trusted orator she named "Fuiono" and charged him to be the spokesman for the village. "Taofinu'u" ("Hold fast the village") was charged with upholding the good of the village. "Soifua" ("life") was charged always to protect the village's well-being. After she bestowed these titles, another prominent orator came running from the village to Nafanua. "I'm sorry, but I have no other *tofi* for you," Nafanua told him. "But look at your fine clothes. I will call you 'Silia laei' [literally, "beautiful clothing"], for you will always beautify the village with your presence.

Nafanua deigned that the village should be led, under Auva'a's direction, by the four paramount orators. The reign of Nafanua ushered in an era of solidarity and peace among the Samoan people. Temples were built to her, and Auva'a became her earthy representative. But before returning beneath the waves, Nafanua left a prophecy: "I have founded a government that will serve you well. But one a day kingdom will come from across the sea that is not of this earth, but of heaven. When it comes, you must enter it." It is largely because of this prophecy that, when John Williams of the London Missionary Society introduced Christianity to Samoa, nearly all of the inhabitants of Samoa converted.

By the time Silia and Lamositele had finished telling me the story of Nafanua, men were starting to launch their canoes by lantern light for night fishing. It must have been nearly 2:00 AM. Lamositele started to rise to prepare his own fishing gear.

"But Lamositele, I still don't understand. I think that is a beautiful story, but why would Fuiono say that I am filled with the spirit of this goddess?"

"Don't you see? Nafanua was not from Samoa. She just appeared out of the sea to fight our battles and save the village from oppression. She loved the rain forest and protected it. Well, we're now under oppression from this sawmill. We have nowhere else to turn to get funds for the school. Suddenly, you appear out of nowhere and want to kick the loggers out. You talk about loving the forest. Fuiono, at least, thinks that in some sense, Nafanua has returned."

I knew that the chiefs' discussion of my proposal would be difficult and protracted. Consensus is required for all major decisions. Absent consensus, there is simply no conclusion. As a result, important decisions can be delayed for weeks until everyone agrees. The morning after my proposal, all of the chiefs in Falealupo district met. Though the subject was perilous and difficult, consensus was reached in only a matter of hours.

It was afternoon when Lilo told me breathlessly of the chiefs' decision. "They accepted your offer! They have agreed to stop all logging if you can pay for the school!"

I offered a silent prayer of thanks. I later learned that Fuiono Senio, Tai'i, Soifua, and Auva'a all championed my proposal, but that Taofinu'u regarded it with suspicion. What would happen after I paid for the school, he wanted to know. Would I gain control of the village lands? Why would I want to pay for a school and expect nothing in return? Surely I must have something up my sleeve.

Tai'i argued that God must have sent me to deliver Falealupo from its terrible dilemma. Auva'a pointed out that the logging company might cut down the whole forest, and there still wouldn't be enough to pay the debt for the school.

Fuiono Senio, sensing that a consensus could be reached, asked Taofinu'u if he couldn't join his fellow chiefs in accepting the proposal.

Taofinu'u, seeing that he was the only holdout, agreed that the village had little recourse if it wished to preserve the forest. They would travel down this new and perilous road together.

Fuiono and the other three paramount orators asked to meet with me so that they could discuss my offer in detail. I told them that I would go to the Development Bank in Apia and immediately have the mortgage on the school signed over to me as a personal obligation. I had arranged for mortgage payments for six months, during which time I would raise in the United States the funds necessary to pay off the mortgage completely. I planned to return to negotiate a covenant protecting the forest forever in return for paying for the school. I would formally renounce any rights to the village lands or forest and would negotiate the covenant completely in the Samoan language with the village. All I asked in the meantime was a complete moratorium on all logging and flying fox hunting during the six-month period.

Fuiono nodded agreement. I spoke again. "I know that this has required a tremendous leap of faith for you and thank you from the bottom of my heart. I will not let you down." As I left, Fuiono muttered, "He is the spirit of Nafanua."

The chiefs' decision to protect the forest rapidly spread through the village, and village representatives informed the loggers. However, the loggers apparently did not believe that such a reversal was possible, and showed up the next day for logging as usual.

Word that the loggers were still cutting the forest in direct opposition to the village decision reached Fuiono Senio, who was visiting friends by the sea. Fuiono ran three miles to the logging site with his machete in hand. Motioning the bulldozers and saws to stop, Fuiono spoke to the astonished group of loggers.

"Don't cut another tree! This forest is now taboo!"

Apparently one of the loggers didn't believe Fuiono and reached for his saw to continue working.

"Don't touch another tree! Try it and watch what happens! You'll turn to dust!"

The head of the logging party spoke respectfully to Chief Fuiono, well aware that any insult given to a Samoan chief in his own village could lead to immediate violence.

"Excuse me, sir, but is there a reason why we should stop cutting these trees?"

Fuiono replied vehemently. "Yes. Let me explain it to you. This forest is now taboo. I am the chairman of the village forestry committee and have authority over the entire forest. And the chiefs' council has decided to taboo the forest. You are all now standing on taboo ground. You should all leave immediately."

The logging company employees, all Samoan, looked at each other. They had heard words that have deep saliency in Samoa: taboo, authority, chiefs' council. To willingly violate taboo is an unthinkable offense. Besides, they had heard Fuiono threaten one of their own workers. They knew that even with all of their machinery, they stood little chance against an entire village. This was clearly a problem for the front office to sort out. Quietly they packed up their equipment and left.

PAUL COX, *former Dean of General Education and Honors, has taught botany at BYU since 1983. Cox is an ethnobotanist, specializing in the uses of plants by indigenous peoples. He received his PhD from Harvard as a Danforth Fellow and National Science Fellow and his MS from the University of Wales where he was a Fulbright Fellow. He received undergraduate degrees from BYU in botany and philosophy. Cox has published three books and over 100 scientific articles. He is currently the director of the National Tropical Botanical Garden, a congressionally chartered group of five gardens in Hawaii and Florida focused on the conservation of rare and endangered plants.*

Questions

1. Why does Cox immediately have the sense of being an outsider when he enters the chiefs' meeting?
2. How does Cox build credibility with the chiefs? How did he prepare himself for this meeting?
3. What means does Cox use to persuade the chiefs? How does Chief Fuiono persuade the loggers to leave?
4. What is the model of negotiation practiced by the Samoans? How does this model differ from other models you have read about? How could some of the principles of this model be applied outside of the Samoan community?

Expanding the Dialogue: Service Learning in Costa Rica and Indonesia

DAVID D. WILLIAMS AND
WILLIAM D. EISERMAN

As David Williams attended conference sessions on service learning, he found that the presenters were focusing their concerns and models primarily on the national level and that there was a conspicuous lack of interest in work being done on an international level. Williams wrote this article to "encourage educators to look beyond the United States" when developing service learning programs. In order to practice what they preached, Williams and colleague William Eiserman did fieldwork together in Costa Rica and Eiserman did solo research in Indonesia. Their article was originally published in The Michigan Journal of Community Service Learning.

A new book on service-learning in higher education (Jacoby, 1996) "provides a historical overview and a context for understanding the essential linkage of service and learning; it describes the current state of practice; and it highlights the relationship between service-learning and institutional education goals"(p. 5). Although the several authors examine predominant assumptions underlying the combining of higher education, offer several illustrative examples from colleges and universities, and explore issues related to designing and administering service-learning programs, the focus is almost exclusively on service-learning in the United States.

But, as the questions are asked and plans are developed for service-learning programs, whether on individual, institutional or national levels, we can learn from the experience of those who have been involved in the development and implementation of service-learning programs in other contexts, too. Existing programs outside the United States may inform service-learning in this country.

Unknown to many, some of the most comprehensive and innovative approaches to service-learning have been designed and implemented in developing countries (Eberly & Sherraden, 1990). In the present study, the University of Costa Rica's compulsory service-learning program, which began in 1975, is compared to a similar, even older program in Indonesia. This article explores the historical roots, program components, perceived outcomes, and strengths and weaknesses of programs in Costa Rica (The Trabajo Comunal Universitario or TCU projects) and Indonesia (the Kuliah Kerja Nyata or KKN projects).

METHODS

A qualitative inquiry approach (Denzin & Lincoln, 1994) was used, allowing for emergent themes to arise in the context of on-site interviews and observations. Qualitative inquiry provides a means for investigators to refine their questions to better reflect the perspectives of all participants throughout a study. Thus, an attempt was made to blend the concerns of students, faculty, administrators, service recipients, the literature, and the researchers through the ongoing refinement of questions in light of concurrent data analyses. New questions arose and were addressed along with questions suggested by literature.

Documents were reviewed and participants interviewed in three KKN projects associated with Andalas University in Padang, West Sumatra, Indonesia. Then, after analysis and review of that experience, eleven TCU projects associated with the University of Costa Rica were studied.

Interviews in Indonesian and Spanish were conducted by the authors with thirteen administrative staff, thirteen participating faculty, and thirty students as well as forty-five community participants (families being served, teachers in the setting, and visitors at museum and display sites). Nineteen questionnaires were also collected from students participating in the Indonesian projects. On-site observations of the KKN and TCU participants at work were also made.

Three forms of data were generated by the authors: a) field notes, which included reconstruction of interviews and observations as well as questions and interpretative comments, b) supplementary data, which included photographic documentation of sites, observable outcomes of projects, and exposure to the various participants, and c) archival data, which included official documents describing the goals and objectives of the programs and their implementation criteria, documents provided to faculty and students regarding participation guidelines, student evaluation instruments, as well as student and faculty reports of individual project activities.

The authors' analysis procedures consisted of searching for patterns across data sources and postulating tentative answers to original and emergent questions. Additional data collection allowed the testing of these tentative answers.

Several methodological standards for conducting qualitative inquiry have been proposed (e.g., Eisner, 1991: Guba & Lincoln, 1989) and were used to guide this study. For example, though each visit was brief (less than a month in each country), the triangulation standards were met by using two investigators, a variety of sites, multiple informants, and complementary collection procedures. Tentative findings were shared with participants and they were asked for their judgements of accuracy and credibility (member checking), and the findings were also shared with disinterested others to discover any blind spots (peer debriefing).

What was learned from participants in these two countries that could help others as they develop service-learning programs and policies in university settings? The remainder of this article summarizes lessons learned around the following questions:

1. What are the historical roots that lead to the formation of these programs?
2. What are the basic program purposes and components?
3. What are the perceived outcomes and concerns associated with participation in these programs from various perspectives?
4. What are some implications for combining service and learning for university students in other countries?

HISTORICAL ROOTS

Both of these "non-military national service" programs developed in the 1970s, beginning in grassroots initiatives and culminating in centralized governmental support and/or mandates.

INDONESIA

Rooted in a rich history of *gotong-royong* (or mutual assistance), KKN had its first observable roots as a program between 1945 and 1949 when Indonesians were struggling for independence from the Dutch. Due to a critical lack of teachers in guerrilla areas at that time, members of the student army were recruited to teach in secondary schools in these areas (Hardjasoemantri, 1981). After the fighting ceased, the organized students felt a "moral commitment" to continue providing teaching services on a voluntary basis and subsequently developed a volunteer project called *Pergerahan dan Penempatan Tenagaa Mahasiswa* (recruitment and placement of students for the purpose of teaching, known as PTM) which lasted until 1962.

In 1966 a major revision of the entire educational system included an institutional service-learning concept that was drawn from the earlier students' experiences with PTM. Several reform objectives eventually emerged from this movement and became the basis for *Kuliah Kerja Nyata* or KKN:

1. Education would become more Indonesia-based in content.
2. Education would relate more closely to the range of skills presently needed in Indonesia.
3. The availability of non-formal education would be increased in order to complement the available formal education.
4. Education would provide greater opportunities for young Indonesians to participate directly in the development of their country in practical and satisfying ways.

With these objectives as a foundation, KKN emerged in 1972 as a formal course which was piloted at three of Indonesia's major universities, including Andalas University. The success of these pilot projects resulted in expansion to all 43 public universities, 90% of which subsequently have made KKN compulsory for all students. Thus the impetus behind service-learning has shifted over the years from a voluntary effort fueled by student initiative to a compulsory "program" mandated by universities.

COSTA RICA

Details from Sherraden & Castillo (1990), Gonzalez (1992), a booklet describing TCU entitled *Informacion General* (1992), and interviews with TCU administrators and university faculty contribute to understanding the historical roots of TCU as a program initiated by several Costa Rican students and faculty concerned about how to make their university more responsive to the needs of their broader society. They believed that because they were receiving many opportunities at the expense of others, they ought to find a way to compensate the rest of the nation. This attitude first emerged in what is described as a small "radically left" group of students and received support from a similar group of faculty during the 1960s and 1970s. Like most modern universities, the University of Costa Rica identifies a three-pronged mission for itself, including teaching, research, and service to the community.

Therefore, in 1974, in an effort to respond to this "service movement," to raise service to the level of importance held by research and teaching and to better integrate the three within the academic mission of the institution, the University of Costa Rica created an Office of Social Action (*Vicerrectoría de Acción Social*) to match its sibling offices of research and teaching, all three of which serve as administrative supports for faculty. Responsible for a variety of service related activities which bridge faculty and students with the community, this office administers several service-learning programs, including TCU, which became compulsory for students in 1975.

BASIC PROGRAM PURPOSES AND COMPONENTS

Costa Rica and Indonesia have many similar objectives and processes for carrying out their service-learning programs, both programs are viewed as a means for bridging university resources with community resources. The emphasis in both is on community improvements and benefits, while benefits to the students, faculty, and university as separate from the community are of secondary importance. They both emphasize students' obligations to society more than student learning, although that is a secondary focus.

In terms of motivation for participating, community members view the program in both countries as a means of obtaining services not otherwise available. These programs are also meant to provide a feedback loop so that society can inform the university about the social realities that academia should address. Thus, the community not only receives benefits but also informs the university via these programs.

Students in both countries are required to participate if they want to graduate (though many of them want to offer their help and do not view this requirement negatively). According to faculty and students interviewed in this study, students who participate in Costa Rica feel some obligation beyond their university requirement to participate because about 60% of them pay almost no tuition. Even of those who do, the highest payments are only about the equivalent of $120 a semester. And in Indonesia, all university students feel some obligation to the rest of their society to help, even though they have to pay tuition and often major costs associated with their projects.

Faculty motivations vary more substantially. In Indonesia, faculty are assigned supervisory roles to projects that may or may not be directly relevant to their teaching and research. They do not appear to glean much professionally or personally from participating. But in Costa Rica, faculty propose their own projects, which may grow directly out of their research and teaching activities. It appears that a major incentive for these professors' involvement is the opportunity to publish.

Administratively, the programs are very similar in that program offices are set up to bridge service with research and teaching rather than make service a separate activity. However, the Indonesian program administration is centralized within the KKN government office and involves service-learning projects for students from many different universities. Though the Costa Rican program has the TCU office and a formal project development and evaluation process (involving reviews of plans, implementation, and outcomes), most of the development and administration are decentralized to academic departments and faculty within those departments. Each academic department in the university has a faculty member assigned to coordinate the efforts of their department with the Office of Social Action. This person helps orient other professors to the Social Action programs, knows the community service projects pertaining to their department, helps solve problems, encourages integration of service with inquiry and teaching, and otherwise searches for ways to meet the Office of Social Action's main responsibility—applying university learning to the society at large.

Both programs provide minimal financial support, although the Costa Rican program appears to provide slightly more. Most University of Costa Rica departments dedicate at least three percent of their budget to TCU-related projects and allow up to 30% overload or faculty release time to participate in these programs. The TCU office provides an assistant for ten hours a week to help faculty members in whatever ways they see fit. That office also provides food, transportation, hourly assistants, materials, and evaluation/accreditation assistance for projects they approve. In contrast, the Indonesian students, in addition to paying tuition, often provide their own financial support for projects, though the program does provide travel funds.

In terms of student requirements and faculty involvement, the TCU programs, translated as university community work, are designed to meet the Costa Rican objectives through compulsory "pass/fail" participation of all undergraduate students, in addition to their traditional course work and departmental practical requirements. Students must complete the equivalent of 300 hours of service by working on a segment of a faculty member's TCU-approved project in less than one year after completing at least 50% of their course work, and taking a class on "national reality" which orients them to the problems of the nation (course contents and activities vary widely as each academic department teaches its own version). They apply to participate in a project after reviewing descriptions of available projects.

These projects usually involve some needs assessment with community leaders or members, span at least three years and are somewhat interdisciplinary in nature. Projects vary widely: efforts to solve health problems, improve literacy, enhance cultural development, preserve historical relics, and preserve native dialects. Projects usually grow out of the faculty member's assessment of what a particular community needs in light of each faculty member's primary research and teaching interests and their ongoing relationships with the community. Thus, the faculty members are usually members of these communities or have strong ties to them, and are willing to dedicate several years to addressing needs there, working with several cohorts of 10-30 students from many different disciplines throughout the project's duration.

The KKN program is also compulsory, occurs subsequent to at least two years of on-campus study, and involves participation in a graded four credit "coaching" class taught for 2–4 hours from January to June within each college. Students are oriented, usually in large groups of up to 200, to the village infrastructure, as well as production, education, social, cultural, and spiritual issues important in village life. Toward the end of this course, students are divided into small teams of 8-10 and are assigned to a participating village. Meanwhile, village leaders are approached by government and university staff to explain the aims of KKN and prepare the villagers to identify needs and prepare for the team to take residence there. Eventually, an initial one day "observation visit" is conducted to allow the students to gather data about the situation and needs of the village. However, rather than a formal needs assessment, this visit only involves introductions, a short tour of the village, and a short meeting to discuss the starting date, housing arrangements, and the expression of hopes for what will be accomplished.

About a week after this initial visit, the student team moves into the village and spends two months developing relationships, working with village leaders to develop a multi-disciplinary work plan and work collaboratively with one another and villagers to address this plan. The students are expected to assume five main roles: sharers of information from outside sources that the villagers might want to use, motivators to encourage village members to make necessary changes, diffusers of national programs and ideas, inter-system mediators between villagers and offices offering technical services within the region, and supervisors of project activities. However, actual roles emerge and are negotiated, often resulting in the students spending considerable time physically laboring on villager-designed projects. The students also spend time each day informally meeting together to talk about their work, challenges they face, and possible solutions.

The projects usually combine several areas of development that reflect local, regional, and national governmental priorities. Some examples include rodent control, building an irrigation canal, reactivating a local chapter of the national family education and welfare organization for women, activating youth through sports, traditional dancing, and drama, renovating a bridge, advising on legal issues, conserving traditional folk drama through education of the youth by knowledgeable villagers, educating on health maintenance and hygiene, conducting a census, and mobilizing funds for economic development. The students are supervised and evaluated/graded at the end of the two months by faculty assigned to their project who do not usually reside in the village with the students, but do make occasional visits. These evaluations include observations of projects, interviews with key village leaders, and review of a final report prepared by the students which describes the village, current problems in it, and students' activities and project outcomes.

One important component of service-learning programs according to the literature is "reflection" by participants on what they are learning from their giving of service. Neither of these programs specify a "reflective' component per se. However, there are many opportunities for the students and faculty in the Costa Rican projects to meet, talk, make decisions, and solve problems together. Thus, there is an emphasis on being thoughtful about what they are doing as they address real problems of their communities. But reflection is implicit rather than explicit. Also, the focus is on encouraging an orientation toward helping others first and on one's education second.

PERCEIVED OUTCOMES

The goals of both KKN and TCU are actually being realized in the practices and experiences of faculty, students, and members of the community. It becomes clear that the service missions of these programs are being expressed in tangible, though somewhat different ways.

While students, faculty, and the university seem to be benefitting in a variety of ways, both programs emphasize community benefits in terms of stated objectives and the planned activities of participants. Members of the communities being served by the university students and faculty reported that they felt understood and listened to by the academics, and that they were usually very involved in identifying their needs, developing the programs that would address those needs and evaluating their success in collaboration with the faculty and students involved. As one Costa Rican community leader said,

> This project has been good. . . . It has helped people to get involved, to listen to one another. Some of our people have volunteered with building a canal here, because of this project. This land, you know, was given to us. This is a problem. People sometimes begin to think other people should always solve their problems. This project has begun to show them that outside help is important, but it requires effort from us. Change requires collaboration. The best outside help is like this, when they help us decide, help us plan, help us accomplish our goals.

With only a few exceptions, most of the university students felt that participation also helped them to develop a realistic sense of civic responsibility, understanding, and caring for others in their society while providing an opportunity for them to refine their skills and apply knowledge obtained through their studies in new and useful ways. As one Indonesian student noted,

> I never realized that the villagers might have a set of customs and beliefs about what the materials can be used for something like a water system and that concrete was not a part of that. This required a great deal of discussion. At times I was frustrated that we could not proceed faster. But I also gained an appreciation for their ability to deliberate on these matters. Without this sort of deliberation, important aspects of the culture could be lost. . . . Those ways might actually be there because they are the most effective. I suppose I did not realize that slow progress may sometimes be appropriate. . . . KKN helped me learn the importance of examining these cultural issues, especially when drastic changes are being suggested. They know their reasons for previous practices and they know some of the barriers to change which outsiders cannot anticipate.

Another student from Costa Rica explained,

> I'm a boy from the city, but now my heart beats to the rhythm of the village. . . . Now I know the condition of many people in my country which I could have easily been shielded from my entire life. It is possible, you know, to pursue your own interests above the needs of people who are suffering nearby. We learn to navigate around them, those people, so well that we remain completely ignorant of their circumstances. But once you know about them first hand . . . then you no longer can only pursue your own interests. TCU helps you accept some responsibility for your society.

Costa Rican faculty who choose to participate are also positively affected. However, Indonesian faculty are more tangential. While the universities in Indonesia which participate receive greater visibility in the communities involved and believe that most of their graduates have a deeper knowledge of and commitment to the society, faculty do not appear to benefit directly, and most curriculum and research programs are not affected directly by the service component.

In contrast, TCU appears to serve as a sort of faculty and university development program for at least a small proportion of the faculty. Participating faculty reported that they benefitted in many of the same ways students did because faculty viewed themselves as learners alongside the students. As one professor reflected,

> This project gives me a chance to go to areas I never would otherwise go. I meet people I never would know and learn about circumstances I have only heard about. It is one thing to have an opinion or a solution in your mind. It is another to confront it, to address the problem just as it exists, with all of the complications. . . . And to do it in the peace of high mountain villages. Well, it is enjoyable and difficult at the same time. It changes you, personally and professionally. It anchors who you are and why you do what you do.

Others noted that participation helped them to be better teachers and researchers and to integrate those responsibilities with service in meaningful ways.

> By blending them, I am not torn between my responsibilities as I would be if I had them all separated.

> Doing different things is a good way to stay interesting to your students. Somehow I think I am more lively now when I teach my courses because TCU has gotten me out into the fresh air, off campus. TCU is a good reminder of what I am really doing as an instructor. It is easy to forget about that.

> For me it has been a good way to integrate research and service . . . and teaching. It has given me many ideas for teaching and research. I am very excited about this research. It is full of surprises.

One of the striking features of the research being conducted in the context of TCU projects is the way research questions arise. Many of the ideas for research projects contextually emerge. Rather than formulating a research agenda out of context and imposing it on "subjects," TCU research projects arise from community needs. For many researchers, this calls for a methodological departure from highly reductionistic, quantitative approaches to more individualistic, qualitative approaches. Several faculty find themselves developing new research skills as they ask new kinds of questions, often more directly bridging their research with practice.

Inasmuch as faculty experience personal or professional development, it is likely the university itself is indirectly upgraded. Faculty indicated that the most apparent way the university benefits from their TCU experiences is that the curriculum is informed by the community-based projects. The strengthened community relationships which result from many TCU projects, including collaboration with various public and private agencies, also are perceived as beneficial to the university. As one student explained, as the faculty have improved through participation in this program, the whole university has benefitted.

> TCU makes the university more realistic. It forces faculty to take their theories into the streets, not just to test them, but to use them. And I think that when they teach, their experience of having used a certain theory or method in a real situation makes their lesson more meaningful to students, more valid. This improves the university generally, I think.

Programs in both countries address real problems of their national and local communities using interdisciplinary teams of students. In Indonesia, this occurs because the teams are created through a mixing of students from a variety of majors; the teams are assigned to villages where the problems to be addressed are negotiated with the villagers and the students are able to call upon their experiences and course work to address those needs. In Costa Rica, faculty focus on real problems faced by communities, and this naturally leads to the use of several disciplines to cooperatively address those problems. The students join the projects from many different majors and in response to requests from the faculty for students with particular expertise.

In both situations, the interdisciplinary efforts break down barriers between people with different academic perspectives while generating better solutions to problems they all face. As one student said,

> I am from the hard sciences. It was helpful to work with social workers on this. I would not have thought to do this, maybe because I was never taught to think that way, that inclusively, in my course work. They helped me understand why people were making the decisions they

> were about how they built their houses; why they did or did not take care of their land like I thought they should. This was necessary to understand if we wanted to get them to change how they did things. It was humbling, I guess you would say, to realize that our solutions were useless until we learned how to reach them. This is why TCU is valuable to me. It is my work to help solve human problems, but in my school, we do not study humans. We study the earth. TCU taught me the human side to geology that never appeared in my books.

And a faculty member noted,

> I have learned many things from this project already. I am a social worker, but I have had to learn about geology and geography, even architecture in order to make the social changes I am interested in making there. None of us can work in isolation when we are applying what we do to real life problems. This has helped me question my methodology and others' methodologies as well. What can it mean when people are working within a single perspective? What kinds of solutions to problems can they offer?

In both countries, service projects are created by the participants to coalesce efforts of all group members around community problems. This approach helps focus their efforts in ways that could not be achieved through individual service hours spent in service agencies. Students are not just giving service—they are part of a team which supports them, challenges them, and helps them see that they are part of something bigger than themselves. They are learning to collaborate as citizens for the common good.

Although the Indonesian students are graded while the Costa Ricans receive pass/fail ratings, both programs include the service curriculum as a separate requirement for students, outside of course work, again emphasizing the focus on community needs first. Interestingly, several of the Costa Rican faculty who were interviewed as well as the TCU administrators, commented on how the aims of TCU depend on the freedom this external placement of the program provides. As one faculty member noted (and this seems to apply in Indonesia as well),

> I think it is better to have TCU separate as well as non-graded. It helps me to achieve many of the objectives of

> TCU related to social responsibility. The interdisciplinary nature of TCU would be much more difficult if TCU were part of specific courses. And how can you respond to community needs if you have to do projects which must operate on the semester calendar? The way TCU works now, students are involved for 300 hours. How those hours are distributed depends totally on the nature of the work to be done for the community. It all depends on the community project. . . . Having TCU non-graded is also very good, at least for me. It helped me to use the evaluation process to achieve the objectives of social responsibility. If I had to grade the students, they would be motivated by a grade rather than by doing something which was meaningful to them and to others. The TCU process is just more real and so is the way they are evaluated. Don't you think it is good to learn how to evaluate your own work in your own terms? And, the students were motivated more than students ever are when grades are a part of it. This is ironic because some people, other faculty, who don't participate in TCU, say that it is impossible to motivate students if you are not grading them. Those of us who are committed to TCU do not find this to be true.

One of the most hotly debated issues regarding university service-learning programs is whether they should be compulsory or voluntary. Many of the outcomes cited above are a function of these programs' compulsory nature. Though this appears to be critical to their success, it also creates some problematic side effects. In Indonesia, because nearly all universities participate in this national program, there are more students needing supervision and guidance than the existing faculty can appropriately serve. So, although many villagers are receiving help, the quality may be uneven. And, because other Costa Rican universities which do not have this requirement have an edge in competing for students, the compulsory nature of TCU is coming under increasing attack by those who want to reduce costs and time to graduation.

Participants in both countries are searching for ways to involve more faculty, to clarify the purposes of the program for potential participants, to obtain greater supporting funds, to improve the quality of the experience for all participants, to overcome negative side effects associated with their programs being compulsory, to have external evaluation assistance, and to conduct research on the processes and outcomes of their programs.

The Indonesians are also seeking to develop more urban projects, and they are searching for ways to place faculty directly in field settings with students.

CONCLUSION

Universities all over the world have continually aligned themselves with a three-pronged mission of research, teaching, and service. While the ways each of these missions are defined may vary from one university to the next, it seems to be universally true that service in academic life remains a low priority, is often ambiguously and narrowly defined, frequently refers only to on-campus service within or between departments, is rarely integrated with research and teaching, and is rarely considered as an equally viable component in promotion and tenure evaluations.

The KKN and TCU programs serve as examples of university programs which promote service, though still as a "third" priority, as a more legitimate part of students' and faculties' academic lives than in most universities in the United States. They do this in different ways, suggesting that variations that respond to cultural, political, and other societal differences are essential to the successful integration of service into the university agenda.

In contrast to the United States, both Costa Rican and Indonesian cultures emphasize the community over the individual. Students participate in service-learning experiences not only because they are required to, but because they feel obliged to their fellow citizens and want to pay back their society.

Regarding faculty motivation, Costa Rica is probably a better model than Indonesia for the United States. Because the central government of Indonesia has required all students to participate in service-learning, they must also require faculty to supervise and guide them; thus, the faculty are motivated by government decree more than by their own desires to serve the country or to combine their service, teaching, and scholarship agendas. But in Costa Rica, faculty volunteer to provide opportunities for the students. With a growing emphasis in the United States on service integrated into the curriculum and finding ways to persuade faculty to build opportunities for students that also benefit their own research, service, and teaching activities, Costa Rica, in particular, provides an instructive model.

The literature (e.g., Kendall & Associates, 1990) in the United States suggests that reflection is essential not only to ensure that students and faculty benefit fully from the service-learning activities but also to make these activities a legitimate dimension of the academic experience. This study found very little explicit reflection occurring in either Indonesia or

Costa Rica, although students in both countries and faculty in Costa Rica spend considerable time discussing their work in various forms that might be described as implicit reflection. Perhaps the Costa Ricans and Indonesians can learn something about the value of explicit reflection from the United States universities' evolving service-learning systems.

Finally, this study suggests that although the context for service-learning in the United States differs from contexts elsewhere, the growing diversity of cultures represented in America and the evolving needs of students, faculty, neighborhoods, and society generally mitigate against a single comprehensive approach to combining service and learning in universities. A host of options should be considered, and educators in other countries serve as excellent resources.

DAVID D. WILLIAMS *is an associate professor in the David O. McKay School of Education, Department of Instructional Psychology and Technology at BYU. He earned his PhD in educational research and evaluation methods at the University of Colorado, Boulder. His master's degree in educational leadership is from Western Michigan University and his bachelor's degree is from BYU.*

WILLIAM D. EISERMAN *earned his PhD in instructional design at BYU. He is currently on the research faculty in the Department of Communication Disorders and Speech Sciences at the University of Colorado, Boulder. Professor Eiserman's research focuses on the needs of families as they adapt to the birth of a child with a disability and on the various ways communities support these families and children. He also has a strong interest in service and experiential learning.*

References

Denzin, N. K., & Lincoln, Y. S. (1994). *Handbook of qualitative research.* Thousand Oaks, CA: Sage.

Direktorate Pembinaan dan Pengabdian pada Maysarakat Ditjen Kikti Depdikbud, 1986.

Eberly, D. J., & Sherraden, M. (Eds.) (1990). *The moral equivalent of war? A study of non-military service in nine nations.* New York: Greenwood Press.

Eisner, E. (1991). *The enlightened eye: Qualitative inquiry and the enhancement of educational practices.* New York: Macmillan.

Gonzalez, M. A. (1992). In Eberly, D. J. (Ed.), *National youth service: A global perspective.* Washington, DC: National Service Secretariat.

Hardjasoemantri, K. (1981). *Study-service as a subsystem in Indonesian higher education.* Unpublished dissertation.

Información General (1992). (General Information). San Jose, Costa Rica: The University of Costa Rica, Vice Rectory of Social Action.

Jacoby, B., & Associates (1996). *Service-learning in higher education: Concepts and practices.* San Francisco, CA: Jossey-Bass Publishers.

Kendall, J. C. & Associates (Eds.) (1990). *Combining service and learning: A resource book for community and public service,* Volume I. Raleigh, NC: National Society for Internships and Experiential Education.

Sherraden, M., & Castillo, C. M. (1990). Costa Rica: Non-military service in a national with no army. In D. Eberly and M. Sherraden (Eds.), *The moral equivalent of war? A study of non-military service in nine nations.* New York: Greenwood Press.

Questions and Writing Activity

1. What is service learning?
2. What are the advantages of learning about international service-learning programs?
3. What questions are Williams and Eiserman trying to answer through their study? What methods do they use to answer these questions? What conclusions do they reach?
4. As a class, consider the kind of international service-learning projects that BYU could be involved in. Write a proposal to the administration of the university or to the Kennedy Center explaining and justifying your proposal.

Renewal through Reciprocity

SUZANNE EVERTSEN LUNDQUIST

In the spring of 1992, Suzanne Lundquist and a group of BYU students and faculty went to the high mountains of Bolivia as part of a three week long service activity among the Aymara (the indigenous people of the Andes mountains). The experience was the second part of a class that began the previous semester where Lundquist and other faculty members had taught a class on service, third-world literature, ecology, archeology, and a wide variety of other topics as a way to prepare their students to "go forth to serve" the Aymara. In this essay that was first published in BYU Today, *Lundquist shows how listening is the first step to serving. Steve Pierce, who works for LDS Humanitarian Services and who accompanied the BYU expedition to Bolivia, says, "Development is finding out where a people think they are and where they would like to go," not simply telling them what they need to progress. Lundquist and the entire expedition are a stunning example of the good that can come from honestly and compassionately going forth to serve.*

We have been waiting five hundred years," says Willaru Huaytu, a *chasqui* (spiritual messenger) from the Incan tradition. "The Incan prophecies say that now, in this age, when the eagle of the North and the condor of the South fly together, the Earth will awaken. The eagles of the North cannot be free without the condors of the South," says Huaytu. "Our generation is here to help begin this age, to prepare through different schools to understand the message of the heart, intuition, and understanding" (McFadden 216). To Huaytu, the fact that a team of faculty and students from BYU went to the high plains (*Altiplano*) of Bolivia to help the Aymara Indians build a school, greenhouses, and a well would be a partial fulfillment of Incan prophecies.

Huaytu's assertion that different schools will be involved in this awakening of the earth also applies to the BYU/Aymara experience. Professors of religion, mythology, anthropology, political science, environmental biology, technology, and linguistics from North and South America have been and are now involved in the development and restoration of the lands of native peoples in Bolivia. What is most important to the Aymara, however, is the idea of reciprocity—mutual give and take, the eagle and the condor flying together. This essay, then, is one story of that flight.

Solutions to the problem of the people on the Altiplano are complex and long-range. The solutions are interdisciplinary and intercultural. It is not enough to say that three faculty members and 29 students from BYU went to Bolivia from April 28 to May 19, 1991, and built wells, greenhouses, and a high school.[1] The members of our BYU Bolivian expedition came home altered—reshaped by working in a Bolivian setting. We came home with something to say about Western notions of education, philosophy, development, community, and ethics. The reclamation of the Altiplano will continue the sacred narrative of the Aymara. The Aymara, however, are not the only characters in this story. Those involved in telling this story are multiple; they are actors, narrators, and writers as well as readers. And "they" are "we."

Prophecies, legends, sacred stories, and rituals still play a large role in the beliefs and attitudes of the Aymara, whether they be of their traditional faith or Christians. Stories of awakening and renewal, however, imply stories of sleep and destruction. Sacred stories dealing with the end of the world exist throughout all cultures. Nevertheless, people from every culture tell their own version. From the many narratives about the world's end told and retold throughout the Andean highlands, several important patterns emerge. Whether Earth is destroyed by flood, fire, earthquake, or drought, when the few survivors go forth to see the condition of the world, they discover that everything has been reduced to savanna; no trees are left. Earth is dry, harsh, and barren. The world has returned to a state of chaos. Fortunately this is not the final condition of the world. Cosmic cataclysms have opened the way for a restoration or recreation of Earth and degenerate humanity.

The symbols for renewal are rain, the growth of trees and grasses, and—through communal effort—the ability to sow and reap a life from the flesh of *Pacha Mama* (Mother Earth). Land, life, and community: these three components must exist in a state of reciprocity— supported by appropriate ritual behavior. This is the message of the ancient stories, the stories that still live. And these are the stories that must be shared beyond the borders of the Altiplano. Native Bolivians—the Aymara and the Quechua—live this story today. However, they are at the point in the narrative where those who have been preserved are looking out upon a land without water, grass, or trees. The tragic reality of this condition can best be measured by the loss of new life; fifty percent of the children in some parts of the Altiplano die before the age of five.

The causes for this condition can be easily enumerated. The Aymara live above 12,000 feet in a flood-and-drought-prone plain. During the day, the sun is relentless. The nights are cold; many areas in the region have frost 260 days a year. Since Spanish colonial times, the area has been deforested and overgrazed. For 500 years, Spanish patrons harnessed the lives of the people to control their resources and labor. In 1952, when the land on the Altiplano was returned to the Aymara and Quechua people, the land was exhausted and the remnant was left to reorganize themselves in a time when the rest of the country was moving into a cash economy. As a result, the Aymara and Quechua struggle to squeeze out an existence on depleted lands.

Today, the people rely mostly on potatoes and sheep to sustain life. Without fruits, vegetables, and adequate health care, the people suffer continuous disease. Illness is both the cause and effect of poverty among cultures that practice subsistence agriculture. To further complicate matters, since the early 1980s, the rains that usually come in late November or December have come as late as March. In 1983-84, when the rains did come, the drought was replaced by flood. And so it goes. The waters that remain and are available to quench the thirst of crops and people are polluted. All the elements of tragedy exist in such a setting.

In the analysis of literature, critics also look at the formal elements of a piece of writing, its component parts—setting, characters, plot, symbols, tone and style, as well as figures of speech. To careful readers of literature, setting is more than mere background or framework. Setting makes things happen. Setting, the place in which events occur, spurs characters to action, rouses specific kinds of positive or negative reactions, or reveals the inmost nature of the human soul. To thwart further tragedies caused by living in a polluted environment, the villagers on the Altiplano need potable water, wells, greenhouses, trees, and knowledge to change their present circumstance. The *campecinos* (farmers) need to reshape their setting. While the *campecinos* might be the central characters in this story, the story also requires other actors, contributors to a better plot line. "They" are "we."

We are all part of the story. How we begin to define the characters in the story, however, will change the outcome. If we view ourselves as outsiders or observers and the Aymara as "Indians," "natives," "pagans," "underdeveloped," "the ones who need help," and ourselves as "the chosen," "civilized," "Christians," "developed," "the ones who give help," the story is already finished. The characters, in this view, need to be recast. We need, as writers, to revise. As any character in a story about revision knows, re-vision generally involves a recreation of being—death, rebirth, and renewal. Recreation of being means repentance or the ability to continually overcome ignorance. Perhaps it also means that we quit dividing up the world in "us" and "them." There are so many ways that we divide and thereby can never conquer.

Not only are the nouns and pronouns we select to tell our story important, so are the adverbs and prepositions. Forward/backward, up/down, in/out are as value laden as the oppositional nouns we use. Such terms imply the same political and moral judgments that West/East and North/South have created. Steve Pierce, who works for the LDS Church's Humanitarian Services and a central character in this story, is particularly interested in the preposition we employ while discussing development. Pierce says "there are a lot of people who do development 'to' other people, or do development 'for' other people, some who even do development 'with' other people." What Pierce prefers, however, are people who genuinely try to do "development 'through' other people."

The episodes and events that are part of the unfolding of the plot of our story also point to the need for a recombination of objects and actions. Who would have thought for example, that two labs, blood, coca leaves, bits of candy, and the idea of a center could create an event that would point to the interdependence between human, animal life, plant life, and the earth. On May 5, as the BYU team prepared to help complete the Ayamaya high school, the members of the Aymara community seemed hesitant. They stood and talked around the center of the school. Some dug a hole in the courtyard, others came with two sheep. Coca leaves and mint were stuffed into the mouths of the sheep, their throats were slit, the rest of the blood was caught in a glass cup. Coca leaves and candies were cast into the hole, and the blood of the lambs was taken into each room and splashed upon the walls.

Following this ritual event, smoke was sent into the air as a messenger to *Pacha Mama.* A request was being made. That Earth Mother would protect the gringos, the Aymara and the work on the school. The sacred powers of the earth and sky were being invited to that village to participate in a wonderful event. The 210 children of Aymara would have a high school, five other village communities could send their Ayamaya. We would work together for the future so that the rising generation of adults could become literate, could learn to work better with the earth, the crops, the sheep, and the community in healing ways. Perhaps the ritual was also a sign of gratitude for the strange, tall, white folk who brought tools, cement, lumber and muscle.

Sacrifice means "to be made sacred." The sacrifice of the sheep came a day following the ceremony of our welcome. As the bus of BYU workers drove up the hill to Ayamaya, the entire village came in greeting. With pan pipes, flutes, and drums, the people of the town came dancing to greet us. And with tears and laughter we stepped off the bus, our hands taken up and held by the dancers. As we tried to step to the rhythm, we were drawn through the streets in an alternating chain of brown and white. This was a scene less than idyllic, however, since dancing at 13,000 feet is nearly impossible for gringos with altitude sickness. The jubilant music was punctuated by gasps for air, moans, and sighs. Some stepped aside to take pictures, others, like Gary Bryner, to hold the children in his arms. Following the dance came a program: an oration by the Secretary General, poems recited by the children, further dancing and speech making. And the feast.

The figure of the suffering "stranger" or anything else we see alien or "Other"—the environment, other cultures, women—shock us into considering another order, another time, another way of being. One way that we can open ourselves to the Other is through storytelling, through conversation. Two elements, time and voice, are always altered in sacred stories of renewal. Many kinds of time and many voices speak in store. As we come to allow the voices to mediate what we see, how we are, what we do, we come to inhabit new worlds. In the Aymara language, for example, time has a "direction orientation." "The future in Aymara is what has not been seen. We cannot see the future." In Aymara, the future is "behind you—you cannot see it." In Aymara, "the past is visible" (Miracle and Moya 33). This means that the walk forward is a walk into the past. The past, however, can only be redeemed through the human voice, through storytelling. Restoration is like a "sacred flashback."

This theme of restoration and renewal was clearly shown members of the BYU Bolivian Project when we spent a Sunday at the ancient temple site of Tiwanuku. Carlos Stumpf, assistant director of archeology in Bolivia, served as our guide. As we stood across from the temple site, Stumpf began pointing out what archeology has brought to the Aymara now living. As we stood overlooking a field of alternating canals, Stumpf said "the most important thing to understand here is that the *Sukakollus* [meaning ditch and hill] were discovered through archeological means." The *Sukakollus* are long, field-length 1-meter high hills, about 4 meters wide, with 2-meter wide canals on either side. As Stumpf continued, he told us that 19 different disciplines are working on the issues of poverty and environment in the Andean highlands. One project, covering 15,000 hectares, involves 25 communities, explained Stumpf. "The average *campecino* produces about two and a half tonnes of potatoes per hectare, and with our ancestors's system, we produce 40 tonnes of potatoes per hectare."[2]

The Andean highlands are cold and harsh. Major periods of frost occur during the agricultural cycle. The canals on either side of the ditches absorb the sun's energy during the day, radiate the energy during the night, and thereby protect against the devastating effects of frost.

As Stumpf led us through the temple complex and the adjoining fields, his recurring theme was the "resurrection of the Andean culture." For Stumpf, this movement is spiritual in nature. It involves understanding and protecting the environment, recovered by research and sustained through ritual, in relationship to the past. The Andean culture is pre-Incan. The Incas existed for only 80 years prior to the coming of the Spanish. The Tiwanacan culture, however, existed for 800 years. It existed as an advanced culture with sophisticated technology. What surprises observers, said Stumpf, is that those working in developments are relying on practices that the Aymara have forgotten. The outsiders are helping the Aymara to remember. This remembering the past restores "dignity to the farmers" because it gives the Aymara a "faith in their own culture," Stumpf explained.

The BYU team spent three hours in the hot afternoon sun with Stumpf at the Tiwanuku Temple site. But the time went quickly as Stumpf moved from one statue to the next, drawing our attention to details. We learned about other ancient practices and the wonders of such an old, long-lasting culture that prolonged drought finally brought to an end. And yet, as Stumpf's arm circled in the air, he recreated the livingness of the past with his words. Through his work as an archeologist, Stumpf recreates the past in the lives of the descendants of the Tiwanacan culture. Stumpf created images of a center as he spoke. He said that Tiwanuku has several names. "But the one that we feel is more realistic is *Tipacala*—which means the rock in the center." At another moment, Stumpf revealed, "We think of the Andes as the axle of the Bolivian country." Inside one of the temples, Stumpf continued to explain, "It wasn't just a temple, but it was also an astrological observatory; we have precise mathematical orientation from the sun and the stars."

At the Sun Gate, we stopped our conversation—the questions, comments, and answers. Stumpf was silent for a time. He called attention to the spiritual tone of the surroundings. "Actually we talk about the Andes Mountains not as something that separates the country, but as something that unites the country." Stumpf spoke of Bolivia being in the middle of many different systems—river systems, mountain ranges, as well as archaeological systems. "It starts here in Bolivia," explained Stumpf. "And so in a way, we are in the heart of the Americas, in every sense."

Drawing from disciplines ranging from science to religion, Stumpf showed the interdisciplinary nature of development. "For an Andean man, the earth is alive and the only way to interact with her is with love and respect. Because of that relationship, the Aymara conduct ceremonies and rituals that are very important." Throughout the afternoon, Stumpf's voice took on the authority of a poet, scientist, and priest. He entered the realm of poet and priest, for example, with such comments as, "Because this project is not just about producing potatoes, but restoring the thoughts and emotions of the Andean man, the only place where the Tiwanaku should be in our culture is in our hearts. It is the only way we can give it life. That is why, if I seem to come across very strong; I am sorry, but that is the only way to convey these feelings. If not, we'd be just a bunch of tourists." Stumpf admitted to being a Romantic. His rewards are certainly not monetary. His desire to help led him toward Aymara. In the face of their suffering, Stumpf responded with what he had to give—his love, time, respect, and knowledge. With such resources, people develop food to eat and renewed pride.

What, then, is development? How can we appropriately help those in cultures other than ours who are in need? Many voices answer this question. Representatives of the Andean Children's Foundation (FAN), CHOICE (Center for Humanitarian Outreach and Intercultural Exchange), and the LDS church's Humanitarian Services all joined the BYU expedition in Bolivia. For two of the three weeks, the BYU team stayed at the Andean Child Survival Resource and Training Center in Viacha, Bolivia. While there, we constructed wells and built greenhouses so that local farmers can come to the center and learn how to improve their own production and health. FAN conducts ongoing programs in 53 villages. "The CHOICE/FAN comprehensive child-survival program includes training of village health workers, nutrition programs, greenhouse and small-plot agriculture programs, safe drinking water development, immunizations and parent education," explain Gary Bryner and Sam Rushforth, both BYU professors and leaders of the expedition. While FAN conducts these ongoing programs in Bolivia, CHOICE organizes volunteer groups from North America to travel to South America to aid in the work of FAN. Because these organizations are not government sponsored, they have the flavor of a people to people operation.

With a doctoral degree from the School of International Service at the American University, Stephen Pierce of the LDS Humanitarian Services was an important actor in the intercultural exchange portion of our expedition. Pierce began his own work among the Aymara at Aymara Village in June 1985 while he was a member of FAN/CHOICE. During the past six years, Pierce has been instrumental in developing health and agricultural programs in Ayamaya. To date, 100 greenhouses have been erected in the village, and local health and literacy programs have been developed. Because of the level of trust already established between CHOICE/FAN and the Aymara, members of the BYU project were invited to live in the homes of the Aymara while working on the high school. Most villagers live in two-room dwellings. One of those rooms was cleared for the use of the BYU visitors.

Pierce's general vision of development is simple. "It is *not* paternalism." According to Pierce, paternalism is "reflected through development agencies as 'we know what is best for you; all you really have to do to develop is to imitate us, copy us.'" Modernization theory—"how to make carbon copies of our society and pass them out to others—has not been a successful approach to development," explains Pierce. Modernization, as part of paternalism, is failing because such a mind-set does not recognize "that the people have the answers to their own problems," says Pierce. "Development is finding out where a people think they are and where they would like to go." Development is also finding out "if there's anything you can supply in the way of technical or credit resources to help." In other words, "development is about providing a wider range of opportunities for people . . . to better their standard of living." However, this approach to development requires work in social, political, scientific, and religious areas. For Pierce, "there is an opportunity for any type of student to learn how his or her field affects development."

One final, but very important, aspect of development is that any technology developed to serve the poor must be accessible. If, for example, the people realize they need potable water to drink and more water for crop irrigation, they need a technology for digging wells that is not expensive. If the people in Ayamaya recognize the need for a high school, they need one that they can build with resources at hand, including adobe, mud, and rocks. One of the greatest resources of the Aymara is labor; their culture could be characterized as being labor-intensive. The men and women in Ayamaya, for instance, are skilled laborers; their knowledge of building adobe walls, rock floor foundations, insulated roofs, and smooth, stuccoed finishes is impressive. The villagers on the Altiplano might be the poorest of the poor in terms of material resources, but they are not poor in their skills or in their desire and willingness to provide for their own.

While driving on rutted Bolivian dirt roads, digging wells, shoveling dirt, or laying on straw mats before sleeping, our conversations turned to questions and answers. Answers usually came in the form of stories— recollections and interpretations: "How did FAN/CHOICE get started in this work?" was a consistent query. Each representative of these organizations had a different version of the story, but the feelings about the events surrounding the foundation of the Andean Children's Foundation were the same. Tim Evans (founder of CHOICE and FAN),

John L. Woods (CHOICE field director and trustee for FAN), Jaime and Terry Figueroa (country directors of FAN's Bolivian projects), and Tony Archer (board member of CHOICE/FAN and on-site mechanic) tell similar narratives about the beginnings of their humanitarian efforts. All served missions among Native Americans in North or South America. All have a great desire to help, and all believe it is both their responsibility and privilege to do so.

Dr. Evans, a Salt Lake City dentist and returned Bolivian missionary, became interested in doing something about the diarrhea problem that was taking so many of the lives of children. Knowing that access to clean water is the key, he began contacting charitable organizations in the United States as well as Bolivian groups that could help establish a technology for hand-dug wells. The response was so great that Evans was forced to split his efforts into two groups—one (FAN) to carry on the work in the Andes and another (CHOICE) to handle volunteer expeditions. One such expedition was in response to the story about Hilda Plata's death. In 1982, Hilda Plata, only four, drank water from a small pond near her mud-brick home; three days later, her body dehydrated from severe diarrhea, Hilda died in her mother's arms. Hilda was an LDS child. So many people wanted to help that the project to build a well for Hilda's family expanded into building a local school. Since 1983, hundreds of wells have been completed, 2,000 greenhouses built, and 20 schools constructed with the help of FAN/CHOICE. The Collegio Mixto in Ayamaya, built with funds raised by Bryner and Rushforth's Honors class, is the largest school built to date. According to Evans, who attended the dedication ceremony for the school, this seven-room structure with its central courtyard is not only a monument to the industry of the Aymara people but to Brigham Young University's humanitarian outreach program as well.

"Our class, Environmental Biology and Policy, is designed to give students an opportunity to experience firsthand what Sam Rushforth and I see as a relationship between environmental problems, poverty, and development—to see that causes and solutions are intertwined," says Bryner. The second purpose of the class is to allow students to become "involved in a project that will be helpful to people." Bryner says he and Rushforth would "eventually like to see all the students at the university have access to some kind of experience that involves them in learning from people who have a much different background than they have. And at the same time get involved in some kind of service project to remind them of the responsibility we all have to be of service."

Bryner and Rushforth's two-semester class has five components. The students are first introduced to environmental biology and policy. In the second phase, students read and write about books from a variety of disciplines concerned with a central theme of the class: "the interaction between environmental degradation and poverty in developing countries."[3] The third component is experiential. Students participate in projects dealing with environmental and developmental issues and are given the opportunity to organize themselves in order to raise money to finance the cost of materials for the work in Bolivia or elsewhere. In the 1991 class students worked on a "reforestation project in Arches National Park, raised funds for UNICEF, wrote reports on conservation, and gave presentations in public schools on global environmental problems such as ozone depletion and deforestation, recycling, and air pollution," explains Bryner. Students raised $10,000 that went directly to the purchase of buildng materials for the work on the wells, greenhouses in Viacha, and a school in Ayamaya.

As a fourth component of the class, a number of guests are also invited to speak on "development theory, the role of women in development, culture and mythology in South America, anthropology, and health care in less developed countries" says Bryner. The fifth component is the actual doing of the work.

None of the 35 of us could have anticipated the effect of the Bolivian project on the lives of the Aymara or on our own lives. This expedition was hard. We suffered from diarrhea, respiratory infections, nausea, altitude sickness, and exhaustion. Dr. Lucinda Bateman, a Salt Lake City physician, donated her services to the expedition and kept the entire group going. But even the illnesses were instructive. We all learned what it is like to be tired, ill, depressed, and harassed by environmental pollution. By the end of two weeks, many wondered if we could endure a third. And yet, humor was the leveler. On one occasion, several students had to come out of the hot afternoon sun. Others were already on their sleeping bags. In the general daze of disbelief that so many people could feel so rotten all at once, Ted Beuhler muttered: "Beam me up, Scotty." Ted's wit brought relief. Yet we all knew, as Dr. Bateman noted, "We can go home; these people *are* home."

Dr. Bateman's skills were extended to the villagers. She cleaned wounds, administered medicines, instructed the local health representative, Jacob Mamani, and was called to the side of injured villagers. One woman, kicked in the chest by a donkey, brought Dr. Bateman to a clear realization of what injury and illness mean on the Altiplano. As Dr. Bateman examined the injured woman, it was evident that she had a skull fracture, broken ribs, and likely broken vertebrae. Without transportation or a local hospital, many people simply die. All Dr. Bateman could tell the woman's loved ones was, "If she makes it through the night, she won't die."

The week after we left Bolivia, the spiritual leader of Kichani, a nearby village, died from appendicitis. For those of us who hiked over the mountains to his remote village, this gentleman had served as host. He showed us the village school, the women's literacy program, and the flowers and trees growing in the yards in the village. He was full of joy at receiving guests from North America.

Each student could tell a story about the family with whom she or he lived. Ricardo Diaz lived with Ayamaya's mayor. When Ricardo left, the mayor sobbed. Ricardo now has two godsons in Ayamaya. The Secretary General, that wonderful orator, sends us messages through Tim Evans. Every BYU student and faculty member now has a home in Bolivia should s/he be able to return. Says Pierce, "By them having the opportunity to share their lives—their culture—with white people, or people from the West who did not spurn them or look down on them, their cultural identity has been reaffirmed. That is what I think has been the real value of this project."

At our final meeting before returning to Provo, Jaime Figueroa detected a sense of helplessness among the comments being made by students. What had any one of us done to alleviate the suffering? In response, Figueroa said, "The school you people helped to build, if this group didn't come, there was no other way we were going to build it. We didn't have the funds to do it. Do you know what it means, a school for Ayamaya? It means the girls are going to school. The girls in the community were going only up to fifth grade because it was too dangerous to send a girl." In Figueroa's understanding of village life, if you educate a woman, whole nations can change. And although Ayamaya presently has only 100 families, down through future generations many more families from Ayamaya and surrounding villages will be affected by this new school.

There are still unanswered questions. Perhaps the question posed by Andrea Jackman is foremost in the minds of those who returned. After a testimony meeting, Andrea sat quietly weeping. "Why was I born with so much and them with so little?" she whispered. What is the theology of poverty? None of us has found an acceptable answer. What we did discover, however, was a glimpse of what it might feel like to live a life of consecration. We have come to understand this more fully as we have returned home. Many experienced depression for several weeks. Perhaps the reason for the depression was that for three weeks we were able to give all of our time, talent, resources, and energy to each other and to the Aymara. Each of us would like to continue to feel as we felt then. As we share our renewed vision with others, many want to get involved. As for the faculty members, this is what a university education is for. The retelling of the story of renewal on the Altiplano has an influence broader than our South American experience. We will go again, often, and anywhere our talents and resources will allow. Spring of 1992 will find the same teachers with new students working in Mexico. We await the unfolding of another story. We invite you to help write new sacred narratives.[4]

SUZANNE EVERTSEN LUNDQUIST *received a BA in English from BYU and a DA in literacy from the University of Michigan. As a professor of Native American and third-world literatures, Lundquist has always strived to take what she teaches in the classroom and put it to use to help the people whom she studies. She has served people in various parts of North and South America (Bolivia, Mexico, and the United States, to name a few places) as well as serving the students in her classroom. Lundquist is known in the BYU English department as a life-changing professor who integrates literature, gospel insights, personal growth, and concern for current social issues into her teaching curriculum.*

Endnotes

[1]Faculty members included Gary Bryner from Political Science, Sam Rushforth from Botony, and Suzanne Evertsen Lundquist from English. Dr. Lucinda Bateman was the physician for the group. BYU students included Stuart Ames, Felicia Alvarez, Angela Ashurst, Wendy Baird, Chyrel Black, Ted Buehler, Valerie Burnett, Richard Crockett, Ricardo Dias, Christine Dix, Cindy Edwards, Jane England, Eric Ethington, Celeste Ghilchrist, Rachel Hokanson, Robert Hokanson, Paul Hudson, Andrea Jackman, Cherstin N. Lyon, Tom Lyon, Michael Marlow, Laurie McBride, Lorraine Paterson, Leslie Randall,Nancy Rushforth (graduate student), Spencer Stevens, Tamara Townsend, Liz Valentiner, Alison Wiltbank. Jed and Sarah Rushforth also went.

[2]Translated into English by Chelita Pate, administrative assistant in the Political Science Department.

[3]Readings include: Miller's *Living in the Environment* (as central text) and Clark's *Adriadne's Thread,* Commoners, *Making Peace with the Planet,* Erlich and Erlich's *Extinction*, Eisley's *The Unexpected Universe,* Fromm's *To Have or To Be,* Hamilton's *Entangling Alliances,* Leopold's *A Sand County Almanac,* and Ornstein and Erlich's *New World, New Mind.*

[4]For information on future BYU-CHOICE/FAN projects, please write: Dr. Tim Evans, Director FAN/CHOICE (BYU Project), 928 East 100 South, Suite E, Salt Lake City, Utah 84102.

Works Cited

Huayta, Willaru. "When the Condor Flies with the Eagle." *Profiles in Wisdom.* Ed. Steven McFadden. Santa Fe: Bear & Company Publishing, 1991.

Miracle, Andrew W. Jr. and Juan de Dios Yapita Moya. "Time and Space in Aymara." *The Aymara Language in Its Social and Cultural Contexts.* Ed. M. J. Harman. Gainesville: University Presses of Florida, 1981.

Questions

1. In what ways does the BYU/Aymara project fit the definition of service-learning articulated by Williams and Eiserman?
2. What are some of the differences that the BYU students and faculty had to negotiate (both within their own group and between their group and those they served)?
3. What principles and values guided how they negotiated and developed solutions?
4. What model for negotiation can you derive from Lundquist's narrative? How could this model be applied in other contexts?

Why BYU? Education and Much More

MADISON U. SOWELL

In 1986, Jeffrey R. Holland, then president of BYU, invited faculty and staff to submit essays on the responsibility and rewards of teaching at BYU. Of the many entries submitted, Madison Sowell's "Why BYU?" was one of six essays President Holland chose as most representative of what a BYU education can be. "BYU has meant a lot to me as a student and as a professor," Sowell states. "It has been a catalyst for profoundly spiritual and rigorously academic experiences." Sowell points out that the freedom to discuss the gospel of Jesus Christ in the classroom liberates students and teachers to recognize the "eternal truths to be found" in academic disciplines. In "Why BYU?" Sowell looks at how a BYU education can be enriching for students and faculty in academic and spiritual ways.

Fall 1969. "*Brigham Young* University, did you say?" Mrs. Simon stared incredulously for several seconds, then mechanically pushed the black-and-silver-rimmed glasses up her pointed nose, fussedly patted the graying bun of hair on her head, and reached for one of the outdated guides to colleges on the shelf above her neat desk. She paused, unable to refrain from drawling, "But why, of all places, *Brigham Young* University?" The emphasis, once again, fell like a blunt ax on *Brigham* and *Young* as if to make dead certain I had correctly indicated the college of my choice. Somewhat intimidated, I muttered what undoubtedly seemed more of an excuse than a conviction: "I have friends who say they've received a great education there." Sighing, the guidance counselor proceeded to draw a comparison between BYU and Vanderbilt University, where many of my Central High School classmates with similar scholastic records were hoping to enroll the next fall. In her mind there really was no comparison; the "Harvard of the South" won hands down because its admission requirements were considerably stiffer than BYU's. Why had I studied Latin, four years of science and math, Advanced Placement American history, and accelerated Senior English only to select a university that would accept me with two-thirds of what

I had accomplished or taken in high school? Still I persisted: "I really believe BYU is where I should go for my undergraduate education."

In reality, the answer to the query, "Why attend Brigham Young University?" was then too personal for me to attempt an explanation in the half-hour allotted by my bewildered high school counselor. Only now, at a distance of just over fifteen years and from my perspective as an associate professor in BYU's College of Humanities, am I fully realizing just how wise my decision to come to BYU was first as a student and later as a teacher. Yet the question (and my awkwardness in responding to it) has not disappeared, although it has been recast, by inquisitive colleagues at national scholarly conferences, as "Why teach at BYU?" After much consideration, I have concluded that the best answer to both "Why BYU?" questions is probably the same: at BYU students and teachers can concern themselves with the traditional curriculum of college education and much more. In the reflections which follow I shall attempt to illustrate what that "much more" can be. While the experiences I seek to share as student and teacher at the Y are particular to me, I know that parallel experiences have occurred thousands of times throughout the school's history.

I first heard of the university during the Vietnam era of the late '60s. I was a teenager living in Memphis, Tennessee, and investigating and playing the organ for the LDS Church. After I was baptized in May 1969, I regularly invited missionaries to my home to teach my friends the restored gospel. One of those missionaries, Elder Andrew Ehat, convinced me that I should seriously consider attending BYU. When one of my relatives (a mathematics professor at a small college in Arkansas) strongly cautioned against my enrolling in any university with such a large student body and so far from home, I became discouraged. The redoubtable Elder Ehat came to the rescue. He assured me that by becoming involved in a student congregation and by choosing carefully from among the most challenging teachers, I would not become a "lost soul" and could indeed receive a first-class college education.

Refortified, I looked up the admission requirements to the BYU Honors Program, which at that time required a separate application for admittance. I shared those requirements with Mrs. Simon; she agreed that they were at least as rigorous as Vanderbilt's general admission requirements. I did apply in the fall of '69 to BYU and soon received an early acceptance and scholarship. I was also admitted to the Honors Program. At that point I made a leap of faith: I decided to attend BYU and not even complete my application to Vanderbilt. I made my decision even though I was a convert of less than a year and had never been to Utah. To familiarize myself with the school and the campus before the regular school year started, I did decide, however, to participate in a three-week Late

Summer Honors Program, an intensive course of study designed for incoming Honors freshmen.

Summer 1970. Brother and Sister Harvey Petersen, the parents of another missionary who had taught the gospel to friends in my home, met me at the Salt Lake City airport and drove me to Provo on a dry, hot August day. I still recall the exhilaration I felt upon reading the motto marking the entrance to campus: "Enter to Learn—Go Forth to Serve." I am sure I wondered *what* I would learn and *where* I would serve, not really fathoming that, under the tutelage of devout and demanding teachers, I would soon be concentrating on *how* to learn and *how* to serve. Within hours I was getting to know bright young LDS men and women from around the country; within one evening Alma Heaton, widely proclaimed professor of fun, had taught us how to laugh together and at each other and, most important, at ourselves; within days Terry Warner, then director of Honors, had kindled within us a "passion for learning" (his very apt term); within three weeks I had made more life-long friends than in my previous eighteen years. I naively thought I had rediscovered an already perfected Zion!

Winter 1971. The fall semester slipped by so quickly that January final exams came and went before I realized my folly in not keeping a journal of the events of the first half of my freshman year. Not all had been bliss: my naiveté as a convert was shattered when, on a dreary afternoon, a quiet fellow at the other end of my Stover Hall floor hanged himself with his belt. Guilt-ridden, I could not recollect ever having spoken to the shy young man in the weeks we had shared the same noisy lavatory and eaten in the same crowded Cannon Center cafeteria. As I pondered the tragedy, I came to realize how one can be quite alone even in a throng of people. I soberly resolved to do better at reaching out to fellow students and not just to my close acquaintances, a resolution that over the years has garnered me new friends in places as diverse as Cambridge, Massachusetts, and Florence, Italy.

Although I had limited success as a BYU freshman in influencing my peers, eight years later when, at age twenty-six, I returned to teach, I decided to interview each of my students at least once early in the semester—a practice I have doggedly continued every semester I have taught. Ostensibly these initial ten-minute interviews serve to resolve any academic anxiety a student may have; they also allow me the opportunity to assess if I have any solitary individuals who require my assistance or need directing to a professional counselor. In one case, a returned missionary, whom I shall call Barry, came in for his interview. He had said little in class but had written a couple of fine papers. It soon became apparent, as he haltingly attempted to respond to my routine questions, that he suffered from a serious problem with stuttering. I encouraged him to return to my office during office hours or to make an appointment with me after class whenever he wished to discuss an assignment on a one-to-one basis. Over time, I noticed that, despite his increased relaxation in returning to see me, his stuttering continued unabated. I carefully reflected on what course to take. When I discovered that the university had a speech therapist trained to work with people who stutter, I bolstered my courage and decided to discuss the problem openly and in the spirit of brotherhood with Barry. To my surprise and pleasure he responded warmly to my suggestion that he contact the BYU therapist whose telephone number I had secured. Soon afterwards I left Provo for a summer of travel and research. When I returned to teach for the fall semester, Barry came to see me. He was smiling. After having suffered almost daily embarrassment through a two-year mission and three years of college, he had, after only a few months of therapy, nearly conquered his problem. Since that experience, I have hardly ever hesitated to recommend professional help to students who obviously could benefit from spiritual, medical, or psychological counseling. I feel that all my students are worthy of a "Christian fellowship," a caring involvement which may prove much more valuable to them than any monetary fellowship I received to advance my own education.

Unquestionably, my closest friend that first year at the Y (1970-71) was George Schober Laird, 3rd, a lanky nonmember from Pennsylvania who delighted in poking fun at my Southern accent. (It was he who first brought to my attention the different pronunciations of *pin* and *pen* which Yankees insist on making but to which I was theretofore completely oblivious!) We ourselves could hardly have been more different. I was a pathetic sportsman, and he had selected BYU primarily for its convenient ski slopes and tennis team, on which he earned a place at the end of his sophomore year. George taught me the fundamentals of what my father, who had died in a car accident when I was eight, would have wanted me to learn years before: how to camp out, box, wrestle, and play tennis. In return I taught my newfound brother what was most meaningful to me: how to gain a testimony of the restored gospel of Jesus Christ. Sister Clara Schofield, our bemused dorm mother, marveled at how George and I never tired of debating religious topics. During the second semester of our freshman year, after a weekend of fasting together, he asked me, an Aaronic priest, to baptize him. He was the first person I ever baptized; the service took place on campus in the Jesse Knight Building, where I currently have my office and teach most of my courses. Participating in George's conversion was instrumental in helping me to decide that, despite my nonmember mother's opposition, I would submit a mission application. My decision meant that I would spend funds long earmarked for my education on a mission instead. I could easily live with that reality, for I had learned that the best education always considers eternity and not just the here and now—a belief I attempt to pass on to my students.

Because only a holder of the Melchizedek Priesthood could confirm George a member of the Church, he asked his favorite teachers—philosophy professor Dennis Rasmussen—to perform that ordinance. Dr. Rasmussen exemplified such a stirring spirit of inquiry that George had taken not only Introduction to Philosophy but also second-semester Book of Mormon from him. Naturally, I yearned to study with him, too, and was able, during the summer of 1971, to take two of his classes, including a course in the philosophy of ethics. A reflective Latter-day Saint who received his doctorate from Yale, Dennis (I call him by his first name because we are now colleagues) taught us not to be afraid to question or disagree with a philosophical idea or notion, no matter how eminent the philosopher or popular the philosophy. Ideas—whether others' or our own—must stand on their own merits. And so it was that during my first year at BYU I was primed, without fully comprehending it, for the challenges of my own graduate experience a few years later at Harvard. Although I would delight in examining many fashionable literary and philosophical theories at Harvard, I had had a strong conviction implanted in me as an undergraduate that I had to draw my own conclusions as to what ultimately constituted the good and the true.

During my second semester as a BYU student I learned from a music major that Professor John Longhurst might have an opening for another student of piano. (This was a few years before Brother Longhurst became one of the Tabernacle organists.) I auditioned with a piece by Mendelssohn, and he indulgently accepted me as a student. When he asked me, for one of my first assignments, to prepare Number 7 of Bach's Three-Part Inventions, the "Andante con moto," I informed him that I had already "done" all the Three-Part Inventions. He smiled and said, "We shall see." At the following week's lesson I nervously started racing through the invention and had almost reached the end of the first line when Professor Longhurst abruptly stopped me. Taking a pencil in hand, he began to trace the various voices which he wished to hear properly phrased and to discuss the value of each note I was playing. He insisted that I slow my playing considerably so that I could better distinguish the separate voices and he could more easily correct my imperfectly stressed notes. He soon had me practicing my scales in octaves in another attempt to slow down my playing. I had studied piano and organ for several years, rapidly mastering (or so I thought) as much repertoire as I could. What John Longhurst taught me in four months of weekly half-hour lessons was how to pause, consider, and interpret what I had long known how to read. Naturally, he also challenged me with musical pieces I had never before attempted, such as Béla Bartók's *Mikrokosmos*. Although it soon became painfully clear that music performance would not play a significant role in my career plans, Brother Longhurst encouraged me to keep my talent alive for subsequent service in the Church. Not until a dozen years later, when I was on a leave from teaching and living in New York City, did I realize how prudent his counsel had been; during that year there was a temporary dearth of LDS keyboard students at Juilliard, and I was called to play the Manhattan Ward pipe organ for sacrament services. Enter to learn and go forth to serve indeed!

Spring 1974. During the fall and winter semesters following my mission to Northern Italy I took onerous academic loads, 23 and 26 hours, respectively. I did so in order to complete a double major in Italian and comparative literature and still graduate in the three years I had planned for my undergraduate education. By spring term, however, I was eager for a saner course load and took "only" one literature course for credit: a four-hour nineteenth- and twentieth-century British authors course from Dr. Karen Lynn. Class met four days a week, two hours at a time, and started promptly at 7:00 a.m. (only at BYU!). Sister Lynn proved to be a master teacher, as sensitive to literature as she was to the viola she played so well. Within a couple of days she had memorized all our names; almost magically she knew how to draw us into discussions that inevitably led to a revelatory insight into the poem or novel under consideration, whether Keats' ode "To Autumn" or Conrad's *Lord Jim.* She left the door to her office wide open during her extended office hours so that we felt more at ease about dropping by to discuss our reading assignments or essays. She had us submit blank cassette tapes with our papers so that she could informally comment on our style, vocabulary, and ideas as she read the papers. She queried us on our goals and aspirations and was the first professor ever to suggest that I apply to an Ivy League school for my graduate program. Her confidence in me gave me renewed confidence in myself, and she became for many of us not only a revered mentor but also a treasured friend. She showed by her service to others, including long hours on the Church Music Committee responsible for the new LDS hymnal, that it is good to be faithful in the kingdom but even better to be faithful and competent. Her ultimate boon to me, however, was only tangentially related to academics: in an Honors seminar she conducted on the "Literary Foundations of Opera" I met my wife-to-be, Debra Hickenlooper; it was Karen who first hinted, rather broadly, that I should ask Debra for a date!

Winter 1975. My final semester as an undergraduate arrived, and I had only one major academic goal yet unfulfilled—to take a course from

BYU's renowned teacher of Shakespeare, Arthur Henry King. Unfortunately, my schedule allowed only a one-hour course from him, a senior seminar in religion rather than the Shakespeare I had hoped for. I soon learned, however, that Brother King, like most great teachers, taught a method as much as a subject. Not unlike John Longhurst four years before him, Arthur insisted that I slow down my reading, only this time the literature was scriptural rather than musical. He insisted that we read the scriptures aloud to attune ourselves to the cadences and emphases. We must have spent a month closely reading one chapter of Genesis—the story of Abraham's attempted sacrifice of Isaac—and equal time on Paul's Corinthian discourse on faith, hope, and charity, and on Jacob's allegory of the tame and wild olive trees. That I can yet recall the scriptural passages we contemplated in that one-hour seminar should be eloquent testimony to the renewed reverence I was gaining for the power and seriousness of the Word.

At one point during the semester Arthur invited the seminar participants to his Orem home, where his wife Patricia served us home-made soup and he regaled us on the piano with witty "Variations on Three Blind Mice." The repast, simple but tasty, and the fellowship that followed, short but sincere, made for two or three memorable hours. Several of us reveled in observing a lighter side of our distinguished professor from Britain; I decided then that, should I ever teach, I would attempt to emulate his example of hospitality, even if on a more modest scale and with considerably less élan. True to my decision, I instituted, within the first year of my return to the Y, annual Dante evenings in the basement of my Provo home. For this event students bring copies of the *Inferno*, either in Italian or in English translation, and we pass the evening reading of ingenious infernal torments; looking at slides of William Blake and Gustave Doré illustrations of Dante's underworld; and eating such niceties as devil's food or, less frequently, angel food cake.

After a number of these *Serate Dantesche* I began to wonder if I should continue to sponsor the evenings, which only became more elaborate with each passing year; I questioned whom they benefited. Then I reflected on Scott, the BYU Italian Club president who had worked so diligently to help me, the club advisor, organize the first such evening in 1979; I thought of the club notice he had placed in the *Daily Universe,* which, to our initial horror and later amusement, was captioned "Professor Reads Dante." (What could be more accurate and more misleading at the same time? Since I had written my doctoral thesis on Dante, some of my colleagues could not resist "congratulating" me on finally getting around to reading the poet!) Notwithstanding the *Universe* miscue, the evening was a great success. One result of the happy collaboration between Italian

Club advisor and president was that Scott soon began to assist me in my scholarly research on Dante, and I helped him get accepted into Harvard where he received his MBA degree. With these thoughts in mind, I could only conclude that such extracurricular events can be of mutual benefit. I also realized that, ideally, student and teacher roles are closely interwoven. Effective teachers really must keep as a touchstone their best memories as students and strive to see that their own students participate in analogous experiences, whether intellectual, social, or religious. To become a mentor and truly affect eternity is not to limit one's influence to what transpires in the classroom but rather to foster learning wherever and whenever possible.

Sharing these vignettes of my experience as a student and teacher at BYU has not come easily, as the stories are quite personal and I relish my privacy. But as I write these words far from the Provo campus—in London, where I direct a Study Abroad program—I feel an overwhelming need to dramatize what an eternal difference BYU can make in a student's life and testimony, as in my own case. Because of the benefits I have derived from the intimate sense of community possible at the university, I wish to affirm that most BYU professors deeply care about student education and much more. Personally, I aspire not only to challenge students to be idealistic but also to nurture them in the realities of life; to stimulate them to realize their potential and face their inadequacies or areas in which they require growth or change; to inspire them to thirst after knowledge and righteousness but also to help them cultivate the ability to laugh at themselves; to teach them, more than the memorization of facts too quickly forgotten, how to learn; to show them how to serve others but not always as they think best and without shrinking from their own duty to be competent. While BYU is not necessarily for every Latter-day Saint, whether student or professor, it can offer an excellent education and much more to the individual eager to prepare not only for the exigencies of today but also for the eternities to come. Of this I testify, as one happy product of and now humble catalyst in the ongoing Brigham Young University experience.

MADISON U. SOWELL *did his undergraduate work in Italian and comparative literature at BYU before going to Harvard University to receive his MA and PhD. After finishing graduate school, Sowell returned to BYU where he has regularly taught Italian and Honors courses and occasionally Book of Mormon courses. Sowell served for nine years as chair of the Department of French and Italian and is currently president of the Italy Milan Mission—the same area in which he served as a missionary.*

Questions

1. Sowell states that he came to BYU in order to study "the traditional curriculum of a college education and much more." What is the "much more" that BYU offers? In what ways have you participated in this "much more"?
2. What has BYU taught you about "how to learn and how to serve"?
3. Write to a friend or relation who might be considering BYU. What can you relate about your experience here that would help them to understand BYU's mission?
4. In what ways can you individually and as groups of students make the BYU experience more meaningful for others?

Topical Index